Italy, the Least of the Great Powers:
Italian foreign policy before the First World War

Italy, the Least of the Great Powers: Italian foreign policy before the First World War

R. J. B. BOSWORTH

Senior Lecturer in European History
University of Sydney

CAMBRIDGE UNIVERSITY PRESS

London   New York   New Rochelle
Melbourne   Sydney

Published by the Press Syndicate of the University of Cambridge
The Pitt Building, Trumpington Street, Cambridge CB2 1RP
32 East 57th Street, New York, NY 10022, USA
296 Beaconsfield Parade, Middle Park, Melbourne 3206, Australia

© Cambridge University Press 1979

First published 1979

Printed in Great Britain
at the University Press, Cambridge

Library of Congress cataloguing in publication data
Bosworth, R. J. B.
Italy, the least of the Great Powers.
Bibliography : p.
Includes index
1. Italy–Foreign relations–1870–1915.
1. Title
DG568.5.B67   327.45   78-18090
ISBN 0 521 22366 0

Contents

Preface *page* vii

List of maps   x

1   Society and politics in Liberal Italy   1

2   New political pressure groups and foreign policy   39

3   The making of a Foreign Minister: Antonino Di San Giuliano   68

4   The *Consulta*: the bureaucrats of foreign policy   95

5   How Italy went to Libya   127

6   How Italy stayed in Libya   165

7   The politics of alliance: Italy in the Triple Alliance, 1912–1914   196

8   The politics of friendship: Italy, the Triple Entente, and the search for a new Mediterranean agreement, 1911–1914   255

9   '*Un cliente maleducato*': Italy in the Dodecanese and Ethiopia, 1912–1914   299

10   Preparing to digest some spoils: Italian policy towards Turkey, 1912–1914   337

11   San Giuliano's epilogue. The realities of European war 28 June to 16 October 1914   377

Conclusion   418

Appendix I The Ten Commandments for Italians abroad   421

Appendix II Pro-memoria on our politico-military situation, by A. Pollio   423

Appendix III San Giuliano's poem about his funeral ceremony   427

Abbreviations used in the notes and bibliography   429

Select bibliography   431

Notes   452

Index   525

For Michal

Preface

On 10 June 1940 Benito Mussolini appeared on the balcony of the Palazzo Venezia and declaimed to the marshalled throngs below that 'destiny' was sounding out the hour for Italy to enter the Second World War. As Greece, North Africa, and finally the islands and peninsula of Italy itself would soon testify, what the *Duce* was really heralding was the end of Italy's role as a Great Power.

In domestic matters, after 1945, the wind from the north may have been diverted; Christian Democratic Italy may owe a large legacy to the Fascist or Liberal past. But the fiasco of Fascist military effort and the changed international balance after the war destroyed at a blow the imperial pretensions, the assertions of greatness made for almost a century by the intellectuals, industrialists and politicians of the 'Third Italy', the 'resurgent' Rome.

No doubt there is a distinct break in continuity between the foreign policy of Fascist Italy and its successors. Is there a similar break between fascism and its predecessor, the Liberal regime which governed Italy from 1860 to 1922? The greatest of Liberal historians, Benedetto Croce, of course declared that fascism was a 'parenthesis', and that Mussolini's regime was different in kind from that of Giolitti or of other Liberal leaders. Croce's theories have often met with withering criticism in so far as concerns Italy's domestic affairs. In foreign policy, oddly, the concept of parenthesis has retained more support. For example the two most notable recent English-language studies of Fascist foreign policy argue respectively that in the nineteen-twenties Fascist foreign policy was new, aggressive and totalitarian and that in the nineteen-thirties Italy was dragged into 'Mussolini's wars'.[1]

However the crowds in the Piazza Venezia on 10 June 1940 had some architectural reasons to doubt if matters had changed so much. Their chants and their uniforms were new; their *Duce* used new words about 'Proletarian and Fascist Italy'. Yet, there in the heart

---

[1] See A. Cassels, *Mussolini's early diplomacy* (Princeton, 1970); D. Mack Smith, *Mussolini's Roman Empire* (London, 1976).

of Rome, the most stridently imperialist atmosphere was not generated by the tinsel of the Fascist demonstration, but rather by the enormous, white, Victor Emmanuel monument which, from the southern side of the square, towered over Mussolini and those who shouted *Duce* up at him.

In the front, splendidly on his horse sat the caddish King Victor Emmanuel II, *pater patriae*, armed for combat; at the very top Winged Victories guided their chariots to glory; on the monument itself mosaics displayed Italian triumphs, bas-reliefs recorded Italian heroism and devotion; below there was the altar of the *Patria*, with its solemn guards. Rows of mock-classical pillars earned from sardonic foreigners the title 'the wedding cake', but, if viewed with appropriate patriotic gravity, outmatched the rivalry of the ruins of the Capitol and the Forum behind. The *monumentissimo*, as the Socialist paper *Avanti!* called it, made Fascist architecture look lean, restrained and even modest.

For the Victor Emmanuel monument was a Liberal structure, planned from 1878 and inaugurated on Sunday 4 June 1911 to celebrate the *Cinquantennio*, the fiftieth anniversary of the Risorgimento. In its size, in its decoration and in its positioning, the Victor Emmanuel monument is testimony to the fact that the ruling classes of Liberal Italy also had an ambition to locate an imperial heritage of 'Roman grandeur' for their Italy, a desire that Italy play a full role as a Great Power.

The book which follows is essentially a monograph. But, in looking at the aims and methods of Italian diplomacy just before the First World War, evidence is produced which is relevant to the wider debate on just what difference fascism made to Italy. In Germany, after the work of Fritz Fischer, it is widely accepted that the diplomatic hopes, and even plans, of Imperial and Weimar Germany differed more in style than in essence from those of Nazi Germany. There is little reason not to believe the same about Fascist and Liberal Italy. Pre-1914 Italy was a Power on the make, looking for a bargain package deal which would offer the least of the Great Powers a place in the sun. The major difference with Fascist Italy lay in the method of diplomacy, in the preference of Giolitti and his Foreign Minister, Antonino Di San Giuliano, for seeking out bargains, for conjuring up paper victories by stealth and diplomacy rather than by bluster or war. Yet, if a relationship is sought with

Preface

the realities of Italian society, with the character of Italian poverty, Liberal foreign policy was as absurd and disastrous as was Fascist diplomacy.

This monograph also produces evidence challenging the theory of a clear-cut turning to imperialism, a *'svolta imperialistica'*, in the sense of one managed by some arch-machiavel, Giolitti, the Nationalist Association or new Italian industrialists from 1908 to 1915. Instead a detailed study of the making of foreign policy illustrates that foreign policy remained basically in the hands of diplomats and leading politicians who were not, in any real sense, the puppets of their 'public opinion' or business community. Italian foreign policy became more expansionist from 1911 to 1914 very much within the domestic and international context. If there was a turning point, it was one prepared, recognised and approved by the majority of the ruling class of Liberal Italy, and one made possible by unusual international opportunity allowed to the least of the Great Powers by the peculiar relationship between the other, more genuine Great Powers just before the First World War.

The interest which produced this book was first stimulated during a Ph.D. thesis on British policy towards Italy, 1902–15, which I wrote for the University of Cambridge. I owe a great debt as supervisor and friend to Professor F. H. Hinsley of St John's College. My other debts to colleagues, librarians and students in Australia, Italy and England can hardly be repaid by a fleeting reference at the end of a preface. But in calming my impetuosity, ironing out my style or cutting through my detail, I must thank, among others, A. E. Cahill, G. Cresciani, G. Filippone Thaulero, C. Halder, G. Harrison, N. Pragnell, F. Stambrook, J. M. Ward, G. White and J. K. Wilton – not to mention Edmund and Mary. I also must acknowledge financial assistance from the Australian Academy of Humanities and the Italian Government's exchange scholarship scheme.

Maps

1 Liberal Italy   *page* 26
2 Libya   153
3 Albania and Montenegro   239
4 Italian penetration of Asia Minor   309
5 Division of Ethiopia suggested to the British Foreign
  Office by Lord Kitchener in May 1913 (from PRO file
  FO 371/1571)   334

CHAPTER I

Society and politics in Liberal Italy

The political and military leadership in the Risorgimento...said that they were aiming at the creation of a modern State in Italy, and they in fact produced a bastard. They aimed at stimulating the formation of an extensive and energetic ruling class, and they did not succeed; at integrating the people into the framework of the new State, and they did not succeed. The paltry political life..., the fundamental and endemic rebelliousness of the Italian popular classes, the narrow and stunted existence of a sceptical and cowardly ruling stratum, these are all the consequence of that failure. A consequence of it too is the international position of the new State, lacking effective autonomy because sapped internally by the Papacy and by the sullen passivity of the great mass of the people.[1]

So, with justifiable anger, Antonio Gramsci scribbled into his *Prison Notebooks* the now classical definition of the foundation of modern Italy, of a process of unification which had brought political but not social change, of a boasted 'national revolution' which was really a *rivoluzione mancata*, of an Italy of transformism where 'If we want things to stay as they are, things will have to change.'[2]

For it had not been by intellectuals, attracted by the ideas of Mazzini and Pisacane, nor peasants moved to rebellion by the 'Imperishable Heroism' of Garibaldi that Italy had been united, but by strategems in the field of diplomacy and war, that is by an exploitation of the 'artichoke', one leaf at a time, policy of dynastic expansion by Piedmont under the leadership of Cavour. Cavour himself was an ambiguous figure, whose modern interest in railways, steamships and agricultural improvements concealed a traditional adherence to many of the credos of a Piedmontese aristocrat. Cavour's definition of war as something which could readily be started and, as easily, stopped, owed much to lingering feudal aristocratic assumptions which had been rendered old-fashioned by the mass participation in Revolution and War from 1789 to 1815. The new Italy, rather like the new Germany, was united by blood and iron, although Cavour's manipulations concealed this fact, and the fact that it was largely the blood and iron of Frenchmen (and Austrians), and not that of Italians, which cemented the Italian state.

Italy, the least of the Great Powers

In the conjuror's hat bequeathed to Italy by its Founder could be discovered not only war, but also treaties made and not made, royal marriages, financial interests, utopian ideals and a large dose of good fortune. Some of Cavour's successors were intelligent and sceptical enough to see that war and good fortune could not always be so readily fused. Depretis' commonsense instructed him to remember: 'Whenever I see an international crisis on the horizon I open my umbrella and wait till it passes.'[3] But commonsense was usually diluted by 'realism' which, invoking Cavour and sometimes also Machiavelli, declared that any achievement was possible if you were sufficiently adroit or lucky. Nitti, that 'new democrat' of 1919, had discovered that international formulas of morality were various, but that, in reality, there was only one that mattered: 'whoever loses is in the wrong'.[4] Cavour had transmitted to his successors, both for foreign and domestic affairs, the lesson that, if the pack was shuffled often or covertly enough, a winning combination would turn up which would be all that was needed until someone else started shuffling. This 'realism', sometimes dressed up under the fancy name of 'amoral familism',[5] lies at the base of much Italian political behaviour before 1945, and even after.

The style and nature of the Risorgimento therefore decreed that Italy would be confronted by a constant gap between appearance and reality, rhetoric and achievement, a gap which could only be denied by a deep-seated cynicism and dishonesty. Italy's inheritance was further blemished from outside. The false 'national revolution' was accompanied by a false 'international revolution' which accorded Italy the status and duties of a Great Power, however unable her armies, her economy and her social and national unity were to bear that burden.

Two factors alone defended Italy's title as a Great Power: her numbers, a population which had reached 35 million by 1912, and her history, or, at least, the history of that 'geographical expression', Italy. By any other criteria, Italy's role from 1860 to 1914 had more in common with that of a small Balkan State or a colony than a Great Power. Even after a decade of considerable economic expansion from 1896 to 1907, Italy's economic indices cannot bear comparison with those of genuine Great Powers. The peninsula was almost entirely lacking in supplies of coal, the basic fuel of industrialisation. By 1914, Italy's annual production was less than one million tons as against Germany's 277 million, Britain's 292 million and even Austria–Hungary's 47 million tons. The development of hydro-electricity was beginning to provide some answer to Italy's energy needs, especially in the North; but hydroelectricity could not fuel the Italian Navy nor much aid the Italian railways in their transport duties in war-time. Shortly before the First World War, almost 88% of Italian energy requirements were met by coal, against the 3.4% provided by hydroelectricity. Great Britain provided 90% of that coal[6] and therefore had a rarely stated, but frequently understood, stranglehold on Italy's ultimate diplomatic options. The elder von Moltke had laid down the dictum: 'Build no more fortresses, build railways', but railways required coal, and Italian experimentation in electrified railways before 1914 extended only to a few lines of industrial rather than strategic use, around Genoa and Milan. It was still coal-powered steam trains which would haul Italian troops to fight on the Entente side along Italy's north-eastern borders after 1915.[7]

Even when Britain sent her coal to Italy, railways did not drive Italy to a firm station among the Great Powers. The network of Italian railways was still incomplete in 1914. Moreover, railways had to combat the difficult terrain of the peninsula and were vulnerable to a gamut of natural disasters from flood to earthquake. The haphazard, foreign-financed history of much railway construction also reduced the potential military value of Italy's lines. Many, in the key north-eastern sector, as in the rest of the country, were only single-track, able to be traversed slowly and uncertainly by antiquated rolling-stock.[8] In war-time, bottlenecks would be certain. No wonder, in spite of von Moltke's dictum, that Italian strategists in 1914 were still dreaming of the completion of fortresses along the Austrian border.

In contrast to her nugatory coal resources, Italy did possess some iron deposits, notably on the island of Elba, and the Italian government soon comprehended the economic and strategic imperative to exploit these. State backing was granted to the iron and steel industry, especially in the famous works near Terni.[9] Yet Terni was an odd site on which to base a major industrial development. Located in the Umbrian countryside, far from enemy naval guns, from supplies and from customers, not even on the main North–South rail-link, Terni was costly and inefficient. Close contacts

3

with the state and politics rapidly created a structure of *sottogoverno* which sometimes made it hard to detect whether the industry's *raison d'être* was to produce iron and steel or to digest government subsidies. Perhaps corruption and incompetence were more a product than a cause of under-development, but, for whatever reason, in 1913 Italy's iron and steel production was one-eighth that of Britain, one-seventeenth that of Germany, and only two-fifths that of Belgium. So far from fully utilising her meagre mineral resources, Italy actually exported a considerable portion of them. A feather-bedded heavy industry did little to stiffen the sinews of war, and although government expenditure on armaments doubled in the two decades before 1914, gross defence expenditure remained chronically less than that of any Great Power, even Austria–Hungary.[10]

Italy's financial situation was no more secure, being afflicted externally by balance of payments deficits with all her major European trading partners, and internally by low levels of liquidity and serious institutional weakness. The Italian economy was propped up only by the invisible assets earned by tourism and emigrants' remittances, factors giving little credit in the international economic system and likely to be cut short altogether if ever there was general war. Inside Italy, the rickety banking structure collapsed entirely in the scandals of the 1890s and was re-erected only through German patronage, which, to some, signalled a further abandonment of Italian independence.

Social indices were equally depressing. In 1911 Italy's illiteracy rate was 37.6% overall, and far greater in the backward regions of the South. Life expectancy was lower than in any major countries except Hungary and Russia, and pellagra and malaria still devastated much of the countryside. Most graphic of all was the problem of emigration. In 1913 almost 873,000 Italians, about one-fortieth of the total population, left the country, the majority for the Americas. This national inability usefully to occupy these emigrants, who were often the most able and independent of the poor, was a further testimony to the limitations in Italy's industrial development. In 1911 employment in 'industry' was less than half that in agriculture, and most industries were small-scale, local, and even familial concerns. Naples, with its almost wholly traditional social structure, was Italy's largest city in that year of the *Cinquantennio*, the

4

celebration of the fiftieth anniversary of the Risorgimento in 1911. Even after all the growth of the Giolittian decade Italy, by any serious standards, was not the economic equal of the other Great Powers.

It was only Austria–Hungary, one of the 'sick men' of Europe, to which reasonable Italian ambition in 1914 could strive one day to equal, but for the moment even Austria had a salutary lead over Italy in most matters. Typical was the 'naval race' between the 'two Adriatic Powers' in the last years before the war. Austria began building two Dreadnoughts at Trieste in the summer of 1910 and was able to launch one in 1911, and the other in 1912. Italy had begun constructing her first Dreadnought, the *Dante Alighieri*, in 1909, but it was not completed until 1913.[11] During the war, despite the crippling losses and incredible incompetencies experienced on the Eastern Front,[12] Austria was able to hold her own militarily with Italy until November 1918. Performance in World War One indicated that Italy was no equal match even for Austria–Hungary, which was easily the weakest of the other Great Powers.

Despite all these figures, and despite Italy's consistently disastrous military record, European statesmen went on talking as though Italy were a Great Power. 'The Concert of the Great Powers', which, notwithstanding its formal demise under Metternich, continued until 1914 to act as a *de facto* steering body for world international affairs, always accorded Italy membership. No international conference could be held without an Italian delegation. If a Great Power force was needed for police duties in Macedonia or Crete, then Italy would be invited as a possible member. Furthermore, when alliances and ententes became the fashion, then Italy was a possible member of this side or that. In the Spring of 1915, most extraordinary of all, many a European statesman awaited with bated breath Italy's 'decisive' intervention in the Great War.

It may readily be admitted that an over-estimation of Italian strength and importance was the most constant factor in European diplomacy from 1860 to 1915 and beyond. It is less easy to find an explanation. Perhaps it was a matter of custom. If your neighbour treated Italy seriously, if Italy sat among the Great, then she must indeed be Great. But also of great significance was Italian history. Every European statesman was nurtured on the classics, on the 'greatness that was Rome'. Most statesmen also desired to be as cultured as possible, and knew that modern culture had begun in the Renaissance, that Florence and Venice had been Europe's most splendid towns, one the seat of an artistic empire, the other the fount of commercial growth and perhaps of modern politics. Conservatives and imperialists alike aimed to recreate new Roman Empires for their own countries. Liberals hoped that modern Progress would develop in their countries a civilisation that might equal that of Florence or Venice.

As young men on the grand tour, and later on holidays, many European statesmen were wealthy enough to visit Italy; to philosophise over the ruins of the Capitol, to find their souls uplifted by Michelangelos or Fra Lippo Lippis, to emerge from the gloom, the power and the puritanism of the North into the 'bright light' of the South.

But this sort of interest in Italy was only another *dannosa hereditas* as far as Italy's role as a Great Power was concerned. For among the ruins and art treasures there also unfortunately lurked modern day Italians, poor, dirty, often importunate, at best merely unreasonably cheerful. The young Theobald von Bethmann Hollweg, a little earnestly and laboriously, summed up the feelings of two generations of travellers to Italy: to be in Rome for two months was 'simply splendid';

It is indescribable what magic hovers over the walls of this eternal city! The great historical past that one encounters at every step through the magnificent ruins imbues everything with a seriousness and a dignity which contrasts poignantly with the life of the present Italian people, and especially with the intrigues of the Catholic Church.

Bethmann was not offended by

this contradiction; it rather lets one feel all the suffering and joy of this world without a touch of sentimentality...The most precious gain one can bring home from Italy is that one learns to suppress sentimentality before the majesty of history and nature.[13]

Experience appeared to demonstrate what racial theory and popular culture was already saying. In the South was Beauty and the Past, but also corruption, backwardness, inferiority; Death in Venice, or Florence, or Rome.

These sorts of sentiments perhaps explain why, running alongside a diplomatic over-estimation, there was very often a profound contempt, as if there was a half-realisation by a statesman of his own error in continuing to treat Italy as a Great Power. Sir Charles Hardinge, fresh from his experiences as Viceroy of India, minced no words in assessing the Italians' role at the Versailles Conference in 1919:

Their incapacity and vanity are extraordinary...they are, in my opinion, the most odious colleagues and allies to have at a Conference...'the beggars of Europe' are well known for their whining alternated by truculence.[14]

Lord Salisbury, a generation earlier, had varied his definition of Italy between 'sturdy beggars' and 'the *quantité négligeable*'. Bismarck had coined the dictum: 'As to Italy, she does not count.'[15] The younger von Moltke told his wife that the Italians who had 'once dominated the world' now were 'a gang of thieves and beggars'.[16] Even Sir Edward Grey grew witty when, in 1909, he minuted on a report of Italian dalliance with Russia that the Italians were 'the blue-bottle flies of international politics: always buzzing when one wants to be quiet. Happily they do not stay.'[17] For many a European statesman the Italians could never be relied to live up to their past, or even, ironically, to their present.

This irritation produced by the separation of past and present, theory and practice, was in turn aroused among the Italians themselves, most famously before 1914 in the intellectuals of the Futurist movement. Marinetti's manifesto proclaimed:

Daily visits to museums, libraries and academies (those cemeteries of wasted effort, calvaries of crucified dreams, registers of false starts!) are for artists what prolonged supervision by the parents is for intelligent young men, drunk with their own talent and ambition...Let the good incendiaries with charred fingers come! Here they are! Heap up the fire to the shelves of the libraries! Divert the canals to flood the cellars of the museums! Let the glorious canvases swim ashore! Take the picks and hammers! Undermine the foundation of venerable towns!'[18]

But intellectual phrase-makers were not the only ones who felt this way. In one of the most important parliamentary speeches shortly before the Libyan War, Francesco Guicciardini, an ex-Foreign Minister, complained that foreigners merely admired 'our sky, our countryside, our cities'. To end this humiliation, he said, Italy must 'less invite the holiday spirit' and be 'more respected'.[19] The British ambassador, Sir James Rennell Rodd, detected in this kind of language an 'adolescent' hyper-sensitivity. As a 'friend of Italy', he found it natural to ascribe Italy's 'inferiority complex' to her growing pains.[20] But neither he, nor anyone else, was very ready to learn when and how adolescence turned into manhood.

For Italian politicians, the sensitivity and self-defensiveness encouraged by Italy's international reputation and record, were made harder to bear by the nature of Italian history. Venetians and Florentines sometimes dreamed of restoring their version of an empire, but all Italy was dogged by the 'universality' that was Rome.[21] No sooner had Italian troops stormed the Porta Pia on 20 September 1870, than Italian politicians began to meditate on the need to find a universal mission which could justify the occupation of the Eternal City. The men of the 1870s searched idealistically and naively for an amalgam of rationality and anti-clericalism which might offer Science and Progress to all humanity.[22] This quest for the universal was endorsed by the Heroes of the Risorgimento: Mazzini had prophesied that 'after the Rome of the Emperors, after the Rome of the Popes, there will come the Rome of the People'; as late as 1874 Garibaldi could be heard to say that

Rome was and will be until the end, the ideal of my whole life...the Roman eagle is no more the symbol of conquest but of work, progress and civilisation.[23]

The august purity of this ideal was soon stained by reality. The 'Third Italy' was not of the people but of the elite who had won out in the *rivoluzione mancata*. The 'Third Rome' owed what progress it made to land speculation and to the growth of its inimitable bureaucracy. Soon words like 'progress' and 'civilisation' merged into words like 'power' and 'international prestige'. Public architecture, said Crispi, must express the spirit of the 'new Rome' so that 'later generations can say that we were great as our forefathers were'.[24] The new Ministry of Justice and the Victor Emmanuel monument were made massy, solid, indestructible. Especially the latter, positioned beneath the ruins of the Capitol, to oversee the ruins of the Forum, proclaimed the inheritance from classical Rome.[25] As once the legions had carried power, so now should the 'Third Italy'. By the 1880s, in imitation of the other Powers, to divert domestic pressure, but also because of the fact of Rome and its history, Italy had betrayed its Mazzinian inheritance and had begun to practice or plot an imperial course. It was the occupation of Rome, the idea of the 'Third Italy' which helped to explain why Crispi's imperialism was so 'passionate, oratorical, without any economic or financial basis'.[26]

Italy's birthright, from the Risorgimento and the decades which followed, was therefore to play out the role of a Great Power, however unfitted she was for that role, either economically or socially. Indeed, to be a Great Power, to have a foreign policy, in the end to be imperialist, became one of the chief *raisons d'être* of the post-Risorgimento State. If Italy could not act as a Great Power, if the falsity of Italy's diplomatic pretensions was revealed, so also might be the falsity of the 'national revolution' at home. If this happened, then Italy might have to be 'made' again, and that could only occur by social revolution.

To act out the role of a Great Power while lacking the means was a most intricate exercise, which could lead easily to embarrassment, humiliation and perhaps worse. Reflecting these problems, Italian foreign policy became intricate, confused, complex, the most unreliable of any European State. The first assumption of the rulers of the new Italy was that they must carry on Cavour's diplomatic campaigns against Austria, the hated *tedeschi* of all text-book accounts of the Risorgimento. For the Risorgimento even after 1870 was incomplete. Italian-speakers, however unenthusiastic they might be about eventual inclusion in Italy, lived in the Habsburg cities of Trieste and Trent and must be 'redeemed'. This thread of Austro-Italian antagonism was soon knotted by domestic doubts and problems. The most ardent advocates of renewed diplomatic and military victory against Austria were precisely the Mazzinians and Garibaldinians whose idealism had been most blighted by the social reality of the Risorgimento. The patriotic excitement, the very national unity, at least in the North, which could be inspired by a war against Austria, let alone the lesson taught in the Paris Commune (and repeated in Russia in 1905) that defeat in war brought social revolution, meant that a contest against Austria, unless cleverly managed, would advantage radicals and republicans, and not the Italy of the House of Savoy.

The South of the new Italy was unimpressed by the idea that Austria was the eternal enemy. The traditional agrarians who had been allowed to keep so much of their power in this region after the Risorgimento (and of whom Antonino Paternò Castello Di San

Giuliano, the major figure in this study, is a fine example) disliked France much more. It was the French who had brought revolution to the 'happy realm' of King Ferdinand IV in 1796. It was in France that there had occurred the terrible Commune, where the spectre of socialism was given flesh, and where peasants and not agrarians owned the land. It was the 'garden of France' whose agricultural products competed most uncompromisingly with the crops of Naples and Sicily. To the new generation of Southerners also, to the lawyers and middle men themselves a pre-industrial rather than a modern middle class, with whom aristocratic Leopards had been forced to share power, France was equally the most obvious enemy in the new game of imperialism. It was France which, in Algeria, Tunisia and Morocco, took for herself the largest and the choicest parts of North Africa, that area which Italian rhetoric already declared must be the '*quarta sponda*', the 'fourth shore' and, in Tunisia, the very seat of Carthage. Thus the Southerners, who were soon to discover that they possessed native abilities which could be exploited in the political life and the bureaucracy of the new state, usually carried with them to Rome the belief that, if Italy was to have an enemy in international affairs, then that enemy was France.[27]

In the decades after 1860, France and Austria became the two poles around which Italy's diplomacy operated, and San Giuliano summed up much about Italian diplomacy in September 1914 when he remarked cynically, but a little wistfully, to a friendly journalist: 'The ideal for us is that Austria should be beaten on the one hand and France on the other.'[28]

If these were the hopes and ideals of Italian diplomacy, military, diplomatic and domestic realities usually added a strong dose of caution. After France seized Tunis in 1881, the next year Italy associated herself in defensive alliance with Germany and Austria, forming the famous Triple Alliance. Successively renewed, the alliance was still in existence in 1914, although its strength was tempered by the implications of the dictum that Italy and Austria must be 'either allies or enemies'. Its value in war as distinct from peacetime diplomacy was rendered highly dubious by many features of Italy's strategic, economic and social character. Moreover, tantalising and difficult of resolution was the famous Article vII, added to the Treaty in 1891, and pledging 'reciprocal compensation for every advantage, territorial or other...giving satisfaction to the interests and well-founded claims of the two Parties' in any alteration of the *status quo* 'in the regions of the Balkans or of the Ottoman coasts and islands in the Adriatic and in the Aegean Sea'.[29] The phrase about 'interests and well-founded claims', from an Italian viewpoint, contained obvious potential reference to Trento and Trieste and made it likely that, whatever factors worked in the other direction, Italian diplomatists would neither want, nor be allowed, to forget that the Risorgimento was incomplete, and that there might come a time when it would be rewarding for Italy to stop being Austria's ally and become her enemy instead.

While there was no war between the Great Powers, Trento and Trieste were left in Austrian hands, and Italy could try her fortune at pursuing the course of imperialism in Africa. In 1885 the Southerner, Mancini, ordered the occupation of Massawa, a port on the Red Sea. It was a poor and dusty beginning, where not even the standard of a Roman legion could be re-discovered, but Massawa was a beginning permitted by the other Great Powers, and a centre for expansion into what would become the colony of Eritrea. On the other side of the Horn of Africa private companies sowed around Assab the seeds of Italian interest which finally bore somewhat arid fruit as the colony of Somaliland in 1905.[30]

The most notorious early Italian example of imperialism was the Sicilian Crispi's effort, in the decade after 1887, to acquire Italian over-lordship of Ethiopia. A gradually deeper involvement in colonial war was accompanied by a tariff campaign against France, and a demagogic attack on the 'social peril' in Italy, as exemplified most flagrantly in the peasant unions, the *fasci* of Sicily. Crispi's recipe, however dated and careless in execution, and however unrealistic in its assumption that Italian peasants could settle the Ethiopian high-lands, and thereby be saved from misery and socialism, was surprisingly successful politically, in the short term. As so often in European states before 1914, and as the fate of the Second International in 1914 would demonstrate so tellingly, many Italian socialists felt the seductive allure of colonialism, power politics and patriotism, and could be induced not to oppose the 'national interest' with too rigid an intransigence.[31]

However the promise of social collaboration or international respect won by imperialism was betrayed by the disaster at Adowa on 1 March 1896. The ambition of Crispi's Italy had outrun both its means and its purpose; foreigners sneered knowingly and socialists regained their internationalist virtue when a force of 16,500 men was routed by the Ethiopians under their Emperor Menelik. Six thousand Italian soldiers died in one battle, more than in all the wars of the Risorgimento, and it was comforting to Italian mothers but not to Italian honour or prestige that many of them were *ascaris*, black troops from Eritrea.

Crispi fell, in disgrace, and Adowa imposed a re-assessment of foreign ambition. Eritrea was taken out of military hands and placed under civilian rule, and there was talk of abandoning it altogether.[32] Emilio Visconti Venosta, a pure blooded Piedmontese who was the lineal heir of Cavour (and the Alfieris and the Solaros), returned to office for the first time since 1876 as Foreign Minister. To him fell the congenial task of austere retrenchment, signalled by the end of both the diplomatic and economic contest with France. Domestically, Adowa had produced deep fissures which threatened to tumble down the entire Savoyard system. In 1898 King Umberto I was driven to appoint as Prime Minister a General, Pelloux, who declared that Italy must 'return to the Constitution' granted by Charles-Albert in 1848. A more modern interpretation of Pelloux's reactionary administration from 1898 to 1900 says that it attempted a 'bourgeois coup d'état'.[33]

However, with the fall of Pelloux's second government in June 1900, and the subsequent assassination of King Umberto on 29 July, reaction seemed to have failed, and Italian history to have passed an important turning-point. In 1901 Giolitti became Minister of the Interior in a new government led by Zanardelli and for the next decade under moderate governments Italy became ostensibly 'a democracy in the making'.[34]

In international affairs the Giolittian decade was one of peace and quiet. Giolitti himself, a master of domestic manipulation, perhaps a genuine conservative reformer and certainly a politician intelligent enough to change things so things could remain just about the same, was at heart a parochial Piedmontese, little interested either in Southern Italy which he visited only once, or in Europe where he travelled for repose or financial advantage. His published papers[35] show that until 1911 he paid almost no attention to foreign policy, unless, as in 1908–9, interest was forced on him by an international crisis. His Foreign Minister after 1903, Tommaso Tittoni, was selected for essentially domestic reasons, as a link man in Giolitti's efforts to wean the Catholic Church from its official hostility to the Liberal State.[36] That Tittoni had contacts with Vatican-backed high finance in the Banco di Roma was naturally also useful.

There was some substance to these changes to Italy's international behaviour under the cool, competent and steadfast Giolitti, but, in any profound or long-term sense, Adowa had produced merely another *rivoluzione mancata*. When economic expansion faltered after 1907, it was soon apparent that the Italian ruling class had not surrendered the desire to give flesh to Italy's role as a Great Power, to take up the inheritance of Rome, to divert the social peril. So important and so powerful did this desire become that in 1911 Giolitti, who, nine years earlier had threatened to resign if Prinetti, the impetuous Foreign Minister, tried to seize Libya, was himself forced or persuaded to lead Italy into colonial war. The explanation of this event, and of the expansionist foreign policy which continued until 1914, is the major task of this book.

According to Article Five of the Italian Constitution, it was the King of Italy who retained ultimate authority over foreign affairs and, from 1900, the King was Victor Emmanuel III. Vittorio Emanuele Ferdinando Maria Gennaro was born, as his last three names might indicate, in Naples on 11 November 1869. Tiny, repressed, malicious and mean, Victor Emmanuel, was married in October 1896 to Elena, the tall, bloomingly handsome daughter of Prince Nicola of Montenegro. It was a match, said Victor Emmanuel's mother, 'for the good of the dynasty'. After his father's assassination, King Victor Emmanuel III reigned through momentous years for Italy until his characteristically begrudged abdication in 1946. The role of this king has been the object of much historiographical controversy, not so much because in 1915, 1922, 1924 and 1943, Victor Emmanuel intervened (as the Constitution allowed him to do) in Italian politics but because on each occasion he did so on the conservative side, and always with unfortunate results. These interventions have supported allegations that the King was the hidden hand behind much Italian policy, especially in foreign affairs.

More evidence may be revealed if ever the Savoy archives are made public, but, at the moment, it seems that the famous self-control[37] of Victor Emmanuel usually concealed not so much

13

a devious Machiavellian mind as a sullen sense of honour and inadequacy, an almost total pessimism and misanthropy. Victor Emmanuel disliked wars, at least in their early stages, because he needed time to gear up his sense of duty to withstand the dangers of defeat and revolution, and the humiliation of public appearances in uniform. Doubtless he knew that the possession of but a grain of wit could encourage his subjects to pun about their King's 'stature'.[38] In October 1911 the King was reported to be 'glum' at the early progress of the Libyan War. In August 1914 he was close to a nervous breakdown with scandal-mongers ascribing his problems variously to the Queen's pregnancy, to 'neurasthenia', 'meningitis', or 'attacks of madness and similar things'.[39]

The King preferred to keep distant from the political hustle of Rome, spending much of his time on his estates at Castelporziano or in Piedmont. In 1910 it was reported that he only visited the capital twice a week.[40] In peacetime diplomacy his interventions were almost entirely conventional, as though he reflected ruling class opinion rather than ruling himself. Typical is the fact that his most openly critical comment to San Giuliano from 1910 to 1914 occurred immediately after Austria published the Hohenlohe decrees which, in 1913, struck at the rights of Italians within the Habsburg Empire. Like most of Italian public opinion, Victor Emmanuel was reminded that whatever value had been gained from cooperation within the Triple Alliance, 'a concert' in the Mediterranean 'with France and England' was Italy's most basic diplomatic requirement.[41] Anti-clerical, bourgeois in his tastes and habits, Victor Emmanuel was too much a citizen of Liberal Italy, in the last analysis, to prefer that ministers dabble in combinations too exotic or intricate rather than concentrating on the more proper policy aim of completing the Risorgimento. In these public moments the King resembles an identikit image of a good, if rather narrow-minded, Giolittian. There is no need to change traditional adjectives and refer to the *età vittorio emanueleana*.

Before embracing this conclusion too enthusiastically it should be noted that much royal influence existed, but in a covert or indirect way. The privacy of a royal audience or the advice of a member of the royal entourage could reveal royal preferences, which were especially powerful in the area of patronage and appointment. King Victor Emmanuel III usually exerted this responsibility in a somewhat perfunctory manner, but, even in his reign, a Foreign Minister was unlikely not to be *persona grata* at court. Tittoni engaged the Ferdinando Maria Gennaro side of the King's sympathies while prefect in Naples; San Giuliano, the *vicerè* from Sicily, may also have appealed to Victor Emmanuel's liking for the South; while that statesman's anti-clericalism, public cynicism, and the fact that both his wife and his daughter-in-law were royal ladies-in-waiting, ought also to have warmed his relationship with the King. Not that royal sympathy necessarily was converted into royal gratitude. After Tittoni's fall from the Foreign Ministry, for example, Victor Emmanuel did not hesitate to make spiteful comments about Tittoni's clericalism and financial dealings.[42]

Royal patronage did not only derive from the King, for there was also an extensive and often ambitious royal family. Victor Emmanuel's queen, Elena, was a good-natured if dull figure, significant only because her Montenegrin birth allowed Italian contacts, especially financial, with Montenegro. More important were the cadet branches of the Savoys, of whom the most famous was Emanuele Filiberto, Duke of Aosta.[43] Nine months older than his cousin, Aosta did everything earlier and better. Tall, handsome, a soldier and explorer, Aosta was married not to a Montenegrin but to a Bourbon of France, and had two sturdy sons before Victor Emmanuel and Elena could conceive a daughter. He was a patron of Nationalist movements, and was strongly rumoured in 1922 to be aiming at replacing his cousin as King. It is doubtful if Victor Emmanuel, who was a good hater, hated anyone more than the Duke of Aosta.

Additionally, there were Aosta's two brothers, of whom one, the Duke of the Abruzzi, made a brilliant naval career, and a half-brother. Descended from Ferdinand, Duke of Genoa, the brother of King Victor Emmanuel II, there was another wing of the Savoy dynasty represented by a number of young princes, the Prince of Udine, and the Dukes of Pistoia, Bergamo and Ancona. The most publicly influential member of the dynasty was a woman, Margherita, who was the daughter of this Duke of Genoa and who had married her cousin, King Umberto, in another example both of the parochialism of Piedmont and of Italy's low status on the royal marriage market. Margherita diverted the frustrations of her marriage with the mechanical King Umberto into illuminating intellectual salons.

There she learned from Carducci or D'Annunzio, or perhaps she had always understood, that socialism was 'an organised brigandage on a vast scale all over Europe'.[44] Margherita, who made no secret of the fact that she found her son pathetic and Elena boring, kept distant from most court activities, but her open contempt for parliament and democracy, and her enthusiasm for imperialism were a constant personal pressure on Victor Emmanuel not to become too ardent a maker of a peaceful and democratic Italy.[45]

One of the major questions about the Savoys relates to their financial operations, but unfortunately most evidence so far in this respect is indirect. The family did carry off a fair fortune in 1946, and before 1914 they and their agents seem to have been involved in dubious enterprises abroad, in Montenegro, Egypt and perhaps Turkey, which may have had some influence on foreign policy. One minor but documented example of royal interest is uncovered by the fashion in which the Italian Foreign Ministry sprang into action in 1910–11 in order to try to regain for the Savoys the fortune of Maria Pia, the Queen Mother of Portugal, whose large estate, it was feared, would attract sequestration from the revolutionary republican government in Lisbon.[46]

Apart from those concerning the royal family, there are also many questions to be asked about the influence of the royal entourage. Urbano Rattazzi, the Minister of the Royal Household, is seen by many to have been the political king-maker of the 1890s, and even the hand behind the bank scandals. King Victor Emmanuel III's *uomo di fiducia* seems, by 1910, to have been his Adjutant-General, Ugo Brusati. Brusati's papers are available at the *Archivio Centrale*, and are a mine of information. They are full of the detail of military affairs, a good indication that Victor Emmanuel took seriously his role as Italy's Commander-in-Chief, however ill-at-ease he was while publicly astride a horse.[47] The King was criticised for not involving himself more actively in the Libyan War, but, after 1915, he would certainly do his best to prove to himself, to his cousin and to the Italian people that Victor Emmanual III was a genuine *re soldato*.

All in all, an analysis of the court's role in the making of Italian foreign policy is a little inconclusive. Victor Emmanuel lacked the panache of William II, and the authority of Franz Joseph, although he was perhaps as devoted as the latter to his bureaucratic desk. One authority describes Victor Emmanuel reading newspapers for three hours every day, pedantically noting down any inaccuracies which he found in them.[48] Signs of positive interventions by him into foreign affairs are rare. Rather, Victor Emmanuel's influence, and that of his family and entourage, was mostly a matter of unspoken assumptions, of an implicit rather than explicit exercising of power.

The chief assumption was a lingering belief, held by almost all members of the ruling elite, in the royal prerogative in international affairs, an assertion that diplomacy was 'above politics'. Foreign Ministers or diplomats should not be radicals, but should be skilled in the traditional arts of the courtier, and, more importantly, should never think too differently from the more conservative section of the ruling classes, and therefore from the court. In the decade after 1896 none of this mattered very much as foreign policy became less immediately decisive than domestic changes and economic growth. But, after 1910, as the Giolittian system fell into crisis, as the more conservative heirs of the Risorgimento grew increasingly alarmed by the 'social peril', and began anxiously to search for diplomatic and even military solutions to domestic problems, so the royal Establishment and authoritarian traditions of foreign policy making regained their significance. In 1911–12 Italy could still try to wage a colonial war on the cheap, and pretend or hope that royal prestige and the institutions of the Savoy state were not totally involved; but after 1915, that group of conservatives which was mainly responsible for Italy's entry into the First World War irremediably linked monarchical institutions to the war. There were, after all, more than personal reasons why Victor Emmanuel abandoned Giolitti for Salandra, and left the royal coin-collections to become the *re soldato*.

If the Constitution allowed the King great powers, which he did not always directly use in practice, the other great centres of authority in the Italian Liberal system, the Prime Minister, the Foreign Minister, the Cabinet, the Senate and the Chamber of Deputies, also hedged in their practice of diplomacy with some ambiguities. The parliament, notably, had severe limitations on its power.[49] For example, it was adjourned both through the months of preparation of the Libyan War, and in the period from the July Crisis to the death of San Giuliano. Debates on foreign affairs were not frequent, and it was expected that they would be couched in gentlemanly language, making obeisance to phrases like 'continuity', 'in the national interest', 'above politics'. Deputies or Senators who spoke on foreign affairs were a select group, and were not expected to push Ministers too hard.

This sense of decorum was threatened in 1913 by the election of five Nationalist deputies, led by Luigi Federzoni, who were willing, and indeed eager, to ask embarrassing public questions. Unused to this variety of impertinence, San Giuliano, in the next months was often flurried by the prospect of having to collect information in order to placate Federzoni and his friends.[50] It was an unlooked for development that this new variety of conservative and monarchist would be sufficiently unpatriotic to probe publicly the government's definition of 'national interest'. This sort of behaviour in the past had been restricted to irredentists, radicals and republicans, parliamentary riff-raff who could not be expected to understand the polite norms of diplomacy.

To deny parliament as a forum where decisions were made in Liberal Italy, is not to declare that parliamentarians did not exercise influence over the making of foreign policy. Rather, within the rules of the Liberal system, and among that small elite which were recognised competent to deal with international affairs, a contest about, and analysis of foreign policy did occur. Parliamentary speeches and whispers in parliamentary corridors by members of the opposition, or, more often, by politicians who were out of office but were willing to be 'transformed' into it, could and did have a considerable impact. During his period in office, San Giuliano had to resist major, if courtly attacks on his policy in November–December 1910, June 1911 and July–August 1914. Thus however docile and manageable the parliament was in appearance, it would be an unwise Foreign Minister who did not keep a sense of its opinions.

By comparison with the parliament, the role of the Cabinet in the making of foreign policy was still more shadowy. Ministers responsible for Posts and Telegraphs or Public Works were often neither socially, intellectually nor even ideologically admissible into the elite of the elite which might address itself to foreign affairs. Liberal Cabinets, assembled by the traditional methods of *trasformismo*, had little sense of collective responsibility. Ministers functioned very much as individuals, impressed far more by their bureaucratic staff or their Prime Minister than by their Cabinet colleagues. The sense of continuity, of royal authority, of being 'above politics', made this all the more true in the field of foreign affairs. Tittoni and San Giuliano (at least until March 1914) were accustomed to be the most conservative members of reforming cabinets. San Giuliano, in return, paid almost no formal attention to domestic affairs, except in the summer of 1914 when his training under Giolitti perhaps stimulated him to urge moderation on Salandra during the social crisis of the *settimana rossa*. From 1910 to 1914 San Giuliano's contact with his Cabinet colleagues was perfunctory. After the foundation of the Ministry of Colonies in 1912, he naturally favoured the Foreign Ministry's cause in demarcation disputes with that new and upstart Ministry; occasionally, too, he had contact with the Army and Navy Ministers, but he was never at pains to keep them or their Chiefs of Staff abreast of the intricacies of Italian diplomacy, and he devoted similarly little attention to fitting Italian diplomacy into the 'realities' of Italy's military or naval preparedness. Though he often addressed himself to the Minister of the Treasury, he usually did so reproachfully, asking why secret funds had not been handed over more gracefully or freehandedly. It was only to be predicted that the Ministers of the Treasury would in turn resent these requests so that, on a number of occasions, Prime Ministers were forced to adjudicate between the importunities of the Foreign Minister and the good-housekeeping of the Minister of the Treasury.

The other major relationship between the Foreign Minister and his Cabinet colleagues, and indeed with other deputies and Senators, was based on the shadier questions of patronage and influence. The archives of both the Foreign Minister and his Under-Secretary are filled with requests for jobs, or deals, or simple *raccomandazioni*, from all kinds of colleagues and friends.[51] No doubt the same is true of the papers of many other politicians who played their part or sought their reward in the history of Italy after 1860.

In these circumstances, enormous potential power lay with the man who assembled the Cabinets, who chose the Foreign Minister; that is, with the Prime Minister, Giovanni Giolitti, the man labelled, unfairly but with some justification, the 'parliamentary dictator' of Italy.[52] War is often the best test of real authority in a country, a test which the German Reichstag failed so dismally from 1914 to 1918. When there was war involving Italy, in Libya from 1911 to 1912, it was Giolitti's power which stood starkly above that of the

King or of the parliament or even of San Giuliano. Although in peacetime Giolitti allowed San Giuliano much latitude, even then, at difficult moments, it was likely either that the Prime Minister would intervene directly or that he would distance himself from San Giuliano, who would then no longer be 'Giolitti's Foreign Minister' but merely another politician for whom a replacement could readily be found. On the other hand, when Giolitti was out of office, and when from March to October 1914 San Giuliano served under Salandra whose power base was most insecure, then the Foreign Minister, strong in his experience and his continued support both from Giolitti and the King, could manifest remarkable personal independence. The power of the Prime Minister therefore was not dependent so much on the office as on its usage. Giolitti's immense authority sprang both from the influence constructed in government and *sottogoverno* during two decades of labour and manipulation, and from Giolitti's undeniable perspicacity and staying power, qualities admitted even by the misanthropic King.[53] 'Dictator' however is not a fair word with which to typify Giolitti who in many ways was growing somewhat old-fashioned in his methods and beliefs by 1914. His very devotion to parliament, to the needs and ideas of lawyers, small-town journalists and intellectuals, of prefects, bureaucrats, and of union officials was not easily tailored to an age of the masses. Even his control and corruption techniques were becoming a little naive and parsimonious for a country granted near universal suffrage. Some demonstration of these failings in the Giolittian system can be seen in the way in which so much of the major press, and the most prestigious intelligentsia, had rejected *giolittismo* by 1914. Parliamentary majorities were no longer a certain base for power as Liberal Italy was confronted by the crisis of World War I. All Giolitti's skills had been unable to repair the gap between politics and society in Liberal Italy, and it was those groups in society which were most anxious to find new or adapted answers to old questions confronting Italy, who were dreaming of relegating Giolitti to the attic of history.

The most obvious alternate source of power to the parliamentary system was the armed forces, that is, the officer corps of the Navy and, more importantly, the Army. Although Italy panted a long way behind, the least of the Great Powers, in gross expenditure on the armaments' race, in the years just before 1914 some 30% of the budget was directed to 'defence', to the Ministries of War and the

Navy.[54] It is no easy matter to understand precisely the role of the military in Liberal Italian society. Theoretically, the Army was 'above politics', loyal to the King and his institutions, but naturally there were other implications behind the simple honour of this phrase. The officer corps was very much a caste, cut off from most ordinary Italian politics and society. Often officers were themselves the sons of officers; pay was relatively low; social contacts were restricted, marriage while still a subaltern, for example, being regarded as a social and economic calamity.[55] Promotion was slow, training brutal and boring, and many officers took refuge from their vocation in alcohol.[56] There was little interest in modern techniques, and one officer complained that his colleagues retained an appropriate Latin distaste for sport, objecting to the demeaning effort of bicycling, and fencing only occasionally.[57]

The first officer corps of united Italy had been composed by officers from the Savoy, Bourbon and Habsburg armies, and regional background and loyalty continued after 1860. General Carlo Caneva, who in 1911 so cautiously commanded the Italian forces in Libya, had begun his career under the Habsburgs, and allegedly was stirred not so much by the thought of the *'patria'* as by his concept of 'the honour of the Army'.[58] Pollio, the Chief of General Staff from 1908 to 1914, was a Neapolitan. But the most powerful section of the officer corps was certainly the Piedmontese with its near, almost familial, relationship to the Savoy dynasty. If an officer wanted to reach the General Staff, it was said, he should be 'noble, blond and in the artillery'.[59] The most famous commanders, of whom three generations of Cadornas are the best example, and many Ministers of War, including Paolo Spingardi,[60] the colleague of San Giuliano from 1910 to 1914, were also Piedmontese.

Regionalism might affect the relations between one officer and another, but it was still more significant in the relationship between officers and men. *Campanilismo* sometimes meant that officers and men literally did not speak the same language, and illiteracy ensured that they did not read it either. Moreover the tradition of local postings to *caserme* scattered throughout the peninsula, preferably in a region which was not the officer's own (in the para-military *carabinieri* this was mandatory), did little to encourage much sympathy between officers and men, who in their several ways felt displaced, away from home, family and real life.[61] There also could be very real problems of translation. One officer spent time in his memoirs explaining the problems caused by the sanitary habits of a brigade from Potenza, delayed at Savona railway station – habits which provoked formal complaints from the mayor of Savona who regarded the men of Potenza as the near equivalent of the Huns or Vandals.[62] In order to overcome these regional complications, Italy's mobilisation plans aimed to prevent the formation of too many regional brigades, and, as a result, seven thousand one hundred trains were required to unite the scattered forces of the Italian Army.[63] Even so, military realities soon failed to share the mathematical precision of the planners, and after the battle of Caporetto, retreating soldiers from the capital of the 'Third Italy' reacted by shouting the ancient huzzah: 'Viva il Papa'.[64]

Mobilisation procedures held only the promise of chaos, but generally the morale of the officer corps was not high. The national military record did not excite optimism, even in colonial wars, and many officers were grateful that Europe was confronting 'an unending period of peace'.[65] It was also regrettable that politicians were not always sensitive to an officer's *amour propre*; in July 1911, for example, Giolitti made no effort to conceal his anger at the stupidity of a General Staff which selected for manoeuvres an insalubrious spot where soldiers fell easy victims to cholera.[66] Military incompetence also inspired a rare flash of wit from Giolitti when he explained that he had preferred Pollio to Cadorna as Chief of General Staff because he did not know Pollio, but did know Cadorna.[67] San Giuliano, too, often had a quip ready about the limitations of the military mind.

Thus although a lot of money was spent on the Army in Liberal Italy, the officer corps was scarcely the puppet master of Italian diplomacy. The caste system, Italy's military record, the phrases of civilian politicians all reinforced the standard belief that officers should have 'no politics', and even that it was praiseworthy not to know the name of the Prime Minister.[68] Such factors also meant that officers, even the Chief of General Staff, should naturally accept the *status quo* in foreign policy, that is the Triple Alliance. Herein lies a great deal of the explanation of the much commented on differences between Italy's military arrangement in 1913–14 and her diplomacy.

In form, then, Liberal Italy was the least militarist of the Great

Powers on the continent of Europe. Even the expenditure figures may have looked larger in the ledgers of a budget than they were in practice. Sonnino later remarked benignly that Giolitti should be hanged for spending the military vote on parliamentary combinations.[69] Whether or not this allegation is true there can be no doubt that much of the Army's vote was spent locally on 'law and order', on the housing and other needs of the officer corps, and on nourishing a favourable press.

However this very parochialness and devotion to domestic responsibilities carried with it a latent strand of influence for the officer corps, in much the same way as it did for the royal family. The purpose and cost of the Army was domestic. Those *caserme* in which gilded lieutenants grew so bored, even the very mobilisation plans, were designed to 'make Italians', to reinforce the unity of the post-Risorgimento State, to repress social and regional perils. As Queen Margherita put it, with her usual crudity, the soldiers were 'the real custodians of Italic virtue... fleeing indignant from all that stagnant water of the political world'.[70] By the twentieth century it was the social peril which had become the graver threat than regionalism to the ideals of the Army. One lieutenant, found reading a book on socialism, was told: 'Whoever deals with matters outside the bounds of his profession, is not a good officer', and that if his interest was known he could not expect much future in the Army.[71] Still more interesting is the fact that a candidate for the officer corps in the 1900s took an oral examination on the theme 'the social question' after having written a paper on the set topic: 'to demonstrate how Nations though fallen into ruin can always rise while they maintain intact their honour and their love of independence and liberty'.[72] The governments of General Pelloux were another indication of the reserve military power which lay behind the Risorgimento establishment.

By 1914 the officer corps was sensing a new crisis in Liberal Italy in much the same way as were other conservative elements of the ruling classes. Officers had already begun to abandon the traditional anti-clerical definition of Italian 'independence and liberty'. In 1907 the garrison of Rome gave an unwonted sign of this by lending a bass drum and cornet to the Vatican's Swiss Guard for use on San Raffaello's day, the *festa* of the Papal Secretary of State, Merry del Val.[73] A rather more serious sign came in 1913 when many high officers supported Federzoni's sensational campaign to purge the Army of Free Masons.[74] In return the Church, which in 1896 had been delighted at the failure of the 'Satanic' Italian armies which at Adowa were paying the 'wages' of a 'divine vendetta',[75] grew much more friendly to the achievements of Italian soldiers. A clerical and Nationalist officer corps not only promised better contacts with the officers of other Great Powers, but also menaced the allegiance of the Army to the social compromises and diplomatic restraint of Giolittian Italy.

Much of what has been said about the Army also holds true for the Italian Navy. The Navy was junior to the Army in terms of its budget, in 1913 taking about 33% of the total military vote.[76] It too suffered under a disastrous combat record, the Battle of Lissa in 1866 being the naval equivalent of Adowa.[77] At times the Navy looked formidable on paper, especially around 1890 when it was third in Europe's lists after Britain and France. However, many European assumptions about real Italian power and abilities must have been confirmed when, at the formal international opening ceremonies for the construction of the Kiel Canal, an Italian ship, the *Sardegna*, ran aground and could not be refloated until some days later.[78] After Crispi's period, naval expenditure fell away, and did not revive until the last years before World War I.

Socially, the naval officer corps was not very different from the Army. One officer has remembered that it was 'a rather gentlemanly calling', although he also complained of the triumph of Southern bureaucratism and timidity which made some captains reluctant to search out 'the living space' needed by Italy.[79] The Navy had a strong aristocratic Piedmontese or Genoese side, typified in 1914 by the Navy Minister, Millo, and the Chief of Naval Staff, Paolo Thaon di Revel.[80] By tradition, and by a natural result of its involvement in the Mediterranean, the Navy tended to be Francophobe, more especially because French sailors rarely concealed their contempt for Italian seamanship. It was also jealous of its own independence, *vis à vis* both the Army[81] and the Ministry of Foreign Affairs. Naval officers disliked socialists, but also could be realistic about war when confronted by the thought of having to compete against an overwhelmingly powerful rival like Britain. One Commission in 1871 suggested that the sandy Italian coasts needed thirty-one naval bases for adequate defence, but by the 1880s an understanding of likely budgetary restrictions had encouraged the Navy to accept the see-no-evil principle of forward defence. 'Coasts', it was now decided, 'are defended on the high seas.'[82] In 1914 the mind of Paolo Thaon di Revel was sufficiently realistic to pose for the first time the problem how Italy's power was to be reconciled with a possible conflict with the united fleets of France and Britain.

Other sources of possible influence by the Navy lay in the activities of the Navy League (which are discussed in chapter 2) and in the contacts of naval officers with the merchant marine and with heavy industry. The most important element in the merchant marine was the Società di Navigazione Generale Italiana, which had been set up in 1881 by combining the Florio and Rubattino groups.[83] The SNGI was in turn linked to those with interests in heavy industry, especially the Orlando family, with their ship-building yards in Liguria. After 1902 the company was assisted financially by the Banca Commerciale Italiana, 'Giolitti's bank'. The SNGI ran its major lines in the Mediterranean, naturally concentrating in realms of 'national interest'. Equally naturally, parliamentary or 'expert' spokesmen for an expanded Navy favoured the further development of Italy's merchant marine in general and the SNGI in particular. Only then, thought one commentator, could Italy take her place as 'the natural queen of the Mediterranean', with Britain, the United States, Germany and Japan (but not France). Italy must be one of the 'five Great Naval Powers',[84] then the phrase '*mare nostrum*' at last would no longer be a bad joke.

Patriotic rhetoric at meetings of the Navy League was given some substance by an adapted and rather twisted version of Giolitti's promises about North–South cooperation. The major shipping interests in Italy, the Florios and the Orlandos, were Sicilian in origin. They might open offices in Genoa, or be received at court in Rome, but their political power base remained Sicilian. Indeed, the two families provided living examples of how real life Mastro Don Gesualdos and Tancredis got on in Italian big business. The Florios, by the third generation, were able to marry into the Lanza family, the most princely of Palermitan aristocrats. A fortune which, on the death in 1868 of the founder of the Florio dynasty, Vincenzo,

1   Liberal Italy

was worth 300 million lire, sweetened the *mésalliance* for the Lanzas. It must also have been comforting when Giulia Florio was recognised as a lady-in-waiting to Queen Elena. By 1900 'Don Ignazio' Florio, apart from his shipping interests, was deeply enmeshed into the politics of the Lanza's city, Palermo, controlling the local newspaper, *L'Ora*, in the interests of Prince Pietro Lanza Di Scalea. It was this Lanza Di Scalea who from 1908 onwards was Under-Secretary of State for Foreign Affairs.[85]

Still more successful were the Orlandos. A scion of the family,

Vittorio Emanuele Orlando, would be the 'Prime Minister of Victory' in 1918. The Orlandos had reached respectability and the North a little before the Florios, establishing their yards outside Genoa after the failure of the 1848 revolution in Sicily. Already in the Sicilian *moto* of 1837 Luigi Orlando and his three brothers had supported the rising, for example collaborating in Catania with Benedetto Di San Giuliano, the father of the man who became Italy's Foreign Minister in 1910.[86] In the succeeding years, the Orlandos were intimately tied to the whole Risorgimento legend: according to an official eulogist, it was from Luigi Orlando's house that Garibaldi left on the expedition of the Thousand. One of the brothers, Paolo Orlando, was Minister of Public Works, an auspicious office, in Garibaldi's first government in Sicily.[87]

Family connections are a rock on which any Sicilian enterprise should be built, and both the Florios and the Orlandos had another sure defence against political perils in *uomini di fiducia* among the lawyers and journalists who belonged to the political elite. One example may suffice: the eulogist referred to above, who was chosen in 1897 to write the official biography of Luigi Orlando, was Primo Levi, a man who had been one of Crispi's most faithful agents,[88] and was probably in need of funds after the Battle of Adowa. After 1910, Primo Levi again became one of the most important officials in the Foreign Ministry.

Family politicians, contacts, 'patriotism' all merged into the great aim of the shipping interests to be rewarded for their loyalty, business acumen and hard-work. But Italian lines in the Mediterranean were not very fruitful, unless, for example, they were utilised under state contract to carry troops to Eritrea or Libya. As far as the shipping companies were concerned, Italy's most profitable potential export, emigrants to America, was never responsibly guided by Italian hands. Instead, the emigration question involved the shipping concerns in a series of embarrassing public controversies with defenders of other 'southern interests', local agents and officials, who believed that the guidance needed for, and profits available from migrants ought properly to remain in their hands.[89] Both shipping lines and ship-building yards were basically inefficient, even parasitic, depending on government subsidies. In the budget of 1913–14 the shipping lines received a government subsidy of almost 20 million *lire*, a more than useful contribution to the SNGI's announced profit of around 3 million *lire*.[90] Whenever the subsidies were challenged, the spokesmen of the merchant marine and of the government could say that the shipping lines ran to the Balkans, North Africa or the Eastern Mediterranean, to 'areas of national interest'. Apart from the SNGI and its hopes and fears in the Mediterranean, in the Adriatic, too, merchant marine interests in Venice were issuing a new challenge to the supremacy of Austrian *Lloyd* and to the Habsburg ports of Trieste and Fiume.[91]

This story of feather-bedding, of 'cooperation' between business and politics, can be found in every aspect of the economy of Liberal Italy. In some ways, its significance can be exaggerated. As A. J. P. Taylor has put it drily, with reference not only to Italy: 'most great men of the past were only there for the beer – the wealth, prestige and grandeur that went with power';[92] so in Liberal Italy, as in Christian Democratic Italy, government and wealth worked together and supported each other. The thickets of the *sottogoverno* which they created became the essential social base of the regime, and the way in which the fissures between politics and society could be repaired or concealed. What the corruption of this system does not necessarily mean is that business was the puppet-master, and government the puppet. Rather, each continued to operate very much in its own sphere. Government did the governing and protected or rewarded industry, just as the social power and wealth of other ruling class groups was also protected.

Moreover, similar to the military or the monarchy, Italian industry, despite its growing involvement abroad before 1914, was still sufficiently under-developed for its real interests to be mainly domestic.[93] At home, industry was confronted by crisis: the growth rate in the economy slumped after 1907; in 1908–9 Italy's weak international diplomatic position was exposed in the Bosnia–Herzegovina crisis. Strikes began to increase, and in 1909 the moderate union organisation, the Confederazione Generale del Lavoro, was under siege from radical elements tired of the compromises of *giolittismo*; CGdL's membership in the major cities actually fell in 1909–10.[94] Then in 1911 Giolitti suddenly announced a 'leap in the dark' to near universal manhood suffrage.

Confronted by these evident challenges, employer groups united in 1910 to form Confindustria. Thereafter, Confindustria became a major spokesman of all anti-socialist causes. The newly united industrialists also began to talk about the economic value of autarky. Politically, the President, Luigi Bonnefon Craponne, who was a French citizen, declared that Confindustria, above politics and even parliament, must seek to control public opinion by its own means. Confindustria became almost a state within a state, and in 1913 Giolitti was driven to the somewhat desperate remedy of threatening to have Bonnefon Craponne expelled from Italy if Confindustria did not moderate its policies.[95]

Nonetheless, until 1914, a certain naivety clung to many of the ideas of Italian business circles. A good example of innocence, gradually lost, is given in the diary of Ettore Conti, one of Italy's leading electrical entrepreneurs, and a man working therefore in one of Italy's most modern industries and one much subject to German competition and assistance. In January 1908 Conti noted:

About politics, I concern myself very little...Luckily we rejoice in a period of peace: Italy asks its citizens to work, and I, by working, know that I am doing my patriotic duty.[96]

Conti, a Milanese, would have been shocked by the 'Southern' methods of Florio or of the Terni works. Brought up with an Italian version of strict Victorian morality, never to lie, always to keep faith in his work, Conti possessed but one brand of politics – patriotism and a hatred of Revolution which undermined Work, Efficiency[97] (and Profits). He believed in all the myths of the Risorgimento, in his own interest, but nonetheless sincerely. From 1910 to 1914 this sort of bourgeois innocence was challenged; Conti's sense of patriotism and of economic advantage were both stirred by the Libyan War; and in 1913, having rejected a Giolittian offer to stand as a deputy in Milan against a 'Radical-Republican-Masonic-Socialist', he comprehended that the bourgeoisie like himself had perhaps in the past kept themselves too distant from politics. 'I think' he confided to his diary, 'that fatally we must organise ourselves as the productive class', and give modern leadership surpassing the style and politics of 'the accustomed lawyers'.[98] On 1 January 1914 he mused that there were two great tasks for industry: 'industrial concentrations in the grand style' which would eliminate 'damaging competition'; and unity among industrialists against 'the increasing demands of the working class' which might destroy the profit motive. Giolitti, he feared, bore grave responsibility in going too far to appease the socialists.[99] Neither Conti's deepening awareness of the crisis of Giolittian Italy, nor the general talk about autarky, nor even capitalists' joy at Salandra's repressive measures in the *settimana rossa*, the social disturbances in June 1914, translated neatly into an advocacy of war and foreign adventures. It is a commonplace that Liberal Italy was less industrialised than it was bureaucratised, but what business interest there was did not react with one voice to the July Crisis and World War. In July, Conti was torn between a proper loyalty to the Triple Alliance and his fears that wars brought Revolution. The beginning of combat also for him disrupted the smooth processes of payments and credit, and it was only reluctantly and belatedly that he joined the interventionist camp.[100]

In such attitudes, Conti and other industrialists shared opinions held by other members of the ruling classes. That they did so does not uncover an 'industrial–military complex' dictating foreign policy; but rather, it shows that there was an elite which ruled Liberal Italy, that it was small and close-knit; and that this elite found by about 1910 that its world view was in crisis. Fears increased that the compromises, moderation and peace of the last decade could no longer blindly continue. It was in this general sense of malaise, of the need to change course, or to return to old ambitions, that industry can be held most seriously to have influenced Italian foreign policy making from 1910 to 1914.

Another segment of Italian society which demands analysis as an influence on the making of foreign policy is agriculture. Agriculture, after all, employed in 1914 twice as many Italians as did industry. If industrialists were the friends and contacts of the Under-Secretary and the Minister of Foreign Affairs, both Scalea and San Giuliano were themselves large landowners. Even Giolitti, with his bureaucratic career and his family contacts with industry (his son, Federico, was an engineering expert,[101] trained in the universities of Rome and Göttingen and, from 1911–19, employed by Ansaldo), devoted much time and affection to his Piedmontese estates. Many Liberal politicians shared this background, either as small landowners and professional notables from the North, or as large landowners from the South.

Much of the story of Italian agriculture is again a chronicle of feather-bedding and protection. Examples can be found in Italy's international treaty arrangements about agricultural products, treaties many of which were renewed in the period from 1904 to 1906. In negotiating the new deals, the Italian government 'did its best for agriculture',[102] disregarding, in the case of the treaties with Switzerland, Germany and Austria, industrialist and banking advice that it was being too kind to rural interests.[103] These treaties remained in force until 1914, and encouraged agrarians to send a large proportion of their exports to Central Europe. As a result, many Southern landowners, San Giuliano being one, talked habitually as though France, whose agricultural product rivalled their own, was a graver enemy to Italy than was Austria. On the other hand, it was sometimes Italy's larger trading partners, Germany and Austria, who were condemned for manipulating the market in their own favour, although, once again, the available evidence does not reveal a neat or inevitable relationship between the economic interests of large landowners and the making of Italian foreign policy.[104]

Many historians have quested for the hidden key to the power structure of Liberal Italy – was it the King, the Army, Big Business or large landowners? Palmiro Togliatti provided what, on the surface, looks like a more original answer: 'The Italian bourgeoisie did have one unified political organisation,...Freemasonry'.[105] However unlikely it may first look to an English-speaking reader, Togliatti's comment does contain more than a grain of truth. Until shortly before the First World War, membership of a Free Masonic association was the nearest thing to a universal factor shared by all members of the Liberal political elite. San Giuliano, Fusinato, Bertolini, F. Martini, Nasi, Marcora, Credaro, Rava, Fortis, Colajanni, P. Villari and Andrea Torre make only a beginning to the list of important Masons.[106] Indeed it is hard to find anyone who was not, except Giolitti, the great exception to so many aspects of Liberal Italy, although the Piedmontese leader's son-in-law, Mario Chiaraviglio, was a leading member.[107]

A question is of course at once raised by Masonry's ubiquity and eclecticism. Was it more than a 'mutual-aid society',[108] a passage through which the funds and offices of Liberal Italy could be equably distributed? Certainly Ernesto Nathan, the mayor of Rome from 1907 to 1913, and ex-Grand Master of Italian Masonry, defined the purpose of his organisation very generally: 'Masonry is not a political association. It is a patriotic and educational association.'[109] Once, the meaning of such phrases had been clear; then, anti-clericalism (and Masonry) had been the touchstone of Italian Liberalism; but by 1910 these old certainties were weakening. The Church no longer counted as the chief enemy of Liberal Italy and despite unremitting anathemas from the Vatican,[110] there were even some Masonic clericals. Masonic purpose was dispersed, and in 1908 there was also schism – in Palazzo del Gesù a rival version of Masonry was set up against the main body in the Palazzo Giustiniani.[111]

On the political scene, anti-clericalism had so faded that in 1913 there occurred the Gentiloni pact and Catholics were permitted to participate freely in the general elections so long as they fought in the anti-socialist cause.[112] Both this political event and the domestic divisions within Masonry were accompanied by a violent attack on Masonry's entrenched position at the heart of Liberal society. Through the pages of *L'Idea Nazionale*, Luigi Federzoni, in 1913, held an informal referendum to demonstrate that Masonry must be cast into the trash-can of history. He was backed not only by Nationalist Association members, but also by some of Italy's most respectable liberal intellectuals, including Croce and Luigi Einaudi. The historian Pasquale Villari lent the weight of his years, pen, and reputation, to the attack, even though he noted that it had been Masonic pressure which had once ensured his election as President of the Dante Alighieri Society.[113] The service Ministers, Spingardi and Leonardi Cattolica were frightened by Federzoni's 'revelations' of Masonic influence in the Army and Navy, and agreed that the knell of Masonry had been rung.[114]

Nathan was duly defeated in the 1913 elections in Rome which saw the local triumph of two Nationalist candidates who were able to plead the zeal of their combat against Masonry, and the purity of their admiration for the Church in order to collect clerical votes released onto the electoral market by the Gentiloni pact.[115]

Despite this setback, and even despite Mussolini's later sensational anti-Masonic campaign, the Masons were able to survive into Christian Democratic Italy. It is reported, for example, that in Genoa in 1977, all politicians of the *arco costituzionale*, except the Communists, are Masons. 'Old Masons never die, they only fade away' might be an apposite motto for Italian history.

What is more significant for the historian of Italy just before the First World War is that Masonry, which had perhaps been the most ubiquitous organisation behind the Liberal regime, was in crisis. In other words, Masonry, like the Monarchy, the Army and the industrialists and agrarians, had evidence to doubt whether the smooth process of Giolittian compromises could proceed without diversion. The Liberal ruling class was small, and its institutions overlapped. But in all its branches, by 1910–11, there was good reason to fear that the comfortable Italy of Giolitti and Turati was no longer the best defence of the ruling classes. In these circumstances, and given as well Italy's own past, and the behaviour of other 'Great Powers', it is hardly astonishing that many in the Italian leadership began to see foreign affairs as a useful detour around domestic troubles. This assertion does not mean in any naive sense an acceptance of the concept of a '*svolta imperialistica*', certainly not one inspired alone by new capitalists. Rather, it was a much wider group, probably the majority of the Italian ruling classes which was worried by a sense of flux and uncertainty, and which was looking to a more expansionist and successful foreign policy in the last years before 1914.

Further evidence for this conclusion can be found, somewhat ironically, in the opinions and policies of political organisations whose power base was not in 'legal Italy' but in 'real Italy'. The Roman Catholic accommodation with the state and Army over foreign policy has already been noted. By 1913 *Civiltà Cattolica* was pleased that Italy now carried 'greater weight in the estimation of other States' and that national unity during the Libyan War had checked the socialist peril. Nonetheless, it warned that there was still the problem that 'democracy' was rising in Italy: 'that democracy which deforms every character...and kills the germs of every moral grandeur'.[116]

Apart from Italian clericalism, what of other groupings excluded from immediate political power in Liberal Italy? Mazzinian radicalism had lost out in the Risorgimento, and, furthermore, the idealistic purity of the prophet's heirs had been diluted by the succeeding years. The Mazzinians had been internationalists at first[117] and had naturally favoured the launching of the international peace movement in Italy. This behaviour had little challenged the assumptions of the Liberal regime which was itself sufficiently 'made by Mazzini' eagerly to join the developing system of interparliamentary contacts (the third Interparliamentary Conference was held in Rome in 1891), and later to sympathise with the Hague Peace Conferences and international arbitration schemes. In 1912–13, for example, Giolitti favoured arbitration to solve the *Carthage* and *Manouba* incidents with France ignoring advice from his chief legal consultant that Italy was likely to be treated unfairly.[118] Italy also provided ideologues for the international peace movement, of whom the most notable was Gaetano Meale, who liked to style himself 'Umano'. In 1889 Meale published a pamphlet entitled *The End of Wars Through the Federation of Peoples*, and in October 1914 he was still proclaiming the values of an international peace movement in *This is the Time for a True Third Rome*. Umano lived on to be nominated for the Nobel Peace Prize in 1925. By then he was a little wary of Mussolini, but his major critique was against that rival internationalism, socialism.[119]

If the opaqueness of Meale's arguments reduced their likely influence, other heirs of Mazzini had weakened earlier in their devotion to internationalism: Giovanni Bovio, one of the leading political Mazzinians of the 1880s and 1890s, had detected by 1893 that both Trento and Malta wanted to reclaim their 'mother', Italy. Hostile to what would come to be called the 'old diplomacy' of 'Machiavellian double-plays', Bovio drifted into a variety of racialism which held that the world was divided into the Slav, Anglo-Saxon and German, and Latin races, the last of which was, unfortunately, the 'least prepared'. Bovio rejected war as 'too terrible', but he predicted a sharpening contest of rival civilisations, and was especially anxious that Italy's colonies, notably in that 'new Italy', South America, should assist the rise of the Latin race.[120]

Bovio died in 1903. In some ways his inheritance passed, in the intellectual sphere, to E. T. Moneta, a writer and organiser of Italian internationalism, who, in 1907, became the only Italian before 1945 to win the Nobel Peace prize. Moneta's works preached a curious combination of peace and of the myth of the Risorgimento. Some wars, he said, if they were liberating, were just.[121] The implications of this assumption were tested sooner for Moneta than for his internationalist pacificist colleagues in other countries. Just as most leading European 'pacifists' could not combat their own sense of patriotism at the outbreak of the First World War, so most Italian pacifists, Moneta among them, supported the government, once Italy had invaded Libya. The Italian delegation formally withdrew from the Interparliamentary Union, after that body had voiced criticisms of Italian methods and ambitions in Libya.[122]

It would be an exaggeration to state that all democrats and radicals rallied to the Liberal regime when its foreign policies became expansionist or were contested from abroad. In 1911–12, Gaetano Salvemini and his friends on the weekly *L'Unità* provided the most scathing critiques of the disadvantages of war in Libya, as they did for the domestic inadequacies and contradictions of the 'Ministry of the Underworld'.[123] In January 1914, the more moderate Radicals, who were members of Giolitti's Cabinet, defected, complaining that the government was spending too much time and money on foreign affairs.

Yet, inadequacies and contradictions were not a trait of Giolitti alone, but also of many Radicals and democrats. Giovanni Amendola, although unconvinced of the economic value of Libya, broke from Salvemini in October 1911, because he accepted the ancient dictum that a mere intellectual was not competent in international and military affairs, and that political debate should only revive after military success.[124] A Radical, some years earlier, had exhibited similar ambiguities in stating: 'Our foreign policy today must be moderate and peaceful precisely in order one day to become proud, and, eventually, belligerent.'[125]

In these circumstances, the most consistent 'opposition' foreign policy was enunciated in the internationalism of Italian socialists. During the Libyan War, for example, the rank and file of the socialist movement in their native opposition to conscription and war,[126] impelled most of the Socialist leadership into rejecting the colonial campaign. Recalcitrant reformist sympathy for patriotism was punished in July 1912 when Bissolati and three other deputies were expelled from the main Socialist party officially for expressing sympathy to the King on his escape from an assassination attempt, but really to demonstrate, even during colonial war, the revolutionary probity of the Italian Socialist movement. This triumph of the Ideal was a prelude to the fact that, in the First World War, of all major Socialist parties, the Italian would stay most loyal to the principles of internationalism.

But in more normal times there were far more points of contact between the definition of foreign policy by the ruling classes and that by the leadership of the Socialist party and by the Confederazione Generale del Lavoro than might be expected from a knowledge only of what happened in 1912 and in 1915. For a long time, for example, many in the often bourgeois leadership of the infant Socialist movement hesitated openly to oppose the colonialism of Crispi. Similarly, in the 1900s the Italian and Austrian Socialist movements developed organised collaboration as a sort of socialist parallel to the Triple Alliance.[127] Even during the Libyan War, there were many signs of compromise and patriotic transformism. Despite the rapid condemnation by the organisation of the Second International, which, on 1 October, declared the Libyan War an 'act of brigandage',[128] Turati and the other Socialist leaders had shown little enthusiasm for the general strike which, theory said, they must summon to stop the war. In fact, a strike had been proclaimed on 27 September, but the job was bungled, in some places not even being called on the right day. Neither the Socialist leadership nor CGdL were too dismayed, Turati having warned of the danger of the 'convulsionary state' ('*stato convulsionario*').[129] The war, with its promise of land, also attracted many Southern 'socialists', of whom the most notable was the Catanian leader, Giuseppe De Felice Giuffrida.[130] It was only the fact that the war dragged on which really allowed the anti-militarism of the rank and file, exploited by the revolutionary wing of the party, to triumph at the Congress of Reggio Emilia in July 1912. For the next two years, as a result of this victory of maximalism, Socialist ideas about foreign policy remained more distinct from those of the ruling class than they had ever been before; but however much in retreat, many of the Socialist leaders and some of the Socialist rank and file still could have their emotions and self interest tugged at by the prospect of national and colonial triumph.

The only other social group which may be deemed to have affected foreign policy, however indirectly, were those people who voted with their feet, that is, the emigrants who streamed out of Italy in the decade before 1914.[131] So constant and severe was the loss of population through emigration that it was natural that much foreign policy came to be discussed inside the parameters of the emigration problem.[132] Tittoni said when he was Minister of Foreign Affairs that emigration was socially useful, a 'safety-valve';

San Giuliano, fearing the depopulation of the South, diagnosed instead a 'haemorrhage' of Italy's best blood; the Nationalist, Corradini, believed that emigration revealed Italy was a 'proletarian nation'.[133] Even the Socialist, Treves, found emigration 'a policy of *pathology*' directed against the proletarian class.[134]

The emigration question lent a new urgency to Italy's problems in being the least of the Great Powers, and in particular lent moral justification to politicians who wanted to defend their conversion to an expansionist foreign policy. There were only a few socialists and democrats who pointed out that the best sort of colonisation for Italy would be internal migration backed by land distribution and campaigns of field improvement, drainage, disease removal and other public works. This judiciousness and commonsense was matched and perhaps surpassed on the other side of the political spectrum by Nationalists who, confronted by problems of foreign affairs, cried out that 'blood' was 'the wine of a mighty people' and that the 'Gods' of History insatiably demanded 'victims, victims and more victims'.[135]

Apart from the fearful, if a little rococo, rhetoric of Nationalist intellectuals in search of employment and power, many in Giolittian Italy, whether formally opponents or supporters of the regime, shared an ambiguous attitude to foreign affairs. In both 'legal' and 'real' Italy the myth that Italy was a Great Power, the allegiance required by patriotism, was persuasive; but on the other hand, almost all Italians feared general, as distinct from colonial, war. Perhaps the best example of these ambiguities in attitudes to foreign affairs is Olindo Malagodi's study, *Imperialism*, published in 1901. There, in contorted phrases, Malagodi declared his admiration for the achievements of Empire, but his dislike of the ideology of imperialism.[136] In a way, Malagodi was giving expression to Italy's eternal diplomatic dilemma – ambition and failure were the two constants of Italian foreign policy from 1860 to 1945. Ambition sprang from history, the class factors of the *rivoluzione mancata*, and international recognition; failure was made almost certain by economics, social and national disunity, and the realities of international power. There was no real escape from this nexus. Mussolini tried fatuously to boast it away in the 1930s. San Giuliano and his colleagues, more successfully, at least in the short term, tried to conjure it away from 1910 to 1914. But Italian foreign policy always remained 'dishonest', tortuous, changeable, exposed perennially to the risk of defeat and humiliation. Moreover, Italy always had to recognise that there would be times when she could not even make her own foreign policy, but must yield to the whims and ambitions of others. As Giolitti put it, with his usual accuracy, Italy 'must always keep in consideration events and situations which it is not in our power to modify, or sometimes not even to accelerate or delay'.[137] International war was a most terrible risk, if only for the budget which would not balance without those peacetime aides, tourism and emigrants' remittances. Journalists might boast in 1914, as Mussolini would do later, that 'Rome has always been a country of conquest',[138] but for Liberal Italian diplomatists (as, in many ways, later for Mussolini) the conquests of the Third Rome would have to be located in the bargain basement. The trappings of greatness were not to be found anywhere else by the least of the Great Powers.

CHAPTER 2

New political pressure groups and foreign policy

The sense of crisis in Italian society and foreign policy around 1910 did not really imply a break with the past. Historians are often too eager to locate turning points to divide history into a story of one parenthesis after another. So, the more they are studied the more blurred become many of the alleged differences in the foreign policies of Fascist and Liberal Italy. Those who favour historical parentheses often search for historical forerunners, for those who play John the Baptist, who signal the turning point on the horizon. In Liberal Italy, the chief harbingers of fascism-to-come are usually seen as that group of intellectuals and publicists who, at Florence in December 1910, founded the Associazione Nazionalista Italiana.

The Nationalists' first hero was Enrico Corradini. According to Fascist historiography, it was in the dark days of the defeat at Adowa, when a few of the 'best men' in Italy felt a new, stubborn stirring of patriotism; then Corradini lit the torch which would guide the way forward.[1] His idea that Italy was a 'proletarian nation'[2] would become the catchcry of many a later opponent of Marxist internationalism, and be deliberately used to divert the masses from socialism to nationalism. This romantic picture of a heroic minority rising, a phoenix from the ashes of defeat, and waxing, uncorrupted, before absorption into fascism is, to say the least, distorted. The originality, the unity and the influence of the Nationalists before the First World War have been greatly exaggerated under the impact of events which came later.

Corradini is only one example. His very idea of 'proletarian nationalism' was borrowed from Giovanni Pascoli, an ex-socialist who had developed into something like the official rhetorician of the Liberal ruling classes.[3] Corradini, himself a second-rate novelist, also admired Gabriele D'Annunzio, Italy's poetic apostle of decadence. Schism, however, was always possible in the intellectual world. Founding a journal, Il Regno, in 1903, Corradini linked himself with

39

younger literary 'rebels' such as Giovanni Papini and Giuseppe Prezzolini, who wanted to excise D'Annunzio's self-indulgent luxuriousness from Italian culture. Corradini continued to write, usually on political themes, and became very interested in the emigration question, visiting Tunis and the Italian colonies in South America.[4] Impressed by his experiences there, by Italy's diplomatic humiliation in the Bosnia–Herzegovina crisis and by the growing threat in Libya, Corradini, Papini and Prezzolini united again to set up the weekly *L'Idea Nazionale*, the first number of which was timed to appear on 1 March 1911, the fifteenth anniversary of the Battle of Adowa.

The story of intellectual critics, of middle-class professional 'rebels', is not a new one in Italian history. In the previous generation Giosuè Carducci and Alfredo Oriani had also violently assailed the post-Risorgimento regime while naturally enjoying their membership of its establishment. The delights of Queen Margherita's salons, and the patronage system in the educational and publishing worlds, were a useful corrective to an unbridled attachment to social revolution. Mussolini too, '*professore* Mussolini', would show a certain benignity to literary rebels, putting up, most of the time, with the flourishes of Malaparte, and in the 1930s tolerating a sort of court literary opposition around his son, Vittorio.

It has long been evident that neither D'Annunzio, nor more extreme intellectual critics like Marinetti and the Futurists, had much direct influence on Italian politics. Both had a certain international reputation and, as a result, were able to prefer the flesh-pots of Paris to serious campaigning. They remained famous, or at least lionised, at home because parochial Italy did not have many international celebrities. They were more the symbols of discontent or of an alternative life-style to Giolitti, than serious actors on the political stage.

It is hard to take the influence of literary rebels like Corradini, Papini[5] and Prezzolini much more seriously, although their lack of an international reputation did keep them within Italy. The first congress of the Associazione Nazionalista met at Florence, and there was much that was rather Florentine in the ideas of Corradini and the others. Their phrases could be beautiful, clearly formulated and perhaps accepted, but it was not from Florence, or just by spinning off elegant or memorable ideas and phrases that Italy would be ruled.

In forming the political organisation (the ANI) and setting up a political newspaper (*L'Idea Nazionale*), Corradini had ostensibly stepped into the political world. But he never entirely accepted that this was what he had done. Lacking the lawyer's skills necessary in an Italian politician, Corradini failed to win the prize of leadership, and slipped again into the uncertain office of Philosopher. Between the creation of the ANI and the formal establishment of the Nationalist party in 1914, Corradini's power fell away. Even as a philosopher, his position was challenged and compromised by Alfredo Rocco who joined the ANI in 1913.[6] It was perhaps predictable that the Nationalist movement would house many opposing ideas. Much historiography has been devoted to the task of unravelling the Nationalists' policy towards irredentism, syndicalism, emerging political clericalism, or towards the Giolittian system as a whole. Paradoxes and simple confusions abound, not least in what Nationalists suggested should be an ideal foreign policy. In the July Crisis, when the ambiguities and opportunities of Liberal Italian foreign policy were most evident, the Nationalists, more than any other group, were unable to make up their minds about their answers to the questions facing Italian diplomacy.[7]

The Nationalists' very conversion to politics was a little uneasy. Organised at a moment when Italy was at last to be granted something approaching manhood suffrage, the Nationalists failed dismally to develop into a mass party. In the 1913 elections they managed to send only five deputies into a Chamber of over 500.[8] Although their social contacts would help usher Mussolini into power, they still only won ten seats in the 1921 elections.

Moreover the character of their successful candidates in 1913 testifies less to the Nationalists' originality than to the solidity of their members' credentials among the establishment of post-Risorgimento Italy. 'Newest' of the deputies, and the nearest equivalent to a leader, was Luigi Federzoni. Federzoni, who became the major ANI spokesman on foreign affairs in the Chamber, and who made himself into a sort of parliamentary mosquito buzzing impertinently around the aristocratic head of San Giuliano, had been born to a bourgeois family in Bologna, his father being a teacher at the local university. Preferring to write under the pseudonym, 'Giulio De Frenzi', Federzoni began his career in *avant-garde* literary circles, taking his laureate from Bologna in 1900. This literary activity was appropriate, bourgeois 'rebellion', since Federzoni, to the dismay of his father, a loyal follower of Carducci, spent his time attacking the inanities of the older generation. After a period of not very successful novel writing, Federzoni turned to more orthodox journalism becoming in 1904 *redattore* for *Resto del Carlino*, Bologna's most important paper. In 1905 he moved to Rome, where, for eight years he worked in a similar capacity for *Giornale d'Italia*.[9]

This rise to politics via literature and journalism was a wholly predictable one in Liberal Italy. Federzoni's first major political campaigns were hardly more original. In 1907 he 'exposed' for *Giornale d'Italia* the accustomed examples of Giolittian corruption in Naples. This ought not to have endeared him to Tommaso Tittoni, about whose prefecture in Naples the most unsavoury stories were still eddying, but, within six years, Federzoni would be enough 'transformed' gladly to accept money from Tittoni's clerical friends.[10] In 1909 'De Frenzi' turned to foreign affairs, publishing *Per l'italianità del 'Gardasee'*, an attack on the cultural baggage brought by German tourists to the area around Lake Garda. Ten thousand tourists, he warned dramatically, provided but 'the copious planting of the hoped-for harvest' (lit. budding).[11] The book, which collected articles written for *Giornale d'Italia*, was blessed by Corradini and by Scipio Sighele, the Crispian elder statesman of 'democratic' nationalism until his irredentism and social radicalism rendered him too unpopular. But Federzoni's comments were also endorsed by Luigi Rava, ex-President of the Dante Alighieri Society, a Giolittian Minister of Education who was devoting his time to a campaign encouraging the name-changing of each *Hôtel Central* to an *Albergo Centrale*.[12] Federzoni's work on *Giornale d'Italia* had turned him into a Roman, and much of his nationalism was devoted to attacking the curious blend of Free Masonic social radicalism and pacifism of Leone Caetani, a princely deputy for Rome.[13] In 1913, it was in Rome that Federzoni won election,[14] defeating another, less radical, prince, Scipione Borghese, who had become famous in 1907 as the dilettante-adventurer who had won an Italian 'triumph' in the motor-car 'raid' from Peking to Paris.[15] In most senses, Borghese, a member of the Italian Geographical Society and the other patriotic bodies, an explorer and in 1914 an interventionist, was hardly less patriotic than Federzoni.

Federzoni's words certainly sounded a little different: 'To fertilise civilisation, hatred is, in fact, no less necessary than love.' 'The new Italian generation, if it possesses the consciousness of its historic mission, can only be nationalist and imperialist.'[16] His actions, too, could be dramatic. In 1913, as a prelude to the electoral campaign, Federzoni went off on a much-publicised tour of the Eastern Mediterranean to urge that Italy make plain her intention to keep the Dodecanese. With memories of Julius Caesar's 'friend and ally', but with a somewhat pedestrian choice of metaphor, Federzoni hailed the 'regaining' of Rhodes as the reclamation of 'an ancient family jewel'.[17] Federzoni also launched in 1913 his attack on Free Masonry.[18] The topic of Masonry might seem particularly old-fashioned, but Federzoni was acting inside a Roman context. Since 1907, to the disgust of the Papacy, the city of Rome had been administered by a junta of Masonic Radicals, under Ernesto Nathan. In the Rome of the Gentiloni pact, nothing could be more likely to win Vatican finance than a campaign against Masons. Federzoni duly got the money from Romolo Tittoni of the Banco di Roma and won his seat in the Chamber.

There can be no doubt that as a political campaigner or a publicist Federzoni's rhetoric on both foreign and domestic affairs was distinct from the stock-in-trade of the Giolittians. In the Chamber, Federzoni was also ready to break rules or assumptions about appropriate gravity and respect. Nonetheless, too much should not be read into the sound and fury of Federzoni's words. One student has reported that, apart from their polemical tone, Federzoni and the other Nationalist deputies were, in practice, difficult to distinguish in the Chamber from more orthodox and older members of the opposition.[19] It can readily be asked whether Federzoni's ideal society would have been very different from that wanted by Prince Scipione Borghese, his erstwhile liberal, Masonic opponent. Despite the attacks on Giolitti and San Giuliano, the real opponents for Federzoni and his friends associated with *L'Idea Nazionale*, in the context of 1913–14, were Sonnino and the group around *Giornale d'Italia*.[20] More than anything else what the Nationalists were aiming at in 1913–14, and then thwarted from by the war, was the succession to the leadership of the 'constitutional opposition'. Given Sonnino's long catalogue of failures in this capacity, it is hardly astonishing that a challenge should come, and come from the younger generation, if still with the usual forms of Italian politics, a newspaper, radical rhetoric, and promises difficult to analyse that 'things must change'.

This suspicion that the Nationalists stood most for the rhetoric of the younger generation is lent more credence by a brief analysis of the other successful ANI deputies in the 1913 elections. One was Camillo Ruspoli, son of a deputy and member of one of Rome's most eminent clerical conservative families; another, Luigi Medici del Vascello, again from an aristocratic household, was the grandson of a Garibaldinian deputy and senator;[21] and a third, Romeo Gallenga Stuart, also a youthful deputy from a parliamentary family, was a count, who rapidly proved transformable into ministerial service during the First World War.[22] The final Nationalist, the most prestigious member of that group apart from Federzoni, was Piero Foscari, a count, a deputy since 1904, President of the Trento and Trieste Society, a new irredentist body which had been founded in 1903. A Venetian, Foscari as much represented the peculiarities of that city as Federzoni, Ruspoli and Medici del Vascello represented those of Rome. Indeed the person in Liberal Italy whom Foscari was most like was Giuseppe Volpi, the financial adventurer used by Giolitti to help negotiate peace with Turkey in 1912. Foscari, proud of his descent from the Doges, had been an officer in the Italian Navy, but had resigned and become a deputy in 1904 after being involved in a dispute between the rival naval yards of La Spezia and Venice. Thereafter an assiduous advocate of the interests of the Venice arsenal, and of local business expansion, Foscari believed that he had a mission to restore the entrepreneurial glories of Venice. He even named his daughter 'Marina' to exemplify Venice's sea-going past. In 1908 he helped stage, and probably encouraged the financing of, D'Annunzio's *La nave*[23] with its famous line 'Arma la prora e salpa verso il Mondo'.[24] Foscari's politics were thus very local, notwithstanding later efforts to see him as an apostle of fascism. His politics were also decidedly odd. His irredentism,[25] while providing the Nationalists with a living symbol of a tradition of past objections to Italian diplomatic passivity, ill-accorded with the trend of Nationalism by 1913 towards an admiration for German philosophy and the diplomatic opportunities allowed by the Triple Alliance. An ideal foreign policy for Venice might not seem so attractive in Florence, Rome or Palermo.

Outside the Chamber of Deputies, the greatest impact by the Nationalists was on the Italian press. In 1911 even the pro-Giolittian papers, *La Stampa* of Turin, and *La Tribuna* of Rome, employed Nationalists, Giuseppe Bevione and Giuseppe Piazza, as their correspondents in Tripoli. More consistently influential was Andrea

Torre, Rome correspondent of *Corriere della Sera*, and himself a deputy since 1909. Although not formally a member of the Nationalist group in the Chamber, Torre was an ardent exponent of many Nationalist ideas. But Torre's Nationalism shaded into more orthodox anti-Giolittism and he had many ties with the more conventional Italian Right. In December 1893, he had succeeded Primo Levi as *direttore* of Crispi's *La Riforma*. He had belonged to a commission investigating the quality of schools abroad, presided over by Pasquale Villari; when Sonnino and Bergamini founded *Giornale d'Italia* in 1901, Torre was for five years among their most zealous collaborators.

Had the Nationalists captured the Press, or the Press the Nationalists? Certainly the Press was remarkably eager to employ patriotic talent. Luigi Albertini, straitlaced critic of Giolittian 'corruption', was an accommodating patron to Gabriele D'Annunzio, whose poetry often appeared in *Corriere della Sera*. On the day that Italy declared war on Turkey, Albertini wrote to D'Annunzio requesting an ode to celebrate 'Tripoli,...our disembarkation on those historic shores,...the magnificent revival of our national sentiment.'[26] Nationalists such as Francesco Coppola or Roberto Forges-Davanzati were also employed by Albertini.

The Nationalists in 1911 favoured the colonial war with Turkey, but then so did many government supporters. Government, Sonninian opposition and Nationalists were all inspired to rhetoric about the 'Third Italy' and the 'new era' by the anniversary celebrations of the *Cinquantennio*. So indeed were officials. When Mario Lago, working in the Foreign Ministry, wrote patriotic descriptions for *La Tribuna*, or published a eulogy about the sculptor of the bas-reliefs on the Victor Emmanuel monument,[27] it is difficult to see what was so distinctive about the Nationalists.

Outside the immediate political arena, the story of the social and political character of the Nationalists is repeated. One young member was Luigi Villari, son of that intellectual Jeremiah of the Italian Right, Pasquale Villari. Luigi survived to act as a propagandist in English speaking countries for Fascism throughout the Mussolinian regime. He was still serving in Salò, and in the 1950s wrote an unregenerate apologia for Fascist foreign policy.[28]

'Liberal fathers, Nationalist sons', is one way of summarising the character of the ANI in pre-1914 Italy; a Florentine love of well-sculptored words, and of dissent from the existing government, is another. But, above all, it is the Romanness of the Nationalists which is most apparent by 1914. Mussolini would one day march on Rome. The Nationalists never could, because they were already there; and one truism which has stood out through centuries of Italian history is that it is not much use marching on Italy from Rome.

Rhetoric apart, the issues contested between the Nationalists and the constitutional opposition to Giolitti were slight. The Nationalists had much more continuity with the Italian past, and a much closer attachment to segments of the contemporary Italian ruling class than has often been assumed. Nationalist ideas were a threat to Giolittian reformism; the more dangerous threat sprang from the fact that the ideas were held not just by a few, noisy, upper-class youths and intellectuals, but by large sections of the ruling class created by the Risorgimento. In the years 1911 to 1914, Italian foreign policy is not, as has been implied,[29] a story of the tail wagging the dog, but the more ordinary one of the dog wagging its tail.

To isolate the Nationalists from other nationalist bodies is, therefore, a misleading process. Well before 1910 Italy had produced a number of ruling class pressure groups advocating particular foreign policies. The earliest of these was the irredentists.[30] Arising directly from the 'unfinished' character of the Risorgimento, the various irredentist societies, often locally based, aimed to direct Italian foreign policy against Austria.[31] The end desired was the reclamation of Italy's *terra irredenta* ('Unredeemed land'). The borders of this was uncertain, but included Trento and Trieste and their provinces, the Trentino and Venezia Giulia, perhaps Dalmatia and its islands, even Ragusa (Dubrovnik) and Albania south to its borders with Greece.

In its origins, irredentism was a left-wing, Jacobin movement, preaching national grandeur in the style of the French revolutionaries after 1789. The ageing Garibaldi was an obvious, if erratic, sympathiser. Domestically, irredentism was linked with Republican ideas, hostile to the Savoyard Risorgimento. In 1877 the Pro-Italia Irredenta Society, founded in Naples, was led by M. R. Imbriani, one of Garibaldi's Red Shirts, 'a fiery, eloquent and irrepressible republican'.[32] A notable sympathiser was Aurelio Saffi, with Mazzini one of the triumvirs of the Roman Republic of 1849, who refused to accept his seat in the Italian Chamber because it involved swearing an oath of loyalty to the monarchical constitution.

In Europe the 1880s mark a strange, partial, but definite shift in the direction of nationalism. Jacobin nationalism did not die overnight, but in relation to domestic politics, nationalism moved from being a doctrine mainly of the Left, to become one mainly of the Right. This change is particularly clear in France. Sometimes individuals switched political base with their ideas. Henri Rochefort fought as a communard, but backed General Boulanger, became an anti-Semite and one of the bitterest anti-Dreyfusards. Paul Déroulède founded his Ligue des Patriotes in 1882 with Victor Hugo as patron, Léon Gambetta as a founding member and a full panoply of Republican respectability. But Déroulède later backed Boulanger and opposed Dreyfus. In 1899 he even attempted what has been labelled, with some reason, the first proto-fascist *coup d'état*.[33] By 1900, however patriotic the Left was in fact, 'nationalists' sat on the Right of the French Chamber.

In Italy the same drift can be discerned. The liking for foreign adventure which the old radical, Crispi, showed when in office after 1887, combined with domestic repression, is an obvious example. But for the irredentists, the situation was complicated by changes in the international spectrum outside Italy's control, changes which placed Italian diplomacy in a particularly murky light between her 'friends' and her 'allies'. Italy's expansionism could aim to win *terra irredenta* back from the hated *tedeschi* of Austria, but it also could be directed towards reclaiming the *mare nostrum*, in which future cries would be heard for Tunis, Nice, Corsica and Malta. Some diplomatic expansion could be won around the Mediterranean, in Libya and Asia Minor, or Albania and perhaps Ethiopia, in peacetime, without a recourse to general war which was needed if Trieste was to become Italian.

Faced with these circumstances, it is not surprising that the old identity between irredentism and nationalism broke down. Some irredentists, such as Imbriani, retained their Mazzinian innocence, and advocated 'self-determination' everywhere. Purer irredentists also never consummated the domestic flirtation with governing circles. In 1913 the leadership of the Trento and Trieste association passed to Giovanni Battista Giuriati, the chief of the Seamen's Union, a radical, who in 1919 would be D'Annunzio's associate in Fiume.[34]

47

In return, governments, doggedly fighting the war before last, continued to treat many irredentists as 'subversives' even when they knew that 'socialists' were their real enemy. San Giuliano favoured police surveillance of the Trento and Trieste association,[35] and saved some of his most scathing sarcasm for his descriptions of the surviving irredentists.[36]

Embarrassment also sprang from the vagueness with which Italian governments sensibly hid their long-term ambitions for Trieste. Opposition, new Right groups, thus never quite made up their mind about irredentism. The ANI was characteristically confused; Federzoni declaimed against the *Gardasee*, and proved his patriotism by slipping past Austrian border authorities put off guard by his pseudonym, 'De Frenzi', in order to address patriots in Trieste;[37] but he was more fascinated by a *romanità* which directed Italy to the Mediterranean not the Julian Alps. Foscari, leader of the Trento and Trieste association until 1913, joined the Nationalist group in the Chamber and seemed ready to divert his irredentism into a search for new avenues for Venetian business expansion. Depressing also was the lack of enthusiasm for irredentism from so many Triestine 'Italians'[38] who, despite subsidies paid by Giolitti himself to patriotic leaders, and the ominous formation of local middle-class 'squads' to deal with the growing, Slovenian population,[39] showed little susceptibility to the attractions of Italy, and regarded Venice, at least, more as a commercial rival than the natural leader of an expanded Veneto. So irredentism lingered on, favoured in Trieste and in Italy by a few social or economic groups for their own advantage, but with little surviving vitality. The significance of irredentism only returned when war revived the belief that Trieste could be regained. Even then, irredentist ideas were simply added to Nationalist, and later, Fascist lore. The idealistic, internationally nationalist, Jacobin irredentism which had won so many hearts in the Risorgimento had become a corpse, annoying only because it had not been wholly interred.

The same cannot be said about organisations which grew initially from the irredentist movement, but which assimilated themselves more readily into the Liberal ruling classes. As these groups swung to the Right, they changed not only their domestic policies, but much of their foreign ambitions as well. Irredentism yielded to imperialism.

The earliest and most long lasting of these groups was the Dante Alighieri Society which was founded in Rome in 1889, in formation direct evidence of an irredentist *rapprochement* with the government. The first suggestion for such an organisation was raised by *trentini* refugees in Rome, Salvatore Barzilai, Enrico Tolomei and Giacomo Venezian.[40] Officially, the Dante Alighieri Society was formed to sponsor Italian language and culture, but it was clearly political in intent. A drive to aid Italian language and culture could defeat what was regarded as Austrian attempts to destroy the *italianità* of the *terra irredenta*.

The very choice of a name was a challenge to Austria, and incidentally to the Vatican, which always continued to be suspicious of the hidden hand of Free Masonry behind Liberal society. Dante had long been selected as one of the 'prophets' of Italian unity. How could the greatest of Italian poets have been anything else? His writings had been searched to prove that the river Quarnaro in Istria, just to the west of Fiume, marked the border of Italy. One day, the Fascist anthem *Giovinezza*, would pay homage to Dante in this role. In the Liberal era also there was something of a Dante cult; Sonnino wrote sentimental articles about his poetry, and Giolitti was attacked for only once citing Dante in the Chamber, and then incorrectly. Other politicians, including San Giuliano,[41] more than made up for the Prime Minister's literary sterility.

An interest in the Trentino, Venezia Giulia and Dalmatia remained basic to the Dante Alighieri Society. In July 1913, the President, Paolo Boselli, complained officially to San Giuliano about the Austrian slavicisation of Trieste. The Society, he said, was working hard there to preserve *italianità*. In contrast to his treatment of the 'subversives' of the Trento and Trieste Society, San Giuliano took Boselli's note seriously, minuting that his officials should contact Bonaldo Stringher, head of the Banca d'Italia to help the Dante Alighieri Society financially.[42]

However the Society had long not confined itself merely to irredentism, but rather was willing to offer support to Italian foreign policy wherever it was, or could be imagined to be, preserving or extending *italianità*. In its foundation, the Dante had already received much 'official' backing. Sponsors were Giosuè Carducci, the patriotic poet; Ernesto Nathan, the London-born Jewish financier, once a Mazzinian, Grand-Master of Italian Free Masonry 1896–1904 and

1917–19, Mayor of Rome, 1907–1913; and Menotti Garibaldi, one of the sons of the great Giuseppe.[43] The Society's first President was the politician and educationalist Ruggero Bonghi. Bonghi was a still more orthodox figure than Carducci, Nathan or Menotti Garibaldi. A Southerner, he had been the *Destra*'s last Minister of Education. By no means an anti-clerical, in the Risorgimento the youthful Bonghi had sat at the feet of Rosmini and Manzoni.

The drift of the Dante Alighieri Society towards the Right was confirmed by Pasquale Villari who was the second President from 1896 to 1903. Despite his admiration for Gladstone and the English liberals,[44] and despite his concern for the wretchedness of living conditions in Italy's South, Villari was a rigid enemy of socialism. More a scholar and a publicist than a parliamentarian, like Bonghi, Villari sat on the Right of the Chamber. A Senator since 1884 and Minister of Education 1891–2 in Rudinì's conservative government, Villari was among those most aroused by the 'subversive' threat of the Sicilian *fasci*,[45] and doubted the ability of parliamentarianism to withstand the socialist peril. So prestigious a figure did Villari become in the Italian Establishment that he was awarded the Collar of the Annunziata in 1910.

Under Villari's aegis, the Dante Alighieri Society extended its membership to 18,000, organised in 241 groups.[46] Villari was well aware of the emigration problem, and hoped for some 'Italian way to imperialism', as Sabbatucci has neatly labelled it.[47] Whether this implied territorial annexation was left vague, but certainly the Society was steered away from Jacobin irredentism. For Villari, Argentina was as much a problem as the Trentino: 'Wherever the language of Italy is spoken we recognise brothers, and wish to tie ever more closely those bonds which Nature has created and which man cannot break.'[48]

Like so many of his generation, Villari spoke the language of Social Darwinism. Nations, he said, were like organisms. Some lived. Some died. Uncontrolled emigration meant the destruction of part of the living corpus of *italianità*.[49] Emigrants, he complained, left without Italian schools and books, were placed at the mercy of hotel-keepers, women, liquor and 'subversive agents'.[50]

After Villari retired as President in 1903, the Dante Alighieri Society moved away from too close an association with the Sonninians, nearer to Giolitti himself. The President from 1903 to

1906 was Luigi Rava, Federzoni's later sponsor, a politician whose career was remarkably flexible even in the era of *trasformismo*. It is notable that as well as being an educationalist, he was president of the landowners' Società Agricola Italiana and a member of the Consiglio Superiore dell'Emigrazione. Covered with official honours he would end his career in 1932 with appointment as Minister of State. Rava's particular cultural interest was the preservation of the Italian language. In 1911, he was also delighted that Italy's first Dreadnought was to be called the *Dante Alighieri*, and declared that the whole history of the Risorgimento had indicated that the 'ideal' could triumph over the 'real'.[51] Italy could be a Great Power yet, he implied, despite the squalor of Sicily or Sardinia.

Rava was succeeded by Paolo Boselli, another educationalist-politician with leanings potentially hostile to Giolittian reformism, who remained President of the Society until 1932. His presidency continued the translation of the Dante Alighieri Society into a semi-official organ. In 1916 Boselli was dragged out of relative political obscurity to head a compromise government, which, in turn, led the Italian war effort to the disaster at Caporetto. Despite this set-back, Boselli was thought to be of sufficient importance to merit being offered one of the first honorary membership tickets in the Partito Nazionale Fascista. He accepted. He also won a Collar of the Annunziata and a seat in the Senate, dying aged ninety-four, as Italy's elder statesman in 1932. Under Boselli's leadership the Dante Alighieri Society continued to grow. By 1911 it claimed over 50,000 members; its active budget was over 400,000 lire per annum, one of its Vice-Presidents was the President of the Banca d'Italia, Bonaldo Stringher.[52] However, the Dante Alighieri Society now lacked a strong political impulse, its closest links being with the embattled 'constitutional opposition'. Just before the First World War it was embarrassed by the attentions of members of the ANI who tried to stiffen the Society's attitude towards Italian expansion. Corradini addressed its Milan branch in 1909. In December 1913 one of the Vice-Presidents, D. Sanminiatelli, had to explain away to an annoyed San Giuliano how a Nationalist motion came to be passed at a Dante Congress. In fact, what the motion said was very much the truth, namely that 'in the new State of Albania the Italian government and the National Dante Alighieri Society will work assiduously for the diffusion of our culture thus complementing the political necessity of an economic penetration, which is employed to affirm the primacy of Italian influence on the other shore' of the Adriatic.[53] The Foreign Minister may have blanched at the word 'primacy', but he was more offended that tacit ambitions should have been expressed openly.

The extravagances of Nationalists apart, by 1914 the Dante Alighieri Society had developed into being little more than a semi-official[54] purveyor of cultural propaganda. Its direction was inevitably patriotic, but there is no evidence that its President, Boselli, or the Society as a whole, could directly influence policy. Much more it acted as a reflection of the opinion of that segment of the ruling classes interested in foreign affairs. Given its concentration on cultural matters, the political area involving the Dante Alighieri Society had become increasingly restricted. It was certainly not as influential as the Pan German League which was, in a way, its German equivalent. The Dante Alighieri Society might preach the lessons of *italianità* and remind patriots of the losses caused by emigration, but others organised and paid for the schools, and dreamed of constructing colonies to save the emigrants for Italy. If the Dante Alighieri Society was any example, it was still the government which made policy, with 'public opinion' being left the supportive role.

More courtly than the Dante Alighieri Society, but like it, potentially of considerable influence was the Italian Geographical Society, officially entitled the Royal Italian Geographical Society after 1913. Founded in Florence in 1867, the Society, which aimed to promote scientific knowledge by organising explorations in the vast unknown territories of the world, sent expeditions to places as diverse as Ethiopia, Morocco, the Congo, Tierra del Fuego and into the Arctic Ocean. In 1907 it was the Geographical Society which backed Prince Scipione Borghese's Peking to Paris 'raid'.[55] Proud of its wide international contacts with other learned bodies of its type, the Society usually left its leadership safely in aristocratic or academic hands,[56] while the more nationalist members of the royal family, the Queen-Mother, Margherita, or the Aostas, were often present at meetings and sometimes absent on expeditions.

However polite in appearance, the Geographical Society, was not solely a body of innocents. When imperialism became fashionable in the 1880s, the Society showed a distinct tendency to divert its attentions towards areas of Italian ambition, Harrar, the Somaliland and the Juba river were penetrated by sponsored 'scientific missions'.[57] The Juba expedition ended with the 'heroic death' of its leader, Captain Bottego, proclaimed by San Giuliano in the Chamber a martyr of the cowardly abandonment of Empire, and later to be an object of Fascist myth making.[58]

In 1906 the Society took a definite step towards politicisation, when it elected as President an active politician, Antonino Di San Giuliano. San Giuliano's travels and his academic pretensions gave him some reasonable claim to the Presidency, although it was only two months since he had left the Foreign Ministry. Never before had the Geographical Society been so openly linked to politics.

San Giuliano who had only joined the Society in November 1904, immediately announced that he wished the Geographical Society to intensify its pro-colonialist programme. On May Day 1906, presiding over his first ordinary meeting, San Giuliano urged that the Geographical Society should have a double aim:

to organise explorations, to study scientifically and practically those regions which for many reasons are of special interest to Italy; to diffuse, using as means publications and meetings, the results and every other theoretical and practical piece of knowledge which might concern [the science of] geography.

He was also anxious that the Geographical Society establish contacts with the other patriotic bodies, the Dante Alighieri Society, the Lega Navale and the Istituto Coloniale. But less than a week later another address qualified the zeal of his devotion to pure science:

Ours is a scientific Society which by preference must carry its scientific study to those countries where Italy has today, and will have in the future, its greatest economic and political interests.

The Society, San Giuliano thought, should pay attention to Italian public opinion, and encourage 'the country' to develop a 'love and recognition' for problems in areas of national interest.

In the grandiose struggle of the nations for prosperity and power Italy must not be the last, and one of the most effective means in order not to be the last is that which diffuses and reinforces in public opinion the consciousness of this necessity and the firm intention to work for this ideal.[59]

The areas which he defined as suitable for Italian 'scientific' expeditions were Asia Minor, Mesopotamia, the Aegean islands,

Ethiopia, Eritrea, Yemen, Benadir, Tripoli and Cyrenaica. His language may have been opaque, but he was presenting a catalogue of Italian imperial ambition.

The small elite group, anxious at that time to revive Italian colonialism, were much in evidence to applaud San Giuliano's rhetoric. Members of the Society in 1906 included Canevaro, De Martino II, Pelloux, P. Levi, Scalea, Martini, Salvago Raggi, A. Scalabrini and Paolo Thaon Di Revel. But they had little time to respond to the fervently imperialist direction given to the Society by its new President. San Giuliano's presidency was the shortest in the history of the Geographical Society and, in November 1906, it was announced that he had resigned to become ambassador in London. His period of office had produced little more than pronouncements of intention.

The new President was Raffaele Cappelli, an ex-diplomat and ex-Minister of Foreign Affairs. Like Rava of the Dante Alighieri Society, Cappelli was a landowner of flexible, moderately conservative, politics. The impulse given to the Society by San Giuliano was diverted. By January 1908 membership had increased to a high of 1,407, a rise, it was boasted, of 65% in twenty-one months.[60] Some eminent Foreign Ministry officials joined (e.g. Bollati and the youngest De Martino).[61] Some colonialist papers were read. But the definition of aim provided for the Society by San Giuliano was blurred. Cappelli was pleased when two new branches opened in 'colonial countries', respectively Tunis and Argentina,[62] but the vagueness of the meaning of 'colony' when used in this sense was indicative of the difference between the new President and his predecessor.

Under the patronage of the King, with an annual budget of 70,000 lire, about half provided by the government, the Geographical Society returned to being a pleasant meeting ground for eminent dilettantes. A few nationalist speakers were heard; but so was the British Military Attaché, Delmé-Radcliffe, an official who was *persona gratissima* at court. It was appropriate that Cappelli's successor as President was Prince Scipione Borghese. Only in the 1920s, that hey-day of Nationalist influence over colonial policy, did the Geographical Society return to the endeavour suggested by San Giuliano, to mobilise the elite of public opinion in favour of colonialism. From 1921 to 1928 Thaon Di Revel, Federzoni and

Scalea were successive presidents,[63] but by then invocations of colonialism were openly made at government request.

Less amateur than the Geographical Society was the Lega Navale Italiana, which was set up in 1897, one year before the more famous German Navy League. The immediate spur to the establishment of the Lega Navale was the battle of Adowa and its aftermath. The League's early rubrics made its intention quite clear.

After this defeat it seems that a strange sense of despondency has fallen upon the Nation, and the faith of public opinion in the effectiveness of our military organisation has been shaken. Groundless was the weakness of this and groundless the fear. In the life of a people of thirty million souls one colonial defeat is only an incident. It is sufficient to change way and direction.

In order to ensure that expansion was not abandoned the League stated 'we want new, strong and virile sentiments to come to reinvigorate our people'.[64]

The first committee was headed by a sailor, Rear-Admiral Renaud di Falicon. The leading politician and founding Vice-President was Antonino Di San Giuliano, who also presided over a special sub-committee on Emigration and Colonies. Among other politicians who joined the Lega Navale were Sidney Sonnino and Giorgio, his elder brother, De Marinis, Cirmeni, Morin, General Bava Beccaris, P. Villari, N. Nasi, Franchetti and Scalea. There were also representatives of the Ferraris and Thaon di Revel families, Salvago Raggi, Chiaramonte Bordonaro and a number of other officers from the consular service.[65]

In comparison with its German or other foreign counterparts, the Lega Navale progressed slowly at first. In 1899 official membership was only 4,000, and a central office was not established in Rome until 1902. In 1907 the League received a Royal charter, and by 1911 membership had reached the respectable height of 15,000.[66] By then Victor Emmanuel III was its patron, the Duke of Aosta its Honorary President; Piero Foscari and Giuseppe Lanza Di Trabia, a cousin of Scalea, were among its counsellors.

Apart from San Giuliano, there were two other particularly interesting members. The Secretary-General, who did most of the work in the early days of the League was Giovanni Limo. Limo, in 1899, reinforced his fame by writing the sensational *La Guerra del 190...*, an early, and Italy's major, contribution to the *genre* of popular scare books about the shape of wars to come.[67] When writing directly about the Lega Navale, Limo's rhetoric had a familiar ring. The sea had a 'poetic' beauty and grandeur, but what was really significant was that nations which did not essay onto the seas 'died'. The Lega Navale, he said, must overcome the 'ruinous struggle' of the classes and unite the nation in favour of expansion. Emigration, social problems and the poverty of the South could be solved by a strong navy and merchant marine. 'The problem of the *Mezzogiorno*', he declared, 'is above all a maritime one.' Once 'our fathers' had called the Mediterranean 'Mare Nostrum!' 'Public opinion' must always be reminded of this and of Italy's potentially incomparable strategic position in the Mediterranean.[68]

Limo directed the League's journal, which was also called *La Lega Navale*, and continued to expend his own rhetoric and encourage the rhetoric of others in conferences often in Rome, but also in other cities where the League had opened offices.[69]

The other particularly interesting member of the Lega Navale was Admiral Giovanni Bettòlo who became President from 1912 to 1916. Also cited on the first membership lists was the Società Anonima La Siderurgica Italiana, symbolic of the attention likely to be devoted to a body which favoured political expansion, a bigger merchant marine and navy, and larger government subsidies to Italian heavy industries. Bettòlo was very much the link man between heavy industry and naval and diplomatic politics. Three times Minister of the Navy, under Pelloux, Zanardelli and Sonnino, Bettòlo was also celebrated as the commander who hauled off the Italian ship which unluckily and disgracefully ran aground during the formal inauguration ceremonies of the Kiel Canal in June 1895.[70] Bettòlo won a different sort of fame in 1903 when he was attacked by the Socialist, Enrico Ferri, for corrupt dealing with the steelworks at Terni. Naval reconstruction, it was alleged, had proceeded under terms unduly favourable to the Terni organisation which had been allowed to charge elevated prices and use poor material in order to recoup its economic fortunes. Bettòlo was forced to resign, and from 1903 to 1906 a parliamentary commission investigated his dealings with Terni until the matter was safely '*insabbiata*'[71] (lit. ensanded, to use the delightful and untranslateable Italian word).

Bettòlo's career suffered from the scandal, and his patriotic rhodomontades in the Chamber were particularly likely thereafter to arouse Socialist hostility. As President of the Lega Navale, Bettòlo declared his intention of creating a 'colonial party' among the deputies, presumably on the model of Étienne's group in France,[72] but he eventually admitted that the nature of the Italian parliament prevented him from succeeding in this task.

What is notable about the Lega Navale, at least in its origins, is its difference in its ideal of foreign policy from the Dante Alighieri Society, and Trento and Trieste groups. For Italian navalism, the major rival down to 1914 was France, the country which many Italians feared, could genuinely talk about a 'mare nostrum'. It was characteristic, however, of the new position in international affairs which Italy was reaching by 1914, that past Francophobia was fading, or at least being joined by new Austrophobia. In 1908 the hated Franz Ferdinand, who was known to be an enemy of Italy, became President of the Austrian Navy League.[73] From 1909, the Italian version of a 'naval race' in Dreadnought building was waged against Austria, not France.[74] The story of the Lega Navale is thus the reverse, but also the parallel of the Dante Alighieri and some of the irredentist groups. From 1910 to 1914 factions in Italian politics would go on favouring France, or Austria, as Italy's major rival, but many members of the ruling classes were turning to the more generic belief that Italy must expand, and that it did not matter so much against whom this expansion was directed, so long as it did occur.

The changing emphasis of the Lega Navale also raises the question of the extent of its influence. Useful as an assembly place for deputies and admirals who did not believe that Adowa was a turning point, or as a forum in which to encourage, and be encouraged by, heavy industry, the Lega Navale lacked the tightness of organisation or size of membership to impinge strongly on government decisions. What the League did do was to reflect the strong current of ruling class opinion which was nationalist *ante letteram*, which never quite understood all the philosophy of the ANI's intellectuals, but which had long been quite clear that Italy must be strong, and anti–socialist.

Similarly anti-French, and therefore anti–irredentist in its origins, but soon preferring a more general expansionism, was the Istituto Coloniale Italiano, numerically the smallest, but also the most powerful of the groups trying to push Italy back onto an imperial course. The Institute was founded after September 1905, when the

Governor of Eritrea, Ferdinando Martini, summoned a colonial conference to his new capital, Asmara. Martini was a most able and influential member of the ruling elite, politically a Sonninian rather than a Giolittian. He also had many literary contacts, and was personally a *belle-lettrist* of wit and urbanity who was to write a book called *Between One Cigar and Another*. In 1914 he took on the job of Minister of Colonies under Salandra, after he had failed as a lyric writer for his fellow Tuscan, Giacomo Puccini.[75]

As Governor of Eritrea, Martini had presided over a policy of retrenchment, and accepted that Eritrea could not be a suitable venue for demographic colonialism.[76] Nonetheless, as his appointment drew to a close, Martini, perhaps encouraged to proper activity by the inevitable allegations of corruption which were being raised against him, decided to sponsor a colonial conference at his new capital, Asmara, where he had done his best to recreate a Tuscan city on the Eritrean plateau. The Conference was summoned with appropriate Liberal fanfare. King Victor Emmanuel III became patron, the Ministers of Foreign Affairs, the Navy, Education, and Agriculture, Industry and Commerce shared honorary presidency; the Geographical Society and other groups, learned or commercial, interested in Italian Africa, pledged their support. Giacomo Agnesa, chief of the Colonial Office inside the Foreign Ministry, San Giuliano, and Primo Levi helped Baron Giorgio Sonnino with preparatory organisation.

It was hoped that the Congress would make it easier for 'all citizens' to visit Eritrea. This experience would then remove the 'diffidence and scepticism' which 'military events' (the unmentioned Adowa) had caused Italy. Once Adowa was expunged, Italy could begin 'a period of fertile economic activity regulated by direct knowledge of the African land which has cost so many noble lives to the *patria*'. In this manner, Eritrea would fulfil its destiny as a 'marvellous garden rich in useful products'.

The Congress was designed to underline Martini's achievements as governor and to extol the values of colonialism. The 'public opinion' which was to be so moved, in practice meant the restricted electorate of Liberal Italy. The definition of the 'citizens' who might marvel at the Eden of Eritrea had a more antique than democratic ring – the registration fee for attendance was fifty lire, about one month's pay for the majority of Italians.

Political pressure groups and foreign policy

First of the themes to be discussed was 'the problem of emigration in its relations with Italian Africa'. Other topics involved the agricultural, commercial and maritime development of Eritrea and methods of further penetration in Africa. Attention was to be given to the encouragement in Italy of colonial studies and the propagandising of 'public opinion' in favour of colonial development.[77] Those who would attend the conference were a familiar group: San Giuliano, Primo Levi and Giacomo De Martino II were among those who travelled to Asmara. Many of the young men of the Foreign Ministry also indicated their interest, notably Mario Lago and Salvatore Contarini, as did Enrico Corradini. Most major Italian newspapers sent correspondents; Rome's Chamber of Commerce, the Banca Commerciale Italiana and Bonaldo Stringher of the Banca d'Italia accorded support. But it was De Martino and San Giuliano who alone had the privilege of staying in the Governor's Palace.[78] One colonialist journalist wittily said that the Conference had turned into a triumph not for the Grand Duchy of Tuscany but for the Kingdom of the Two Sicilies.[79]

The conference's major decision was to set up the Istituto Coloniale Italiano to 'coordinate' Italian 'colonial action'. Collaboration was urged with other Italian colonial and geographical groups since 'pacific Italian commercial penetration in the Mediterranean basin must meet ever greater success', specifically in Tripoli, Cyrenaica and Ethiopia. The emigration report, signed jointly by San Giuliano and De Martino II, noted that Eritrea could take more emigration, but not all of it. The government must commission urgent studies to see how to overcome this loss to the nation.[80]

In 1906 the Istituto Coloniale Italiano was formally constituted in Italy, with its central office in Rome. Ironically, given further events, this was located in the *Assicurazioni Generali* building in the Piazza Venezia,[81] directly opposite the Palazzo Venezia, from the balcony of which Mussolini would later preach imperial grandeur. To the south both structures were shadowed by the rising Victor Emmanuel monument.

The Institute organised iself in the same fashion as other pressure groups. Local branches had considerable autonomy. A journal *Rivista Coloniale* was published, usually once a month. Its *direttore*, Renato Paoli, was a colonial expert, whose enthusiasm was mixed with realism, which later proved unacceptable to the Society. The Institute was not a mass organisation, only two hundred and twenty nine people attended the foundation meeting in Rome.[82] What was far more significant was the nearness of the membership to those who made foreign policy. First President of the Institute was Giacòmo De Martino II; as Vice-Presidents were two former Ministers of Foreign Affairs, San Giuliano and Guicciardini; and Ignazio Florio, the chief of the family which controlled the *Società di Navigazione Generale*. Giorgio Sonnino, the brother of Sidney, was the final Vice-President. Other leading figures in the Institute included Primo Levi (a counsellor), Scalea (who succeeded San Giuliano as Vice President in 1907), Bettòlo, Angelo Scalabrini (a counsellor), Martini (Vice-President in 1909), and Luigi Borsarelli Di Rifreddo (who replaced Scalea as Under-Secretary for Foreign Affairs in March 1914). Foscari, Rava, Pirelli, Salandra, S. Crespi, Andrea Torre, Giuseppe Volpi, Franchetti, Agnesa, Imperiali, Stringher, Camillo Ruspoli, Nathan, the youngest Giacomo De Martino and even Daniele Varè were early members.

De Martino II remained as President until Sidney Sonnino and Guicciardini appointed him Governor of Somaliland at the beginning of 1910.[83] Until then, he had been a firm leader, defining closely what he regarded as the Institute's aims. The language was familiar: the *Rivista Coloniale* would systematise the thinking of 'public opinion' about colonies, emigration and the *patria*; in the past, opportunities had been missed; now Italians must supervise more closely their colonial actions if they wished 'to leave the narrow bounds of our present activity and...develop wider forms of life'.[84] The *Rivista* specifically denied any 'imperialist' intention in these ostensibly menacing phrases. 'Serene objectivity' and 'reasoned discussions' were its simple aims, and, if science led to imperial action, then that was not the Institute's fault.

Early articles in *Rivista Coloniale* cast doubts on the genuineness of this pious declaration. One writer pointed to the desolation of Italy's current international situation, and the impossibility of standing by while other states expanded.[85] An anonymous archaeologist wrote about 'Antiquity in Tripoli and Cyrenaica', asserting that 'Archaeological explorations...must follow and not precede the occupation, armed or pacific, of the country'.[86] In Italian archaeological circles, the *romanità* of the Mediterranean inspired a not infrequent argument that either the spade should follow the flag, or the flag the spade. More circumspectly, Mayor des Planches, the Italian ambassador to the United States, wrote of the prejudices held there against 'Dagoes' and 'organ-grinders'.[87]

De Martino's presidential pronouncements also showed a singular lack of a pure devotion to science for its own sake. In April 1907, for example, he urged the federation of the 'four, great, related societies', the Dante Alighieri Society, the Geographical Society, the Lega Navale and the Istituto Coloniale. These, he noted optimistically, were

all signs of a promising reawakening of public opinion which would like to drive Italy, in its reborn industrial and commercial prosperity, towards those remote regions where the most powerful nations of the world are contending for primacy, attaining by pacific conquest an admirable increase in power and prosperity.

The major, present struggle, De Martino observed, was between the 'Anglo-Saxon' and 'Germanic races'. In this contest, 'woe to the weak'.

The colonial policy of struggles and economic conquests will thus represent the blood which flows and re-flows through the veins in the great body of the nations; and the isolated and secluded State, like an atrophied and useless member, will perish.[88]

De Martino did not succeed in uniting colonialist opinion. Indeed, briefly the Institute was challenged by Franchetti, always a law to himself, who set up an Istituto Agricolo Coloniale in Florence. But, with Primo Levi acting as negotiator, Franchetti was eventually persuaded to join the senior body.[89]

Meanwhile, De Martino was refreshed by a safari along the coasts of North Africa. He returned to invoke the image of Carthage regained by the 'new Italy', and to report a meeting in the sands with an Anglo-Indian who used at length the same Social Darwinian arguments about imperialism of which De Martino himself was so fond. 'Italy talks and England works, here is the secret of our peoples and their contrasting colonial performance', said De Martino to close the discussion.[90]

De Martino's hope for a united colonialist bloc, an Italian *parti colonial*, had not disappeared. To the 1908 Annual General Meeting he announced that the patriotic bodies were combining to hold a

'Congress of Italians Abroad' for which Tittoni had pledged government financial assistance, and encouragement from Italian officials stationed in foreign countries. Associated too would be the usual politicians, Salandra, Giorgio Sonnino, Martini, Boselli, and Scalea.[91]

While preparations for the Congress began, De Martino's eloquence in favour of national expansion matched Corradini's. When it was announced that a branch of the Institute was to open in Palermo, De Martino proclaimed: 'Sicily, strong mother of our best colonisers, is a worthy seat of an Institute which has among its main aims the expansion of Italy abroad.'[92] In June, De Martino travelled south to open the branch, and told the Palermitans of his regret that Tunis, the pride of his 'race', had fallen to foreigners. A 'biological law' operated for nations as well as individuals. Herein some change was possible: 'France has a happier present; Italy a more promising future.' Above all, Italy must develop the consciousness of being a Great Mediterranean Power and must

know how to pick the occasions which certainly are not lacking, to affirm her own influence and her own hegemony over the northern regions of Africa where the traditions of the past and the realities of the present called her to exercise an active policy.

Look, for example, he said, to Tripoli, 'a land so near to us as almost to be able to see it, a land fertile, rich, once a happy and prosperous colony of the Greeks and Romans'. Nearby lay the plateau of Cyrenaica, 'a real Eden'. Italy, thus, he declared, needed a new policy for new conditions. The 'four great patriotic societies' were working and must work to awaken national consciousness to these new ambitions.[93]

The Congress of Italians Abroad duly assembled in Rome in October 1908.[94] King Victor Emmanuel III listened to another of De Martino's orations proclaiming 'the greatness of Italy working outside its borders' but, this time, the tone was official. Dante, Galileo and Christopher Columbus were cited more than the *romanità* of Tripoli and Carthage.[95]

Naturally the Congress was very concerned with Italian emigration, which had gone on increasing each year. To meet the problem, the Istituto Coloniale was given government support, and Tittoni promised that Italian diplomats would sponsor Institute activities. Emigrants too were to be encouraged to use Institute branches as their major advocate with foreign governments.[96] As a further initiative, in association with the Dante Alighieri Society, the Institute established a Commission to investigate Italian schools abroad. Primo Levi and Angelo Scalabrini were members.

If a revival of *romanità* was most likely to be challenged by France, *italianità* was always opposed by Austria. By chance, the First Congress of Italians Abroad was reminded of the ambivalence of Italy's diplomatic position. The assembled patriots were shocked by Austria's annexation of the provinces of Bosnia and Herzegovina in October 1908. Despite Article VII of the Triple Alliance, Italy received no compensation for Austria's advantage. Rather, the awkwardness of Italy's ties to her rival 'friends' and 'allies' were still more embarrassingly plain than they had been at the Algeciras Conference two years before.

These events point again to the 'natural' character of the revival of Italian pretensions to be a Great Power by 1910. The Asmara Congress had been held before the Algeciras Conference or the economic downturn of 1907;[97] so the First Congress of Italians Abroad was planned before there was any knowledge of the Bosnia–Herzegovina crisis. Far from being the fount of Italian nationalism, the events of 1908 only underlined the meaningfulness of what 'patriots' had been saying for years.

Was the Istituto Coloniale by 1908 a mouthpiece of Italian business and financial interests in the way that Étienne's *parti colonial* was in France? The answer to this question seems to be definitely no. There were some important businessmen, involved in Italian 'economic imperialism', who did belong to the Istituto Coloniale – Volpi, Besso, I. Florio, Foscari, Crespi, Stringher. Far more often, the members who were not prominent politicians were 'intellectuals' or publicists – botanists, archaeologists, lawyers, economists. The Institute remained a tiny, elite body, proud when its membership passed 300.[98] It represented not a particular interest within Italian society,[99] but the general acceptance by many in the Liberal ruling classes that Italy needed to think anew about colonialism, imperialism and foreign policy.

Symbolic of this new or revived ambition for the Third Italy were to be the great patriotic *feste*, planned for 1911 to mark United Italy's Fiftieth Anniversary, the *Cinquantennio*. The Istituto Coloniale announced that there would be a second, larger and more vibrant Congress of Italians Abroad. The accustomed names joined an organisational committee, De Martino, Canevaro, Cappelli, Scalea, Boselli, Fusinato, Martini, Salandra and Stringher.[100]

Another structure, long planned, was due to be completed in 1911. This was the Victor Emmanuel Monument, begun in 1882, as yet without winged victories and the tomb of the Unknown Soldier, but still a decided demonstration that Italy had taken up the mantle of Rome. Positioned in the area of Rome most redolent with the relics of the classical past, the very presence of the monument seemed to contemporaries a demonstration that Italy could acquire a place in the sun. *Corriere della Sera* set the tone of the inauguration day when it enthused over the monument risen 'amid the immense ruins of ancient Rome', affirming the 'imperishable hope of Latin blood' as it symbolised 'the epic dawn of the Third Italy'.[101]

The future had hung more heavily over Italy at a *festa* in Turin one month before. On that occasion, a parliamentarian, in the presence of the King and Queen, had told 6,000 children assembled in a '*festa* of the future' that

the strong and ancient trunk which gave to Rome, mother, the branches tightly bound about the axe, thus making the lictor's *fascio* the symbol of the supreme power and of strength in unity, seems to us to grow green again . . . by the miracle of renewed youth in the era of the Third Italy.[102]

Only the Socialists, whose paper *Avanti*! sardonically talked about the Victor Emmanuel '*monumentissimo*',[103] and Giolitti,[104] remained relatively immune to such rhetoric.

However exemplary of the nationalism of the Italian ruling classes in the months before the Libyan War, the popular celebrations of the *Cinquantennio* were rather outside the original aim of influencing 'public opinion' as defined by the Istituto Coloniale. With San Giuliano in the *Consulta*, De Martino II in Somaliland, and Martini puzzling over lyrics in Tuscany, the Istituto Coloniale drifted more and more into becoming another semi–official body. The government made a generous grant of 40,000 lire to the expenses of the Second Congress of Italians Abroad.[105] In return, the Istituto Coloniale acted as a useful channel of unofficial diplomatic information during the Libyan War, and, thereafter, in Albania, seconded the government in its cultural and commercial contest with Austria.[106]

Political pressure groups and foreign policy

De Martino II had been replaced as President by Guido Fusinato, an expert on international law, who would be one of the negotiators of the Treaty of Lausanne in 1912. Fusinato had the appropriate training for a leader of the Istituto Coloniale – he was Under-Secretary of State for Foreign Affairs 1899–1901, 1903–5. His own ideas about foreign policy were conservative, and markedly triplicist.[107] Fusinato did not leave much imprint on the Istituto Coloniale and in 1912 he was replaced by Bettòlo who was at the same time President of the Lega Navale and who announced again the intention of forming a united colonialist party.[108]

In fact, the triumph in Libya had appeased the immediate ambitions of many members of the Institute. San Giuliano, in office, was not interested in sponsoring too many public exhibitions of Italian planning of a road to imperialism. The *Rivista Coloniale*, therefore, did not echo the criticism of Nationalists or Sonninians that Giolitti and San Giuliano had not prosecuted the Libyan War energetically or openly enough.[109] Instead it limited itself to warnings that, after the 'little war', a 'big' one was coming, for which the nation should be ready.[110] Roman names, it was meanwhile argued, should be restored in Libya to help Italians recall their heritage.[111] Ethiopia too was mentioned again as part of a 'geographical and political entity' naturally belonging to Italy. The 'ten commandments for Italians Abroad' were listed,[112] but no more plans were made to hold exhilarating emigrant congresses in Rome.

In May 1914, paralleling the change in government, there was a change in leadership at the Institute. Sonninians and Nationalists began to play a more prominent role in the flagging Institute, which still only boasted 678 members. The new President was the young and energetic Ernesto Artom, a pro-Salandran deputy, who had once been Visconti Venosta's secretary, and who soon declared that the Institute must become a more vocal defender of *italianità*.[113] Andrea Torre, Elio Morpurgo (twice a Sonninian Cabinet Minister) and Giovanni Colonna Di Cesarò (another anti-Giolittian, Mussolini's first Minister of Posts and Telegraphs) were Vice Presidents. Of the younger generation, Federzoni and Gallenga Stuart became Councillors.

Before Salandra's government could be encouraged to new imperial action there was war. Given its triplicist leanings, its large establishment membership, its refusal to attract mass support, and its ties to the government, the Institute was embarrassed by the Great War which it had once predicted. Limping behind the government, it refrained from advocating Italian intervention until 1915.

The final equivocation of the Istituto Coloniale highlights a predominant feature of all the pressure groups which tried after Adowa to encourage Italian colonialism. In advocating colonialism, none of the groups, probably including the Nationalists and irredentists, understood that goal in mass terms. The Victor Emmanuel monument, the Congress for Italians Abroad, did not yet have as many democratic, 'liturgical' overtones as did fascist architecture or assemblies. The 'public opinion' which was so eagerly courted was not that of the people, of a State with universal suffrage, and certainly not of a State with genuine democracy. The Istituto Coloniale, the Royal Italian Geographical Society, the Lega Navale Italiana, the Dante Alighieri Society, still viewed their Italy as that narrow, Liberal one created by the Risorgimento.

It is also notable that most of the elite interested in foreign policy did not recognise a democracy in the making in Giolitti's Italy. The colonialist societies agreed that socialism and democracy were hostile and dangerous, but they shared a certain confidence or lassitude in believing that the traditions of government by the existing ruling classes could survive so long as Italy became appropriately nationalist, expansionist and colonialist. The traditions of the continuity of foreign policy, the importance of the royal prerogative, the 'decencies' which meant that Foreign Ministers should not be too directly criticised, all died hard. With one of their number in office, with the success in Libya, all of the pressure groups except the Nationalists, became rather less ardent in their advocacy of expansionism than they had been from 1905 to 1910.

At the same time, the distinctiveness of the Nationalists should not be exaggerated. So much of their rhetoric was for domestic consumption, and indeed was directed at winning a particular conflict for control of the major 'constitutional' opposition to Giolitti. One day, the Nationalists, despite their enormous and much underestimated role in Fascist foreign and domestic affairs, would ironically find themselves under attack by another, rather more rudely popular, group of 'outs' from within the Fascist party. In the nineteen-thirties many ex-Nationalists were left to retreat into the surviving but 'fascistised' versions of the Geographical or Dante Alighieri Societies, the Lega Navale or the Istituto Coloniale. Then, in the Second World War, Fascist methods would destroy the foreign policy ambitions held by so many of the Italian ruling classes after 1860. For what is most significant about the Nationalists and the other pressure groups before 1914 is not their differences, but their similarities. Politicians, journalists, bankers, industrialists, agrarians, young and old, were all agreed that Italy was and must be a Great Power. Adowa, Algeciras, Bosnia–Herzegovina, an economic crisis or downturn, could produce short-term temporising or advance. But all the Liberal elite, which now held Rome, which dreamed of a new, universal ideology for the 'Third Italy', and which chose the site of, and erected, the Victor Emmanuel monument, were anxious that the 'new Italy' play a major role on the international stage.

A large-scale consensus in the ruling elite was one thing; the practice of Italian foreign policy was another. Victor Emmanuel III, in one of his lapidary moments muttered that it was 'bayonets and not Dante Alighieri' which made Italy.[114] After 1910 it would not be the bayonets, nor the Dante Alighieri Society and the other pressure groups which 'made' Italian foreign policy in any real sense. In so far as Italy took initiatives of her own, the centre of her foreign policy making process remained in the Foreign Ministry, and therefore in the man who from 1910 to 1914 was incumbent there, Antonino Di San Giuliano.

CHAPTER 3

The making of a Foreign Minister:
Antonino Di San Giuliano

His efforts in promoting new enthusiasm for the Geographical Society, Lega Navale or Istituto Coloniale scarcely seem enough to win Antonino Paternò Castello Di San Giuliano immortal fame. The fact that he was Italy's Foreign Minister in July 1914 has also granted him little recognition outside Italy. His Christian name is often misspelled; even his term of office is mistaken. The major English textbook on modern Italian history dismisses him as 'timid and pro-German, the one politician whom the King really appreciated'.[1]

Inside Italy, by contrast, San Giuliano's defenders have outnumbered his critics. One of his more intelligent juniors, Carlo Galli, looking back decades after San Giuliano's death, discerned that 'after Cavour there certainly has not been any other Minister of Foreign Affairs of a higher ability, of a more ardent spirit and of a further vision' than San Giuliano.[2] From the senior Italian diplomatic historian of the period San Giuliano has earned the assessment 'excellent', in reference both to his ability and training.[3] The Fascist historian, Francesco Salata, even depicted San Giuliano, the seer, prophesying in 1914 that Italy would fight another great war 'twenty or thirty' years later.[4]

The motivation of such defenders was rather more patriotic than objective. For example, Galli was already a friend of the Nationalists, before 1914 a patriot and a Fascist-to-be. Augusto Torre has been the epitome of the official writer, having pursued an unbroken pedagogical career from 1913 to the 1970s. San Giuliano's reputation seems to rely on his success. While foreign affairs were under his administration Italy conquered Libya and suffered no international fiascoes. His death in October 1914 was fortunate because his policy had been sufficiently opaque until then for most later historians, depending on their tastes, to find in the archives either that he was an interventionist *tout court*, or that he was a sensible neutralist.

Antonino Di San Giuliano

This somewhat fortuitous reputation as one whose career was successful or ambiguous enough to be deemed a patriot by most[5] is made manifest by town planning in Rome today. The Viale Antonino Di San Giuliano, 'diplomatico', carries buses full of minor bureaucrats and zealous research-students from the Tiber to the Farnesina. This white, rectangular building, famous for its echoing corridors, was erected to be the headquarters of the Fascist party, but today houses the Ministry of Foreign Affairs and its archives. This is itself something of a symbol of much Italian writing on diplomacy. But there are other symbols, outside. San Giuliano was not the only patriot acceptable to those nominating the street names in Republican Italy. Other streets recall Salvatore Contarini, by reputation the last professional, the man who ruled the Ministry before 'Fascistisation'; Marshal Armando Diaz, *Duca della Vittoria*, leader of Italian armies to their final victory in the First World War and Mussolini's first Minister of War; Count Giuseppe Volpi di Misurata, Venetian entrepreneur, advocate and banker for Italian imperialism, servant both of Giolitti, and, as Governor of Tripolitania and Minister of Finance, Mussolini; Mario Toscano, until his death in 1968, doyen of Italian diplomatic historians, member of many an international commission, a Jew whose writing of patriotic history was interrupted but not changed by the last days of fascism. The official way of looking at things has proclaimed San Giuliano worthy, a statesman who would be acceptable in a national *paradiso*.

If Volpi, Contarini, Diaz and perhaps also Toscano, are to be accorded celestial patriotic pleasures, then San Giuliano is a worthy partner. For what San Giuliano, or Volpi, or Contarini or the others best represent is the continuity of Italian history. Compared to Berchtold or Jagow, Grey or Sazonov, San Giuliano was a clever diplomat. He was also a most equivocal one, in aim, in motivation and in background. San Giuliano, the diplomatist, the nationalist, the anti-socialist, is a better symbol of the nature of Liberal Italy in 1914 than many official historians have seen.

Antonino Di San Giuliano, sixth *Marchese* Di San Giuliano, fourth *Marchese* Di Capizzi, fourth *Signore* Di Motta Camastra, sixth *Barone* Di Campopetro, third *Barone* Di Pollicarini 'etc.' was born at Catania on 9 December 1852. The urban geography of Catania opens up rather different vistas about San Giuliano to those revealed in the streets outside the Farnesina. The main piazza of Catania is

69

that of the Duomo of Sant' Agata, and in it stands the symbol of Catania, a grey antique elephant in its colour reflecting the city's special relationship with Mount Etna. Along the Via Etnea lies the next piazza. There stands the administrative heart of Catania where the *Municipio* and the University administer to the body of the city the lay equivalent of what Sant' Agata and the elephant do for the soul. There is one further major building in the square. It is the *Palazzo San Giuliano*, on the outside pink, balconied, baroque; on the inside grey lava, the colour of workaday Catania. In the passage-way there are plaques celebrating visits in 1881 of King Umberto I, Queen Margherita and young Prince Victor Emmanuel, and in 1909 of King Edward VII, Queen Alexandra, Maria, Empress of Russia and Princess Victoria.

Behind the sculptured iron of the balconies lived the San Giuliano family from the early eighteenth century. The pink baroque vindicated their boast to be princes of the aristocracy of the Kingdom of the Two Sicilies, and the grey lava reminded them too that they belonged to Catania. The family was Norman, and had branches all over Sicily.[6] But, after something like a Catanian version of the politics of *illuminismo*, in which they won a conflict over the right to erect the Palazzo San Giuliano on a site owned by the Jesuits before the great eruption of Etna in 1693, the San Giulianos were the most famous and powerful family in the city. Later, Federico De Roberto, a local novelist of the *verismo* school, would write a trilogy about the family calling them the *vicerè*, the Viceroys.[7] A local proverb defined the social position of these viceroys rather more succinctly: 'Birritti e Cappeddi nun si juncinu.'[8]

Naturally the San Giulianos often held high rank in the administration of the Bourbon state, although perhaps the most famous member of the family had been the *Marchese* who in 1784 murdered his wife and her maid, missing the nurse who then revealed all. As punishment, the Palazzo San Giuliano had a squad of Bourbon troops stationed in it, although the erring nobleman had been allowed to escape by sea 'to an unknown destination'. Thereafter, one window in the Palazzo, facing the piazza, was walled up reminding locals of the San Giuliano crime and giving rise to further macabre rumours about what had gone on in that room.[9]

The heir of this ill-fated union, also called Antonino, was a reactionary who bitterly contested the abolition of feudal dues in

1812 and who died, shocked by the disasters befalling the Bourbon dynasty, on 6 January 1861. In the meantime he had been powerful or adroit enough also to obtain office in the Catanian versions of the anti-Bourbon *moti* of 1820 and 1837.

Antonino's son, Benedetto Orazio, was sufficiently involved in the 'revolution' of 1837 to be exiled for a while to Malta. He was amnestied in 1844, but again became a Colonel of the National Guard in 1848. He was, however, attached to his class and its interests and married the daughter of the Prince of Cassaro who was Foreign Minister in the 1830s to the Bourbon King, Ferdinand II, 'Bomba'. Although it was the yellow flag of Sicilian particularism and not the green-white-red tricolor which had waved over Catania in 1837, Benedetto found no discomfort in the Risorgimento. Indeed he was another Sicilian willing that things should change so that they could remain the same. The new *Marchese* Di San Giuliano accepted nomination to the Italian Senate on January 20 1861, precisely a fortnight after his Bourbon father's death. *Trasformismo*, it seemed, was not something which Sicilian aristocrats would find difficult to learn in United Italy. In the *rivoluzione mancata* which was the Risorgimento in Sicily, the 'unification' of Italy had been won for (if not by) men like Benedetto Orazio Di San Giuliano. Fifty years later, when Antonino Di San Giuliano, the grandson of the Prince of Cassaro, promoted to be his Secretary-General, Giacomo De Martino, the heir of the family which had been Bourbon consuls in Tunis, almost uninterrupted from 1816 to 1861, and which had provided the last Foreign Minister of all in the Kingdom of Naples–Sicily, it may be asked whether a student is better qualified to study Italian foreign policy by a knowledge of theories of economic imperialism, or of 'the moral bases of a backward society', and of 'honour and shame' in a Mediterranean familial community.

To make sure of the rewards of his political good sense, Benedetto needed an heir. After a series of family deaths, Antonino was the only surviving child and family attention was concentrated on keeping him alive. Later Antonino regretted his cosseted youth:

the only son, after the almost simultaneous death of all my brothers, delicate of health, loved too much by my father, flattered by everyone in the narrow circle of Catanian aristocracy, belonging to a family to which everyone admitted an unarguable local superiority, I came unconsciously to consider myself the centre of the universe.[10]

Often restricted to bed, prevented from mixing with other children 'because my father feared either that they would injure me or expose me to draughts and other dangers', San Giuliano grew up a melancholic and introverted child, who was often treated as if he were feeble-minded 'not able to take decisions, not able to do manual work'. With the onset of middle age, he would philosophise, a little self-consciously: 'I read in Rousseau: "souffrir est la première chose qu'il doit apprendre et celle qu'il aura le plus grand besoin de savoir". Here then is the great gap in my education.'[11]

The sixth *Marchese* Di San Giuliano was left with a weak constitution. From 1882 he suffered regularly from what was called gout,[12] a term which must have covered a number of physical and nervous ills. When he died he was not yet sixty-two, still a young man by the standards of Italian politics, ten years younger, for example, than Giolitti. His 'gout' meant that he often suffered from atrocious pain. In 1914 the contorted state of his corpse appalled even the most urbane mourner.[13] While he was alive, San Giuliano comforted himself with cynicism; the trouble had lain with his mother, he said. If only she had not been 'honest', the faults of generations of inbreeding might have been overcome by the introduction of new blood.[14]

This misanthropic, somewhat ungentlemanly, cynicism was what immediately struck contemporaries about San Giuliano. They also noticed a prodigious memory and a passionate love of work. Beneath the cynicism, some detected what might have been expected in a man of San Giuliano's background and upbringing – a compulsive search for admiration and success, for that Power which belonged to the *vicerè*, but which had been more and more threatened by the processes of modernisation occurring through San Giuliano's lifetime.

To a certain level, political involvement and achievement came effortlessly to a San Giuliano. A helpful family story was spread, after the event, about Antonino's first essay into the political world. Too young to fight in the Risorgimento, the boy San Giuliano, prompted by his mother, was alleged to have made his choice for Italy by shouting 'Viva l'Italia' down from the palazzo balcony to the conquering *Garibaldini* in 1860. Whether or not this was so, in 1866, the sickly non-combatant teenager composed a *Hymn to War* for those Catanians unlucky enough to be marching off to the inglorious campaign against Austria. The rendition of the *Hymn* by the town band in the Bellini gardens may have been facilitated by Benedetto's career as *sindaco* and Senator. The young Antonino meanwhile continued writing, producing some political poetry, a patriotic hymn to Italy, two liberal odes to the First Republic in Spain and a satire on the French, perennial objects of suspicion to the Sicilian ruling class.[15]

An interest in bad poetry was soon replaced by one in modern philosophy. In 1871 San Giuliano descended the stairs of his palazzo and crossed the road to enrol at the local university. There, apart from not altogether unexpected academic success, he found that the great names of contemporary political philosophy – Comte, Spencer, Darwin, J. S. Mill and even Marx – were known. San Giuliano is reported to have read and re-read them, copying whole pages into a commonplace book. From 'positivism' and 'sociology' he learned that world events occurred because of laws which were rational and inexorable and which man must try to discover.

Throughout his political career, San Giuliano would look wistfully back to academic life. Perhaps he was envious of Salandra, Orlando or Nitti, Southern politicians who all held university posts and who fitted the Italian tradition recently followed by *professori* Fanfani and Moro, and once aped by that erstwhile school-teacher of French, *professore* Mussolini. Certainly San Giuliano liked to meditate on the intellectual constructs which lay behind politics:

Perhaps I should abandon politics, and since life without hope of fame would be too burdensome for me, I should dedicate myself...to science. Sociology on the other hand has always attracted me, and there are two fundamental concepts in this science which I would like to deepen and clarify in their various examples and consequences; that is the identity of the laws of nature in all their varied phenomena from mechanical to social, and progress.

Some years later, San Giuliano reverted to this theme, pondering whether he should write a book entitled *The Future*, wherein he

would try to foresee the consequences of the two causes which most powerfully act and modify the current state of man and society, that is first, the Darwinian law of selection with all reasons which support and oppose it, second, the rising, irresistible domination and spread of the positivist spirit.[16]

Perhaps, all in all, it is as well that politics became his calling. But, however jejune were these ideas, San Giuliano continued to hold them. As Minister of Foreign Affairs he would look for patterns and laws into which Italian expansionism could be fitted. Much of the mind of the Foreign Minister was made at the parochial University of Catania in the 1870s.

At the university he duly completed his laureate in law, writing on 'State and Church' from an anti-clerical and rationalist stand-point. Reflecting his society, his Freemasonry and his ancient family rivalry with the Piazza del Duomo, San Giuliano derided post-conciliar contemporaries who thought internal reform could restore the Church to ancient purity or power. 'Reconciliation between Church and State', he wrote solemnly, is 'neither possible nor desirable'.[17]

His anti-clericalism having defined his 'liberalism', San Giuliano was duly launched into local politics. In 1876 the *Gazzetta del Circolo di Cittadini* was good enough to publish two speeches delivered by the young *Marchese* who, it averred, 'possesses the serene gravity of an English *leader*'. The reference to England was apposite because San Giuliano, apart from an obligatory citation from Dante, used John Russell and Herbert Spencer to argue an extension of the suffrage to those who had reached the culture of the fourth *elementare*. Any further move, he regretted, would only encourage clerical reactionaries.[18]

Fortified by his career in public speaking, in 1879 San Giuliano became *sindaco* of Catania at the minimum legal age. Despite a dispute about the appropriate embellishment of the elephant statue and its fountain with De Roberto who would have preferred a new monument to Bellini,[19] in 1882 San Giuliano ran for the Chamber of Deputies when still below the minimum age of thirty. Local interests were attracted by San Giuliano's defence of the *Circumetnea* railway, the building of which had been recently suspended. References from Horace and Dante assisted a learned case that the railway would help Catania's port and its trade in rivalry with Messina.[20]

San Giuliano also spoke more generically to his '*cari cittadini*'. He stood, he said, for the Savoy dynasty, for 'order with liberty', for 'stability with progress'. He favoured a firm foreign policy, hostile to France, against whom Italy must keep her powder dry and 'prepare' militarily, economically and diplomatically. 'Blessed is the money which is spent on the army and fleet.' More governmental attention and funds should be given to the countryside. For the cities it was Bismarck's social policy which he thought to deserve admiration and emulation. Italy should learn above all to conjoin order and progress, and oppose both 'the black flag of Satan' and the 'red one of social liquidation'.[21]

The rhetoric was successful. Hats were thrown and handkerchiefs waved at the most exhilarating moments of the speech. In the election, the twenty-nine year old was triumphant, and went off to Rome to plead a legal case until his thirtieth birthday made him a deputy *de iure* as well as *de facto*.

In parliament San Giuliano was soon busy and rapidly established himself as a man to be watched. The youngest deputy in the Chamber (with a father in the Senate), as representative of the capital of eastern Sicily, San Giuliano had a strong power base. Much of the young deputy's interest was parochial. The sociologist *manqué* was soon loyally urging that Catania be promoted to join the first rank of Italian universities.[22] His maiden speech had also addressed itself to local matters, pleading Catania's special case on railway tariffs compared to the rival cities of Messina and Caltanissetta. San Giuliano politely remarked that he and all his citizens loved all Italian cities with equal affection, but he did not want to see fall to the noble city of Messina an advantage in trade beyond that achieved by Catania.[23]

The following debate rapidly degenerated into an exhibition of the disunity of Sicily. Crispi, from the heights of his experience as a statesman, rebuked the newcomer's parochialism. The Minister for Public Works, Baccarini, produced complacent laughter in the Chamber when he noted that San Giuliano and the deputy for Messina were using the same statistics to put opposite views. When, in reply, San Giuliano was called short by the President of the Chamber for over-indulgence in quotations from Juvenal,[24] to the merriment of his colleagues, the limitations of the maiden speech seemed complete.

However these were merely initiation rites. In his first full year in the Chamber, San Giuliano was made *relatore* for a report on the law of 30 May 1883, on strikes. In 1886 the report completed, he spoke at length in favour of the legislation. Defending the government from attacks from both the Right and *Estrema*, San Giuliano argued that the toleration of trade unions was 'a first step towards

...social conciliation' and would lead to a gradual improvement in the living conditions of the working classes. Italy's lack of industrial development meant that, so far, she had not experienced as bitter a social struggle as had other European states. 'Before these conditions worsen', San Giuliano declared, 'it is proper to eliminate or reduce as much as possible the causes of such a worsening with an act of salving and wise justice.' The State should intervene to help the weak against the strong. Strikes were now perfectly legitimate as long as they did not involve 'violence, threat or fraud'.[25] The only problem with all this liberal rhetoric and legislation was that, in the practice of the local prefect and *maresciallo* of the *carabinieri*, it was the 'violence, threat or fraud' which was the most emphasised.[26] Whether the deputies knew that their phrases at Montecitorio would lack a certain reality at Vercelli or Palermo must remain an open question, if a question which can be asked about most varieties of liberalism.

Meanwhile San Giuliano made a number of speeches on the theme of 'Progress and Order', and could quote with the best from Juvenal or Horace, Comte or J. S. Mill and naturally acquired a reputation as a Dante scholar. In 1886 San Giuliano undertook another electoral campaign in Catania. He found what he described as a 'kind and spontaneous initiative', a banquet organised in his honour by the local electoral committee, which was presided over by Duke Enrico Paternò Castello. His message remained that Italy should have a strong foreign policy ('Woe to that nation which others believe they can offend with impunity'), and that the rising social question should be met with 'Progress and Order'.[27]

San Giuliano's comment on the 'social question' was timely in view of the social changes occurring, not merely in Northern Italy, but also in the South. In Sicily, Catania itself was undergoing spectacular modernisation; its population doubling in the first thirty years after the Risorgimento. De Amicis, the patriotic writer, hailed Catania as the Sicilian city with the most hope in the future.[28]

A hope in the future was not something which could easily be fitted into the career of the *viceré*. The portents were ominous. A new style of local politician and journalist had begun to appear to challenge the effortless supremacy of Antonino Di San Giuliano. The radical Napoleone Colajanni, was one who, in the 1880s, made his career in Catania and Caltanissetta provinces. Another was the novelist, De Roberto, whose stories in another age could have been suppressed as guilty of *lèse majesté* towards the San Giulianos. Worse still were the people who had started to call themselves 'socialists', who talked about 'the working class'. In 1889, the local police dutifully reported that a group called Unione Operaia was 'the cause of continual disorders in the city'.[29] Such groups also had an impressive local leader, Giuseppe De Felice Giuffrida, who had risen to local fame in the 1880s by leading a campaign against financial irregularities in the municipal administration, during the time when Antonino Di San Giuliano was *sindaco*.[30]

A certain sense of urgency began to creep into the political statements of San Giuliano. To combat the situation he decided to set up a new party. Venturing north to Milan, no doubt hoping for an influx of funds from Lombard businessmen, San Giuliano announced the formation of the 'Progressive Constitutional Party'. An excellent leader, he implied, could be found in Antonino Di San Giuliano. A reiterated interest in Bismarck's answers to the social question, and annual trips to the spas of Wiesbaden had encouraged San Giuliano to widen his customary English references and to argue now that the discontent of the working classes could be typified as a sort of Faust, whose real problem was psychological. To confront this, the opponents of socialism must 'cut the grass from under the feet' of the socialists, either by riches as in the U.S.A., or by social legislation as in Germany. Italy must also have a strong foreign policy especially in the Mediterranean, 'which our fathers called *mare nostrum*'. Perhaps enthused by his own rhetoric, San Giuliano ended on a Triumphal March of words about the Roman sunset which he had learned to love, about the greatness of Rome's past, and the need for Rome to have a great future. Horace, he said, had pointed the way in the *Carmen Saeculare*: 'Alme Sol!... Possis nihil urbe Roma Visere maius.'[31]

Unfortunately for San Giuliano, the Progressive Constitutional Party did not bear rich fruit. It was true that in 1892–3 San Giuliano was rewarded with his first ministerial experience, as Under-Secretary of Agriculture, Industry and Commerce in the short-lived first government of the rising star of Italian politics, Giovanni Giolitti. It was true also that this step was something of a Catanian declaration of independence as San Giuliano did not and would not serve in the governments of the virtual alternate Prime Ministers, the western Sicilians, Crispi and Rudinì. But, in other areas, life was turning a little sour for the sixth *Marchese* Di San Giuliano. As a Giolittian Minister, San Giuliano ought not to have been too surprised at being involved in the contemporary bank scandals, and in being mildly censured in November 1893 by the parliamentary investigatory commission,[32] whose report precipitated the collapse of the Giolitti government. It was not so much in the political field as in the social that trouble was mounting for San Giuliano. The activities of the Unione Operaia had spread outside Catania, and the whole of Sicily was being enveloped by a movement of peasant trade unionism called the *fasci*. San Giuliano found his own estates involved, and heard himself labelled, along with the Lanzas and the Rudinìs, as a 'class enemy'.[33] That comfortable proverb 'Birritti e Cappeddi nun si juncinu' was turning into a fearsome Marxist battle cry.

In 1892 the social threat also loomed over San Giuliano's political ambitions. De Felice Giuffrida contested one of the seats in Catania but, whether through arrogance, or trusting in the power of direct government aid, San Giuliano remained in Rome. There he received importunate letters from his wife who was horrified to learn that the women of Catania had gone out onto the piazza to cry: 'Viva De Felice, Abbasso San Giuliano'. 'All your co-citizens have gone completely *mad*' she reported, before reiterating her usual advice that her husband give up politics and return to Catania to preserve his health and his patrimony, and to be instructed by her piety.[34] Despite all Giolitti's efforts, De Felice won one of Catania's seats, leaving the other to San Giuliano.[35] Equally depressing was the fact that the University of Catania, of which San Giuliano had once been the proud advocate, was now rumoured to be dominated by 'socialists'.[36]

Sensational events followed. In 1893–4 the Crispi government decided to repress the *fasci*, and did so with great violence. De Felice, who had become the leader of the *fasci*, was gaoled for twenty-two years. In 1895, though still in gaol, he was returned triumphantly by his loyal Catanians as a Martyr-Deputy, but the election was declared void. Amnestied after Adowa, he was at length allowed to resume his seat in the Chamber, but he continued his radicalism. In a famous incident, in June 1899 he broke the voting urns in the Chamber as a gesture of defiance against the reactionary Pelloux government, in which San Giuliano was then serving.[37] By the 1900s De Felice had become boss of Catania, but, his radicalism fading fast with power, he supported the Libyan War and interventionism, and eventually flirted with the forces which would become Sicilian Fascism before his death in 1920.[38]

As a landowner confronted by the *fasci*, San Giuliano had a more direct taste of the 'social peril' than most of his contemporaries. De Felice had wrecked the power of San Giuliano over the local administration, and severely damaged his national political ambitions. It was notable that Giolitti, who had done all he could to thwart De Felice in 1892, rapidly thereafter sought an accommodation with him. In reaction, despite his service as Under-Secretary in 1892–3, for the next decade San Giuliano became an opponent of Giolitti, or at least a friend of his enemies.

It had been a bad moment to launch the Progressive Constitutional Party but San Giuliano went on endeavouring to uphold his preferred mixture of Liberty and Order. In a book, *Le condizioni presenti della Sicilia*, which he published in 1894, he evinced a studied moderation. Characteristically, he favoured a greater profundity in the analysis of the social crisis, justifying his argument by quotations from Marx and De Tocqueville. Hoping perhaps to regain his power as *padrone* of Catania, San Giuliano tried to stem the tide of history by denying that the *fasci* problem had really been one of class. Instead, he averred, it was a Sicilian question, and must be resolved by further aid to, and research on, Sicily.[39] In the Chamber, San Giuliano's message had been less statesmanlike. The *fasci*, he warned, threatened the 'gravest dangers'. The government must not be weak:

As far as I am concerned that liberalism and that democracy which deny to the Government the means to safeguard the security of property and person are a false liberalism and a false democracy.[40]

Order, it seemed, more than Progress, was what Italy and her *vicerè* needed.

Given the gradual erosion of his power base in Catania, it is not very surprising that San Giuliano turned more and more to foreign affairs. Many a European aristocrat had taken the same course, escaping the immediacy of the social peril by turning his hand to the agreeable *métier* of diplomacy. Perhaps too, in asserting the primacy of external politics there might be a last chance to divert the domestic evils of modernisation and socialism.

This new world to which San Giuliano now directed his attention was not an alien one, for his social position had always demanded a certain interest in foreign affairs. While still a student, he had been sent to visit London in 1872 and Vienna in 1873, although the contacts he made were of the second-rank, ambassadors and politicians, not Europe's leading statesmen.[41] As a deputy, he had occasionally directed his mind to diplomacy, usually parroting the catch-cries of his class and region.[42] Italy must be strong; France was the greatest danger. In a characteristic speech, San Giuliano welcomed the Triple Alliance as a counter to France in the Mediterranean, that sea 'which was once called *mare nostrum* which we wish [to be] *mare liberum* and which we cannot at any cost allow to become *mare alienum*'. After a series of Latin quotations, and apposite references to Dante, Hegel and Ricardo, San Giuliano produced so patriotic a peroration that the listening deputies applauded him with shouts of '*Bravo!*' and '*Bene!*'. Italy, he declared, seemed 'splendid and glorious', 'despite transitory troubles'. 'It [is] the power of the principles which Italy represents...; the principle of nationality and that of the freedom of the Mediterranean' which would overcome her difficulties and ensure that Italy could anticipate a greater future.[43]

San Giuliano was initially not very enthusiastic about colonialism. In the 1880s, emigration was more a Northern than a Southern problem, and, in any case, the *viceré* was above such tawdry issues which brought political and pecuniary gain not to great landowners but to those middling classes, shipping agents, clerks, journalists and hotel-keepers, who were the political enemies of a San Giuliano.[44] In 1886 he told his Catanian electors that 'Our garrisons on the Eritrean coast can never...serve as a base for a worthwhile colonial expansion'. On the other hand, San Giuliano did not want to renounce Italian power, especially in the Mediterranean. So he argued that Italy eventually must plan an outlet where emigrants could preserve their nationality and language.[45]

In his speech to the Milanese audience in 1890 about the virtues of the Progressive Constitutional Party, San Giuliano took a similar line. He repeated his usual scornful remarks about France, whose military expenditure demonstrated that a 'republic is not a cheap form of government'. He noted the usefulness to Italy of the Triple Alliance, and expressed his special admiration for Britain. He regretted the always increasing emigration, which was an 'enormous force, decisive for the future of our race, of our language, of our position in the world...' Internal emigration back to uncultivated land was, he said, one possible solution, but, in the end, it must be recognised that Italy would have overseas needs.[46]

By 1890 foreign affairs were thrusting themselves into the attention of any ambitious deputy as Crispi discarded restraint and became an advocate of colonial conquest. In 1889, the Benadir coast, south of the Horn of Africa, had been placed under a protectorate. To the north, in 1890, Italian possessions were formally acknowledged and named Eritrea.

If Crispi was now an 'Africanist' his main opponent in Sicily, Rudinì, remained critical of unnecessary foreign adventures. San Giuliano, who wanted to distinguish himself from both Crispi and Rudinì, in order to demonstrate his own potential as leader of the Progressive Constitutional Party, not surprisingly took something of a middle line. Still doubtful about Eritrea, he nonetheless regaled the Chamber with a disquisition on the special abilities as colonisers of the 'Latin races'. Most important, he said, 'is to assure to our emigrants territories where in the shadow of the flag of the *patria*, they can preserve their national language and remain Italian'.[47]

This middle position probably earned San Giuliano nomination to the Royal Commission set up in 1890 with the task, attractive for civilians, of investigating military achievement and corruption in Eritrea. A more delicate problem was posed by the fact that not only Crispi, but King Umberto I and the royal family were ardent and financially committed advocates of an Italian future in the Horn of Africa.[48] The membership of the Commission was predictably respectable, but not very distinguished. The President was a Piedmontese Senator, Giuseppe Borgnini, who could be relied on by the court. There were five other deputies on the Commission, among them Ferdinando Martini, who, following some recent sarcastic remarks in the Chamber about the value of Eritrea, was regarded as an anti-colonialist.[49] On 9 April 1891, assisted by soldiers and interpreters, the Commission sailed from Naples, reaching Massawa via Alexandria a fortnight later. After a tour of Eritrea, the

Commissioners left Massawa on 17 June, before the summer became too torrid, and were back in Brindisi on 28 June.

The most clamorous result of the venture was the conversion of Martini to 'Africanism'. In a book, *Nell'Affrica Italiana*, which was still selling in its tenth edition in 1935, Martini exulted at the liberating effect Africa had on a man's soul. It was a joy to be away from debilitated Europe. Nights hardily spent in the open reinvigorated body and soul. (The climate of Massawa, said Martini, was comparable to that of a Tyrrhenian Sea resort.) In Africa there were no visiting cards, no *coups d'état*;[50] and, one must suspect, no socialists. Martini was also unashamedly racist, noting that Italy was crowded and 'needed' space in empty Ethiopia. Martini had other plain words to say:

Now colonial conquests are a necessity [for Italy's] selfish national interest; but let us not talk about bringing civilisation. Whoever says that he is bringing civilisation to Ethiopia is lying or joking. Race must be substituted for race: either this or nothing...'[51]

The Commission's report, which San Giuliano, as *relatore* drafted, was not so blunt. Nevertheless, it was the emigration problem which received the most attention as it was 'of so vital and decisive importance for the political and economic ends of the Italian nation'. The report argued that emigration involved a contest in which Italy was being defeated. Nations lost their sons if they remained emigrants for more than two generations. In the last eighty years the English speaking population of the world had risen 310%, the Russian 133%, the German 73%, the Spanish 71%, but the Italian only 55%.[52]

Perhaps not all the Commissioners had found African nights as invigorating as Martini proclaimed. Certainly the report was most cautious about the attractions of the area around Massawa. Progress, rather, lay in the inland plateau, and in Ethiopia beyond. There, the Commissioners reported, 'the future is open to Italy; it is not an Eldorado, but a virgin and fertile land is awaiting the labour of Italian farmers'.[53]

In the Chamber, the report was received without many recriminations. Absolute anti-colonialism was not at first strong in Italy, even among socialists. They, in any event, were disarmed by the Commission's partial endorsement of the parasocialist schemes of

Franchetti aimed at establishing a variety of share-cropping in Italy's colonies; small scale, 'demographic', rather than 'capitalist' colonisation.[54]

But hardly had the report been tabled, when its cautious optimism appeared misplaced. The protectorate over Ethiopia, which Italy had won in the Treaty of Uccialli of 1889 was denounced by the Ethiopian Emperor Menelik, and Italy's whole position in East Africa tottered. Back in government in 1893, Crispi, always more a rhetorical than an active coloniser, began the combination of threats and refusal to send adequate military reinforcement which would lead to Adowa.

In the years from 1892 to Adowa and its aftermath, San Giuliano became the most open spokesman in the Chamber of Deputies for a tough-minded colonialism which was carefully distinguished from Crispi's enthusiasm or Rudinì's renunciation. In 1892 he deplored Rudinì's concealment of the damage occurring to Italy's position in Eritrea. In 1894 he warned Crispi that colonial policy needed to be more decisive, adding an apposite quotation from Virgil, which justified Italy's need not to surrender the *italianità* of her emigrants.[55]

San Giuliano took his campaign into semi-learned journals. He continued to uphold the Eritrea Commission's belief that Eritrea could become a new United States, Canada or Australia and that 'it is the highest national interest that [Italy] does not lose the Italian imprint (*l'impronta italiana*)'. But there were also phrases which recalled Martini's racism, and San Giuliano's own training in Social Darwinism. People might want peace, he said, but questions existed 'which only the sword can resolve'. Italy must be ready for the day of 'the great conflict' and recall that in the past two centuries Britain had climbed on the backs of others to imperial greatness by using military victories in Europe to take over already developed colonies in the wider world. In East Africa, Italy must be machiavellian, play off one chief against another. Italy must also be ruthless. When natives were in the wrong, no clemency should be shown since the 'Future' lay not with them, but with the Italians. This clarity of mind was what Italy needed, not Crispi's policy of 'unprepared waiting'.[56]

There was another problem. Just as the *fasci* threatened the ideal social system, so San Giuliano now found danger in the rising tide of anti-colonialism favoured by men like Colajanni or De Felice

Giuffrida. Perhaps the Liberal system itself needed amendment to allow greater coherence in the all-important arena of foreign affairs.

The direction of colonial policy should not be subordinated to the changing needs of transitory parliamentary and electoral situations, in the interests of a ministry or of a party, but should proceed with a constant and continuous programme, looking to the future and thinking exclusively of the permanent interests of the country.[57]

In increasing personal isolation, supported only by Franchetti and Giacomo De Martino II, San Giuliano went on objecting not to Crispi's African programme, but to its method of execution.

Meanwhile Crispi abandoned a policy of unprepared waiting for one of unprepared action. As a result, on 1 March 1896, a colonial army led by General Baratieri was routed at Adowa by Ethiopian forces. In Rome, Crispi fell and was replaced by Rudinì, amid demands that Italy end all colonialist ventures. In three brief years, San Giuliano's ideas on domestic policy had been overthrown by the *fasci*; now his ambitions for Italian diplomacy had been disgraced at Adowa.

San Giuliano tried to soldier on. When the Chamber reconvened to debate the provision of credit for the Eritrean campaign, San Giuliano was first on his feet to demand that government policy now be one of reorganisation and victory. Otherwise, he argued, in the Mediterranean which had been the '*mare nostrum* of our fathers', Italy's whole position would be shattered. In the future there should be retrenchment, but not renunciation:

For many years we must follow a very prudent and circumspect policy, and one above all based on the potentiality of the national economy, but without ever losing sight of the ultimate end.[58]

Apart from Franchetti, few agreed that Adowa could be converted into a victory. Sarcastic questions whether or not the government had an African policy went unheeded. The Chamber did not listen when San Giuliano prophesied darkly that in the Mediterranean Italy might lose 'a position of the greatest importance in the vast and world theatre of the great struggle for hegemony between the Slav race and the Anglo-Saxon race'; nor was it impressed when he argued that Ethiopia was a key area 'in the struggle for hegemony and expansion between the great civilised peoples'.[59] When Martini went to Eritrea as Governor in 1897, one of his first steps was formally to abandon any surviving idea of 'demographic' colonisation.[60] Italy would keep Eritrea, but the colony would do nothing to save *l'impronta italiana*. In 1913, the grand total of non-military or bureaucratic colonists in Eritrea was sixty-one.[61]

Domestically San Giuliano had further defeats to experience. In 1899 he was finally elevated to ministerial rank, in charge of Posts and Telegraphs in the second, more reactionary, Pelloux government. One congenial task in this minor office was to favour the continuance of state subsidies to the Società di Navigazione Generale for its shipping lines which called at ports in Cyrenaica and the Near East.[62] There were few such pleasures to savour. Already San Giuliano's patience had shown signs of wearing thin when, a few months before, as a *grand seigneur*, he had publicly dismissed a Sicilian Radical's attack on him as provoked by an unbridgeable 'difference in manners and training'.[63] As a Minister, he confirmed his move away from Giolittian moderation, becoming the Sicilian ally of Sonnino. He and his colleagues in Pelloux's cabinet, Salandra, Bettòlo and Boselli, hoped 'to return to the Constitution', to stem the social peril by repression, and a re-evocation of the 'heroic principles' which had driven the Savoy dynasty to unite Italy. But this too failed. Pelloux and Sonnino lacked sufficient nerve to be successful reactionaries, and in June 1900 the Ministry collapsed like any other. In July the King was assassinated, and a few months later the young King, Victor Emmanuel, brought in a new liberal Ministry headed by the radical and irredentist, Zanardelli. Six months before, San Giuliano had already expressed his disillusionment to his old colleague Martini, 'Our parliamentarism is the fount of great woe to the country.'[64] In 1901, again the *grand seigneur*, he scornfully opposed the equalitarian tax reforms suggested by the new government.[65]

San Giuliano's wife had died in 1897, cutting another link with Catania which, in any case, was now hopelessly in the hands of De Felice Giuffrida. It was not in Catania but Rome that real power lay, as far as San Giuliano was concerned. He had complained before that 'the provincial intellectual environment suffocates me, oppresses me, asphyxiates me'.[66] In 1904, ironically it was in Catania that events threatened to give the *coup de grace* to all San Giuliano's ambitions. In the general elections, San Giuliano unwisely decided to run as a Sonninian, a member of the 'constitutional opposition', thus surrendering any hope of aid from the government's agents. With somewhat desperate bravado, San Giuliano stood both for his own seat, Catania I which was contested by a Radical, Auteri Berretta, and for Catania II, the seat held by De Felice Giuffrida. It was an exciting campaign. De Felice's entry to the city was greeted by revolver shots and a knifing incident.[67] The result for San Giuliano was predictable: a clear defeat by Auteri Berretta and an overwhelming one by De Felice. Catania, which only two decades before had been a family fief was no longer loyal to Antonino Paternò Castello Di San Giuliano.

Amid these domestic disasters, San Giuliano had restricted his interests more and more to foreign affairs. From an assiduous politician he turned into a traveller, writing romantically and self-consolingly in 1897 that 'the wandering nomad instinct and the warlike impulses of the pirate' sometimes surfaced in his Norman blood.[68] In the next eight years he journeyed widely, visiting Tunis and Tripoli, the Balkans, and the United States of America in search of Roman greatness, and a place in which *italianità* could be saved for Italy.

In the Chamber, he continued to try to remind the deputies that Adowa must not be a turning-point. Mainly he summoned his listeners to old campaigns against France. In Tunis, he said, Italians were persecuted because of Italy's inadequate consular service. 'The balance of power in the Mediterranean, or better, what is left of it' was dominated by France because her foreign policy was not a prey to party squabbling. 'It is very sad for Italy', he lamented, 'to possess the first element of grandeur and power, which is the tendency of its population to increase, and to see it converted into an element of weakness.'[69]

Italy's levity was wasting 'the necessary laws of nature and history'. As matters were, the imminent collapse of the Turkish Empire would only benefit the Franco-Slav alliance. Italy's friends, Britain, Germany and the United States, could not treat her as a partner, unless she learned *serietà*. History was uncovering stern laws which would apply to Italy:

Peoples who do not know how to fit a parliamentary regime into the iron exigencies which the laws of history impose on modern politics will find themselves confronted by an inexorable dilemma; either to renounce the parliamentary regime, or prematurely to declare themselves defeated in the great

86

struggle of nations for wealth and for power, which today more than ever ought literally to be called the struggle for life.[70]

After the fall of the Pelloux government, San Giuliano openly rejected the reconciliation with France favoured by his old colleague, the Minister of Foreign Affairs, Visconti Venosta. In his enmity towards France, as in his lingering ambitions for a real colony in Eritrea, San Giuliano again was fighting on the losing side.

In 1901, Sonnino tried to rally the 'constitutional opposition', using a new daily paper, *Giornale d'Italia*, directed by Alberto Bergamini. San Giuliano became the equivalent of the Shadow Foreign Minister of this group.[71] Broadening his interests away from traditional Bourbon Francophobia in the Mediterranean, San Giuliano was encouraged to visit the Turkish territory of Albania, where Italy's rival was Austria, not France. San Giuliano's reports were published in series by *Giornale d'Italia*, and in 1903 collected in book form as *Lettere sull'Albania*.[72]

Albania was becoming an area of developing interest for Italy as the *ravvicinamento* with France restored some stability to Italy's overall diplomatic position. In 1900, another of Sonnino's friends, the fellow Tuscan, Francesco Guicciardini, had visited the area and reported that Albania had a great economic potential. 'Albania', he declared, 'is destined to possess, as once in the time of the Roman Empire, one of the great commercial routes in Europe.' Here was another area in which Italy must stand ready for the future:

In Albania, as in Tripoli, [Italy] should respect the *status quo* while it lasts; but since the *status quo* does not give many guarantees of lasting, [Italy] should prepare...a diplomatic situation from which she can create an arrangement of Albanian affairs conforming to Italian interests.

For, Guicciardini argued, in Albania more than anywhere else, the gravest strategic issues were involved. The port of Valona, he declared, should be deemed part of Italy:

this gulf controlled by a military and naval Power, would be not only like Bizerta, a threat to our country...[but] it would be a loss already sustained since the master of that gulf is already in fact master of the Adriatic and virtually of the richest part of Italy, of fertile Puglia.[73]

San Giuliano was not a close friend of the stylish and rather frivolous Guicciardini. But in formulating a policy on Albania, San Giuliano's conclusions were much the same. Naturally he was

87

moved to moralising by the sight of ruins, testimony to struggles lost and won:

Our immortal and suggestive Rome! From her glorious records can spring either the vain talk of a beguiling rhetoric, or encouragement to fruitful work. To modern peoples a great past can be power or weakness, danger or help.

San Giuliano too believed that Albania had to be considered in terms of the potential disintegration of the Turkish Empire, for 'the *status quo* can either last many years...or collapse from one moment to the other'. The parallel with Bizerta was again invoked. Valona was the key to the Adriatic and must not fall into hostile hands.[74]

It was characteristic of San Giuliano's seriousness and his growing dedication to the fine print of foreign affairs that he added more detailed political, strategic and economic suggestions. Trade bonds between Italy and the Balkans must be strengthened. A bank, post offices, schools and railway lines should all be weapons in the friendly but serious competition in which Italy must engage Austria in Albania. San Giuliano declared himself moved by the sight of Albanian children singing the *Marcia Reale*, but the government must spend more money to spread Italian culture. Once again San Giuliano declared the matter urgent:

This is perhaps the critical and decisive moment for the future of Italy in a sea which was hers; great would be the responsibility of him who let it pass, and perhaps irreparable the damage.[75]

San Giuliano, once the parochial Sicilian antagonist of France, now even showed signs of flirting with irredentism. Journeying north from Albania, he noticed the Italian population in Dalmatia, 'where *italianità*, embattled and battling, hopes with good cause for more warm and effective sympathy from Italy'.[76] From an Africanist, San Giuliano was changing into a nationalist.

Domestically, the loss of his seat at Catania forced San Giuliano to further readjustments. Only fifty-one years old, he was anxious to have a political future, still very much the man who in 1894 had sighed over a victorious general: 'What a lucky man! I do not believe that there now is a greater happiness than to win a battle! It must be a supreme, inebriating joy.'[77] So, San Giuliano, described by a colleague as an 'aristocrat who knows his time',[78] changed political tack once more. He had fought alongside the Sonninians in 1904, and lost; it was time to 'transform', to rejoin Giolitti. In 1905 he therefore accepted nomination to the Senate. That same year, he joined the Second Cabinet of Alessandro Fortis, a lieutenant of Giolitti, whom San Giuliano had previously derided as leading 'the ministry of mothers in labour (*puerperio*)'.[79]

1905 had been San Giuliano's most hopeful year for a very long time. Democracy had, after all, not run amuck. The Lega Navale and the Geographical Society were being extended into the much more powerful Istituto Coloniale. The Asmara Conference had been blessed by the Giolittian Establishment, and San Giuliano had been able to earn the reputation as the most statesmanlike figure in attendance. Meanwhile, the emigration problem grew worse and worse belying the hopes of Giolitti and Tittoni that it would go away of its own accord. San Giuliano became the most public opponent of leaving what Tittoni called the 'safety valve' open no matter what the consequences.[80] Instead San Giuliano proclaimed emigration a national disgrace, or worse. On a visit to the United States he saw Italians crowded into cities like Pittsburg, which he described as Dantesque hells of 'flame and smoke'. The Southern question, he said, was intimately bound to the colonial one. Italy, was 'wasting her seed' in the great struggle:

While the other great and prolific peoples possess either vast territories or extensive colonies, where their sons can conserve the national language and the ethnic imprint in which language is the preponderant factor, Italy disperses to the benefit of others that precious force and...will become, compared to the others, a nation always less important.[81]

After his criticism of Crispi's unpreparedness, his lonely struggle against renunciation after Adowa, his hard work in the various pressure groups, it might have been expected that San Giuliano would be regarded as a somewhat sensational addition to Fortis' Ministry in December 1905. In fact, it is hard to see much of a break in continuity. For one thing, San Giuliano was only in office over the Christmas holidays, before Fortis' Ministry fell in February. He thus scarcely had time to read his files. During his period of office San Giuliano did not speak in the Senate. In the Chamber his only task was the formal one of commemorating the death of the King of Sweden. No new public direction was given to Italian foreign policy. Contemporaries remarked mainly that San Giuliano had never held major office before. The fact that Fortis had had to choose such a second-rank figure[82] must mean that the Ministry would not last much longer.

Inside the *Consulta*, San Giuliano did little more. His major step was to change the delegate selected for the Algeciras Conference; then, under heavy and open pressure from the ambassadors of France and Britain, San Giuliano removed Giulio Silvestrelli and replaced him with Emilio di Visconti Venosta.

Silvestrelli, the ambassador in Madrid, was an obscure diplomat, rumoured by the French ambassador, Camille Barrère, to be a Crispian and a triplicist. Initially, Silvestrelli's appointment had seemed logical as the other nations were reported to be sending their ambassadors in Madrid to Algeciras.[83] From one of Rome's leading families, related to Tittoni, Silvestrelli was most unlikely to adopt a radical stance at the Conference. In fact, he turned out to be a fussy minor figure, more interested in the size and state of hotel rooms and the number of secretaries needed by his delegation, than in creating for Italy a new and independent policy. When dismissed by San Giuliano, Silvestrelli telegraphed his pleasure at avoiding a difficult journey at a time when his children were sick.[84]

The presence of Visconti Venosta at Algeciras was much more likely to make the limelight fall on Italy. Visconti Venosta was the elder statesman of the Italian Right. He had been first choice as Foreign Minister in the Cabinets from 1863 to 1876. In 1896 he had returned to the *Consulta*, serving as Foreign Minister in three more Cabinets before 1901, during which time he was the architect of Italy's *rapprochement* with France. Barrère, a strong-minded ambassador, who often liked to feel that he controlled Italian foreign policy, had happy memories of co-operation with Visconti Venosta. The slippery Tittoni he thought to be far less satisfactory.[85] It seems to have been Barrère who first raised the idea that Italy should be represented at Algeciras by Visconti Venosta.

The suggestion was applauded by anti-Giolittian circles in Italy, which, as Sonnino naively put it, were anxious to see a more 'coherent' foreign policy.[86] San Giuliano may have been more pleased that Visconti Venosta's eminence would give Italy a properly prominent part at the Conference, although he must have been astonished suddenly to be *persona gratissima* with Barrère.[87] In this regard, San Giuliano did his best to fracture his pro-French image by telling the Austrian ambassador the reverse of what he said to

Barrère. This was a technique of diplomacy in which San Giuliano would later develop great skill but, for the moment, the graver problem lay with the appointment of Visconti Venosta. The last thing which Italian policy needed at Algeciras was the limelight. Allied to one group of rival powers, friends of the other, Italy could hope for little more than to be forgotten. Despite the fact that, once at Algeciras, Visconti Venosta did his best to be cautiously impartial, Italy was put in difficulty by her conflicting ties. The Kaiser rewarded Austria with the title of Germany's 'noble second', but ostentatiously omitted to mention his other ally, Italy.[88] Perhaps more embarrassing were France's exaggeratedly grateful thanks for assistance given.[89] The humiliation of Italy's position had been all the greater given the expectations raised by Visconti Venosta's appointment. San Giuliano had been given a useful lesson for an Italian statesman, that it was most unfortunate to prefer the shadow to the substance.

The only other potentially interesting step which San Giuliano took as Foreign Minister, on 25 January 1906, was to request from the Chief of General Staff, Saletta, a clarification of Italy's very obscure military obligations to the Triple Alliance. San Giuliano, it seemed, was still willing that Italian troops be promised eventually to join their allies on the Rhine.[90] He was too no doubt anxious to assert the prior claims of the Ministry of Foreign Affairs over any defence experts on confronting strategic issues. But the government fell before anything could be done properly to unravel these threads of Italian defence policy.

In retrospect it is still odd that San Giuliano, after all his preparations, was not a more authoritative Foreign Minister in 1905–6. But what the history of Liberal Italy often demonstrates is that differences between the makers of foreign policy were more apparent than real. Tittoni who was a most quietist Foreign Minister, happily endorsed Italian expansionism when an ambassador, and, given his ties to the Banco di Roma, had a nearer economic interest in imperialism than many Italian politicians. In office with Fortis, a 'lieutenant' whose government would be bound not to last long, San Giuliano was in a way serving an apprenticeship. If his reputation did not suffer during his tenure of office, and it did not, if he managed to please both the King and Giolitti, and it seems that he did, then he could hope to return to office on a rather more serious occasion.

Replaced at the Foreign Ministry briefly by Guicciardini and then again by Tittoni, San Giuliano returned to the task of organising colonialist influence on 'public opinion'. Perhaps embarrassed by this open politicking, in October 1906, Tittoni removed San Giuliano from the Italian scene by sending him as ambassador to London. Now San Giuliano could test the ideas which he had long held, that 'we cannot and must not forget the permanent solidarity of vital interests which binds us to England regarding the safe-guarding of the Mediterranean equilibrium'.[91] By abandoning the political scene for an Embassy, and leaving the pressure groups to which he had contributed so much, and which now tended to languish into merely official bodies, San Giuliano appeared to have committed another political error. Moreover being an ambassador was frustrating, as Tittoni kept his staff under a tight hold and his relations with San Giuliano were cool. At the height of the Bosnia–Herzegovina crisis, Tittoni found time to complain that an article had appeared alleging that San Giuliano felt that diplomatic life in London was very difficult and that Tittoni did not discuss policy with his diplomats. San Giuliano was instructed to send a telegram of denial to the journal, via Tittoni, not, he explained, because he did not have unlimited faith in San Giuliano, but because, from the distance of London, San Giuliano was not able to understand the political manoeuvrings of Rome.[92]

San Giuliano also learned directly of Italy's humble international reputation. Britain might be sympathetic in the end, but immediate support could only be won after much hard work by an ambassador.[93] San Giuliano's background meant that he was often more independent as a diplomat than a professional bureaucrat might have been. He was fascinated by the domestic scene, admiring the 'marvellous good sense of the English people' which allowed them to find 'practical and wise' solutions to social disputes.[94] With his training as a publicist San Giuliano was interested, too, in public relations, and tried to build contacts with the British press.[95] He declared that, unlike his colleagues, he made particular efforts to mix not just with the most elegant section of society but with all classes.[96] He founded an Anglo–Italian association and favoured the 'penetration' of Italian culture into British intellectual circles.[97]

In the more formal areas of diplomacy he was generally a clear-sighted and intelligent ambassador. He foresaw the coming of the Anglo-Russian entente, and predicted rightly that it would produce ever closer contacts between Britain and Russia.[98] The economic laws of history, he argued, meant that Britain and Germany must drift further apart, and Italy should not, therefore, exaggerate the significance of temporary flirtations.[99] He continued to admire the achievements of Empire, and desire Britain as a friend – but he urged that the weakness of the British army and the growing German challenge to the Royal Navy should warn Italy not to rely on Britain totally.[100]

In December 1909 Giolitti's government fell. Tittoni left the *Consulta* and the new Prime Minister, Sonnino, appointed Guicciardini as his replacement. In a major reshuffle of embassies, San Giuliano was transferred to Paris, an unlikely spot for an old Africanist Francophobe. It was perhaps Sonnino's way of rebuking San Giuliano's 'transformation' of four years before.

Before he left London, probably hoping more to organise his own mind than to impress the Foreign Ministry, San Giuliano wrote a long despatch detailing his thoughts on Anglo-Italian relations. Britain, he decided, was a conservative power, anxious that the international equilibrium remain steady. The traditional friendship between Britain and Italy was strong, but its usefulness should not be exaggerated:

The truth is that in England, because of our artistic and literary glories, the beauty of our country and our climate, the recent memories of our Risorgimento, there is for Italy a sincere sympathy, but it has very little influence on practical policy.

Rather 'Italy…is considered weak militarily and uncertain in its political aspirations'. Italy's importance would be better believed if Italy tried 'to give here the impression of being a country politically, economically, militarily, and above all morally, strong'. Britain wanted Italy to stay in the Triple Alliance. In colonial questions she was sympathetic, but thought Italy basically incompetent as a colonial power. Eritrea had still not been developed. Therefore, he concluded:

in my opinion, there really exists a sincere Anglo-Italian friendship, but it would be dangerous for us to have too many illusions about its practical weight or to let weaken the guarantees which safeguard our interests through the loyal interpretation and application of the Triple Alliance.

The best motto for Italy was 'to be and to seem strong'.[101]

San Giuliano did not have much time to become accustomed to Paris. Before he was settled into his new Embassy, he was summoned back to Rome since Sonnino's government had fallen after another hundred days, to be replaced by one led by Luzzatti. San Giuliano was invited to become Minister of Foreign Affairs. He would not leave the *Consulta* again until he was dead.

By 1910, San Giuliano had had the most complete training, in the Chamber, in journalism, in the pressure groups, in his travels and in the Embassy in London, of any Foreign Minister in the Liberal era. The once ambitious *vicerè* had also learned much from domestic affairs, from his personal failure to cope with modernisation, or with the social question in Catania. He had learned that diplomacy was the last refuge of an 'aristocrat who knew his times'. He had learned also, or understood by his nature, that it was best, in office, to be cynical, to believe in 'prudence, reserve, secrecy'. A victory for Italy in the great battle of the nations which was to come, a survival of the sixth *Marchese* Di San Giuliano, would have to be won by stealth, and would certainly be lost if Italy's hand was declared. San Giuliano still wanted to refight the battles which he had lost in the 1880s and 1890s, but he recognised that they were best fought privily. Settling into the *Consulta*, at first timidly, as though half expecting soon to be out of office again, he began to write memoranda on the colonial question, and to select staff who would help him search out a method to open the way to an Italian path to imperialism and real Greatness.

CHAPTER 4

The *Consulta*: the bureaucrats of foreign policy

Tourists have traditionally passed by the ochre-stained *palazzo* on
the wrong side of the Quirinal hill. The *Consulta* has merely formed
a convenient backdrop for the water-colours of Vanvitelli or for the
clicking shutters of millions of Yashicas and Leicas today. The statue
of the *Dioscuri* and its fountain, the magnificent view over Rome
beyond, the papal, royal and then presidential palace of the *Quirinale*,
or the nearness of Bernini's *Sant'Andrea*, divert attention from yet
another Roman palace.

Nonetheless, the *Consulta* is a distinguished building. Set in what
used to be Constantine's imperial gardens, it was built in 1730 by
Fuga for Pope Clement XII. It was to house the Tribunal of the
Sacred Consulta or Supreme Court and Administrative Power of
the Pontifical Government. There were also barracks for the papal
guard.

When Rome became capital of the united Italy after 1870, it was
this building which was chosen to house the Foreign Ministry of the
new state. Apart from its architectural beauty, the *Consulta* was also
appropriately situated; only a step across the road from the *Quirinale*,
the royal palace, it was a reminder that Charles Albert had retained
many prerogatives in the constitution which he had granted in 1848.
In the era before the telephone, messages of advice and instruction
could pass to the *Consulta* more easily from the *Quirinale* than from
Montecitorio, the parliament building, where deputies debated, or
from the *Palazzo Braschi*, where Prime Ministers had their offices.
The *Consulta* was positioned to demonstrate that the foreign policy
of Italy was not to be too different from that of the Kingdom of
Piedmont – Sardinia. Not that King Victor Emmanuel III was more
gracious to diplomats than to any of his other servants. 'Ambassadors
are more or less all spies', he was heard to remark on one occasion
with his accustomed misanthropy.[1] It was only Mussolini who
publicly broke with the assumptions of royal control when, in 1922,
he transferred the Foreign Ministry to the *Palazzo Chigi* just next to
the parliament buildings.[2] The *Consulta* was relegated to having the

honour merely of housing the Colonial Ministry and a Colonial Museum.

For the denizens of the *Consulta* in Liberal Italy, as in many another pre-war European chancellery, 'life was sweet before the revolution'. Young clerks or attachés worked none too hard, spending much of their time polishing their social graces and epigrams. The work of deciphering and transcription was so boring, recalled one clerk, that soon 'I decided that it was not worth the trouble to go to the office to sleep when I could sleep more comfortably in my own bed or pass my time in more interesting or more amusing tasks.' The clerk moved on from puzzling over the difference between *distinta, ben distinta, alta, altissima* and *profonda* on letters of *raccomandazione* received in the personnel office, to more serious diplomatic work in Paris which occupied him each day from noon to 5 p.m.[3] Another young attaché has recalled that when he hurried eagerly to his first assignment abroad, he was greeted by his ambassador with sarcastic comments about his excessive zeal, and then given almost nothing to do.[4] One ambassador is reported to have spent only fifteen days in a year in residence at an unwelcome posting.[5] Daniele Varè, who defined himself as the 'laughing diplomat', alleged that he joined the *Consulta* to help out a friend whose marriage made him need a passage to East Africa, which Varè had booked for himself.[6] Once in the Ministry, Varè found that juniors were treated with affectionate contempt. Asked to submit a 'half yearly report on some subject appertaining to...official duties', Varè wrote a sonnet on Zanardelli, the *Consulta's* cat. This work was solemnly returned by the Foreign Minister, San Giuliano, with the curt note: 'In fourteen lines, you have made six errors in prosody!'[7]

In this world of laughing diplomats, clerks rejoiced at such splendid eccentricities in their seniors. Hard work and seriousness were a little *outré*, best reduced to another funny story:

I do not know if General de Verdy du Vernois would have accused the Duke Avarna of taking himself too seriously. Certainly he was no laughing diplomat. I have rarely known a man so absorbed in his work...Typical of his absorption was his way of playing golf...He always played alone and never seemed to bother where he was going. He just hit the ball along towards any hole that happened to be in sight, choosing the right club and using it not unskilfully. He would finish up just any where. If he had not been...Ambassador [in Vienna],...I doubt whether they would have allowed him thus to violate almost every rule of the game. But it was obvious that his thoughts were not on the game at all. He enjoyed the exercise; it did him good and nobody else any harm. Not all of us can say the same of our pleasures.[8]

There were certain drawbacks to being a gilded Italian in the *belle époque*. Diplomatic staff from post-Risorgimento bourgeois families, or from princely Sicilian stock, who had a glorious past but no money at the moment, found it a trifle wearisome to learn the social graces of the Habsburgs. Foreigners' sneers could also be readily provoked in remembering the most famous *bon mot* of bluff, King Victor Emmanuel II. The two things which he had been unable to refuse to anyone were a title of nobility and a good cigar. Contemporaries understood when, a little later, *Punch* mocked: 'BROTHER: "Well, how did you like Venice?" SISTER (an heiress): "Oh top-hole! Had proposals from three Italian Counts." BROTHER: "That's nothing. At the present rate of exchange it's about equivalent to one British commoner." '[9]

Being involved in the conduct of Italian foreign policy also had its disappointing side. Still, if an Empire was hard to win, Italian diplomats could study the skills of hunting, shooting and fishing, and then reduce it all to another joke:

In the early morning, I sometimes rode in the Villa Borghese, round the so-called *galoppatoio*. One day, my horse shied at a double sheet of foolscap paper that fluttered down the wind from the neighbouring dairy, where some people were having breakfast. There was something familiar about the typewritten sheet and I stopped to look down at it from the saddle. To my astonishment, I recognized the well-known signature 'Avarna'. It was a report to the Foreign Office from our embassy in Vienna. I dismounted, picked up the report and looked round to see where it could have come from. Then I saw San Giuliano sitting at a little table at the Vaccheria. With his gouty hands, he had difficulty in holding papers. The Duke Avarna's report had slipped through his fingers and the breeze had carried it away. I took the report back to the Minister, who accepted it without much gratitude. He seemed to think that if I had left it on the riding-track, it would not have mattered very much. 'But it is marked "Strictly Confidential" ', I said, pointing at the words at the top of the page. 'They always put that', answered San Giuliano. 'But generally, what they write to me as strictly confidential was all in the evening papers of the day before.'[10]

The diplomatic world of the *belle époque* was not just an endless whirl of waltzes, or an anthology of good stories. Notwithstanding the glitter and the jokes, the diplomats of Liberal Italy came from definite social classes, with definite social and diplomatic ideas and assumptions. Even Daniele Varè, the 'laughing diplomat' himself, was the son of a hero of the Venetian Risorgimento. Varè was also proud of the impetus given to his career by his contacts with Crispi, and was enthusiastic about the expansionism of the 1890s.[11] Italian diplomats naturally came from the ruling classes, which in Liberal Italy either meant the Northern gentry, and industrial bourgeoisie, or the Southern nobility. The diplomats were, as naturally, politically conservative, and patriotic. Almost all would welcome Mussolini's restoration of law and order to the body politic, and of promotion to the diplomatic service after 1922. In 1910 the Italian Foreign Ministry in fact reflected, in its developing nationalism, and in its social hopes and fears, the same ambiguous movement towards a Fascist future as did the ruling classes generally. Under San Giuliano, much of this movement became more apparent.

On 11 June 1907 a Royal Commission had consolidated the career structure of the Foreign Ministry. Candidates for either the diplomatic or consular branch of the service had to take an examination. Raffaele Guariglia, who entered the consular service in October 1909, remembers four days of written exams, in English, French and German, law, history and political economy, orthodox enough areas by contemporary standards and a system of examination which would remain for the next thirty years.[12] But entry was not just competitive. To be accepted as a candidate a young man had to have completed his compulsory military training, to be physically fit and to have been always 'of praiseworthy conduct and gentlemanly behaviour'. The archaic language of this last phrase was an index of the political test which it required; a social radical was a *persona non grata* in every European Foreign Ministry.

Educational requirements further limited the field. Candidates were obliged to hold a laureate in *giurisprudenza* from an Italian university, or a comparable diploma from traditional diplomatic training grounds such as the Social Science Institute at Florence, or the School of Commerce at Venice. Jurisprudence, the degree traditionally taken by aspirants to political or bureaucratic life, was much the most usual degree. The admission of social sciences and economics was, on the other hand, some testimony to the bourgeois base of the Risorgimento and to the industrialisation of Giolittian

Italy. Nonetheless the typical Italian diplomat remained much more likely to publish semi-learned articles on Dante than on the balance of trade. Uncles and cousins might sometimes deal in the more tawdry side of life, but many Italian diplomats remained contemptuous of commerce.

To be accepted as a candidate for the written exams there was also a heavy property qualification. The aspiring attaché had to control a personal fortune of over 8,000 lire per annum (3,000 lire for the consular service). In a country where the mean daily wage was 3 lire, only the wealthiest classes could hope to send their sons to the *Consulta*. Salaries were low, not exceeding 8,000 lire until ambassadorial rank was reached.[13] While remaining an attaché the official was not paid at all.

The 1907 Commission also suggested reforms to guide the careers of successful candidates. Promotion was to be *a scelto*, by merit, as decided by a Committee of Five. In practice this principle was rarely followed. Qualifying clauses had removed the temptation to allow careers based too narrowly on ability. Before being considered for promotion, staff had to spend five years in each category of the service. In 1910 there were eight categories, so, theoretically, a career based on the most rapid possible promotion would take thirty-five years to move from attaché to ambassadorial rank. An official who joined the service at twenty-five would reach the highest rank when he was sixty, when, usually, he was ready to retire.

In fact promotion was often given within the five-year limit, but almost always strictly in terms of seniority. Under San Giuliano, in a diplomatic staff of about one hundred and twenty, only one officer gained a remarkable rise, and four others received notable minor adjustment. The most influential bureaucrat in the Ministry, Giacomo De Martino, stayed in his official rank: in January 1914, when Secretary-General of the Ministry, he was still only listed no. 23, among those officials with Envoy Extraordinary and Minister Plenipotentiary (second class) status.

This image of social order and administrative form is a little misleading. Traditionally, there was another side to bureaucratic life in Italy, the side of the *raccomandazione*, of political and social influence. If such influence could naturally play some part in the assessment of the written entry papers, it was still more valuable in the oral examinations in which a candidate discussed a set thesis, but in which inevitably he was judged by his social standing, and by the number of recommendations from important people which he had been able to muster.[14] Sometimes, there might even be more to it than that. Salvago Raggi, unusual in coming from a clerical family (his cousin became Pope Benedict XV), has many stories to tell of clientalism and corruption. He alleges that he was failed at the first attempt in the entry exams because of his refusal to use the client system in a year when a successful candidate was typically the cousin of the then *capo di gabinetto* in the Ministry. He returned to Rome the next year to be crammed by intellectuals as distinguished as Antonio Labriola, only to refuse to attend seminars when he found that he was being indoctrinated with 'socialism'. Another false step followed when his friend, Andrea Carlotti, revealed the sure path to examination success. A prominent politician had introduced him to a Masonic lodge. Carlotti had made absolutely sure of election to the diplomatic service because, in addition, he had promised to give a donation of from 5,000 to 6,000 lire to the Masons. Salvago Raggi's clericalism would not let him surrender his soul so blithely, and his career prospects seemed dismal, but he then discovered that a bribe of 6,000 lire could be paid directly to a prominent political personality, and his clericalism need not be sullied by the evil touch of Masonry. Salvago Raggi detected classic cheating methods in the written exam (he picked up pages of a text book in the toilet), but nevertheless he had found the route to academic success. He duly joined the diplomatic service, although it was Carlotti who topped the examination, and Salvago Raggi continued to believe that his career was hampered by the presiding Masonic influence at the Ministry.[15]

Too much should perhaps not be made of Salvago Raggi's stories, clouded as they are by a combination of personal disappointment and extreme clerical fascism reflecting the decade of the thirties in which he was writing. Yet the particular revelations do make the valid general point of the essence of clientalism to the Italian political and social system. There is no doubt that the members of the Italian diplomatic service based their careers on *raccomandazioni*, and on being a nephew, or a cousin, or a cousin's cousin.

The skills of a client were not necessary merely for admission to the lowest ranks of the bureaucratic hierarchy. Ambassadors too needed friends. The Italian ambassador in Constantinople, Mayor des Planches, was abruptly and insultingly recalled in 1911, allegedly because Giolitti still bore him a grudge for his loyalty to Crispi whose private secretary and diplomatic factotum he had been before 1894.[16] Ambassadors were often direct political appointments, the careers of San Giuliano and Tittoni being excellent, and by no means unusual, examples. The court too, across the road from the *Consulta*, naturally had a heavy influence in the selection process. Prime Minister's interventions are also easy to find. An excellent illustration of Giolitti's influence can be found in the career of Camillo Garroni, promoted from the prefectural corps to succeed Mayor as ambassador in Constantinople. Garroni had long been a most important aide of Giolitti, earning fame by his adroitness during the strikes in Genoa in 1901, and afterwards being one of Giolitti's most renowned 'managers.[17] In defence of patronage, it could perhaps be argued that the abilities needed in the prefectural service would be of more value in Constantinople after 1911 than would be the traditional, and criticised, *faiblesse* of Garroni's aristocratic predecessors, Mayor or Imperiali.[18]

There were also other versions of clientalism which were a natural accompaniment of life in the Italian Foreign Ministry. A student of modern Naples has alleged that the Southernisation of the Italian bureaucracy began with the corporate state, and a commentator on Italian foreign policy has explained some of the mistakes of Ciano's foreign policy by his creation of a personal Cabinet of his Roman friends,[19] yet both processes have in fact deep roots in Italian history. This is not merely a tale of fathers and sons, as when Visconti Venosta took his elder son, Enrico, as his private secretary to Algeciras, later replacing him with the younger son, Giovanni.[20] In the story of the 'making of Italy', there are rather more profound strands of clientalism which are neatly revealed by a study of the Italian Foreign Ministry in 1910. At that date the tide of Piedmont, of the conquest of Italy by the Savoys, was gradually being diverted by the return of the 'Bourbons', by a tide of Southern control of the bureaucracy which has certainly not been shifted by fascism or Christian Democracy.

Bare statistics begin to tell the story. In 1909, there were 376 career officials in the Italian diplomatic and consular service. Less than 20% of these had been born in Southern Italy (thirteen in Sicily, one in Sardinia); another 15% were Romans. The greatest number were Piedmontese or Tuscans.[21]

The pattern of royal patronage is thus clearly marked among

diplomatic personnel. In 1910 the highest ranks of the Ministry could easily have been serving any Savoyard King or Duke. Of the first seven, six had laureates in jurisprudence from the University of Turin; five were Piedmontese born and the other had come from abroad. The only non-Piedmontese in the group was Giuseppe Avarna, Duke of Gualtieri, the Palermitan who had been ambassador in Vienna since 1904. Avarna, an official of the old school,[22] was also the only senior ambassador who did not possess a laureate.

Five of the leading group held noble titles. The exceptions were Alberto Pansa, the doyen of the service, and Giulio Melegari, the ambassador to St Petersburg. Pansa was a Torinese of great distinction who had joined the *Consulta* in 1865, after obtaining a youthful laureate in 1864. His ideas were like those of Avarna, 'of the old school', and he rejected, for example, any idea of a revival of colonialism.[23] Melegari, who had joined the Ministry as an attaché in 1877, had also been born in Turin and had obtained a laureate from his local university. His family had played a distinguished role in the Risorgimento, one member, Luigi Amadeo Melegari, being Secretary-General of the Foreign Ministry in 1862, an ambassador, and then Minister of Foreign Affairs in 1876–7.[24]

Important posts were also held by more junior officials, but the pattern of their careers did not vary from their seniors. The ambassador in Paris, recalled in January 1910, was Count Giovanni Gallina, a Torinese with a laureate in jurisprudence from Turin university. The Ministry's Secretary-General was Riccardo Bollati, from Novara, with a laureate in jurisprudence from Turin. His predecessor, Giacomo Malvano, who had retired in 1907 after being Secretary-General for more than a decade, was also a Piedmontese. Further down the list was the Minister to the Hague, *nobile* Giuseppe Sallier de la Tour, *duca* di Calvello, who had been born in the province of Turin and had gained a degree in jurisprudence from the University of Turin. He could boast descent from Sardinia's Minister of Foreign Affairs from 1822 to 1835.

Thus, apart from the political appointment to the Embassy in London, Antonino Di San Giuliano, the background of Italy's most senior and successful diplomats at the end of 1909 was remarkably homogeneous. Italy, it seemed, did not so much have a Foreign Ministry; Piedmont did. Most of these officials had joined the Foreign Ministry while King Victor Emmanuel II was still alive.

Their character is testimony to the powerful conservative and parochial influence which he had on the Risorgimento.

Yet, by 1910, to isolate these most senior officials is misleading. Lower in the hierarchy, Piedmontese domination was weaker. Many of Italy's most distinguished Foreign Ministers (e.g. Mancini, Crispi, Rudinì and Tittoni) were not Northerners. Since 1887 the only Piedmontese to hold the Foreign Ministry for an extended period was Baron Alberto Blanc, who served as Crispi's rubber stamp from 1893 to 1896. Foreign Ministers were usually from the nobility, but even this tradition was not unbroken as Mancini, Crispi, Prinetti and Tittoni exemplified.

Among the bureaucracy the process of the geographical unification of Italy had also begun. Of the twenty-two other officials with Minister Plenipotentiary rank below the most senior seven, apart from Bollati, Gallina and Sallier, only three were Piedmontese. Fifteen had noble titles. By 1926 the distribution of the birth places of staff fitted tidily into the national pattern. Then only 35% were Northerners, and about the same percentage were Southerners. Rome, the centre of political activity, and perhaps of imperial inspiration, provided a further 20%.

San Giuliano inherited a Ministry in which this change had begun. Under his aegis, the process of change was given a personal twist. Although postings were made in consultation with a Committee, the Foreign Minister had considerable powers of selection and promotion, and San Giuliano made a sparing but careful use of this prerogative. The area which seems least to have concerned him was the appointment of ambassadors, in which the role of the King and of Giolitti was still strong. The selections for major Embassies from 1910 to 1914 were thus largely predictable. To Paris, San Giuliano sent Tittoni, a posting which left Tittoni available to return as Foreign Minister if San Giuliano made any disastrous mistakes, and which certainly allowed Tittoni to continue his private political and economic speculations in Rome.[25] To Berlin went Bollati, of impeccable social and political background, an old style Piedmontese bureaucrat, 'cold and reserved,...a high class clerk, no more'.[26] Bollati was also useful because he was a loyal triplicist who rapidly associated himself with Avarna, the correct and reactionary ambassador in Vienna. To St Petersburg in 1913 went Salvago Raggi's contemporary, Andrea Carlotti, *Marchese* di Riparbella, a Veronese with laureates from both Bologna and Padua universities. Over-educated by bureaucratic standards and rumoured to have an artistic temperament and 'the delicate soul of a poet',[27] Carlotti had been an able ambassador in Athens, but does not seem to have felt at home in St Petersburg. Perhaps his old Masonic ties made him ill at ease in the court of Rasputin and the Tsarina. To Constantinople went the political appointment, the *Marchese* Camillo Garroni. The only major ambassador who was a Southerner was *Marchese* Guglielmo Imperiali, whose transfer from Constantinople to London had been listed by Guicciardini. Imperiali, born in Salerno, with a laureate from Naples, was excitable and rhetorical, frequently and openly derided by San Giuliano. Imperiali's none too successful experience in Constantinople from 1904 to 1910 had left him with a personal interest in Asia Minor. He too believed in Italy's need for expansion in the Mediterranean, although his effectiveness as an ambassador was limited.

In any case, as San Giuliano had himself discovered, ambassadors rarely made Italian foreign policy. In office, San Giuliano often circulated his ambassadors asking for their opinion on this or that policy. But he almost always did so with an ulterior motive, usually that of procrastination, so that he could tell a presumptuous foreign ambassador in Rome that Italian policy could not be settled at that moment, and would have to remain unsettled until the loyal Foreign Minister had loyally consulted his loyal ambassadors. In fact, the ambassadors' advice rarely seems to have been taken. San Giuliano, like many other European Foreign Ministers, readily, and not irrationally, believed that ambassadors tended to represent the view of the countries in which they were stationed. The ambassadors with equal justice, often believed that policy was conducted behind their backs and that they were rarely fully informed.

In the busy and rather disorganised world of the *Consulta*, ambassadors were little more than postmen and reporters, and offers to them of independent action were as dangerous as Greeks bearing gifts. Once again a Varè story has a ring of truth about it. Varè alleges that Imperiali was sent the following despatch by San Giuliano:

You will receive, every now and then, long despatches on colonial matters, giving you precise and detailed instructions as to what to do. These despatches will bear my signature. But I advise you not to take any notice of them. The department which looks after the colonial matters in this Ministry is composed of well-meaning and hard-working officials. They know much more about colonies than I do. But political sense they have none! Unfortunately I have not time to read all they bring me to sign. I put my signature at the bottom of the page and hope that my Ambassadors will do what they think best. So, if the instructions that you receive from me appear reasonable, act upon them by all means. If they seem useless, leave them alone. If they appear utterly unwise, write me a note and I will see what can be done.[28]

If San Giuliano could be this sarcastic to his ambassador about his officials, he could be just as sarcastic to his officials about his ambassadors. The diplomatic world of despatches and telegrams, cyphering and decyphering, went on, but policy was made in Rome, by the Foreign Minister, by the Prime Minister, or by the effects of the Powers greater than Italy.

If the hand of San Giuliano cannot easily be detected in ambassadorial appointments there are more signs of his influence in the selection of the junior staff of the Foreign Ministry. Thirty candidates passed the examination into the diplomatic service between 1910 and 1914. Gaps in Italian reference books make it impossible to trace the careers of four of these. Of the remaining twenty-six, fifteen were Southerners, a proportion remarkably higher than the Ministry average. Seven of the fifteen were Sicilian. Of the remainder, two were Romans, five were Northerners and four had been born abroad, in Gorizia, Fiume, Prague and Argentina. Of the Northern five, one was a Visconti Venosta; another was the son of a deputy prominent in foreign affairs debates; a third had a brother already in the diplomatic service. Seventeen of the intake had noble titles, and eleven had deputies in their immediate family. One odd example was Ugo Cafiero, from the same Barletta family which had produced Bakunin's unlucky financier, Carlo Cafiero. Two other attachés who must have had an easier time with the examiners, were Prince Giuseppe Lanza Di Scordia, from the elder branch of Scalea's family; and *Marchese* Gaetano Paternò Di Manchi Di Bilici, from San Giuliano's own Catanian aristocracy.

Italy's universities shared the training of the successful applicants. Only one had a laureate from Turin, then Italy's most stimulating and Marxist university. He, ironically enough, was Augusto Rosso who was ambassador in Moscow when Italy declared war on Russia in 1941.

Italy, the least of the Great Powers

In their careers after San Giuliano's death, the attachés show an interesting consistency. Despite their upper-class background, which in another profession or in another country might soon have brought death in the trenches, none died on service in the First World War. The Fascist achievement of power also brought no 'parenthesis' to their careers. None retired for political reasons in 1922, and only one rejected the assumption of the dictatorship in 1925. By 1930, five other diplomats had died, or retired for orthodox reasons. Only one was a Southerner, Lanza Di Scordia, who succeeded to his titles and left the service.

There were some casualties in the nineteen thirties, during the 'Massacre of the Innocents', and more especially when Ciano began to exert his personal brand of patronage. Then a posting to Quito, Havana, La Paz or Asuncion was sometimes taken as good grounds for retirement. There were successes as well, such as Ottaviano Armando Koch, who was elevated to the title of *Ambasciatore* and made Director-General for Propaganda in the Ministry of Popular Culture. Koch's membership of the famous Roman banking family perhaps made his abilities especially obvious to Ciano. Among other survivals were Raffaele Guariglia, Augusto Rosso, who in 1961 was still a member of the Republic's Council for *Contenzioso diplomatico*, and the *Marchese* Francesco Maria Taliani del Marchio, who, after being Chief of the Ceremonial Office, 1929–32, became the ambassador at the Hague, and in June 1938 was tranferred to Chiang Kai-Shek's China. He remained there through troubled times until 1945. Recalled to Rome, in 1946 he was reappointed to the Office of Chief of Ceremonial where he continued to assist the infant Republic adjust to its past until 1951. His final posting was as ambassador to Franco's Madrid before he retired in February 1952, Italy's most senior diplomat. In retirement he has peaceably written books on China and on Cardinal Gasparri, suitable topics for the last years of a clerical nobleman from the Abruzzi.

Among those who joined the consular service under San Giuliano the same pattern evolves. Twenty-eight young men were appointed between 1910 and 1914. None died in the war; none had retired by 1930, perhaps illustrating the greater economic impulsion behind those who went into the lesser wing of the service. Indeed their careers prospered, favoured by a typical Mussolinian sleight of hand which offered formal promotion by creating the new rank of

Ambasciatore, superior to the old title Envoy Extraordinary and Minister Plenipotentiary First Class. In fact the number of ambassadors was almost the same as those who in the past had been First Class Ministers.

Seventeen of the twenty-eight survived to retire under the Republic. One, a Sicilian, Luigi Sillitti, did not leave the Foreign Ministry until 1957. Another, Francesco Fransoni, a Calabrian, became Secretary-General of the Ministry from 1948 to 1949. During San Giuliano's Foreign Ministry, both in the diplomatic and consular service, appointees tended to be Southerners, and tended to be men whose bureaucratic skills and political and social background and ideals would not be disturbed by Italy's future.

Apart from seeing that the examination process worked with due propriety, there were also other areas in which a Foreign Minister could exercise patronage. One was promotion. Italy's diplomats were strictly ranked, and movement in the ranks was rare. Under San Giuliano, there were few changes, but the changes which did occur have some significance.

The most rapid and significant example was Salvatore Contarini, who gained five places in seniority from 1910 to 1914. Contarini was a Palermitan, with a laureate in law from Palermo university. His family was from the petty aristocracy, grown wealthy with the Risorgimento. One member, the *Marchese* Luigi Contarini, had been a deputy, albeit of the variety who preferred financial to parliamentary activity. Although a Sicilian, Luigi Contarini, like San Giuliano, never became a Crispian. He sat in the centre of the Chamber and usually supported Rudinì. By his efforts, the Contarini family gained large holdings in the Banco di Sicilia, which in turn became prominently involved in Italian economic imperialism. In social, political and economic ideas the Contarinis and San Giuliano had much in common.

Contarini had joined the Foreign Ministry in 1891 on the recommendation of Rudinì, in the humble capacity of clerk.[29] He was promoted to attaché rank two years later, but, unusually, and at his own request, he remained almost exclusively in Rome, preferring bureaucratic activity to gilded diplomatic life abroad. His only foreign posting had lasted three months in Athens in 1895 before, in 1912, he was made ambassador in Lisbon, allegedly as a penalty for antagonising Giolitti. On the outbreak of the First World

War, he was rapidly recalled to Rome, rising in January 1920 to replace De Martino as Secretary General. He retired in March 1926, aged fifty-eight, amid doubtful allegations that he had been forced out because of policy differences with Mussolini. Contarini complained that the ex-Nationalists, Federzoni and Rocco, had too much influence over the *Duce*. Famous for his irascibility, Contarini was always an unlikely working companion for Mussolini. He had had the time to coin the best of all witticisms about Mussolini. Objecting not to Mussolini's ambitions but to his crude manners and interference in bureaucratic life, Contarini remarked to his delighted juniors: 'As for Mussolini we must use him like the blood of Saint Januarius. Exhibit him once a year and only from far off.'[30]

Contarini had been prominent in the revival of colonialism before 1910. He attended the Asmara Conference in 1905. He was an early member, and later Secretary, of the Istituto Coloniale Italiano, sharing office with the more urbane Mario Lago, another career diplomat, who became Mussolini's Governor of the Dodecanese Islands for more than a decade after 1924. With his testy and efficient temperament, Contarini was a powerful figure at the Ministry. His personal importance, however, should not be exaggerated. There is no evidence for claims that it was Contarini who was the grey eminence who pushed Italy into the Libyan War.[31] What is significant about Contarini is that his Mediterranean oriented expanionism, his nationalism, accorded well with the changing tone of San Giuliano's Foreign Ministry.

Among other promotions were Baron Carlo Fasciotti, Antonio Chiaramonte Bordonaro and Vittorio Cerruti, who each rose three places, and the most successful of the new attachés, Raffaele Guariglia, who gained six. Fasciotti and Cerruti were Northerners. Fasciotti, born in Udine, belonged to a family prominent in the diplomatic service and the Chamber. He seems to have had a taste and ability for the more obscure Giolittian financial dealing. San Giuliano sent him as Minister to Bucharest, an important position for both Italian politics and, potentially, economics.[32] There he remained eight years before moving to Madrid, his most senior post. Cerruti, a younger Piedmontese, did better, rising to be Mussolini's ambassador in Berlin and Paris.[33] He too had ties to the colonial and nationalist revival, having been personal secretary to Guido Pompilj,

Under-Secretary for Foreign Affairs, 1906–9, a Giolittian with an interest in Eritrea and the Istituto Coloniale.

Chiaramonte Bordonaro and Guariglia fit more closely to the pattern of San Giuliano, Scalea, De Martino and Contarini. Chiaramonte Bordonaro was another Palermitan, but had a diploma in social sciences from Florence. He joined the consular service in 1899, not transferring to the diplomatic side until 1908. From 1910 to 1913 he was personal secretary to his fellow Palermitan, parliamentary Under-Secretary, Prince Pietro Lanza Di Scalea. He was succeeded by Contarini's friend, Mario Lago, who had previously been Scalea's secretary in 1906 and in 1909–10. After the rise of fascism, Chiaramonte Bordonaro stayed in the service, replacing Contarini as Secretary-General from 1926 to 1927, until the suspicious Mussolini again suppressed that dangerously influential post. Chiaramonte Bordonaro was then transferred to the Embassy in London. He retired in 1932, aged fifty-five, in the 'Massacre of the Innocents', that sudden and partial Mussolinian effort to 'fascistise' the diplomatic service.

Raffaele Guariglia, Baron of Vitusa, was also a Southerner, born in Naples with a laureate in jurisprudence, awarded in 1908 by his local university. He too had joined the diplomatic service via the less socially demanding consular wing. He transferred in 1912, allegedly because a friend who was Salandra's nephew saw the chance to take over Guariglia's post and remain in Paris which 'he adored'.[34] Once again, San Giuliano had promoted a young man with a fine career in front of him. Like the others, Guariglia possessed the Southern aptitude for the grind of bureaucratic work and the flexibility of bureaucratic politics. As an old man he would remember piously that, in 1922, he held no political opinions except that the national interest should be raised above party squabbles.[35]

By then Guariglia had become a fixture at the Ministry where he remained from 1919 to 1932. In the crucial years 1935–6 he was recalled to Rome as Chief of the Special Office for Ethiopia. Mussolini's ambassador variously in Madrid, Buenos Aires, Paris, the Vatican and Ankara, Guariglia survived to become Foreign Minister in Badoglio's first post-Fascist government. He revived the post of Secretary-General,[36] appointing to it one of his fellow attachés under San Giuliano, Augusto Rosso. After his retirement (officially not until October 1946) Guariglia lived on into the Republic, writing his memoirs, a Senator and pillar of Lauro's corrupt and Neapolitan Monarchist party. Guariglia could reasonably claim that his ideas had remained unchanged by the political and social vicissitudes of fifty years of Italian history.

But the key positions in the Foreign Ministry were not really decided by the formal system of promotion. Theoretically, the chief aide to the Foreign Minister was a politician, the Under-Secretary. Until March 1914, the Under-Secretary was in fact another Sicilian, Pietro Lanza Di Scalea, who had also held this office under Sonnino and Guicciardini in 1906 and 1909–10. Scalea fitted easily into the 'Southern' Ministry. Although he belonged to a cadet branch, the Lanza family were more distinguished scions of the Sicilian aristocracy than were the San Giulianos. Born in Palermo and a great landowner, Scalea was rumoured to be friendly to the Mafia and certainly was to Southern business and shipping interests.[37] Politically he was conservative, with dilettantish artistic tastes. During the war he became a prominent supporter of the Italian aeronautical industry. After 1919 he moved formally into Nationalist ranks but was adroit enough to serve Facta as Minister of War in 1922 and to return under the Fascist regime as Minister of Colonies from 1924 to 1926,[38] Minister of State and Senator. Before 1914 already a prominent member of the Geographical Society and the Istituto Coloniale, Scalea became President of the Royal Geographical Society, and of the Aero Club of Italy under the Fascists.

On foreign policy, Scalea's exact influence is hard to trace. Few memoranda bearing his name remain in the archives. The Under-Secretary traditionally had an influence on the selection of personnel, but differentiations in this process are not easy to detect along the Catania–Palermo Axis. Typical was the nomination of Scalea to preside over a Commission set up in June 1913 to consider the 'reorganisation of the Central Administration of the Ministry for Foreign Affairs'. Typical also was the fact that 'the practical results [of the Commission] were undoubtedly none'.[39] Throughout his career Scalea's greatest interest was not so much in bureaucratic reform as in the defence of the social structure of the Sicilian *latifondisti*. His career in Rome helped him to ensure that any changes there could be deflected to the advantage of the great landowners. A position in foreign policy was useful because Italian expansionism had its political and social attractions to the *latifondisti*, and because the Under-Secretary of the Foreign Ministry held one of those positions least exposed to the 'democratic' parliamentary process.

The most important bureaucratic office in the *Consulta* was that of Secretary-General. Indeed this post, the equivalent of the British Permanent Under-Secretary, allowed such power to its holder that the position was repressed by Crispi and then again by Mussolini when those statesmen were anxious to appear to be running their own foreign policy. In 1910 the Secretary-General was the safely respectable Bollati. After he was transferred to the Embassy in Berlin in January 1913, San Giuliano promoted to Secretary-General Giacomo De Martino. By that date De Martino had already become the Foreign Minister's closest associate in the making of foreign policy.

Just as San Giuliano's grandfather had been a Bourbon Foreign Minister, De Martino's family reached directly back to the diplomacy of Naples–Sicily. Giacomo had been born in Berne in 1868, and had a diploma from the School of Social Sciences in Florence. His background, however, was Neapolitan. His grandfather, Giacomo I, had been born in Tunis into a diplomatic family from the court nobility of the Bourbons of Naples.[40] Still more ancient strands were woven into the De Martino clan by a member of the family who had set up a double menage in Egypt and become one of the most trusted servants of the Khedives. In 1908 a Giacomo De Martino Pasha was still Minister of the Khedival house in Cairo.[41] This association with the royal family of Egypt must have helped the De Martinos to be *persona grata* in the court of Victor Emmanuel III who, throughout his life, would continue to build ties with Egypt, and would go into exile in 1946 to Alexandria.[42]

Among the family who remained on the Italian side of the Mediterranean, Giacomo I had entered the diplomatic service under King Ferdinand II, and represented Naples–Sicily in Rome, London and Paris. He earned a reputation as a man able to be on two and perhaps three sides at once, although his abilities were of no use to King Francesco II who appointed De Martino Minister of Foreign Affairs in the last Bourbon government before Naples fell to Garibaldi.[43] With the disappearance of his Kingdom, Giacomo I retired from diplomacy but was rapidly assimilated into the Piedmontese system as a ministerialist. In 1865 he was elected a deputy for Sorrento and the railway town, Foligno, north of Rome. His choice of seat was significant for he was already engaged in the agreeable and appropriate task of founding a second family fortune as director of the railway system of Central Italy.

His son, Giacomo II, was elected deputy for Naples in 1892, and collaborated with San Giuliano and Franchetti in the small group of non-Crispian but patriotic deputies in favour of a more ordered prosecution of African expansion, joining Rudinì's cabinet after Adowa as Under-Secretary of Public Works. In 1901 he returned to a ministerial post when for six months he was Under-Secretary for Foreign Affairs to Prinetti. He was the first President of the Istituto Coloniale, and a Senator much given to expansionist rhetoric. In 1910 he became Governor of the Somaliland, and in 1919 Governor of Cyrenaica, dying in service at Benghazi in 1921. An admirer of the British Empire, De Martino was the closest Italian equivalent to an imperial viceroy.

It was his nephew, Giacomo III, who was San Giuliano's selection as Secretary-General in 1913. Giacomo III had returned his family to its diplomatic traditions, joining the Ministry of Foreign Affairs in 1891. His first important posting occurred in 1901 when he became his uncle's personal secretary. In 1907, befitting his family's Mediterranean heritage, he was made Agent and Consul-General in Cairo. There he had a somewhat difficult time given squabbles within the Italian community. He also was driven to complain that Tittoni did not keep him informed of Italian policy, and had despatched the wrong sort of agent to inspire among the Egyptians a love of Italians. De Martino presumably preferred that ties with Italy, and Italian funds, passed in an orthodox fashion through the branches of the De Martino family.[44] Where Tittoni had frowned, San Giuliano smiled on the youngest De Martino. In July 1911 he was deliberately selected by San Giuliano to be *Chargé d'Affaires* in Constantinople, with the task, by his own account, to see that war was not avoided.[45] In October, after Italy had invaded Libya, De Martino was recalled as *Chef de Cabinet* at the Ministry. Promoted again in 1913, he retained his post as Secretary-General until 1920, then serving Mussolini as ambassador in Tokyo and Washington, before retiring in 1932 after forty years in the service. In staying power he had matched his grandfather.

In the world of San Giuliano, Scalea, De Martino and Contarini, it was no wonder that contemporaries believed that the *Consulta* had fallen into 'Sicilian' hands.[46] 'Bourbon' might have been a more accurate adjective.

Yet, to be a Southerner was not the only formula for success in San Giuliano's Ministry. It was also useful to be a believer in Italian expansionism. The most graphic case exemplifying this point is the career of Primo Levi who, in August 1910, was nominated Director-General of Commercial Affairs, an office of great potential importance given San Giuliano's belief that trade should be the 'secular arm' of diplomacy.

Levi, a Ferrarese, had for twenty years been Crispi's closest newspaper associate, *redattore* of Crispi's personal paper, *La Riforma*. He was an enthusiastic Africanist, loving, it is reported, '*dannunzianamente*' to sign his articles '*Italicus*'.[47] *La Riforma*, in characteristic rhetoric in 1896, warned against the threat that Italy 'become an extended Switzerland, that is in winter a house of pleasure for foreigners,...and in summer a...bathing establishment'.[48] Levi had wide artistic contacts, and also was well regarded by the powerful and important men of the shipbuilding companies and merchant marine.[49] In 1895 Crispi had appointed his friend and colleague director of the new 'Office for the Colony of Eritrea and the protectorates'. After Adowa, Levi retreated into relative anonymity by being admitted to the consular service. However, he attended the Asmara Conference and became a prominent member of the Geographical Society and Istituto Coloniale. In 1908 Tittoni gave recognition to his special abilities by sending him on a delicate mission to Egypt where Levi was able to build up an excellent relationship with Giacomo De Martino III. There was no danger that Primo Levi, even though a Northerner, would feel out of place in the 'Southern' Ministry of Antonino Di San Giuliano.

In January 1911 San Giuliano made another interesting choice, this time for the new post of Director-General of Schools Abroad. The idea of Foreign Ministry control of a national cultural drive was not new. The Directorate-General of Schools Abroad had been dissolved after Adowa, but Prinetti had re-established the post of Inspector-General in 1901.[50] Given San Giuliano's repeated declarations of his belief that commerce and culture were linked weapons for a nation's foreign policy, the increase in stature given to the office is interesting. So was the choice as Director-General.

The new Director-General was Angelo Scalabrini, born in the province of Como, and a school-teacher by profession. In June 1893 Scalabrini had been summoned to join what was then called the Directorate-General for Schools Abroad. In January 1896, Crispi made him Inspector-General, but the post lapsed after Adowa. In the 1900s Scalabrini was another at the forefront of the development of the Geographical Society and the Istituto Coloniale.

Scalabrini was not just a returned Crispian. In France it has long been known that anti-clerical Ministers at home were willing to cooperate with Roman Catholic missionary organisations abroad in areas of French colonial interest, particularly if the missionaries belonged to French-based organisations. In Liberal Italy, that usurper State which kept the Pope a 'prisoner in the Vatican', it has usually been assumed that such cooperation did not exist. Yet Angelo Scalabrini, the man appointed by the anti-clerical Crispi and the sarcastically anti-Catholic San Giuliano, was the devoted brother of Giovanni Battista Scalabrini, Bishop of Piacenza, founder of the Scalabrinian missionary fathers. So loyal a brother was Angelo that at the request of Giovanni Battista he had turned down the offer of election to the Italian Chamber. He had also used his contacts within governmental circles to help the Scalabrinian cause.[51] After his brother died, Angelo piously collected and published the writings of the bishop whom he described as the 'apostle of religion and *patria*'.[52]

The Gentiloni pact of 1913 demonstrated the reconciliation of many Catholics to the Liberal State. Catholic preference was then not for Giolittian reformism so much as for socially conservative nationalism.[53] Giovanni Battista Scalabrini had urged these attitudes two decades before. 'Religion and *patria*', he said, were the 'two supreme aspirations of every noble and gentle heart.' Emigration was 'a safety-valve given by God to this society in travail...a conservative force much stronger than all the moral and material pressures, planned and enacted by legislators to safeguard the political order and to guarantee the life and property of citizens.'[54] Above the Scalabrinian missionary foundations among Italian emigrant communities waved the green, white and red tricolor with '*religione e patria*' emblazoned on it. The Lateran pacts may not have been signed for another generation, but in her revived colonialism, Italy had as sympathisers many Italian churchmen. San Giuliano's appointment of Scalabrini was thus an early, diplomatic equivalent to the Gentiloni pacts. Italian ambitions in Libya, Ethiopia, the Balkans or Asia Minor might yet, it seemed, be worth a mass.

These images of the personnel of the Foreign Ministry do not surprise. Apart from the special process of Southernisation, Italian diplomats, like their equivalents in other European countries, came from an elite, wealthy and often aristocratic group within the already tiny Italian establishment. Politically, diplomats liked to talk about diplomacy being 'for the professionals', above politics, but, in fact, they were staunchly conservative and fearful of socialism. Italian diplomats believed that Italy must be a Great Power, especially in the Mediterranean. Their nationalism had far more similarities than differences with that of Crispi or Mussolini. Some of the gilded youth may have been laughing diplomats, but more joined San Giuliano in planning how Italy should take up as much as possible of the white man's burden.

Changes in the personnel of the *Consulta* were quite coherent under San Giuliano but coherence can be far less readily discovered in the organisational structure of the Ministry. Traditionally, bureaucratic reform was difficult to achieve in Liberal Italy. There were twenty-seven Foreign Ministers from 1870 to 1914 and only a few, Visconti Venosta, Mancini, Tittoni and San Giuliano, were in office long enough, or often enough, to make much of a personal imprint on Italian foreign policy. Several tried to tinker with the administrative structure of foreign policy-making. This tinkering reached its most major, and destructive, level from 1887 to 1896 when the Prime Ministers Crispi and Rudinì had rival structural schemes. Twice, Crispi abolished the overweening office of Secretary-General, and twice the less firm Rudinì restored it.[55]

After this excitement, the next Foreign Minister to have any major impact was Tittoni who, in 1908, produced an organisational structure of the Foreign Ministry which lasted until 1920, although San Giuliano did some tinkering of his own in 1910, and was planning major changes in 1914. By then, the Foreign Ministry was theoretically divided into sections under the control of, respectively, the Foreign Minister, the Under-Secretary of State for Foreign Affairs and the Secretary-General, the last being a bureaucrat not a politician. Both the Minister and his Under-Secretary had their own cabinets which were duly headed by a career official with the title *capo di gabinetto*. The politicians were also provided with private secretaries, often young men whose appointment promised them a considerable future. As long as they did a reasonable job, secretaries could expect their careers to be followed with the interest and support of their *padroni*.

In theory, there was little differentiation between the material sent to Foreign Minister and Under-Secretary, but, in practice, the Foreign Minister usually played a dominant role, and used his junior merely to escape the more formal and irksome diplomatic or parliamentary tasks. Foreign Minister and Under-Secretary appeared from time to time in both the Chamber and the Senate, no matter to which of the two houses they formally belonged.

The great coordinating post in the Foreign Ministry was that of Secretary-General, an office originally established by Cavour in the 1850s on older Sardinian traditions. Cavour had seen the position as essentially one of overseer of all administrative work,[56] but it was soon apparent that the Secretary-General would need to be expert in all aspects of foreign policy. This total role provided a continuity amid falling Ministries, but created suspicions among politicians like Crispi, who disliked bureaucrats knowing more about foreign policy than they did themselves.

The office of Secretary-General was at once restored by Rudinì after the Battle of Adowa, but the politicians protected themselves in the next decade and a half by appointing grey bureaucrats, Giacomo Malvano (1896–1907) and Riccardo Bollati, to the post.[57] It was San Giuliano who brought about a change in 1913 by promoting Giacomo De Martino, as a *uomo di fiducia*, very close to the Foreign Minister himself.

In 1914, the Secretary-General, theoretically, ruled over only four offices, those of the Press and Translation, the Cyphers, of Correspondence and of Law and Passports. But, in fact, as if to prove Cavour right, he oversaw almost all business.

Apart from the autonomous offices, the Ministry was split into a number of 'Divisions', usually under the control of a Director-General. Division I, moved back by San Giuliano to direct dependence on the Secretary-General, dealt with accounts, pay, subsidies and the general administration of diplomatic property. Division II looked after personnel and ceremonial matters, the Archives and the Library. Supervising Division II was the Director-

General of General Affairs. Much more significant was the Director-General of Political Affairs, who dealt with most day to day diplomacy. His Division III was further split into sections dealing with Europe, the Levant and Africa, the Far East and America, and colonial affairs. The tasks and power of this last were much reduced by the creation of a Ministry of Colonies in 1912. The Director-General of Political Affairs also dealt with Division IV which was concerned with claims by Italians on foreign governments, and police matters.

The Director-General of Commercial Affairs headed Divisions V and VI concerning trade and financial matters of all kinds from railways to tariffs. A Director-General of Private Affairs looked after Divisions VII and VIII which assessed questions of extradition, disputed nationality, pensions and inheritance. He also had responsibility for the Legal Office, the *Ufficio del Contenzioso e della Legislazione*.

Separate from all were the council of '*Contenzioso Diplomatico*', comprised largely of elder statesmen, and of uncertain advisory function, and a *Commissariato Generale* of Emigration. In 1911 San Giuliano provided a new segment by elevating the officer who looked after Italian schools abroad to the rank of Director-General.

There was no hard and fast differentiation between the clerks at the *Consulta* and the diplomats abroad, although there was inevitably some grumbling from the more stay-at-home at the short terms worked in Rome by some of the more gilded youth. Primo Levi, for example, complained in very up-to-date parlance that the turn-over at the Ministry was like 'a kalaeidoscope or cinematograph'. Manzoni, the Director-General of Political Affairs, proposed formally that Directors-General stay in their position for at least four years, and Chiefs of Offices for two.[58] On the other hand, the *Consulta* was flexible at its highest levels. Both Bollati and De Martino, after being Secretary-General, went off to ambassadorial posts abroad, and Contarini's love of work in the Rome office, and dislike of foreign postings, was rare enough to excite comment.

There was a distinction between the diplomatic and consular service, in entry, examination, pay scales and posting. As in other European countries, by 1914, this difference was provoking criticism, especially when it was alleged that diplomats paid far too little attention to what was really important, i.e. financial and commercial questions.[59] In practice, the divisions seem to have been less rigid than in some other countries, and certainly in the early stages of a career it was not unusual to find officers moving from the consular to the diplomatic service, although formally only two officers each year could apply to transfer.[60]

This picture of sensible harmony and neat organisation existed rather more on paper than in practice. Any student familiar with the orderliness of the British Foreign Office after the reforms of Sir Charles Hardinge will be dismayed by the lack of order at the *Consulta*. Certainly there was no regular passing of a despatch up the hierarchy of bureaucrats before a final summary reached the Secretary of State's eye as at the Foreign Office. In San Giuliano's period at least, only very occasionally did Directors-General write memoranda which could have had a serious influence on the making of policy. Before 1913 significant advice was rarely given, even by Bollati, who was then Secretary-General.

It is undoubted that an enormous administrative burden and enormous administrative power rested with the Foreign Minister. Italy's weakness meant that opportunities for individual initiatives in foreign policy were relatively rare, but from 1910 to 1914 what initiatives there were were made by the Foreign Minister. The only possible candidates for *eminences grises* in the *Consulta* were De Martino, who had had his career made by San Giuliano, and the Director-General of Commercial Affairs, Primo Levi, who had had his career remade by the Foreign Minister.

Perhaps not surprisingly, in Liberal Italy there was little enthusiasm for modern technology in the diplomatic service. One later attaché was told that no typists had been formally appointed to the *Consulta* until the outbreak of the First World War.[61] In several posts abroad, there were rumours of unsanitary Embassies, and of ambassadors who did the work themselves without secretarial or typing assistance.[62] In May 1914 San Giuliano appealed for a further grant of 80,000 lire *per annum* to reorganise his office. He noted that he had been able to appoint four extra clerical assistants during the Libyan War, and now would like to promote the two surviving men who deserved support since they were 'fathers of families'. A third assistant would also be of great benefit. Although San Giuliano asked for Salandra to intervene in his favour with the Treasury, nothing was finalised before San Giuliano's death in October.[63]

In these circumstances, although telegrams and despatches were duly typed, and copies sent to King, Prime Minister, Foreign Minister, Under-Secretary, Secretary-General and archives, San Giuliano preferred to do most of his work in an execrable long-hand. He occasionally apologised about its indecipherability, which he usually complained had been caused by the inadequacies of his gouty fingers. San Giuliano was enormously hard-working. Apart from the earlier story of him working over his breakfast in the Borghese Gardens, archival evidence can be found of him jotting diplomatic ideas on the back of his menu at his club. For a man already wasted by disease, the task of being Italy's Foreign Minister was exceedingly onerous and must have contributed to his early death. His illness, his workload, his personality and the style of his diplomacy encouraged many visits to spas, usually to Fiuggi, just south of Rome, from where he could leave the importunities of parliamentarians, journalists and foreign ambassadors to the Secretary-General and Under-Secretary, and go on plotting his personal version of Italy's way to greatness.

Given Giolitti's reputation as the master-corrupter of the press, it might have been expected that Liberal Italy would be adept at enrolling the cohorts of the press behind foreign policy. As in other European chancelleries, there were rumours that the *Consulta* readily disbursed 'subventions' to the Italian[64] and foreign press. However, in passing, it may be worth asking whether Giolitti deserved his reputation as the puppet-master of the press. His rather old-fashioned way of working through prefects and the police may have still been effective electorally with the minor local press, but, to a considerable degree, the crisis in the Italian intelligentsia's attitude to Liberal Italy by 1911 reflected a world of journalism which was no longer doing as it was told. Indeed it was the hostility to Giolitti in the major papers, *Corriere della Sera*, *Giornale d'Italia* and *L'Idea Nazionale* which was the best indication of the new fissures in the political structure of Liberal Italy.

As far as foreigners were concerned, Italy was prepared to make disbursements to sympathetic journalists, but rarely did so with the flair[65] or generosity[66] of the French. For one thing, as Mussolini would later find, foreign journalists who were willing consistently to admire Italy, were neither many nor prominent.[67] Moreover Liberal Italy lacked a propaganda structure which could assist the propagation of information or funds to the foreign press.

The relevant office in the *Consulta* with the task of pleasing foreign journalists was the *Ufficio Stampa*. Daniele Varè remembered that conditions there were somewhat primitive and disorganised:

In the old days [the Press Bureau] was housed in three rooms, in a sort of garret, looking out on to the Consulta's courtyard. Under the papal regime, those same rooms had been used as a gilded prison for the young nobles of the papal guard, who misbehaved themselves...[The Office] boasted of one typewriter, and the work...consisted in preparing a few extracts from the Italian and foreign daily papers, on matters connected with international affairs...No journalist came near the *Ufficio Stampa*. They got their information elsewhere. Even the reports from abroad, concerning the press in foreign countries, went direct to the political and commercial offices and were never shown to poor old Deciani [the Chief of the *Ufficio*]. His office was a press-cutting agency and nothing more.[68]

Given the part he had played in the revival of colonialism and given his repeated references to the importance of 'public opinion' it might have been expected that San Giuliano, in office, would work zealously to modernise the *Consulta's* primitive relationship with the press. But before reforms could occur, there were also other issues to be considered. Unsure of the strength of his position as Foreign Minister, naturally preferring work in the dark to the light, with none of the jocularity and ease of personal relationships which might allow him to make contact readily with journalists, San Giuliano was also very aware of the danger of public fiasco which always hung over Italian foreign policy.

Therefore, in his first two years in office, San Giuliano worked to keep journalism and diplomacy apart. During the *Cinquantennio* celebrations, for example, he regarded excessive patriotism with anxiety. When Foscari's Trento and Trieste Society held its seventh national Congress in Rome, its activities were kept under close surveillance by public security officials.[69] In March 1911, San Giuliano addressed an alarmed memorandum to his new Prime Minister, Giolitti, pointing out the possible hindrance to foreign policy which could come from speeches by members of the government during the various *feste*. In an ideal world, he said, there would be no speeches at all. This was regrettably impossible; but the Cabinet should be instructed to show the greatest public reserve, and to be very careful of those with whom they shared platforms. Prefects should be told to keep the local press as quiet as possible.[70]

This fearful, even timid, San Giuliano was the one who earned the ire of the Nationalists. Quarrelling as much with Giolitti as San

Giuliano, it was also in the summer of 1911 that the Nationalists and some of the anti-Giolittian press joined in condemning the appointment of Garroni to Constantinople. Andrea Torre wrote that, instead, a 'young, active and energetic' diplomat should be sent, and *Corriere della Sera* declared that the affair was 'the culminating story of the moral decadence of our parliamentary mores'.[71] The extraordinary naivety of these comments cannot have impressed San Giuliano with the profundity of either the Nationalists, the opposition or the press.

Despite his timidity before the Libyan War, San Giuliano had continued to talk about the need for a more useful 'public opinion'. Naturally enough, he went on 'subventioning' the domestic and foreign press as Tittoni had done. He also promised his officials abroad that during the *Cinquantennio* they would be sent more detailed examples of national 'intellectual and economic' life so that they could answer possible criticisms of the Italian performance.[72] The extent to which this promise was carried out, however, may be questioned. In December 1912, even in so key an area of Italian interest as Albania, the local official can be found complaining of the total inadequacy of the information which he was receiving about Italy.[73]

Meanwhile, the Libyan War had given an enormous boost to the interest of 'public opinion' in foreign affairs and to San Giuliano's confidence in Italian performance. During the war, special Ministry of the Interior funds had been released by Giolitti to the Foreign Ministry to encourage sympathy for the Italian cause. Perhaps reluctant to surrender the bureaucratic advantage thus won, in February 1913 San Giuliano suggested that the *Consulta* continue to have the funds at their disposal. The Minister of the Treasury, Tedesco, doubted the propriety of such usage, but was overruled by Giolitti. San Giuliano was granted continuing money to encourage his 'good disposition towards our political aims' in Albania.[74] Whether through bureaucratic impulsion, or because of the basic character of the 'cold war' with Austria, San Giuliano continued to appeal for more and more cash to help Italy win the contest for the hearts, minds and bank accounts of Albanians.[75]

The covert style of the press campaigns in Albania appealed naturally to San Giuliano. He was a less fervent advocate of a role for 'public opinion' in more public forums, for example, after

Austria published the Hohenlohe decrees for Trieste in August 1913, or in the atmosphere of the general electoral campaign in November. San Giuliano had hoped rather naively that journalists could easily be persuaded to speak out or keep quiet as the 'national interest' demanded. But the various excited press campaigns in the latter half of 1913 provoked the *Consulta* into re-thinking its policy toward the press. De Martino drafted a forty-eight page memorandum on the state of the *Ufficio Stampa* and the need for reform. Only with complete re-organisation, the Secretary-General noted, could there be liaison between the Foreign Ministry and the press as there already was in other countries. Reiterating what San Giuliano had often said, De Martino pointed out that 'public opinion' could be an indispensible element in the making of diplomacy. The *Cinquantennio* and the Libyan War had illustrated the strength of Italian patriotism, which would sustain the government in a forward ('*ardita*') policy. Already 'public opinion' was proving itself a very effective instrument of diplomatic action in current disputes such as the *Carthage* and *Manouba* incidents, or in assisting Italy's efforts to continue her occupation of the Dodecanese.

The old school, De Martino complained, saw the press as an unfortunate necessity. But these archaic prejudices had been abandoned in other countries. The Foreign Ministry must deepen its contacts beyond those with *La Tribuna* and *Il Messaggero* in Rome and *Corriere della Sera*. The profession of journalism was an important and useful one; journalists were busy men, and ought to be treated efficiently. The Foreign Ministry, therefore, needed officials available for interviews daily. Some journalists would still have to be excluded from these briefings. De Martino was not specific about whom he meant, but he did note that Nationalists ought to be permitted consultation. The existence of Pan Slavs and Pan Germans, he argued, had helped Russian and German policy. The Nationalists could 'fulfil a necessary function, because that complex organism which is public opinion, to function as it must, needs a certain amount of exaggeration'. De Martino did not feel it necessary to add the obvious – Nationalist exaggeration was preferable to that of socialism's pacifist internationalism.

De Martino concluded these comments by declaring in favour of the formation of a large and powerful *Ufficio Stampa*. Journalists, as well as diplomatic officials, must be on its staff. The journalists

selected would have to be vetted carefully to see that they had no
dangerous preconceptions towards the Triple Alliance or the Triple
Entente. They must be 'neither Francophile nor Triplicist...but
simply Italian'.

The director of the Press Office would need to be the Minister's
intimate, wholly *au courant* with diplomatic correspondence, in other
words, presumably, the Secretary-General. De Martino pointed to
Albania as an example. There, even when the Albanian State was
properly established, Italian 'vigilance' must be 'intense'. 'Public
opinion' must in the future be kept fully informed about Albania,
and Italian interests there. Another example, De Martino minuted,
was Asia Minor, where Britain and Germany were rivals to Italian
influence.[76] In short, the *Ufficio Stampa* should protect and develop
Italy's interests. It should propagate Italian nationalism.

In his long analysis De Martino had used most of the arguments
raised by San Giuliano eight years before when he had been nursing
Italian colonialism back to life. Moreover the memorandum was
soon followed by public and private declarations from San Giuliano
that Italy had abandoned a remissive policy and must be accepted
as an equal by the other Great Powers. But despite this, a re-
organisation of the Press Office did not take place. In February 1914,
De Martino again presented San Giuliano with a memorandum
suggesting a development of the Ministry's information services.
Again he relied heavily on the competitive argument, pressing that
Italy should not fall behind the other Great Powers.[77]

It was characteristic of San Giuliano that despite his minuted
agreement with the report of the 'valorous collaborator' on whom
he relied so much, he did not hasten the plan into action, merely
passing it on to the investigatory commission under Scalea and then
to the new Under-Secretary after March 1914, Borsarelli. In
practice, when he wanted Italian press support for national policy
in Albania and Asia Minor, San Giuliano appealed to De Martino
to arrange matters.[78] But, in his heart, especially after the fall of
Giolitti in March 1914 had changed the bases of his position as
Foreign Minister, San Giuliano preferred the *de facto* to the *de iure*.
He continued to want 'public opinion' to be marshalled behind
Italian policy, but Italian policy must not surrender to the superficial
and public idiocies of Federzoni.[79] Expansionism was better left
surreptitious than a subject of open discussion. So a formal change

in the *Ufficio Stampa* had to await the impact of war and, in 1917, the belated creation after Caporetto of an Under-Secretaryship for Press and Propaganda.[80]

The story of the *Consulta's* relationship to the business world is very similar. Again San Giuliano can often be found in his memoranda noting the importance of an economic side to diplomacy. Only six months after he had taken office, he showed an anxiety to define the relationship between business and foreign policy. He asked his Ministry to inform him of the 'way in which the commercial information service' was 'regulated by Italian diplomats and consuls', and how the 'material furnished by the agents...was utilised and brought to the knowledge of the business class'. Equally, he noted, the Ministry should discover how best its officers could correspond, perhaps even on a personal level, with Italian companies, public or private. In general, he argued, diplomatic agents ought to be instructed 'to support and protect the initiatives and undertakings of a commercial and industrial nature [taken] by Italian citizens'.[81]

But, San Giuliano quickly saw, sometimes the government would have to give the lead:

It is clear that we have a business segment, underdeveloped ('*giovane*') and not yet wholly independent of other countries; hence, at the moment, we should not aspire to emulating equally...the three great States [Britain, Germany and France], economically so much stronger than us...But in spite of this, given the marvellous steps taken by the Italian economy in these fifty years of national unity...some financial expansion ought to be allowable even to us, not only without risk to our markets but with advantage...[e.g.] to our political credit...I say political since it is well known today how foreign policy and international finance are intimately bound together...But Italian Capital is timid and slothful: it is thus necessary that the encouragement to act should come from above. Therefore I rely on Your Excellency [Giolitti] whom I trust is convinced of this truth: there cannot today be an effective foreign policy unless the vigilant, constant and zealous action of Ministers, diplomats and consuls is backed by a combined economic and financial expansionism, demonstrating that the words of the rulers are the expression of the positive results achieved by the country.[82]

This hortatory desire for support from Big Business, remained a constant in San Giuliano's foreign policy. It was also echoed in reports by permanent officials at the *Consulta* like Manzoni, the Director-General of Political Affairs, and especially, and characteristically, by Primo Levi.[83] Some funds certainly were handed over by the *Consulta* to 'national' business organisations abroad.[84]

Once again, in practice, the increased interest in the commercial side of foreign policy was not turned into anything concrete. San Giuliano remained most anxious to help, and to be assisted by business, which he called 'a kind of secular arm',[85] but cooperation in real terms continued to come as it had in the past from Giolitti's ties with the Banca Commerciale and the Banca d'Italia. It was in Albania, and under the urging of De Martino, that Liberal Italy came closest to a full-scale organisation of economic imperialism. Already in May 1913 San Giuliano had set up an unofficial Albanian Office under Scalabrini.[86] In April 1914, given the continued competition with Austria, De Martino asked for more. Austria, he said, had established a successful pro-Albanian committee, but had drawn its membership chiefly from the aristocratic and academic worlds. 'The Italian Committee must instead get its support essentially from the financial world', De Martino claimed. Included, among others, should be the president of the Chamber of Commerce, the directors of Italy's principal banks, the presidents of Italy's leading business and trading concerns, representatives of the Italian State Railways, representatives of any Italian shipping lines touching on the Balkans, the principals of technical schools and the presidents of national patriotic institutions such as the Royal Italian Geographical Society and the Istituto Coloniale Italiano.[87]

San Giuliano, as usual, approved his lieutenant's scheme, but the committee had hardly time to come into operation before the priorities of Italian foreign policy were changed by the outbreak of the First World War.

One final curious office in the *Consulta* was the Directorate-General of Colonial Affairs whose real power lapsed with the creation of a Ministry of Colonies in 1912. The main task of the Director-General of this office had been to try to paper over the personal bickering which was always likely to break out between civilians and soldiers involved in the administration of Italy's desert colonies. It was also as well to have a place in which the charges of corruption, which followed the careers of Martini and Salvago Raggi in Eritrea and De Martino II in the Somaliland, could be hushed up. Despite the evident disadvantages of his office, Giacomo Agnesa, the long-term Director-General of Colonial Affairs, was as nationalist as anyone else at the *Consulta*. In the First World War, he won fame by advocating an extent of Italian colonial expansion which was scarcely equalled by the more enthusiastic Fascists during the decades which followed.[88]

In its organisation as in its staffing, the *Consulta* from 1910–14 reflected both continuity and the changes occurring in the assumptions about Italian foreign policy. The formation of pro-colonialist pressure groups, continuing emigration, the economic growth of the decade to 1907 and then its relative falling off, the granting of near-universal suffrage for the elections of 1913, and the new opportunities allowed by the state of the international Concert, alerted Italian diplomatists to some of the ramifications of what would soon be called the 'new diplomacy' whether of the democratic, Fascist, or Bolshevik variety. San Giuliano's *Consulta* was aware of the process of modernisation, and the energetic De Martino was especially anxious to do something about it. Yet the *Consulta* itself, in its staff, in its Ministers, in its workload and in the success of its policies, remained isolated enough from modern troubles to be largely traditional in its practice. The Italian Foreign Ministry in 1914, although holding ambitions which Mussolini would recognise, possessed an organisation which had fitted the style of Cavour.

CHAPTER 5

How Italy went to Libya

When San Giuliano was recalled from Paris in March 1910 he cannot have expected to hold office for long. During the previous decade Italian politics had developed a clear pattern. Giolitti was Prime Minister for most of the time, and always controlled a parliamentary majority. When he was not in office, succession passed briefly to the more conservative, more scrupulous and more blinkered Sonnino, or to one of Giolitti's 'lieutenants', Alessandro Fortis or Luigi Luzzatti. Fortis and Luzzatti were eminent politicians, with careers and ideas of their own, but they possessed neither Giolitti's power base, nor Sonnino's 'principles'. A number of Cabinet Ministers held office from one government to another, but Foreign Ministers changed with fair regularity. Tittoni worked with Giolitti,[1] Guicciardini served Sonnino. San Giuliano was Foreign Minister for Fortis or Luzzatti.

Luzzatti's government had no particular foreign ambitions. Salandra, disappointed not to find a place in the Ministry when he was available, complained that Luzzatti was too pro-French. Barrère, he noted sulkily, was the real creator of the Ministry.[2] It was true that Luzzatti had ties to the traditions of Visconti Venosta and the Francophilia of the *Destra*, but these were no longer important in 1910. Indeed the garrulous Prime Minister, a Jew, a financial expert and an intellectual patron of many congresses, was as friendly to Germany as to France.[3]

During his career Luzzatti had commented intermittently on foreign affairs. He had disliked Crispi's 'grand design', but he congratulated Prinetti for his convoluted treatying in 1902. 'We must renew the Triplice and observe it loyally', he had noted, 'we must bind ourselves always more in friendship with France. And I believe that both are feasible'.[4] Luzzatti resented French arrogance at Algeciras. He saw the Bosnia–Herzegovina crisis as an alarming example of German irredentism but was always anxious that Italo–Austrian relations remain peaceful. He was to applaud the Libyan War once it was inevitable. In 1914 he was to be a neutralist, one of his reasons apparently being that he feared devastating attack from Switzerland, and in 1915 he was an interventionist.[5] Perhaps his views were best summed up by his statement to the Chamber in 1907: 'Unbreakable faithfulness to the Triple Alliance, sincere friendship for England and France, and cordial relations with the other powers always remain the bases of our foreign policy.'[6] In 1908 too he pledged himself a friend of the Young Turk Revolution. No country, he maintained, desired more than Italy the territorial preservation of the Turkish Empire.[7] In any case, in 1910, his would only be an interim government until Giolitti was ready to return. His Foreign Minister could also expect to be in office briefly. San Giuliano would not have time to do much more than preserve the continuity of Italian foreign policy.

While the Luzzatti administration was being assembled, the German Chancellor, Bethmann Hollweg, was in Rome, having formal discussions with Guicciardini. On 2 April 1910 Bethmann met the new Foreign Minister, San Giuliano, and they exchanged pious remarks about their dedication to the *status quo* in Europe in general, and in the Turkish Empire in particular. Like any other Italian statesman consulting the senior member of the Triple Alliance, San Giuliano tried to sound German attitudes to Italo-Austrian relations. Was Italy equal to Austria in German eyes, or just a messenger boy? In asking the question it would also be useful to highlight any faults in recent Austrian policy. So San Giuliano, innocently but obviously, told the German Chancellor that there had been rumours, which naturally the Italians scarcely believed, that the 'ambitious designs' of Archduke Franz Ferdinand included a general discussion of the Triple Alliance, and of possible compensation in the Balkans. Bethmann had been briefed about such comments, and was not ingenuous enough to rise to the Italian bait. Instead he murmured blandly that Aehrenthal and Franz Joseph were pleased by the improvement in Italo-Austrian relations, and by the reduction of public irredentism in Italy.[8] If the Austrians had Franz Ferdinand's war party, the Italians had the irredentists.

Bethmann then tried a tack on the German side. Seeing San Giuliano had expressed such friendship for Germany and Austria, why not publish an official version of their talks emphasising the new sympathy existing between Italy and Austria? San Giuliano was too shrewd not to cover this German move. He pointed out that the suggested statement was too frank, and might make it appear that the Triple Alliance needed new assurances.[9] The diplomatic fencing exhibition over, both statesmen rested content at their opponent's skill and inaction.

The new Italian Foreign Minister had made no mistakes in his first, not very difficult contest. Despite his rumoured Triplicism, San Giuliano had made a very distinct differentiation between Italo-German and Italo-Austrian relations. Despite his dislike of domestic irredentism, he had not hesitated to mention again the concept of territorial change in the Balkans, with the inevitable corollary that an Austrian advantage must be accompanied by the raising of the Trento–Trieste question. San Giuliano had been neither amateur nor ideological enough to break the continuity of Italian foreign policy.

The summer months of 1910 passed relatively quietly, almost as if Europe had decided to concentrate on enjoying its last great set-piece of monarchical celebration, the funeral of King Edward VII in England. Italy, as if for once accepting her secondary power status, sent only a royal cousin, the Duke of Aosta, to that event. He was well down all protocol lists.

In Rome, San Giuliano had occupied himself with agreeable but minor tasks. He instructed his ambassador in London, Imperiali, to look more favourably on the meetings of the local Dante Alighieri society.[10] He tried to adopt a firm line with the French ambassador, Barrère, when that 'maker of Italian Foreign Ministers' persistently asserted French ownership of the Farnese Palace. Barrère won this particular point, the French Embassy is still in the Farnese Palace today, but San Giuliano was able to give an international demonstration of his independence from the French ambassador.[11] The overall tone of San Giuliano's early weeks in office was best summed up by the naively honest British ambassador, Sir James Rennell Rodd. He wrote home to London in June: 'I almost feel as if I were not earning my salary. There is so little to report here.'[12]

If the representatives of the Triple Entente were hardly living through a maelstrom of diplomatic activity in Rome, San Giuliano was showing a characteristically greater preoccupation with the Triple Alliance. He at once endeavoured to get on easy terms with the new Austrian ambassador, Kajetan Mérey von Kapos-Mére who was often unpredictable and sometimes truculent in his dealings with Italy, a more peremptory character than the retiring ambassador,

Heinrich von Lützow. With Mérey, San Giuliano tried the soothing balm of long and 'open' discussions, and was at pains to note how outdated irredentism was, and how annoying to any Italian government were all irredentist demonstrations.[13] Dealing with the other ally, Germany, was a simpler process and in May, San Giuliano quickly reciprocated Bethmann Hollweg's trip, by visiting Berlin. It was an untroubled journey, and San Giuliano circularised his ambassadors with a report that Germany had indicated its 'friendship and esteem' for Italy, but perhaps the serious achievement was better summarised by a clerk in the British Foreign Office who commented sardonically: 'It means o from a political point of view.'[14]

In August and September San Giuliano went on to talk with the Austrians, meeting Aehrenthal both at Salzburg and at Turin, but the discussions were formal. The fact that the exchanges had occurred looked like newly enthusiastic triplicism on the part of the Italians, but, if San Giuliano showed a greater anxiety to identify the character of Italy's partnership in the Triple Alliance,[15] old preoccupations about Austria did not disappear. The pro-Austrian ambassador in Vienna, Avarna, early advised San Giuliano that he believed Austria had no desire to attack Italy.[16] This was encouraging advice on the one hand, but, on the other, the very mention of a possible attack was hardly testimony to profound or untroubled friendship. Avarna, and certainly San Giuliano, were sensitive to possible Austrian meddling in the Balkans. Following a predictable line, San Giuliano was always ready to ask if this could bring compensation for Italy 'towards' the Isonzo.[17] A typical meeting between San Giuliano and the Austrian ambassador, Mérey, occurred on 11 May 1910. With accustomed indirectness, San Giuliano noted that it was not now necessary to examine possible compensation for Italy, because it was known that Austria did not intend to reoccupy the Sandjak of Novi-Bazar. 'But', he added, 'if such a reoccupation becomes probable, it will be necessary to consider the compensations before it takes place. But our zealous desire is that it will not take place, and the *status quo* will be maintained.'[18] Both Mérey and San Giuliano understood that Italy would be unhappy about further coups in the style of Bosnia–Herzegovina. Italy preferred peace and the retention of the *status quo*, although, if there was to be territorial change, the last thing Italy wanted was 'clean hands'.

San Giuliano also chipped away at the familiar problem of

Austria's treatment of its Italian minority. Using a weapon he would wield with increasing expertise, he warned the Austrians that Italian 'public opinion' was hyper-sensitive on the issue, registering every friendly or unfriendly incident.[19] While trying to use 'public opinion' in his diplomacy, San Giuliano kept it under careful leash at home.[20] In December 1910 Italy's prefects were told that it was 'indispensable absolutely to prevent demonstrations by students or anyone else against Austria and absolutely to prevent affronts to the Embassy or to Austro-Hungarian consulates, and the burning of [Austrian] flags'.[21]

One problem, in retrospect very grave, which San Giuliano ignored, was the Austrian reinforcement of her border with Italy, begun under the aegis of Conrad von Hötzendorf in the summer of 1910.[22] There is no evidence that San Giuliano paid any serious attention to this, or to Austria's plans to construct two Dreadnoughts in Trieste itself, in a naval build-up obviously directed at Italy.[23] This remarkable detachment of civilian and military affairs is characteristic of Liberal Italy, and was repeated in the planning of the Libyan War. The basic assumption on which Italian diplomacy was posited was the continuation of European peace. If there was to be a war, there were two more implicit beliefs in the Italian version of the 'short-war illusion': firstly, crisis signs could be read long enough ahead to allow soldiers the 'easy task' of military preparation; secondly, once war began, the generals (and perhaps the King) would take over, and diplomacy would become irrelevant. The appalling military record of the Italian Army and Navy, the jealous separation of Ministries, and the absence of a genuine Cabinet or Committee of Imperial Defence system of discussion, allowed these beliefs, so extraordinarily false in a technological age, to remain. Not until May 1915 would Italy start to learn lessons about the links needed in a modern society between military and diplomatic planning. The lessons were still not mastered in June 1940.

In his own fief of diplomacy, San Giuliano had tried to set the bounds of Italy's relationship with Austria, but had done little to alter its basic lines. Of course he had very little ground on which to manoeuvre. In 1910 Italy's ambassadors to both Russia and Britain reiterated what San Giuliano had learnt for himself in London, that the Triple Entente powers preferred that Italy remain in the Triple Alliance.[24] There were no rewards to be offered for breaking with

Vienna. Instead, conflict with Austria offered the prospect of the gravest dangers abroad and at home. In 1910 the ancient slogan 'either allies or enemies' was still the base of Italo-Austrian relations,[25] and of Italy's whole international position.

As the end of the year approached, San Giuliano could look back on his tenure of office as a period of consolidation in which the alarums of 1908–9 had been quieted, and the fears of an imminent collapse of the Turkish Empire had proved false. He even had the time to begin the congenial task of re-organising more effectively the Foreign Ministry's commercial, consular and information services. No war clouds were on the horizon and the Darwinian contest of nations, about which San Giuliano had previously so often commented, could be waged comfortably in trade and influence, especially in the Eastern Mediterranean.

In his first meeting with Bethmann Hollweg, San Giuliano had pledged Italy's determination to defend 'the integrity and independence' of Turkey.[26] In the following months, there was no variation on this theme. When the British ambassador suggested Great Power intervention in Constantinople to discourage a Turkish boycott of Greek produce, San Giuliano demurred, pointing out that he would have to consult his German ally.[27] At the same time he rejected a suggestion from Mayor des Planches, Italy's ambassador in Constantinople, that this might be an ideal opportunity to take traffic away from the Greeks.[28] *Quieta non movere* seemed to summarise Italo-Turkish relations by October 1910.

Two months later the situation had changed radically. On 2 December 1910 San Giuliano told Mayor that Italo-Turkish relations had reached a crisis point. On one of his rare appearances in the Chamber of Deputies, San Giuliano had made appeasing statements about Turkey, but these had been received 'not just coldly' but with a sort of 'hostility' which he had not previously experienced as a parliamentarian. The discontent with Turkey was 'more profound and widespread' than he could have believed. Given the character of the institutions of the Liberal regime, neither he nor the government could carry through a policy opposed by 'the country'. There was now 'an absolute necessity' for Turkey to give 'tangible proof' of a change in her attitude. The current situation could 'not be prolonged without danger'.[29]

It is somewhat ironical to find the old apostle of Italian expansionism writing such a flurried note when confronted by what would be the beginning of a new episode of Italian expansionism. The advocate of the 'creation' of public opinion as an aide for foreign policy, suddenly found public opinion running along ahead of him.

San Giuliano's troubles in the Chamber had begun on 30 November 1910. The circumstance was the usually innocuous debate on the budget of the Ministry of Foreign Affairs. On this occasion, however, the Foreign Minister was subjected to a strong attack by Errico De Marinis, a relatively minor Southern Giolittian *ascari* and a Mason, ten years younger than San Giuliano, who had begun his parliamentary career in the 1890s among the Socialists, but had 'transformed' into a Giolittian after attending the funeral of King Umberto I. He had briefly been San Giuliano's colleague in the Fortis Ministry of 1905–6. De Marinis was known for his interest in foreign affairs; in 1901 he had given an important speech, hostile to the renewal of the Triple Alliance, but his radicalism had later faded. He was a prominent member of the Istituto Coloniale, and had attended Martini's 1905 Asmara conference as president of the small Società Africana d'Italia. But what was most important for San Giuliano was that, on 2 December 1908, De Marinis had presented an eloquent defence of Tittoni's much criticised policy during the Bosnia–Herzegovina crisis. Although there is no documentary evidence to prove it, there can be little doubt that De Marinis' attack was, and was seen by San Giuliano to be, an effort by Tittoni to return from Paris and replace San Giuliano at the *Consulta*. It was also perhaps an indication that Giolitti was potentially no longer as hostile to Italian expansionism as he had been in the past.

De Marinis' speech was wide-ranging, and indeed attacked San Giuliano over most of the very initiatives on which the Foreign Minister prided himself (and on which incidentally he had distinguished himself most clearly from Tittoni). De Marinis began by noting 'the lack of any economic programme' related to national foreign policy, and the isolation of Italy's general diplomatic position. Italy's troubles were greatest in the Mediterranean and in Asia Minor. There, private enterprise had done what it could but 'all that we have conquered in the Mediterranean and Asia Minor must be marked down to private initiative, not backed by the government, and sometimes even hindered [by it]'. Turkey was now showing new hostility towards Italy, and the government was doing nothing about it.[30]

De Marinis' rhetoric made considerable impact on the Chamber. Many deputies rose and went over to congratulate him amid loud applause. Two old Crispians, subsequently transformed into Giolittians, Roberto Galli and Carlo Cavagnari, spoke up in agreement with De Marinis. When the debate was resumed on 2 December, there were great signs of attention in the Chamber as Ferdinando Martini rose to speak, but the Chamber's expectation that he too would attack his old friend and colleague proved false. In fact Martini only gave some predictable descriptions of the potential wealth of Eritrea, which had not been revealed by Italy's incompetent administration of the colony.[31] No doubt relieved that Martini had not joined his critics, San Giuliano closed the debate. With probable reference to Tittoni, the Foreign Minister recalled that he was not animated by 'a dangerous desire for personal successes'. His foreign policy was 'calm and tranquil' but not 'humble and remissive'. Its 'main goal' was 'the maintenance of peace and the territorial *status quo*'. Only in peace could there be

the continuation of the gradual work of development of all the economic resources of our country, of our internal civil reforms, of the gradual economic and intellectual amelioration of the working classes, of the social concord and of the solidity of the national structure which is the necessary consequence of it, of the gradual development of our military potential, in proportion to our economic potential.

Despite what De Marinis had said, San Giuliano was making every effort not to reflect patriotic excitation. It was true, he agreed, that the Turks were causing some difficulty in Tripoli. But 'another [cause] of this is the attitude of part of our press and some of our politicians'. In any case it had been a mistake for Italy (i.e. the clerical Tittonian Banco di Roma) to concentrate so much in Tripoli and Cyrenaica, and financial opportunities had been missed as a result. 'The Turks', he declared, 'have still not succeeded in understanding one thing, although it is very clear. Italy does not wish to take Tripoli and desires that it remains Ottoman.'

Having made such an apparently blunt abdication of interest, San Giuliano did not conclude his speech. As he went on, his tone became confused, and his organisation wandering. At one point he even had the sitting suspended for ten minutes so that he might compose himself. In conclusion he returned to rebut De Marinis' allegation that he had ignored economic matters, affirming rather that they were the basis of 'the foreign policy of modern states', and indeed revealing that he himself had long been working to get some major institution of Italian finance to establish an office at Constantinople. His peroration noted that all deputies were patriots who loved Italy and would serve it, in its 'great cause of civilisation, of peace and of progress with which the cause of Italy itself has been, is, and always will be identified and fused'.[32]

It had been an embarrassed, and almost cravenly official speech. The Catanian aristocrat in San Giuliano had long disliked the Chamber in which he now cut so irrelevant a figure. He also always believed, in office, that diplomacy was to be worked at and not talked about. But he would have to do better than this, if he wanted to remain Foreign Minister. His despatch to Mayor des Planches in Constantinople seems to indicate that San Giuliano himself was aware of the fact.

San Giuliano's troubles arose not merely from the deteriorating relations between Italy and Turkey, but the always increasing exposure of one of the tap-roots of Italian public and diplomatic imperial ambition, the area of Tripoli and Cyrenaica, soon to be called by the Italians, Libya, in imitation of the nomenclature of ancient Rome.[33] Italian ambition in Libya dated back to Italy's beginnings as a nation. Indeed, even before the Risorgimento, both the Kingdom of the Two Sicilies and the Kingdom of Piedmont–Sardinia had been interested in colonial acquisition in North Africa (and Ethiopia).[34] In the 1870s Libya was variously suggested as possible Italian compensation if the Turkish Empire collapsed. In 1878 Foreign Minister, Corti, could probably have dirtied his 'clean hands' at the Congress of Berlin by establishing a protectorate over Libya.[35] At the time Italy was more interested in Tunis, which was nearer, richer, had more Italian settlers and, with the ruins of Carthage, remains more redolent of classical Roman greatness.

In 1881 however, in an act from which Italo–French relations never wholly recovered, France took Tunis from under Italy's very nose. In the next decades, patriotic speakers would almost always use that loss of the port of Bizerta to argue that Italy should not be behindhand in acting in Libya, Albania, Ethiopia or elsewhere. With the establishment of the British protectorate over Egypt in 1882,[36]

Tripoli and Cyrenaica also became the only segments of the Mediterranean African coast not occupied by Great Powers. If Italy had any pretension that the Mediterranean was her *mare nostrum*, then she had to remain interested in Libya.

Already in 1883 Italy had threatened to act in Tripoli, preparing to send a warship until pacified by the recall of the local *Vali*.[37] But, in the decade after this, Italian attention focused more on Ethiopia than on North Africa. In any case, the moment for action had passed as the Great Powers turned their attention away from North Africa. Instead Italy began, characteristically, to 'prepare' for action by tortuous diplomatic soundings. Often these soundings had an illusory quality about them as European statesmen, scornful of the 'beggars of Europe', yielded on paper to Italian importunities, but then continued to believe that nothing concrete had been extracted. Libya, it was widely assumed, could not fall to Italy except in the case of the general dissolution of the Ottoman Empire. So great and dangerous an event would that be, that most European statesmen held the tacit belief that, in such circumstances, promises granted to a state as weak as Italy might be forgotten or overborne by events.

Germany, master of the Triple Alliance and the most easily approached patron, was the first state to weaken before Italian appeals. During the 1887 renewal of the Triple Alliance, Germany and Italy signed a separate protocol that Germany would support Italian action in Libya, if France upset the North African *status quo* in Morocco.[38]

The deterioration in Italy's international position after Adowa, and the return of interest in Libya after failure in Ethiopia, produced new Italian initiatives around the turn of the century. The reconciliation with France was crowned by the exchanges of 14 and 16 December 1900 between Visconti Venosta and Barrère, in which France and Italy pledged a reciprocal lack of interest in Tripoli and Morocco.[39]

Prinetti was a much more indefatigable builder of houses of diplomatic cards after he became Foreign Minister in February 1901. He talked restlessly about an Italian future in Libya. On New Year's Day 1902, the British ambassador reported a rambling conversation with Prinetti, who had

said that the possession of Tripoli would be of great value to Italy and would afford the only possible outlet for emigration under Italian rule. He did not know whether it would be possible to make an arrangement with Turkey. He did not at present contemplate any attempt to obtain possession of Tripoli by force; but his own idea, which, however, was not yet matured, would be an occupation of the country on the same terms as England held Egypt or Cyprus.[40]

For Prinetti, a Milanese businessman, as for so many of Italy's Northern and Southern ruling classes, Adowa had not marked any long-term abandonment of imperial ambition. Yet Prinetti was also right to admit that his ideas were not 'mature'. There is no evidence whatever that his Prime Minister, Zanardelli, would have contemplated action in Libya; the most powerful man in the Cabinet, Giolitti, threatened to resign if Prinetti seriously envisaged the launching of foreign adventures.[41] There was no military preparation. But Prinetti kept up his action, or verbiage, on the diplomatic front and in March 1902 was rewarded with a note from the British which declared that any alteration in the *status quo* in Libya 'would be in conformity with Italian interests'.[42]

Prinetti apparently regarded this as a major concession, and it has been so treated by a generation of patriotic Italian historians. It is doubtful if the Foreign Office saw it that way. One month later, Under-Secretary of State for Foreign Affairs, Viscount Cranborne, told the House of Commons that Britain was completely without obligation to Italy in Tripoli.[43] In 1911, when reminded of the 'agreement' by Imperiali, the Foreign Office had to hunt through its files to find out exactly what had been said.

Meanwhile, having 'won over' the British, Prinetti continued to build on his paper structure. On 30 June 1902 the famous Prinetti–Barrère agreement was secretly reached, making more definite that, in any territorial change, France should have Morocco, while Italy should have a free hand in Libya.[44] In the further renewal of the Triple Alliance, which had occurred two days previously on 28 June, Prinetti extracted from the Austrians a promise that

the Austro-Hungarian Government, having no special interest to safeguard in Tripoli and Cyrenaica, has decided to undertake nothing which might interfere with the action of Italy, in case, as a result of fortuitous circumstances, the state of things now prevailing in those regions should undergo any change whatsoever.[45]

'Four down, one to go', Prinetti can almost be imagined to have sighed. The approval of the last Great Power, Russia, was not attempted until 1909. Then, the usually cautious Tittoni accepted the heritage of Prinetti and approached Izvolsky, the Russian Foreign Minister. Izvolsky, who had been shown the text of the 'secret' Prinetti–Barrère exchange by his French ally, agreed, at the Racconigi meeting with Tittoni in October, that Italy had special interests in Libya, should there be an alteration of the *status quo*. Italy, in return, declared her sympathy for Russian aspirations to remove restrictions on the passage of Russian ships through the Straits.[46]

Italian politicians in 1911, and many Italian historians since, have argued that all these arrangements made Italy's eventual annexation of Libya wholly legal.[47] In so doing they have obscured the major issue whether the Great Powers, apart from France, were bound to regard a change in Morocco, rather than a general break-up of the Ottoman Empire, as giving Italy the right to act. They also have obscured the extent to which the other Great Powers had signed simply to pacify Italy's apparently insatiable desire for verbal agreements which would never be acted on. The words of diplomatic agreements are important, but so are the motives with which they are made.

Nonetheless, after the Racconigi meeting, any Italian statesman could argue that the diplomatic preparations for action in Libya were as complete as they were ever likely to be. San Giuliano had written and talked much about the need for an economic accompaniment to foreign policy. By 1911, to some extent, Italy had this accompaniment in Libya, if not with a setting planned by San Giuliano, or particularly pleasing to him.

An Italian economic interest in the Ottoman Empire had begun seriously in the early years of the new century, as perhaps the inevitable result of the Giolittian combination of industrialisation and 'democracy in the making'. San Giuliano, for example, had spoken in favour of the economic penetration of Libya already in 1903.[48] The group associated in the Istituto Coloniale had also defended and encouraged any Italian moves towards economic imperialism. Giacomo De Martino II had enthused in 1908:

Tripoli opens her arms and is waiting. The land is the same as that of Tunis, if not more fertile; the climatic conditions are the same...; minerals, there must be...[there] as in Tunisia...[but] what is needed is a government which acts, or is willing to assist action.[49]

Meanwhile the Dante Alighieri Society had done its bit for culture and finance by setting up branches in the provinces of Tripoli and

Cyrenaica. Not to be outdone by the threat of anti-clerical education, in 1907 the Church blessed the passage of the protectorate of Franciscan missionaries in Cyrenaica from French hands to Italian.[50] But to inspire this battle for souls and minds in Libya, there was also the continuing chorus of news about coming economic advantage. 'Africa', learned professors, archaeologists and politicians reminded their audiences, had once been the greatest grain-producing province of the Roman Empire, but ironically while there was talk of minerals, there was none of the one product, oil, which has eventually made some Libyan deserts bloom.[51]

After 1905, the first initiatives for a serious economic presence in Libya came from an appropriate source. The chief agent of 'peaceful penetration' was the Banco di Roma,[52] which had been founded in 1880 mainly using the funds of the 'black', clerical aristocracy. The Banco di Roma thence followed a course predictable in Liberal Italy, making its first advances by speculating on building development in Rome. Noteworthy figures on the staff were from 1891, the vice-president, Romolo Tittoni, and, from 1903, the president, Ernesto Pacelli. After 1900, having absorbed another smaller Catholic bank, the Banco di Roma began a new expansion in the decade of Italy's great industrial growth, and started to look for further investment beyond national shores, but in areas of 'national interest'. It opened an office at Alexandria where there was a considerable Italian emigrant population, and in 1905 participated in the foundation of the Bank of Ethiopia. In 1906 it also opened a branch in Malta, and joined in the establishment of the state bank of Morocco at Tangiers.[53] One year before the Banco di Roma had become interested in Libya, and in 1907 it began major investment in the province of Tripoli. It was a time of great development for the Bank, its capital growing from 30 million lire in 1905 to 200 million in 1912.[54]

There has been some debate whether the bank's investment in Libya was on its own or government initiative.[55] No hard evidence exists of government direction, yet the pattern of association is evident – there was a personal link between the Bank's officer, Romolo Tittoni, and his brother, Tommaso, Foreign Minister, 1903–5, 1906–9; there was the increasing domestic *rapprochement* between clericalism and the Liberal regime;[56] there was the simple fact that the Bank used Italian capital and Italian staff, and saw economic advantage in areas where Italian statesmen had also seen potential diplomatic and imperial advantage. By 1911 the old divisions between clericals and anti-clericals were no longer the greatest in Italian society, and certainly were not the greatest in Italian finance.

The Banca d'Italia had also made some small initiatives in Libya, but was no competition to the Banco di Roma.[57] Despite the suspicion of the local Turkish authorities, the Banco di Roma had financed some railways, construction on the port of Tripoli, a coastal trading service, agricultural improvements, hydraulic works and even olive oil production.[58] By 1910, Italian imports from Tripoli were worth 9.8 million lire, her exports to Tripoli 4.4 million, the imports especially having increased greatly since 1905.[59]

In world terms, these figures were still very small, a fact which is always true of Italy's efforts to ape Great Power imperialism. The style of Italian interest can be gauged from a long despatch sent to San Giuliano by Italy's Consul-General in Tripoli in February 1911. Pestalozza reported that, from the scarce information available, he had discovered that imports to Tripoli came mostly from Britain, then in order, from Italy, Austria, Turkey, France, Germany and Tunis. Exports went most to Britain, then to Turkey, France, Malta, the United States, Greece and Italy. Eight Italian banking and commercial concerns existed in Tripoli, of which by far the most important was the Banco di Roma. There were also two Turkish banks, two British banks, one Greek and one French. Of 22 [sic] foreign commercial representatives, seven had Italian nationality (of these four were local Jews); seven were British (of whom six were Maltese or locals), five were French, three German and two Austrian. Pestalozza added proudly that Italy owned the largest mills, had a Roman Catholic mission, was the only foreign country to possess sponsored schools in the province, and had the most professional men (e.g. three Italian doctors against one Maltese; two Italian engineers against no other foreign ones). All in all, Pestalozza believed Italian interests were 'the greatest'.[60]

The Young Turk revolution of 1908 infused a new nationalism into Turkey's attitude to all foreigners. In October 1910 this was discernible even in Tripoli, where a new *Valì*, Ibrahim Pasha arrived, and immediately began to attack the most obvious foreign presence, the Italians. Always aware of competition, whether it existed or not, Italian public opinion began to be affected by rumours that German or French or British or Austrian investment would now be preferred by the Turkish administration.[61] On 8 November 1910 Pestalozza warned darkly that Tripoli might be moving towards the destiny of Tunis. San Giuliano minuted his dismay at the prospect of being Foreign Minister on an occasion when Italy would suffer another humiliation at the hands of the French.[62]

Unlike Tittoni, San Giuliano had no personal links to the Banco di Roma, and at first he did not realise the seriousness of the new Turkish actions, and the greater seriousness of the Italian reaction. However the parliamentary debates of 30 November and 2 December alerted the Foreign Minister. Nor was there any sign of improvement in Italo-Turkish relations; on the contrary, Mayor des Planches advised from Constantinople that Ibrahim Pasha must in fact be acting on the instructions of the Turkish government.[63] A series of other incidents excited further press comment and deepened the dispute. A sambuk flying the Italian flag was seized by Turkish authorities at Hodeida on the Red Sea. An Argentinian journalist named Guzman was allowed to return to Tripoli from which he had been expelled previously at Italian insistence, after it was alleged that he had traduced the manhood and strength of the Italian Army.[64]

Recovering from the embarrassment of his parliamentary performance, and his statement that Libya must remain Ottoman, if still having no clear policy, San Giuliano began to talk generally to foreign ambassadors about Italy's irritation with Turkey.[65] In particular, he warned the German and Austrian ministers that Italy would soon have to take 'an energetic action' to drive the Porte to compromise.[66] Despite having reproved the wild talk of press and politicians in his speech to the Chamber on 2 December, San Giuliano at once began to demonstrate to foreign representatives the exacerbated state of this 'public opinion', and the difficulty which he would have 'in a Liberal state' of controlling it. Italy, he asserted, could not tolerate concessions in Tripoli passing to non-Italian concerns.[67] As the weeks passed, San Giuliano grew more emphatic. The Turks should clearly note 'the continued demonstrations of discontent by our press because of the attitude shown by the Turkish authorities towards us' in Tripoli. The press illustrated 'the real mood of Italian public opinion'. If the Turks continued to block Italian ambitions then the Italian government might find itself unable to resist the justified pressure of its own public opinion.[68]

There is no evidence that San Giuliano was doing more than

talking. No serious diplomatic and no military planning had begun. However the pressure of public opinion continued to build up. On 3 December 1910 the First Congress of the Italian Nationalist Association opened in Florence, and announced a new generation's political rivalry to the Liberal regime in Rome. It may be that many Nationalist phrases were merely rhetorical, but the rhetoric was certainly emphatic and declared a total challenge to the old generation and its system. Much of their attention was concentrated on foreign affairs. San Giuliano, they said, was the worst Foreign Minister Italy had ever had. Enrico Corradini, the ANI's chief ideologue, enunciated to the Congress his new 'principles of nationalism':

We are an emigrant nation, that is to say... in order to obtain work and our daily bread, we are obliged to leave the country of our fathers and disperse all over the world... We must start by recognising the fact that there are proletarian nations as well as proletarian classes... [and that] Italy is, materially and morally, a proletarian nation... Nationalism... must become, to use a rather strained comparison, our national socialism. That is to say that just as socialism taught the proletariat the value of the class struggle, we must teach Italy the value of the international struggle. But international struggle means war. Well, let it be war! And let nationalism arouse in Italy the will to win a war.[69]

Corradini, who had been touring Italian migrant communities in South America, and had only returned to Italy in 1909, now also argued that it was '*Africa purissima*' where Italian emigrant problems could be solved. San Giuliano's statement to the Chamber that Tripoli must remain Turkish, Corradini specifically condemned.[70]

In his memoirs, Giolitti does not admit that the Nationalists had any special role in the fomenting of Italian action in Libya, and implicitly denies that their rhetoric occasioned government policy.[71] However this may be, there can be no doubt of the Nationalists' concentration on Libya, and their use of the running crisis there to encourage their own growth within Italy.[72] In January 1911, sections of the ANI had opened in Milan, Genoa, Florence and Venice. By March, they had their 'imperial presence' with branches in Tunis, Malta and Benghazi and Tripoli.[73] On the fifteenth anniversary of the defeat at Adowa, 1 March 1911, the Nationalists were united, numerous and wealthy enough to begin publishing a weekly, *L'Idea Nazionale*.

In the second number of this paper, on 8 March 1911, Corradini proclaimed that 'Tripoli is the fulcrum of Italian foreign policy'[74]

In the next months, a war for Libya was openly advocated as Nationalist 'policy'. Luigi Federzoni, another prominent Nationalist intellectual with definite political ambitions, demanded

the most complete suspension of every irredentist vindication,... and the immediate mobilization of all the energies [of the country] for the colonial conquest in Africa.[75]

Corradini visited Tripoli from June to August, and sent back excited despatches which were later assembled into the resonantly entitled book *L'Ora di Tripoli* ('The hour of Tripoli').[76] From March 1911, other Nationalists were also employed by major Italian papers to report on the character and prospects of Libya. The pro-Giolittian *La Tribuna* and *La Stampa* sent Giuseppe Piazza and Giuseppe Bevione to assess the value of Libyan sands.[77] Their reports reflected their Nationalism. Tripoli, said Bevione, was 'the jewel of Africa and the most cherished prize ('*pupilla*') in the Mediterranean'.[78] Editorials were more general and inconsistent than their correspondents' reports but they too showed a deepening determination to act. *La Tribuna* remembered that classical Rome had dominated the Mediterranean. *La Stampa* believed San Giuliano's foreign policy lacked virility. By 12 July 1911 *La Stampa* complained that unless Italy showed independence in Libya she would 'renounce also this time and perhaps for ever the honours and the privileges which come from being a Mediterranean Power'. On 11 September, Bevione was allowed to publish an article in *La Stampa* under the caption 'Now or Never'.[79]

Bergamini's *Giornale d'Italia*, the organ of the critics of Giolitti around Sonnino, in January 1911 still employed Federzoni on its editorial staff and continued to publish articles by Corradini. In September 1911 the paper was confident that 12,000 Italian troops would be enough to conquer Libya.[80] Luigi Albertini's *Corriere della Sera*, after a period of doubting, also favoured the colonial campaign and offered public opinion the luxurious backing of the patriotic poems of Gabriele D'Annunzio.

In assessing the influence of the ANI on Italian foreign policy in 1911 it is important not to take the Nationalists too much at their own ideological face value. As a group they were formidably literate, but they were also small, and, it was soon plain, divided on issues of foreign and domestic policy. They were divided on their attitude to irredentism. They were divided on their attitude to clericalism and to parliamentarism.[81] Corradini never made a serious political career, and Federzoni's depended heavily on his personal ability.

Also, in foreign policy at least, their ambitions were not so different from the stock-in-trade of the Italian ruling class. If Corradini wanted emigration to flow somewhere fruitful for Italy, so had San Giuliano and many other Italian statesmen. If Corradini thought Libyan deserts would flower under fertile Italian ownership, so had Guicciardini, San Giuliano and many another Liberal commentator. The fact that Nationalists were employed so widely by the press in 1911 is a testimony to their influence among young men bold enough and rich enough to be employed as overseas correspondents by Italian papers, but also that their ideas were not radically out of tune with those of their employers. The patronage of Bergamini, Albertini and the Sonninians is testimony to the growing domestic crisis of Liberal Italy. It is still more significant to find that Frassati, the *direttore* of *La Stampa*, positively encouraged Bevione's articles. The fact that *La Tribuna* and *La Stampa* were 'Giolittian' papers, yet ones which could criticise a Giolittian Foreign Minister, is also evidence of the deep-seatedness of the assumption of the ruling elite of Italy in 1911 that a newly decisive action had to be taken in Libya.

The impulse to patriotism from the economic and social crisis of Liberal Italy in 1911 was given public sponsorship by the series of patriotic *feste* which opened on 27 March and culminated in the formal inauguration of the Victor Emmanuel monument in Rome on 4 June. The economic penetration of Libya, the ideology of the Nationalists and the 'threat' of social democracy may have encouraged Italy to take imperial action in Libya, but so too did the whole culture of the Liberal leadership, its assumption about the nature of the Risorgimento, its assessment of Italy's role among the Great Powers and its belief in the *virtù* inherited by modern Italy from the Roman Empire. The style and the positioning of the Victor Emmanuel monument beside the ruins of the Capitol, was visual testimony to this belief that 'now' was the moment for the 'Third Italy'.

The charge so often made, that Giolitti was cynical in manipulating both Nationalism and nationalism in 1911,[82] thus needs to be considered against the evidence that 'public opinion' (that is, the opinion of the ruling class), both young and old, did genuinely see Libya as a chance, and perhaps a last chance, for Italy in 1911. If Giolitti did not act, then the Sonninians, Tittoni, and perhaps the Nationalists would.

What worried those in control of Italian foreign policy most about the Nationalists was not their ambitions, but their suggested methods. Blithe talk of the value of war was not readily accepted by politicians who remembered the fate of Crispi and others in the catalogue of Italian leaders ruined by the long series of military or diplomatic defeats. Giolitti was especially scathing about this Nationalist foolishness. He told Guglielmo Ferrero that

The Nationalists imagine that Tripoli is the territory of a poor black simpleton whom a European State can dethrone when it wishes. But Tripoli is a province of the Ottoman Empire and the Ottoman Empire is a great European power. The integrity of what is left of the Ottoman Empire is one of the principles on which is founded the equilibrium and peace of Europe...Is it perhaps in the interests of Italy to shatter one of the cornerstones of this old edifice? And what if, after we attack Turkey, the Balkans move? And what if a Balkan war provokes a clash between the two groups of Powers and a European war? Is it wise that we saddle ourselves with the responsibility of setting fire to the powder?[83]

All San Giuliano's assumptions about foreign policy were in agreement with his Prime Minister's contention. San Giuliano, the aristocrat who knew his time, wanted Italy to advance, but to do so cautiously, without risk to Italy or to San Giuliano. Retained, somewhat surprisingly, as Foreign Minister in March 1911, when Giolitti returned to office on a programme of domestic reform which would be the culmination of the 'Giolittian decade', San Giuliano had at once urged his Prime Minister to restrain their colleagues from too many flowery displays of patriotic rhetoric at national *feste*. Worried no doubt especially about irredentism, San Giuliano commented drily that it would be best if there were no patriotic speeches at all.[84] At the same time, the Foreign Minister instructed his agents abroad to emphasise publicly the Progress illustrated in the anniversary celebrations. Italy was now 'a precious coefficient, indispensable in modern international life'.[85] Both Giolitti and San Giuliano believed that Libya would have to be won first diplomatically and then militarily. Diplomatic victory had to be won on the diplomatic front; military victory in real war. For both, 'public opinion'[86] carefully used might have advantages. But for both in a real crisis, public opinion would be largely irrelevant.

Throughout the spring and early summer of 1911 Italo-Turkish relations remained tense over Libya, but there was no sign of serious Italian government planning for action except that Giolitti sent a personal agent, Enrico Insabato, to scout out the terrain in Libya. Once again it was in the Chamber of Deputies that there was voiced the most significant condemnation of San Giuliano's *attenteisme*. On June 7, only three days after the excitement of the inauguration of the Victor Emmanuel monument, the Chamber met in a brief summer session. A major debate was held on foreign affairs. The key speech in this debate was made by Francesco Guicciardini who had twice been Foreign Minister in the short-lived Sonnino administrations of 1906, and 1909–10. Guicciardini was still polite, but his meaning was clear. Drawing directly on the experiences of the *feste* of the *Cinquantennio*, he complained 'Foreigners admire our sky, our countryside, our cities, praise our economic progress and search out and love our country as a place of repose and meditation.' This sort of attention was humiliating. Now 'there rises in our spirit the desire less to invite the holiday spirit (*'festeggiati'*), but be more considered and more valued'.

At this point in his speech, Guicciardini was interrupted by shouts of *'Benissimo'* from the deputies. Obviously Guicciardini was not alone in recalling that in the last three months of the *Cinquantennio* foreigners had often been condescending at best about the achievements of the 'Third Italy'. As if emboldened by his reception, Guicciardini became more direct in his criticism. There was the current dispute over Libya. Italy, he noted, had had a 'dolorous tradition' of diplomatic failure since 1881, and now the Turkish regime was openly discriminating against Italians. Foreign Powers were using the opportunity to encroach on Italian rights; the French were gradually moving into the very territory of Tripoli from their base in Tunis. Both Italy's 'friends' and 'allies' were adept at offering kind words and no more:

We are allies, we are friends, but notwithstanding alliances and friendships, honourable colleagues, we must say the sad word, we cannot save ourselves from the impression of being completely isolated in Europe'.

There was only one way out. In Libya, Italy must take 'a more energetic and more decisive ('*risolutiva*) action'.[87] Although one of his most recent claims to fame was having scandalised the court by wearing a light blue tie at a ceremony in Milan in 1906,[88] Guicciardini spoke from an impressive background in foreign affairs. Like San Giuliano, if more intermittently, he had always advocated Italy's need for some kind of colonialism. He had been a founding Vice-President of the Istituto Coloniale. As early as 1900 he had visited Tripoli, and written a prognostication of Italy's destiny there for the ultra-respectable fortnightly, *Nuova Antologia*. 'Luminous' Roman ruins, and an Arab population devoted to the Italian *patria* and *nome*, he said, only made more worthy, Libya, a province

so rich with historical memories which bind it to our *patria*, so abundant in land which only awaits the fertilising work of man to return it to its old productivity, so lacking in population, so important for the future trade-routes of the continent of Africa.

Turkish rule was in tatters: 'the end of Turkish government in Tripolitania can only be a matter of time; but it will happen. Who will be the heir?'[89]

There can be no doubt that 'Italy' was then the answer to Guicciardini's question. It is true that, during his short periods as Foreign Minister, he made no serious attempt to turn words into action, but that difference between language out of office and policy in has also been seen in San Giuliano. Probably Guicciardini, had he been in office in 1911, would also have been cautious. But certainly his speech on 7 June represented a major attack on San Giuliano's foreign policy, and therefore on the whole Giolitti government. It was a virtual declaration that the small but powerful conservative wing of the Liberal establishment agreed with the Nationalists that something should be done, and done soon, in Libya. This was all the more serious because of the conservative social traditions of the making of Italian foreign policy, which gave so much importance to the monarch and his few 'statesmen' advisers. Now one of Italy's major 'statesmen' had spoken.

Guicciardini's words were applauded from the usual quarters. Oldest of the Nationalists, Piero Foscari, also rose in the debate in the Chamber to make a violent, if long-winded, speech, which a number of times stung San Giuliano enough for him to object to particular points.[90] Guicciardini's speech was also praised editorially

by *Corriere della Sera*, a not surprising event given that Guicciardini
was a close friend of the paper's *direttore*, Luigi Albertini. On 8 June,
Andrea Torre, *Corriere*'s pro-Nationalist political correspondent,
reported from Rome that 'many' had agreed with Guicciardini that
Italy gained less from her friends and allies than anyone else did,
and so was losing out in the great international contest.[91] The next
day an editorial picked up the themes of this report. 'National
feeling', it declared, had seen Italian policy in the last months as
'typically weak' and 'confused'. It must be made 'more
coherent'.[92]

From July, parliament was closed down and did not meet until
February 1912, after the invasion and indeed annexation of Libya.
This is sometimes regarded as a more serious piece of cynical
Giolittian manipulation than it really was. It is true that there was
no parliamentary opportunity for the more democratic deputies and
especially for the Socialists to declare their opposition to Italy's
revived imperialism. Indeed, immediately after the war began, a
Socialist request to reconvene parliament was refused on bureaucratic
grounds.[93] But the social traditions of Italian foreign policy were
all against such popular intervention, and Liberal Italy was often a
state where parliamentarians but not parliament held power. To be
taken seriously, criticism of San Giuliano's foreign policy would
have to come from within the ruling elite. Guicciardini's speech,
picking up what De Marinis had already said in November, had
made it quite clear that the only likely alternative government,
whether backed by Tittoni or Sonnino, would favour a 'forward
policy' in dealing with Turkish obstinacy in Libya.

These themes were reiterated in one more formal patriotic
celebration in the summer of 1911. That was the meeting of the
Second Congress of Italians Abroad which opened in Rome on 11
June, on the next available Sunday after the inauguration of the
Victor Emmanuel monument. Carefully planned by the Istituto
Coloniale, the Congress was meant to focus on the whole purpose
of Italy's renewed colonialism, and especially on the connection
between the always increasing national emigration figures, and the
never increasing figures of colonial territory gained. The Congress
was favoured by the very heights of the Italian social and political
world. Both King and Queen attended, to be greeted by a speech
from San Giuliano himself. The Foreign Minister spoke carefully

and indirectly, pointing out only that Italy's population density made further emigration inevitable.[94] There were no references on this occasion to 'haemorrhages of blood'. The new President of the Institute, Guido Fusinato, was more expansive, bewailing the 'suffering' but having no doubts for the future about the 'glorious vitality' of Italian 'stock' (*stirpe*). One motion passed, which may have pleased the young Starace who had come home from New York to attend the conference, affirmed: 'the urgent necessity for an energetic action on the part of the government, enough to guarantee securely our rights and interests in Tripoli'.[95] Reviewing the ceremonies, *Corriere della Sera* remarked sourly that the Congress had been a further demonstration of the government's 'failure' to solve the emigration question.[96]

There was one further, more covert strand of conservative attack on the Giolitti government in the summer of 1911. Giolitti had taken office on a strongly reformist programme, which included the nationalisation of life insurance companies, a step very alarming to many Italian businessmen,[97] and a move towards universal male suffrage, advocated by some conservatives in the past but now seen socially as 'a leap in the dark', and described with misgiving by Salvemini as being like dinner at 8 a.m.[98] Moreover Italy's economy in 1911 was having its worst year for a decade, re-emphasising the problems which had begun to occur in 1907, after the end of the best years of industrial expansion. The reformism of the Italian socialist and trade union movements, which had been so encouraged by Giolitti's past adroit social policy, was under deepening threat from extremists.[99] Strikes, which had fallen in number in 1908-9, increased again in 1910-11.[100]

Worker radicalism was matched more ominously by new action from employers who, with their greater immediate power, began to undermine the Giolittian system of a neutral State holding the ring in disputes between workers and capitalists. An 'Industrial League'[101] had first appeared in Piedmont in 1906, but in May 1910, twelve employer groups joined to form Confindustria to be the (anti-) trade union of employers pledged to safeguard 'the freedom to work'. In January 1911, the president of Confindustria, Luigi Bonnefon Craponne, openly advocated an independent social policy for industrialists, with the threat of competition against the very parliamentary bases of the Liberal system:

We are not a party, nor do we wish to give life to a party nor can we even bind ourselves in alliance with political parties; our scope must be vaster and more complex: it is not so much in parliament that we must make our ideas accepted, as in the consciousness itself of the nation, in the so-called public opinion that we must try to instil the exact idea of what our industry means to the national life.[102]

It was not until 1912 (when it declared that it favoured 'autarky')[103] that Confindustria made major pronouncements on foreign policy. But, formed as another competing institution calling on Italian 'public opinion' to prefer industrial expansion to the Giolittian definition of social justice, Confindustria was an additional dangerous threat to the whole Giolittian system. It was a further indication of the new discontent felt towards Giolitti by many of the Italian ruling class, and can hardly have not been united in Giolitti's mind with the colonialist agitation, especially given the ties between industrial interests and the press.[104] In 1911, Giolittian Italy was either in crisis, or nearer to a crisis than ever before. In similar circumstances, a relatively cheap colonial war was an idea which had occurred to many politicians in the social milieu of pre-1914 Europe.

Whatever the impact of industrialists' manoeuvring, the new Nationalist ideology of the bourgeois young, or the long-standing expansionist cultural traditions of the Italian ruling elite, the final decision to go to Libya had to be made by Giolitti and by San Giuliano. It was made also in the immediate diplomatic context.

In his memoirs, Giolitti claimed that he had returned to office in March 1911 'with the firm intention of taking the first opportunity...[of finding] the solution to the Libyan problem'.[105] Except in the most general sense, there is very little evidence which can be adduced to support this claim. It is possible that Giolitti's retention of San Giuliano as Foreign Minister was a hint that a forward policy was favoured. But equally San Giuliano's statement to the Chamber on 2 December could scarcely have been a clearer indication of his caution in actual policy making. Alternatives to San Giuliano, such as Tittoni[106] and Guicciardini, scarcely opposed some sort of activity in Libya. There was no sign of military preparation and no untoward action on the diplomatic front until well into summer. Some sort of improved economic penetration of Libya may have been envisaged, but the decision for a colonial war was made very late indeed, in fairly specific diplomatic circumstances.

In serving Giolitti rather than Luzzatti, San Giuliano had not undermined the continuity of his own foreign policy. He continued to reject suggestions for more open intervention in Constantinople, for example by using an Italian naval force to prod Turkey into acting effectively in Albania.[107] He showed no sympathy whatever when the Montenegrins wondered whether Italy would be interested in their campaigning against the Turks.[108] Indeed incidents in Albania or Montenegro were further reminders of the connection of one part of the Ottoman Empire with another, and further encouragement to Italy to be restrained in Libya; or else there could be the most dangerous involvement with Austria.[109] San Giuliano occasionally complained hopefully to Britain or Germany that these most disinterested friends and allies did not realise how serious the Balkan problems could be,[110] but real government intention was better evidenced by the constant police surveillance of Ricciotti Garibaldi's pro-Albanian groups, and all Nationalist assemblies.[111] Neither San Giuliano nor Giolitti had yet unlearned the ancient axiom that Italy must not provoke the break-up of the Ottoman Empire.

Indeed, while the *Cinquantennio* celebrations were at their most enthusiastic, diplomatic interest in Libya waned. In March 1911, San Giuliano had threatened vaguely that 'public opinion' might force him into 'coercive acts' against Turkey,[112] but, on 7 June, Mayor des Planches was able to report that Italo-Turkish relations were 'good'. 'Italian enterprises', he advised, were 'no more systematically opposed' than those of other countries, not even in Libya 'where they [the Turks] were most suspicious of us'.[113] On 15 June now speaking in the Senate in reply to criticism from Leopoldo Franchetti, San Giuliano said that for Italy the colonial question was about the development of what she already had, of getting 'all the advantages which [existing colonies] could give to the country'.[114] Even more than his Foreign Minister, Giolitti also refused to be drawn by opportunities to be expansive about the greatness of Rome or Italy.[115]

The crucial change for Italian policy occurred after a development on the international scene. On 1 July 1911, the German gunboat, *Panther*, landed at Agadir. The long-running dispute between France and Germany in Morocco was now in crisis. For Italy this changed two factors; it became increasingly apparent that France would take Morocco, and thus legally Italy could argue that her previous diplomatic arrangements, especially the Prinetti–Barrère and Prinetti–Visconti Venosta exchanges, gave grounds to demand a *quid pro quo* in Libya; also, and perhaps more important, in the area of *Realpolitik*, the crisis divided the Concert, and gave the weakest of the Great Powers the opportunity for individual action. Most temptingly, Austria would not be able to show serious hostility to Italy, because Austria's ally, Germany, had her hands full with France, and was most unlikely to risk a quarrel with even so weak a power as Italy.

There was a further impulsion to act. France was always the nation likely to treat Italy with the least respect. If France took Morocco without Italy seeking compensation, then the diplomatic castles built by Italian statesmen for three decades would collapse like sand. Such a public humiliation could hardly be risked, especially given the heightened colonialist and nationalist enthusiasm of the *Cinquantennio*.

There is evidence that both Giolitti and San Giuliano were quickly aware of the opportunity, and perhaps also the necessity, to adopt a clearer policy on Libya. The first steps were cautious. On the very day of the *Panther* incident, San Giuliano suggested to Giolitti that, in the light of the Franco-German dispute, Italy should make 'a calm appraisal of the line of conduct to be taken and of the eventual resolutions to be prepared'.[116] These were opaque words, and Giolitti did not react.

San Giuliano, still alarmed by the concept of war, and reluctant to commit himself too far, given his weak and threatened position as Foreign Minister, did begin diplomatic preparations, using a tortuous mixture of hints and prevarications in which it would soon be apparent he was so expert, and which had often been the hallmark of the least of the Great Powers. Naturally San Giuliano first approached Great Britain, usually Italy's most benevolent patron, and the major Power not directly involved in the Moroccan affair. Reminding Rodd of the possible connection with Morocco, he suggested that perhaps the Great Powers should mount a naval demonstration against Turkey over 'vexations' suffered by Italy in Libya.[117] Later in the month, after Imperiali broached the subject again with Grey, Italy received a reply more favourable than can have been expected from the Foreign Secretary:

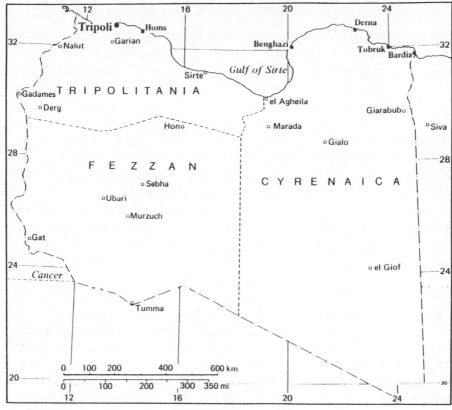

2   Libya

I desired to sympathise with Italy, in view of the very good relations between us. If it really was the case that Italians were receiving unfair and adverse economic treatment in Tripoli – a place where such treatment was especially disadvantageous to Italy – and should the hand of Italy be forced, I would, if need be, express to the Turks the opinion that, in face of the unfair treatment meted out to Italians, the Turkish Government could not expect anything else.[118]

The Italians read these words as a green light to act as they wished, a meaning which Grey had not intended. Imperiali's report of the meeting was scored over by San Giuliano's red pencil and sent off to Giolitti.[119] More doubtful noises about Austria's probable reaction were not as important as this apparent British support.[120]

In these same days there was a changing of the guard among the Italian diplomats working in key positions in the Ottoman Empire. On 17 July Mayor des Planches was recalled. The announcement of his replacement by Camillo Garroni, ex-prefect of Genoa, and an old crony of Giolitti, was received with disgust by the nationalist press which preferred that a younger diplomat be sent and that he be not so tied to Giolitti. On 24 July *Corriere della Sera* complained that San Giuliano had surrendered utterly to Giolitti, although this was anything but true, a fact which was underlined by the development of events more precipitately than the government in Rome had expected. Garroni had still not reached Constantinople when the Italo-Turkish war broke out. In the interim, during the crucial months from July to September, the Italian embassy was in the hands of the *Chargé*, Giacomo De Martino III.

De Martino has written his own account of these months, but unfortunately he did so in 1937, and he then dressed his actions up as a Nationalist triumph, signalling to Mussolini waiting in the wings. The ground for colonial success, he said, had been prepared inside parliament by the 'combative nationalist group' and outside by the new ideology of youth and their 'incipient passion' for sport.[121] However, he admitted, at base, two men made Italian foreign policy in the summer of 1911: Giolitti, who wanted a pacific solution in Libya; and San Giuliano who first saw the need for military action.[122]

De Martino also said that his posting to Constantinople had been given with instructions to take a 'new line' towards Turkey. In an interview with San Giuliano, De Martino alleged that he realised that a pacific solution would be a mistake, and 'alluded to the political and moral benefits for our country from a victorious war'. San Giuliano yielded nothing before this prodding from his junior, but gave his consent with his eyes.[123] De Martino then went off to Constantinople to ensure the final breakdown in Italo-Turkish relations.

Similar allegations are made by Carlo Galli who reached Tripoli on 29 July 1911, designated by San Giuliano to be 'the last Italian consul' there. Galli had met San Giuliano on 22 July, and been told that the Foreign Minister did not want to revive Crispi's dreams, but that the Moroccan crisis meant that the Libyan situation could mature in four to five months. England, Russia and France would not object. The only danger might come from Italy's allies. Galli also met Under-Secretary, Pietro Di Scalea, and two Foreign Ministry officials, Mario Lago and Salvatore Contarini, who were openly exultant at the thought of Italian action over Libya.[124]

Galli, and especially De Martino, have made too much of what they have seen as a difference between Giolitti and San Giuliano. There is no strong evidence that either was thinking of immediate action in Libya and, in 'four or five' months, Garroni would be in Constantinople. That action would come sooner, no-one foresaw. De Martino's particular role in Constantinople was thus not planned, although his selection as *Chargé* had undoubtedly occurred because he was, of all the staff in the Foreign Ministry, most San Giuliano's *uomo di fiducia*.

The diplomatic ramifications of the Moroccan crisis in connection with Libya had become more and more apparent to San Giuliano. On 22 July amid general diplomatic information sent on to the Prime Minister, San Giuliano noted that Italy might be driven towards action in Libya.[125] In the Ministry, San Giuliano was also preparing a longer, and much more serious memorandum on events in North Africa.

As he was accustomed to do when it was hot, when his gout was particularly bad, or when he was least anxious to be subject to the attentions of the press in Rome, San Giuliano retreated to the hill resort of Fiuggi, in the Apennines, south of Rome. There he completed, and, on 28 July, sent a long and crucial memorandum to Giolitti.[126] Although still using his habitually cautious language, San Giuliano now explained that he thought it 'probable that, in a few months, Italy could be constrained to go forward with its military expedition to Tripoli'. The crucial word 'military' had been uttered. Italy must not think only of diplomatic manoeuvre, but also of war, even if only of the colonial variety. The first danger as always came from Austria. There was 'a probability *not* [sic] certainty' that if Italy acted in Libya, so would Austria in the Balkans, which would produce an alteration in the *status quo* there, harmful to Italian interests, and intolerable to Italian 'public opinion'. Therefore if Italy was going to act, she must act quickly. Morocco had provided the essential legal opportunity:

France cannot, by treaty, oppose [us]; England, Austria and Germany will see such an act of ours with displeasure, but will have no way of preventing it, all the more so if it is rapidly done.

There were further pressures to act. Events in Morocco must soon see the 'Tunisification' of that region which would end the

French side of the Prinetti–Barrère agreement, and potentially undermine Italy's whole Mediterranean position. The Triple Alliance was due for renewal in 1912. It would be best to act before those negotiations began, as Germany and Austria might simply demand the abandonment of the Prinetti–Barrère agreement. The Balkans might explode at any time, and Italy must move in Libya before that happened. If not, in any peacemaking, Libya might be offered as Italy's compensation, while other Powers (i.e. Austria) made gains in the Balkans. With Turkey, Italy could only have friendly political and, importantly, commercial relations once the Libyan incubus was removed. 'Public opinion' was aroused and was likely to stay aroused, believing 'the national energy should affirm itself vigorously in some way'. Bettòlo, Sonnino's old Navy Minister and President of the Lega Navale, had suggested the occupation of Tobruk, but San Giuliano believed in the need for a more extensive action which would seize both Tripoli and Benghazi (i.e. both Tripolitania and Cyrenaica should be taken.) San Giuliano's thoughts even ran ahead to warn of the need to think closely about what kind of sovereignty to aim for in Libya; Italy could use the local dynasty, or establish the sort of protectorate familiar in Bosnia and China.

As if he had caught himself dreaming illicit dreams, San Giuliano's concluding words were again very careful:

To discuss all this [i.e. the best type of regime] is premature today; today it is enough to keep in mind the probability that the whole expedition will soon become inevitable: and from now on to aim at the double goal of avoiding it on the one hand while at the same time taking every possible step for its successful outcome if, as seems always more likely, it becomes, against our will, inevitable.

From 28 July 1911, however foggy his language, Italy's Foreign Minister had decided to begin manufacturing a colonial war.

Giolitti did not reply at once to the memorandum. Like San Giuliano, he had discreetly retired from Rome to pass the summer in Piedmont, presumably reckoning that it was better to leave the first steps of diplomatic preparation to the Foreign Minister. If there was a difficult reaction from the Great Powers, San Giuliano could no doubt be disowned.

San Giuliano certainly began to move on the diplomatic front. Convinced that Britain was, or could be alleged to be favourable, on 29 July, San Giuliano carefully told his German and Austrian allies that the Turks had allowed further 'atrocious calumnies' to be published in Tripoli about the Italian Army. Italy could only repeat that if Turkey continued to treat her so discourteously, she would be driven to take 'energetic action'.[127] There are a number of interesting factors about this despatch. Italy had approached Austria and Germany jointly, no doubt hoping thus to restrain any strong Austrian reply. The language had been even more indirect than that used with Britain. The incident chosen by San Giuliano for complaint, whether intentionally or not, was not likely to produce more than a guffaw in Berlin and Vienna – 'Atrocious calumnies' against the performance and standard of the Italian Army were common in every European Chancellery and indeed every European hostelry.

San Giuliano had nonetheless given his allies warning. Naturally he did not approach France, whose potential reaction, he gauged, was still more likely to be hostile than that of Austria. France would be told that the Prinetti–Barrère agreement was being applied, only when it really was. Nor did San Giuliano make an effort to check if the Russians still held to the Italian version of the Racconigi pact. A sounding in St Petersburg would at once be passed on to Paris. Or, as San Giuliano preferred to explain to his ambassador: 'the internal situation and administrative condition of the Empire' prevented Russia at the moment from 'becoming again a powerful factor in European international politics'.[128]

On 9 August San Giuliano wrote again to Giolitti, still on holiday at Bardonecchia. He began by making some sardonic remarks about rumours that Pacelli had said that if the government did nothing, the Banco di Roma would be forced to sell out to a foreign concern in Libya. San Giuliano recalled that he had himself talked to Pacelli only a couple of weeks previously, and that then the Bank had been considering expanding its Libyan interests, being convinced that, 'willing or unwilling', Italy would soon be driven to occupy Libya.

San Giuliano, having demonstrated his proper anti-clerical distaste for 'black' Tittonian conspiracies, then went on to presume that 'by now' Giolitti had had a chance to read the memorandum of 28 July. In the last ten days, San Giuliano said, the international situation had developed in the way which he had expected. France was to get a free hand in Morocco. Turkish–Italian relations had deteriorated again, as the information received from Giacomo De Martino demonstrated. The hostility of Italian public opinion was clear in *La Stampa*. Although Italy still need not decide formally one way or the other, preparations were necessary, and must be secret. Eventually action would have to be as rapid as possible ('*rapidissima*'). In a long post-script, San Giuliano analysed the likely international reaction. As it was, it was best not to approach the other Powers, until a clear decision had been made.[129]

In this second memorandum San Giuliano does seem to be pressing Giolitti. Why, he asks, have there been no military preparations? Yet San Giuliano's own fears are very close to the surface. In a country like Italy, how would 'secret' large-scale military preparations be possible? The Foreign Minister was most anxious to go to Libya, to fulfil a colonialist dream, but he was also still haunted by memories of colonial, military and diplomatic disasters of the past.

The officials of the Foreign Ministry were doing their best to stiffen San Giuliano's nerve. In addition to the colonialist spirit of De Martino, Galli, Contarini and Lago, on 13 August formal advice came from the Under-Secretary, Pietro Di Scalea. Intervening with unaccustomed directness Scalea couched his letter in the strongest terms:

I maintain that now it is no more possible to delay resolving [the Libyan question.] If you, who have reviewed the question in the *promemoria*...[of 28 July] with so much clarity of thought, do not decide to carry the issue resolutely before the Cabinet and do not make it an issue absolutely bound to your life as a Minister, you cannot in any way justify before public opinion the reasons for inaction at a time when all the civilised nations bustle about increasing their territorial possessions and at a moment in which the situation in the Mediterranean is being radically modified, and has already been transformed so much to our disadvantage alone.[130]

A copy of this letter was also sent on to Giolitti. San Giuliano, and Giolitti were being spurred on by what was almost the equivalent of a Cabinet revolt. De Martino in Constantinople also did nothing to seek out a compromise. On 11 August, for example, he reported that, although the Turks had agreed to recall Ibrahim Pasha, the offensive *Valì* of Tripoli, an improvement in Italo-Turkish relations could only be short-lived.[131] Four days later De Martino provocatively warned that he believed the Turks were about to reorganise the military defences of Tripoli, and were already sending more powerful cannon there.[132] On 21 August he declared that experience said that agreements with other Powers could 'lose value with the passage of time', Italy should rather take the opportunity to bury the 'Adowa myth' and illustrate the renewed efficiency of the Italian Army.[133] On 1 September a long despatch analysed the other Great Powers' economic penetration of the Ottoman Empire, always to Italy's loss, although, naturally, De Martino said, it was San Giuliano who had to decide how to restore Italo-Turkish relations and how to safeguard Italy's 'huge' interests in the Empire.[134]

It is doubtful if the officials of the *Consulta* were right in believing that there was a potential difference between their views and those of the 'Cabinet' (i.e. Giolitti). This 'pressure' appeared at least partly because of the way in which Italian politics were played. Just as Giolitti was allowing San Giuliano to take initiative, which could perhaps be disavowed, so the excited telegrams of relative juniors like De Martino could be disavowed if sudden pressure was put on Italy not to go to Libya. Indeed it is not the division, but the unity of the Italian policy making elite which is most apparent in August 1911. Both Garroni and Mercatelli, more senior men, who were waiting in Rome eventually to replace De Martino and Galli when the heat of the summer was over, agreed that Italy should go to Libya. And both, most unusually, were shown all the relevant despatches by San Giuliano.[135]

Where there were grounds for different opinions was not in ambition, but in method. San Giuliano himself and Giolitti both still had not set a timetable for action. Indeed both watched the international diplomatic scene, as if half-waiting to be convinced that Italy was not going to be able to act easily. Although repeatedly told by the military attaché in Constantinople that 'now' was the military moment to act,[136] San Giuliano procrastinated again by taking the mildly and suspiciously participatory step of circulating his ambassadors to sound their opinions. The naval manoeuvres were allowed to continue from 5 to 15 September, and then to end without any reference to a coming colonial war.

Replying to San Giuliano's request for comment from St Petersburg, Melegari reported that Russia was fearful of possible repercussions in the Balkans, but would not complain if Italy took Libya, and believed that it was best if Italy acted in a 'prompt and resolute' manner.[137] Pansa, from Berlin, said that he personally opposed foreign adventures, but that Germany could not prevent Italy from acting; nonetheless, the nature of the final German reaction would be determined by whether or not Italy was successful.[138] From Paris, Tittoni said more tersely that Italy must act in Libya, or France would.[139]

By now San Giuliano was sending Giolitti memoranda almost daily. On 31 August he repeated his request for rapid preparations,[140] but was not more specific. Some hint of the possible timing was made on 2 September, when Giolitti was told that the deputy Chief of Naval Staff believed that Italy must act before December.[141] On 13 September, San Giuliano prepared another long memorandum concentrating on the problems of the renewal of the Triple Alliance, as if he sensed that this issue would soon be raised. Italy would have to go to Libya before that; and there was the additional problem that France could use the opportunity to abandon the Prinetti–Barrère agreement. If Italy already had Libya, the Triple Alliance could be more easily and more effectively renewed.[142]

The next day San Giuliano and Giolitti met secretly in Rome, and probably agreed on military action for November: 'now, to act before the Austrian and German governments know it, is as necessary for us, as in my opinion [it will be] welcome to them'.[143] Giolitti at once returned to his estates at Cavour in Piedmont, but was greeted by an anxious note from San Giuliano that 'October' would probably be the best time to act, given the calm seas of the equinox, and the probable international situation.[144] A decisive step had been taken. On 17 September Giolitti met King Victor Emmanuel privately on the royal estates at Racconigi, and informed him of the decision. Returning to Cavour, he now urged at last that events should move as rapidly as possible.[145]

Two pressures had made action urgent. The Moroccan crisis was now unambiguously close to a solution, although the Franco–German agreement was not formally signed until 4 November.[146] Worse, San Giuliano's sixth sense, or secret service, had been right. On 21 September the Central Powers suggested that the Triple Alliance should be renewed early. San Giuliano at once told both Giolitti and the King. It was, he said, an indication of the Austro–German desire to improve their position in Turkey, and must affect Italian policy with respect to Libya.[147]

The day before, Aehrenthal had already expressed his annoyance to Avarna at 'what happened in Italy' over Libya.[148] Once again the old spectres were rising of the domestic impact on diplomacy, of Italy's relationship with Austria. If, either directly or indirectly, by negotiation on the Triple Alliance, Austria publicly thwarted Italy in North Africa, the whole base of the Liberal regime was threatened. Upper-class youthful Nationalism would be wedded to popular radical irredentism; the Triple Alliance would be broken, and Italy might have to fight a European war for her very existence.

Little could now be done about the previous failure to ensure proper military readiness for a colonial war. Instead San Giuliano and Giolitti together began to make frantic, if still secret, preparations for a coup in Tripoli. Galli was advised, on 21 September, to 'prepare the ground' for a decisive 'action'. San Giuliano was already preparing ground of his own by immediately requesting that Giolitti hand over secret funds to the Foreign Ministry for use in Turkey and Libya.[149] Three days later Giolitti sent on to the King a formal request by San Giuliano that an ultimatum to Turkey be authorised. No satisfactory reply was envisaged: 'If Turkey does not reply, within twenty-four hours a declaration of war.'[150]

Searching as usual for the briefest and most jejune reply, the King agreed that this would be in the 'best interests of the country'. Giolitti had to appraise wider domestic matters. On 25 September he assured the King that internal opposition to the war would not be significant:

I do not believe that the socialist movement is important. A number of socialists are favourable to the undertaking, and this morning Barzilai came to tell me that the Republicans do not approve of the socialist hostility and will not cause any trouble.[151]

San Giuliano meanwhile made the proper diplomatic arrangements. Still preferring not to be open, on 24 September, he informed his ambassadors that Italy was being driven 'to take energetic measures' in defence of her co-nationals in Libya.[152] Avarna received an extra telegram remarking that San Giuliano was confident that Austria would adhere to the accord of June 1902; in case of difficulties, a copy of the text was enclosed.[153] Avarna also repeated in Vienna Italy's loyal desire to see the Triple Alliance renewed. Pansa was sent a more expansive note. He was instructed to wait the opportune moment and then explain very clearly the only motive for which we have delayed speaking to them about [Libya] is our friendly desire not to put the allies in a difficult position, and to give them a way to reconcile their interests in preserving the friendship of Turkey with the spirit and duties which reciprocally unite the Allies.

On the general question of Libya, San Giuliano was

confident... that the attitude of Germany in this situation so decisive for the future of Italy and her position in the Mediterranean will aim to reinforce always more the bonds of the alliance and of the friendship between the two nations.[154]

Returning to the Austrians two days later, San Giuliano instructed Avarna to use any means to impress on Aehrenthal Italy's pleasure at renewing the Triple Alliance, once the Libyan imbroglio was over.[155] That night, 26 September 1911, the ultimatum to be passed on to De Martino was drafted. De Martino himself had already been instructed that he could expect as much money as he needed for local 'subventions', but that what was really important now was to secure a *fait accompli*.[156]

Italy's military readiness was all the poorer because of the suddenness with which the crisis had arrived, and its immediate diplomatic causation. San Giuliano and Giolitti never showed much enthusiasm for military affairs, and the events of September 1911 had been so rapid that most rudimentary military preparations had not been made. On 3 September the conscripted class of 1889 had been allowed to disband. Neither the Minister of War, Spingardi, nor the Chief of General Staff, Pollio, was kept abreast of events, even after 17 September. Even after the very ultimatum had been despatched to De Martino, Pollio did not believe that action was possible before 10 October. That an advance guard of sailors reached Tripoli on 4 October, and substantial numbers of soldiers landed on 11 October,[157] was something of a miracle of improvisation.

The ultimatum had reached De Martino early in the morning of 28 September. He presented it to the Grand Vizier at 2.30 that afternoon. Turkey appealed to Germany, but the Central Powers did not intervene, and prompt at 2.30 p.m. on 29 September, De Martino presented Italy's declaration of war. The first Italian ship was already in the Mediterranean bound for Tripoli.

The reasons for this decision to go to Libya say much about Italy's deepening social crisis in 1911, much about the impact of nationalist and conservative 'public opinion', but most about the cultural traditions of post-Risorgimento Italy, and the diplomatic methods and assumptions of the weakest of the Great Powers. On 20 July 1911 Camille Barrère, reviewing Italy's *Cinquantennio* celebrations, remarked on the 'nationalist disease' which had struck 'young Italy' and which had been further developed in all the *feste*.[158] On 3 August the British Ambassador, Rodd, confided to his diary that if France gained Morocco, Italy would be very likely to take Libya.[159] Both ambassadors were right.

In 1911 the state of mind of Italy's ruling elite was more unitedly patriotic than it had ever been before, the peculiar rhetoric of nationalists and conservatives being only the most obvious side of this patriotism.[160] Yet to convert perennial ambition and a new lust for imperialism into action was a slow and difficult task. San Giuliano and Giolitti were never simple adventurers, and had too many memories of Mentana, Lissa, Dogali and Adowa to be reckless. All major Italian statesmen in 1911 had eventual colonial ambitions in Libya; none thought action in Libya was near until the *Panther* went to Agadir.

Even after that, planning was notably uncertain, a definitive step being left to the future. Indeed, the final decision to go to Libya was not made until late in September 1911, when it became apparent that Italy's ancient dreams were threatened by Franco-German, and especially Austrian actions. The diplomatic cheques which decades of Italian statesmen had prepared, with such effort and difficulty, had to be cashed after 21 September, or they would never be cashed at all. Since the Risorgimento, Italian statesmen had boasted so often that they were clever enough to write diplomatic cheques; that Italy's reputation was grave and fearful enough for her to be accorded the status of a Great Power, that, given the diplomatic opportunities and imperatives of September 1911 there were not many alternate options open to San Giuliano and Giolitti.

In a speech in the Theatre Royal at Turin on 7 October 1911, Giolitti declared that Italy's invasion of Libya had been provoked by 'historical fatality'.[161] Usually these words, or, for that matter, his private claim that he worked in perfect harness with San Giuliano,[162] have been treated with cynical derision by commentators and historians, as another example of Giolitti's habitual dishonesty. Yet, in fact, much that Giolitti said was true; as Croce, acting as semi-official historian of Liberal Italy put it so naively, Giolitti, after weighing up the diplomatic position, as a man

who had about him nothing of the visionary or the rhetorician, but understood what Italy wanted, like the father who sees that his daughter is in love and therefore, after due inquiry and precaution, takes steps to secure for her the husband of her choice.[163]

That Croce could write such extraordinary phrases when he had had time to reflect on the valuelessness of the Libyan deserts and on the damage done by the war to the Italian body politic, is the final evidence needed to deny that, in any real sense, the Libyan War was a turning point[164] in Italian history. There are few signs of a conspiratorial change of direction in Italy in August–September 1911. No doubt Giolitti and San Giuliano had private differences about the likely value of Libya to Italy. But, in the final analysis, both Prime Minister and Foreign Minister stumbled into action because there was little else that they could do. In September 1911 Italy 'went to Libya'; manufactured a colonial war with Turkey, using, in the eventual ultimatum, the most cynical and blatant means, because Italy was the least of the Great Powers. Italy's very political system was tied to the assumption that Italy was a Great Power. As Scalea had advised six weeks earlier, 'all the other civilised nations bustle around increasing their territorial possessions'. That was a belief basic to the ruling class created in Italy by the Risorgimento. Usually there was little Italy could do about it, but in the peculiar condition of the Concert of the other Great Powers in 1911, Italy at last for once, as perhaps later in 1935,[165] had what she saw as a chance.

CHAPTER 6

How Italy stayed in Libya

By 11 October Italian forces were firmly in control of the town of Tripoli, and by the end of the month all the major coastal centres, Tobruk (on 4 October), Derna (18 October), Benghazi (20 October) and Homs (21 October) had fallen to Italian arms. So much was military triumph. But, among the troops, the first cholera victim had died on 11 October,[1] and contrary to the optimistic predictions of Galli, De Martino, and the press, the local Arabs did not flock to enrol beneath the banners of the new Rome. Instead, with sporadic help from the Turkish authorities, they resisted Europeans who had come to take away their land and their religion.

Victory by the seizure of a few towns, by 'sending a gunboat', if that was what Italian public opinion and politicians had expected, thus proved illusory. As Giolitti had himself earlier warned, a short war against 'poor black simpletons' was not enough. There were international ramifications.

Indeed, potentially, Europe was now confronted by a major contest between two acknowledged members of the Concert of Great Powers, even if their power was more titular than real. It was the first war between historically Great Powers since before the Congress of Berlin. The coup in Bosnia–Herzegovina, the struggle for influence in Morocco, the Boer War, the Cretan revolution, the various Balkan skirmishes, even the Russo-Japanese War, involved different diplomatic assumptions, and were different in kind from a real war between Italy and Turkey. Rapid action in Libya was perhaps tolerable. But a full-scale Italo-Turkish conflict would strike at the very basis of the Concert. The Balkans might erupt, and the massive Ottoman Empire might disintegrate. That awful problem two generations of European statesmen had pondered, sometimes with lustful dreams, but always in the end had postponed. The complexities of effecting an equable distribution of Turkish territory, satisfactory to all the Great Powers, let alone the Small, were too great for diplomatic settlement. The downfall of the Ottoman Empire, it was widely assumed, must involve all Europe in war.

Italy, the least of the Great Powers

It was characteristic of the methods and nature of Italian diplomacy that, although Giolitti and San Giuliano understood these problems, they had not made any effort to prepare a national policy before them. Italian policy was always one of prodding away at areas of 'national interest', almost to see what would happen, and certainly with the basic belief that nothing irreparable would. The sudden move to Libya, the abrupt conversion to action, after generations of diplomatic planning and dreaming and of military inertia, had left Italy virtually without a policy, either military or diplomatic. So Italy had gone to Libya; what came next? And what if the coup was not won at the tables of diplomacy, was not a matter of minutes,[2] but had to be won over weeks and perhaps years?

In October 1911 San Giuliano and Giolitti had no answers to these questions. They had an early, Italian, 'least of the Great Powers', version of the short-war illusion.

Finding a Libyan peace was thus an immensely more complicated task than launching a Libyan war. It was not even clear geographically exactly what 'Libya' was. The borders with Egypt and Tunis were reasonably fixed, but where would the Italian flag cease to wave in the interior, in the desert tracks which led to Lake Chad? Militarily, the problems were still greater. How could European soldiers conquer such a country? The 5,000 Turkish troops in the provinces were only the beginning of the problem. What towns there were could be seized and garrisoned. If they were on or near the coast, and could regularly be supplied, they could probably be retained, but then what? If the nomadic local population was hostile, and it soon was, how could it be pacified? In the 'sand-pit' of Libya, as the critics of the war labelled it, how was it possible to stop the sand running through your fingers?

Although Italy was soon widely accused of atrocious military methods of 'pacification'[3] in Libya, no answer to these questions was found until Fascist 'firmness'. Indeed, in 1921, the Italian state controlled little more of Libya than it had by 21 October 1911.[4] In the actual war, military progress was extremely slow. The Italian commandant, General Caneva,[5] like Cadorna and Diaz in the First World War, was well versed in the dangers of the Italian military tradition, and feared impetuosity would lead to another Lissa or Adowa in the Libyan sands. Unless there was dramatic pressure from the politicians, Italy's generals were unlikely to look for dramatic victory.[6] No such dramatic pressure came from a statesman like Giolitti, who had neither love nor respect for generals. Soldiers could not win the peace in Libya; politicians would have to win it in Rome, or in the other European capitals.

But which capitals? With whom should Italy treat? Libya had not been the brightest jewel in the Turkish Empire, nor did the province receive the most direct government from Constantinople.[7] Throughout 1911–12 Turkish officers continued to try to assist the resistance to Italy, but most fighting was done irregularly by the local Arabs. The unity thus evidenced in the Ottoman Empire was not so much political as religious. To prevent a holy war, how should Italy deal with the religious allegiances of the Moslems of Libya? In Tunis and Egypt, France and Britain had *de facto* colonies which retained the political forms of a local reigning dynasty and religious ties to the Caliph in Constantinople. Should Italy do the same? And if Italy did not, would the Caliph stir up a *jihad* against Christians in all the Near East?

Colonial officials from Tangiers to Delhi contemplated this prospect with alarm, and added their pressure to the demands that Italy finish the job quickly. The Italian assumption that the war would be short, the European assumption that it must be short, Ottoman detachment from the immediate contest in Libya, and the accustomed methods of government in the Near East, all discouraged urgency in the Turkish reaction to Italian peace offers. What reason did Turkey have to hurry to submit to Italian terms? The war was not costly to Constantinople, and it could be assumed, with reasonable certainty, that Italy could not risk the Great Power wrath which would follow an attack on some more vital part of the Ottoman Empire. Politicians in Rome found that an immediate diplomatic settlement was as difficult to win as military triumph was in Libya.

For the Prime Minister, domestic problems were added to the unlooked-for troubles of the military and international situation. Giolitti had had these closely in view in the months before military action, but his final assumption that war would rally widespread popular support soon proved false in fact. If the war had been launched to lance the boil of adolescent Nationalist criticism, it did not do so. Instead the military and diplomatic style of the war confirmed the Nationalists in all that they believed wrong in the

Liberal system. Dying of cholera in a camp outside Homs was not the sort of heroism envisaged as glorious, cleansing war by Papini or Marinetti. Giolitti's version of war was not the 'hygiene'[8] they had looked for. ' *Tripoli, bel suol d'amore* ', 'Tripoli, fine soil of love' said the popular song, but its lyrics were more compelling sung in Bologna than in Benghazi; some soldiers, at least in letters made public in the press, exulted in a land as rich as 'America', where the Arabs were like 'animals' to be shot at like 'snakes',[9] but private letters home told instead of heat, disease and brutal officers.[10]

The 'hour of Tripoli' had thus not sounded in the way Corradini had apprehended; neither was 'the promised land' giving Italy the Moses which some Nationalists believed was needed. Indeed, the short-term effect of the Libyan War on the Nationalist group was to exacerbate the existing tension between the 'democratic' and reactionary factions. In the Congress of Rome, held soon after the end of the Libyan War, in December 1912, the reactionary elements around the staff of *L'Idea Nazionale* triumphed, purged the movement of its more moderate sections and declared its unremitting enmity to 'the whole system of public life'.[11] Certainly the Libyan War had not transformed the ANI into Giolittians, although, by the end of 1912, it was not evident what sort of future existed for the strident radicalism of the right to which the ANI was now wedded.

Nor did the Libyan War reconcile to *giolittismo* the friends and patrons of the Nationalists, those conservative members of the 'constitutional opposition' whose power base was so near the heart of the Italian ruling elite. Hardly a week after the war began, Sonnino and Guicciardini arrived in Tripoli, and were described as being as happy 'as school-boys on holiday'. But this moment of exhilaration soon passed, and was diverted into the more familiar themes of criticism of Giolittian methods.[12] From Paris, Tittoni, in his feline way, continued to present his own good offices to run a better diplomacy than that of San Giuliano.[13] In *Giornale d'Italia*, Sonnino took up and doggedly pursued the argument that the trouble with Giolitti's domestic and foreign policies during the Libyan War was that they were not 'firm' enough. Luigi Albertini, in *Corriere della Sera*, also had not forgiven Giolitti, the hated 'parliamentary dictator', and continued to attack the government, endorsing, for example, the nationalist reports from the front, written by war correspondent, Luigi Barzini.[14] Both Giolitti and

San Giuliano blocked one avenue for criticism from the 'constitutional opposition' by refraining from calling parliament. When the Chamber did assemble, San Giuliano tried to disarm conservative hostility by invoking the proprieties of foreign policy making. In the present circumstances, he said, the war should be treated as an administrative matter so that the deputies'

eloquent silence... [could demonstrate] one more time to the entire world the firm and unbreakable intention of the Italian nation [to go on with the campaign]

Nonetheless Guicciardini who, like Tittoni,[15] still thought of himself as an alternate Foreign Minister, did not miss the opportunity to reiterate his profound nationalism, as the Sonninian spokesman on foreign affairs. In Libya, he believed, the government's 'temporising tactics' could damage Italy's 'renewed prestige' and injure 'our magnificent affirmation of energy and will'.[16] In war, as in peace, the methods of Giolitti did not appeal to the heirs of Crispi or Pelloux. Inside the Italian ruling class, there was still a definite alternative to the Giolittian system.

If the war did not assuage political tensions in 'legal Italy', it was equally unable to bring new unity to 'real Italy'. Colonial war was unlikely to appeal to all Catholics or all socialists, those potential mass groups of Italy's democracy in the making. The government had its greater success with the Catholics, who were given a special interest in the campaign by the Banco di Roma. *Corriere d'Italia*, a newly Catholic paper, partially financed by the Banco di Roma,[17] was one of the earliest and most fervent advocates of Italian action in Libya.[18] Once the war began, the Jesuit journal, *Civiltà Cattolica*, was delighted to be able to ally with elements in the Liberal regime against socialism. The Italian conquest of Libya, it preached, would be 'a great advantage for civilisation and progress'.[19] Not all the hierarchy was willing to give such open endorsement to actions by the 'infidel state'. *Osservatore Romano*, which, throughout the *Cinquantennio* celebrations, had devoted itself to snide comments about Liberal Italy's faithlessness and superficiality now rebuked the patriotism of *Civiltà Cattolica*.[20] Other Catholic papers opposed the war altogether.

The attractions of comradeship in war and imperialism did further the processes which were leading to the 'Gentiloni pact' when, in 1913, clericals and anti-clericals made newly public their harmony, in contesting the general elections under the new, near universal, male suffrage, and in combating the 'red peril'. But this too brought little short term benefit to Giolitti, since Catholic votes tended more to favour the 'constitutional opposition' and even the Nationalists, those unsullied warriors against Free Masonry and internationalism, than they did the Giolittians.[21]

The war, even if mildly waged, also could not hope to placate Italian Socialists. Already, social changes evident in the formation of employer groups and greater economic troubles, had undermined the Reformist hold on Socialist organisations. The Libyan campaign provided words like 'war' and 'conscription', which were condemned by Marxian heritage and whose use could guarantee popularity to an ambitious and demagogic revolutionary like Benito Mussolini.[22] Reformists, like Bissolati, might embarrassedly defend the war, or, at least, uphold the manhood of Italian soldiers when their virility or heroism was traduced. More dedicted Socialists, like Filippo Turati, were also inconvenienced by their, in fact, considerable patriotism, and could only explain the war as 'resulting from an error'.[23] For this, both reformists and moderates were bitterly attacked by the extremists. *La Lotta di Classe*, Mussolini's earnestly entitled paper in Forlì, branded together in its attacks, Reformists, Giolittians and '*tripoleggianti*' (Libya lovers). By the end of the war, Turati and his old friends, the moderate unionists of CGdL were isolated from their political and social base in the Socialist movement.[24] The party's Congress at Reggio Emilia in June 1912 formally expelled the reformists Bissolati and Bonomi, ruining Turati's efforts to keep the party united. Mussolini, the most rhetorically vivid of the extremists was raised from relative obscurity to the editorship of *Avanti!*, Italian socialism's major organ. Outside immediate party politics, strikes and social violence, provoked by the war, in turn encouraged trusts and employer organisations to tighten their grip on economic and social power, and to grow more determined to undermine the toleration accepted in the Giolittian decade.[25]

The domestic effect of the war thus did not strengthen Giolitti's power base, but instead encouraged the process which led to the 1913 elections, to Giolitti's resignation in March 1914, and to later events in Italy, in 1915 and 1922. However the conduct of foreign policy continued to be kept oddly and strikingly detached from any direct connection to these domestic contests. To a considerable degree, even in war, the assumption held that Italian diplomacy was 'above politics'. A fine example of this tradition was provided by the young democrat, Giovanni Amendola. Amendola, who, in association with Salvemini, had opposed the coming of the war on the sensible grounds of Libya's uselessness, once the war began broke with Salvemini in an agonised debate, precisely on that issue – the war had begun; it was therefore no longer appropriate to criticise. For Italy, action had moved from 'the area of current affairs' to 'that of history'; 'from now on there are only diplomatic and military issues [to be resolved]; our sense of duty (*serietà*) forces us to recognise our incompetence' in these areas.[26]

In retrospect, Amendola's line of argument seems extraordinarily naive, but there can be no doubt that his words echoed the deeply held beliefs of many in Liberal Italy. However embattled at home, the Libyan War notably increased the authority of the Prime Minister, Giolitti, over foreign affairs, sometimes to the extent of him having his own policy and agents, separate from San Giuliano and the professionals of the *Consulta*. Contemporaries noted how spry Giolitti was, despite his 72 years; and the Prime Minister was enjoying himself enough, to savour a *bon mot*, when he graphically described war diplomacy as a 'dance on eggs'.[27]

How San Giuliano viewed either the excitation of public opinion or the intrusions of the Prime Minister is somewhat unclear. For the Foreign Minister, the more immediate problem was foreign opinion, which soon reacted to the war with a combination of derision, paternal superiority and moralising which might have been predicted. Italy would experience similar, if more justified, reactions in 1935–6. In 1911 some foreigners restricted themselves to sarcasm; Jagow, the German ambassador, opined that Italy would collapse into revolution after three months of a military campaign; in Constantinople, German and Austrian officers were overheard exchanging pleasantries about those 'clowns', their Italian colleagues; the French military attaché in Rome reported to Paris that there were few chances that the Italians would actually manage to win a war, even in Libya.[28]

To Italian dismay, the most hostile public reaction occurred in England, that hoped for 'disinterested patron', which had the least immediate interests involved and where opinion was least shackled by government control. *The Times* had summoned all its magisterial pomposity to excoriate England's erring friend and client:

Even in this country, where Italy counts so many true friends and where the stanch friendship of the Italian nation is so warmly appreciated, public opinion will be unanimous in its disapproval...The step...[Italy] has now declared her intention of taking seems...out of all proportion to the grievances of which she complains, and to bring the peace of Europe into more imminent danger than has threatened it since the annexation of Bosnia and Herzegovina.[29]

Admiral Jackie Fisher snorted more decisively that the expedition was 'damnable rascality'.[30]

When stories spread of Italy's 'atrocious' war methods, even so loyal and sentimental a friend of Italy as G. M. Trevelyan, the historian who had just put the finishing touches to the last volume of his romantic and epic trilogy on Garibaldi and the Risorgimento, was moved to pained rebuke. He wrote to *The Times*:

The English love of Italy, which is very sincere and a real factor in European affairs, rests much on sentiment, a sentiment of affection for a people who have won freedom at a price and have hitherto not abused it at the expense of others, as the Magyars are held to have done. Of the effects of too great severity upon the ultimate relations of the Italians to the inhabitants of Tripoli, whom they have undertaken to govern, I can only judge *a priori*: but of the effect on English opinion, if a policy of cruel repression is begun and persisted in by the Italians, I can only speak from a knowledge of my countrymen.[31]

The Italian government viewed these criticisms with alarm and unease as a threat to Italy's whole Libyan policy. The meaning of 'traditional friendship' needed clarification; San Giuliano summoned up his own version of 'public opinion' to provide this. After Imperiali's initial satisfactory talk with Grey on 28 July, both the ambassador and San Giuliano had continued to probe gently at Britain's probable reaction to a Libyan war. As so often, the ambassador, Rodd, was a reliable advocate of the Italian cause. On 4 September he had informed Grey that:

we must be prepared for the eventuality of a move in Tripoli, and the direction which...[Italy's] sympathies will thereafter incline, with its important bearing on Mediterranean questions will depend on the attitude which...[the Triple Alliance and Triple Entente] powers adopt towards her action. With Egypt on the one hand and Tunis on the other, the goodwill of Great Britain and France will be of paramount importance to...[Italy.] The bidding for Italian friendship at the international auction may have to be rapid.[32]

But Grey had many more pressing problems to define than perennial Italian ambition.[33] When, therefore, the ultimatum to Turkey was framed, Imperiali came at once to inform the Foreign Office, and to ask for that 'moral support' which he believed or averred that Italy had been promised in July. Grey and his Under-Secretary, Sir Arthur Nicolson, were surprised and puzzled. 'I may have used the words "moral support"', Grey minuted, 'but I do not remember them.' Britain, he now said, could not back a forceful Italian action in Libya 'which must cause great disturbance, and the indirect consequences of which may spread beyond what any one can foresee'. Vaguely, Grey recalled the Lansdowne–Prinetti agreement of 1902: 'Reference should be made to our own agreement with Italy. I am not sure what bearing it has on the point'.[34]

However initially unprepared he had been for Italian rhetorical importunities to turn into fact, Grey rapidly found a policy. On 29 September he told Imperiali that the 1902 agreement did apply, and meant that Britain could not oppose Italian action in Libya. Despite this, Grey hoped to encourage a compromise; Britain

regarded the annexation of Tripoli by force as an extreme step, the indirect consequences of which might cause great embarrassment to other Powers, including ourselves, whose Moslem subjects were so numerous. It was therefore my earnest hope that affairs would be so conducted that other Powers would be embarrassed as little as possible.[35]

Italy could scarcely have expected greater benevolence. Probably San Giuliano had never taken too seriously Grey's phrase about 'moral support'; and must have been delighted and a little disconcerted when Grey did act to restrain the British press from too fervent a moral condemnation of Italy's imperial war.[36] By 2 October, Giolitti noted briefly, but comfortably, to the King that there was 'nothing to fear from that [Britain's] quarter'.[37]

Meanwhile, as if jolted by British press criticism, San Giuliano drafted a long memorandum for distribution to Italy's agents abroad, underlining the justice of Italy's cause. Britain was to be reminded especially of Italy's manifest friendship and tact during the Boer War.[38] Whether impressed by these arguments or not, and occasionally indulging in acerbic exchanges with Rome on particular events, Grey had undoubtedly decided that nothing could be done to remove Italy from Libya – British policy must wait on events, and hope that somehow Italian arms, or wiles, could drag Turkey to the peace table before the feared, more serious eventualities occurred.

At first Italy had even less diplomatic opposition from her most dubious friend in the Triple Entente, France. A final settlement between France and Germany in Morocco was not signed until 4 November, and, before that date, France could not risk abrogating the Prinetti–Barrère agreement, lest such an act devastate her relationship with Italy, or, more seriously, endanger the whole Moroccan arrangement. On 2 October, therefore, Tittoni could afford self-congratulation as he wrote from Paris that no-one there contested Italy's right to Libya:

The prudent and serious policy which we have conducted for eight years resisting the impulsiveness of our public opinion and the extravagances ['*bizzarrie*'] of our political parties', he declared 'has produced its fruits'.[39]

San Giuliano was no doubt pleased to read this, if wrily amused by hearing Tittoni, his old rival, continued political conspirator and 'friend' of the Banco di Roma, write such appropriate diplomatic phrases about the vices and superficiality of politicians and journalists.

Inside the Triple Alliance, Italy also had more and less reliable contacts. Germany was willing to accept the *fait accompli*; Austria was less likely to be accommodating. Here lay the most worrying questions of all Italian diplomatic constructions. How jealously would Austria view Italian expansion, even in remote Libya? How could Austria be prevented from compensatory action in the Adriatic, with the certainty that this would expose the bases of the Triple Alliance, Article VII and the meaning of the word 'compensation', and thus the Trentino–Trieste question, and all the linked problems of irredentism?

In the last analysis, Giolitti and San Giuliano had acted so suddenly in September 1911 for fear that Austria was about to uncover these very issues by the indirect method of suggesting the renewal of the Triple Alliance. Italy had scarcely treated Austria with good faith in the last days of planning the expedition. While the ultimatum was being drafted, Avarna had tried merely to appease Aehrenthal with vague words about the need to find the proper mode for renewal of the Triple Alliance.[40] Once it was clear that Italy had decided on military action, Avarna was abruptly summoned to the *Ball-hausplatz* and given a dressing down by Aehrenthal. The Austrian Foreign Minister expressed 'his regret that...[Italy] had abandoned [so] soon the field of diplomacy'. Austria would not place immediate difficulties in front of Italy, but he called Avarna's attention to 'the eventual repercussion such an action as this could have in the Balkans'. Was it necessary to remind Italy that the Triple Alliance was founded on the principle of 'the maintenance of the *status quo* of Turkey in Europe'?[41]

This last phrase was the escape clause, and, in fact, Austrian reaction could have been very much worse. It soon became so, when, that very day, the first naval action of the war threatened direct Italo–Austrian hostilities. An Italian squadron, commanded by the King's cousin, the Duke of the Abruzzi, operating in the Adriatic, sank two Turkish torpedo boats off Prevesa. Shots were also exchanged with some Austrian steamers running to Turkish Albania.

San Giuliano had prepared a note to his ambassadors warning that, before accepting the neutrality of the Balkan littoral, Italy would at first need to take action in the Adriatic, and that the initial reaction to this might be unpleasant, but it would all be over in a couple of days.[42] He had underestimated the extreme touchiness of Austria. Aehrenthal, whose own policy of improved relations with Italy was under constant domestic attack, reacted very strongly. Avarna was again summoned, and told that it was 'urgent' that Italian operations in the Adriatic end; if they did not, the whole Balkans might be in danger. Brushing aside Avarna's explanation that Italy felt threatened by Turkish torpedo boats so close to her coast, Aehrenthal demanded 'assurances of a positive kind' that Italy would limit her future action to the Mediterranean.[43]

Characteristically, San Giuliano first tried the effects of soothing verbal assurances. Avarna was instructed to tell Aehrenthal that Italy had received the 'best impression' from Austria's 'loyal reaction' to events in Libya. It would all prove to be 'an antidote to irredentism' and 'another step on the path of always more cordial friendship between Italy and Austria'. Reaching the nub of the question late in the telegram, San Giuliano added that commanders had been told not to act in the Adriatic unless 'absolutely unavoidable'.[44]

This was not enough for Austria. Indeed Aehrenthal can hardly have been much gratified to receive patronising remarks about his loyalty, from Italy of all places. Austria showed no desire to accept the Italian compromise suggestion that action be limited to emergencies.[45] San Giuliano may have tried to keep talking, but foreign policy was not in his hands alone at this stage in the war. Indeed every major despatch went on to Giolitti who offered frequent advice and instruction to San Giuliano and the diplomatic staff. Giolitti, the King, and the Navy Minister, Leonardi Cattolica, shared San Giuliano's anxiety to avoid a breakdown in Italo-Austrian relations.[46] On 8 October, in something unusually approaching a Cabinet decision, San Giuliano, Leonardi Cattolica, Giolitti and Spingardi, the Minister of War, formally agreed to accept the neutralisation of the Adriatic, northern Ionian, and Red Seas, throughout the course of the hostilities.[47] A week later, Italo-Austrian relations were still tender enough for Avarna to deny officially rumours that Austria had begun menacing military preparations against Italy.[48]

In bowing to Austrian pressure, and accepting a fairly tight territorial limitation on her war with Turkey, Italy had given a public demonstration of the potential weakness of her position. On the immediate combat level, the superior Italian Navy could hardly be used for punitive action designed to drive Turkey to the peace table. The expeditionary force in Libya could continue to occupy sand, especially if within reach of Italian naval guns, but the way to peace was no nearer.

In the very first days of the war, Germany had made available her good offices, but neither Italy nor Turkey had reacted. There had also been, perhaps under Turkish sponsorship, a murky private mission from Constantinople to Rome led by Alberto Theodoli, Italian delegate to the Ottoman Public Debt,[49] but the time was not yet ripe for the success of such manoeuvres.

Italy, in particular, had an urgent need to define her war aims. Under Austrian pressure, she had set geographical boundaries to the war which she would wage, but what was intended in Libya itself? No clear decision had been reached about this before the campaign was launched, the closest thing to planning of the government of Libya being San Giuliano's brief mention of possible alternate administrative systems in his memorandum of 28 July. Now in the last days of October, Italy did decide on a policy.

Bearing the imprint of Giolitti's toughness, rather than San Giuliano's preference for permanent flexibility or duplicity, the decision made was a firm one. On 5 November Italy issued a royal decree formally annexing Libya,[50] which was to be administered directly as a colony of the nation, and not to be governed by a local dynasty, nor through some form of protectorate as Tunis and Egypt were, or as had been the case in Bosnia–Herzegovina.

The motives behind this decision are nowhere defined, but seem to have sprung from Giolitti's incisive understanding of Italy's international situation which would become dangerously fragile if a decision on the legal ownership of Libya was too long delayed. Once the campaign had begun, the other Powers had not been slow to realise the lack of definition in Italian war aims, and soon were asking embarrassing questions. Thus San Giuliano was at his most blunt in replying to the Austrian ambassador, Mérey, on 10 October. Italy, San Giuliano asserted, could not at the moment have anything to do with Turkish peace feelers:

Our intention is to resolve the Tripoli question in a way which can no longer be a perennial source of conflict between us and Turkey, and of international complications.

Italy would consider 'with serenity and objectivity' Mérey's suggestions that the nominal sovereignty of the Sultan be retained, but

the actual state of Italian public opinion did not seem...to make very probable a solution different from the extension pure and simple of Italian sovereignty over those regions.[51]

San Giuliano however had not set a timetable for annexation. After the meeting with Mérey, he did no more than draft a despatch to all Italian diplomats exhorting them to work on foreign governments and the foreign public to encourage acceptance of Italian annexation 'with assiduous but inconspicuous propaganda'.[52]

As this last phrase suggests, San Giuliano continued to look fearfully over his shoulder at foreign reactions, whether by governments or by the press. Reports on the Balkans were alarming;[53] as was the present attitude of the Austrian military leadership.[54] Both Germany and Russia made apparent their preference for a swift peace,[55] and thus increased the pressure on Italy.

San Giuliano went back to his diplomatic parleying, for pressure on Italy could be reduced by diplomatic pressure from Italy. Italy's friends and allies, he now pointed out, could win 'the sincere friendship of the Italian people' by exerting their influence at Constantinople in Italy's favour.[56] With an enjoyment which he had shown before and would show again to sift through the dust of diplomatic despatches to see if any nuggets had been left behind, San Giuliano now was bold enough to ask Avarna whether Austria would tolerate wider action against Turkey, if it could produce peace.[57]

San Giuliano and Giolitti, contrary to what has sometimes been alleged, [58] thus showed no particular difference over the ambition of outright annexation, but it was Giolitti, perhaps recognising his Foreign Minister's habitual preference for procrastination, who, on 25 October, told King Victor Emmanuel III of his intention to 'proclaim the absolute sovereignty of the Kingdom of Italy over Tripoli and Cyrenaica' once there had been some more military gains.[59] Ten days later enough of these were adjudged to have occurred for the annexation decree to be formally promulgated. Italian agents abroad were circularised with the information that a less radical solution would have built up trouble for the future. 'The solution adopted by us', the advice to diplomats magnificently and optimistically ran, 'is therefore the only one which safeguards definitely the interests of Italy, of Europe, and of Turkey itself.'[60]

There was some truth in these words, at least in so far as Italy was concerned. As Austrian reactions had already indicated, if Italy made do with half-measures in Libya, she would leave herself open to diplomatic pressure in every succeeding European crisis. The weakest of the Great Powers, let alone a Power with ultimate ambitions on Trento and Trieste, could not afford an unclear legal position in Libya, which others could point to when they wanted to deny Italy future compensation, or ask Italy to clarify her position between her 'friends' and her 'allies'. There was not only Austria to be suspected in this regard, but also France. The timing of the annexation decree was indicative of Italy's hopes and fears. 5 November was one day after the formal Franco-German treaty was made, ending the Moroccan crisis and therefore returning to Austria her great ally, and giving back to France her diplomatic independence, and arguably ending the legal application of the Prinetti–Barrère agreement. It was just as well that the 'military situation' now allowed Giolitti to publish the annexation decree.

Once again, the *coup de main* by Italy was received with annoyance in European chancelleries, and with sarcasm by the European press. Even Britain made frigid references about the need, posed by annexation, to discuss previous commercial and extra-territorial rights.[61] In places as distant as Berne and New Haven, Connecticut, under the *Consulta*'s patronage, the Dante Alighieri society was called on by the government to repair the damage to Italy's reputation abroad.[62] Yet press campaigns could scarcely alter Italy's policy. Indeed, the annexation had also lessened the chances of successful Great Power diplomatic pressure for a compromise of any kind. Having taken such a formal step, no Italian government could allow itself a future retreat, except in the most extreme circumstances, a fact which Giolitti, if not San Giuliano, always thereafter recognised. To be successful, pressure for such a step from another Great Power would have to be so great as to destroy for some time that Power's relationship with Italy. If the pressure came from France or Austria, then there might even be risk of a war.

At the same time, the annexation was a very difficult public loss of face for Turkey to accept. Any Power which tried to influence Turkey towards peace, would also have to risk a drastic loss of influence at Constantinople. Given the economic contest for penetration of Asia Minor, waged with such zeal by all the Powers, there was little likelihood that any Power would want to alienate Turkey by action on Italy's behalf. So, during the next eleven months, the five major Powers, for the most part, watched helplessly as the war dragged on, always fearful that the Balkan nations would use the opportunity to throw Turkey out of Europe, but always unable to do anything about it. And when peace was finally reached, it was too late.

In the last months of 1911, there was one curious effort to promote a Turco-Italian peace. This was the so-called 'Charykov Kite', named after the Russian ambassador in Constantinople.[63] Reviving themes traditionally dear to Russian foreign policy, Charykov put forward the idea of a guarantee of the Turkish Empire in return for a free abandonment of the restrictive clauses imposed after the Crimean War, and a consequent opening of the Straits to Russian shipping.

In fact the complicated Russian scheming came to nothing, being received unfavourably by every Great Power since Charykov had raised too nearly the old spectre of defining each Power's interest in the Ottoman Empire. This was perhaps just as well for Italy in the circumstances of 1911. A general settlement of the Turkish problem would very likely have involved a reconsideration of Italy's position in Libya, as well as the usual grave dangers latent in the Balkans. Had the Russian initiative prevailed, it would have proved all the more embarrassing for Italy given that, at Racconigi, in 1909, Italy had promised to sympathise with the Russian desire to have free access through the Straits. Open hostility to the 'Charykov Kite' in Rome might encourage the Russians to renounce their side of the Racconigi agreement, and even perhaps take Turkey's part in any further negotiations. San Giuliano must have been relieved from a further twinge of anxiety, since trouble with Russia might promote the cause of his rival, Tittoni, who had found a conspiratorial soul-mate in Izvolsky, the Russian ambassador in Paris. Tittoni could certainly be imagined offering himself as the 'saviour' of Italo-Russian relations, if San Giuliano became too openly remiss in remembering what had been promised at Racconigi.[64] In fact, San Giuliano did not have to worry too much about such a scenario since the 'Charykov Kite' found no favourable breezes from any European quarter, and Italy was allowed to continue her campaign. Russo-Italian relations were not left entirely amicable; Italy resented Russia's touchy independence in some later incidents during the war, especially when Russia's grain trade through the Straits was blocked. Traditionally Italo-Russian relations had been minimal, but, around this time, Russian affairs bothered San Giuliano sufficiently for him to christen his most assiduous, and pro-Russian, bureaucrat '*Contarinov*', perhaps not wholly as a joke. Certainly, San Giuliano enjoyed restraining Tittoni's stratagems with the rebuke 'there is no motive at all for us to give Russia today more than we have given her at Racconigi'.[65] But, with more long-term importance, the unusually direct contact between Italy and Russia during the Libyan war prepared the way for increased comment on the 'Slav problem' by San Giuliano and other Italian diplomatists in 1913–14, although this comment remained inconsistent, and never became the mainspring of major Italian policies.

Italo-Austrian relations remained tender, although they had endured surprisingly well the successive stresses of the invasion of Libya and the annexation decree. Aehrenthal, who was worried by what he regarded as a generally deteriorating European situation, and was also anxious to assert that Austria was not just Germany's 'noble second',[66] had adopted a largely sympathetic policy towards Italy. The triumph of his policies over its domestic critics was publicly signalled on 30 November, when Conrad von Hötzendorf, the Italophobe Chief of General Staff, who, in a secret memorandum in September, had advocated a preventive attack on Italy while its armies were preoccupied in Libya, was relieved of his office.[67]

The Italians, who knew that Conrad was no friend of Italy, were anxious to do nothing to harm their relationship with Aehrenthal's Austria. In November–December 1911, in a series of despatches, San Giuliano consulted Avarna and Pansa about the best way of ensuring the happy renewal of the Triple Alliance. Italy, San Giuliano was at pains to argue, was anxious not to convey an unfriendly impression at Vienna. These pious words spoken, all the Italian diplomatists arrived without labour at the logical conclusion that nothing could be done about the renewal of the Triple Alliance until the Libyan War was over. As San Giuliano put it in official rhetoric:

The Italian Nation is determined to obtain at all costs its ends [in Libya] and we for our part have no haste in bringing the war to a finish; moreover the position of Italy in the world will be so much more renowned and strong as the greater will be the proof of the tenacity which she will know how to give. And she shall give it.[68]

Instead of further difficulty with Austria, the New Year soon brought increased tension with France. Italo-French relations had seemed uncharacteristically cordial in the first months of the Libyan War, but this appearance had been created by France's serious involvement with Germany over Morocco, and thus her helplessness in the face of Italian action. Once the Moroccan crisis was over, it was predictable enough that Italo-French relations would soon grow more tense. The issue, to become a familiar one in the First World War, involved the rights of neutral shipping. On 16 January 1912, the *Carthage* (in name an appropriate opponent of the 'Third Italy'), a French postal steamer, was suspected of carrying an aeroplane to be used by Turkish forces in Libya, and was therefore stopped by Italian naval action. The aeroplane was duly found, and the *Carthage* was ordered to sail to Cagliari in Sardinia to be impounded. The ship's release was agreed to only after strenuous protests from Paris, which declared that the aeroplane had been destined not for Tripoli but for Tunis.

Two days later, another ship, the *Manouba*, was also stopped. Twenty-nine Turkish officers were aboard, a fact which appeared to justify the Italian case, at least until the French blandly asserted that they were officials of the 'Red Crescent',[69] the Turkish version of the Red Cross. When, on 25 January, a third ship, the *Tavignano*, was seized, taken to Tripoli, and then shamefacedly released when no contraband was found, Italo-French relations fell to a lower ebb than at any time in the previous decade.

The politicians of both countries, and especially the press, reacted very bitterly. In Italy there were even rumours that the Navy at La Spezia and the Army stationed along the Alps were making ready to oppose a French attack.[70] It did not calm French susceptibilities that the German Foreign Minister, Kiderlen Wächter, should be present in Rome, during the very days that the *Carthage* and *Manouba* were boarded. Raymond Poincaré, the patriot from Lorraine, who led a staunchly nationalist government in Paris, took a very firm line, very publicly. Tittoni was instructed to inform San Giuliano that the incidents had been 'really dangerous for the good relations of the two countries'.[71] On 22 January Poincaré addressed the French Chamber of Deputies and scathingly rejected the Italian suggestion that the *Manouba* incident be sent to the Court of Disputes at the Hague.[72] The British ambassador in Paris, Bertie, reported back to London:

Though there may be talk of affinities of race and of sympathy for Italian democracy there is at heart here intense distrust of Italy. The attack on Tripoli is regarded as pure brigandage and satisfaction is felt at the difficulties in which the Italian Government find themselves.[73]

From London, the influential French ambassador, Paul Cambon, used the opportunity to point out that he had long not seen the point in Barrère's efforts to extract Italy from the Triple Alliance:

L'Italie semble une alliée moins utile qu'embarrassante, elle nourrit contre l'Autriche une hostilité latente que rien ne peut désarmer et, s'il s'agit de la France, nous avons des raisons de penser que, dans le cas d'un conflit, elle resterait neutre ou plutôt elle attendrait les événements pour prendre un parti.'[74]

The *Carthage* and *Manouba* incidents were soon formally over. The Italians, despite an initial reluctance to abandon their 'rights' under pressure,[75] kept their heads, and Barrère was a usefully soothing aide. On 24 January, San Giuliano reported that for ninety minutes, he had a 'courteous and cordial' conversation with the

French ambassador. Barrère, San Giuliano believed, had been deeply impressed by the claim that 'eight-tenths' of all his work to restore Franco-Italian relations had been wiped out by the *Manouba* incident.[76]

Mollified by Barrère's diplomatic courtesy (so often such a marked contrast to the domineering unpredictability of the Austrian ambassador Mérey), Italo-French leaders soon relocated a *modus vivendi*. Despite the *Tavignano* incident, by the end of January a compromise had been agreed whereby Italy liberated her prisoners from the *Manouba*, with, however much incredulity, acknowledging that indeed most of them were legitimate Red Crescent officials. The question of the legality of the seizure of the vessel, and of possible compensation passed to the Hague Court. No further French ships were stopped.

It is customary to regard the *Carthage* and *Manouba* incidents as an important turning-point in Italo-French relations. Malgeri, for example, has described the 'sense of stupor and bitterness' aroused in Italian 'public opinion' by the French attitude.[77] It is also customary to note the encouragement given by the affair to the imperialism and triplicism of the Nationalists. Yet the press excitation was as great in the traditional as in the Nationalist press.[78] No dramatic break in continuity had occurred but rather the incidents had brought into the limelight what many Italian public figures had long known; as San Giuliano would later bluntly put it, in 'the ideal [battle] for us, there would be beaten on the one side Austria, on the other, France'.[79] In the fluid diplomatic situation from 1912–14, this ancient hostility between Italy and her 'Latin' '*sorellastra*' (step-sister) would often be apparent.

The *Carthage* and *Manouba* incidents had again not assisted an Italo-Turkish peace. Indeed, the public hostility between France and Italy, combined with new uncertainty about Austria after the death of Aehrenthal on 17 February,[80] and the underlying and continued Great Power concern at news of Balkan troubles of any kind[81] further encouraged Turkish delaying tactics. To overcome the sense of lassitude about the war and its diplomacy, Italy began to look for a new means of driving Turkey to the peace table. In March 1912 the Libyan War entered what has been defined as its 'third phase'.[82] In this phase, Italian effort would be intensified on land and sea, and also in the back alleys of diplomacy.

Throughout the war, Giolitti had continued to pay the closest attention to Italian foreign policy. He had also never restricted his information to that received through the official channels of the *Consulta*. In October 1911, for example, he had persuaded Bonaldo Stringher, the *direttore* of the Banca d'Italia to use his influence on German and British financial circles in a way that would favour Italy's cause.[83] Giolitti had also employed, directly or indirectly, a series of agents who attempted to make contacts, and presumably distribute bribes, in Constantinople. One major contact was Count Giuseppe Volpi, the Venetian entrepreneur, who had a developing interest in the Ottoman Empire especially through his company, the Società Commerciale d'Oriente. Volpi regularly forwarded to Giolitti information received from Bernardino Nogara, the agent of the Società Commerciale d'Oriente, who was still working in Constantinople.[84]

These reports became important when, on 24 February 1912, an Italian naval squadron commanded by Admiral Paolo Thaon di Revel sank a Turkish torpedo boat off Beirut and briefly bombarded the city. Neither in the initial promises to Austria, nor in frequent general discussions of such matters, had San Giuliano pledged Italy to avoid naval action off the Mediterranean coasts of the Ottoman Empire. Nevertheless, the Italian action alarmed the French who had already appealed to Britain and Russia to make plain to Italy that the Triple Entente Powers would object to any Italian attack on the Dardanelles.[85] However, when Grey suggested that Italy be asked to give such assurances formally, Rodd joined Barrère and the Russian ambassador, Krupenski, in order to delay any appeal to San Giuliano.[86] Rodd warned Grey dramatically that such an act might 'definitely throw Italy into the arms of Germany and Austria, who are making every effort to conciliate their ally'.[87]

Meanwhile the news from both official and unofficial contacts on the Beirut incident encouraged Italy to take further action. Nogara wrote to Volpi that 'such small events' as the bombardment had made an enormous impression. Nogara did not know what were the intentions of the Italian government, but he did not see how the war would be brought to an end without an extension of the blockade and the threat of a raid on Constantinople. The Turkish government, abetted by the Turcophile ambassadors of the Great Powers in Constantinople, would not yield to less.[88] A fortnight later, Nogara returned to his advice that, for the moment, parleying with the Turks was impossible. The Turkish Minister of Foreign Affairs would not grant him an interview. There were limits, it seemed, to the value of Italian 'subventions', even in Constantinople. The Italian fleet would have to be used.[89] While these suggestions reached Giolitti, San Giuliano was being told much the same by Andrea Carlotti, Italy's ambassador in Athens, which was used as a near listening post to the Ottoman Empire.[90]

Perhaps the most influential report of all was sent on 11 March, again through unofficial channels. Its author was Guido Fusinato. Fusinato is one of the most shadowy, but important figures in the Giolittian decade. Usually described as one of Giolitti's most faithful agents,[91] Fusinato was much more than one of the fabled '*ascari*'. An eminent jurist, he had a long and distinguished career in the Italian Chamber, notable for his service in many ministries. He had been Under-Secretary of Foreign Affairs under Pelloux and Saracco, 1899–1901, and had returned to this office when Tittoni became Foreign Minister in November 1903, remaining in both the Giolitti and first Fortis Ministry. In 1906, he was for a short time, Minister of Education in Giolitti's third government.

Fusinato had been prominent in the foundation of the Istituto Coloniale, and in 1910 had become the Institute's president. He had spoken at the 1911 Second Congress of Italians Abroad, and had recently been used by San Giuliano to defend Italy's legal position in the *Manouba* incident.[92] In February 1912, with Martini, Luzzatti, Cappelli and Stringher, he had formed, in the Istituto Coloniale, a special Tripoli Committee to encourage the coordination of Italy's economic activities in Libya under the Banca d'Italia and the Banco di Sicilia.[93] On 21 March 1912, he was to resign the presidency of the Istituto Coloniale to become one of Giolitti's main personal agents in attempting a peace settlement with Turkey. His expertise in foreign affairs, in law, and in finance all recommended him as a peacemaker.

Fusinato's advice to Giolitti, therefore, bore the stamp of great authority. Fusinato could be reliably taken as the spokesman of the views of the Italian ruling class, from the very heartland of *giolittismo*. On 11 March he told Giolitti that, from everything he heard, both inside Italy and out, '*peace will never* be obtained by a *formal act*' [*sic*]. Italy and Turkey had taken up positions which did not allow conciliation. 'We cannot make any concession in the area of political sovereignty', Fusinato wrote, 'and Turkey can never recognise our sovereignty.' In a metaphor not very surprising in Liberal Italy, Fusinato went on to explain: 'The Pope has still not renounced Avignon, and the Sultan too is a Pope; even more of a Pope than ours.' Italy should thus try to find a tolerable *de facto* situation, which then could be gradually consolidated. Two lines of action were necessary: intensive naval effort, 'doing all that we can', and secret negotiations with Turkish agents 'paying under the counter what is necessary'.[94]

It soon became apparent that Giolitti had accepted Fusinato's advice, and that this 'third phase' of the Libyan War would be based on a double policy of treatying, and of naval raids. By 18 March, the Navy Minister, Pasquale Leonardi Cattolica, had begun preparations for a surprise attack on the Dardanelles.[95]

With trepidation, the diplomatic and political ground was also made ready for action. From 24 to 26 March, Kaiser William II was due to exchange royal embraces with Victor Emmanuel III on a state visit to Venice – just the right romantic setting to inspire as much as possible the Kaiser's sense of historical sentimentality, and therefore his current geniality towards Italy. The monarchical meeting was therefore a great success; William II forgot, and Victor Emmanuel III forebore to remember that, some years before, the Kaiser had summarily dismissed the King of Italy as 'the Dwarf'. More significant than the temperature of royal friendships was the fact that Italy was accorded a public demonstration of the excellent state of her relations with her most powerful ally, Germany.[96]

In the Chamber, the debate on 27–28 March, and especially Guicciardini's speech, was a further stimulus to action. But, on the diplomatic front, despite the pleasing emotions released at Venice, Italy lacked enough confidence to launch a *coup de main* without another sounding of the terrain by what the British called 'mysterious hints' about the project.[97] It was the Austrians who most openly expressed annoyance at inspired leaks from Rome.[98] San Giuliano, still in the accustomed groove of his policy, then appealed to Berlin that Italy could 'very well sustain' that Article VII of the Triple Alliance was not relevant to Asia Minor and its seas.[99] On 10 April he wrote a long note to Avarna, making still more distinct the revised Italian line. Article VII, he now argued, did not apply in a campaign the object of which was Libya. Italy had full liberty of action in the Aegean, and the expressed fears of repercussions there were exaggerated. It was not good enough 'to give Austria the right to limit our freedom of action, prolonging the war, and damaging an Allied Power in finance, in prestige and in loss of men'. This all risked the stirring up 'in Italian public opinion of a resentment capable of compromising the alliance, and the noteworthy progress made in Italo-Austrian friendship'.[100]

Before either Germany or Austria had much time to consider the ramifications of San Giuliano's statement, Italy acted. On 14 April news services reported a large Italian fleet steaming east. On 18 April attacks were launched on the forts off the Dardanelles. Turkey reacted at once by closing the Straits to all shipping. Not taken aback, on 28 April, Italy continued her firmness and seized the island of Stampalia off Asia Minor; in the next month, the rest of the Dodecanese, and the island of Rhodes were occupied. Giolitti had followed Fusinato's advice for a naval action, on 'doing all that we can'.

Both the attack on the Dardanelles and the occupation of the islands provoked international reaction. Turkey's closure of the Straits especially affected Britain and Russia, who experienced a serious interruption to their trade. Russia was inclined to blame Turkey,[101] while Britain, more reasonably, believed the fault lay with Italy. Yet neither Power could really bring much pressure to bear on Italy. On 28 April San Giuliano declared abruptly that Italy could not accept any limitation on her actions in the Aegean Sea.[102] To the British, he had already enunciated the remarkable statement that the attack on the Dardanelles had been accidental. In view of the planning of the last month, it was an argument of doubtful veracity, to say the least, but one which the British found very difficult to rebut. Rodd's telegram reported:

Minister of Foreign Affairs is anxious that accidental character of engagement should be appreciated. He fears that Turkish Government may try to close Dardanelles, and wishes to preclude any representations here from His Majesty's Government which might have unfortunate effect on Italian public opinion, which has been prepared by German and Austrian press to anticipate possible [Entente] intervention. Position of Italy is as follows: She had not intended any attack on Dardanelles at present time; she must reserve to herself liberty to attack Turkey in any way to her advantage, and Turkish apprehensions on account of Dardanelles are an asset to her: but in practice such an attack is not likely to be realised either soon or at any time.[103]

Rodd ended by believing the argument that it had all been an accident – either because he could not think quickly enough to break out of the toils of San Giuliano's words, or because he was satisfied by the partial promise not to do it again. Officials in London, however, did not share their ambassador's optimism or ingenuousness.[104] They were still less impressed when the British military attaché in Rome, Delmé-Radcliffe, who was a close confidant of King Victor Emmanuel, revealed that Italy had even contemplated forcing the Straits.[105]

Seeing through Italy's policy did not resolve the problem of what could be done about it. Hostile intervention in Rome, as San Giuliano had repeatedly stressed, carried the risk of alienating Italy completely. In any case Turkey had laid the mines, and only Turkey could remove them. Despite deepening Russian disgust, this was not done until 20 May. Italy savoured both her enemy's embarrassment, and the difficulties of the Great Power ambassadors in Constantinople.

However pleasant an episode for Italian diplomatists, the 'accidental' naval manoeuvres did not bring peace. Another, rather half-hearted, but again 'accidental' raid was attempted by Italian torpedo boats under Captain Millo on 19 July, but this time Turkey called Italy's bluff by not mining the Straits in reaction. As a result, on 27 July Giolitti warned Leonardi Cattolica that there should not be any more raids, given 'what Italy had done in the Dodecanese',[106] where Italy's 'temporary' occupation had already produced complaints from France and Britain, and ominous Austrian suggestions that Italian ownership of the islands 'in the Aegean' might carry an arguable legal corollary from Article VII of the Triple Alliance, that Austria be granted compensation 'in the Balkans'. In the naval operations Italy had pressed her power, and perhaps her luck, and could not, without retribution, continue indefinitely tweaking the other Great Powers' tails.

Many Italian political leaders were by now extremely frustrated at Italy's inability to finish off the Libyan War. They were not won over by the parliamentary promise that Giolitti intended to create a Ministry of Colonies, even though this was a further indication that Italy would accept no compromise in Libya. Nor were they reassured when San Giuliano grew more than usually vibrant in his patriotic rhetoric:

How Italy stayed in Libya

I hope today that the great events in the Mediterranean have reawakened in Italy the colonial consciousness and have imprinted on the minds of all Italians the profound conviction of the necessity for Italy to pursue a colonial policy with adequate and effective means.[107]

On 29 June the Chief of General Staff, Alberto Pollio, who had grown increasingly offended by the politicians' continued domination of war policy, made a rare intervention into civilian administration by sending Giolitti a long memorandum.[108] Pollio complained that Italy's progress was being unjustifiably restrained in the Eastern Mediterranean. Although he did not know the details of Italian diplomatic commitments, he did know that the war could not be won simply by piling up military victories in Libya. The Turkish Empire, he declared, was doomed to collapse. Italy could not and should not go out of her way to prop Turkey up, but rather should prepare an attack on Smyrna. If this meant that Austria took the Sandjak of Novi-Bazar, then Italy could perhaps find compensation in Albania.

Pollio's very suggestion of a cavalier acceptance of the destruction of the Ottoman Empire was indicative of the distance even the highest Army officers were kept from foreign policy planning, and Giolitti received the suggestions for extended military action very coldly.[109] But Pollio's words were also an indication of the growing domestic rejection of the style of Giolitti's war-making. Although neither Giolitti nor San Giuliano yet had discovered a clear path toward peace, Giolitti was now encouraged to increase his unofficial contacts with the Turks.

On 13 May Giolitti had already instructed Volpi that peace moves should be continued, though with 'the utmost prudence'.[110] Carlo Garbasso, the First Secretary who had stayed in Constantinople until July 1912, in charge of the Italian Embassy, was also distributing funds and lubricating connections which might help the Italian cause.[111] On 6 June Volpi himself had set out on a mission to Constantinople, and talked there with Turkish officials from 10 to 16 June. His reports to Giolitti underlined basic Turkish intransigence, but added the hopeful information that Turkish determination had been sapped by Italian naval action in the Aegean. Generally, Volpi believed, Turkey was 'a country which continues its fatal path towards its end', without honourable men who might be able to stop the rot.[112]

Such philosophising was of doubtful value to Giolitti. Messages from Carlotti that Wangenheim, the German ambassador sent to Constantinople to replace Marschall, was very friendly to Italy[113] or from Stringher, that the Turks were finding credit increasingly difficult on the Paris *Bourse*,[114] equally offered no short-term solutions.

However, Volpi's mission had born unexpected fruits. The Turks, after all, were willing to talk. Nogara and Joel both so informed Volpi.[115] After some discussion where the ideal venue would be,[116] on 12 July 1912 unofficial Turkish and Italian delegations began meeting in the Hotel Gibbon at Lausanne. (Once again the building of the Empire of the new Rome was being favoured by the auspices of an ironically suitable name.) The Italian delegation was composed of Volpi, Fusinato and Pietro Bertolini, soon to become Italy's first Minister of Colonies, and believed by some to be Giolitti's designated political heir.[117]

The exclusion of San Giuliano is sometimes seen as demonstrating the failure of his policy, the thread of which had been lost in the tortuous maze of his politicking.[118] But the differences between the Prime Minister and Foreign Minister should not be exaggerated. Giolitti had been in evident control of foreign policy since the campaign had begun. The informal side of treatying had been accepted as necessary by both San Giuliano and Giolitti,[119] and probably indeed was, given the international situation and the nature of the Turkish government. In the summer of 1912, San Giuliano also had personal reasons for being out of the limelight: his gout and stomach troubles were still more painful than usual; his only son and heir, Benedetto, had recently died.[120] For a Sicilian aristocrat, proud of his Anglo–Norman descent, and a Darwinian believer in the rise and fall of a species, this death of his first-born was especially hard to accept. The San Giuliano family now consisted only of children and pious women. First the *fasci* threatening his estates, then radicals and socialists taking away his family seat in the Chamber, and now his only son dead, Antonino Paternò Castello Di San Giuliano was left to fight alone his personal battle between embittered cynicism and his definition of a patriot's sense of service.[121]

Meanwhile the unofficial delegates found the talks in Switzerland to be long and complicated.[122] On 28 July the original Turkish delegation was replaced by another, and the meeting place was moved to Caux and then to Ouchy on 4 September. On the diplomatic front, San Giuliano had to deal with Balkan alarums, notably discouraging a Bulgarian suggestion that Italy back a Balkan uprising.[123] Giolitti kept up his advice to his diplomatists. He rejected Fusinato's idea that the inland Libyan territory of Fezzan, where Italian troops had hardly penetrated, might be left independent.[124] He also warned San Giuliano to ensure that the talks in Switzerland were as secret as possible, and urged San Giuliano to be as firm as possible in the face of mediatory blandishments from the other Great Powers, so that no encouragement could be given to the Turks.[125] San Giuliano immediately resorted to such firmness when, contrary to Carlotti's earlier advice, Wangenheim made pro-Turkish noises in Constantinople.[126] Firmness appeared likely to be a difficult line for Italy to follow when, on 13 August, Berchtold raised the idea of a general reform scheme for Turkey under the auspices of all the Great Powers. Italy could not afford to disregard an idea which carried the potential danger of renewed Great Power interference in her diplomacy, and, after some delay, both San Giuliano and Giolitti, blandly and unenthusiastically, declared that they were willing to associate with any positive steps which Austria might take. To Italy's relief, the other Powers had been equally unimpressed by a reform which might appear to give Austria hegemony in the Balkans, and Berchtold's initiative lapsed.[127] Italy could safely go on running her own war and her own diplomacy.

As far as the negotiations in Switzerland were concerned, Giolitti retained his conviction that Italy should show the strength and majesty of a real Great Power, and not resort to unseemly bargaining. San Giuliano and his Secretary-General, Bollati, both advised that there could be some concession in the area of religion, suggesting, for example, that the Caliph could be left some rights still in Libya. Giolitti rejected this out of hand, arguing that Turkey (and thus, potentially, the other Great Powers) could not be permitted the right to interfere in the domestic arrangements of an Italian colony.[128]

Lubricating funds, those ideal accompaniments of strength and majesty, were also not assisting the wheels of Italian diplomacy to turn any faster. Nogara, in Constantinople, remarked that he needed more detailed information on how the *Consulta* intended to keep money flowing through to him.[129] In Switzerland too, an Italian journalist complained that the real problem was no longer financial but political.[130] On 29 August Volpi reported that the discussions were 'deadlocked'; Bertolini and Fusinato also reluctantly agreed that they could not see any present exit from the diplomatic morass.[131]

Ignoring these complaints and San Giuliano's fears about new Adowas, Giolitti turned back to the military for news of more victories, but received no joy from the cautious and pessimistic Minister of War, Spingardi.[132] Achieving a peace on her own, either at the tables of diplomacy or on the field of battle, remained a most onerous task for the least of the Great Powers.

The question whether Giolitti had been right or not in refusing all compromise was now made irrelevant by events outside Italy's control. The situation in the Balkans had deteriorated,[133] and on 30 September the member states of the secret Balkan league began mobilisation. The Ottoman Empire was not just losing Libya, but was menaced by total dissolution.

San Giuliano naturally was aghast at this prospect, and prophesied a general Balkan war, with the ever present danger of Austrian action and its corollary, an overwhelming domestic Italian demand for Trento and Trieste. San Giuliano turned back to the value of negotiating, urging compromise on Giolitti. 'The best solution for us', he warned,

would be the rapid conclusion of peace even at the cost of some sacrifice on our part, provided that it does not infringe the indisputable right of our full and complete sovereignty over all Libya.[134]

Volpi, with the flair and boldness of a captain of commerce, disagreed, believing that the Balkan situation could be used to Italy's advantage, and indeed might be the only means of forcing Turkish domestic opinion to accept any peace with Italy.[135]

Having retreated to Piedmont as was his custom, Giolitti, away from the attentions of the Press, decided on a show of strength. Acting on his instructions, on 2 October Italy threatened to call off her negotiations with Turkey; and Rechid Pasha, the current Turkish negotiator, was given eight days to find a solution.[136] San Giuliano was summarily instructed that any talk of Italian concessions would only produce further delays and hinder an eventual peace.[137]

On 4 October San Giuliano was delighted and perhaps relieved to learn that Germany had at last intervened at Constantinople, criticising Turkey's procrastination. It now seemed that Turkey would be willing to come to a settlement. Full powers were prepared for the secret negotiators to sign a pact, although San Giuliano, still anxious about the Balkans, privately repeated his fearful advice that Italy must compromise if necessary.[138]

The Balkan situation worsened again when, on 8 October, Montenegro formally declared war on Turkey. Nogara, still in Constantinople, suddenly perceived how grave a prospect was confronting Italy and Europe. Demonstrations had occurred in front of his house and concerned to preserve his own life and property, he now despaired of finding peace in the excitement of a general Balkan war. Negotiating an end to the Libyan War was, he said, 'the punishment of Tantalus'.[139]

On 11 October, still searching for concessions, Turkey tried to suggest one last modification of the terms which Italy had offered. It was again Giolitti who showed no signs of weakness, and who instructed Bertolini to warn that further Italian naval action would follow any breakdown of the peace talks.[140] There were even rumours that Italy contemplated military action in Smyrna, or a landing in European Turkey.[141] Certainly a memorandum was drafted, detailing Italy's grievances against Turkey, to be presented to the other Great Powers if further military action turned out to be necessary.[142]

Germany, Austria, France and Britain were now thoroughly dismayed by events in the Mediterranean. On 14 October both Germany and Austria agreed to counsel Turkey to accept Italy's peace terms.[143] On 15 October Britain reached a similar decision;[144] and at 6 p.m. that evening a preliminary accord was initialled at Ouchy.[145] Three days later the Treaty of Lausanne was formally signed.[146] The Great Powers hastened, in predictable order, to recognise Italy's ownership of Libya; first Germany and Austria, then Russia and Britain, and last France.[147] Bertolini was rewarded with an offer of the position of first Italian Minister of Colonies.[148]

It was ironical, given the firmness which he had displayed in contrast to many of his advisers, that Giolitti had still not satisfied everyone. The Nationalists, as usual, were reminded by the peace that Italy had not behaved heroically enough.[149] Journalists like

Albertini and politicians like Sonnino also preferred to remember their criticisms of Giolitti's methods rather than their delight at Italy's triumphant expansion of her Empire. Giolitti, however, could enjoy his own moment of triumph in that still loyally Giolittian forum, the Italian parliament. In the Chamber of Deputies, the Treaty of Lausanne was ratified by 395 to 25 on 26 October, and, in the Senate, by 157 to 2 on 14 December.

Giolitti was perhaps fortunate in obtaining so victorious a conclusion. By September 1912, Italy's unofficial and official diplomacy had not progressed far towards finding an exit from the Libyan War. The door to peace had not been opened by Italian arms but by the military action of the small Balkan states. Moreover, the cost of victory was high. Neither Italy's social unity, nor her future military power had been given stronger foundations by participation in a colonial campaign. Hegemony over dissident intellectuals had not been won back by the Liberal state. Equally unfortunate were the diplomatic ramifications. The Balkan Wars, which Italian action had indirectly done much to unleash, damaged the Concert, and both frightened and annoyed Austria. All in all, there was a heavy price to pay in the long run for the assuaging of some of Italy's colonial ambition in the sands of Libya.

That was in the long run. In the short term, the Libyan War, and even its diplomatic results, greatly increased Italian confidence. At last there was a time when '*l'Italia farà da sè*' had proved an apt phrase. Certainly, on a personal level, San Giuliano soon imbibed this new draught of confidence. Shrugging off his personal disappointments of July, and forgetting his diplomatic timidity of September–October, on 31 October San Giuliano drafted a long memorandum to all Italian diplomatic agents which detailed the glories of Italy's victory. Now was the moment to emphasise to all Italians abroad 'the bonds of brotherhood', which united them to the '*madre patria*'. 'The situation of the Exchequer,' he boasted,

the revenues of the State, the level of savings, the financial and industrial concerns, trade abroad, public works, State railways, electricity stations, the improvements of our greatest port, the progress of Rome, the Capital, the condition of public health and hygiene –

all could be cited as matters of pride so that 'our brothers in all the world' can see 'how fine it has been to feel themselves and to show themselves Italian'. They were sons of a country which was 'strong in the enterprise of war, hard-working and fecund'.[150]

Buoyed up by the experience of presiding over diplomacy while Italy actually won a colonial war, San Giuliano had come close to introducing into the making of diplomacy the rhetoric which he had used when out of office. The Libyan crisis had also shown to San Giuliano that his basic assumptions about international diplomacy were right. Austria, and France as well, were the Powers most likely to challenge Italian pretensions to be a Great Power. Relations with either of these States were never likely to be cordial in the fullest sense of the word. Events had also shown that when the other Great Powers were as seriously involved as they had been in the Moroccan crisis, and would be in the Balkan Wars, they found it less easy than usual to restrain Italian ambition by public rebuke.

The war over, Giolitti's supervision of foreign affairs was reduced. He had enough problems to consider at home, where an easy but slow transference to democracy had not been helped by the stresses provoked by military action. San Giuliano, more confident than in the past, now could run most of his own diplomacy, assisted by staff of his own stamp at the *Consulta*, where, in the early days of November 1912, he effected the changes which brought Giacomo De Martino III, his 'valorous collaborator', to the powerful position of Secretary-General. Moreover, there were many opportunities left for diplomatists to plot the planting of future bases for the greatness of the 'Third Italy'. The Triple Alliance had to be renewed. Some replacement for the Prinetti–Barrère, Prinetti–Lansdowne and Racconigi arrangements should perhaps be negotiated with Italy's 'friends' in the Triple Entente. A method of handing back, or retaining, the Dodecanese had to be found. There was the question of Albania. Now that the Libyan problem was out of the way, there would be new economic possibilities in the Ottoman Empire, especially in Asia Minor. There was always Ethiopia to be kept in mind. In each of these areas, in the last two years before the First World War, San Giuliano, De Martino and their associates made Italian diplomacy more busily intrusive than ever before.

CHAPTER 7

The politics of alliance: Italy in the Triple Alliance, 1912–1914

'A pointless farce'[1] – the blunt summation by General Conrad von Hötzendorf of the value and character of Italy's membership of the Triple Alliance is corroborated by events. Italy, after only the briefest hesitation, did not join her allies in war in August 1914, and before that month was out negotiations had begun on the terms by which Italy would instead enter the war on the Triple Entente side against her old allies.

The firm base of our foreign policy is, as is well known, the Triple Alliance...I am able to affirm that no point of disagreement...[between Italy and Austria] can be seen on the horizon today, with respect to any great international questions.[2]

In retrospect, San Giuliano's words to the Chamber of Deputies in December 1910, repeated in similar phrases at almost weekly intervals in the following three and a half years, seem almost ludicrously false, another example of Italy's habitual diplomatic deviousness and dishonesty.

Yet the issue is by no means so clear. Indeed, it is controversial enough to have encouraged a greater volume of analysis and commentary than any other aspect of Italian foreign policy just before the First World War. Interpretations have varied considerably. The major Austrian diplomatic historian, A. F. Pribram, writing in the 1920s, agreed with Conrad that the Triple Alliance was always worked in Italy's favour, and that Italy never had any intention of loyally limiting her ambitions within it.[3] Italian historians on the other hand have been inclined to defend San Giuliano's triplicism as part of his nationalist achievement,[4] or to regret that the Liberal regime had not been tough-minded enough to see Austria's essential perfidy, and to 'prepare' Italy better for the 'inevitable' Austrian attack. Salvemini and Albertini presented the other side of this coin by condemning San Giuliano both for triplicism and for confusion, for generally failing to take up early enough a public stance hostile to the aggressive intentions of Germany and Austria. There have been more sophisticated arguments. Luigi Salvatorelli, in the first major Italian study of the Triple Alliance, argued that the alliance differed from many other treaties in that it had greater 'elasticity'.[5] To begin with, the German–Austrian relationship, formed already into a bilateral alliance in 1879, was always different from Italo-German or Italo-Austrian relations, so that even though by 1913 the Triple Alliance had grown more solid than it had been for decades, that basic 'elasticity' remained. All Italian historians are in agreement that the Italian abandonment of the alliance in 1914 was not a betrayal, but a valid interpretation of the Treaty, given Austro-German actions in the July crisis.[6]

Too much discussion of the Triple Alliance has been set in terms of morality, judging who betrayed whom, and in its corollary, legalism, searching for an 'accurate assessment' of the meaning of the treaty's clauses, especially Article VII, with its promise of no alteration in the Balkan *status quo* without compensation. The point which needs, rather, to be explained and emphasised is the basic distinction between the assumptions of Italy's diplomacy, in day to day actions, while peace between the Great Powers continued, and her likely policy if ever again Europe was to see a general war.

The concentration by Italian or Austrian historians on defending their own country's policies has also distorted the nature of the alliance, and the way it fitted into the context of the European Concert. In their earnest patriotism, such historians forget the obvious fact that the ultimate centre of the Triple Alliance was not in Rome or Vienna, but in Berlin. Italy was the weakest of the Great Powers, Austria, the second weakest. In assessing the Triple Alliance, it is often German policy which first demands clarification – more needs to be known about German motivation in preserving Austria as a 'noble second', and keeping up the appearance of tolerating Italian membership in the Triple Alliance, despite Italy's manifold *giri di walzer*. One reason for the longevity of the Triple Alliance was certainly a negative one – by 1910 Britain (and France) usually understood that Italy was best left a member of the Triple Alliance, and, indeed, Italy's many invitations to seduction were blandly ignored in London where clear minds knew that the existing division of the Concert was preferable to any likely *rimpasto*. There were positive reasons for Imperial Germany working along with Austria since the 'brotherhood' of the 'German Powers' averted any danger of the breakup of Austria–Hungary, and the subsequent influx into a Greater Germany of Vienna's Catholics and socialists. Italy had no such positive attractions domestically, and, even in international affairs, her old role of a contact with London was unconvincing in the state of diplomacy just before the First World War. Therefore, in any final analysis, Germany retained the Triple Alliance, and could still be gentlemanly to her Italian client, simply because her efforts to precipitate diplomatic changes in the Concert had failed so dismally in 1906, 1908–9 and 1911. As a 'Great Power', Italy had to be somewhere; she was Germany's ally because no other country wanted her, and because Germany had been unable to force another country to replace her; Italy's membership of the Triple Alliance was a *pis aller*.

Within the Triple Alliance there was also the problem that, however much Austria relied on Germany in all respects, and however much Italy did in day-to-day diplomacy, both Powers from time to time sought to assert their independence, to ask Germany not to be too suffocating in her patronage. One corollary of efforts at independence by Austria or Italy was, almost inevitably, an effort to draw closer to the other ally, that is an improvement in the bilateral Austro-Italian relationship. On the Austrian side this was particularly noticeable during the career of Aehrenthal. Before the Bosnia–Herzegovina crisis and later during the Libyan War, Aehrenthal favoured better Austro-Italian relations as a method of increasing his freedom of action from Berlin.[7] The Italian situation was more complicated, but similar. From 1910 to 1914, and especially in 1912–13, San Giuliano emphasised improved Italo-Austrian relations as a means of demonstrating Italian independence from Berlin as well as from Paris and London. It is perhaps evidence of the distortion in the Concert in the last years before 1914 that each of the two weakest among the Great Powers should pursue similar policies at much the same time. It says much, too, of the ambiguities and failure of German policy that Austria and Italy were not pulled into line by use of the prestige of Germany's overwhelming power.

The Triple Alliance was first signed in 1882 and then amplified in successive renewals. In 1887 the key Article VII was added, particular reference to Albania being decided in 1900 in a bilateral Italo-Austrian exchange. In 1902 the Treaty was renewed, and again for a fifth time in 1912, the eventual expiry date by then being 1926.[8]

Italy's original membership of the Triple Alliance had been, to a considerable degree, accidental. Reconciliation with Austria occurred largely because of short-term irritation with France, after the French took Tunis in 1881. Bismarck, too, viewed the arrangement with Italy with more than usual cynicism, first encouraging the French move to Tunis, and then using Italy in the Triple Alliance as a sort of messenger boy to Britain. Italy's role in this regard was especially plain in the Mediterranean negotiations of 1887, promoted by Bismarck as part of his complicated structure to ensure French isolation.[9] When Italy tried to act as a Great Power, and put on the clothes of imperialism in Africa from 1887 to 1896, she received little sympathy from Berlin. Under Crispi, Italian policy was centred on hostility to France, and trying to shake patron Britain into attention of her client long enough to precipitate definite rewards for Italy. Thus Crispi passed for a triplicist more because of Britain's close ties with the Triple Alliance at that time than from any assistance offered by Berlin to Italy's African ambitions.

After Visconti Venosta began the *ravvicinamento* with France in 1897, Italy's evocations of the Triple Alliance became less frequent. Italy's new policy of 'friends' and 'allies', to back up her general low profile on the international scene, was made plain in the successive agreements of 1900 and 1902 with France, the 1900 agreement with Austria on Albania and the 1902 renewal of the Triple Alliance. The fact that the Triple Alliance was renewed a mere two days before the Prinetti–Barrère exchanges of 30 June 1902 was a good index of Italy's total unreliability should there be a general European crisis. Parallel to this diplomatising, in 1901 King Victor Emmanuel III and his Chief of Staff, Saletta, in talks with the German military attaché appeared to admit the difficulty of Italian troops serving outside their own country. Perhaps not altogether understanding the gap between military and foreign policy in Italy, the Germans thereupon abandoned their previous hopes that the Triple Alliance meant that Italian troops would be ready, if needed, to serve on the Rhine.[10] Saletta, by contrast, believed that a possibility of Italian troops associating with Germany still existed, and even that

Italy might have to violate the neutrality of Switzerland in order to have a maximum impact on a war against France.

By 1902 Lord Salisbury was by no means the only European statesman who believed Italy to be a '*quantité négligeable*'. Bülow, the German Chancellor, polished his aristocratic sarcasm on Italy by noting that the Triple Alliance could tolerate Italy's *giri di walzer*, since it was known that the 'wife' would remain loyal to the 'marriage' as she had nowhere better to go.[11] The general contempt then felt towards Italy was all the more clearly displayed by the fact that Bülow, a *littérateur* with classical interests, ex-ambassador to Rome, married to an Italian, was in temperament and sentiment just the sort of European politician who usually over-valued Italy out of respect for the glories of the three Rs (Rome, Renaissance and Risorgimento) of Italy's past.[12]

After 1905 it was widely accepted that Italy was little more than a member of the Triple Alliance *pro forma*. Her embarrassment between 'friends' and 'allies' in the Algeciras and Bosnia–Herzegovina crises did little to change this appearance. If anything, Britain's *rapprochement* with France, and the creation of the Triple Entente still further undermined the likelihood that Italy would ever be a loyal soldier of the Triple Alliance. That at Racconigi Italy even signed an entente with Russia completed the picture.

Yet, most likely in the short term, there were also factors working in the other direction. The very creation and use of a second international bloc, the Triple Entente, lent new respectability to the older Triple Alliance, potentially to Italy's advantage. In day-to-day diplomacy the manifest deterioration of Germany's direct relationship with Britain made it possible to imagine that Italy's original value as a line to London could be revived. Moreover, as long as Germany continued to be unable to decide the priorities of her foreign policy between rivalry to France or Russia or Britain, Italy could hope to be an intermediary, and even, ideally, a paid one. For the Germany who found her policies were making her always more unpopular, an unreliable Italian friend and ally, for the time being, was better than no friend or ally at all.

Changes in Austrian foreign policy by 1910 also meant that Vienna took Italy more seriously than before as a diplomatic aide. Austria's entente with Russia over the Balkans had been destroyed by the annexation of Bosnia and Herzegovina. For the moment, if

Austria wanted to be anything more than a German puppet, then Italy became the logical ally in Balkan affairs. It was characteristic of Austrian, as well as Italian, diplomacy that the Racconigi meetings were followed rapidly in November 1909 by Tittoni–Aehrenthal exchanges agreeing on an 'explanation and supplement' to the Triple Alliance which pledged new cooperation in the Balkans.[13]

It is important not to assess the Triple Alliance too much under the influence of what happened in 1914–15. Although war eventually occurred, most diplomatic action before 1914 was posited on the continuation of peace. In peacetime, and in the ordinary labour of diplomacy, the Triple Alliance had acquired a certain vitality from the simple fact that it had survived so long.

Of course no treaty functions purely in legal or diplomatic terms. What were the domestic factors encouraging the survival, and also the fragility, of the Triple Alliance? In so far as the weakness of the Triple Alliance is concerned, the most notorious and important problem was irredentism, the fact that Austria–Hungary continued to rule in Trento and Trieste, Istria and Dalmatia, a population which was partially Italian. Irredentist movements remained active in these territories, with nourishment from Italy, into the twentieth century.

However, by 1910, irredentism was weakening, at least on the surface, and certainly was changing. The Risorgimento had been won against Austria, the 'old tyrant', the 'hated *tedeschi*'; after Italy was united, it was natural that this hostility to Austria should continue. Indeed, the lack of a genuine social revolution in the creation of the Liberal State made the teaching of the myths of the Risorgimento all the more important. Certainly, state education had to do all possible to obscure the fact that Austrians had not been particularly unpopular masters before 1848, and, in most objective senses, had governed Tuscany and Lombardy better than the Italians themselves managed after 1860.

Nonetheless, the need to oppose Austria was soon diffused by other matters. The move to 'common sense' conservatism was symbolised by the very signature of the Triple Alliance in 1882, and, after that, public irredentism became the cause of the dissatisfied heirs of the Risorgimento, Jacobin radicals and Mazzinians, who often associated their irredentism with a general attack on the institutions of the Savoyard monarchy.[14] Irredentism was married to republicanism and was therefore officially regarded with as much worthy horror by the Italian ruling classes as was subversive catholicism or subversive socialism.

If republican irredentism contained strands both hostile and favourable to the Triple Alliance so too did the newer variety of Nationalist irredentism, which was beginning to appear in pre-1914 Trieste and Fiume. As a prelude to provincial fascism, the cities of Venezia Giulia were already producing middle-class, Italian, 'squads',[15] financed by Italian businessmen, who detected advantages in combating Slovene workers, perhaps less because they were Slovenes than because they were workers, and workers whose Socialist votes were treated sympathetically by the Austrian Governor of Trieste, the 'Red Prince' Conrad von Hohenlohe-Waldenburg-Schillingsfürst.[16] The local *triestini* reaction against Austria's pro-Slovene policies led to a renewed sympathy for irredentism, and promised an eventual merger with nationalism and fascism. Nonetheless, before 1914, matters had not proceeded so far. Most *triestini* viewed their struggle as one occurring within the Habsburg Empire and disliked the prospect of being 'saved' by Italy.[17] There were some Italian irredentists already attracted to the Nationalist movement, but their standard bearer, Piero Foscari, a Venetian entrepreneur who saw himself as the heir of the Doges in Dalmatia, and who combined commercial, social, patriotic and personal rivalry with Austria,[18] was more a pleasing link to the past than the man who dominated the Nationalist group. Rather, for most Nationalists before August 1914, imperialism was more important than irredentism; an imperialism to be conducted in harness with Austria (and more important, with Germany), and against France, and, perhaps eventually, Britain.

Beyond the Nationalists, newer and more genuinely popular forces in Italian society were by no means irredentist, as they by no means accepted the Liberal delineation of the myths of the Risorgimento. Organised political Catholicism, naturally enough, was pro-Austrian. At the most simple level, the Pope and his hierarchy preferred the solid piety of Franz Joseph's monarchy to the 'godless' anti-clericals of Republican France. *Osservatore Romano* did not even find particular fault when, in August 1913, Prince Hohenlohe issued his famous decrees, expelling from employment in Trieste all the *regnicoli*, Italian citizens who found working inside the Habsburg Empire more profitable or comfortable than it was in the Kingdom of Italy.

In contrast to the middle-class Jacobin irredentism of some radicals, Italian socialism also was not particularly hostile to the Triple Alliance. The German S.P.D. was the most admired of Socialist parties, and Italian Socialists had many ties with their comrades in the Habsburg Empire. In Trieste, the birth of middle-class nationalist squads had not been celebrated by the local Italian Socialists who were led by V. Pittoni. Pittoni declared nationalism a 'political narcosis', and distinguished 'bourgeois irredentism', which thirsted for war, from 'proletarian irredentism', which knew the cost of war, and instead favoured progress to socialism through a federation of peoples.[19] Between 1905 and 1914 a kind of unofficial parallel Socialist Triple Alliance was created with negotiations, meetings, and even virtual treaties between Pittoni, Adler, the Socialist leader in Vienna, and Bissolati, and later Turati in Rome. Not all Socialists agreed with this reformist fabianism, just as not all Socialists agreed with their leadership's usual failure before 1912 to have a very strong line on foreign policy. The demagogic and radical intellectuals of the party, of whom the young *'professore'* Mussolini counted himself one, often flirted with irredentism as a way of demonstrating that they were carrying on the torch of Mazzini and the other anti-establishment heroes of the Risorgimento.[20]

However unimportant irredentism was as a public force by 1914, however much it had been overtaken by social and diplomatic events, it must not be imagined that serious Italian statesmen had in fact abandoned the desire to regain Trieste and the Trentino. Rather, this desire always remained the most basic one in all Italian diplomacy should there ever be a war. There is no particular reason to believe that Giolitti or San Giuliano were exceptions to this rule, nor were the staff of the Foreign Ministry. Daniele Varè tells a story, which like so many of his, *se non è vera è ben trovata*. He recounts that, while a bored young attaché at the *Consulta* in 1907, he was copying and deciphering judicial notices, when suddenly he happened to notice a document dealing with citizens in the commune of...Trieste!

Suddenly all my sleepiness vanished and I stared open-mouthed at the name of the locality where the notification had to be effected...So, in the year of grace 1907, the Imperial and Royal authorities admitted that Trieste belonged to Italy! All our irredentist aspirations were considered legitimate? Alas! It was merely a clerical error. Before the Italian flag could float over the castle of San Giusto, the greatest war in history had still to be fought and won. So the document [concerned]...was returned to the Ballplatz. I prepared a covering Note, with the remark that 'there was no commune in Italy of the name Trieste'. As I copied it out, I wondered what would happen if this innocent phrase were preceded by the words 'as yet'.[21]

Thus although Italo-Austrian relations blossomed between 1910 and 1914, there was something unnatural about the spring. A war party flourished around General Conrad and Archduke Franz Ferdinand in Vienna, and Italy knew it.[22] For both Powers 'friendship' was very often a way simply of claiming German attention. And, in any case, as shall be illustrated in successive pages, Italo-Austrian diplomatic collaboration in the Adriatic, or in Asia Minor, very often concealed a more deep-seated and abiding political and economic cold war between the Powers in those very areas.

If a study of domestic political factors amplifies but does not alter the evident ambiguities of Italy's relationships inside the Triple Alliance, what of commercial affairs? Here again, conspiracies have been detected, long term factors have been analysed. In the most common theory, first enunciated during the *intervento*, then with the motivation of damning Giolitti, commentators from F. S. Nitti to the Nationalist, E. M. Gray, alleged that the Giolittian regime had been propped up by German business.[23] Italy, it was claimed, moved back towards the Triple Alliance before 1914 because of the hidden pressure of German financiers and industrialists.

In attributing hidden motives, it is as well to begin by remembering Sir Edward Grey's caution:

A Minister beset with the administrative work of a great Office must often be astounded to read of the carefully laid plans, the deep, unrevealed motives that critics or admirers attribute to him. Onlookers free from responsibility have time to invent, and they attribute to Ministers many things that Ministers have no time to invent for themselves, even if they are clever enough to be able to do it.'[24]

Grey, himself a railway director, was perhaps a little too palpably ingenuous (he was often irritatingly so) but what he had to say also had relevance to a Giolitti or a San Giuliano. The further Italy's commercial ties with Germany or Austria are studied, the deeper the investigation of the *sottogoverno* of foreign policy, the less clear become the direct influences on foreign policy.

Table 1. *Trade figures in thousands of lire*

Country	1910	1911	1912	1913
Austria–Hungary				
Imports	289,746	288,914	294,479	264,660
Exports	164,581	184,754	219,191	221,147
Total trade	454,327	433,668	513,670	485,807
Germany				
Imports	524,634	550,159	626,284	612,690
Exports	293,139	301,249	328,236	343,444
Total trade	817,773	851,408	954,520	956,134
France				
Imports	333,957	327,182	289,591	283,356
Exports	218,296	206,168	222,570	231,481
Total trade	552,253	533,350	512,161	514,837
Great Britain				
Imports	476,269	509,831	577,130	591,776
Exports	210,356	222,797	264,406	226,050
Total trade	686,625	732,628	841,536	817,826
United States				
Imports	363,968	415,280	515,347	522,722
Exports	263,816	247,230	261,938	267,892
Total trade	626,784	662,510	777,285	790,614
Total imports	3,245,976	3,389,296	3,701,922	3,645,639
Total exports	2,079,977	2,204,273	2,396,927	2,511,639
Total trade	5,325,953	5,593,569	6,098,849	6,157,278[25]

In overall trade with both Germany and Austria, Italy had a negative balance of payments. However this was endemically true of her commerce with all countries, her budget being restored by the invisible assets of tourism and emigrants' reimbursements. Germany was Italy's largest trading partner, and trade was expanding. But trade with Britain and the United States was not markedly less, and the expansion rate of trade with the United States was greater between 1910 and 1913. Italy's trade with Austria was tending to expand, and was becoming more balanced. The general position can be seen in Table 1.

In the wider sphere, Italian trade in the Balkans and Asia Minor was also increasing, although this increase must be considered in the context that Italy's exports to Serbia, Bulgaria and Romania combined were hardly 2% of her overall trade.[26] The statistics of Italian commerce, therefore, prove nothing at all, except that commercially Italy was as much between the Powers as she was diplomatically.

Advocates of the suffocation theory have not so much concentrated on general trade figures as on more particular areas. The German role in Italian banking, especially as related to Giolitti himself, cannot be gainsaid. Following the collapse of the Banca Romana, the reformation of the Italian banking system was achieved largely on the German model, and with direct German technical and capital assistance. Most important of the new banks was the Banca Commerciale Italiana, which, in the first decade of the twentieth century was intimately concerned in the whole Giolittian system of industrialisation and modernisation. So intimate were the ties between bank and politician that in 1910 it was the capital of the Banca Commerciale which secured for Giolitti the key Roman newspaper, *La Tribuna*, in direct contest with Giolitti's political enemies, Andrea Torre and Luigi Albertini.[27] In the subsequent months both Giolitti and San Giuliano often consulted Otto Joel, the bank's German born director, about particular aspects of foreign policy. Yet Joel was hardly the hidden puppet-master of Italian diplomacy. Often indeed, like many another 'new citizen', he was almost pathetically anxious to prove himself a good Italian. In 1914 in his conversations with Bülow, Joel maintained that Italy could 'not let pass this moment without requesting the territorial advantages to which our people believe themselves to be entitled'.[28] In other words, for Joel as for anyone else, Trieste and the Trentino became, in war, a necessary claim.

If German traditions and expertise had great influence on the Italian banking system, the Banca Commerciale was not the only bank in Italy. It had been the Vatican-financed Banco di Roma which had become most involved in Tripoli before 1911, although it certainly did not dictate Italian policy there. French capital also was attracted to Italy, as it was to other European countries. Eventually Salandra would use French money and skills to favour the creation of the Banca Italiana di Sconto to threaten the Giolittian system, and challenge the role played by the capital of the Banca Commerciale,[29] but, even in these circumstances, the decisions of Italian foreign policy in the *intervento* were not made merely at the behest of French capital.

Beyond banking, German expertise also played a major part in numerous Italian industries before 1914, especially in newer industries such as the electrical and chemical ones. But, in this regard as well, contact and involvement brought in their train challenge as well as imitation, resentment as well as admiration. Using these facts, one commentator has recently turned the 'suffocation' theory on its head, arguing that Italian rejection of German pressure, and direct examples of German dumping,[30] encouraged thoughts about 'autarky', and therefore played a major role in Italy's new enthusiasm for an imperialism competing against Germany. The argument about imperialism is debatable. What is certain is that German economic influence did not directly dictate Italian foreign policy, in either a positive or a negative sense. The functioning of the Triple Alliance from 1910 to 1914 rather occurred within the traditions of Italian foreign and domestic policy as affected by the current state of the European Concert.

San Giuliano, when he regained office in 1910, already had a reputation of being something of a triplicist. His initial friendly exchange with Bethmann Hollweg, and the subsequent meetings in the summer of 1910, first with Bethmann, and later Aehrenthal, confirmed Italy's interest in the Triple Alliance. Indeed, throughout the period from 1910 to 1914, many a commentator would detect that San Giuliano had a weakness for 'the charm of Berlin'.[31] Equally San Giuliano notoriously possessed the most profoundly sarcastic attitude towards the social and political skills of traditional irredentism. It was typical of his political methods and intentions that, in August 1910, he hastened to inform Vienna in advance that the Italian navy would soon commence manoeuvres off Venice, and that the Italian government would use 'all means possible' to prevent on-shore offensive demonstrations against the Habsburg Empire. He even suggested that Italian consuls in Trieste and Innsbruck should restrain over-zealous irredentists from returning to Italy as it was 'the firm desire of the Royal Government to give proof, in this, as in all other circumstances, of its sentiments of absolute loyalty' towards Austria.[32]

In this first year in office, San Giuliano displayed little interest, either, in a forward policy in the Balkans. There was much truth in Avarna's remark to Aehrenthal in January 1911 that Italy found nothing to object to in Austria's Balkan policies, and that the lingering dissidence between the two states was based simply on

Austria's treatment of her Italian minorities.[33] In April, when confronted by troubles in Albania, San Giuliano repeated his belief in a degree of Italo-Austrian cooperation which would exclude

any ambition whatever of territorial gains in Albania and will consider as the basis of...policy the maintenance of the territorial *status quo* and integrity of the Ottoman Empire and of the Balkan states.[34]

The harmony of Italo-Austrian relations should not be sounded in too melodious a way. San Giuliano's greater use of the Triple Alliance in ordinary diplomacy was basically the predictable product of the fiasco into which more passive and pro-French policies had led Italy during the Bosnia–Herzegovina crisis. As ambassador in London, San Giuliano had seen at first hand that Britain (and therefore France) had little to offer Italy at that moment, and were instead hopeful that Italy remain as meekly as possible within the Triple Alliance. In any case, the Italo-Austrian *rapprochement* of 1910–11 continued in minor key, with the discords of the past and the future never far away. Italy was still more worried by rumours of imminent military combat with Austria than with any other state. The irredentist question, if ignored as far as possible, had not gone away. Even in Albania, San Giuliano's appeals for Italo-Austrian cooperation, rendering already a theme to be heard later of direct military association there,[35] were also accompanied by planning in the *Consulta* how best to compete with Austrian influence across the Adriatic.[36]

The equivocation of Italy's triplicism in 1911 was again evident in her decision to go to war with Turkey over Libya. The first major diplomatic impulse for the Libyan War came from the Agadir crisis, and the resultant probability that French ambitions would succeed in Morocco, and that, as a consequence, the Prinetti–Barrère agreement would no longer be valid in Libya. Nevertheless, the immediate spur to action came from rumours reaching Rome in late August and early September that Germany and Austria favoured an early renewal of the Triple Alliance. Fearful that such discussions would mean that Italian gains in Africa would have to be compensated by Austrian gains in the Balkans, a development which would carry the corollary of a domestic underlining that Italy had opted for expansion in the Mediterranean rather than regaining the 'unredeemed' provinces, Giolitti and San Giuliano hastened their preparations for war against Turkey. In going to Libya, Italy acted out of fear both of the friendship of her friends and the alliance of her allies.

The ultimate origins of the suggestion to renew the Triple Alliance are a little obscure. The alliance was not due for renewal until 1914, although there had been a tradition in the past, for example in 1906, to agree early to discuss the continuation of the treaty. There had not been a formal consideration of the clauses of the alliance since 1902, so, almost a decade later, there was good reason on all sides to examine the alliance's validity. There were also personal reasons for action. The Italian ambassador in Vienna, Avarna, was a doughty Austrophile, who regarded the improvement of Austro-Italian relations as his life's work. As early as October 1910, he had tried to interest San Giuliano in a full-scale survey of the Triple Alliance, especially as regarded either the question of compensation under Article VII, or of Italy's traditional special relationship with Britain,[37] the significance of which had been so altered for the Central Powers by international events since 1902. The domestic struggle in Austria between the relatively Italophile Aehrenthal and the known Italophobe Conrad also gave impulse to Italian interest in the renewal of the Triple Alliance.

It is traditional that it was Italy which first hinted at the idea of renewal during the summer of 1911.[38] It may be, as some commentators have averred,[39] that half-hints were made from Rome in order to soften Austro-German objections to Italian preparations against Turkey; but, whatever the case, there can be no doubt that the first clear suggestion of the early renewal came from the Central Powers, as an attempt to stop Italy from acting in Libya. Aehrenthal naturally disliked the prospect of Italian advantage, the Kaiser seems to have been obscurely convinced that Italy was acting as Britain's puppet, and Marschall, Germany's powerful ambassador in Constantinople, was dismayed by the probable effect on Germany's position in Turkey, if Germany's ally, Italy, seized Libya.[40]

Once raised, the idea of a re-affirmation of the Triple Alliance was not likely to be dropped by the Italians. Indeed, on 13 September 1911, with the timetable for action in Libya still not set, San Giuliano had already written a detailed memorandum to Giolitti on the problem. Attributing information on Austrian interest in renewal to Avarna, San Giuliano made plain his belief that Italy should act in Libya before opening general negotiations with the Central Powers, noting obliquely that Italy might be asked to give new guarantees of the Mediterranean *status quo* which could pose great difficulties if Libya were not yet 'resolved'. However San Giuliano also expressed strong support for the idea that Italy should define her attitude to membership of the Triple Alliance by next spring at the latest. Austria, he reasoned, probably had no alternative but to continue the alliance, given what San Giuliano saw as the 'irreducible and fatal antagonism' to her of Russia in the Balkans. This rather negative explication of Austria's general diplomacy was accompanied by an equally negative assessment of the bases of Austro-Italian relations. San Giuliano had 'no doubts on the utility to us of the renewal of the Triple Alliance', but he also believed that there were new signs of a genuine Austrian distrust of Italian irredentism, that ancient hindrance which, contrary to the wishes of Italian statesmen, could still excite Italian public opinion. Irredentism was a nigh hopeless problem, for Austria would not set down a timetable for a cession of the Trentino and the Isonzo valley, and, even if she did, Austria knew that this would not end irredentism.

San Giuliano's exploration so far had been little more than the traditional line of *pis aller*, 'either allies or enemies', but in examining the general international situation he did see some new aspects. Italy's Mediterranean rivalry with France was increasing, he averred, adding a judicious philosophical aside about the tendency of France to military and demographic decline. Russia, he believed, could not soon recover from the 'calamity' of corruption and revolution, and Britain, despite its naval power, was really a defensive Power. In any case, he had learned while ambassador in London that Britain and the Triple Entente did not want Italy. Militarily, even without Italy, the Central Powers would have a probable supremacy over their opponents. Strategic considerations only reinforced the other regrettable fact that Italy would not receive 'sufficient compensation' for her interests if she joined the Triple Entente. Avarna had been not entirely unjustified, San Giuliano concluded, in suggesting that Italy should re-adjust the balance between her friends and her allies.[41]

Although he had not written with limpid clarity, San Giuliano had gone far toward defining the bounds of Italian foreign policy. If Italy wanted to pursue a more active diplomacy, and she did, then, for the moment, there were more prospects of doing so within the Triple Alliance than by leaving it. If Italy wanted to preserve as far as possible her security, and put off the last war of the Risorgimento with Austria, and she did, then, again, the Triple Alliance was more useful to Italy than would be a movement of uncertain end toward the Triple Entente. Italy remained a member of the Triple Alliance in 1911, not especially because of habitual disloyalty, but because there was no serious alternative.

In the days before the Italian ultimatum to Turkey, San Giuliano had made it clear that Italy had accepted the idea of the renewal of the Triple Alliance, but was refraining from positive diplomatic action in order, responsibly, to save embarrassing the German and Austrian position in Constantinople. As Avarna put it, Italy accepted 'in massima' that the Treaty should be renewed, but, in the present conditions, found delineating a mode of procedure difficult.[42]

Once military operations began, it was as unlikely that a renewal of the Triple Alliance could be made, as it was that there could be serious negotiations with the Triple Entente about a Mediterranean pact. From time to time in the next months, there were soundings between the allies, but Germany and Austria were as reluctant as France and Britain to support definitely, or appear to support definitely, either Italy or Turkey.

The greater tendency to action came from Austria. At the very beginning of the Italo-Turkish war, Aehrenthal had made it abundantly clear that Austria would not tolerate Italian action in the Adriatic. Italian verbiage assuaged Aehrenthal's irritation, but Conrad, the Austrian Chief of General Staff, resumed his urging that Austria wage a preventive war against Italy, exploiting the admirable opportunity offered while Italian defences were dispersed by her invasion of Libya. In November 1911 there was an open conflict between Conrad and Aehrenthal, whose friendship for Italy was stimulated by his anxiety to assert Austria's independence from Germany. When, at the end of the month, this conflict was resolved by the dismissal of Conrad, the Emperor, Franz Joseph, explained, still not altogether to the comfort of the advocates of the Triple Alliance:

My policy is a policy of peace...It is possible, even probable that...[an Austro-Italian] war may come about; but it will not be waged until Italy attacks us.[43]

Though Avarna may not have known these details, he was well-enough informed about the general situation, and, in customary collaboration with Pansa, the ambassador in Berlin, he took the opportunity to suggest again that now might be the best moment to renew the Triple Alliance.[44] With indirect but obvious reference to the Conrad affair, Pansa seconded the idea, given the delicate state of Franz Joseph's health, and the fearsome character of his successor, Archduke Franz Ferdinand, a close friend of Conrad, a clerical, who was rumoured to favour the raising of the Slavs in order to balance the Magyars among the nations of the Habsburg Empire, and therefore further to attack Italian pretensions in Trieste and Dalmatia.[45]

San Giuliano, however, was particularly clear-sighted about the opportuneness of renewal while the colonial war continued. He wrote back to his ambassadors that he favoured renewal, since the age and health of Franz Joseph counselled haste, but that such a diplomatic action could not be kept secret. If it was revealed, there might well be objections from Italian 'public opinion' at a time when 'national unanimity' was particularly important. He also feared that such a choice, or apparent choice, in wartime would 'alienate' France and Russia, and arouse pro-Turkish sympathies in Britain. More sinisterly, there were unfortunate potentialities in the discussion of compensation for Austria, arguable under Article VII, or, if that was averted, of binding strategic limitations on Italy's participation in the Triple Alliance. Moreover, there were other, more hopeful reasons to procrastinate – Italy's adamantine decision to follow the Libyan campaign through to its end, and 'at whatever cost' to assert the annexation of Tripoli and Cyrenaica, would ensure, at the end of the war, that Italy had a 'more elevated' international reputation. Then she would be treated with more respect in any negotiations.[46] Perhaps moved by this patriotism, Avarna submitted to the advantages of delay,[47] and Pansa, who had always disliked colonial adventures and was therefore less susceptible than Avarna, reiterated his fears about Franz Ferdinand, but admitted that a serious negotiation of terms could not be made while Italy was at war.[48] From Paris, Tittoni weighed in with the sensible advice that nothing could be done for the moment, but that Italy must hasten to renew the alliance after the war, in order to demonstrate that she was not an adventurist power, and to deflect the zest for war, which he attributed to the Nationalist party, noisy, bold, blown up with pride by the conviction which they have (wrongly, but it matters little) that they were the author of the Tripoli expedition.[49]

During the course of the Libyan War in 1912 the situation remained basically the same. Neither the visit to Rome of the German Secretary of State, Kiderlen Wächter, in January,[50] nor the effusive exchanges prompted by the Kaiser's visit to Venice in March, altered the state of the Triple Alliance. Rather than being offered a renewal, San Giuliano had to endure complaints from both Mérey and Jagow that Italian 'tergivisation' about the ideal method to win triumph in Libya was creating a bad impression. Italy, the ambassadors declared, ought to state plainly that she wanted to put off all discussion of the Triple Alliance until the end of the war. San Giuliano turned this injunction aside with technical suggestions about possible alterations to articles nine and ten of the Triple Alliance, while protesting as usual that he only wanted to be loyal, but that Germany and Austria must remember the susceptibilities of Italian public opinion.[51] Neither the *Carthage* and *Manouba* incidents, nor the death of the sympathetic Aehrenthal on 17 February, brought any change to the independent line of Italian policies. Just as in November 1911 the annexation decree had been decided without reference to Italy's friends or allies, so now the 'accidental' raid on the Dardanelles and the subsequent 'temporary' occupation of the Dodecanese paid no attention to the wishes of other Powers. As for the graver symptoms produced by these blows towards the heart of the Ottoman Empire, San Giuliano asserted bluntly to his ambassadors that Balkan troubles had nothing to do with Italian actions in the Aegean, but were the result of 'events of years long past'.[52]

It has sometimes been argued that the distance between Italy's actions and those desired by the Central Powers during the Libyan War damaged the Triple Alliance beyond repair.[53] Yet, however unilateral were Italian policies, and however much Italian freedom was disliked in Vienna and Berlin, the end of the war at once returned the Triple Alliance to the position which it had reached in September 1911. Indeed, the hostility of Austrian public opinion, and the pro-Turkish plotting, especially of Marschall and Wangenheim in Constantinople, merely presented San Giuliano with weapons from the past when, in subsequent months, he wanted to combat allegations of Italian disloyalty. Avarna had quickly detected the levity of Berchtold, but he knew as well that Austria had not abandoned the desire to pursue policies of her own accord, an independence which suited Italy.[54]

The events surrounding the last days of the war indicated considerable vitality left in the Triple Alliance. It was France, not Germany, nor Austria, which delayed recognising the Italian victory. Berchtold rather took the opportunity to visit Italy, and, at Pisa, was given what was described as the warmest reception received by an Austrian minister for twenty-five years.[55] This moving event, and common sense, signified the pressing need that Italy re-examine the question of the renewal of the Triple Alliance. The outbreak of the Balkan Wars, and the peril, at once evident, that Serbian advantage could provoke Austrian action, made continuing Italian membership of the Triple Alliance still more important. The phrase 'either enemies or allies' would remain the absolute basis of Italian policy, as long as the Balkan conflict continued, and while Austrian 'intransigence' still threatened what San Giuliano called euphemistically a *'pericolosissimo'* development.[56]

San Giuliano was not slow to see the ramifications for his diplomacy. Mérey, compounding his usual lack of timing with a failure to obey the most elementary diplomatic courtesies, as soon as Berchtold had gone home to Vienna, told San Giuliano abruptly that the Triple Alliance should not be renewed before the Balkan Wars ended, as otherwise Austria would only present Italy with limitless opportunities to talk about compensation. San Giuliano who, a month previously, had remarked on the need to watch Austrian reaction to any Balkan outbreak, used the opportunity to point out that Mérey was apparently acting on his own initiative, and that Italy was most anxious to act in harmony with Austria as long as it was understood that Italy, too, had Balkan interests.[57] San Giuliano naturally reiterated this opinion to Berlin, and followed the problem up with a personal visit to the German capital. Thence he wrote to Giolitti, that he had found 'complete faith' in Italy from the German government, which had been impressed by his pledges not to sympathise with Serbia against Austria.[58] Germany was either worried or excited by the prospect of an Austrian *coup de main* and Bethmann Hollweg earnestly proclaimed his anxiety that Italy and Austria preserve their *modus vivendi* in Albania.[59] San Giuliano telegraphed Giolitti:

International situation is improving. Our situation very delicate but hope rising that we could guarantee our interests against eventual excessive Austrian claims through continuing to improve our relations with both the allies.[60]

Mérey greeted San Giuliano's return to Rome ungraciously with complaints about Italian public opinion and general policies, but, on 19 November, San Giuliano, sure of German support, formally announced Italy's desire to renew the Triple Alliance.[61] In the next fortnight there were a few minor complications; the German ambassador, Jagow, tried to establish the significance of the apparent gap between government policy and Italian 'public opinion', which was regrettably cheering the victories being won by the Balkan powers;[62] and there were alarming rumours that irredentists would use the moment to protest against Austrian repression;[63] San Giuliano, on his behalf, was worried lest the Central Powers renounce their previous guarantee of the North African *status quo*.[64] But basically the negotiations were amicable, and by 2 December Jagow even shed his previous fears that Italian public opinion would seriously sympathise with Serbia. Two days later, San Giuliano learned from Mérey that Berchtold desired 'to continue to proceed in intimate agreement with Italy' in the Balkans,[65] and that it had been mutually agreed to favour a Great Power conference on the Balkans to assemble in London. On 5 December the Triple Alliance was formally renewed.

Finally achieved almost eighteen months after it was first raised, the renewal did not mark a change in the traditions of Italian foreign policy. Indeed, no serious Italian statesman could have refused or sensibly delayed the renewal of the alliance, given Italy's military preoccupations in Libya, and the urgent need to encourage as far as possible peaceful cooperation with Austria over Balkan alarums. In the immediate circumstances of December 1912, the accompanying desire to act more independently, to play a middle role between friends and allies, had a secondary influence.

The Triple Alliance remained a diplomatic arrangement likely to work in peace and not in war. None of the ultimate inconsistencies were resolved by the renewal. That irredentism remained an issue hidden rather than overcome, was plain in Avarna's letters during the very days of the renewal. In Austria, Franz Ferdinand remained the heir to the throne and a feared 'enemy' of Italy. Worse, on 12 December, a mere week after the renewal, Conrad von Hötzendorf resumed the position of Chief of General Staff, though for the moment his war–mongering was directed more against Serbia than Italy. San Giuliano, too, was most careful that the re-signature of the Triple Alliance did not cut Italy's wire to London, or even to Paris. On 10 December he told Barrère that the Triple Alliance contained no new clauses, and, more importantly, that it was compatible with Italy's other Mediterranean agreements.[66] The Prinetti–Barrère accords were not denounced; Italy would continue to have 'friends' as well as 'allies'.

In renewing the Triple Alliance on 5 December 1912, San Giuliano was not a partner in, and probably did not know of, the current German pledges of unswerving loyalty to Austria should she be troubled by Serbia or Russia, and of the German discussions, at the highest level, which many historians have regarded as heralding a major step towards the deliberate provocation of a preventive war in the East.[67] Ironically, in so far as Italy's claims to be a Great Power were concerned, there is also no evidence that Germany, even as she graciously renewed the Triple Alliance, was pondering deeply about Italian hopes and fears in diplomacy, or how Italy could be most suitably rewarded in a war.

On the military and naval level, in contrast to the subtleties and independence of her diplomacy, Italy offered comfort and even conceivably encouragement to German ambition. Pollio, the Italian Chief of General Staff, had a tidy mind, and, in December 1912, prompted perhaps by a German hint of interest in reviving military talks,[68] he used the announcement of the renewal of the Triple Alliance to probe into the accretions of time on Italy's military and naval arrangements with Germany and Austria. Recognising Italy's exhaustion from the Libyan War, and the military commitment still needed in Libya, where the signature of the Treaty of Lausanne had not been accompanied by an Arab surrender to Italian 'pacification', Pollio admitted, what the Germans thought Saletta had declared long ago, that Italy could not promise to send troops to the Rhine as envisaged by an Italo-German convention in 1888.[69] However, at the same time, Pollio wrote privately to his German counterpart, von Moltke, promising immediate Italian mobilisation alongside Germany; if a *casus foederis* arose, Italy would move energetically against the Alpine border with France, and perhaps the Italian Navy would disembark troops in Provence.[70]

Pollio also encouraged the ambitious, and sometimes anti-French

Naval Chief of Staff, Thaon di Revel, to raise again the idea of a Triple Alliance Naval Convention, first initialled in December 1901, but subsequently allowed to become a dead letter.[71] In June 1913, after long discussions in Vienna,[72] an Italo-Austro-German naval agreement was signed, envisaging cooperation between the Triple Alliance fleets in war against the Triple Entente.[73] With German support, Italy was able to persuade the Austrians to agree that their fleet should leave the Adriatic in war-time and unite with the Italians off Messina, in order to save the Tyrrhenian coast from French attack. The convention was duly ratified and came into effect on 1 November 1913. Thaon di Revel, supported by the new Navy Minister, Millo, the youthful hero of the raid on the Dardanelles, pressed ahead in private talks with the Austrians, contemplating, for example, a possible joint blockade against Greece. In 1914 technical cooperation grew still closer. By July of that year Germany was preparing a joint signal book for use by Triple Alliance fleets, and intelligence had been circulated about the possible 'enemy', Britain and France. Italy's planned naval manoeuvres for Autumn 1914 involved some combined exercises with Austria, envisaging France as Italy's opponent.[74]

There were similar devopments on the military side. In September 1913 Pollio attended the German manoeuvres, and managed to impress Conrad, who, as a 'loyal second', was also there, with his devotion to the Triple Alliance. After the manoeuvres, the three Chiefs of General Staff met, under the presidency of the Kaiser, to discuss again Italy's possible military contribution to her allies. To the amazement of his colleagues, Pollio expatiated on the necessity that 'the Triple Alliance must act as one State'. Another amateur political philosopher, Pollio explained that the next war would be 'terrible', and a veritable struggle for 'existence'. In this Darwinian *Götterdamerung*, Italy would have two spare divisions of cavalry which could be put under the Germans on the Rhine. By December, Pollio, still more expansively, had left the possibility open that Italian troops would be sent against Russia.[75]

Back in Rome, Pollio received the endorsement of King Victor Emmanuel, Giolitti and San Giuliano for these plans, which, in March, 1914, were extended into a formal promise that Italy would send two cavalry divisions to the Rhine in the event of a conflict. Their passage to the front, it now seemed, would have to be through

Austria, for Swiss neutrality was to be 'severely respected'. The Italian forces were to be positioned on the left wing of the German Army in anticipation of offensive action between Épinal and Belfort. In April a convention was signed in Vienna agreeing to the transport of this army across Austrian territory to Germany.[76] And, indeed, during the July Crisis formal military preparations against France were put in process on 29 July and were not stopped until 3 August.[77]

What is the historian to make of these naval and military arrangements which appear to imply a grave Italian commitment to the Triple Alliance? The answer is probably very little, except to highlight the strange role played by the military in Liberal Italy, and the basic failure of Italian diplomatists to accept Clausewitz's dictum that war is a natural state for mankind. Despite the technical agreements with the Central Powers, such military preparations as were made by Italy in the period 1908–1914 were directed towards her north-eastern borders[78] and were strictly defensive. Similarly, despite the recurring squabbles with France, Italian Dreadnoughts were constructed in rivalry with Austria.[79] Thaon di Revel, more clear-sighted than Pollio, or perhaps forced nearer to realism by the existence of the British Navy, tried to interest Salandra in a clarification of the relationship between technical planning and financial means for the Navy,[80] and even while the naval talks with the Central Powers were in progress Thaon had remained a little sceptical about the relevance of such strategic 'planning'. The discussions were extraordinarily wide-ranging, including, in a matter-of-fact way, not only such grandiose ambitions as the seizure of French North African colonies, but also an attack on Malta and the acceptance of the French bombardment of Savona, Genoa, Livorno and Elba. Another piece of bravado or rhetoric dismissed the significance of the Russian fleet on the evidence that it would take 'ten or twelve' days to reach the battle zone. Still more incredible was the easy Italian concession that the combined Italo-Austrian fleets, once joined off Messina, should be commanded by the Austrian Admiral Haus.[81] Either the Italian naval staff was afflicted by a short-war illusion of quite stupendous proportions, or the negotiations went so far and so easily because in their hearts neither the Italians nor the Austrians really believed in them. If this was so, it still remains puzzling that statesmen so adroit as Giolitti and San Giuliano should both know and not oppose the new agreements with the Central Powers. No doubt Italian diplomacy was always likely to be tortuous – both Giolitti and San Giuliano could recall that the previous military and naval talks with Germany and Austria had occurred from 1900 to 1902, the years of the exchanges with Barrère and of the culmination of the *rapprochement* with France.[82] Certainly, in 1913–14, in so far as planning for war was concerned neither Giolitti nor San Giuliano were able or perhaps anxious to iron the equivocations out of the policy of the least of the Great Powers.

For, as always, Italian diplomacy remained posited on peace. It is characteristic that, despite enormous and increasing expenditure on armaments just before the First World War, Italy showed few signs of catching up with the Greater Powers.[83] Nor did Salandra's Italy resolve the ancient necessity for the Army to preserve law and order at home. In July 1914, the Minister of War, Grandi, reflecting on the wastage of military resources during the *settimana rossa* (and on the continuing 'pacification' of Libya), protested that, despite the huge military vote, there were scarcely enough funds for the Army to afford to keep public order.[84]

Making still more hallucinatory Pollio's technical schemes was the complete failure of Liberal Italy to develop any unity of planning between her soldiers and her politicians. In the Army itself, in peacetime, it was by no means certain who commanded, the King, the Minister of War, or the Chief of General Staff.[85] All officials, whether civilian or military were extremely jealous of their own prerogatives. Pollio was most anxious to exclude civilians from his discussions with Moltke and Conrad. In return, politicians and diplomats treated soldiers with contempt. San Giuliano and his predecessors did not reveal the terms of the Triple Alliance to Pollio,[86] let alone keep him informed of more complicated policy. Military schemes which talked blithely about the *casus foederis* were signed in total ignorance of what the *casus foederis* would be. The only person in a position to change this situation, to unite the diverse strands of Italian military and diplomatic planning, was the King. It is a useful corrective to common allegations that Victor Emmanuel was the hidden hand behind many events in Liberal Italy to note the absence of any evidence that he attempted this logical and urgent task. His acceptance of advice from Pollio to draw closer to the

Central Powers was as 'constitutional' and automatic as his acceptance of advice from Giolitti or San Giuliano. In grave domestic crises, such as those of 1900, 1915, 1922, 1924 and 1943, Victor Emmanuel's power was important in Italy; in normal times it was far less so.

Thus, despite the military and naval conventions, it is in diplomacy that the real temperature of Italian membership of the Triple Alliance must be measured.

The outbreak of the Balkan Wars had at once raised, for all of the Great Powers, but especially for Italy, the question of Austria's reaction to advantage won by the Slav States, Serbia and Montenegro. If Turkish power in the area known as Albania collapsed, then Serbia or Montenegro, or perhaps the two combined, could conquer an Adriatic littoral, escape from Austrian economic tutelage, and threaten a Russian (or perhaps Italian) sponsored naval station in an area of particular Austrian vulnerability. They could also provide a serious rival attraction to the Habsburg Empire's own Slavs. Austrian policy, if somewhat inconsistent under Berchtold's weak guidance, was basically opposed to such an alteration to the Balkan *status quo*. At its simplest, the Austrian solution was to favour the creation of the independent state of Albania, the border of which was to run from Austrian Dalmatia to Greece. On 28 November 1912 Ismail Kemal duly proclaimed Albanian independence relying on Austrian support.[87]

The future independence of Albania had long been an object of interest to Italy. The traditions of the Risorgimento, and the existence of Italo-Albanian communities in Apulia and Sicily, of which Crispi was the most famous son, encouraged a Jacobin, irredentist attention to Albanian affairs. Even in 1911 the closest security watch was kept on Ricciotti Garibaldi lest he lead volunteers across the Adriatic to favour Albanian independence.[88] More serious Italian statesmen were also interested in the area. Both San Giuliano and Guicciardini, for example, had been there, and had reported on the Roman tradition of the province and its obvious strategic relevance to an Adriatic power. For over a decade, a commercial and cultural contest had been fought out in Albania between Italy and Austria,[89] if sometimes in a rather absent-minded fashion. By 1911, the contest was becoming more serious, but it remained one where agents of one Power were inclined to attribute victory or near-victory to the other Power, *pour encourager les gouvernements propres*.

On a strictly legal level, Austria and Italy had agreed, in 1900 and 1909, to recognise their mutual interest, and to pledge that neither Power would seek to surpass the other in Albania. Both instead would favour the *status quo*, the survival of the Turkish adminis-tration. It may be suspected that agreements of this variety are very often made because of the intention of both parties to try to steal a march on the other, but, in 1910–11, despite his previous interest in the area, San Giuliano showed few signs of wanting to deviate from a passive support for the *status quo*. However, in 1911 another of the perennial spring risings in Albania alarmed Rome. In April San Giuliano wrote to Avarna proposing that, if Turkish rule collapsed, and the need arose, Italy and Austria should agree on joint military action, although any such action would necessarily be temporary. As usual, San Giuliano probed nervously at the question whether Austria would mount another sudden *coup de main* in the Balkans. This, Italian 'public opinion' could not tolerate;[90] another Bosnia–Herzegovina affair and San Giuliano would lose office. The *Consulta* remained very anxious about Albania throughout the summer of 1911. In June San Giuliano sufficiently misjudged an alarmist report from Durazzo unilaterally to send the Italian warship *Varese* to that port. Fortunately, Aehrenthal treated the Italian error graciously, though he did take the opportunity to use some appropriate words about 'unfortunate precedents' from Italy's failure to provide Austria with prior information.[91]

During the Libyan War, Italy naturally wanted to avoid all Balkan complications, and San Giuliano paid no public attention to occasional hints of support from Balkan states, such as Montenegro, for Italy's struggle against Turkey.[92] Avarna, too, sometimes added comforting advice that Austria's policy in the Balkans remained 'essentially pacific and based on the maintenance of the *status quo*'.[93] Italian policy, however, was by no means one of complete disinterest. Minor consular agents especially kept up a sniping campaign against Austrian penetration. When, in August 1912, Berchtold made his suggestions to Constantinople for a decentralisation policy in Macedonia, Italy at once asserted her right to be included in any discussions. Carlotti, from Athens, explained that Italy had 'become a [Near] Eastern Power of the first order' in the Balkans,[94] and San

Giuliano wrote hastily to Giolitti emphasising that Austria was trying to ingratiate herself with the Balkan people; despite the Libyan War, Italy should not abandon her 'normal role as a Great Power'.[95]

With the end of the Libyan War, and the simultaneous commencement of general conflict in the Balkans, Italy was naturally at pains to assert her special interest in Albania, as well as her rights or duties as a Great Power. At the same time, there was no reason to believe that Italian policy should not continue to involve diplomatic cooperation with Austria. Italy's squabbles with France, and her staunch desire to keep Greece in her place, both over the Dodecanese and in defining the southern border of Albania, confirmed this policy. Thus, in the first crisis of the Balkan Wars, coinciding with the renewal of the Triple Alliance, Italy had every reason to act in concert with Austria. By 10 December Italy had already been rewarded with Austrian support in condemning Greek moves against Valona.[96] In joining the Conference of Ambassadors assembling in London, Italy enjoyed this Austrian backing; and the prestige of being a Great Power and not a small one. It was unlikely that it would be Italy which would want to renounce her ties with Austria (or Germany) at such a moment.

The problem for Italy in the next months was to diagnose whether or when Austrian hostility to Serbia and Montenegro would turn into armed action. Already, in October 1912, Austria had partially mobilised, to the extent of retaining under colours conscripts due for release after three years service.[97] In the next months, from March to May 1913, in July, in October, and then in January 1914, Austria seriously contemplated military action in the Balkans. On each occasion Italy was put in a most embarrassing position, given her pressing need to work within the Triple Alliance, but also because of the obvious fact, which Scalea had already expressed to Rodd in December 1912, that nothing could be more unwelcome in Italy than being dragged into a war on Austria's side.[98]

In the initial crisis, Italy had soon indicated to Germany that she was not an adamantine opponent to a Serb outlet to the Adriatic, and thoroughly disliked the concept of using force to drive Russia into abandoning her patronage of the Slav peoples of the Balkans.[99] It was following all the customs of Italian foreign policy that San

Giuliano should reiterate, to the German ambassador, Austrian inconsistency and intransigence.[100] Yet, in her own interests, Italy was being as loyal as she could be to Austria. San Giuliano sent detailed instructions to Imperiali in London that he associate with Austria, and, more specifically, that he consult beforehand with the Austrian and German ambassadors, Mensdorff and Lichnowsky, to work out 'a common language and a common attitude' on all Albanian issues. Any differences should be returned to their governments for resolution, rather than being exhibited at the Conference.[101]

Despite this, it was undeniable that some of the equivocations of Italian policy remained. When, in February 1913, Berchtold implicitly rebuked Italy for talking in too friendly a manner to the Russians, San Giuliano's reply was neither 'loyal' nor even conciliatory. Italy and Austria, he declared blandly, should collaborate directly 'to eliminate every cause of mutual dissension and to make the alliance always more popular in both countries'. But there were limits, since he could remember Russia's 'exceptionally friendly' conduct during the Libyan War (in implied contrast with Austria's behaviour at that time). Italy, he added, would stand by Austria at the moment, but 'we could not follow her in an action against Russia over questions in which our action is not bound by any obligation'.[102]

In the privacy of the *Consulta*, San Giuliano had still more complicated thoughts. Noting reports from London on Austria's peremptory demand that Scutari be included in Albania San Giuliano mused that the result of the Balkan War had been a victory for Italy and Russia, as any further Austrian expansion was blocked by the expansion of Serbia and Montenegro. But, he minuted:

this result could be compromised if Austria makes war, and to stop Austria from making it, to stop the military party from prevailing over the pacific tendencies of the Emperor, it is necessary that Austria obtains at least some apparent satisfaction.

There were further reasons why Italy should currently sympathise with Austria. Between Italy and Austria in Albania there was 'a struggle for influence', 'pacific and courteous' but real enough. Now that Serbia, Montenegro and the other Balkan States had won great gains, Italy would not want it to appear in Albania that only

Austria wanted to restrict these gains and defend Albanian ownership of Scutari. That might be fatal to Albanian admiration for, and submissiveness to, Italy. In addition, the Balkans must not be regarded too narrowly for there was the further problem of Asiatic Turkey and the general Mediterranean balance. There, it was necessary

that Austria is not weakened too much and that our relations with her, as a result of this crisis, are reinforced and not damaged, and that Germany becomes aware of the necessity to keep a serious account of the interests of Italy in the problem of the Mediterranean balance.

If Italy gave the appearance of more *giri di walzer*, then Germany might consider only her own interests 'in the day perhaps not too far off' of the collapse of Asiatic Turkey. Given the current position of France, and the stationing of her fleet in the Mediterranean, Italy must not allow Balkan changes to turn her independence into isolation.[103]

It was an opportune time to ponder the full ramifications of national policy, because the military situation in Northern Albania had deteriorated. Serbia and Montenegro had besieged the ruined fortress of Scutari, which Austria was absolutely determined should remain Albanian. Confronted by this rigid stance, the Ambassadors Conference in London overrode Russian objections, and, on 13 March, the Great Powers ordered Serbia and Montenegro to retire. Montenegro, smallest, most obdurate and ambitious of the Balkan States, refused to do so. Germany thereupon proposed that 'one or more' of the Great Powers should carry out a naval demonstration to enforce the decision of the London Conference.[104]

San Giuliano's initial reaction was to joke sarcastically about the likely inadequacy of naval demonstrations against a mountainous country like Montenegro.[105] But there were also far more serious questions involved. What if the mandate was entrusted to Austria alone? What if Austria acted before being formally awarded a mandate? As San Giuliano had very good reason to know, Powers which occupied territories for temporary reasons sometimes stayed there for a long time. Equally, if Austria used force to attain her wishes in Northern Albania, what of the Italian ambitions in Southern Albania (the Dodecanese and Asia Minor), which had been so neatly tied to the Austro–Slav dispute? A conflict over Scutari was fraught with the most perilous potentialities for Italy.

One possible policy might be to lie doggo and pray that the crisis went away. But San Giuliano rejected the attractions of passivity, and instead declared, with a sense of the proprieties of Great Power status, that Italy must reserve her own right to act analogously, should the actions of any power question Italian interests in the Balkans.[106] The implied danger of a direct Italo–Austrian confrontation was lessened when Mérey proposed a joint Italo–Austrian demonstration against the port of Antivari. San Giuliano, who had already mentioned such an action to Berchtold in January, wrote at once to Giolitti suggesting that Italy agree, as 'a territorial occupation on the part of Austria...must be avoided at any cost'.[107] Giolitti, who previously had not shown much interest in Balkan alarums, was not pleased by the idea; perhaps fearing outbursts of irredentism at such public Italo-Austrian collaboration, he telegraphed San Giuliano:

I am absolutely contrary to taking part in a naval demonstration. This will either finish in ridicule if it is not followed by the landing of troops, or it will constitute the beginning of a European war if a military action is begun.[108]

But San Giuliano objected to his Prime Minister's policy of masterly inaction, and warned that, if Austria was allowed to act alone, the result would

compromise our entire situation in Albania and the Adriatic as happened to France in Egypt in 1882, and it would put us, even in matters concerning the Mediterranean, at the mercy of the Triple Entente because our relations with the allies would be compromised for a long time.[109]

There was, therefore, an unusually open difference of opinion between San Giuliano and his Prime Minister, who was again in Piedmont. But, just how real the difference was, is open to debate. Basically, Giolitti was rejecting bilateral action. Yet Germany had requested a mandate from the London Conference for any move by a Great Power, and it is hard to believe that San Giuliano, with his well-known ability at procrastination, would not have waited for a mandate.

Whether this is so or not, San Giuliano, in contrast to his timid yielding in 1911, was now confident enough to turn aside Giolitti's criticisms. His methods were subtle and appropriate. First, he pointed out, with a tidy recognition of constitutional propriety, that the King should be consulted. Next, he declared that both the King and the Minister of War, Spingardi, agreed that Italy must 'not compromise [her] political situation in Albania and in the Adriatic to the exclusive advantage of Austria'.[110] Giolitti, convinced, or aware of subtleties which he had not realised before,[111] now telegraphed that for Italy and Austria to act together on behalf of all the Powers would be justified.

San Giuliano's fertile mind had meanwhile been appraising other alternatives. Perhaps Austria could act against Montenegro; and Italy, separately, but in association, against 'some other part of Albania so that we do not find ourselves in a position of inferiority with respect to Austria'. Seeing the point of Giolitti's objections, San Giuliano also tried to establish without a shadow of doubt German support for a mandate from the Powers. Jagow did agree to make this point in London, although, ominously, given the future, he refused to take any steps in Vienna to dissuade Austria from acting unilaterally.[112]

San Giuliano appealed to Giolitti to return to Rome, but persevered in his belief that Italy must prepare to act. When Giolitti wrote reproaching his Foreign Minister with the allegation that Mérey was trying to provoke a war, San Giuliano replied firmly that Mérey had little influence but that more threatening were 'clerical interests' who were trying to give Austria a 'preponderant position' in Albania as a means of bolstering the Habsburg monarchy.[113] While appearing, ironically enough, almost to be willing to tolerate a war on Austria's side in order to assert Italy's rights in the Adriatic against Austria, San Giuliano worked systematically through the processes of diplomacy to prevent an Austrian coup. On 22 March all his major ambassadors were circularised with a strong note stating that Austrian action without a mandate was contrary to the spirit of the Italo-Austrian accord and would not assist the aims of Italo-Austrian policy. San Giuliano also wrote specifically to St Petersburg warning against the danger of general war.[114]

On 28 March Russia agreed to accept a naval demonstration by the Powers against Montenegro, although Russia would not herself join it. The danger reduced, Giolitti still urged caution, encouraging San Giuliano to advocate a five Power force, rather than just acting with Austria,[115] since, he reiterated, there must be no confrontation between Triple Alliance and Triple Entente. But, expert in the art of bluffing, Montenegro, until a reward was paid cash down, continued to ignore the orders of the Great Powers. A five-Power fleet, commanded, to Italy's pleasure,[116] by an Englishman, assembled off the Albanian coasts on 3 April and, a week later the port of Antivari was tightly blockaded. But Montenegro, with her forces inland before Scutari, was not, as San Giuliano had first prophesied, impressed by a fleet. San Giuliano had proposed the more appropriate way of bribery, money being reputed a sure way to King Nicola's heart, but Italy's suggestions in both Paris and Berlin that Austria pay the Montenegrins to retire, were rejected by the honourable Great Powers.[117] On 23 April the Montenegrin forces broke through the last Turkish defences and occupied Scutari. Montenegro, weakest of the Balkan states, had scorned the panoply of the Great Powers assembled in the naval blockade, and again cast Europe into the most dramatically dangerous condition.

In the weeks before, Austria had grown more and more dismayed and irritated by Montenegrin arrogance. San Giuliano zealously assembled all information which might clarify how far Austria would accept a check to her policy in the Balkans, and much of the information was highly alarming. Germany, Bollati reported on 5 April, would definitely back any Austrian action, since Austria's 'dignity' and 'legitimate interests' could not be allowed to suffer. Bollati, loyal as ever to his allies, deduced that Italy must, in any circumstances, march with the Central Powers.[118] In Rome, Mérey asked bluntly to what extent was Italy willing to cooperate with Austria. But San Giuliano was trying not to define his policies, and, with a certain intrepidity, went on believing that there would be no general war.[119] He fobbed off Mérey with a statement about the limitations of his own authority. By the time he had telegraphed Giolitti to receive approval for the proposal that Italy note her loyalty to previous Italo-Austrian Balkan accords, but reject isolated action which could endanger European peace,[120] San Giuliano could avoid replying to Mérey at all as Grey had announced the formal commencement of the blockade.[121] Just in case there were mistakes San Giuliano had explained to Giolitti, who was still most reluctant to be caught in any crisis on Austria's side, that he well knew the need 'to interpret the *casus foederis* in the way most convenient to free us from any obligation of taking part in a European war', but, San Giuliano repeated, the graver immediate task was to remove the danger of such a war.[122] Moreover, always sensitive to the manifold currents of his policy, he had not forgotten the more easy and congenial tasks of stimulating 'financial compensation' to Montenegro,[123] or of soothing the Russians with the advice that, whatever the present, in the future a Serb-Montenegrin union was 'inevitable'.[124] Nor did San Giuliano forget to remind that ally and patron, Germany, that, by any just standards, Greece's behaviour in South Albania was as relevant as Montenegrin obstinacy in the North.[125]

The murky light cast by these policies flickered, when Montenegro occupied Scutari. Mérey, in outrage, proclaimed that Austria was likely to act even at the cost of a European war, which, he added with little comfort to the Italians, would not last long.[126] Again the opaqueness of Italian diplomacy would have to be adjusted to absorb the twin perils of war, or Austrian unilateral diplomatic (or military) triumph. Unabashed, San Giuliano proceeded with his now customary policies, but there was a new urgency to some of his remarks, at least within the Triple Alliance. Flotow, the German ambassador, had his attention drawn both to the limits of San Giuliano's loyalty given that Giolitti wielded ultimate authority, and to Italy's traditional friendship with Britain, a Great Power which, San Giuliano now reported, Giolitti desired to associate in any Italo-Austrian landing in Albania.[127] More discouragingly still, Mérey was told that Italy could not accept unilateral Austrian military action or diplomatic advantage, and reminded of the compensation clauses in Article VII, a first, gentle hint that Trieste and the Trentino had not been forgotten. If Austria acted alone, San Giuliano murmured icily, Austria must accept the consequences alone and, in these circumstances, even an Italo-Austrian war was not out of the question.[128] Treading more warily elsewhere, San Giuliano instructed Imperiali to state in London that Italian cooperation with Austria could not altogether be discounted because Italy could not tolerate Austria winning a preponderant position in Albania and the Adriatic.[129]

At first, the London Conference seemed helpless before the Montenegrin occupation of Scutari, and by 2 May Austria had begun a *de facto* mobilisation of her forces in Bosnia and Herzegovina.[130] San Giuliano, still cool, reacted by reopening, as an obvious effort to delay Austria, discussions whether Italian cooperation with Austria should be direct or occur in other parts of Albania.[131] It must have been some comfort to learn that both Grey and Sazonov had detected some of the implications of Italian policy and declared that parallel Italian action in the Adriatic would render a great service to peace.[132]

Apart from continuing to ponder and nurture diplomatic opportunities and complications, Italy also had begun military preparations. San Giuliano and Brusati even appealed to Pollio to begin a 'secret mobilisation'. Pollio, justifiably, was baffled by this concept, and took the opportunity to complain again that he was not aware of the character of Italy's treaty relationship with Austria.[133] Nonetheless, some military preparations did commence, and the Italian fleet duly assembled off Sicily, as though Italy were about to go to war against France.[134] Ironically, while the military, confusedly but happily, was acting as though Italy was about nobly to carry a shield for her allies, San Giuliano's diplomacy was separating Italy further from the Central Powers, at least by implication, should there be war. Told abruptly by both Berchtold and Jagow that Italy could not legally apply Article VII to the present crisis, San Giuliano insisted that Italy must be granted 'compensation' for any Austrian profit.[135] Tittoni in Paris wrote words which San Giuliano did not dare to express, but probably nonetheless accepted:

The day in which Austria would try to disturb in any way and by any means the balance of power in the Adriatic, the Triple Alliance would cease to exist.[136]

Rejecting the need yet to accept such an alarming prognosis, San Giuliano merely repeated to his allies that Italy would move in South Albania, with or without Austrian approval.[137]

While San Giuliano's diplomacy was being driven to a more anti-Austrian position in Albania, Italian (and Austrian) military authorities, ignorant of the intricacies of diplomacy, methodically reached an accord on the details of a military action in Albania.[138] France was scarcely gratified to hear rumours of such collaboration and began to speak openly of her objections to an Italo-Austrian division of Albania.[139] Overlooked by all, the character of Albania itself promised hazards which might confront an Italian military expedition to that 'small, muddy town' of Valona – or to its hinterland. Experts in transport in the Italian Army ought to have feared the prospect of invading a country, where as one contemporary journalist put it:

no region of the world except perhaps Tibet and the equatorial jungles has roads in such a shocking condition as does Albania.[140]

All in all, on strategic, political and logistical grounds, San Giuliano ought to have been most relieved when, on 4 May, Montenegro at last agreed to evacuate Scutari. Certainly San Giuliano hastened to point out to the Germans that this event rendered all further military action unnecessary,[141] and disarmed Rodd with the information that Italy did not covet one yard of Albania, and had only been preparing to act in order to secure hostages against Austrian designs.[142] Some days later, San Giuliano was still emphasising to an unimpressed audience that Italy had played a great part in securing peace during the Scutari crisis, and that her moderation had not been sufficiently appreciated; Italy herself had no designs on Valona.[143]

There are so many puzzling features about Italian policy during the Scutari crisis that a commentator despairs altogether of resolving them. Indeed, it can scarcely be believed that San Giuliano himself had resolved all the complications and potential complications. For Italy, the Scutari affair threatened very nearly a re-run of the Bosnia–Herzegovina crisis, and San Giuliano's active if tortuous policies carried as many possibilities of failure as had Tittoni's in 1908. Nonetheless, in the event, San Giuliano's policies did not meet with disaster, and his confidence proved justified that Europe was dealing with a diplomatic and not a military crisis. Whether favoured more by skill or good fortune, San Giuliano's policies had led neither to military adventure nor to diplomatic defeat.

Where did San Giuliano's ultimate loyalties lie in April–May 1913? This question has been often asked without very satisfactory reply. What, for example, should be made of those preparations for armed collaboration with Austria, at a moment when Italian diplomacy was threatening to act independently of Austria, and even against Austria? Immediately after the crisis, San Giuliano, speaking to the British and Germans, congratulated himself on pursuing policies which had averted an Italo-Austrian conflict.[144] Had he only known of later additions to the vocabulary of politics, he might have waxed eloquent about the virtues of Italy's 'complexifying'. In so doing, there can be no doubt that Italy's policy of 'either enemies or allies' reached its most extreme form from March to May 1913, when, to avert a crisis with Austria, Italy was willing to accept or proclaim a loyalty to the Triple Alliance which was at times so steadfast as almost to threaten war with the Triple Entente. The extent of this working within the Triple Alliance is still surprising. Is this then San Giuliano's often notorious 'triplicism' in its naked state?

Such an interpretation is possible, but is predicated on very shifting ground. If Italy was acting within the Triple Alliance, she was also acting very much in her own interests. To begin with, San Giuliano never lost sight of the connection between the Scutari incident and Italian ambitions in the Corfu Channel, in the Dodecanese and in Asia Minor. And San Giuliano also never lost sight of Italy's own direct interests in Albania, for which, one month after the crisis (and despite his pious words to Rodd on 8 May), San Giuliano coined the policy dictum: 'No Power in Albania, but if others [try to] we [go] to Valona immediately.'[145] Before and during the Scutari affair, the *Consulta* increased its efforts to give more definite form to Italian commercial penetration of Albania, and there can be no doubt that this commercial penetration was directed against Austria.

Some other aspects of Italian policy throughout the crisis deserve further comment. It is odd, given their apparent serious difference of opinion, that Giolitti preferred to remain in Piedmont, and not come to Rome in order to give San Giuliano closer guidance. Very probably, the eagerness with which San Giuliano spoke to Mérey and Flotow of his problems with his Prime Minister indicates that San Giuliano (and Giolitti) were using the 'difference' to give Italy policies and not a policy, to render Italy both 'reliable' and 'unreliable' at the same time.

What then was Italian policy about? The most convincing answer is that Italian policy desired at base to delay Austria from acting unilaterally against Montenegro or Serbia. All means could be used to this end, even mobilisation, but Italy at no stage envisaged a war between the Great Powers. The difference between Giolitti and San Giuliano, had the crisis become too ominous, would have allowed Giolitti an escape route by sacking San Giuliano, and resuming 'his own' policies. Thus, there is paradox built upon paradox: Italian loyalty to the Triple Alliance was directed against Austria more than against any other Power, reaching its extreme position at the beginning of May when San Giuliano talked about helping Austria militarily in Albania whether she liked it or not; but, usually, Austria and Germany were meant to understand that Italy could be relied on diplomatically, that San Giuliano could be relied on personally, but that there were limits beyond which Italy could not follow the Central Powers. San Giuliano's curious emphasis during the crisis, especially to Flotow, on personal matters, on his depression and tiredness, on the difficulty of being a loyally triplicist Foreign Minister, amplified this picture. Italian diplomacy, promising military assistance, was reliable as long as military assistance was not really needed, although the Italian military, unaware of even the simplest norms of diplomacy, were themselves willing to act.

If, however half-understood by the protagonists, these were the lines of Italian policy, it must also be said that the use of complications as a delaying technique, accompanied by a pursuit of national interest, led the least of the Great Powers into dangerous territories. If San Giuliano's bluff had been called, either by Germany, or by the Triple Entente, then Italy would have been in a very embarrassing, and possibly perilous position. For what was Italy to do, if some of the other Great Powers did not want to delay, or if they treated Italian 'national interests' with the contempt which they perhaps deserved? What would happen then Italy would discover in another Balkan crisis, one year later, after the assassination of Archduke Franz Ferdinand.

The Montenegrin evacuation of Scutari meanwhile gave only temporary respite from Balkan crises. The victors among the small Balkan states fell out over the Turkish spoils, and in June war broke out anew between Bulgaria on one side, and Serbia, Greece and Romania on the other. Once again Austria's position in the Balkans deteriorated. In these circumstances there occurred the second of the major Balkan crises in 1913–14, the so-called 'Serb war scare' of July 1913 which has won particular notoriety in Italian historiography because of Giolitti's revelation of it in December 1914 as the signal of the beginning of his unsuccessful campaign to remove Salandra from office and put off Italy's entry into World War I.[146]

It seems likely that Giolitti's revelations have given the events of

July 1913 greater importance than they deserve. What Giolitti was looking for in December 1914 was a neat example of the difficulties facing Italo-Austrian relations in 1913. The famous fact that he misdated the crisis by one month illustrates that he was none too choosy about what example it was, as long as it could be depicted dramatically to the Chamber and the press, and would be as embarrassing as possible to Salandra.

As the story later went, in July 1913 San Giuliano, *en route* to Sweden, passed through Germany by train, and there was suddenly informed of an Austrian threat to attack Serbia, because of Serbia's refusal to reach a peace with Bulgaria. San Giuliano's immediate reaction was to tell the Germans that, in these circumstances, the terms in the Triple Alliance of a *casus foederis* would not arise. When he reached Stockholm, he telegraphed Giolitti on 8 July to ask if this was the right policy. Giolitti replied briefly that Italy could not favour such a 'very dangerous adventure' and, as she had no interests involved, must make it clear that an Austrian coup against Serbia could not be a *casus foederis*.[147]

Giolitti's image of Italy nobly restraining Austrian madness is tarnished by the facts that Austria was also receiving no sympathy from Germany, where William II was engaged in one of his recurrent flirtations with Greece, and that Berchtold's plans to support Bulgaria were not favoured by Franz Joseph, who objected to a confrontation with Romania. If Italy seriously believed that Austria was contemplating action, and Mérey had certainly been spreading rumours to that effect in Rome,[148] then Italy was ill-informed.

From the Italian side, what is important is the clarity of the position taken in July 1913, a clarity surprising after the opaqueness of Italy's stance in the Scutari affair. Some significance may be attributed to Giolitti's phrase that no Italian interests were involved in an Austro-Serb clash, in a war away from the Adriatic coast, and from the key area of Albania. Many Italian publicists were not hostile to Serb expansion,[149] and San Giuliano himself was fond of saying, usually to the Germans, that Serb irredentism was unlikely ever to be controlled while Serbs remained within the Habsburg Empire.[150] These comments with their obvious implied reference to the latent problem of Italian irredentism, confirm the validity of the interpretation made above on the tactical and even anti-

Austrian character of Italian loyalty to the Triple Alliance during the Scutari affair.

Italy, then, had made no secret of her likely position should Austro-Serb relations threaten general war. But, on neither side did this halt collaboration either at the Conference of Ambassadors, or in the general diplomacy of the Great Powers towards the Balkans. Austro-Italian diplomatic association was confirmed also by the distance currently existing between Germany and Austria. The vagaries of German policy in the Balkans, especially the attraction exercised on William II by King Constantine of Greece, pleased neither Rome nor Vienna. Despite the plain evidence in July 1913 that Italy would not follow Austria into a European war, despite the reiterated evidence provided, in August, by the Hohenlohe decrees that the irredentist question remained unsolved and unsolvable, despite the constant commercial competition in Albania and Asia Minor, Italy and Austria continued to collaborate with each other in Balkan diplomacy, if only because there was no other way of defending their immediate interests.

The final crisis during the Balkan Wars began on 17 October when Austria issued a unilateral ultimatum to Serbia to get out of areas of Albania as defined by the Great Powers.[151] Italy at first reacted coolly to the Austrian action, pointing out to Berlin and Vienna Italy's 'reservations' about the consequences and dangers of 'reckless' Austrian action against Serbia.[152] But, by 20 October, confronted by renewed German backing for Austria, Italy had associated herself with Austro-German representations in Belgrade. San Giuliano, however, lost no chance to reiterate his view that Greece was as recalcitrant in Southern Albania as Serbia was in the North.[153] By 30 October, Italy, whether by nature or design, had again confused the Austro-Serb issue and persuaded Austria to join with Italy in a summons to Greece to abandon Southern Albania by the end of the year.[154] San Giuliano naturally used the occasion to remind Vienna of the damage done to Italo-Austrian relations by the Hohenlohe decrees, warning Avarna, for example, on 1 November, that Italy would inevitably have to move back closer to France because of Austria's intransigence.[155] He also was happy to remind Germany, privately, that Austria had acted badly towards the Triple Alliance by the peremptoriness of her ultimatum, and could only expect further trouble from Serbia.[156] To the other

Powers, notably France, San Giuliano, with customary exquisite tact and sense of the main chance, preached the unanimity of the Triple Alliance on all Albanian problems. There was not the slightest danger of war between the Great Powers, he noted, with a due assertion of probity, since none wanted it, and, yet, Italy and Austria should not forego their preparations for bilateral armed action as the London Conference might be remiss in enforcing its decisions on the delimitation of Albania's borders in the North, and in the South.[157]

There, it was Greece which was behaving with the immaturity which San Giuliano could have predicted from a small Power. Therefore, he quickly maintained, the precedent of possible Austro-Italian action against Montenegro or Serbia should be adapted to suit Italy's interests, and directed against Greece. On 8 November he wrote to Giolitti that Italy and Austria must again think of joint military or naval action against Greece in early January if Albanian territories were not by then evacuated. He had received from the Navy Minister, Millo, a note that the Naval Staff had a plan ready to act against Greece, but needed to know more details of what was envisaged. Once again, as in the Scutari crisis, San Giuliano argued that combined action by the 'two Great Adriatic Powers' was directed as much against Austria as anything else. Ignoring the obvious fact that Austria had never contemplated acting against Greece, San Giuliano explained that Italy must not allow Austria to act alone as then she would be 'destroying at a blow the edifice on which is built our Adriatic and Albanian policy and ruining our international prestige'.[158]

Having thus, by sleight of hand, turned an Austrian rebuke of Serbia into an Italian challenge to Greece, San Giuliano found some difficulty in preserving the credibility of his magic-making. Germany was already suspicious of Italian policy in Asia Minor and was displaying unpleasant signs of seeking a *rapprochement* with Greece.[159] Austria, too, viewed the role of Italy's 'noble second' in Southern Albania as somewhat demeaning, and on 31 December 1913, the ultimatum to Greece was formally extended for another eighteen days, and then allowed to lapse pending the application of an easy promise by Venizelos that Greece would evacuate Southern Albania. The creation of the Albanian state and the selection of the pro-Austrian William of Wied to be its prince made it newly clear that

Italy's main rival in the Adriatic was not really Serbia nor Montenegro, nor even Greece, but Austria. Thus, in the early months of 1914, a marked coolness was evident in Italy's relationship, with Austria, and within the Triple Alliance.

The ambiguities of the Triple Alliance had never been entirely concealed by the 1912 renewal, or, subsequently by the frequent incidence of Italo-Austrian diplomatic collaboration in the Balkans. To a very considerable degree, the apparent warmth of Italo-Austrian relations throughout 1913 had been caused by the continuation of real war in the Balkans. While the small Powers fought, there was imminent and obvious danger that the Great Powers would join them, and the meaning of the traditional phrase 'either enemies or allies' could be understood even by the simplest mind. Moreover, in the atmosphere of permanent crisis, Austria had remained anxious to be independent of Berlin, and therefore had a further motive to listen, at least sometimes, to Rome. But, with peace of a kind restored in the Balkans, these factors slipped away, and the old tradition of irredentism, and the newer one of commercial rivalry re-emerged. Ironically, the danger of war for Italy as a Great Power increased as open war between the small Balkan states ended.

Commercial and cultural rivalry between Italy and Austria in the Balkans had a long history. For over a decade, the Powers had engaged in an often obscure contest for the economy of Montenegro in which the power of Viennese banking was matched by Italy's royal relationship with King Nicola and Crown Prince Danilo, and by the special business skills[160] of those rebuilders of the Venetian Empire, Piero Foscari and Giuseppe Volpi. As far as Italy was concerned the most glamorous prospect was in Antivari, where Volpi had a contract for port improvements and even, bizarrely, for a tourist hotel to be named the Hotel Marina, doubly symbolic of Volpi's daughter who bore that name, and of the glorious sea-going traditions of Venice.[161] More exciting was a railway contract which could make Antivari the *entrepôt* for much of the trade from the East,[162] although there must be some suspicion that Italy's most honourable motive in entering Balkan railway schemes was merely that of being the least of the Great Powers, and therefore having to be in any scheme, with little reference to such tawdry concerns as completion of railway works or real, as distinct from subsidised, profit. In all railway affairs in the Balkans, Italy, as one commentator has coldly but not inaccurately put it, ran 'true to form, oscillating uneasily between the camp of her allies and the embrace of her friends'.[163]

If Italian involvement with the Slav state of Montenegro had inevitable anti-Austrian overtones, and indicated that Italy had never accepted Austria's objections to Montenegrin or Serb expansion, the heartland of Italo-Austrian rivalry was in Albania. In his philosophising about the coming great struggle of the nations, San Giuliano often remarked that it was on commerce that a modern nation's growth and achievement depended. In the very first of his *Lettere sull'Albania*, written from Brindisi on 28 June 1902, he prophesied that the 'decisive moment' was at hand for Italian interests in Albania.[164] The *status quo* must be preserved as long as possible, but

in the meantime, rather, shipping lines, post offices, consulates, commercial agencies, schools, institutes of charity, insurance, credit, eventual backing for railway construction, in the final analysis, all the peaceful and civil means compatible with a loyal respect for the sovereignty of the Sultan are necessary to maintain and extend our influence in Albania.[165]

Given these opinions, it is no surprise to find San Giuliano, after he became Foreign Minister in 1910, trying to reorganise the commercial side of the *Consulta* and to use business, his 'secular arm', however infant was its development, and however much to work at all it required lifeblood and subsidies from the government. In no area of the world was San Giuliano more anxious to see collaboration develop than in Albania.

In particular the unexpectedly easy triumph in Libya had spurred San Giuliano on to greater confidence in the independence and advantage permitted to Italy as least of the Great Powers. It was therefore in 1913, just as his political diplomacy seemed to be taking Italy more tightly into the embrace of the Triple Alliance, that San Giuliano returned to his emphasis on the need for commercial and cultural expansion in rivalry with Austria. In the very days of the Scutari crisis, while Giolitti worried lest San Giuliano was ready to conceive participating in general war on Austria's side, San Giuliano drew his Prime Minister's attention to economic questions. 'In Albania', he explained,

there is everything to play for and that Power which will know how to take up its position in time both with civil and commercial institutions and with the winning over [literally *accaparramento*, lassooing], of influential persons, will gain a genuine political and economic supremacy.

Italy's rival was, naturally, Austria, which had unfortunately done consistently better than Italy in Albania, by establishing a 'faithful and fanatical clientele'. The government must hand over to the Foreign Ministry 250,000 lire, as a modest estimate, to facilitate the development of a countering influence which was an 'absolute political necessity'.[166] A few days earlier, San Giuliano had already written to Bianchi, the Director-General of Italy's State-owned railways, requesting that he sponsor preliminary studies to allow Italian railway development in Albania.[167] On 6 April San Giuliano repeated to Giolitti his plea for money. Returning to the metaphor of lassooing, San Giuliano observed that Ismail Kemal, the chief of the Provisional Albanian government, had made it known that 20,000 lire would be a useful way to preserve his 'good disposition' towards Italy. If she handed over the sum requested, Italy would only be following Austria which subsidised Albanian personalities 'very considerably'. By 15 April, the money had been found from secret government funds.[168]

Increasingly, San Giuliano was looking to a more considered policy than one merely of occasional bribes. He won collaboration, for example, from Giolitti and Stringher of the Banca d'Italia, in order to achieve an Italian presence in the capital of an Albanian bank. It would be most regrettable, he noted, if Austria was left to have a free hand in investing capital in Albania. Stringher duly bowed to San Giuliano's importunities on the understanding that it was a question of 'great political importance'.[169]

Since the Scutari crisis luckily did not produce a new, Bosnia–Herzegovina style humiliation for Italy, San Giuliano, on 9 May, again approached Giolitti about the 'urgent' problem of extra funds to combat Austria in Albania. There, he explained, all Italy's diplomatic actions must not produce merely a 'platonic' affair, but genuine political supremacy. Readily recalling some of his personal anti-clericalism, San Giuliano declared that, by tradition, Austria used the Roman Catholic Church to spread her influence in Albania, yet Italy could counter that well by exploiting the existence of her own Italo-Albanian community. Repeating his phrases of six weeks earlier, San Giuliano explained again that Austria had built up a 'fanatical clientele', not merely from the convictions of piety but from *largesse* and by sending agents 'to all corners of Albania'. 250,000 lire was thus urgently required. It was far below what

3   Albania and Montenegro

Austria spent, but San Giuliano well understood Italy's pressing need for economy. When the funds were granted he intended to establish a special Albanian office in the *Consulta* under Angelo Scalabrini, the Director General of Schools Abroad. This committee would deal with political, administrative and economic matters and mediate between Italian and Albanian individuals and institutions. These measures, he emphasised, would ensure the maintenance in Albania 'as a matter of fact of that parity with respect to Austria which we claim as a right'.[170] Scalabrini's presence also promised Vatican sympathy in the labour of weaning some Albanian priests from too slavish an admiration for Austria.

For both Italy and Austria, the main agents in the contest for influence were, however, consular officials who dealt with the day to day business of cultural prestige and financial largesse. Italy had agents in Scutari, Janina, Elbassan, Durazzo and Valona, who well understood that Austria was Italy's permanent opponent in the Adriatic.[171] Equally, the stimulating advice which reached Rome was usually that Italy was doing badly in comparison with Austria, or at least had a long way to go. In 1911, for example, Labia, then Consul in Durazzo, reported a long Austrian trade lead over Italy in the territory of Albania, although he did admit that Italy's position had improved in the last decade.[172] It is typical, both of the vagueness of statistics about the area, and also of the variety of semi-colonial cold war existing there, that the Austrians should receive a report from their agents at the same time saying that Italy had surpassed Austria in trade with Albania.[173]

In the summer of 1913, San Giuliano made an interesting new appointment to his consular staff in Albania. To watch over the proceedings of the international force occupying Scutari he sent Carlo Galli, able, literate, with the closest ties to Trieste, a friend of the Nationalists, whom, two years before, San Giuliano had despatched to be his 'last consul' in Tripoli. Interviewing Galli before his departure, San Giuliano made it plain that Austria was Italy's rival in Albania, but, since Italy could hardly attack her ally directly, she should use internationalisation to defend her own interests and avert direct confrontations. 'We must not,' he reasoned, 'ourselves undermine the Triple Alliance but make it work for us.' Austria must not be allowed to essay a coup as she had done in Bosnia–Herzegovina, to prevent such an eventuality was for Italy a matter of 'life and death'.[174]

The style of Italy's working with her 'friend of today' as San Giuliano had described Austria to Galli, was soon further explained to all Italy's consular officials in Albania. Austria, it had been learned, was willing to come to an economic accord, an admission of Italian equality naturally delightful to San Giuliano, as he explained in detail:

in all those affairs which call for a concession and a privilege from the Central Albanian government and which would give to the concession a special economic preponderance in the country, for example in railways, ports, roads, public buildings, communications, privileged banks, mining rights, the exploitation of forests etc. etc.

While negotiations proceeded, and after, the consuls must do all they could in these areas to allow Italy to catch up to Austria.[175]

In the next months examples multiplied of efforts to produce a real Italian presence in Albania. San Giuliano suggested the payment of 30,000 lire to new pro-Italian newspapers at Valona, Durazzo or Elbassan;[176] there was the continuing byzantine tale of Italy's efforts to secure a concession to the forests of the Mirditi in Northern Albania;[177] and by 1914, the *Consulta* would even be building a little file on the financing of a cinema at Scutari, which Galli hoped would combat the two existing Austrian-owned cinemas by showing films with an Italian or Italo-Albanian basis.[178] He did not explain whether any of the latter existed.

It was never very clear whether these descriptions of possible commercial advantage were well matched with reality. Certainly, there is room for doubt in the story of the Mirditi forest concession which involved a Milanese businessman, Vismara, who enjoyed his government subsidies and was a little reluctant to clinch his deals in Albania; and the Albanians, Prince Bib Doda (a man whose local soubriquet was 'Northern Albania's good epicurean')[179] and Abbot Primo Dochi,[180] neither of whom seem to have had clear legal rights to the forests which they offered for exploitation. The ease with which the spectres of Britain, France, Germany, and especially Austria, were raised as rivals to Italy in the deal also stimulates enquiries about the sincerity of the business participants. Bib Doda, too, had wide-ranging political ambitions, and was known to be in touch with the Montenegrins across the border, with a possible view to establishing an autonomous Mirditi state. It was true, however, that age and good-living had tempered Bib Doda's nationalist zeal.

His travels abroad, often to Paris, were reported to have left him with 'a somewhat indolent disposition', although he could still send shivers down listeners' spines by remarking, coolly, at dinner parties:

If Albania is to be ruled peacefully, three persons ought to be hanged: Ismail Kemal, Essad Pasha, and myself. If all three of us were dead, Albania would fare much better.[181]

Despite Bib Doda's obvious drawbacks as a client, and despite his brazen admission that he needed money for the *'divertissements'* of Paris,[182] San Giuliano asked no questions about his or Vismara's financial probity (Vismara's reluctance to be dragged away from a comfortable cure at the spa of Montecatini does not impress as an example of his commercial zeal), and was perfectly happy to scrounge funds for Vismara's deals from the Treasury, the Banca Commerciale or the Banca d'Italia, always giving the explanation that the Mirditi forests were a 'national interest'. Typical was his explanation to Salandra shortly after the fall of the Giolitti government in March 1914:

As you know we have taken in Albania a most noteworthy moral and political stand: and Austria, which has worked for a century with great moral and economic means to establish her supremacy in these regions, has had to recognise our parity both in the economic and political field. But this parity, obtained with great effort, will naturally be annulled in practice...if political action is not supplemented by economic actions...The failure of [the Vismara] business would not only put us in an undignified position towards our rivals who are trying again by every means to oust us, but would destroy at a stroke our prestige in that region, making us look to [Albanian] eyes not only incompetent but poor, two negative qualities for anyone who wishes to exercise influence abroad; influence which in this case has a political importance of the first order.[183]

Despite his reiteration, in almost Marxist language, of the importance of economics, San Giuliano was a traditional Sicilian nobleman who had little real idea how business worked. What he wanted was something which could be seen on paper, and which he could use in his diplomacy to appeal for continued recognition of Italy's rights in Albania, and which would avoid a new Bosnia–Herzegovina.

The sincerity even of such an aim in the long term may also be doubted. In August 1913, San Giuliano's chief of Commercial Affairs in the *Consulta*, Primo Levi, who was an old Crispian with long experience in the Balkans, produced a devastating memorandum declaring that Albania was a wholly artificial state without moral, political, religious, or geographical justification. In the future, Levi wrote ambitiously, the area was destined to play the role between Italy and Austria that the Duchies of Schleswig-Holstein had once played between Austria and Prussia. Naturally, in this contest, Italy's would be the part of Prussia, although for the moment the conflict should be delayed as along as possible. San Giuliano minuted his approval of Primo Levi's ideas, adding that it was in the economic sphere where Italy could best now act. But he remembered the phrase about Schleswig-Holstein and used it to the German ambassador in April 1914, when it was becoming increasingly plain that Triple Alliance unanimity in the Adriatic was breaking down.[184]

In the succeeding months down to July 1914, the *Consulta* kept up its efforts to out-manipulate Austria in Albania by sponsoring some sort of financial coup, or, perhaps, preferably, a series of small financial coups. San Giuliano's underlining showed his approval of a suggestion from Galli that Italy could best outdistance Austria by dogged application. 'Economic penetration', Galli had declared,

is not a matter only of great enterprises and major works, but above all [is won] by the small, continuous and uninterrupted infiltration of little, minute interests, which being less apparent do not induce fear and opposition but on the other hand constitute the solid, secure and indestructible basis of a greater influence.[185]

In October 1913, pointing to the Vismara affair, San Giuliano had reported to Giolitti that Italy was getting better value for her money in Albania than was Austria.[186] During the next month, he wrote congratulating Joel that the Società Commerciale d'Oriente, with finance from the Banca Commerciale, had set up an agency in Scutari. 'The current relations between [the *Società*] and the... government', he wrote graciously, 'have accustomed us to consider it as an essentially Italian institution, which the...government is ready to favour and prefer to others' because of its association with the general cause of 'the economic expansion of Italy.' Trade of such a kind, he noted with emphasis and customary metaphor was 'for us...a kind of *secular arm*'[187] to Italian foreign policy.

In 1914, if anything, San Giuliano's attention to 'little minute interests' increased as Italo-Austrian relations deteriorated. When Austria reduced her postal tariffs in Albania, San Giuliano's pressure at once made Italy do the same.[188] The *Consulta*'s 'secret' Albanian fund rose to 500,000 lire for a year, and De Martino used this generosity to argue that the real need was for 1,000,000.[189] When Austria planned a trading exhibition at Scutari, Italy proclaimed her intention to equal or better it, by using the good offices of the Istituto Coloniale Italiano.[190] On 7 June Galli could report that Italy's National Day had been locally celebrated by an uplifting *festa*. Foscari had promised to create an association which would unite in a solid *fascio* all local Italians and a branch of the Reale Museo Commerciale di Venezia was duly opened that afternoon amid congratulatory telegrams from Chambers of Commerce all over Italy.[191] Back in Rome, when it was revealed that Austria had set up an Austro-Albanian society to popularise Austrian culture and ideas among 'all classes' of Albanian society, De Martino soon drew up a memorandum urging that Italy act similarly. His advice was typical of much of the ambition of Italian foreign policy under San Giuliano. The Austrian committee, he advised, had been drawn largely from the aristocratic and academic worlds, but Italy could do better by relying 'essentially on the financial world' (an argument which earned the marginal note '*giusta*' from San Giuliano).[192] In Albania, the *Consulta* proudly announced, business, culture and diplomacy would unite to give flesh to Italian ambition, but it was business, sponsored, and subsidised, by the government which must come first.

World War broke out before victory could be won by Italy or Austria in the contest for Albania. Before this event, the last days of peace were familiarly devoted to sorting out a particularly bitter dispute between the rival consuls in Durazzo. San Giuliano behaved with what must have been by now natural duplicity. To Aliotti, the Italian consul, San Giuliano was all pacifying wisdom, explaining that momentary difficulties had been caused because Löwenthal, the Austrian representative, had been maligned by the press. Italy's interests, he added gravely, dictated the maintenance of 'good relations with Austria'. But, lest Aliotti grew too moved or incredulous at this noble exhibition of statesmanship, San Giuliano concluded by admitting that an Italian consul's real task was to spread 'our influence without waking...Austrian vigilance'.[193] Message understood San Giuliano duly resisted Austrian pressure that Aliotti be summoned home, and was gratified soon to learn that Löwenthal would be recalled by Vienna.[194] Aliotti remained in office to preach in September that 200,000 Italian colonists could make Albania 'live'.[195]

The story of Italian commercial ambition in Albania during 1913–14 is thus complicated and even, at times, grotesque. For all the plotting in the *Consulta*, for all the grand schemes devised to extend Italian influence, or to activate the 'secular arm', Albania remained a most unpromising area for the expansion of trade let alone of Empire. Apart from the Venetians, Italian capital, given the problems of the economy at home, was reluctant to become too involved in Albania, or elsewhere in the Balkans. By 1914, San Giuliano was obtaining still more money for Vismara's forests from the Banca d'Italia by the curious expedient of talking sternly about 'reasons of international policy', and then not answering more pressing letters from Stringher requesting an explanation of just what had happened to the Bank's money.[196] The Foreign Ministry also met predictable opposition and rivalry when it requested further Treasury funds for Albanian *pour-boires*.[197]

Moreover, the general Albanian situation was not working to Italy's advantage. The Austrian nominee as Prince of Albania, William of Wied, had proved unable to provide any credible administration. But Austria showed marked hostility to his main local opponent, Essad Pasha, who, in return, received sympathy, and probably funds, from Italy.[198] San Giuliano was very embarrassed by the ungovernability of Albania, which continually threatened to expose the inconsistencies and even incompatibilities of his public and private diplomacy. In the spring of 1914 he was left to re-assert his old dictum that Italy must stand diplomatically alongside Austria in Albania, if only thus to stop an Austrian coup in the style of Bosnia–Herzegovina. For this reason, he continued officially to support Wied, although his intelligence had told him that Wied's regime was not likely to last long.[199]

The alternatives remained that, if Austria moved, Italy must 'go at once to Valona', either unilaterally, or with, or even against Austria. By June 1914, in contrast to the past two years, it was beginning to become apparent that it was the last course which was the most likely. By the spring of 1914, Italian diplomacy was challenged by the unpleasant prospect of an ever-deepening Austrian (and German) *rapprochement* with Greece, which threatened to destroy the carefully constructed position which Italy had established not only in Southern Albania, but also in the Dodecanese and Asia Minor. Despite San Giuliano's blunt and rather despairing remark that the Kaiser, the German government and Flotow were the only people since the beginning of history who believed in Greek integrity,[200] Italy was unable to continue to impose the anti-Greek line on her allies. San Giuliano's attempts to revive the atmosphere of the London Conference and organise further international action in Albania were received with a marked lack of enthusiasm in Berlin and London,[201] although, in mid-June, international ships were eventually sent to Durazzo, in order to rescue William of Wied from yet another revolt.

In these circumstances, San Giuliano's strategems began to look more and more hollow. Moreover, Italian policy in Albania had never quite lost the naive, childish, almost petulant, image of imitation imperialism, of a new Roman Empire, not of marble, nor even of tufa, but of *papier maché*, credible only so long as the skies did not become cloudy. After all, even an Italian agricultural and scientific mission to Albania was honest enough to admit that there could be found only political anarchy, an un-navigable transport system, and no social necessities such as schools. 'It seems incredible,' the offical report ran, 'at so few hours' distance from Italy to find oneself in such primitive conditions.'[202] Given the contemporary state of Sicily, Sardinia or Calabria, that was saying something. San Giuliano's Italy had not really found a solution to the problems of planning an imperial future in an unpromising area, with unpromising means, and in an international context that could not always remain promising. For an Italian statesman, it was always important to remember another Varè *bon mot*: 'nothing fails like success'.

In addition, San Giuliano, in 1914, began to talk more and more about an ancient strain in Austro–Italian relations, that is about irredentism, about Italian 'public opinion's' hostility to Austria, about a Liberal State constructed on the myth of the Risorgimento, and therefore needing the ambition of one day gaining Trento and Trieste, almost to justify its own existence. San Giuliano even began to say that his own position as a triplicist Foreign Minister was endangered by criticism from Italian public opinion, although given his frequent ambition to use the state of public opinion in order to contrast his own innocence and reliability with the dangerous world outside, San Giuliano's assessment should be read cautiously. Blessed, he was saying, should be the meek Italian Foreign Minister, who should thus inherit some of the earth now. But there also can be no doubt that by the spring and summer of 1914 irredentism was reviving in Italy, and that it was doing so because the Italo-Austrian *rapprochement* in 1912–13 had never been sincere nor profound enough to strike at the basic issue of contrast between the two countries.

The *Consulta* had always paid strict attention to, or at least been sent, many reports about Austria's treatment of the Italian-speaking population within the Habsburg Empire.[203] An excellent example of the difficulty of compromise lay in the ancient question of the establishment of an Italian university or faculty, either in Vienna or Trieste. Although some arrangement was favoured by the Austrian Ministry of Foreign Affairs, and especially by Aehrenthal, it was blocked by anti-Italian Habsburg officials, and by the general rivalry of the nationalities in the Empire.[204] Before such conflict, no alleviation came from occasional ceremonies of fraternity, such as a football match between the two nations in 1913, attended by Avarna, and solemnly reported to the *Consulta* as arousing friendly feelings in Vienna – perhaps especially because Italy had 'lost but with honour'.[205]

The gravest issue remained Trieste, and Austria's continued patronage of non-Italians in the city and all Dalmatia. Italian consuls never tired of condemning the 'slavicisation' of Italian lands.[206] Patriotic, Establishment groups, like the Dante Alighieri Society, never tired of appealing for government funds to subsidise the defence of *italianità* in Trieste.[207]

However, by 1913, Italian foreign policy was more complex than simply postponing or preparing war against Austria and the Liberal regime had more matters to deal with than preserving the myth of 'redeeming' national borders. But it was precisely at this moment, when, at least superficially, Italy and Austria were acting diplomatically in the closest harmony, that there was another difficulty in Trieste. In August 1913 Prince Conrad von Hohenlohe, the close friend of Archduke Franz Ferdinand[208] and governor of Trieste, issued 'the Hohenlohe decrees' which sacked all Italian citizens from public employment in the city. To almost all Italians, Nationalist or not, such high-handedness merely covered a new Austrian effort to block Italy forever out of her unredeemed patrimony.

San Giuliano at once protested energetically to Vienna,[209] and kept on protesting. He told the Germans that an Italian Minister could not now reciprocate Berchtold's visit to Pisa of the previous year, unless the Hohenlohe decrees were rescinded. All this triplicism for three years had been 'for nothing', San Giuliano declared bitterly, and threatened, implausibly, to test the legality of the decrees at the Hague Court of International Justice, and, more menacingly, to have Italy's prefects instructed that they should be lenient to anti-Austrian demonstrations.[210] Berchtold, seconded by Avarna and Mérey, argued that the decrees were purely an internal affair,[211] but San Giuliano continued to bombard Vienna with reproofs, noting acidly that in a Liberal state like Italy, public opinion could not be controlled. The whole basis of Italy's relationship with Austria and the Triple Alliance, he remarked in mortification, had been undermined.[212]

In the next weeks, the issue showed no signs of disappearing. Rival demonstrations duly occurred in Italy and Austria, and, on 19 September, San Giuliano repeated his message to Berlin and Vienna jointly that the decrees had rendered 'impossible a real friendship between Italy and Austria'.[213] Giolitti himself began to wonder about the best means to save the *italianità* of Trieste.[214] When the Germans replied blandly that they had endeavoured to use their good offices in Vienna, but had not been successful, and that, in the past, the Triple Alliance had overcome greater problems,[215] San Giuliano reacted angrily by renewing discussions with Barrère and Rodd about a Mediterranean agreement, and announcing to the ambassadors of the Central Powers that he had done so. But Germany showed depressingly few signs of being alarmed at this prodding, and San Giuliano was left to grumble that the question had been raised how the continuance of the Triple Alliance could be reconciled with Italy's political structure in being a Liberal, parliamentary state.[216]

It was very difficult to see what Italy could do except protest rhetorically. Italy's Adriatic policy, and beyond that her policy in the Eastern Mediterranean and Asia Minor, had been constructed on the basis of working within the Triple Alliance, at least during the crisis in the Balkans and when the Triple Entente showed no strong desire to want Italy on their side. Thus, while Giolitti and San Giuliano agreed that the Hohenlohe decrees were 'disastrous', San

Giuliano tried to tone down the enveloping hostility of the Italian press.[217] Even San Giuliano's efforts to attract German attention by talking about Italy's fears in the future of the 'Slavic flood', and, therefore, of the continuing need to preserve Austria,[218] did not produce milder Habsburg policies in Trieste.

The failure to resolve the Trieste question, or even attain a reasonable *modus vivendi*, was therefore another reason why Italo-Austrian relations drifted into dissonance in the early months of 1914. Equally, Germany's deafness to Italian appeals over the Hohenlohe decrees was hardly encouraging behaviour from a hoped for patron. There were also other problems which cut away the artifice of the Italo-Austrian *rapprochement*. General Conrad von Hötzendorf had been left in little doubt by the military attaché in Vienna that Austria would not get military support from Italy in the event of war, and that the technical military negotiations were window dressing. The best he could say, pithily, of the Italians was that they were reliable only in the sense that they were reliably unreliable.[219]

On the diplomatic front, San Giuliano took the moment to raise a problem which was not likely to be received with joy in Vienna. Still trying to put off Balkan complications by talking about them, San Giuliano began to say publicly that, in the end, a Serb-Montenegrin union, and thus a Serb outlet to the Adriatic, was 'inevitable'. Despite this, Italy could not accept a countervailing Austrian gain, for example, the seizure of Mount Lovcen and believed emphatically that any Austrian move south would be 'absolutely incompatible' with the Triple Alliance. The only way to avert open Italo-Austrian conflict would be 'compensation' for Italy elsewhere.[220] There was no doubt that 'elsewhere' meant, and was understood to mean, Trieste or the Trentino. Thus the auspices were not good for the meeting at last arranged between Berchtold and San Giuliano, even though it would be held at 'unredeemed' Abbazia on the Adriatic, a concession to Austrian sovereignty by San Giuliano, which had brought formal protests from the Nationalists of the Trento and Trieste Society.[221]

San Giuliano and Berchtold duly began their meeting at Abbazia on 14 April, and continued discussion until the 18th. The tone of the meeting was set at the very beginning when San Giuliano immediately raised the problem of the Hohenlohe decrees, and requested that an Italian law faculty be set up as soon as possible '*in terra italiana*', that is in the 'Italian lands' of the Empire. However Berchtold showed no sign whatever of being accommodating and San Giuliano was left to report gloomily that 'a noteworthy change in such policy on the part of Austria is not to be hoped for, now or for a long time yet'.[222]

On 15 April San Giuliano and Berchtold turned to the general problem of Albania. Berchtold drew attention to the portents of the total collapse of the Ottoman Empire, giving Kaiser William II as his source, but then, irritatingly, from the Italian viewpoint, turned back to the more immediate question of the union of Serbia and Montenegro. Neither Italy nor Austria, Berchtold opined, could approve the Slavicisation of the Adriatic. At least according to his own account, San Giuliano now took the chance to display his notorious cynicism. Serb–Montenegrin union would not mean an extension of Slavism, as they were both Slav anyhow, he remarked brightly. For Italy, the more immediate source of the Slav peril was on Austria's other borders. Having out-witted his dull opponent in dialectics, San Giuliano used the opportunity again to plead that Austria not be so ready to irritate Italian public opinion. The best he could offer on Albania was some stipulation of mutual interests, and he was not attracted by the concept of a general settlement there. By the end of the day, the two ministers were left to mouth platitudes about 'keeping together' in Albania. Most major issues placed, so depressingly, in the 'too hard' basket, the meeting proceeded with technical discussions until, on 18 April, the very last day of the conference, San Giuliano was impelled himself to raise the question of Greece. (To the King he privately expressed his disappointment that it had been Italy and not Austria which had been driven to do this.) Again some kind words were exchanged, but San Giuliano won no success in trying to persuade Berchtold that Italy and Austria should make more detailed plans for military intervention against Greece,[223] and, more generally, in trying to burst asunder the tender new relationship of Greece with the Central Powers.

The Abbazia meeting had produced no open split, but it had made no evident progress. Given the strong negative undercurrent, which had always been close to the surface of the Austro–Italian *rapprochement*, no progress at Abbazia in fact meant that Austria and Italy continued to drift apart. The Italian press, always anxious that Italy achieve ostentatious recognition of her power, was notably critical.[224] An interesting accompaniment was the gradual recognition by diplomatists that Russia would not again easily permit any Austrian *coups de main* in the Balkans. Bollati, from Berlin, had written a long despatch on 15 April pointing out the increased threat of general war from future Balkan troubles and although his advice remained that Italy should work within the Triple Alliance, he resolved no dilemmas by adding that, in a general war, Italy must naturally get the Trentino and other Italian-speaking lands.[225]

Despite a continued willingness to use phrases like 'the Slavic flood' to select audiences within the Triple Alliance,[226] San Giuliano's policy had long aimed not against Russia but rather to delay any Austrian coups. But, at Abbazia, Berchtold had hardly risen to the familiar bait of Italy's association of the Southern Albania, Greek problem with the Northern, Slav issue. Back in Rome, San Giuliano did not hide his disappointment that 'nothing' had been achieved at Abbazia.[227] Indeed, in the next weeks, Italian policy showed every sign of hardening against Austria: discussions on the Trieste question remained brusque;[228] in Albania, though he acknowledged Aliotti's bad behaviour, San Giuliano took no steps to recall him; to the Germans, he again stated that Italy could not permit any Austrian move against Mount Lovcen.[229] From 1 May the old safety valve of the Mediterranean pacts was again pressed into action, after San Giuliano complained to Flotow that Italy's loyalty to the Triple Alliance in the Adriatic had damaged Italy's traditional friendship with Britain.[230]

Thus, although, in mid-June 1914, Italy's desperate efforts to preserve the façade of the Concert in Albania were rewarded with the despatch of an international fleet to Durazzo, the Italo-Austrian relationship, and Italy's position within the Triple Alliance, was more fragile than it had been at any time since 1910. San Giuliano was devoting much work to reviving recognition of Italian importance, especially in Berlin, but, on 13 June, asked by Flotow whether there were circumstances in which Italy could tolerate Austrian gains in the Balkans, either if Albania was partitioned between Serbia and Greece, or directly between Italy and Austria, San Giuliano himself dared to say what was always obvious but never stated: if Italy was to get compensation anywhere, it should come in the 'Italian lands' of the Habsburg Empire.[231] Unfortunately for San Giuliano, once again the Germans were unimpressed, as they had been by his revelations about a new Mediterranean or North African agreement. By the last weeks of June 1914, San Giuliano had been left to make accustomed and rather half-hearted recourse to telling Flotow that it was only the noble Foreign Minister, who preserved the Triple Alliance, obstructed by Salandra, who was not 'in his heart' pro-Austrian, and by the press and the Chamber, by a public opinion which was 'the real sovereign' in Italy.[232]

In general, therefore, by the summer of 1914, the Triple Alliance was not working well for Italy. Despite the continuing military exchanges and even Pollio's apparent conversion to the attractions of preventive war, be it against Russia or even Britain,[233] Italian diplomacy was moving away from both Austria and Germany. For Austria, the end of the Balkan Wars saw the disappearance of the most urgent reasons to continue to accept collaboration, procrastination and restraint from Italy, and the ever-present troubles in Trieste did nothing to improve matters. Odder perhaps is Germany's failure, by May–June 1914, to pay attention any more to Italian blandishments, to treat Italy seriously as an equal member of the Triple Alliance. The easy German acceptance, and indeed support for the revived Mediterranean talks was a strange sign of a new impatience by Germany toward the eternal subtleties of her ally. It was almost as though, by decision or by lack of decision, Germany had said to herself that it was time that international relations became simpler and clearer.

Clarity and simplicity were, naturally, the last qualities San Giuliano wanted applied to Italy's international position. In June and July 1914, he did his best to save Italy from the exposure which would come from the establishment of clear lines within the Concert. On 28 June 1914 he was given new grounds for hope with the death of Franz Ferdinand, the Italophobe friend and patron of Conrad von Hötzendorf and Hohenlohe. The death of the Austrian Heir Apparent also meant the end of another of Italy's numerous frustrating efforts to regain the national artistic patrimony,[234] since Franz Ferdinand, in recent years, had stubbornly resisted efforts by the Italian State to buy from him the baroque Villa d'Este at Tivoli. In any event San Giuliano was gratified enough by the news from

Sarajevo to exercise his wit. He telephoned Salandra, his dull Prime
Minister, who was at work, that Sunday afternoon, on State papers:

'Is that you Salandra? Do you know what? We're free of that tiresome affair of
the Villa d'Este.'
 'What's that?'
 'This morning at Sarajevo they've assassinated the Archduke Franz
Ferdinand.'[235]

Though history has made this into the most famous example of San
Giuliano's sarcasm, it is not the best example of his profundity. For
Italy would receive more than the Villa d'Este from the events which
would follow the assassination of Archduke Franz Ferdinand.

Between 1910 and 1914, and especially during the course of the
Balkan Wars in 1912–13, Italy had attempted to activate her role
in the Triple Alliance, as part of her efforts generally to follow a
less 'remissive' foreign policy. In Albania, as in Asia Minor, Italy
strove for a public recognition of her interests, both present and
future, by proclaiming her loyalty to the Triple Alliance, even, in
the Scutari crisis, and after, to the extent of contemplating, and
certainly having it known that there was contemplated, military
action in some form of association with Austria. Yet this triplicism
never became too blind or simple. Difficult though it is to distinguish
all the multifarious strands of San Giuliano's policies, and difficult
though it may be sometimes to believe that he himself, or Giolitti,
understood, or was in control of, all these strands, it is nevertheless
evident that San Giuliano's triplicism was always accompanied by
doubts and reservations. One constant accompaniment for example,
with links to the Dodecanese and Asia Minor, was Italy's determination to assert her superiority over Greece, as a 'Great Power'
should against a 'small Power'. Despite occasional rhetoric to the
contrary, San Giuliano always had it clear in his own mind that
for Italy the Greek peril was more an immediate problem than any
Slav threat; and Italy's position towards Greece was completely
different to Germany's, or, by June 1914, to Austria's.

There were also other, still graver reservations within Italy's
long-term loyalty to the Triple Alliance. For all his adroitness, San
Giuliano could never overcome, nor really hope to overcome, the
nationalist problem at the root of the Hohenlohe decrees. In 1914,
the concept of a Liberal Italy, constructed by a Risorgimento against

Austria, and still incomplete, was too strong to be removed, despite some currents to the contrary. Italy's economic ambition, and especially what San Giuliano hoped, after appropriate subsidy from the government, would become Italy's economic ambition, also presaged a conflict with Austria which was not likely to be overcome, and which San Giuliano did not, in the final analysis, aim to overcome.

From 1912 to 1914, San Giuliano hoped that he was improving Italy's position in the Concert of the Great Powers should the 'great struggle between the nations' come nearer. As the Triple Entente Powers showed no desire to help him in this task, it was natural that most of his diplomacy was conducted within the Triple Alliance. His weapon in forging a better power base for Italy was to assert an imperial destiny to go with the old national one as justification for being a Great Power, and build the foundation of an Italian Empire in Libya, Albania, Asia Minor, the Dodecanese, even Ethiopia. But the bricks of Italian imperialism were too obviously made of straw, or better, of memoranda on paper, for minds as realistic as those of San Giuliano, Giolitti, or other Liberal statesmen, not to accept in their innermost corners that, in a real crisis, if peace turned into war, Lake Tsana was not as important as Trieste, nor the mines of Eraclea as significant as the banks of the Isonzo. Imperialist triplicism was a new, short-term, diplomatic, peacetime policy; but the 'completion of the Risorgimento', if ever the opportunity came with war, was, in many ways, what Liberal Italy had always been, and was still about.

CHAPTER 8

The politics of friendship – Italy, the Triple Entente, and the search for a new Mediterranean agreement, 1911–1914

On 2 August 1914 King Victor Emmanuel III initialled military plans for action by Italy on her north-western borders, that is against France.[1] That very day the Italian government was preparing its declaration of neutrality, which was issued the next morning. After this decision had been made public, San Giuliano talked frankly with Olindo Malagodi, *direttore* of *La Tribuna*. Italy had not joined her Triple Alliance partners in war, he explained, because British naval strength had to be recognised as the *force majeure*: 'our decision depended necessarily on that of England'.[2]

No doubt the contrasting royal initials were more a product of the automatic machinery of bureaucracy than the serious making of foreign policy around a strategic plan. Yet, the apposition of potential military conflict with France, and wholly necessary naval peace with Britain, is most striking. At the great crisis point, with war imminent, with the most crucial foreign policy decision in her history demanded, Liberal Italy acted as though a contest with Britain was out of the question, but a fight with France was possible, and perhaps not unattractive.

Many Italian statesmen of the post-Risorgimento regime would not have been surprised at that apposition. If sometimes obscured by the greater threat from Austria, the strand of hostility to France had been a constant one in Italian diplomacy since unification. The questions of Trento and Trieste always carried the extra danger of exacerbating domestic irredentism, and thus Mazzinian republicanism hostile to the Savoyard regime. But any Italian government looking to the Mediterranean immediately ran into the rivalry of France, that 'Latin sister' often dubbed the *sorellastra*, the nasty step-sister, by sensitive Italians. Then, the loss of Tunis in 1881, of Nice in 1860 and of Corsica in 1768[3] were recalled as rankling memories. There was much that was consistent in Italy's foreign policy towards France from 1860 to 1914, and beyond.

Italy, the least of the Great Powers

Yet, in contrast to 1860 or 1890, by 1912 much had changed in the general European diplomatic context in which the Franco–Italian relationship was set. In 1860 and 1890, Cavour and Crispi had been able to count on the fact that France was Britain's major European rival; in 1912, France and Britain were all but official allies.

Italy's relations with her 'friends' of the Triple Entente had thus become at least as complicated as those with her allies in the Triple Alliance. *Entente Cordiale* would perhaps be more accurate a description of this grouping than Triple Entente, because Italy's relations with Russia remained distant. Back in 1898, San Giuliano may have predicted that the great struggle of the future would be between the Anglo-Saxon and Slav races,[4] but that prediction looked unlikely after 1907. From 1910 to 1914, San Giuliano may have occasionally talked of a growing Slav peril, and may even have read of the fears of Roberto Michels, that Trieste could one day be claimed as an outpost of a Slovene state or a Slav empire,[5] but in his diplomacy San Giuliano gaily used Russia as likely friend or dangerous enemy depending on his immediate needs. Both he and Giolitti seem to have clung more tenaciously than most European statesmen to the belief that the Russian Empire was emasculated by the defeat in 1905 and by its continued domestic troubles, or, as San Giuliano put it wittily, that Russia was the great '*impotenza*'.[6] Russo-Italian relations were not much assisted by Anatol Nicholaievich Krupenski, the Russian ambassador to Rome, who was described by the admittedly malicious Bülow as 'known all over Europe in diplomacy for his huge nose, deep voice, and impetuous gestures'.[7] It was perhaps the last quality which most worried San Giuliano, who, in the *intervento*, would make plain his belief that Italy should avoid dealings with Krupenski, who could not be trusted to understand what matters Italy wanted made public and what never revealed.[8] From 1912 to 1914, San Giuliano made no effort to renew the relationship achieved at Racconigi in 1909, and Italo-Russian relations were left to the fertile but somewhat capricious minds of Tittoni and Izvolsky, the architects of Racconigi who now, as ambassadors in Paris, like twin souls, plotted their own triumphant reappearances as Foreign Ministers.[9]

With Russia basically discounted as a major present Power, Italy's diplomatic world was bound largely by her contacts with Britain and France on the one side, and Germany and Austria on the other. Within this world, the familiar problem remained that Britain and

Germany, the two more powerful states, who were the richer and potentially more accommodating patrons, persistently drifted into deeper dissidence. No diplomatic or military masterpiece could be constructed whereby Italy could be seated at a victor's table, and consume at once Trento, Trieste, Albania, Corsica, Nice, Tunis and pieces of the Ottoman Empire. Indeed, far more likely was the embarrassing prospect that in war either France or Austria could use their powerful allies to rob Italy even of dreams of grandeur. Italian policy was thus complicated and complicating, and dependent on peace.

In the 1890s Italy had quarrelled bitterly with France, as Crispi looked to build an African Empire. The external result of Crispi's policies was Adowa; the internal result was the worsening of economic depression during a trade war between the 'Latin sisters'. After Crispi's fall, Italian statesmen strove to mend fences with France, recognising that Italy's European bargaining position was extremely weak. This softening in Italian attitudes coincided with the accession to the French Foreign Ministry of Théophile Delcassé, and the passage in 1898 to the Rome Embassy of the ex-Gambettist, Camille Barrère. Delcassé and his diplomatic circle were engaged in gradually pushing France into reconciliation with Britain, and to a reinforced acceptance of the old view that Germany was France's major potential enemy. The corollary was the '*ravvicinamento*' or *rapprochement* between Italy and France, cemented in exchanges between Barrère and the Italian Foreign Ministers, Visconti Venosta and Prinetti, in December 1900 and June 1902.

In the next years, Tittoni's policy of low profile preserved this *ravvicinamento* with France. Contemporaries spoke of the witty and tough-minded Barrère as the hand behind much Italian policy, for example during the Algeciras Conference. To some later commentators it has seemed that by 1909 Italy's Mediterranean policy had been converted into an Adriatic one 'by the work of Barrère'.[10]

This is an exaggeration. The relative calm of Italo-French relations in the first decade of the new century was deceptive, having more to do with Tittoni's and Giolitti's definition of Italy's immediate needs, and to successive French governments' definitions of their needs, than to any long-term change. An enhanced display of nationalism by either country would soon raise for Italy the familiar problem of France's greater Mediterranean power.

The rise of Poincaré in France by 1911 soon made Barrère's job more difficult in Rome. San Giuliano's Southern traditions also made him no native friend of France. As a boy, he had written anti-French odes; as a young politician, he had rejected the aims neither of Crispi's Africanism nor of economic conflict with France. No Southern Italian diplomatist had ever liked the fact that at least the Western Mediterranean was France's *mare nostrum*. Moreover a tired nobleman, an aristocrat of Norman blood who 'knew his times', saw little to bring him joy in the 'democracy' or republicanism of France.

These personal factors perhaps had some influence. Barrère rapidly lost ground as Rome's favourite ambassador. If anyone was to be caustically witty at the *Consulta* from 1910 to 1914 it was to be San Giuliano, not the French ambassador. Yet, as usual, San Giuliano was acting inside the traditions and needs of Italian foreign policy and in accord with the spirit of his times. Illustrative of how inevitable were disputes with France, once passivity was abandoned, is a long despatch sent by Tittoni from Paris in January 1911. The erstwhile 'agent of Barrère' now argued that for France 'Mediterranean supremacy and colonial expansion have become the real substance of foreign policy'. All recent diplomatic developments, but especially the *Entente Cordiale*, had turned French expansionism towards the Mediterranean: 'And with this [situation] in the Mediterranean the ring of iron is bound...always more tightly about us.'[11] It was this sort of fear which later in the year helped encourage Italy to go to Libya. French success in Morocco had to be accompanied by compensation for Italy in Libya.

Nonetheless, even in these circumstances diplomacy did not act alone, unaffected by other domestic currents. In the fields of business, the press and public opinion, streams ran muddy and able to be diverted, as was predictable in the Italian situation, but also carrying matter hostile to France.

The economic impulse behind Italian policy, be it in the imperial realms of Asia Minor, or, more directly, affecting Italy's relationship with Austria or France, is a particularly unclear and debated one. On the simplest level, Italian trade with France had increased steadily since the end of Crispi's tariff war, although it never regained pre-1890 levels. In overall terms, it was considerably less than Italian trade with Germany, but a little more than that with Austria.[12] In any case the volume of trade is not a particularly important index. Italy's commercial dependence on Germany brought competition and resentment as well as knowledge and friendship. Pre-1914 France exported finance more than she did industrial products, and this was especially true with regard to Italy. French concerns held about three-quarters of the Italian national debt,[13] which was always increasing, given Italy's chronic imbalance of payments.

In contrast to government borrowing, since 1894, Italian private banking had relied most on German money and expertise. The Banca Commerciale with its German origins was 'Giolitti's bank'; Joel, Toeplitz and Stringher, with their German sounding names were Giolitti's bankers. It was rather the *nouveaux* Perrone brothers of the Ansaldo company who looked to France.[14] That Ansaldo also provided finance for *L'Idea Nazionale*,[15] in peace-time strident critic of France and, in the July crisis, at first zealous advocate that Italy do its duty, join the Triple Alliance and fight France, does not corroborate arguments that in pre-1914 Italy there was a neat connection between economic affairs and foreign policy. Pierre Milza is surely right to argue that there was no single-minded economic motivation behind Italy's change of policy in the *intervento*.[16]

The realm of opinion is still more amorphous. Was Liberal Italy, 'by nature', a friend of France, or of Germany? This question has proved very hard to define. There is some evidence uniting Italy to the empires to her north. For example, many historians have seen similarity between the plans of Giolitti in 1911 for universal suffrage and nationalised life insurance, and the earlier 'state socialism' of Bismarck. Whether this be true or not, there is evidence that Giolitti admired the 'efficiency' which many contemporaries mistakenly saw in the Wilhelmine Reich.[17] But too much should not be made of passing comments by the Prime Minister who was an essentially parochial figure, if anything more Piedmontese than Italian. For society, similar equivocations were present. San Giuliano personally was more at home in Berlin than in Paris or London. Italy was also, of course, a monarchy, and on gala occasions such as the *Cinquantennio*, Italy's self-definition seemed nearer to the states 'imperial and royal' than to Republican France. King Victor Emmanuel himself, with monarchical sagacity, can be found warning that the untrustworthy French habitually tried to place Italy in an *imbroglio*.[18] But all this sort of evidence is of fleeting significance;

Italian society was more parochial, more *sui generis*, than a devotee of Paris or Berlin or Vienna. Italy was neither an empire, nor an absolute monarchy. King Victor Emmanuel, the son of an Italian who had married his own cousin, the husband of a Montenegrin princess, was neither socially, physically nor indeed intellectually likely to want to join the yachting expeditions at Cowes of the grand-children of Queen Victoria. Nor was the presence of the Savoys much desired at many royal gatherings. The Kaiser, who was less restricted by taste and manners than many European princes, openly called Victor Emmanuel 'the dwarf' or 'the little thief' and Elena 'the daughter of a Black Mountain cattle thief',[19] and, indeed, it was very doubtful if Queen Elena had enough quarterings of nobility to be properly invited to one of Archduke Frederick's more respectable Habsburg balls in Vienna.

If the Savoy family gave little assistance to Italian pretensions to Great Power status, the Italian aristocracy was also not well known in the salons of 'Europe before the lamps went out'. Few Italians mixed freely at Marienbad or Monte Carlo. The Southerners were often too poor, concentrating instead on making the Italian bureaucracy their own. The Romans were too 'black', more loyal to the Papacy than to the Liberal state. In Northern Italy, the post-Risorgimento regime was based more on notables, as in France, than on land owning aristocracy.

Paradoxes and recurrent parochialism also recur in the attitudes to foreigners of Italian intellectuals. Croce read Marx and Hegel, and tried to systematise Italian thought into the patterns of German philosophy. But to many Italian intellectuals, Paris was still *the* City. In the decade before 1914, D'Annunzio, who was almost the only figure in the Italian literary world to gain fame outside his country's borders, spent much time in France, and, even in the year of the *Cinquantennio*, preferred that his scandalous *Death of Saint Sebastian* open in Paris rather than Rome.[20] The pique of Marinetti and many lesser Italian intellectuals against France, has usually some source in their failure to win international recognition and acclaim in Paris.

The Italian Left had once gained its inspiration from Paris, City of the Revolution – Garibaldi had still been loyal enough to France to fight for her in 1870. This sympathy had weakened by 1914. The orthodox Italian Socialist party looked more to Victor Adler's Austrian Socialists and especially to the SPD, than to Jaurès or

Guesde. The new Nationalist movement on the Right borrowed much of its politics from Barrès, Maurras, Sorel and Bergson, but did 'not like to be reminded of foreign sources',[21] and was usually vociferously anti-French.

Slightly less vague, but still confused, were the attitudes of the Italian military. The traditions of the Italian Army, and often the very generals themselves, were Piedmontese more than anything else. Piedmont sometimes saw itself as the Prussia of Italy, and in any case, most officers in pre-1914 Europe deeply admired the strength and success of the German armies. Although a Neapolitan, Alberto Pollio, Italy's Chief of General Staff until his death on 30 June 1914, was notorious for his preference for Berlin and even Vienna, and enthusiastically pressed on with the task of formally strengthening Italy's military bonds to the Central Powers.

At the same time there were countervailing factors. In 1911, the Italian Army, which had in the past usually bought its armaments from Krupp, began to buy also from the French firm, Déport.[22] Naval contracts, also, were the subject of a bitter competition between the French financed Ansaldo company and the older iron-works at Terni whose financing came from the Banca Commerciale, and whose political ties were Giolittian. Despite its own debt to Schneider-Creusot and Nobel, Ansaldo cashed in on the public fact of Giolittian ties to German finance by declaring that contracts with Ansaldo would mean 'the emancipation of our country from a dangerous subservience to foreigners in the field of naval armament'.[23] For Ansaldo, German money was 'foreign', and French money was not.

One commentator has seen such dealings in terms of a 'military–industrial complex' and argued that

in the years between 1911 and 1915 in the armaments sector, as...in a number of other fields of Italian industry the prevailing attitude was of bitter rivalry with Germany and of cooperation with Great Britain and France. The production of Italian arms was directed towards the Entente powers well before the government took the initiative to change sides.[24]

But the causal connection between business, and foreign and military policy has not been made. Italy's new military and naval arrangements with the Triple Alliance were as serious an event as armaments contracts. Pollio's loyalty to the Central Powers cannot be doubted and, if anything, the Italian admirals were still more anti-French. The *Carthage* and *Manouba* incidents did not increase love between the two navies, and by 1914, for many high officers in the French Navy, Italy was the most serious immediate enemy. On the Italian side, in 1914, Naval Chief of General Staff, Admiral Paolo Thaon di Revel, greeted the new Prime Minister, Salandra, with a series of Francophobe reports, pressing the need to increase Italy's naval building programme.[25] On 15 July he briefed Salandra generally on the state of the French Mediterranean fleet. Morale was high, and was based on victory in a contest with Italy. Vice-Admiral Augustin Boué de Lapreyère, the ex-Navy Minister who commanded the French Mediterranean fleet, was reported to have participated in a ceremony on the new battleship, *France*, in which a bronze group had been exhibited showing Brennus having at his side two chained Roman legionaries with the title '*Vae Victis*'.[26]

To assert blandly from a study of business contracts that 'in this epoch almost no-one in Italy thought of a conflict with France',[27] is thus true only in the sense that Italy's military and naval planning was not well harnessed to her foreign policy, and that generally the assumptions of all Italian statesmen were grounded on peace between the Great Powers. If there was no war plan to deal with a Franco-Italian military conflict, so also Giolitti and San Giuliano have been bitterly criticised for not doing more about Italy's defences on her north-eastern border. On the naval side, Italy's hostility to France was usually tempered by a recognition of the power of the British Navy. Italy's strategic planning towards France, and indeed much of Italy's foreign policy, is well enough indicated, mathematically, in a report by Italy's Navy Minister, Pasquale Leonardi Cattolica, in 1913. Then it was advised that Italy's Dreadnought ratio towards Austria be kept at 1.33:1, while towards France it should be 0.66:1.[28] No other nations were considered in direct comparison.

The press was also the scene of many squabbles between Italy and France from 1911 to 1914. The formation of the Lega Franco-Italiana in 1912[29] on the initiative of French politicians as eminent as Pichon, Loubet and Clemenceau[30] was more an index of the loss of France's natural leadership over her little Latin sister than a sign of developing friendship. A minute study of newspaper reactions has demonstrated that Franco-Italian hostility was profound and widespread. Nationalist rhetoric was louder, but not different in kind from the more established press,[31] which carried, for example, the vividly critical articles of Benedetto Cirmeni, who wrote for the pro-Giolittian *La Stampa* in Turin. Cirmeni was a Catanian and had shared office with San Giuliano under Fortis. He had been a Crispian, and had later joined the Istituto Coloniale, being nominated to the organising committee of the Second Congress of Italians Abroad. Cirmeni also acted as a mouthpiece of Ameglio, the military governor of the Dodecanese, in order to advocate Italy's retention of those islands against what was then offical government policy.[32]

Oddly contrary to the strongly anti-French line of the Italian press is the fact that the French Embassy almost certainly 'subventioned' more Italian journalists than did any other foreign agency. Barrère, with his training from Gambetta and in the French prefectural service, undoubtedly found bribery an easier matter personally[33] than did Rodd or Mérey. The Italian Foreign Ministry, Giolitti, and many Italian banks and business concerns also gave money and loans to journalists, and Giolitti has been accused of spending almost as much money subsidising French newspapers as he did on Italian rearmament.[34] But, in both countries, the corruption of the press was more part of the social system than likely to produce direct influence on policy decision. It is symbolic that the most notorious example of bribery in Liberal Italy, the passage of French money to Mussolini in autumn 1914, is still disputed in detail, and is rarely believed in any case to have been a decisive influence on Mussolini's abandonment of the Socialist party.[35]

The story of Italian press and public attitudes from 1911 to 1914 is thus neither of entailment to France nor of 'suffocation'[36] by Germany. Italian opinion was more anxious to be independent, to be nationalist, than anything else. Perhaps it is all best summed up by the career of one of Italy's most brilliant entrepreneurs, Camillo Olivetti, who had begun to look technologically to the United States, rather than to Europe. On the new Olivetti typewriters, ordered by the Ministry of Posts and Telegraphs in 1913, was stamped a picture of Dante, the great symbol of the Italian nation, who had said, it was believed, that Trieste must be regained, that Italy's borders lay on the Quarnaro before Fiume, and who generally represented Italian greatness.[37] In war Italy's chief task would be to regain the *terra irredenta* from Austria, but there was *terra irredenta*, both European and colonial, in French hands too, and in peace-time, and perhaps in the future, Italy would have to consider how best to remind France of her unpaid debt. Meanwhile, the step-sister would need constant persuasion to treat that aspiring 'adolescent', Italy, with sufficient respect.

The most serious restraint on Italian independence towards France was undoubtedly the *sorellastra*'s great friend, Britain. After the creation of the *Entente Cordiale*, Italian disputes with France were inevitably tempered by the uncertainties of possible British reaction. For Italians, whether publicists or diplomatists, Britain generally was something of a *deus ex machina*. Although watering English *milords* helped found many Italian football clubs in the decade after 1900, and although English tourists patronised also less popular forms of Italian culture, Britain's interests and habits impinged far less directly on Italy than did those of Austria, France or Germany. British trade with Italy also seems to have been less aggressive and contentious than was that of the other Great Powers. The British attitude to Italy combined a sentimental admiration for the Great History and Blue Skies of the South with a magisterial distaste for the dirt and confusion of modern Italy.[38] The British 'friend' of Italy was perhaps best typified by the historian,[39] G. M. Trevelyan, who always had some difficulty in understanding what had 'gone wrong' with Italy since the time of Heroes in the Risorgimento, and could best explain his puzzlement by asserting that the character of Liberal Italy should be understood by historical reference to the times of the Duke of Newcastle or even of King Henry VIII.[40] Britons were readily dismayed by charges of corruption or parliamentary malpractice by Italian leaders, and often preferred the 'honesty' of Sonnino to the deviousness of Giolitti whom some called a parliamentary dictator. Sonnino's attractions were perhaps enhanced by his British ancestry, and the fact that he made a gentlemanly point of speaking English to English visitors,[41] always likely to be at a loss in a foreign tongue.

Such attitudes were extremely superficial and seem of very doubtful importance. So too do Italian attitudes to Britain. The most notable Italian Anglophile was Luigi Albertini, who perhaps saw himself as something of an Italian version of Leader of the Opposition. Albertini had received his training with the London *Times*,[42] and he aspired afterwards to make *Corriere della Sera* an Italian *Thunderer* which would cast lightning bolts against the corruption of the 'dictator' Giolitti. Albertini and many other Italians, including San Giuliano, Giacomo De Martino II and even Giolitti, saw much to admire in the British Empire. This admiration was usually coupled with a realistic assumption that it would be some time before the 'Third Italy' could hope to match British imperial achievement. King Victor Emmanuel III's first governess, with whom the sickly rachitic prince allegedly had his closest childhood relationship, was English.[43] The long-term effects of this may be doubted, and, indeed, it may be questioned whether they would make the King Anglophile or Anglophobe, but certainly Victor Emmanuel spoke English well, and admired both British success and British 'simplicity'. One commentator at least thought Italy's choice of sides in the First World War was influenced by the fact that the royal daughters in turn had English governesses.[44] King Victor Emmanuel III, however, was less likely to be influenced by governesses than was that *pater patriae*, Victor Emmanuel II. Of greater possible influence was the British military attaché, Delmé-Radcliffe, to whom the King was probably closer than to any other diplomat, but whether this friendship ever influenced the repressed little king's decisions is extremely difficult to say.

The usual phrase employed to describe Anglo-Italian relations, and summoned on official occasions, or when Italy wanted something, was 'the traditional friendship'. Rhetoric then certainly required memories of the Risorgimento, and could go back in time to Lionel of Clarence,[45] or even Julius Caesar, if necessary. Thus stated, 'the traditional friendship' seems no more than another polite cliché. Yet, it was more than that. Oddly, it defined how the Anglo-Italian relationship usually fitted in to the diplomatic constellation. In, or perhaps immediately after, the Risorgimento, British sentiment and interests decided that the existence of Italy was useful, and should continue. Italy, in the complexity and fragility of her domestic and international position, her very survival threatened by the Papacy's stubborn or unrenounced desire to regain temporal power, and always likely to be confronted by threats from Austria or France, needed a final reliance on Britain in order to be able to conduct any credible diplomacy. Although they were both

Great Powers, members of the Concert, Italy's real strength was so much less than Britain's that in a way Italy was client and Britain patron.

Patrons do not like their clients to be too importunate, and Italy was rarely not importunate. Crispi had pushed too hard and gone close to isolating Italy entirely. Later statesmen, of whom Prinetti was the most notable, had been ready instead to garner kind words from Britain, without examining too closely their sincerity.

By 1910 the basic state of Anglo-Italian relations was thus very much what it had usually been. A few Nationalists muttered about Malta or Egypt;[46] San Giuliano himself pointed out that there was a limit to the sense of collecting only kind words from your patron; but if war came, the Italian coast was still prostrate before a superior fleet. The Alps and the Apennines made military resistance imaginable, even before stronger armies. Italy's sandy coastline, lacking almost entirely secure harbours, made naval resistance most unlikely. Before a dominant fleet, Libya would be cut off, but, more importantly, so would Sicily and Sardinia. Genoa, Naples, Palermo, Bari and perhaps also Ancona and Venice could not be protected for long against the Royal Navy. Italy might be sundered into its regions, and even its cities might not be loyal. Thaon di Revel, for all his hostility to France, made just these points in a report to Salandra on 1 August 1914. The Triple Alliance's chances in a Mediterranean naval campaign against the Triple Entente were, he believed, slight. The population of Italy's coastal cities was especially hostile to war on the Triple Alliance side and they had reason since their defence could not be guaranteed.[47]

War reduced Italian diplomacy, and indeed the whole Liberal regime, to its bones. In peacetime, such dangerous clarity was not demanded, and therefore there was no need to be subservient to Britain, to observe the proprieties of a client. San Giuliano had already suggested in 1909 that Italy should try to assert greater independence towards Britain, and, from 1911 to 1914, much Italian policy was not fitted in to Britain's desires, and even, at times, risked irritating the Power which commanded the Royal Navy.

On the other hand, British policy towards Italy was based on clear, if usually undefined, assumptions. After the formation of the *Entente Cordiale*, it was believed in London that the 1902 Prinetti–Barrère exchanges ensured that Italy would not participate against Britain in any imaginable war. Prinetti had promised that Italy would not join any aggressive action against France; and Britain would not support any French aggression. All in all, given Italy's restlessness, but also given other possibilities, it was best that Italy remain in the Triple Alliance. The Permanent Under-Secretary at the Foreign Office to 1910, Sir Charles Hardinge, put it most neatly: 'The longer the Triple Alliance can be maintained in its present condition the better it is for us and France.' Despite the 1907 Anglo-Russian settlement, a nagging fear always remained in London, that Russia could not be relied on. If Italy was inveigled out of the Triple Alliance, 'a more formidable combination might take its place',[48] that is, a new *Dreikaiserbund*; and then Liberal Italy would be no substitute for Russia. British policy before 1911 was thus consistently opposed to Barrère's ambitions formally to remove Italy from her ties with the Central Powers.

The Libyan War, by probably ending the Prinetti–Lansdowne agreement and casting doubt on the Prinetti–Barrère exchanges, confused the issue of Italy's legal relationship both with Britain and France. In Britain, this change occurred at a time when British foreign policy was running into many difficulties. Britain's differences with Germany grew ever more serious, as international crisis followed international crisis. Moreover, British foreign policy was under less skilled control. Italy, as a country of secondary importance, was usually dealt with in London not by the Foreign Secretary, but by officials at the Foreign Office. Hardinge's departure to become Viceroy of India in 1910 brought in as Permanent Under-Secretary, Sir Arthur Nicolson, who had a less incisive mind than Hardinge, and by 1914 was also not on good personal terms with Sir Edward Grey.[49] In handling Italian manoeuvering, Nicolson was less sure and less decisive than Hardinge.

Beyond the Libyan War, or Nicolson's fumbling, another event threatened change in Italy's relationship with her 'friends' of the Triple Entente. In 1912, separately, but as an undoubted by-product of the increasing solidity of the *Entente Cordiale*, Britain and France decided to redeploy their fleets. The French Navy, acting on expert advice given repeatedly since 1906,[50] concentrated much of its fleet in the Mediterranean, weakening its forces in the North Sea. France's new role in Morocco, new Austrian naval construction, and the possible death throes of Turkey, all justified the decision. But so too did the belief that Italy must now be treated as one of France's major potential enemies. Certainly Italy saw the French move as motivated by this idea.

Britain, by contrast, weakened her Mediterranean fleet, in order to concentrate on the North Sea. This deployment was clearly to counter Germany, and reflected the fear induced in Britain that the widening of the Kiel Canal could leave British cities vulnerable to rapid and devastating attack by German Dreadnoughts. In memoranda explicating these points, British officials and politicians mentioned Italy merely as a reference in debate – 'Italy' was a potential 'enemy' or 'friend' depending on the argument being constructed. When Winston Churchill, for example, wanted to speak in favour of the move out of the Mediterranean, Italy was listed as a potential enemy. When McKenna wanted to oppose Churchill, then Italy was a friend.[51] Churchill reserved his greatest eloquence, if not his greatest respect for Italy, in trying to persuade the Canadian Prime Minister, Sir Robert Borden, that his Dominion ought to contribute to Imperial defence. 'Although Italy and Austria are very much opposed from the point of view of policy', he warned,

yet they are in alliance. Nothing but fear of Austria forced Italy to join the alliance, and one can never be certain that at the vital moment the terror which forced Italy to join the alliance may not operate to force her to make good the pact which she has signed.[52]

But, debating points apart, Italy was not strong enough to play any major part in planning in London. The move out of the Mediterranean was decided without serious concern for its strategic effects on Italy.

The naval redeployment, on the other hand, had an immense potential effect on Italy. The relative withdrawal of the British brought more into the open the running Franco-Italian hostility. On an immediate strategic level, the French build-up of her Mediterranean fleet induced Italy to increase her naval ties with the Central Powers, and the 1913 Triple Alliance Naval Pact was the direct result of the 1912 Anglo-French changes. In diplomatic terms, the weakening of Britain's direct influence on Italy encouraged still greater Italian independence, and refusal meekly to obey French bidding. That would be in peace time. If there was war, the old influences were if anything greater. Imperiali, from London, defined the position accurately from the Italian viewpoint. He was not sure, he wrote, if the sending of French naval reinforcements to the Mediterranean had been a result of a secret deal with Britain. Grey had said that it was not, 'but the agreement, if not on paper can be said to exist in practice (*virtualmente*)'. However, it was also evident, Imperiali noted, that, if France was attacked by Germany or even provoked into war,

there would be every reason to hold that this Government and the great majority of Parliament, with the exception of the known group of Radicals hostile to Grey, would consider it a vital English interest to draw themselves up alongside the friendly nation.[53]

However unsure he was of the British decision in the July crisis, San Giuliano never forgot the corollary that, in the last analysis, in terms of strategy and simple power, for Italy, the Royal Navy was the *force majeure*.

Such basic laws applied in war; but diplomacy was conducted in peace. From 1911 to 1914 it was important for San Giuliano to act in freedom from Britain and France, but also to ensure that the wire to London and Paris never broke down completely.[54] The method of insurance which San Giuliano used was the prospect of a new Mediterranean pact.

The invasion of Libya, Giolitti's 'premature' annexation decree, France's settlement in Morocco, and the imminent renewal of the Triple Alliance all implied potential or real modification of Italy's ties with Britain and France. The Prinetti–Barrère exchanges had referred directly to North Africa, but, in addition, Prinetti had promised that Italy would remain neutral in a conflict between the Powers where France was the victim of aggression. (He privately defined this generously as having occurred at Fashoda, and in the Ems telegram and Schnaebele incident.)[55] Generally, it was understood by the agreement that there were no differences in 'the respective interests [of the Powers] in the Mediterranean'.[56] Prinetti also promised that his signature in no way infringed Italy's other agreements, and, in particular, the Triple Alliance. In so arguing Prinetti had formed the legal, but tendentious case that the exchanges with Barrère referred to the 'Mediterranean', while the Triple Alliance was relevant to 'Europe'. In subsequent years, the international situation was never such that Italy was required to define where 'Europe' stopped and the 'Mediterranean' began. In fact such definition would only come in war.

Despite their evident legal fragility, the Prinetti–Barrère accords were of considerable use to France and Britain. Their vagueness and lack of time limit, if anything, only added to this value. Italy could be left in the Triple Alliance, where she would be less of a nuisance and would be unlikely to be replaced directly by Russia. But also, the Prinetti–Barrère exchanges meant that Italy's 'friendship' had some sort of written and even, arguably, legal base, which could be referred to in moments of crisis, or when government policy was attacked too fiercely by domestic Italophiles.

The Libyan invasion struck at these comfortable assumptions. Given that France now had Morocco, and Italy was taking Libya, did the general clauses of the 1902 accord have any surviving legitimacy? Would it not at least be useful to clarify Italian 'friendship' because, if Britain and France did not, Germany and Austria might do so when the Triple Alliance was renewed? If there was no agreement between Italy and the *Entente Cordiale* dealing with the 'Mediterranean', then might not the Triple Alliance change Italy's previous definition of 'Europe' also to cover the 'Mediterranean', and therefore the whole question of succession to the Ottoman Empire?

These questions occurred first to two men devoting an unusually and, to their contemporaries, unnecessarily large amount of time to Italian affairs – the British and French ambassadors in Rome, Sir James Rennell Rodd and Camille Barrère. Barrère has always been the more famed of the two. Back in 1905, he had already raised the idea of a Mediterranean agreement, to which Britain as well as France and Italy would be signatory.[57] But it would be unwise to underestimate the significance of Rodd in the period 1911 to 1914, even though there were times when the honest British ambassador was manipulated either by Barrère or by San Giuliano.

Rodd was not entirely a fool to be readily gulled. He was not a member of the inner circle of the Foreign Office and, although capable of Darwinian comments about trade rivalry between Britain and Germany, he was too Liberal and too cosmopolitan to share the intensity of suspicion of Germany held by Crowe, Bertie,[58] Nicolson or Hardinge. Rather Rodd fitted better that type of ambassador who is the friend and advocate of the country to which he is accredited. Rodd, an 'old Balliol man', whose career had survived a youthful dalliance with Oscar Wilde,[59] on an intellectual level was a devout Italophile; described generously by Barrère as:

charmant de physique et de manières, infiniment plus cultivé que ne le sont en général les diplomates, helléniste, italianisant et italophile, rempli de talent et de moyens, sympathique à la société et au monde politique.[60]

A poet who drew from classical and Mediterranean traditions, a medievalist and a historian, Rodd, in 1912, helped to found *The Journal of Roman Studies*; in retirement he wrote a scholarly, semi-historical guide to Rome. He was proud of an amateur interest in art painted under 'the bright skies of Italy', and, as ambassador, spent much time trying to secure Sir Henry Layard's great collection for Britain. It was at least partially appropriate that during the summer of 1914, and until late in the July crisis, Rodd was out of Rome, touring the hill-towns of Tuscany. *Persona gratissima* with San Giuliano, Rodd was also a close friend of Bülow, if rather more of a gentleman than either of them. Certainly more able than many previous British ambassadors in Rome, Rodd never really understood what he regarded as Italy's 'adolescent' ambitions in foreign affairs. He rarely tried to clarify San Giuliano's habitual subtlety and duplicity; as he had puzzled earlier, 'strange place Rome, nothing is what it seems'. If Italian dishonesty or ambiguity was sometimes a trial, Rodd was a natural British 'friend of Italy'; on personal, intellectual and professional grounds, Rodd would be likely to act as an advocate of a Mediteranean pact.[61]

Perhaps stimulated by the blandishments of Barrère, certainly it was Rodd who made the first move. On 16 October 1911, less than a fortnight after Italian troops landed at Tripoli, Rodd wrote to London suggesting that Britain should negotiate a pact with Italy similar to the Prinetti–Barrère accords. Whatever could be said about the legal bases of Italo–French friendship, it was clear, Rodd argued, that, after the Libyan War, the Prinetti-Lansdowne exchanges would have no more validity. Adriatic events suggested that an Austrian clash might not be far away, and, in an ominous aside, Rodd added that the diplomatic situation in the Mediterranean might be revolutionised 'though Ministers here brush away any reference to Tobruk as though they were quite outside the range of practical consideration'.[62] Rodd was hinting that the acquisition of Libya might enhance Italy's naval power, or, more dangerously, her naval value to the Triple Alliance. Tobruk could be a strategic harbour athwart the route to India. But if Rodd expected London to pay attention to innuendos about Italy's future power, he was mistaken. A private letter to Nicolson urging that Britain reconsider her policy towards Italy in the Adriatic had no greater effect.[63] Rodd received no reply at all to his initiatives.

On 25 October Rodd returned to his theme, now clearly in collusion with Barrère.[64] He spelled out what he had hinted at before. There should be a new Mediterranean agreement which would pledge to preserve the *status quo*. In favour of such an agreement, he now phrased his thesis less dramatically and more realistically:

Tripoli will undoubtedly prove a serious responsibility to Italy, and will greatly add to her vulnerability, as well as contribute to her importance as a Mediterranean power, and an arrangement which would eliminate any menace to her new acquisition...would no doubt offer an inducement to her to give us certain guarantees in return.[65]

France, as a Moroccan settlement neared completion, also thought again about Italy. In London, the French ambassador, Paul Cambon, favoured some new arrangement, warning Nicolson that otherwise Italy might accept a German guarantee of her new territories.[66] But the Foreign Office had decided, sensibly, to have little to do with diplomatic machinations concerning Italy during the Libyan campaign. Italy's annexation decree confirmed this opinion. On 14 November Grey told Rodd that he opposed the launching of any scheme while hostilities still occurred in Libya: 'We cannot ask anything from Italy without implying a promise of support in her Tripoli venture: and that we cannot give.'[67]

Rodd tried to keep his idea afloat in a defensive reply noting that he had not been 'contemplating anything immediate in the way of a definite understanding', but that

it was only a suggestion as to a possible combination to which the inevitable force of circumstances might conduct in the future and in view of which it may be in our interests to keep in mind the extreme sensibilities of this hypersensitive and excitable race, which is essentially friendly to us and attaches much weight to our goodwill and good opinion.

Grey read the despatch and minutes laconically 'interesting'.[68] There was nothing more to be done, at least for the moment.

There is no sign that the Italians had played any part in the formation of these ideas. San Giuliano would perhaps be interested if the subject was ever broached by Rodd or Barrère. Already, in his memorandum of 13 September, the Italian Foreign Minister had noted that, after her success in Morocco, France had no reason to keep her previous agreements on Tripoli. He had also been anxious to allay the press storm against Italy in Britain, and had been ready to pledge that Italy would never damage British interests in the Mediterranean.[69] During the war, rumours of a new pact might be suitably discouraging for Turkey, although Italy would always have also to think about the reaction of the Central Powers.

Meanwhile, the *Carthage* and *Manouba* incidents gave both ambassadors another chance to return to their idea. Barrère, in particular, was dismayed that his whole achievement in Rome had been ruined.[70] But it was Rodd who first put pen to paper. On 5 February 1912 he wrote again to Grey. In the past, he noted, Britain and, more recently, France, preferred that Italy remain in the Triple Alliance. But now strategic considerations, especially potential strategic considerations, meant that Britain should think seriously what her policy was towards the renewal of the Triple Alliance.[71]

In opining that Italy should be removed from the Triple Alliance, Rodd's arguments ran far ahead of policy-makers in London and Paris. The *Carthage* and *Manouba* incidents had not changed the belief, as Paul Cambon drily put it, that 'Italy seems an ally less useful than embarrassing'.[72] San Giuliano too lessened any chance of success the scheme may have had by noting, on February 17 in a conversation with Barrère, that he believed the Prinetti–Barrère accords still to be in effect.[73] San Giuliano had probably decided that, while the colonial war continued, negotiations with the *Entente Cordiale* would only endanger Italy's already complicated relationship with the Central Powers. Rodd and Barrère were left to ponder another opportunity to begin definition of a Mediterranean pact.[74]

Franco-Italian relations, and the personal hostility between Poincaré and Tittoni,[75] meant that once more initiative passed to Rodd. The Italian incursion against the Straits prompted Rodd to a still more detailed explanation to London of his hopes and fears. On 13 April he wrote a long letter to Grey pointing out that the Triple Alliance was tightening its grip around Italy: 'The position which France commanded in this country at the beginning of the war has been lost, in a sense perhaps irretrievably.' Britain was well regarded 'certainly by all those whose opinion is of consequence' but 'the old theory that popular feeling and traditional friendship would override all other influences, has been somewhat shaken'. Sharpening his prose, perhaps to meet the tastes of the Foreign Office, Rodd warned that the Central Powers were using every opportunity:

unremitting efforts are made by the agents of the two allied Empires to draw Italy into their orbit and no opportunity is missed by the press of those two countries for utilising the 'suppressio veri' and the 'insinuatio falsi' to our detriment, while the Italians are constantly reminded that in the Triple Alliance is now their only chance of salvation.

If Italy became a 'vassal' of the Central Powers, Malta would be exposed; 'Pan Germans' aimed eventually to conquer Egypt and open the route to India and the East. To counter these designs there should be a new North African agreement as

there might... be real advantages in thus to some extent safeguarding the Mediterranean situation, while the realisation of such a scheme might have further consequences than those immediately apparent.[76]

Rodd was never comfortable in the role of the machiavel. His final hint about a change in the Triple Alliance was not likely to arouse interest in London. Another month passed, and again Rodd received no reply. On 14 May the ambassador left Rome for a private visit to London. He would, he assured Barrère, again ask Grey and Nicolson about the Mediterranean scheme.[77]

Grey received him politely. Rodd's trip had coincided with the Italian seizure of the Dodecanese Islands, and with general discussions in the Committee of Imperial Defence about the Mediterranean. Grey now told Rodd that a North African agreement seemed a good idea.[78] Nicolson too had advised Grey that, although the concept obviously derived from Barrère, if the Triple Alliance were renewed, it could be that 'the question is an important one – especially when we keep in view the serious diminution which we are contemplating of our naval forces in the Mediterranean'. Grey, perhaps less concerned by such arguments than his ultra-Tory Permanent Under-Secretary, minuted back: 'I do not see that we can do anything while war is going on.'[79]

Another Tory, Kitchener, in Egypt, pressed on Grey the danger of too great a deterioration of British Mediterranean naval strength.[80]

Paul Cambon had also developed an interest in some form of new arrangement with Italy to counterbalance the likely hostility to be produced by naval redeployment.[81] On 6 June Grey revealed to Bertie that he had been converted to favouring a Mediterranean pact, although it would probably be negotiable only when the war ended. He had, he said, been influenced by Cambon's fear that the Triple Alliance might be extended to the Mediterranean and a coaling station supplied there to the Central Powers. Therefore, Grey believed, some new version of the Prinetti–Lansdowne exchange might be drafted:

we might propose to Italy some reciprocal arrangement under which we would guarantee not to disturb her *status quo* in Tripoli if she undertook not to disturb the *status quo* in Egypt and Tunis. Such an agreement would give her security, and deprive her of the motive for extending the Triple Alliance to the Mediterranean, that she would have if she were afraid of being disturbed by us.[82]

Grey had not really abandoned his earlier belief that nothing be done while war continued, and did not follow up his idea with action. Rodd and Barrère were again left to be its lonely and pertinacious advocates.[83] In this role, Barrère was no more successful than Rodd. Paul Cambon's conversion to his scheme seems to have been a personal one. More importantly, a pact negotiated in Paris was much more unattractive to Italy than one made in London. The French would be less susceptible negotiators than the British to Italy's problems, and the Central Powers were also more sensitive to direct Italo-French talks than to Italy's almost inevitable friendship with Britain. When, late in May, Poincaré twice spoke to Tittoni about the need to find an arrangement which would restore some harmony to Franco-Italian relations, the news was received very coldly by San Giuliano.[84]

Any slight chance that the Mediterranean negotiations may have had at this time was ruined on 8 July, when the London *Daily Graphic* leaked the news that plans were being formulated for an Anglo-Franco-Italian pact.[85] Italy could not risk such publicity during war-time, when the Triple Alliance was still not renewed, and when it would still be possible for Austria to start talking about compensations in the Balkans. On 9 July San Giuliano told Imperiali, severely, that 'he could be neither contrary nor favourable to a project of which he did not know the terms'. However, reluctant to abandon altogether a concept of which he had previously been only vaguely appraised, and in which there might be some advantage to Italy, he did not altogether privately discourage the idea, at least in the sense that it might be recalled when the war was over. Imperiali indeed almost rebuked his chief's love of the devious by emphasising properly that Italy should

avoid as much as possible, with the Powers belonging to the other group, subsidiary and parallel accords of the type which could bring upon us in the future, embarrassments and trouble even more serious than those in which we have at times found ourselves and which by fortune in the past we have succeeded in overcoming.[86]

Such splendid morality for the moment was appropriate because the war went on and, once again, negotiations lapsed. On 10 September the formal announcement was made that France was concentrating most of her fleet in the Mediterranean. Poincaré was persuaded belatedly to swear to Rome that 'the eventual concentration of French squadrons in the Mediterranean was not at all inspired by diffidence, let alone hostility towards Italy'.[87] San Giuliano, not appeased, remarked tartly that it could be a decisive moment in Franco-Italian relations. There would be 'bitter memories' if France did not assuage Italy's suspicions about the stationing of more ships in the Mediterranean, for example, by showing more 'loyalty' to the 1902 arrangements, and perhaps intervening to help an Italo-Turkish peace. On San Giuliano's initiative, De Martino, the *Chef de Cabinet* in Rome, at once told the Austrian *Chargé* that now might be the time when Italy and Austria should 'search for an agreement on the development of their naval power...to face each future eventuality'.[88]

With respect to the Mediterranean scheme, the next initiative came from Britain. On 20 September, with the end of the Italo-Turkish war at last in sight, Grey kept his promise to revive the idea of a Mediterranean or North African pact. He pledged that the French transfer of their fleet did not mean any change in British policy. 'As a matter of fact', he wrote to Dering, the *Chargé* in Rome,

after the war between Italy and Turkey was over, we should have no difficulty in reassuring Italy that we did not wish to disturb her in North Africa; and she...would give us the same assurance. We would rather be assured directly in that way than by taking any other measures.[89]

Grey told Paul Cambon more frankly that he had made the suggestion to illustrate 'that there were other ways of securing...[Italy's] position in North Africa than by an extension of the Triple Alliance to the Mediterranean'.[90]

Imperiali, despite his previous criticism of *giri di walzer*, liked the idea. The German Counsellor in London, Kühlmann, also did not object to an Italo-British agreement, no doubt seeing advantages in an Italo-British agreement rather than a Franco-Italo-British one. San Giuliano, however, was not impressed by the vague and ill-defined British idea. His sense of irony may have savoured the fact that he could now reject British advances with kind words:

I can only say that I strongly desire that relations between Italy and England are always warm, friendly and cordial as is the ancient tradition and I shall work constantly to that end.[91]

To be able to snub Britain, even if gently, was certainly a change for an Italian statesman.

This Italian independence has sometimes been seen as an indication of San Giuliano's triplicism at that time.[92] Perhaps it was, but, given the state of the war with Libya and the pressing need to end what had become long postponed plans to renew the Triple Alliance, it is hardly surprising that San Giuliano did not jump at the nebulous suggestions which reached him. Imperiali had surely been right in his earlier advice that too many agreements weakened rather than strengthened Italy's diplomatic cause. Moreover, in September 1912, who could be certain that Italian negotiations with Britain and potentially with France, would not push Austria belatedly into thinking about compensation in the Balkans in return for Italy's advance in Libya and the Dodecanese? Therefore, when Rodd reminded San Giuliano of the Mediterranean pact, he was told only that Italy could not pronounce on 'so vague a scheme'.[93] The Libyan War ended with a Mediterranean agreement no nearer than it had been when Rodd first raised the matter a year before.

For both Rodd and Barrère, Italy's victory in Libya added still further urgency to their idea. France's belated recognition of the Italian conquest had underlined the hostility between the 'Latin sisters'. Moreover, peace meant that Italy was certain to think about renewing the Triple Alliance, and she might well be inveigled into extending it from Europe to the Mediterranean. Rodd warned that there was no time to lose, and was seconded again by Paul Cambon.[94] Barrère's deputy, Laroche, had meanwhile discovered that Giolitti favoured a North African agreement.[95] Poincaré, in turn, emphasised his fears that Germany be accorded some strong point in the Mediterranean, but also stressed the need 'to control' Italian ambitions which inevitably had been stimulated by their recent success. Poincaré was all the more wary of Italian allurements given that the outbreak of the Balkan Wars had meant an overall increase in international tension.[96]

French concern did bring a reaction from Grey. After Paul Cambon asked that Britain formally begin talks with Italy,[97] Grey approached Imperiali, although without much optimism. He wrote to Rodd: 'I will feel my way a little more with Imperiali, and let you hear again about the proposed African Agreement.'[98]

It was not a good moment for an *Entente Cordiale* initiative. On 2 November San Giuliano was due to depart for Berlin to negotiate the renewal of the Triple Alliance, and he showed no wish to repeat Prinetti's breathless dexterity of 1902. The British were again fobbed off with the remark that they clarify their suggestion. San Giuliano also moved more directly to quieten Barrère. Interviewing the ambassador on 31 October, San Giuliano stated that the Triple Alliance was about to be renewed, but that the renewal would be without modification and would be consistent with the Prinetti–Barrère accords.[99] San Giuliano had thus implicitly repeated Italy's belief that the 1902 agreement was still intact.

Barrère did not like leaving matters 'implicit' in Rome. Using the opportunity presented by San Giuliano's absence in Berlin, he repeated the old news to Paris that Giolitti allegedly favoured a North African agreement. In case the message was not clear, he underlined it: 'The Minister of Foreign Affairs does nothing without the preventative approval of the President of the Council.'[100] Rodd was a predictable ally, but the Foreign Office staff noted coolly that they would be interested should Barrère be successful.[101] In fact, there was little sign of a division between San Giuliano and Giolitti. On his return, San Giuliano merely repeated his view that the 1902 agreement was still in force. If there was to be a new agreement then he must be presented with concrete details. As exuberant as ever, Barrère told Paris such a response meant San Giuliano's approval, and duly began to draft terms.[102] San Giuliano, in contrast, revealed for Giolitti's benefit a sinister scenario in which 'a certain foreign Power', that is France, was endeavouring 'to create difficulties' between Italy and Austria and was even ready to use financial means 'in certain ambients' to achieve its purpose.[103]

Rodd had still not seen that progress was unlikely and requested immediate British action to lure Italy out of the Triple Alliance. The Foreign Office, in contrast, was satisfied by the implicit continuance of Italy's 1902 promises, and Nicolson told Imperiali that Britain would favour a North African agreement, but not one generally extended to the Mediterranean.[104] Obviously, Britain believed that the latter could provoke all the old fears about a change in membership in the Triple Alliance. San Giuliano, meanwhile, was the soul of diplomatic propriety in Rome. He informed Rodd that, if there was to be any agreement to restrict the possible area of future warfare, he would have to consult his allies. And, in any case, where were the definite proposals?[105]

Paris had discovered again that there were certain difficulties in the 'implicit' in dealing with Italy. In contrast to San Giuliano's soothing loyalty, Tittoni apparently told Poincaré that Italy might still be bound to support Austria in a Balkan war, even if both Russia and France were involved. Disgusted by this appeal to the Triple Alliance, Poincaré asked abruptly for an explanation.[106] But Barrère was unable to use the opportunity to push his Mediterranean agreement. Indeed to demonstrate there were no splits in the Italian government, it was Giolitti, on 25 November, who informed Barrère that Tittoni had not been authorised to make his statement, and that there was no inconsistency between Italy's other arrangements and the 1902 settlement.[107] In other words, as formally as was likely, Italy had announced that the terms of the Triple Alliance had not been changed, and still applied to 'Europe' and not to 'the Mediterranean' and therefore, in so far as such matters were foreseeable, to peace and not to war. For all Italy's alleged triplicism at the end of 1912, the norms of Italian policy remained. There were still 'allies', and still 'friends'.

San Giuliano was less polite in dealing with Rodd. He told the British ambassador sarcastically that Italy could not see the point of a neutralisation scheme which must collapse on the only occasion when it might have any value, that is, in war.[108] Rodd could have remarked that the same applied to almost all Italy's treaty arrangements, but instead he wrote defensively to the Foreign Office, painting a black picture of Italy's current diplomacy. The Central Powers, he feared, 'knowing the mercurial temperament of the southern partner' would take advantage of Italy's bickering with France by 'rivetting the fetters' of the Triple Alliance.[109] Poor Barrère was 'very low' at the failure of his life work. A Mediterranean agreement could change the whole situation:

It is argued here that the manner in which the formula is drafted will make all the difference. Meanwhile I don't like to put anything concrete forward without more definite guidance.[110]

There were few reasons for London to offer guidance. Crowe had explained, in his usual accurate way, what insurance the Prinetti–Barrère accords provided. The renewal of the Triple Alliance had not changed the position in the Mediterranean.[111] Paris, too, must have been encouraged to learn from its military attaché in Rome that despite Aehrenthal's triumph over the 'war party', Austrian strategic planning was still directed against Italy.[112]

Yet, whether because the concept of some sort of agreement with Italy had now developed its own momentum, or whether to restrain further initiatives from Rodd and Barrère, Crowe's draft of a North African pact was sent to Rome on 20 December. In so doing, Grey reproached his ambassador for his past independence, complaining that he had been 'led on' by San Giuliano. Italy's real intention, he explained, was to find out how far any Mediterranean scheme would affect her relations with Germany. Britain, in any case, did not want an Anglo-Franco-Italian Mediterranean pact. 'The Franco-Italian Agreement of 1902' he reminded Rodd,

may be presumed – although we do not know its precise provisions – to safeguard this country against Italy joining in hostilities against Great Britain arising out of aggressive action on the part of Germany.

Therefore the terms which Grey was suggesting were limited to North Africa:

Recognising that the preservation of peace and tranquillity in the North African territories washed by the Mediterranean, and the security of their borders from external attack, which are essential conditions of the welfare of the native populations and of the prosperity and progressive development of those territories, are bound up with the maintenance of the authority of the European Great Powers now severally exercising therein rights of sovereignty, protection or control:

The British and Italian Governments declare that they are firmly resolved, on their part, to maintain their respective rights [in and] over the aforesaid territories. Each Government will refrain from any political or other action of a nature to endanger or embarrass the authority of the other in those regions.

The two Governments declare at the same time that they are not bound to any third Power by engagements conflicting with the foregoing undertaking, and that they will not enter into any such engagements in the future.[113]

Crowe had drafted skilfully. From London's point of view, the sting was in the last paragraph, where an Italian acceptance would remove almost completely any lingering British doubts about any menace in Italy's membership of the Triple Alliance.

Grey still did not encourage Rodd to instigate hasty diplomatic decision. He was anxious that, in dealing with Italy, Britain should keep in step with France. However, Paris had no immediate fears about the Triple Alliance, now that it had been renewed without change, and, in February 1913, Rodd reported dispiritedly that Franco–Italian relations were 'quiescent'.[114]

San Giuliano too had not leaped at the chance for an agreement with Britain. He met Rodd's soundings by the ironically legalist suggestion that 'in and' should be omitted from the final draft. On 6 February Grey formally instructed Rodd not to do anything further unless the Italians took the initiative.[115] An appeal by Rodd that Barrère thought the moment opportune for a general Entente initiative was, not surprisingly, rejected.[116] Once more, the hopes of Rodd and Barrère that Italy be made at least an associate member of the Triple Entente had not fitted the general international position.

While Britain and France had decided that no new insurance scheme with Italy was worth signing, in the first nine months of 1913 Italy's public policy moved closer and closer to the Triple Alliance. As a corollary, Italy's relationship with France grew worse and worse. On 22 February 1913 San Giuliano took the opportunity to make a rare major speech to the Chamber of Deputies, proclaiming the triumph of Italy in the Libyan War:

Not only did we wish to assure Italy's position in the Mediterranean...but...also to show to the world and to ourselves that Italy could resolve by herself and with her own might alone the first great problem...placed before her.

After expending some kind words on Austria, San Giuliano pointed out that Italy's future lay in the Mediterranean which 'no-one today has any more, nor will ever have, the right to call *mare nostrum*'. Italy now was 'a Great Mediterranean Power', and must play out her destined role, especially should Turkey collapse. Warming to his subject, San Giuliano presented the Chamber with one of his set pieces of combined Machiavellian and Social Darwinian philosophy:

The Libyan War has been a great national education and the lessons it has given to the Italian people must lead it to judge foreign policy not as a matter of little incidents but of great and permanent interests. Sentiment is a factor which should not be set aside, nevertheless it must remain secondary. People and Government must have a clear vision of the great and complicated interests of the country; and look at every question not only by itself, in isolation, but connected to all the others... This is always necessary, but it is even more so in the present period of history; a period of great transformations which will be decisive for a long time with respect to the grandeur and prosperity of various nations and assign to them for more than a generation their relative place in the world.

In this great contest of the peoples which is a factor of civilisation and progress because it assures the prevalence of the best and drives individuals and peoples to develop all their faculties and to intensify their efforts, Italy has already demonstrated that it is worthy of a high place and that it is determined to keep one at any cost.

When San Giuliano sat down, the Chamber broke into an uproar of enthusiasm. Many deputies left their seats, to go across to the Foreign Minister and shake his hand.[117] A fortnight later, in the graver atmosphere of the Senate, San Giuliano repeated the message of Italy's new independence, if this time with appropriate references to the impulsion to take up the Roman heritage.[118]

San Giuliano's speech was read then and later as a declaration of triplicism. The French hastened to complain about its tone, and the nature of the Italian newspaper and public reaction.[119] San Giuliano was not impressed. On 28 February he drafted to Tittoni a long despatch detailing his disappointments at current French policy towards Italy. Personally, San Giuliano said, he was motivated by the friendliest attitude towards France, but it was difficult to forget the *Carthage* and *Manouba* incidents, as the Chamber's reception of his speech had shown. Always, France interpreted her agreements with Italy narrowly, in her own interests, and even 'with chicanery', as, for example, in the way France had applied the Prinetti–Barrère accords during the Libyan War. Characteristically blaming France for an ambition in fact held by Italy, San Giuliano alleged heatedly that France was agog so to divide Asia Minor in the event of Turkish disintegration that France would be assured 'the almost absolute supremacy in the Mediterranean'. Generally France displayed

an insufficient acceptance of-the consequences which necessarily derive from the fact that Italy is a Great Mediterranean Power. It seems to me that it is necessary to make this understood to France while there is still time, thus avoiding a conflict between the two countries and preparing an eventual entente between them.

Italy, Germany and Austria–Hungary could not sit by and let the Mediterranean become an 'Anglo-French lake'.[120]

In the same month, a secret *Consulta* memorandum set the bases of Italian policy in the Eastern Mediterranean. San Giuliano saw an essential need to act inside the Triple Alliance. In so far as France was concerned, he emphasised the naval rivalry with Italy:

What the views of France are on the Mediterrranean balance of power we have again seen in the recent declaration of that government which has said that it is determined to have a fleet superior to that of Italy and Austria combined in order to assure to France the *domination* [sic] of the Mediterranean.[121]

At the same time, it was perhaps on *Consulta* initiative, and certainly with *Consulta* approval, that Italy made new pledges about her naval presence in the Triple Alliance.

Yet too much should not be made of the naval talks, nor of San Giuliano's recriminations against the *sorellastra*. If the *Consulta* favoured the naval agreement, it was not publicly involved in it, and at no time released the clauses of the Triple Alliance or of Italy's other pacts to the military and naval chiefs. The naval agreement was thus, to use a phrase later favoured by Aldo Moro, a 'convergent parallel', and could be denounced, or better ignored, if the diplomatic situation so demanded. Moreover, even the soldiers, for all their public triplicism, continued to hold sensible doubts on the practicalities of an Italian military push up the Alps against France, even in summer. As Cadorna put it in a memorandum to Pollio, such an operation could take 'months'.[122] In contrast to their sailors, French soldiers also rarely thought of Italy as a likely enemy.[123]

Italy's manoeuvres in the Eastern Mediterranean, although undoubtedly conducted within the Triple Alliance, were often as directed against her partners, especially Austria, as towards them. In many ways, what is most striking about the deterioration of Franco–Italian relations in 1913 is its openness. France openly urged Italy to retire from the Dodecanese islands; Italy openly complained about French patronage of the Greeks in Albania. The words which San Giuliano spoke in the Chamber, and the much stronger words which he drafted to Tittoni, were of a kind which he would not have dared to have used against any other Power. Similar words addressed to Vienna would very likely have meant war. Within the rhetoric of '*sorellastra*' and 'adolescent' Italian sensitivity, it is most significant that San Giuliano never abandoned his earlier promise that the Prinetti–Barrère accords remained in force.[124] In a way then, Italy's improved relations with Austria and worsened relations with France were more apparent than real, and more than anything else demonstrated the diplomatic means needed at that moment to re-emphasise Italy's new independence, to pursue Italy's new expansionism.

Of course, as time passed, while the Dodecanese remained in Italian hands, and Italian penetration of Asia Minor increased, at least on paper, the improved relationship with Austria began to seem more and more useful to San Giuliano. In September 1913 he instructed Giolitti that Italy's most pressing need was a definite agreement with Austria on Asia Minor. Italy could even give up some of the territory marked out for her to Austria as

it would commit Austria to the Mediterranean balance, introduce into the Mediterranean a new political and military factor opposed to French or Franco-English hegemony, increase our power and influence as much in the bosom of the Triple Alliance as opposed to the Triple Entente, [and] guarantee us against the tyranny of France, always disposed to abuse her power against us when she knows us to be weak.

Austria could be diverted from the Adriatic to join the guard being assembled against a French *mare nostrum*. This was triplicism indeed, if it should also be taken in association with San Giuliano's cynical statement earlier in the memorandum:

Naturally in this division [of Asia Minor] we must seek to get the biggest and best part and possibly give to Austria–Hungary the zone which will most put her into conflict with the Triple Entente.[125]

But, if San Giuliano had momentarily become a real triplicist in the autumn of 1913, his hopes far outran events. The King had expressed doubts about the policy. Most importantly, Austria showed few signs of wanting a genuine Italian alliance. On 24 August the Hohenlohe decrees in Trieste had sparked Italian diplomatic protests which continued in a developing storm of public and press hostility. Only a week after he had dreamed of a new Triple Alliance Empire in Turkey, on 19 September, San Giuliano was driven to appeal against Austria to Berlin:

The Hohenlohe decrees and the attitude of the Austrian government…make impossible a true friendship between Italy and Austria.

The Germans must understand that the Italians who could not 'put ourselves in serious conflict with both our neighbours', would now have to seek a new accord with France. The Germans did nothing, and, a fortnight later, San Giuliano repeated the warning: Italy could not be 'in conflict even simply diplomatically with both Austria and France at the same time'.[126] He complained to Bollati that Austria was only playing on Italy's need for diplomatic support against France. In reply, San Giuliano's mind turned back to the vague ideas of Barrère and Rodd of seven months before, schemes which had aimed at redefining Italy's relationship with her friends of the *Entente Cordiale*.

On 12 October the long-serving *Chargé* in Paris, Mario Ruspoli, raised with Poincaré the concept of a new accord with France. These were the most delicate soundings, and sparring began as to which country would take, or appear to take, the initiative. Barrère, naturally delighted at the rebirth of his cherished scheme, wrote optimistically that San Giuliano was irremediably opposed to Austrian hegemony in the Balkans. Giolitti, too, was again detected to be a natural supporter of a new Mediterranean agreement.[127] The major difficulty which Barrère foresaw, was whether the accord should cover only North Africa, or the Mediterranean as a whole.[128]

San Giuliano was not anxious to move forward with unseemly haste. Talk of a new Mediterranean agreement might well be a better Italian rebuke for Germany and Austria than a signature would be. It was another ideal moment to appeal for advice from Italy's ambassadors. Bollati, in Berlin, always a timid triplicist, could be relied on to be depressing. The Kaiser at that moment, it seemed, was very Italophile, but would be likely to change his views upon hearing of a new Mediterranean agreement. What is more, the change might be prolonged and even irreparable. 'Now I reason thus,' Bollati wrote, 'if we wish to maintain the Triple Alliance, it is clear that the current state of tension with Austria cannot last long.'

To overcome it, Austria might 'do something which up to a certain point can give satisfaction to our national feeling'. However, this was not likely if Italy turned back to France. A Mediterranean accord might be justifiable in the letter of the Triple Alliance, but what of the spirit of it? *Giri di walzer* should no longer seduce Italy from her real allies.[129] San Giuliano respectfully circulated Bollati's advice to the King and Giolitti. A Piedmontese like Bollati, advocating reliance on the Triple Alliance, might sound more convincing to the Piedmontese King and Prime Minister.

While he was awaiting advice from above, San Giuliano made no effort to clarify the old confusion whether a North African or Mediterranean pact was envisaged. Always preferring to work in the dark than in the light, San Giuliano argued that it was not for Italy to define her case. Not wholly frankly, he told Giolitti that the original advances had come from France and Britain. It was therefore up to them to make concrete proposals, and these, he surmised, would be difficult to formulate. The King, San Giuliano pondered, favoured the agreement, but then he too disdained *giri di walzer*. In any case, Italy had once before asked Grey if he would mind that Germany and Austria were kept informed, and Grey had raised no objections. Having covered most possibilities, San Giuliano ended his report with a deliberate mixture of platitudes and confusion:

If you approve...it seems to me that we can persevere in this attitude, although a different attitude would undoubtedly put us too much at the dependence of Austria, because it would exacerbate our relations with France. What always makes our situation difficult and delicate is that, in different ways, we are always exposed to surprises on the part of our two neighbours, Austria and France, and out of necessity we must avoid the danger of finding ourselves at the same time on bad terms with both.[130]

San Giuliano was thus hardly a zealous advocate of a premature conclusion to talks on the Mediterranean. However, when Barrère wooed him, he did not absolutely say no. Indeed, according to Barrère, San Giuliano had been charmed by the idea of a tripartite accord guaranteeing no change in the Mediterranean *status quo* without mutual discussions beforehand. It was true, Barrère admitted, that San Giuliano had also said that an exchange limited to North Africa might be of more advantage.[131] To ensure that Barrère's courting was met with gallantry and delay, San Giuliano now reminded his ambassadors that he would be interested in their opinions of the French proposals. He cannot have been very surprised by what he learned in reply. Bollati and Avarna, in Berlin and Vienna, feared complications with the Central Powers. Ruspoli, Imperiali and Bordonaro, in Paris, London and St Petersburg, favoured improved relations with the Triple Entente.

Potential German reaction threatened to be the most difficult. Bollati advised that he had been told that Bülow had had 'great difficulties in defending our policy of *giri di walzer* and had not succeeded wholly'. Zimmermann had pointed out 'the painful impression' made in Berlin by rumours of Italo-French talks.[132] Whether or not he had expected his ambassador to talk so frankly to German officials is not clear, but San Giuliano now used the attempted German snub to his own advantage. He wrote to Avarna, with deliberate naivety, that Austria could now be informed of the Mediterranean negotiations which, however, probably would 'not lead to any practical conclusion'. In any case, he added innocently, Italy's very discussions with France had sprung from the need to have good relations with her, given that the Hohenlohe decrees had put Austro-Italian relations in jeopardy.[133]

That same day, a despatch to Berlin was worded slightly differently. San Giuliano ingenuously remarked that he could not understand how talk of a Mediterranean agreement could produce a 'painful impression' in Berlin. The ideas were Barrère's, and he had still not put them into a formula. Naturally if he did, Italy would at once inform Germany. Had not Rodd had similar ideas which Germany had known about, some months before, but been unable to find a satisfactory formula? Therefore, it was 'very probable that the step taken by Barrère will not lead to any practical conclusion'. But the troubles of Italy's situation needed comprehension. She did not want to change the Mediterranean *status quo*, nor did she want to see it changed: 'It is our vital interest that it remain unchanged as long as possible.' Similarly in all matters, Italy wanted to proceed with her allies. Yet her honesty and loyalty were not always reciprocated. Austria sometimes almost did not seem to want Italy as an ally, and Italy depended on Germany to restrain Vienna. After all, San Giuliano repeated in now hackneyed refrain, little Italy could not be put 'in conflict at the same time with both her neighbours'.[134]

In a way that was becoming familiar to the European Concert, San Giuliano had thus cheekily held his ground. He may even have encouraged Zimmermann's original 'painful impression'. Certainly, once these words were reported, San Giuliano had deftly parried them, and turned the discussion on to how Austria might be persuaded to be a more honourable and responsible member of the Triple Alliance. Once again, San Giuliano had displayed Italy's new diplomatic independence. Such sleights of hand would be difficult in any real crisis, but then so would any Italian diplomacy.

While San Giuliano paraded Italy's virtues and desires before Berlin there were few signs of progress in the scheme for a Mediterranean agreement. San Giuliano told Giolitti that Italy could proceed 'calmly' in the matter, while loyally paying attention to the feelings of her allies.[135] San Giuliano collected memoranda from his ambassadors commenting in some confusion about a possible agreement on North Africa, the Mediterranean, and even Asia Minor.[136] But Barrère was getting nowhere with Paris, and Paul Cambon had reported that 'Grey is ready to listen to the Italians but will let them speak [first.]'[137] The French Foreign Minister, Pichon, meanwhile heard rumours that the Triple Alliance had been extended to the Mediterranean. Via telegrams intercepted by their secret service, the French had knowledge of the Triple Alliance Naval agreement, and believed that Articles VI, VII and IX of the Triple Alliance had been altered to include the Mediterranean.[138] The public side of Franco-Italian relations at once deteriorated again, and the *Quai d'Orsay* exposed to London and St Petersburg this new and culminating evidence of Italian duplicity.[139]

Rhetoric on both sides expanded. Even King Victor Emmanuel III, formally addressing the first session of the Italian Chamber to meet since the electoral reforms, drew a picture of new national greatness, especially in the Mediterranean. Federzoni, triumphantly elected for one of the divisions of Rome, presented the Nationalist case in vivid terms and increased the pressure of 'public opinion' on San Giuliano.[140] San Giuliano's own rhetoric, whether spoken or written, was also not appeasing. In December 1913 he circulated his ambassadors with a long despatch, re-emphasising Italy's new nationalism: 'Italy is today a power politically, economically and militarily stronger than it was some time ago.' Some states were slow to recognise this. That was predictable, but Italy must now make it plain that she followed a policy fitted to her own vital interests. 'It is necessary,' he asserted bluntly,

both abroad and at home that all should know it and all should understand it; for Italy the days of a submissive policy are gone for ever! And they will never more return![141]

San Giuliano then went on to demonstrate the backing of his favourite historical laws to Italy's new pretensions to greatness:

History is a great contest the outcome of which is progress: some nations have reached earlier a high level of power and development, others, like Italy, later.

Now Italy needed to find riches and influence in proportion to her strength. If this meant a modification of the position of older nations then that was 'the effect of an eternal law of history', which was to the advantage of all and to the damage of none, as people eventually learned how to adapt to a changed situation. After Libya, Italy was on 'a rising path' but, qualifying his conversion to nationalism, San Giuliano noted that, naturally, this would be followed 'with a spirit of conciliation, with prudence, with moderation but [also] with perseverance'.[142]

In fact, as usual, San Giuliano's policy had a second side to it. Despite his own nationalism, he disliked the over-exuberance of the press. When *Gaulois* wrote complaining that Italy had taken the path of Mediterranean imperialism, San Giuliano sent detailed instructions to Tittoni how to reply.[143] He also successfully asked Giolitti to intervene with Frassati to moderate Cirmeni's anti-French polemics in *La Stampa*.[144] San Giuliano was particularly concerned when he was told by Imperiali that French 'knowledge' about the Triple Alliance was taken seriously in London.[145] Russia too had intervened to protest at the extent of the Franco-Italian press storm.[146] San Giuliano usually had a good sense of the limitations of Italian diplomacy, and he was clearly anxious that 'public opinion' should not get out of hand. He now announced to the Chamber that he remained a friend of France, and that there had been in fact no modification of the Triple Alliance. Significantly, a despatch to Tittoni urged the same points, promising to restrain the Italian press, declaring that the Triple Alliance had not been changed, and that Italy always wanted a friendly relationship with France. Lest this be giving too much away, San Giuliano added that France should admit that Italy was now a much greater Mediterranean Power than she had been in the past.[147]

Franco-Italian relations settled back into their accustomed uneasy mutual suspicion. Again the concept of a new Mediterranean pact disintegrated, as Italy concentrated on her probing in the Dodecanese, Albania and Asia Minor.

In these areas Italy was proving tiresome not only to France, but also to Britain. Indeed, it briefly seemed possible that Britain might be driven to cast aspersions on the strength and utility of the 'traditional friendship'. The Naval Attaché in Rome, Captain W. H. Boyle, on 13 December, sent a long report to London the tone of which contrasted with the usual sympathy for Italy of the ambassador, Rodd. Boyle underlined the unchanged strategic realities for Italy: 'Far from having strengthened her maritime position' in Libya, Italy had in fact 'much increased her dependence upon the sea and, consequently, her vulnerability to attack from that element.' If Italy wanted to expand in the Mediterranean, then it would have to be at the expense of Britain and France, but any move south also took Italy away from the interests of Germany and Austria. There was, in any case, no chance that Italy could win a contest with France in the Mediterranean. 'The resources of Italy', he observed,

either as regards finance or ability to build and arm ships, greatly as these have increased in recent years, are not, and cannot be for some generations, such as to render possible a competition with France in the development of a preponderant naval force in the Narrow Sea.

Generally, Boyle concluded,

it cannot be said that the future of Italy in the Mediterranean is very bright, and if military needs must eventually dictate the foreign policy of the country, it would seem as if the near future might see Italy cultivating an understanding with the maritime nations, of whom she is essentially one, rather than protract an unnatural alliance with the military Powers whose attention is occupied to the north, east and west, and whose ability to aid her is limited.[148]

However Boyle's very evidence of real Italian weakness was just that which would make the Foreign Office most reluctant to accept any advice that Italy should be moved from the Triple Alliance. Rodd's recent actions had also not furthered his case. Perhaps having read too many Italian newspapers, Rodd spoke at Livorno publicly in praise of the new Rome's 'new aspirations'. Paul Cambon protested officially at what might be construed as anti-French sentiments, and the Foreign Office noted curtly that Rodd was 'acting on his own initiative'.[149] It was not an appropriate moment for Rodd to hint again that San Giuliano might be willing to talk about a new Mediterranean pact.[150]

Even Grey had grown irritable at Italy's diplomatic methods. When, in January 1914, Imperiali presented him with a note on French press criticism of Lloyd George, Grey scribbled his disgust at this 'childish' attack. Imperiali, he noted,

> might have added an eloquent page contrasting with the petulance of the French press, the wonderful patience of the British S[ecretary] of S[tate] for Foreign Affairs in view of the fact that Italy after having annexed Tripoli by an act of violence and still retaining Aegean Islands was claiming a concession difficult to reconcile with the rights of the only British Railway Company in Asia Minor and was also laying claim in the event of the breakup of Abyssinia to Lake Tsana, which is vital to the Blue Nile and therefore vital to the Sudan and Egypt. This patience in the face of these facts is striking proof that we are as strongly attached to friendship with Italy as Italy...is to friendship with us. It is time that Italy gave some equally striking proof of this friendship to us.[151]

Even Rodd's Annual Report, perhaps trying to regain some ground in London, admitted that Italy could no longer be used as a moderating force in Europe.[152]

Yet Britain, and even France, were curiously unwilling to move from irritation with San Giuliano's untrustworthiness to an open condemnation of Italian policy. Once again, the Italian assumption held that the general international situation allowed Italy unwonted freedom of manoeuvre. In contrast to what he minuted in private, Grey continued to treat Italy politely. When Luigi Albertini visited the Foreign Office on 16 January, an interview with Tyrrell, Grey's private secretary, produced the usual verbiage about Britain and Italy having reciprocal roles in the Triple Entente and the Triple Alliance, and being best left there.[153]

In Rome, Barrère's mood had grown darker. On 20 January he explained to Doumergue that San Giuliano's idea of a European Concert seemed to be '*une cloison étanche*' between Italy and Austria, with Germany as the third factor. San Giuliano had once been a serious statesman, Barrère complained, but now, lacking success, he seemed to grow more and more nationalist. His policy of greatness was a brilliant facade, but, based on 'artifices and passing combinations', it concealed Italy's real weakness.[154]

What Barrère said was, of course, essentially correct, but neither France nor Britain could see what to do about it. In case France was too alienated, on 18 February San Giuliano did remind Barrère that there were no clauses in the Triple Alliance offensive to France, there was no longer a military protocol in existence, and that the Prinetti–Barrère agreement was still valid. While he was talking about military matters, San Giuliano added that it was only reasonable for the Italian Chiefs of Staff to envisage all possibilities in which Italy could be engaged.[155] With not unprecedented obliqueness, San Giuliano was hinting at military discussions currently occurring, which were completed on 10 March by a new agreement with the Triple Alliance. Chief of General Staff, Pollio, restored Italy's old commitment to provide troops on the Western Front in the event of war with France.[156] Naturally, from the Italian point of view, the agreement was only technical, and must be kept subordinate to what was regarded as the higher field of diplomacy.

Meanwhile San Giuliano had remained Foreign Minister in the minority government formed by Salandra in March 1914. He had done so only after considerable persuasion by Giolitti.[157] That Giolitti had so involved himself was testimony to San Giuliano's standing with him, and presumably with the King, but most of all was evidence of the wide acceptance of San Giuliano's policy by the Italian governing elite. Only the Socialists, or Federzoni,[158] disagreed.

Political complications resolved, San Giuliano's mind returned to the Mediterranean agreement. On 6 March Italy had reached a preliminary settlement with Britain on the railway rivalry in Asia Minor. More importantly, the meeting with Berchtold at Abbazia in April proved difficult to organise and eventually again demonstrated that the course of Italo-Austrian relations did not run smooth. This time it was Imperiali who first 'informally' mentioned the idea of a Mediterranean pact. His language was, to say the least, vague. Grey wrote:

The Italian Ambassador observed to me today that, after England and Italy had been friends for 54 years, it might be possible to do something to show that, whatever might happen, a conflict between them was out of the question. He did not propose that Italy should shift her position, or that we should shift ours;

Alliances and Ententes would remain, we would stay where we were, and Italy where she was.

Imperiali hastened to add that Italy always had troubles with France:

He said at once that there would be difficulties about a triple arrangement. There was no lack of goodwill on the part of Italy to France, though France had not lately shown such good feeling to Italy; but, if Italy brought France into the matter, German susceptibilities might be aroused.

Grey received all this suprisingly calmly, perhaps believing that Italian probing could best be limited by some sort of agreement. There were, he said, still the two possibilities, either a Mediterranean, or a North African agreement. The former could not proceed without France, but, in the latter, Italy and Britain might be able to have bilateral talks if there were no French interests involved.[159] This sounded like a concession by Britain, but, as in the past, hopeful words did not mean action, and, for the moment, nothing happened. When Rodd tried to hasten matters, he was met by Crowe's usual refusal to do anything until Italy found a formula.[160] Rather than such decisive action, San Giuliano was again mending fences with France. In a speech to the Senate he declared that the *Carthage* and *Manouba* incidents were now closed; and in any case 'the great lines' of Italian foreign policy were 'not influenced by incidents and episodes' but were 'determined only by the great and permanent national interests'. Italy would work with Austria to resolve any Adriatic problems, and with Britain in the Eastern Mediterranean and Asia Minor. In general, Italy was now more respected than she had been for many years.[161] At the same time, San Giuliano took up a suggestion made by Doumergue in February for a legal agreement on the capitulation rights of Italians in Tunis and Tunisians in Libya.[162]

On 1 May San Giuliano added the formal step of suggesting to Imperiali and his other ambassadors that some sort of North African agreement be revived alongside the capitulation discussions. There were still many uncertainties. Britain would be likely to want France included and this might annoy Germany, although a bilateral Anglo–Italian agreement would be welcomed in Berlin. Perhaps even Spain might be associated given 'the solidarity of Latin civilisation'.[163] Leaving that aside for the moment, on the more familiar question of French participation, perhaps Britain might let something slip in Italy's favour in Berlin? France too could show her goodwill in the talks on Libya and Tunis, by treating Italy with less contempt than usual. In any case, Italy's freedom of action was quite clear. 'Italy', San Giuliano declared,

so far as the Mediterranean is concerned, is not bound by any special conventions. The Triple Alliance, of which the purely defensive scope is clear, has been renewed without modification.[164]

San Giuliano had perhaps been slightly more open than before, but it is difficult to detect much of a turning point in his policy. Rather, the revival of talks with the *Entente Cordiale* fitted the changes in the general international position. San Giuliano had succeeded in securing for Albania, at least theoretically, the southern border which Italy wanted. He had acknowledgment from both Britain, and the Central Powers, of Italy's new interest in Asia Minor. He had not surrendered the Dodecanese. But there were still many areas where Italian ambitions were as yet unfulfilled. Ethiopia, still larger aims in Asia Minor, the running cold war with Austria in Northern Albania – these were all good reasons for returning to the strategy of discussing a Mediterranean pact, and seeing what would happen.

At first it seemed nothing much. France and Italy rapidly reached their capitulation settlement, which was formally signed by San Giuliano and Barrère on 29 May.[165] But such matters were hardly the nub of European diplomacy. San Giuliano's efforts to inspire Britain with a zeal to be Italy's agent in Berlin or Paris[166] were not getting far. In London Crowe, in particular, was not anxious to talk to the Italians at all. Indeed his prose grew quite apoplectic when he considered the enormity of Italy's cheek:

I naturally enquired [of Imperiali] what was the nature of the agreement contemplated by the Italian Government. To this simple question I absolutely failed after an hour's vivacious and voluble explanation from the Ambassador to get any intelligible answer... But he continued to urge that some formula should be found, and that I, in particular, should sit down and find it. So far as I could understand the ambassador, his Government wanted to do something quite platonic, practically empty and meaningless, which yet would have the effect of reconciling France and Italy, and with his usual way of approaching such a subject, he wanted to prove that such a reconciliation was very much to the interest of England, from which it followed, according to his Italian reasoning, that it was really our duty, that is England's duty, to discover and invent this precious formula which would bring about the practical realisation of a vital British interest.

Rodd's 1912 North African agreement had been, Crowe remembered, 'really quite valueless for any practical purposes'. So now he advised that Britain should do nothing:

Italy wants us to square the circle without exposing herself to a charge of breach of faith, she wants to remain in the Triple Alliance and yet not go to war with France in accordance with its stipulations. No Anglo-Italian 'formula' can solve this ethical question.[167]

Crowe's spleen was undiplomatically phrased, but not surprising. Indeed, although Salandra noted that he favoured a Mediterranean agreement as a demonstration of Italo-British friendship, and an affirmation of Italy's power in the Mediterranean,[168] there were the gravest reasons to doubt whether San Giuliano was a genuine convert to the idea of an early settlement. As before, despite his pleading that Britain take up Italy's part in Berlin, he had in fact kept Germany informed.[169] To a large extent, San Giuliano was merely repeating his design of autumn 1913, aimed basically at getting Berlin to restrain Vienna, or, at least, at illustrating Italy's moral superiority and better claims to be regarded by Germany as a 'noble second', who might even deserve reward for her efforts and honesty. On 4 June Grey and Imperiali made little progress when they met again to discuss the hypothetical pact. The Italian ambassador was told that Britain believed that France must be a part of an agreement on 'Mediterranean Africa' and that Italy must find the formula.[170]

What turning point there was came rather from the German side. Reluctantly and belatedly, Bollati, on 13 June, asked Jagow about the current German attitude to a new Mediterranean agreement. In contrast to the previous November, Jagow now said that he was 'rather favourable'. Germany supported anything which would strengthen Anglo-Italian ties, and, although he was less enthusiastic about the association of France, he realised that Britain could not proceed without her.[171]

The motives for this statement are not clear. Perhaps it is testimony to the new warmth of Anglo-German relations in the summer of 1914. Perhaps Jagow was merely acting impulsively, and without sufficient briefing. On the other hand, perhaps the always rash Germany had tired first among all the Great Powers of San Giuliano's unappeasable importunities, and was ready to admit openly that Italy was not a reliable member of the Triple Alliance. If this is so, it is an interesting prelude to Germany's policy towards Italy one month later, when the failure to consult Italy after the assassination of Archduke Franz Ferdinand in the way that had been done in the Balkan crises of 1913 would be very striking.

Whatever the reasons for Jagow's action, he had breathed fleeting life into the dormant Mediterranean scheme. On 10 June Barrère and Paul Cambon agreed that now was the moment to improve Franco-Italian relations.[172] San Giuliano at once took the opportunity to encourage France to find a formula, alleging that he had British backing. Nicolson swiftly disabused Paul Cambon on that point.[173] Since they still had the Italian cypher, the French were probably not too surprised.[174] In any event, as Italo-Austrian relations worsened, France had been showing less interest in the Mediterranean scheme.

San Giuliano, therefore, turned again to London where Grey still favoured a settlement on North Africa.[175] San Giuliano had told Barrère that he was newly interested in a Mediterranean pact,[176] but, receiving no answer, on 6 July he saw Rodd, and said that he

was of opinion that if we were to enter into such agreement it would be well now not to delay it. The terms would be anodyne in character but...would undoubtedly have a good effect on the general situation.

Perhaps sensing the great crisis enveloping Europe, and the fragility of his diplomatic card house before a real storm, San Giuliano was at unusual pains to be accommodating. He was ready, he said, to settle the Lake Tsana issue in Ethiopia, and indeed to resolve any differences between Italy and Britain.[177] The only thing which might seem ominous about that was that he had not yet stated his price, although the mention of Lake Tsana might reasonably be taken as evidence that it was likely to be in Ethiopia. In any case, San Giuliano's discussions with Rodd were soon lost in the July crisis. Nothing further was heard of a new Mediterranean or North African settlement. Even on 6 July progress had not been rapid. No formula was put forward, nor had it been decided who would do the drafting, and San Giuliano in the past had shown a desire to manoeuvre a great deal before making such a definite commitment.

The main historiographical analysis of the whole story of the abortive Mediterranean pacts has seen them as an index of the failure of San Giuliano's triplicism, which, it is argued, was 'without limitation or wavering'.[178] Perhaps this interpretation underestimates both San Giuliano's skill and his uncertainty, as well as his final realisation that Italo-Austrian relations were unlikely to be permanently good.

In this story of an agreement which never occurred, San Giuliano's policy was defined by two basic events. After the invasion of Libya, Italian policy paid more attention, in the short term, to the Mediterranean than to anywhere else. In the past such attention had usually meant an Italian quarrel with France; but, in 1912, Italy was confronted by the new problem of the *Entente Cordiale*, which seemed so solid that it could allow mutual naval redeployment. 'Traditional friendship' with Britain, and a strand of traditional enmity with France were thus very difficult to weave together.

San Giuliano was an expansionist, but he understood that Italian expansion had to come by diplomatic means – really, given Italian weakness, by diplomatic conjuring. To be a successful conjurer, it is necessary to be quick, to change the scene often, and thus to prevent anyone from stopping the show and pointing out that the tricks lack a real basis. This essentially was San Giuliano's policy, 1912–14, both within the Triple Alliance and towards the Triple Entente.

While the Libyan War lasted, the Mediterranean pact really had no chance whatever, and was only favoured by Rodd and Barrère, ambassadors whose office in Rome distorted their understanding of the general international situation. After October 1912, San Giuliano took up the idea of a Mediterranean pact whenever talk of such a scheme, or even of a simple North African agreement, could help his diplomacy. If times grew too hard because of Barrère's 'friendship' or Mérey's hostility, San Giuliano could always make plain to France that the 1902 accords continued and therefore, in practice, that a new arrangement was unnecessary. On other occasions, the suggestion of a new Mediterranean pact was useful to remind France, but especially Britain, that Italy was a 'friend', or to remind Germany and Austria that Italy had friends as well as allies.

In contrast to previous Italian policies of trying to reach as many agreements as possible, a line adopted most clearly and naively by Prinetti (and later favoured by Mussolini), San Giuliano found interesting advantage for Italy in not reaching too many agreements, in genuinely playing on the policy of having 'allies' *and* 'friends'. This was not triplicism, nor indeed was it a conscious dedication to anti-Austrian imperialism. Neither the agreements signed with the Triple Alliance, nor those not signed with the Triple Entente should be taken too literally. San Giuliano wanted to push Italy up a rising path in what he saw as 'the great contest of the nations'. The only method which he believed to be possible was to stir the diplomatic pot, and to do it so covertly and so persistently that the Greater Powers would reward Italy with any rabbit which popped out. While peace lasted, who knew what possibilities there were?

Very few in the Italian ruling classes disagreed with these ambitions. As the King would later put it:

problems like those of Malta, Nice [and] the Canton Ticino should never be let go. There's nothing to be done at the moment... But one never knows. Situations can change... something which seems absurd today, does not tomorrow.[179]

In the 1930s Italy's policy became too distinct, too committed, too apparently ideological, for these or other ambitions to be achieved, and, in the end, Italy was foolishly and disastrously committed to war. San Giuliano did not make the mistake of clarity in his version of expansionism in 1911 to 1914. His manoeuvres were for peace time. Then, if there was war between the Great Powers, he understood that the Royal Navy was still the *force majeure*, and Italy in real terms would still not be able to make good the ancient boast that *Italia farà da sè*.

CHAPTER 9

'Une cliente maleducato': Italy in the Dodecanese and Ethiopia, 1912–1914

A. J. P. Taylor, in one of his throwaway lines, has noted: 'there were few real secrets in the diplomatic world [before 1914], and all diplomatists were honest, according to their moral code'. He then adds a cautionary footnote: 'It becomes wearisome to add "except the Italians" to every generalisation. Henceforth it may be assumed.'[1]

On the surface this comment is absurd, a typical example of Taylor's rhetorical excess. Yet, as so often, Taylor's absurdity contains a grain of truth. Italian diplomatists were, naturally, as personally honest as any of their counterparts. Yet the basis of Italian diplomacy, the simple ambition to act as a Great Power, was so far from the reality of Italian strength as to be, in the last analysis, dishonest, and often produced policy which was ambivalent, tortuous and again, crudely dishonest.

There have been many efforts to search for the key to Italy's newly enthusiastic expansionism between 1912 and 1914. The domestic machinations of Giolitti, the personal frustrations and ambition of San Giuliano, the new philosophy of the Nationalist Association, the *Drang nach Osten* of new Italian capitalism, all have had their advocates, and all indeed had a role to play, an influence on policy. Yet, above all, Italian policy was decided, in the sense of being set in context, by the assumption of the majority of her ruling class after the Risorgimento that Italy was a Great Power and needed to act, distinct from lesser states, as a Great Power. Usually a limit was set to ambition by the reality of the reaction of the other Great Powers, whose strength was so much greater than Italy's if ever there came the time for the test of war. But between 1912 and 1914 the state of the European Concert, the existence of the blocs of Triple Entente and Central Powers, and the tenderness of many of the relationships between the blocs, and inside the blocs, allowed Italy unparalleled freedom of action. In the last months before the assassination of

Italy, the least of the Great Powers

Archduke Franz Ferdinand, the other five Great Powers all feared that a European war was near, and, at the same time, they all feared that a war would not occur, but instead a diplomatic incident which, dexterously manipulated by some rival, would produce a new division of the Great Powers, more damaging than the existing alliance system. In its most simple form, these fears are reflected in the British decision not to woo Italy into the Triple Entente for fear that in gaining Italy, Russia would be lost. The alliance system, which seemed so formal, and yet could also appear so fragile, was the root of the new freedom and ambition of Italy, the least of the Great Powers.

Just as Italy was not really a Great Power, so she was not really, or at least not reliably, either a loyal 'friend' or a loyal 'ally'. Most often this meant trouble for Italy, 'clean hands' at the Congress of Berlin, insults at the Algeçiras Conference, and, ultimately, being disregarded in the July Crisis. However, in the brief years between the Libyan War and 1914, Italy was able to act with new independence; San Giuliano, with sometimes breathtaking negotiating skill and *Schadenfreude*, was able to build a card house of Italian advances, which ought to have been enough to satisfy the most insatiable longing of any Italian Nationalist. Covertly, sometimes no doubt even to himself, turning one way and then another, and with essential dishonesty, San Giuliano strove to establish an Italian presence in any area of the world where such a presence could be imagined; and none of the other Powers called Italy up short. In this continued manipulation, San Giuliano's most important weapon was the Dodecanese Islands.

The islands first came into Italian hands, almost by chance, during the course of the Libyan War. After the 'accidental' raid on the Dardanelles in April 1912, in the following weeks Italy tried a new method of driving Turkey to accept the loss of Libya by gradually occupying the group of Dodecanese Islands off the coast of Asia Minor. Stampalia was seized on 26 April, and there was a disembarkation of an Italian force on Rhodes at dawn on 4 May.[2] Twelve more islands, some very tiny, were taken under Italian control. There is evidence that the military feasibility of these actions had been studied well beforehand.[3] San Giuliano had also probed diplomatic possibilities in early April when he was at pains to sustain with his Central Power allies that an Italian occupation of

300

islands off the coast of Asia Minor would not allow Austria to invoke Article VII of the Triple Alliance.[4] However, the first and basic reason for action against the Dodecanese was unquestionably the tactical one of securing peace in Libya. The Dodecanese were chosen because, of the myriad of Aegean Islands, they were the farthest away from the Balkans, and therefore least likely to provoke the Balkan nations to war, or allow Austria to move further south-east. If Rhodes and many of the other islands had Venetian remains to delight imperially minded archaeologists and historians, if the islands lay near the coast of Asia Minor in an area where Italy was anxious to join the Great Power race to dismember Turkey, so much the better; but the decisive interest was still Libya. And Italy would hardly be allowed or want to keep islands of Greek population and direct Turkish ownership.

The occupation of the islands was accordingly accompanied by a series of disclaimers that Italy intended more than temporary control.[5] Only Russia showed any sign of pleasure,[6] although the other Powers acquiesced, as usual with somewhat bad grace, to the independent Italian action. Austria did not regard an Italian advance in the far-off Aegean as a serious danger, and perhaps hoped for advantages to the Triple Alliance.[7] Poincaré ought to have been concerned by Tittoni's promise that Italy would extend good administration to the Christian population, but he contented himself with the statement that it was '*très douteux*' that a Power should treat occupied territory as annexed before a peace settlement.[8] Indeed the readiness with which the Italian action was accepted is a useful corrective to the argument that Europe's major foreign policy interests in the period were in Asia Minor. The occupation was tolerated because all the Powers had decided that they should do nothing to prevent most Italian action during the war with Turkey, so long as a total Balkan collapse was not immediately precipitated.

Apart from the general fear that Italy was hastening the demise of the ailing Ottoman Empire, it was the supreme naval Power, Britain, whose interests could have been most affected by the occupation of the Dodecanese. These islands, in a powerful hand, could be an enormous threat to Britain's trade routes to Russia through the Dardanelles, and to India through Suez. Italy herself could hardly be imagined to pose that threat; but Italy had allies who perhaps could. In the anti-German atmosphere among the bureaucrats of the Foreign Office in London, it is not surprising to find some who detected sinister overtones in the Italian action.

Acting with due ceremony, the Foreign Office appealed to its military advisers to define the grounds for a policy with respect to the Dodecanese. General Wilson, the Director of Military Operations, replied that the temporary occupation of 'Astropalia' did not offend British interests. He added without comment that the islands would provide a suitable base against the provinces around Smyrna. The clerks in the Foreign Office were not pleased by this military simplicity. Sir Robert Vansittart minuted that it would have been more relevant to have had an assessment on the permanent occupation of the islands.[9] The Assistant Under-Secretary, Sir Charles Mallet, warned:

I do not think that Italy will ever retire from Rhodes or has ever had any intention of retiring. It looks as if the occupation of these islands had the tacit support of Germany, if indeed she was not privy to the Italian designs.[10]

Permanent Under-Secretary, Sir Arthur Nicolson, was in one of his recurrent black moods. The Mediterranean situation, he wrote fearfully, was being 'revolutionised'. The Triple Alliance might be extended to the Mediterranean 'and we shall then be faced with a very formidable naval and military combination in those waters'. The Dodecanese would either become 'a dozen little Cretes' or 'if on the other hand Italy retains possession of one or two of the more important islands, she will be the dominating factor in the East Levant'.[11]

Despite Nicolson's ample and remarkable fears, Britain accepted Italy's declaration that the occupation was temporary, and at first did nothing to try to make the pledge more formal. Under pressure from France,[12] the Foreign Office merely appealed to its military advisers to clarify the significance of the islands. In case there should be further misconceptions, Grey spelled out the problem for the Admiralty: 'What we want to know', he wrote,

is whether it is inconsistent with British strategic interests that Italy should be allowed to retain permanently any Islands in the Aegean or whether it should be an object of British policy to secure at the end of the war the evacuation by Italy of all the Islands seized and occupied by her during the war.[13]

The Admiralty took some time to draft its reply, but, when it came, it was clear. Given the unforeseen nature of the future, the occupation of the islands should be taken seriously. Operating from a base in the Dodecanese, a hostile state could undermine the British position in the Dardanelles, in all Asia Minor and in Egypt. 'It may be confidently asserted', the memorandum ran:

that the possession by Italy of Naval bases in the Aegean Sea would imperil our position in Egypt, would cause us to lose our control over our Black Sea and Levant trade at its source, and would in war expose our route to the East via the Suez Canal to the operations of Italy and her allies.[14]

Italy, it was obvious, should not be allowed to keep the Dodecanese.

Grey was hamstrung by his desire not to appear to interfere while Italy was still at war with Turkey, but, on 6 August he did try gently to warn Italy off. The Italians, he hoped,

would not pass any decree about the Aegean Islands or commit themselves about them: for any Great European maritime Power to keep one or more of these Islands, that might form a naval base, would give rise to difficulties.

Imperiali, with the usual immediate desire to mark out where the lines of potential negotiation lay, remarked that he believed Austria and France were 'sensitive on this subject'. Deadpan, Grey intervened to say that Britain also was 'sensitive about the naval situation in the Mediterranean'.[15]

Apart from Britain, France was also unhappy about the prospect of a lasting Italian occupation of the Dodecanese. When Poincaré asked point-blank to be told Italy's plans, Tittoni declared that 'the occupation of the islands was for us only a means of pressure on Turkey to compel her [to accept] peace'.[16] Barrère, for one, believed that Italy was under no illusions that the islands must be surrendered at the peace table.[17] By no means all French politicians were as sanguine as their representative in Rome about Italian trustworthiness, but France, with the exception of occasional flurries of irritation, was usually willing to accept British guidance over the best policy to employ towards Italian ambitions in the Eastern Mediterranean.

Of her two most uncomfortable rivals, it was Austria rather than France, which, at first, put pressure on Rome. In late May 1912, the news leaked from Berlin that Austria might contemplate invoking Article VII of the Triple Alliance if Italy really intended to make territorial gains in the Eastern Mediterranean.[18] San Giuliano at once enquired of Avarna what this was all about, and was told that Berchtold had had 'an unfavourable impression' of Italy's unilateral naval actions. Berchtold declared that Austria certainly had a legal case to justify an appeal to Article VII, and would be unable to hold back if Italy took any further steps forward, for example by occupying the island of Chios.[19] Berchtold was unimpressed by Avarna's explanation that the Dodecanese were not in 'the Aegean' but were properly part of Asiatic Turkey. He also showed little enthusiasm for the Italian case that the occupation was 'temporary'.[20] Thwarted on these points, San Giuliano fell back on his reiterated theme that 'a delay today in our operations in the Aegean would seem and would be a victory for Turkey against us'. If Italian 'public opinion' thought that this was the result of Austrian policies, then it would be most unfortunate and even dangerous for the well-being of the Triple Alliance.[21] Nevertheless, after further soundings in both Vienna and Berlin, Italy abandoned her probable intention to add Chios to the list of the islands which she had seized.[22]

Austria continued to be unhappy about the Italian naval action, although Berchtold was unable to see that much could be done about it. Negotiations with Avarna proceeded on the wording of the Italian promise to evacuate the Dodecanese with Berchtold making plain his hardly unjustified suspicions that circumstances might arise which, 'unfortunately', could prevent Italy from keeping her word that she had no 'interest nor desire to prolong the occupation of the islands beyond what [was] necessary'.[23] Mérey, too, had weighed in with his usual scant courtesy, noting the Italian ability to find 'pretexts when they were necessary'.[24]

Confronted by such criticism, San Giuliano and Giolitti both ingenuously declared their certainty that the islands would one day be surrendered by Italy; Giolitti, for example, instructed his peace delegates in Switzerland to give no welcome to any Turkish offers about the islands – their retention would simply be a useless expense.[25]

Yet, despite these good intentions, equivocations began to appear. Establishment journals began to publish articles about the historic ties between the Dodecanese and Italy.[26] Moreover, there was the problem that the inhabitants of the islands were not Turkish, but Greek. Could Italy allow Christian people to be handed back to possible retribution by the 'abominable Turk'? As early as 17 June some of the local population had declared their desire to become an independent, or at least an autonomous, Aegean state. With the usual ambition of the agent abroad, the Italian military governor of the Dodecanese, General Ameglio, sympathised with these pleas for national liberation.[27] Rumours of his patronage of the local Greeks became serious enough for San Giuliano to have a denial issued in Vienna.[28] In Switzerland, the Italian peace delegates diverted their boredom by dreaming up new methods of using the islands to influence the Turks to accept a peace treaty, only to be met by a bland Turkish statement that Italian behaviour there was quite irrelevant to the main Libyan issue.[29] Giacomo De Martino III, in Rome, also was thinking of future possibilities. He drafted a memorandum, implying that Italy could do something for the local Greeks. After all, he said, scrutinising earlier despatches with care, Italy had promised Austria only to restore the '*status quo ante*' in the islands, and had therefore omitted the adjective '*politique*'. Some political, as distinct from strategic, changes could thus be legally argued and even allowed.[30] When a formal peace was reached in Libya, there might be continuing military difficulties. As San Giuliano pointed out to his reluctant Prime Minister, Italy could not evacuate the islands until all the Turkish troops had left Libya, an event likely to be far-off.[31] San Giuliano was also interested in the relevance of the schemes, of which he had been told by Berchtold, to encourage the decentralisation of the Turkish Empire. Italy had an obligation to see that the Greek population of the Dodecanese was not mistreated, and some sort of semi-autonomous set-up might have value, although he added hurriedly, Italy did not want to keep any of the islands, and was occupying them solely for military reasons.[32]

So the situation remained until the Treaty of Lausanne. But, as the months passed, the complications of possession increased, as did potential plans for the use of the islands. No definite policy had been formulated, and Giolitti was particularly hostile when approached about schemes for the islands, but Italy was beginning to drift towards proving the old adage 'possession is nine-tenths of the law'.

Giolitti's hostility was undoubtedly based on the assumption that the Great Powers would not permit Italy to keep the islands, once the peace treaty was signed. In September, Grey had repeated his warning to Imperiali that Britain wanted the islands returned, although he toned down the original French request for a brusque *démarche* in Rome.[33] San Giuliano also believed that Austria would not tolerate any Italian retention of the islands, and was still mulling over the worse probability that Austria might use such a retention to apply Article VII in her favour in the Balkans.[34] France continued to be adamant that Italy should not conduct an independent policy in the Aegean.[35]

On 15 October 1912 the Lausanne agreement was duly signed. By Clause 2 of the treaty, Italy promised to return the islands. In London, Vansittart, then a youthful clerk in the Foreign Office, minuted Britain's satisfaction.[36] He should not have been so readily pleased. Whether consciously or not, San Giuliano had written himself a dateless cheque. He had remembered his earlier remark. The islands were not to be surrendered until all the Turkish troops were out of Libya. Given the style of the Italian military occupation, and the difficulty of distinguishing in the sands of Fezzan a Turkish soldier from an Arab insurgent, it was extremely unlikely, unless the Powers did something, that the simple course of events or mere legal pressure would induce Italy to return the islands.

It is possible that, at first, San Giuliano did not plumb to the depths the opportunities for the future. Both Rodd and Barrère readily believed in Italian innocence. Neither Bertie, who perhaps remembered in Paris his training as ambassador in Rome, nor Poincaré were so ingenuous.[37] But once again international events made Great Power intervention in Rome difficult. The beginning of the Balkan Wars had revived the question of the Greek nationality of the population of the Dodecanese. Graecophiles as diverse as Sir Arthur Evans in England, and the Italian ambassador in Athens, Carlotti, began to argue that, given the alteration already occurring in the *status quo* of the Eastern Mediterranean, the islands should go not to Turkey but to Greece.[38] San Giuliano was not slow to begin sounding the terrain on his own behalf. On his instructions, Imperiali underlined the incomplete nature of Clause 2 of the Treaty of Lausanne by warning Britain to prevent any Egyptian relaxation on the passage of troops or contraband to Libya. The Italian ambassador also opened new vistas by gently raising in London the concept of the Dodecanese becoming an autonomous unit under Turkish suzerainty.[39]

Meanwhile the Balkan Wars had had a different impact on Italian policy. The Dodecanese ceased being only a matter of Italo–Turkish relations, or of Italy's position among the Great Powers, and now involved directly Italo–Greek relations.

Italy's relationships with smaller Powers were always inclined to be precarious. Smaller Powers rarely treated Italy with the respect which she considered her due, and with no Power was this more true than with Greece. However much weaker than Italy in real terms, Greece had an imperial past which could rival Italy's own, and, moreover, the legacy of Byzantium could be found all over the Eastern Mediterranean and even in the Adriatic, in the very areas which Italy remembered most vividly had once been part of the Roman Empire. The Greek-speaking elements of the population of Asia Minor or Southern Albania were a *Graecia Irredenta* which directly threatened Italy's own interests. Italy therefore viewed with the gravest suspicion Greek gains in the Balkan Wars.[40]

It was in the Adriatic that the real heart of Italian foreign policy always lay, and it was therefore in Albania that Italy most openly defined her hostility to Greek advantage. By December 1912 rumours reached Rome that Greece intended to advance far to the north of her present territories, and perhaps intended to occupy the island of Saseno, off the port of Valona, and always regarded by Italian strategists as one of the keys to the Adriatic. It was no comfort to learn from Vienna that, if Italy and Austria could not reach an accord on Albania, the territory should best be divided among the small Balkan states.[41] San Giuliano at once declared his joy at the prospect of collaboration with Austria, and bluntly told the Greeks that they must avoid all actions along the Albanian coast.[42] In the next weeks, San Giuliano frequently reiterated this masterful advice, underlining Italy's superiority by the claim that Austria and Germany stood behind her.[43]

It was to deal with just these sort of problems that, in January 1913, the Conference of Ambassadors assembled in London to consider Balkan questions. But, from the Italian viewpoint, there was the extra benefit that Italy's membership of the Concert gave her a great advantage. Italy was a Great Power whose wishes would have to be respected by all; Greece was a little Power, at war, and ultimately would have to accept the advice of the Concert.

In so far as Italy was concerned, there were two major issues involving the Greeks. The first was the question of Southern

Albania, or 'Northern Epirus' as the Greeks preferred to call it. The second was the 'Aegean Islands' – not just the Dodecanese, but the problem of the ultimate ownership of the multitude of islands scattered over the Aegean Sea from Crete to the most tiny. To a mind as logical as San Giuliano's, there was an obvious parallel to be exploited. In addition to keeping the Dodecanese until Turkish troops had retired from Libya, Italy could not also refuse to think of Greek ownership of the ethnically Greek Dodecanese until Italy had her way on the question of the border of Southern Albania. Moreover, there was a second, still shadowy possibility. Soon Sir Edward Grey and the ambassadors were locked in detailed and protracted discussion of the 'Aegean Islands'. But what precisely did that phrase, 'Aegean Islands', mean? Did it, for example, include Cyprus? Did it really include Rhodes and the Dodecanese, which anyhow were covered by the separate legal provisions of the Treaty of Lausanne? Italy did not ask these questions, and was also pleased that nobody asked them of her. Rather, in much of the discussion which followed, the confusion or ambiguity was most useful to Italy. The small Power, Greece, would be encouraged to make a bargain, and then find that Great Powers like Italy expected to be paid on time, but did not always pay their own debts as quickly.

In London, all began with appropriate orthodoxy. Early in January, San Giuliano wrote to Imperiali that Italy was in accord with the Triple Alliance, but believed that Crete should go to Greece, that the islands near the Dardanelles should be kept by Turkey, and that the other islands should have autonomy under ultimate Turkish sovereignty. Accepting the Albanian–Dodecanese bargaining point, Grey told Imperiali that 'new Cretes' could not be allowed, but that he would consider any proposal to guard against a Greek threat to Turkey. Perhaps the Dodecanese could be demilitarised?[44] San Giuliano was unlikely to be attracted by such legal niceties; instead, believing any figure to be negotiable, he began to consider how many islands should go to Greece and how many could be retained by Turkey. Rodd was pleased:

On one point identical views seem to exist. (San Giuliano]...said that Italy would be ready to sign an agreement that none of the great powers should acquire or retain any island and categorically assured me that Italy had never contemplated doing so.[45]

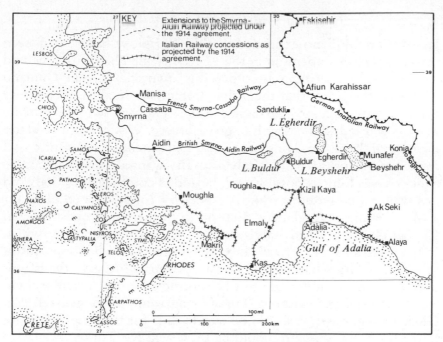

Map labels: KEY — Extensions to the Smyrna-Aidin Railway projected under the 1914 agreement. Italian Railway concessions as projected by the 1914 agreement.

LESBOS, CHIOS, Manisa, Cassaba, Smyrna, French Smyrna-Cassaba Railway, Sandukli, Afiun Karahissar, German Anatolian Railway, L. Egherdir, Aidin, British Smyrna-Aidin Railway, SAMOS, ICARIA, Egherdir, Buldur, Munafer, Konia, L. Buldur, L. Beyshehr, Beyshehr, PATMOS, NAXOS, LEROS, CALYMNOS, Foughla, Kizil Kaya, Ak Seki, Moughla, AMORGOS, NISYROS, Elmaly, Adalia, KYTHERA, ASTYPALIA, SYMI, Makri, Gulf of Adalia, Alaya, TELOS, RHODES, Kas, CARPATHOS, CRETE, CASSOS, Eskisehir

100ml / 100 / 200km

4   Italian penetration of Asia Minor

In case such pledges seemed too yielding, Italy also at once asked for embarrassing reciprocal undertakings that France had no designs on Syria. In case, too, a mere ambassador grew too authoritative at the London Conference, San Giuliano warned Grey against believing everything that Imperiali said: 'the Ambassador in London was given to talking and writing too much – it was his temperament – and people who talked too much very often said ill-considered things'. Having prepared that way, San Giuliano now said what could be construed as 'ill-considered things' on his own account. If Turkey was to be partitioned, Italy would claim a part. Furthering the confusion about which islands were being discussed, Rodd sighed that the Italians had put 'objections...to every possible mode of approaching a discussion on the island question' and that the *Consulta* was 'entirely under the control of the Triple Alliance'.[46] Could it be that the Dodecanese were not just to be used in 'Southern Albania', but also in Asia Minor?

San Giuliano couched his phrases differently when talking to his allies, but continued to enjoy using the word 'islands' to mean different places at different times. To the German ambassador,

309

Jagow, San Giuliano explained that the 'Triple Alliance' had 'seen through' Greek expansion in the Aegean, which had Russia behind it. Moreover, ascribing to others his own views, San Giuliano expressed the belief that the Triple Entente were already counting on the future collapse of Asiatic Turkey. This was why the Entente Powers wanted all the islands to go to Greece. Would it not be better if 'some of the islands lying next to the Dardanelles and Asiatic coast' remained in Turkish hands? Italy naturally wanted Turkey to be able to survive as long as possible and, he added confidentially, Italy did not want to be seduced from her allies by Anglo-French plans for a Mediterranean agreement. Returning to the island question, San Giuliano distinguished Italy's position on the Dodecanese, which Italy currently had to retain in order to get Turkish troops out of Libya. Also, Italy had signed a treaty promising to give the islands back to Turkey, and could not be so disloyal as to surrender them to another power without Turkey's agreement. In general, San Giuliano suggested, it would be worthwhile for the Triple Alliance to see how many islands could be preserved for Turkey.[47]

San Giuliano came close to clarifying his policy. Slightly adapting his conversation with Jagow, he told his ambassador in Berlin that the Germans were insisting that some of the islands should go back to Turkey.[48] Giolitti had not objected to his Foreign Minister's line. Indeed it was the Prime Minister himself who invoked the parallel with Cyprus. Britain, he believed, had promised, when taking Cyprus, to defend Turkey's provinces in Asia Minor. Turkey should now be reminded of this, and the potential connection of this precedent to the Dodecanese, which geography clearly linked to the mainland and not to Greece.[49] After a Russian inquiry, Italy's ambassadors were circulated with the information that the Triple Alliance and not just Italy thought that it would be best if the Dodecanese were returned to Turkey.[50] Imperiali was carefully instructed by San Giuliano to work in all matters with his German and Austrian colleagues: 'I repeat that the Triple Alliance is the fundamental base of our policy. On the whole island question you must stand firm against the Triple Entente.'[51]

While San Giuliano dreamed up new snares for Greece, the Balkan Wars showed no signs of abating, and the London Conference laboured on. At the ambassadorial meetings, San Giuliano was anxious to have it known that Italy continued to act within the Triple

Alliance. Time and time again, he reiterated his desire to work with Austria in Albania, and made plain to Germany that whatever happened to the other islands, the Dodecanese should go back to Turkey.[52] At home, San Giuliano increased his plans for what he now seemed to think was the imminent collapse of all Turkish power, and announced his intention that, with Triple Alliance backing, Italy be inserted into any distribution of territory in Asia Minor. Numerous despatches told of his fears that, otherwise, the Mediterranean would become an 'Anglo-French lake'.

San Giuliano's triplicism seemed complete. In March, when discussions were resumed in London on the Southern Albania question, Italy and France took up radically different stances. Paul Cambon declared that Franco-Italian views were 'irreconcilable'. Grey, far less firm towards Italy than were the French, was anxious to find a compromise but was not helped by vague advice from his strategists that 'the channel between Corfu and the sea possesses great strategic value for a fleet watching the exit from the Adriatic', but ending with the French case that the strait was dominated by the Albanian coast, and so the border should 'probably' be north of Corfu.[53] All that was really established was the supremacy of the Great Powers. On 23 April the Balkan states were informed that the delimitation of Albania and of the Aegean Islands must remain solely an issue for the Great Powers.[54] Nicolson, as usual, dolefully, advised surrender to Italy:

I am sure that we shall have very great difficulty over the southern boundaries of the future Albania, and Italy is raising many difficulties on the subject. To my mind I think she is too anxious not to allow Greece to possess the littoral facing Corfu. Greece is ready to give any assurances and submit to any condition which would render the sheet of water quite harmless and innocuous. However both the Italian naval and military staffs are very decided that it would be impossible to leave the whole of the [Corfu] Channel in Greek hands. Apparently they have said their last word on the subject and I suppose we shall have to endeavour to persuade the Greeks to give in.[55]

Nicolson, it was plain, wholeheartedly accepted the difference between Great Powers and small, and was willing to admit, however resignedly, that Italy, despite her weakness, must get her way as a member of the Concert.

If Italy was still working within the Triple Alliance, this was more for tactical reasons than out of guileless dedication. In February, Italy had already shown an interest in flirting with Russia, if Russia was willing to flirt with her, and had to explain away her conduct before Austrian enquiries. In the same month, an ambassadorial exchange sent Carlotti to replace the feeble Melegari in St Petersburg, and transferred the enthusiastic young Balkan expert, Alessandro De Bosdari,[56] to Athens. The latter at once began to consider ways of improving Italo-Greek relations,[57] but, according to his own account, De Bosdari was soon discouraged by San Giuliano from being too friendly to Greece, and even told to threaten Greece with war if she grew too obdurate in Southern Albania.[58]

It was not however so much Austria's *beaux yeux*, nor ambitions in Asia Minor, which nourished San Giuliano's triplicism. Rather, the Italians well understood that the Balkan Wars created more strongly than usual the need for Italy to stay close to Austria, lest alliance be exchanged for enmity. Throughout the Balkan conflict, Italy experienced the always present fear that gains by the smaller Balkan states, either with Russia behind them, or, almost as bad if Serbia was involved, gains on their own part, could provoke Austrian intervention. In late March and early April 1913, the delicacy of Italy's position was made manifest in the Scutari crisis. If Italy had strategic ambitions in Southern Albania, so did Austria in the North. Only by continuing to link the two sides of the Albanian question could Austria be kept at the peace table, and Italy saved from that most dangerous and embarrassing choice between 'allies' and 'friends', perhaps even between peace and war.

Amid Balkan alarums, the formal preparation of the Italian case on the Dodecanese continued. Throughout 1913, the *Consulta* collected all information on Turkish troop movements in Libya, and was able, from time to time, triumphantly to demonstrate that troops had reached Italian territory from Egypt or Tunisia.[59] On 16 March the Italian Foreign Ministry also received a long and detailed *pro-memoria* from the General Staff defining Italy's needs in Albania. Although warning that Greece could eventually be a direct menace to Italian interests in the Ionian Sea, the generals remarked, moderately, that in Albania what was most necessary was that the border not be north of Santi Quaranta, at the far north of the Corfu Channel. A fortnight later, these opinions were revised after discussions with Italian colonial and naval officials. Thaon di Revel, the Chief of Naval Staff, and Spingardi, the Minister of War, now advised that Italy should insist that the border divide the Corfu Channel.[60] San Giuliano, with still more vehemence, was able to write to Imperiali that the Greeks would have to accept a border south of the Corfu Channel. The Austrians, he declared bluntly, must support Italy, and the Germans must learn to abandon the illusion that Greece could be subtracted from the influence of the Triple Entente.[61] A couple of days after this display of firmness, in order to illustrate his renewed moderation and good faith, San Giuliano declared Italy's willingness to accept a more northern border, at Cape Stylos, in the middle of the Corfu Channel, so long as Greece formally abandoned any claims on the island of Saseno and agreed to neutralise the straits of Corfu.[62]

With the Scutari issue closed for the moment, San Giuliano quickly recalled the potentialities of the Dodecanese. On 10 May he told new German ambassador, Flotow, that he was ready to surrender the islands, but only if Italy got her way on an Albanian border at Cape Stylos. He would however prefer not to make an official and public commitment. When Flotow interrupted stolidly that this would mean a solution purely at the expense of the Turks, San Giuliano, the new Bismarck, 'replied simply that this was the Fate of the vanquished'.[63]

Italy was now reminded also of the existence of her other patron, Britain. Alerted by the apparent end of the Balkan conflict, and backed by emphatic French and Russian advice that none of the Great Powers should keep any islands and by new Greek rumours that Italy might contemplate war, Grey suggested directly to Rome that the Aegean islands might be used as a means to make Greece reasonable on Southern Albania.[64] San Giuliano at once tried to set the discussion in Italy's favour. Britain, he surmised, did not altogether appreciate the moderation with which Italy had treated the Southern Albania question. But, at this time he did not see how Italy or Austria could retreat from the Cape Stylos border; why, he cautioned confidentially, there was even an unfortunate danger of a confrontation between Triple Alliance and Triple Entente. There was a further possible ambiguity. In Rome, San Giuliano preferred to talk about the 'Aegean islands', although, in London, Imperiali had promised that Italy was ready to give up 'the Dodecanese...to facilitate an Albanian settlement'. In case he should be thought more unyielding than his ambassador, San Giuliano explained his own good sense and straight-forwardness to the British ambassador. Rodd described their conversation:

[San Giuliano] said that, speaking not as a Minister, but altogether personally, he was often a good deal irritated by the attitude of the official mind in Italy – not in his own Department, where broader views existed, and there was a better knowledge of foreign countries, but it was especially the Colonial Office to which he referred. He said that the old traditions of Machiavellian schemes contemplating future eventualities and combinations with which we [the British] were credited could not be eradicated from the mentality of a large number of Italians, and the appellation 'Perfide Albion' which Napoleon had, if not invented, successfully exploited, still exercised the sinister influence that such catch-words do on the ignorant. He was constantly combating this misguided predisposition, but was not always successful in convincing minds that were prone to suspect motives. His own knowledge of English methods and dealings had taught him that they were simple, direct and straight-forward, and the difficulty he had in making this understood often caused him considerable annoyance.

Rodd was easily impressed by this melodramatic picture, and the Foreign Office, too, asking no questions, welcomed the Italian climb-down.[65] Even France felt Italy was showing unwonted moderation, and the Ambassadors' Conference was formally presented with the proposal that Greece get her way on the islands, provided that she accept the Italian requests on Southern Albania.[66] It might have interested London to know that, in these very same weeks, Italy was reaching an agreement with Germany on economic interests in Asia Minor, and negotiating with the government in Constantinople for a railway line north-east of Adalia, which happened to be in an area already conceded to a British company.

It certainly did soon become apparent that the Italian surrender of the Dodecanese was further off than might have been imagined. Imperiali explained a technicality. Yes, Italy would give up the islands, but, legally, they must be restored to Turkey first – then the Powers could decide what should be done. Perhaps Turkey should be consulted. It was the Turks, after all, not the Italians, who might prove obstructive.[67]

Thus another moment of possible Italian surrender had passed. The new financial negotiations with Turkey made it still more unlikely that Italy would easily give up the islands to Greece. Now Italy not only had troops in Libya to consider, but also an economic motive not to damage Italo-Turkish relations. The French were naturally outraged by this new Italian perfidy,[68] but Grey refrained from public doubting of Italy's good faith. Rightly understanding that Southern Albania was the first issue to be solved, he warned Greece that if she continued to be obstreperous, Italy and Austria might take matters into their own hands. He tried to calm the annoyance of France and Russia, and suggested an international commission to limit Albania's borders.[69] Being nice to Italy did not produce many rewards. When rumours spread from Athens that Italy intended to keep one or two of the occupied islands, and San Giuliano was asked if this could be his intention, he replied sharply that Italy had no direct negotiations with Greece. That same day he also reminded London that no Turkish troops had left Cyrenaica.[70] It was an ominous concatenation.

Once again it was not altogether certain that San Giuliano was irrevocably committed to keeping the islands, or even to using them in any possible negotiations. If he was firm to London and Paris, he pressed moderation on Berlin. Austria, he thought, should not be allowed to go to war merely because of a few kilometres of Albania's inland borders. When the German ambassador, Flotow, pointed out that Italy had been talking about war with Greece over the Southern Albanian coast, San Giuliano merely said that, if a case was raised, it was best to act as if it was backed by all possible force. At the same time, he tried, as usual, to discourage German sympathy for Greece by emphasising the reliability of the Hohenzollern King Constantine, but also his powerlessness and the unreliability of his politicians.[71]

Outside events now freed San Giuliano from the danger of public condemnation from both Germany and the Triple Entente. The Balkan Wars flared again. Driving back Bulgarian forces, Greece and Serbia made big gains. Neither Italy nor Austria were likely to be pleased by Greek and Serb advantage. Imperiali and the Austrian ambassador, Mensdorff, moved still closer together at the Ambassadors' Conference. Imperiali made it clear that Italy believed 'the amount of territory that Greece was now obtaining would make some difference with regard to the Islands'. Italy no longer saw how the Dodecanese could go to Athens.[72] In Rome, San Giuliano pointed out to Flotow that new Austro-Serb differences over Albania were likely, and that, although Greece was promising to be moderate, Italy regarded as 'too far-reaching' suggestions, which he attributed to Paris, that all the Dodecanese should be given to Greece. He appealed again generally for Triple Alliance unity behind Italy's policy.[73]

Italy's policy on the Dodecanese had now grown so complicated that San Giuliano sat down and tried to clarify it in a memorandum sent on to Giolitti. Clarification was not so easy to achieve, and instead San Giuliano provided a meandering summary of Italy's hopes and fears. He began with a favourite theme: 'In view of the attitude of a section of Italian public opinion' to think about 'some sort of sovereignty', in the Dodecanese, it was necessary to make plain that, without unforeseen circumstances, such a gain was unlikely at the moment. After all, Italy faced the 'irreconcilable opposition' of the Triple Entente, and worse, the problem of Austria and Article VII. 'Italy alone could not abandon the principle that no Great Power obtain a territorial advantage from the current crisis', he noted properly, 'if this principle is abandoned, European peace would be placed in grave danger.'

Having painted in the grand themes in a statesmanlike manner, San Giuliano turned to the more immediate problem. What should be done with the islands? The best which Italy could hope for was to return them to Turkey in exchange for some sort of admission of an Italian sphere of interest on the mainland of Asia Minor. Hopefully Germany would provide support. Ambition, it seemed, was still lurking, despite the danger to 'European peace'. For, as San Giuliano now mused, matters 'can change', and perhaps it would be best if Italy delayed 'as long as possible the solution to the problem of the islands'.

San Giuliano quickly put this machiavellian thought behind him. It was possible that even delay could cause problems. Perhaps Turkish troops remained in Cyrenaica because Italy still kept the islands? Also, it must never be forgotten that Southern Albania was Italy's major present interest and Italy must always be ready to cede some or all of the islands to facilitate a settlement with Greece. In any case, any advantage to Italy in her present condition, breaking the principle of the unity of Asiatic Turkey, might well do more harm than good to Italy's long term interests. No doubt, San Giuliano added politely, Giolitti would be better able to assess this than a mere Foreign Minister. The King too should be consulted.

But, in the wandering course of his *pro-memoria*, San Giuliano was

316

reluctant to end in such a weak position. All these manoeuvres, he added, were really subordinate to greater problems. Italy could not hope to play a dual role in the event of the 'perhaps not far off *débâcle*' of Turkey,

if we do not hasten to strengthen our position by means of a serious economic activity in the zone which we will be able to reserve without much difficulty for Italy.[74]

The whole *pro-memoria* indicates a justified nervousness on San Giuliano's part that Italy was over-playing her hand on the Dodecanese, and could have her quite outrageous bluff called. Yet no-one had called the bluff, and San Giuliano was not going to abandon easily his ambitions of inserting Italy into the 'great struggle of the nations' which he had so often predicted, and which now he thought would occur imminently in Asia Minor. He appealed to Giolitti against Cabinet colleagues who disliked the expense of a 'peaceful penetration' of the Turkish mainland.[75] Just as he had asked Giolitti and the King for their advice and support, so he now turned to the *Consulta* for its expert assessment. His *uomo di fiducia* did not disappoint him. In a full-scale report on 22 July, De Martino picked up many of the arguments which San Giuliano had used to Giolitti, or which were implicit in past policy, but gave them a much more resonant note. Greek advantages in the Balkan campaigns meant that Italy should be especially careful before yielding to her. Italy must emphasise that this was not only her policy but Austria's as well. Towards France, the most obdurate of the Powers, Italy should say clearly that the Dodecanese were a matter of bilateral decision with Turkey. Generally, it was important, and it would be easy once the facts were known, to convert international public opinion to Italy's side. Then, when things were going her way, it was very probable that Italy would be able to preserve some sort of *lien* on Rhodes and some of the other islands. Naturally, Italy could not annex the islands, which would break international principles of behaviour towards Turkey, but Italy must get 'some lasting benefit' out of her prolonged occupation. Perhaps an Italian functionary could be given special responsibilities over the islands?

De Martino concluded his report by reminding San Giuliano of the strands of cultural imperialism which he had so encouraged in the Istituto Coloniale. While the international situation remained uncertain:

the Ministers of War, of the Navy, of Education and of Commerce must work without delay to intensify every measure which encourages the assertion of *italianità* in the islands. Scientific missions, industrial initiatives, shipping lines, able to face any competition, banking offices etc. etc. are all means to put at once into operation in order to create a substratum of fact on which can afterwards be raised the albeit undeclared political claim, that the islands once occupied by Italian troops and then returned to Turkey, nevertheless stay under Italian influence.[76]

San Giuliano had retreated from the Roman summer to Fiuggi, where he nursed his gout, and the ambiguities and successes of his foreign policy. He did not reply directly to De Martino's frank report, but did encourage his Secretary-General to exercise much freedom of action in Rome, delaying again any immediate decision of his own on the islands.[77] At the same time, San Giuliano did all in his power to try to hurry the economic negotiations in Turkey.

On the Dodecanese, the next initiative came from Britain. On 30 July Grey proposed to Paris and St Petersburg that Albania be settled by a commission, and the Dodecanese separately by the Powers, although Italy should undertake to evacuate them and give them back to Turkey.[78] Italy was to get her wishes in Southern Albania, and would not even have to pay with her bargaining card. Imperiali at once hinted at the future by saying that Italy could not return the islands until Turkey honoured the Treaty of Lausanne. Grey snapped that this was the equivalent of a 999-year lease. Imperiali did not deny it, and an enquiry to Rome merely brought the further statement that Italy could not surrender her hostages until Turkey carried out her obligations.[79] San Giuliano had also at once appealed to Germany, treating Flotow to another display of 'appalling frankness'. Italy, he said, could not 'let a pawn slip from her hand', especially when it might be useful against Russian ambitions and to help Greece towards the Triple Alliance.[80]

It is not clear whether the Germans believed such an outrageous argument from their ally, although De Bosdari used the opportunity from Athens to pick up the theme of the possibilities of Greek friendship, which seemed to him a useful counter in the Adriatic to the perennial rivalry of Austria.[81] But it was Britain which now grew irritated with Italy, and which briefly threatened to unravel San Giuliano's diplomatic maze. Under continual French pressure, Grey at last bluntly warned Rome that Italian obstinacy was the only reason for the failure of the Ambassadors' Conference, and that, if Italy did not mend her ways, he would have to say so publicly.[82]

This was at once taken as a very serious threat by Italy. The last thing which San Giuliano and any Italian diplomat wanted to have to explain to the press was how Italy could be in conflict with Britain, Italy's old patron and traditional friend, the Britain which possessed the coal, needed so desperately by Italian industries, and the Royal Navy. Imperiali at once became apologetic. He pledged his personal good faith 'in every possible way' that Italy would abandon the islands, so long as Grey did not make his disapproval public.[83] In Fiuggi, San Giuliano drafted a new memorandum, which at least began by being piously innocent. He had long not believed that Italy would be able to keep the Dodecanese. Now British opposition confronted Italy 'either with a diplomatic check ...or with grave complications'. 'I have spent about four years in England', he continued in responsible vein, 'and I saw for myself a special strain of the English mentality which in this case can become very dangerous for us.' Once the main chance became visible, the English mentality was to press ahead, regardless of potential complications: Italy still had time, but she now must prepare to abandon the Dodecanese, and make Italian public opinion understand what was happening; and that it was 'our supreme interest that the principle remains unaltered that *no Great Power should draw territorial advantage from the current Eastern crisis*' [sic]; San Giuliano, or better Giolitti, should take the occasion to say this publicly in parliament, at a banquet, or in an interview with an Italian newspaper. Then, the immediate British objections would be overcome. Indeed, San Giuliano added brightly, it would even allow Italy to prolong her occupation, although naturally not indefinitely when this was so contrary to Italian interests. Ultimately the islands should go back to Turkey, or perhaps Greece, if that Power in fact showed signs of sympathy to the Triple Alliance as Germany believed. In the meantime Italy should not forget to profit from the uncertainty of her position by pushing on with economic schemes in Turkey.[84]

So there were still combinations to be dreamed of, possibilities to be explored. And this was all the more true because, after all, it seemed that Grey had gone back on his decision to be tough with Italy. Indeed having once vented his irritation, Grey, remarkably, became almost apologetic. He took the surprising step of writing to Rodd for transmission to San Giuliano a personal appreciation of Imperiali. San Giuliano, straight-faced, received the information that the ambassador, whom he had earlier warned should not be taken too seriously because of his garrulous temperament, was now '*persona gratissima*' in London. Still more surprisingly and encouragingly, Grey's praise spread even to Italian policy. San Giuliano must understand

how much I [Grey] appreciate the attitude that Imperiali has taken here. He has never failed to present the point of view of the Italian Government with vigour; but he has also never failed to make me feel that he was working for agreement, and that any influence that I could use to get other Powers to go half-way towards the Italian point of view would meet with a correspondingly conciliatory attitude on his side.[85]

This was really a quite extraordinary moment to choose to woo Italy with fair words, and, clearly, San Giuliano only half believed his luck. Although Rodd had begun again to warn that Italy might be engaging in 'tacit collusion' with the Turks on the Dodecanese, and that this would not be 'altogether alien to the diplomatic instincts of the Italian',[86] the ambassador was again easily baffled by one of San Giuliano's more circuitous discussions. Generally, San Giuliano said, he 'hoped and felt' that Grey would be convinced by Italian sincerity:

But there was one point on which he felt a certain nervousness. The English mentality was different from the Italian. Englishmen took words at their face value. Italians read subtle intentions and significances into phrases, and he was haunted by the dread of some misapprehension arising which might have the very consequences which it was his greatest object to avoid, namely to occasion a feeling of irritation between the two nations owing to the excessive susceptibilities of the Italian people. He wished to appeal to me [Rodd] to place his views before you [Grey], because I knew what that Italian mentality was, and he thought that in all probability you, accustomed to deal with the simple and direct mind of the English, might not have realised how readily a word, which in itself, and as used by an Englishman, meant no more than its literal significance implied, might become a stumbling block and a cause of offence to the excitable Italian.

Philosophising on national character over, San Giuliano at last reached the point: 'Nothing should be said which could possibly be interpreted here as implying pressure or menace, in regard to the islands.'[87]

San Giuliano need not have worried. Britain still refused to show any strength towards Italy. A categorical statement by Giolitti that Italy had no intention of going back on her word[88] was believed or accepted in London. As the weeks passed, Nicolson and some of the other Foreign Office officials, not to mention the French, again expressed their doubts, but Grey continued to state that Italy would give up the islands.[89]

The crisis over, San Giuliano pressed ahead with plans for Asia Minor. Italy's independence there alarmed even the Germans, who were also not pleased by new Italian obduracy towards Greece, despite San Giuliano's promises, only weeks before, that he sympathised with the aim of winning Greece over to the Triple Alliance. San Giuliano formally denied to Germany that he had any secret dealings with Turkey over the islands, producing German bafflement as to the real purposes of Italian policy.[90] On exactly the same day, San Giuliano wrote again to Garroni emphasising the likelihood of the collapse of Turkey and the urgent need for Italian economic preparations.[91]

Rumours of Italian intentions in Asia Minor continued to annoy all the Great Powers, but Italy's most open deceit had been towards Britain. In London, belated news was received of Italy's plans for a railway line which would conflict with the previous concession granted to a private British company to build a line from Smyrna to Aidin. San Giuliano at once promised to meet British wishes on the subject, and, at the same time, showed new interest in the Mediterranean agreement. But he was also quick to hint at something more. Although 'there should be no question which could in any way cause friction between Great Britain and Italy in [the] Mediterranean', San Giuliano said, in a 'half-apologetic manner', that Italy 'like Germany' was a latecomer to Empire; Italy should be treated like 'an unexpected guest at dinner for whom space must perforce be made' and Britain must realise Italy's 'legitimate desire for expansion of her commercial interests'.[92]

Meanwhile Italy's relationship with Greece had deteriorated once again. Confronted by new evidence that Greece was not evacuating the 'Northern Epirus' and that Austria was growing newly agitated about how to digest the results of the Balkan Wars, San Giuliano urged on Giolitti the firmest policy. On 8 November, without any more mention of the possibility of surrender of the Dodecanese, he suggested that Italy prepare a naval expedition to be launched against Greece if Albanian territory was not abandoned by 31 December.[93] In the next weeks, in tight collaboration with Austria, Italy maintained this strong line, ignoring all British and German suggestions for moderation.

On the Dodecanese, both Barrère and Flotow sent new advice how to cope with Italian intransigence.[94] Flotow thought Italian intentions changeable, but advised that, in the last analysis, they depended on Britain. And it was indeed Britain which was soon confronted by a new suggestion for a combination. Repeating yet again the statement that Italy was going to give up the islands, San Giuliano indicated that this might most rapidly be effected by British intervention to further Italy's economic ambitions in Asia Minor. Indeed, he told Imperiali that Italy could not consent to another solution of the Dodecanese or any other Mediterranean problems without having recognised her 'vital political and economic interest' in Turkey.[95]

Given Italy's current attitude to Greece, as well as signs that a conflict with Britain could develop over Ethiopia, it was not a good moment to appeal to Britain for sympathy. Grey had just told Cambon that as only a dozen Turks remained in Libya, it was about time that Italy applied Clause 2 of the Lausanne Treaty.[96] When economic spheres in Asia Minor were mentioned, the Foreign Office bureaucrats and Grey thus had their breath taken away by this new evidence of Italian immorality. Grey telegraphed angrily to Rodd:

It will not do to connect schemes of Italian expansion to mainland of Asiatic Turkey with the question of Italian evacuation of the islands...Italian Government has given us repeated and solemn assurances, which we cannot now be expected to treat as contingent on extraneous conditions under which Italy would obtain compensation in some other form elsewhere.

Britain was completely hostile to economic 'spheres of influence' in Turkey 'which would be tantamount' to an admission of 'the disintegration of the Ottoman Empire'.[97]

San Giuliano shrugged off these admonitions. In any case, strong words were once again followed up by weak, as the next day Grey half-accepted an old Italian case by formally suggesting to the Great Powers that the Dodecanese should be returned to Turkey, but granted autonomy.[98] Giving nothing away, San Giuliano at once told Flotow that he thought an early return of the islands unlikely; Italy must receive some sort of financial compensation to repay the expense which was incurring in the islands, and since Turkish troops remained in Libya.[99] In case the message was not understood, San Giuliano circulated his ambassadors with the information that

Italian public opinion could not tolerate weakness in South Albania, and adamantly believed in the need for serious economic concessions to Italy in Asia Minor. Italy did not want to sponsor a Graeco-Turkish war, but, in the end, that was a secondary matter compared to the above interests. Taking up an old position argued by De Martino, San Giuliano affirmed that, as for the Dodecanese, even after they were handed back, Italy would probably need to retain there some sort of 'counsellor'.[100]

Still no-one rebuked Italian adventurism. Austria, indeed, offered 'complete support' on the Dodecanese question.[101] The French were difficult, but that was not unusual, and, in any case, San Giuliano was still relying on London. As he told Tittoni with unwonted confidence:

The English government is so impatient to see us evacuate the islands that they will probably favour an agreement...[on the Smyrna-Aidin railway] to obtain this end.[102]

Germany also was not enthusiastic about Italy's policy, warning of the 'extreme distrust' felt towards Italy in London. But, the Germans said, the Dodecanese were Italy's affair and Germany would not interfere.[103]

San Giuliano had grown used to ignoring such warnings. Instead, on 30 December, Garroni in Constantinople again asked for British support in getting concessions in Turkey.[104] The next day, San Giuliano instructed his ambassador to press on with the Italian case to obtain 'the most possible' from the release of the islands.[105] Giolitti, holidaying in Piedmont, was sent the same news.[106]

San Giuliano was becoming blunter and blunter. Although he promised Rodd that it was 'almost certain' that Italy would accept the British idea of the future autonomy of the Dodecanese, he instructed Imperiali to point out that Italy would not release the islands until she received economic concessions in Adalia.[107] De Martino was sent to London to add his own persuasions.

Ignoring German efforts to restrain her contumacious ally,[108] San Giuliano, on 11 January, treated Rodd to that variety of Bismarckian bluntness which he usually reserved for Flotow. Backed by a detailed case from the Ministries of War and Colonies, which he had requested a fortnight previously,[109] San Giuliano now had a new argument to present to Rodd: 'The point upon which he enlarged with great emphasis', Rodd noted, was that while Italy did not wish to retain 'even a stone' in the Aegean, the date for her withdrawal must depend on the Turkish Government. The legal advisor of the Government had furnished them with a clearly reasoned argument establishing that Italy was forced to remain in the islands by the non-compliance of Turkey with the terms of the Treaty of Lausanne...He repeated that the occupation cost £3,000 a day; that in all some £6,000,000 of expenditure had been incurred since the signature of the Treaty. Even now new arrivals of Turkish officers in Cyrenaica were reported, and he was tempted to believe that Turkey did not wish the islands to be restored until she had sufficiently advanced her naval preparations to be able to prevent a movement in those islands in favour of annexation to Greece...I [Rodd] observed that it was a new principle in international law to claim compensation for the cost of military occupation. He replied that there were continual new developments in international law. It was in any case beyond doubt that no Government in Italy could withdraw from the occupation of the islands after what had taken place without some form of indemnity. He seemed to imply that a service had actually been rendered to Turkey by the occupation, which had prevented the islands from falling into the hands of the Greeks. The country would not tolerate the presentation of the huge bill upon a simple withdrawal. They did not ask for any financial indemnity. They only asked to be admitted to participation as a Great Mediterranean Power in those commercial enterprises in the Mediterranean area of the Turkish Empire, in which other Powers had obtained their share. In their case it would only be a small proportionate share, as they were a power which had come to maturity late in the family of nations. But without some such participation, the country would never allow the Government to surrender the only lever they could bring into action. The present Government were probably more disposed to carry out the evacuation promptly than other Governments might be, because the Prime Minister had definitely pronounced upon the question and was personally anxious to carry it through. He therefore hoped that the negotiations which had been initiated for the harbour works at Adalia would have our encouragement and lead to definite results.

Rodd was willing to accept this remarkably brazen argument, but the bureaucrats in London were less fond of Italy. Crowe was the most scathing:

After all this shuffling in the matter of the evacuation and restoration of the islands, one thing stands out quite clear, that the words and professions of Italian governments are not to be trusted.

For, he added as an afterthought,

It would of course be in accord with their views that the desired 'compensation' to Italy for carrying out her pledges and treaty obligations should be made at the expense of British interests in Turkey as far as possible.[110]

On the Dodecanese issue, Italy had thus reached a position of diplomatic rugged independence which was quite unparalleled for the least of the Great Powers. Italy still kept the islands, 'accidentally' conquered, and pledged over and over again for evacuation, against the wishes of all the other states except, perhaps, Turkey. German sympathy for Italian ambition in Asia Minor was, at best, lukewarm, and Italy's contempt for Greece hardly accorded with German policy in the Balkans. France was so hostile that most reports to Paris about the Dodecanese received the closest ministerial attention,[111] and only respect for British seniority in dealings with Italy seems to have restrained the French from issuing a peremptory order to Italy to get out. By March 1914, so experienced an ambassador as Jules Cambon could remark in disgust from his post in Berlin that the Dodecanese could in the future provide the Triple Alliance with an admirable naval base, and, still more irritating for the moment, 'more and more the Triple Alliance seems conducted by Italy'.[112]

San Giuliano had even been able to ignore the accepted processes of Cabinet government in Giolittian Italy. In January 1914, some Radicals withdrew from Giolitti's Cabinet at least in formal protest at the continuing expense over Libya and the Dodecanese.[113] The Radical move prompted the fall of the Giolitti government in March, but San Giuliano was allowed to pursue his policies without any reference to this opposition. Indeed, it was Giolitti who personally intervened to see that San Giuliano retained his post, and even was given increased freedom of action in the new Salandra administration. That Giolitti did so is undoubted evidence of the admiration and sympathy which San Giuliano had won by his policies since the Treaty of Lausanne. Before the picture becomes too sentimental, it may be that Giolitti did not mind tolerating a period in which a distinction could be made between his own ideas and those of the ailing San Giuliano. After all, when he returned to government as he planned to in six or nine months, Giolitti might well want to seek new contacts with the political Left in this Italy of near universal male suffrage, and that might make it useful to drop from the Cabinet a Foreign Minister who was an expansionist, however covertly, and who was a conservative aristocrat, even though one who 'knew his times'.

Diplomacy proceeded as though these domestic possibilities did not exist. Inside the Concert of Great Powers, it was with Britain that Italy was least restrained by the usual conventions of power. The client, once easily dismissed as a 'sturdy beggar', was failing to show appropriate respect for the patron's wishes. If Grey stubbornly continued to insist that Italy must evacuate the Dodecanese, San Giuliano was equally stubborn in agreeing, and then showing no signs of carrying out his promises. By January 1914, San Giuliano was not only appealing to the Turks to reward Italy for 'having saved' the islands from Greece;[114] but also bluntly telling the Greeks that the Powers insisted on the evacuation of Southern Albania, and that this issue no longer had anything to do with the evacuation of the Dodecanese, which instead must await an Italian economic concession in Asia Minor.[115]

When Britain tried a tougher line towards Italy, that too brought no feeble submission. Grey had finally persuaded himself to express to Imperiali the resentment so long felt towards Italy in the Foreign Office. As he wrote to Rodd:

I said that, if it was a question of being patient, the Italian government must remember our point of view. Italy had annexed Tripoli, and this had excited Mussulman feeling in Egypt; but, owing to our secret agreement of years ago, disinteresting ourselves in Tripoli, though it did not contemplate any actual change in the status of Tripoli, we had felt bound to stand on one side. In the course of the war, the Italians had occupied some islands, assuring us that the occupation was only temporary. After the war was over, the conditions of the Treaty of Lausanne were attached to the evacuation of the islands, and now further conditions were being made. The Italian Government had selected the district close to the Smyrna-Aidin Railway to acquire a concession, and, had it not been for friendship to Italy, I should have opposed that concession unconditionally, instead of trying to find a way to reconcile it with the interests of the British company, which I must protect. In addition, the Italian Government were now claiming that, if Abyssinia broke up, they were to have Lake Tzana [sic], the control of which we regard as essential to the waters of the Nile. In fact, in one way or another, during the last year or two the Italian Government had encroached more upon British interests than any two European Powers put together.[116]

If Grey hoped the language of Salisbury would return Italy to dutiful clientship, he was soon disappointed. He had waited too long; the Italy which San Giuliano had said at the beginning of the previous year would be submissive to no-one, paid no attention. San Giuliano denied any sins on Italy's part; and complained that domestic opinion would be soured by such criticism. He warned that

Britain was forgetting the rules of the Concert and that Turkey would exploit any apparent Anglo-Italian difference. He complained to Germany about the tone of the British rebuke, and actually had Grey admit that the message had sounded worse in translation than had been intended.[117] Thus, when on 6 March, experts initialled a conditional agreement between the Smyrna–Aidin Railway Co. and their Italian rivals,[118] the Dodecanese had produced a second yield. Britain, and therefore the Triple Entente, had recognised the Italian right to a participation in at least the economic dismemberment of Turkey. And still the Dodecanese were in Italian hands.

In the next months, the Dodecanese, and indeed Asia Minor, took a secondary place in Italian foreign policy as the new state of Albania slipped further into chaos. San Giuliano concentrated on his deteriorating relations with Austria, and perhaps Germany, and on getting irregular Greek troops to accept *de facto* the *de iure* promise of their government that the Graeco-Albanian border was at Cape Stylos. When the Dodecanese were mentioned, it was still apparent that an Italian evacuation was not imminent. On the very day that the technical agreement was reached between the railway companies, De Martino raised again with Imperiali his favourite idea of Italy keeping some sort of inspectorate in the islands after they had been returned to Turkey.[119] Britain too would hardly have been exhilarated to learn that San Giuliano gave instructions that Italian 'public opinion' should learn of the excellence of Anglo-Italian relations as demonstrated by the agreement, and by the likelihood that Britain would continue to favour Italian economic interests in Asia Minor.[120] In May, San Giuliano was still worried about the question of the appearance of Britain's relationship with Italy, but he also made it clear that the handing over of the Dodecanese could not occur before the 'conditional agreement' on Asia Minor became 'formal'.[121] In June and July, had the British Admiralty only known it, there were still more sinister moves afoot. The Italian Minister of the Navy, Millo, who was none other than the hero of the 'accidental' raids on the Dardanelles,[122] sent a confidential agent, Baron Giuseppe Lazarrini to tour the Dodecanese and there to sound out proprietors who might be willing to sell their land to the Italian state. The Ministry of the Navy was pondering the establishment of a coaling station in the area, but they accepted San Giuliano's instructions that the matter be kept secret and that, above all, the

Foreign Ministry must remain 'ignorant' of the affair.[123] When Nationalist journalists, a few months later, proclaimed the Dodecanese were the 'sentinels'[124] of a grandiose Italian future in the area, they were only in fact declaring what governing circles had long known or intended.[125] Paradoxically, Nationalists who loved to state Italian ambitions, often failed to understand the virtues and opportunities allowed by 'ignorance' or concealment.

For, there were dangers in all these machinations about the Dodecanese, and about the linked questions of Albania and Asia Minor. Italy's independence, by July 1914, had begun to fray her ties not so much with her 'friends', Britain and the Triple Entente, but with her 'allies', Germany and Austria. In Asia Minor, the assertion of an Italian presence always posed potential difficulties. Towards Greece, Italian severity had never been favoured by Germany, but had been tolerated because of the skill with which San Giuliano kept Austria by his side. By June 1914, there was every sign that this policy was breaking down. Repeated despatches from the *Consulta* warned with alarm that a *rapprochement* was occurring between Austria and Greece.[126] So serious had Italian fears become of this, and of the accompanying possibility that Austria would attempt an anti-Italian coup in the Balkans, that, on 23 June, a *pro-memoria* was prepared again to demonstrate that Italian retention of the Dodecanese could not allow Austria to apply Article VII of the Triple Alliance.[127] Before Franz Ferdinand reached Sarajevo the lines of Austro-German policy towards Italy in the July Crisis were becoming evident.

With the outbreak of war, and the '*intervento*', the importance of Italian interests in the Dodecanese became less immediate. In war, the Adriatic undoubtedly was more relevant than the Eastern Mediterranean. Yet Italy had not forgotten her 'accidental' and 'temporary' possessions. When Churchill told Imperiali that the Admiralty opposed an Italian retention of Rhodes on strategic grounds, but that the objection would disappear if Britain and Italy were allies, San Giuliano showed interest at once.[128] In his list of negotiating terms with the Triple Entente, after the Battle of the Marne, San Giuliano asked for Italian possession of the Dodecanese and the whole province of Adalia should Turkey enter the war on the other side.[129] By his death on 16 October, there seemed no reason to believe that, in the Dodecanese, San Giuliano had not triumphantly proved the old adage: 'possession is nine-tenths of the law'.[130] Italy might seldom win real battles, but, in diplomacy, if she were brazen enough, in the circumstances of 1912–14, the least of the Great Powers could hold the Concert to ransom.

As well as in Albania, Asia Minor and the Dodecanese, there were even some shadowy indications of a similar policy in Ethiopia. After the defeat at Adowa in 1896, Italy at first seemed likely to abandon all ambitions in East Africa. If some members of the ruling elite, including the Prime Minister, Rudinì, held this view, it was not shared by the King, nor by the majority of establishment 'public opinion'. The despatch of Ferdinando Martini to be Governor of Eritrea in 1897 could be explained as an assertion of civilian over military control, but it also demonstrated that Italy had not lost interest in her colony, nor indeed in its hinterland. The able and indefatigable Martini, in his long term of office from 1897 to 1907, by a policy of severe but intelligent retrenchment, set a basis of organisation in Eritrea. His creation of the capital inland at Asmara, with its pseudo-Renaissance arcades, was a public affirmation that Italy should consider Eritrea as a settlement colony. It was also a probable indication that Italy should hope one day to resume a 'positive policy' towards Ethiopia.

As usual Italy was not behindhand in making verbal preparations. From 1902 onwards Italy began to remind the Powers that the succession to Emperor Menelik in Ethiopia was anything but clear, and that the unity given to the Ethiopian state by the great Emperor might well only last one generation.[131] Britain duly showed sympathy for some sort of arrangement, if for the usual unflattering reasons. As the then ambassador in Rome, Bertie, put it: 'As to concessions in Abyssinia, Italians may not be desirable concession-aires, but as concerns British interests would not Italians be more acceptable to us than Frenchman, Germans, or Russians?'[132]

By 1906 Britain had assuaged French fears that too much be conceded to Italy, and, on 13 December, a Tripartite Anglo-Franco–Italian agreement was signed on Ethiopia.[133] Secret clauses defined spheres of interest for the Powers, should pledged efforts to preserve the integrity of Ethiopia be ruined by its internal collapse. The Italian ambassador who initialled the agreement in London was Antonino Di San Giuliano.

There the matter rested for the time being. Rather as in Libya,

Italy had secured a paper approval for her future interests or intentions. Aside from the words of diplomacy, after 1906 Italy showed no particular interest in Ethiopia. Martini's replacement in Asmara from 1907 was the Marchese Giuseppe Salvago Raggi, a clerical career official with experience especially in China and Egypt. At least retrospectively, his major ideas about policy seem to have been how to thwart the machinations of the Free Masons and divert allegations of corruption and incompetence. The economic interest of Italian business evident in Libya, Albania and Asia Minor, was also not strong, except in the most primitive fashion, in either Eritrea or Ethiopia. More than any other area of Italian ambition, Ethiopia also set ringing alarm-bells of public opinion hostile to imperialism.

Ethiopia was thus a most barren area for political scheming, yet San Giuliano had not forgotten his training in the 1890s. If the Concert allowed Italy to plot elsewhere, why not in Ethiopia also? Moreover, after 1909, the very conditions of collapse which San Giuliano was always predicting in Turkey were in fact occurring in Ethiopia. Like many another great feudal chief, Menelik had long outlived his greatness. His health was already deteriorating when he suffered strokes in 1904, and by August 1908 he was stricken with general paralysis. From 1909 until his eventual death in December 1913, Menelik was almost completely incapacitated, a prisoner in his palace, a prey to rival factions competing for the succession. The victor in this contest was his grandson, Lij Yasu, violent, debauched, fond of personally strangling his enemies and even his friends, and, what was worse, of doubtful loyalty to the Coptic Christianity of the Amharic state.[134] By 1911 European representatives, confined to their compound as the bullets of warring chiefs literally whistled over their heads, began to remind their Foreign Ministries that Ethiopia might not have a future.

It was only in the summer of 1913 that San Giuliano concentrated any segment of his mind on Ethiopia. He reported to Giolitti on the internal crisis of Menelik's empire, and noted the need to preserve Italian interests. He deprecated any intention of action. He was, he said, 'not motivated by ideas or plans of our expansion in these regions: but solely by the need...not to be surprised by possible events'. Therefore, he explained, he had had Gaetano Manzoni, the Director-General of Political Affairs in the *Consulta*, draft a *pro-memoria* on Italian policy towards Ethiopia. What Manzoni had to say was not altogether surprising. Italian foreign policy was based on preserving the *status quo* and on the 1906 settlement. But should Ethiopia disintegrate, Italy must be ready. Especially economic activity should be encouraged in order to enhance Italian pretensions to a zone in Ethiopia which would link Eritrea and the Italian Somaliland. Manzoni duly provided a map marking out this sphere of influence, and he warned that Italy should see to it that foreign 'interests' did not establish themselves in that area.[135]

Following the accustomed processes of her diplomacy, Italy duly communicated a version of this information to London. In the last months, Britain had been paying sporadic attention to possible Italian policy in Ethiopia. All authorities in London agreed that what was most important was that Lake Tsana, at the headwaters of the Blue Nile, should be in a British and not an Italian sphere of interest.[136] To say the least, the Foreign Office believed that there were more important problems for British diplomacy, and their opinion on Lake Tsana was not communicated to Rome until 4 November.[137]

Italy had been devoting somewhat more attention to Ethiopia. In a despatch to Garroni on 22 August, San Giuliano listed 'Ethiopia', along with Asia Minor, Libya, the Somaliland and Eritrea, as areas which provided Italy with 'a colonial dominion' sufficient for her economic potentialities.[138] The new Minister of Colonies, Bertolini, was anxious that Italy define her policy in Ethiopia, if only to assert the rights of the bureaucrats in his Ministry and of Salvago Raggi over the staff of the *Consulta*.[139] The Italian Minister in Addis Ababa, Colli, also took time off from reporting tribal in-fighting and contesting Salvago Raggi's reliability and seniority to warn against French rivalry, and France's failure to show scrupulous loyalty to the intention of the 1906 agreement.[140]

But it was Britain's eventual reply to the Italian questions of July which encouraged San Giuliano to display Italian ambitions. Told by Grey that Britain regarded Lake Tsana as a matter 'of the utmost importance',[141] Imperiali remarked blithely that, from the Tripartite agreement, Lake Tsana was clearly in the Italian zone. Grey replied, accurately, that it had not been settled where the connecting line between the Italian colonies would run, and there could be no doubt about Britain's claim to Lake Tsana.[142]

This bluntness provoked quite a reaction in Italy. Bertolini, contrary to his usual reputation for grey moderation and respectability, and perhaps prompted by his official, Giacomo Agnesa, was especially perturbed. He complained formally to San Giuliano of the 'grave and irreparable damage' threatened by Grey's 'new interpretation'.[143] In a subsequent note, Bertolini declared that Italy was confronted with 'betrayal' from both France and Britain in Ethiopia.[144]

San Giuliano's diplomacy was less rhetorical. He replied innocently to London that he was surprised that the question had been raised, as he had no information that Ethiopia was about to disintegrate. Any Anglo-Italian disaccord was simply a matter of misunderstanding. The question about Lake Tsana had been decided by Italian treaty rights in Anglo-Italian exchanges of 1891, and not in 1906.[145] It was characteristic, given the explosive nature of the word 'Ethiopia' in Italy, that San Giuliano kept Giolitti closely informed of the stance which he had taken.[146]

There was no sign of urgency from either side on the Lake Tsana problem. The Foreign Office even believed that Rodd could safely be left to negotiate, although there was no willingness meekly to accept the Italian revival of clauses signed in 1891.[147]

In January 1914 the information at last reached Europe that Menelik was dead, although his demise was being kept secret in Ethiopia. The Annual Report for 1913 of the British Minister, Thesiger, dolefully commented that all Menelik's achievements had been 'of one man'. In passing, Thesiger also predicted a deterioration in Italo–British relations in Ethiopia as Italy was working with new zeal to reinforce her position there.[148] The Italian Minister, Colli, also predicted imminent trouble and even civil war. Italy was respected by Lij Yasu, he said, but it was time the Ethiopians gave 'tangible proof' of their friendship to Italy, especially in the economic area.[149].

At the same time there was the gravest Italian suspicion that it was in fact Britain which was seeking economic supremacy. Should rumours that Britain wanted special rights on Lake Tsana be true, this would, according to Colonial Office officials, 'devastate' the future prospects of Eritrea and throw the whole state of Anglo–Italian relations into jeopardy.[150] San Giuliano thereupon suggested to London that it was time that Britain and Italy 'deliberate' the whole question of Ethiopia's disintegration.[151] Naturally, San Giuliano also again pointed out that Italy only wanted to see the *status quo* maintained in the territory, and had no intention of intervention unless pacification was called for.[152] Perhaps San Giuliano meant what he said this time, but the language was very much that which he habitually used on the Turkish issue, and it is hardly surprising that Grey and his officials, in the spring of 1914, found Italy's policy in Ethiopia as tiresomely intrusive as it was elsewhere.

Meanwhile, other sorts of investigations were begun. San Giuliano formally requested from his Chief of General Staff, Pollio, a report on the likelihood of military operations in Ethiopia at that time. He was told that the rainy season was near, and that that ought to avoid any threat to Eritrea.[153] Still making appropriate preparations, San Giuliano also told Salvago Raggi that reinforcements would be sent to Eritrea. Italy, he said, must do the 'utmost possible' to prevent 'provocation' in Ethiopia, but also must ensure that her colonies were respected. From the Colonial Ministry, Bertolini continued to press stoutly onwards, as did Martini when he took over the Ministry on March 20. De Martino declared that Italy should not intervene, but, at the same time, cautioned that she might need to, if there was an explicit request from the Ethiopian government.[154]

Nothing too sinister should be read into these despatches.[155] There was a genuine threat to Eritrea from armed and lawless Ethiopian bands, and San Giuliano's preparations were sensible. He also quite properly appealed to Britain and France to apply the cooperative clauses of the 1906 agreement, and, in fact, the three Powers did intervene in Addis Ababa to exhort Lij Yasu to control the xenophobia of his friends and enemies.[156] Martini, too, established at the Ministry of Colonies, was anxious that Italy aim to maintain Ethiopian integrity and the 1906 agreement.[157] In June 1914, San Giuliano told the Chamber of Deputies that this preservation of the *status quo* was Italy's policy.[158]

San Giuliano's Ethiopian policy had thus in the main been no more than could have been expected. But there were also other currents present. One had come to the surface in the Italian memory of her rights in Lake Tsana, and her appeal to the long-lost situation of 1891. Further evidence of long term interests in Ethiopia also came in June 1914 as San Giuliano was publicly asserting his loyalty to the *status quo*. Writing privately to Salandra, he had other points to make, identical with his policy in Asia Minor. In Ethiopia, he noted, Italy's

333

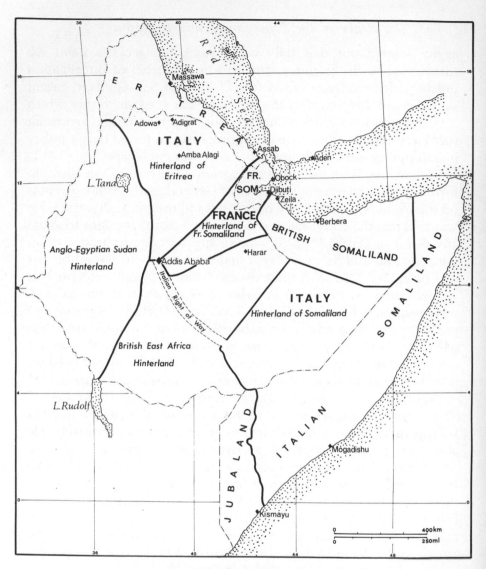

5 Division of Ethiopia suggested to the British Foreign Office by Lord Kitchener in May 1913 (from PRO file FO 371/1571)

position was confronted by 'grave dangers'. Italy should be clear, 'in view of the probable not far off complications' there, that she should 'make effective those theoretical rights which have been guaranteed us'. From the 1906 agreement, when Ethiopia disintegrated, Italy would obtain hinterlands which would unite her two colonies. But this prospect depended 'absolutely on having known

334

how to develop Italian economic interests' which in the future could be 'claims' for union. If not, Italy could lose her 'territorial rights' and gain only 'a *mere railway* [sic]'. The Banco di Roma, favoured by government support, should make a start, as they were the only consortium likely to be able to risk investment in Ethiopia at the moment.[159] There the matter rested as Franz Ferdinand went to Sarajevo.

After war broke out, Ethiopia became a still less influential issue than the Dodecanese. Indeed, Italy's military situation in Eritrea deteriorated badly as troops were needed in Europe, and anarchy enveloped Ethiopia. Lij Yasu, before his deposition in 1916, had officially declared himself a Moslem, entered the First World War on Turkey's side, and announced that he would drive Italy (and Britain and France) into the sea.[160] It did not take long in Eritrea, or elsewhere, for the fragility of the military base of Italian colonialism to become apparent.

Ethiopia was even omitted from the first list of possible Italian entry terms sent to the Triple Entente on 12 August.[161] But it was remembered again as the war dragged on, and in a later context it is hard not imagining that San Giuliano would have made clear his desire for a mandate.

In both the Dodecanese and the by-products which they gave, and, in more muted colours, in Ethiopia, San Giuliano was pursuing with skill the ancient Piedmontese concept of the 'artichoke policy', of an Italian growth to greatness, an assertion of Italian imperial rights by the constant pursuit of little interests day by day. Nothing was given up, despite promises to the contrary. In reality, also, perhaps nothing much was won. In the summer of 1914, Albania was in chaos, Eritrea was under military threat, Libya was still unconquered, and genuine Italian economic imperialism was far from equalling that of Britain, France or Germany. But these military and financial realities are, in a way, irrelevant, or were not, at least, regarded as relevant by San Giuliano, his officials and much of Liberal Italy's ruling class. Diplomacy was a matter of paper houses, but these paper houses were regarded as far more important than real houses in Palermo or Potenza.

Apart from the habitual falsity of Italy's Great Power policies, what is most striking about the story of the Dodecanese and the other areas is what San Giuliano was able to get away with. Partly, this is because none of the other Great Powers, except perhaps France, could believe that Italy's unreliability was as absolute as it in fact was. Partly, this is because in day to day policy, San Giuliano's diplomacy was often a *tour de force* of subtlety, of possibilities and half-possibilities, often probably not even recognised or admitted by their author himself. Partly, also there is the simple fact that for a Concert confronted by numerous grave problems, Italian ambition was not to be taken too seriously. Yet, in diplomatic terms, as long as there was no general war, it is still surprising that Italy could keep up a buzzing independence for quite so long, and in so many different places. Perhaps the freedom allowed to the least of the Great Powers is most of all testimony to the malfunction of the European Concert by 1912–14. And, if in the Dodecanese and Ethiopia, Italy could use this malfunctioning to circumvent the wishes of the Greater Powers, especially those of the *Entente Cordiale*, in Asia Minor she pursued the same policies, but there to the damage especially of the Central Powers. San Giuliano's Italy was an importunate and undutiful client both to her 'friends' and to her 'allies'.

CHAPTER 10

Preparing to digest some spoils: Italian policy towards Turkey, 1912–1914

In June 1905, during his maiden speech to the Senate, San Giuliano had noted Italy's need to have a 'world policy' which, with his usual philosophic wisdom, he argued would allow her to join 'the always more intense and grandiose struggle' of the nations which was occurring in the areas of trade and of politics.[1] Although the phrase is indicative of the extraordinary extent of Italian ambition, a 'world policy' is a little difficult to find in the practice of Italian diplomacy.

In the Far East, Italy limped behind the Greater Powers, her hopes but also her weakness being displayed in her particularly inglorious record during the Boxer rebellion. Then, in the race to the Forbidden City, Italian troops, humiliatingly if appropriately, beat only the Austrians.[2] By 1914, 2.4% of Italian trade was directed to the Far East, 274 Italian citizens lived in China,[3] and 22 Italian firms were in operation there. Italy continued to assert her Great Power role in the area, San Giuliano boasting in June 1914 that Italian success in Tien-tsin had been unexpectedly great,[4] but fiasco was never far away. Even in commerce, Italy's balances of trade were consistently unfavourable. The only real example of successful 'Italian imperialism' in the Pacific and Indian oceans remained the work which Roman Catholic missionaries had continued over the centuries.[5] There was some Italian interest in the empty lands of Australasia, either as a possible venue for, or model of, colonisation, but only a few thousand Italians had emigrated to Australia before 1914. Italy had its usual negative balance of trade with Australia. The most important diplomatic incident in the period occurred when the Australian press published salacious stories on the death of a royal mistress, Duchess Eugenia Litta. This tasteless invasion of royal privacy was deplored by the *Consulta*, discussed, but then not answered.

In the Americas, Italy had a much greater interest because her migration to the United States, Argentina and Brazil was so much larger than in the Pacific. To a probable majority of Italians 'America' continued to mean 'paradise', even if emigrants in reality often found Beatrice hard to attain on the other side of the Atlantic. As the most recent student of Italo-American contacts has brilliantly put it: 'The Italians were the nightmare of the American dream ..."You don't call an Italian a white man?" a construction boss was asked, "No sir," he replied, "an Italian is a Dago".'[6] Official Italy remained curiously ignorant of the United States whose main significance seemed to be rhetorical, useful to demonstrate the evils which sprang from undirected emigration as, for example, when San Giuliano's visit taught him that industrial American cities were 'Dantesque hells'. The United States had already begun to send its tourists, its expertise and its heiresses to Italy. The Paternò Castello family could rejoice in 1912 at a marriage of one of their scions to a Bianca Weithword of New York, while the cousin of Pietro Lanza Di Scalea had earlier enriched his stock with a Martina Potter-Jones of Cincinnati. But, these affairs of individuals and interest aside, Italian diplomatists, even more than their other European counterparts, continued to underestimate or simply ignore the growing might of the United States.[7]

Italian diplomacy paid more attention to South America, no doubt because Italian pretensions to power could seem less absurd there. To begin with, Brazil and Argentina were possible dumping grounds for the excess products of Italian industrialisation, and Italian trade could hope to readjust its perennial deficits from commercial dealings in South America. Argentina was one of the few states in the world with which Italy had a favourable balance of trade although Italy's relative trade position in the area was weakening.[8] Many South Americans still called themselves 'Italians' and, in 1895, Italians made up one-eighth of the entire population of Argentina.[9] Despite this potential new aspect to a world policy, most Italian dealings with the South American states kept an old-fashioned air. Visiting Italian journalists, Luigi Einaudi or Enrico Corradini, loved to talk about the 'new Italies' which had arisen south of the Equator; in 1900, Luigi Luzzatti proudly called the emigrants 'blood of our blood, sinew of our sinew'.[10] But official Italy did little to cement these bonds. For one thing, the colonists' political innocence was off-putting. The largest Italian paper in Argentina, *La Patria degli italiani*, remained true to a Mazzinian past, and praised radicals, socialists and even anarchists.[11] This sort of pre-Risorgimento naivety and patriotism was hardly likely to engender paternal enthusiasm in Rome. Italian contacts with South America thus remained a concern of publicists, of Scalabrinian brothers working for *religione e patria*, and of the Congresses of Italians Abroad, which strove to preserve Italian language and culture and to encourage emigrants still to buy Italian. The results of this indirect imperialism could often be two-edged. Notably in Argentina, already before the First World War, there was resentment at the cultural independence of Italian immigrants and demands that they choose between Argentinian citizenship, and persecution or perhaps expulsion. In 1911 of all years, the Argentinian government declared that it would ban future Italian migration. This prospect was scarcely pleasing in Rome and the ubiquitous Primo Levi warned that Italy would finish by 'not counting for anything at all, as much in Latin America as in the rest [of the world]'. If Argentinians were permitted to treat Italians with contempt, and the 'second generation' allowed to stop being Italians 'double [would be] the damage, double...the danger deriving for us from that stream of emigration'.[12] The following year, Ferdinando Martini was sent on an official visit to use his charm and syntactical accuracy to calm down the ruffled Argentinians and to allow some survival of *italianità*.

Despite the flaming words of journalists, the hard-sell of businessmen, the patriotic piety of missionaries and the occasional intrusion of politicians, the real story of Italy and the Americas before 1914 is a social one, of the labouring lives of millions of men who were not so much Italians as *paesani*, who, so often, one day returned to their *paese* there to be revered for the brief surviving years of their lives as the local *americani*, men who had come back from the strange and enticing *Eldorado* which lay across the seas. *Mamma mia dammi cento lire che nell' America io voglio andar!*[13]

In contrast to this foreign policy experience of the poor, the official lack of interest in the Americas is another sign of Italy's frequent relative slowness to realise and accept changes in the world. It is this traditionalism which in 1935 lent such an old-fashioned imperialist character to Mussolini's war in Ethiopia, despite the press trumpeting of Fascist modernity and technology. Before 1914, then, a 'world policy' for Italy certainly could not be understood in the way that it was for Germany, Britain or Russia. Italy's self-definition remained European, her world was the *mare nostrum*. One of the ironies of the 'Third Italy's' imitation of the First Italy was precisely the re-evocation of the 'Roman empire', which was doubtless a boundless and absurd ambition, but which also turned Italian eyes away from the real and wider world of the twentieth century in which there were perhaps sometimes opportunities for Italy. An Italian 'world policy', therefore, if it meant anything, meant merely a more concentrated interest in the Mediterranean, what has been called an Italian '*Drang nach Osten*'.

In 'Turkey', the Balkans, Asia Minor and North Africa, there were enough memories of an 'Italian' past, of which Libya was only the most unlikely and accessible example. However denied by anti-clerical 'Liberal' Italy, the most vital continuing presence of past Italies was probably the Roman Catholic missions, which were located all over the Mediterranean, but especially in the Holy Land. Given the quarrel between the Vatican and France, after 1904 Italy's pretensions to obtain at least equal protectorate rights there were accorded much sympathy from the Vatican. For decades before, the Vatican, which traditionally conducted all its diplomatic business in the Italian language, had been becoming more and more aware of its Italianness. Bearing some similarity to the fate of other cosmopolitan bodies in pre-1914 Europe, the Vatican was not immune to the attractions of nationalism. It never wholly succumbed to that disease, but, in 1913, that electoral year of close contact between clericals and Nationalists, even *Osservatore Romano*, that erstwhile prophetic castigator of the sins of the Liberal state, can be found remarking that it would be best if Italy were granted 'an increased influence in the Mediterranean'.[14]

Apart from religious and social matters, there were also economic reasons nourishing Italo-Vatican collaboration in the field of foreign affairs. The 'non expedit' had remained firm rather longer politically than it had financially. Vatican money lay behind many Italian banks, of which the Banco di Roma is the most famous example. Its activities in Libya have already been noted, but the Banco di Roma also had important contacts in Egypt, and believed that it had a role to play in Constantinople, where characteristic is the story of successive Italian delegates to the Ottoman Public Debt. In 1905 the Roman Chamber of Commerce elected as Italy's representative on the international commission which supervised Turkey's finances, the youthful Don Alberto Theodoli, who came from a cadet branch of one of Rome's most distinguished 'black' aristocratic families. Three of his sisters were nuns. To avoid the corruption of Masonic Italy, Theodoli had been schooled abroad, in engineering at Freiburg and Lausanne. He had 'come out' in Roman society on the last day of *Carnevale* in 1895 at the Palazzo Lancellotti where, piously and publicly, the main palace doors remained closed from 1870 to 1929, in sign of political mourning at the violation of temporal power. Theodoli served his apprenticeship in business on a visit to Constantinople in 1899, as an employee of a Belgian-based clerical company; in 1901 he was sent to St Petersburg to favour the opening of glass factories financed by the Banco di Roma; and in 1903 he went on a mission to the United States to negotiate a deal about Vatican property which had been seized in the Philippines without recompense by the U.S. government after its war with Spain. Theodoli had thus been a sort of unofficial travelling commercial attaché for Rome-based clerical financial interests, adept at persuading foreigners to render to the Vatican that which was the Vatican's.

In 1905 Italy's Foreign Minister was Tommaso Tittoni, who had his own intimate ties to the Banco di Roma. Theodoli on his election to the Ottoman Public Debt, confident in a good *raccomandazione* from Tittoni, hastened to make his peace with the Liberal state. To denote this he was received by King Victor Emmanuel III, whom Theodoli, as a 'black', had never met before. Despite the King's dislike of priests and their friends, the two had a cheerful conversation about the historical ability of the Theodolis and the Savoys to change sides at the right moment. These pleasantries exchanged, Theodoli, though formally having accepted a supra-national position in Constantinople, nonetheless did not underrate the value of instruction from Tittoni. The Foreign Ministry kindly provided detailed information how Theodoli could expect best and least openly to further Italian national interests. Once arrived in Constantinople, Theodoli could effortlessly locate other useful contacts. The Italian ambassador, Imperiali, was of course friendly, as another Italian in high office, and since he was kin to Theodoli's mother.

In fact, it may be doubted that Theodoli's mission was especially productive for Italian interests in the Ottoman Empire. Whether through his personal failings or Imperiali's, Italy found herself consistently out-witted in Constantinople, notably by the French, who, for example, readily turned aside Italian rivalry over the coalmines of Eraclea, a site replete with the most inspiring classical allusions and said to be of great economic potential, once a suitable infrastructure was provided. Theodoli was left to take refuge in his memoirs, where he hinted that the French ambassador, Constans, cheated at bridge, and, still more deplorably, leafed through the memoirs of Casanova at an Embassy mass, while giving the impression that he was reading the Holy Scriptures.[15]

Theodoli's career in Constantinople came to an inglorious conclusion in the early days of October 1911. Probably at the instigation of Roman Catholic business interests in Constantinople, Theodoli carried to Rome the idea of a compromise settlement of the Libyan dispute. It may be that the Turks too saw a propaganda advantage in Theodoli's peace mission, all the better to savour given Theodoli's nationalism (at least in his memoirs he alleges that he had passed much time in the previous months riding along the shores of the Bosphorus with De Martino III discussing and planning Italy's future in Libya). Giolitti was not a man who could be ensnared so easily, and Theodoli's vague peace move met a cool reception in Rome. Giolitti remarked briefly that Italy intended to annex Libya, and a recognition of this was the *sine qua non* for the commencement of any other negotiations. Theodoli then had nothing better to do than to return meekly to Constantinople there to be upbraided by the Turks with the fact that he had evidently joined 'that band of Sicilian brigands' which controlled the *Consulta*.[16]

This episode finished Theodoli's career in Constantinople and, in the next year, he was expelled as a *persona non grata*. Back in Rome he continued to have a large hand in Vatican finances, and showed the way the wind was blowing by standing as a deputy, despite Giolitti's opposition, in the 1913 elections. The validity of the election was contested, but in 1914 Theodoli still sat in the Chamber as a fervent Salandran.[17]

Meanwhile, in 1912, the Rome Chamber of Commerce had made a most interesting choice to replace Theodoli as delegate to the Ottoman Public Debt. The man elected was another engineer, Bernardino Nogara, who was already establishing himself as perhaps the most important middle man in Italian overseas ventures before the First World War. Director of the reorganised Società Commerciale d'Oriente, Nogara worked easily with Volpi, Joel and the Giolittians of the Banca Commerciale. But Nogara's election by the Rome Chamber of Commerce, which was presided over by Romolo Tittoni, was no sell-out to the Liberal regime by clerical interests. Nogara in fact had a most suitable number of high-placed relatives in the Vatican: one was an archaeologist, the other an administrator of missions – almost the perfect combination for clerical imperialism. In 1929, it was Bernardino Nogara who was called, in a most difficult moment, to help re-organise Vatican finances.[18]

There was much that was insubstantial about Italy's membership of the Ottoman Public Debt, which, as so often for Italy, had been accorded in recognition of Italy's status as a Great Power, and not because of any real financial investment in Turkey.[19] Under Theodoli, this air of unreality and amateurism had not been altogether dissipated, but Nogara was a new style of delegate, and an indication of both Liberal and clerical Italy's new enthusiasm for speculative ventures abroad.

The course of Italo-Vatican relations had always run more smoothly outside than inside Italy. Given the traditional rivalry with 'schismatic' Russia, and the new quarrel with that 'godless Republic', France, the Vatican was ready to applaud when an Italian consular official or commercial agent found his readiest ally in the local priestly representative of the 'other Rome'. By 1914 efforts to restore a Roman Empire were often accompanied by happy collaboration between Church and State. After all, it might be cynically maintained, it was hardly necessary to teach the Roman Catholic Church the meaning and advantages of imperialism.

Priests and their financial advisers apart, modern Italians could pick up the heritage of other 'Italian' empires in the *mare nostrum*. Venice and Naples had left their subjects, now known as Italians, scattered over the coasts of the Mediterranean.[20] In 1911 there were 30,000 Italians living in the Ottoman Empire, about two-thirds of them in the Balkans. Some 10,000 lived in Constantinople itself, where an Italian Chamber of Commerce had opened in 1885. Over 40,000 Italians lived in Egypt and there were perhaps 130,000 in Tunis.[21]

Moreover, many of these Italians held important or influential positions. On mission to the Constantinople of Abdul Hamid, an

343

Italian visitor found that most of the court gardeners, carpenters and musicians were Italians, as was the official court painter. Italian words were said to be used most frequently in Arabic to describe matters of technology and love.[22] Perhaps for the last reason, Oriental potentates seem also to have had a weakness for Italian doctors, recalling the days when Italy had been the world's most scientifically advanced country. Italian engineers, road and bridge-builders too worked all over the Mediterranean hinterland, in testimony to those skills in which Italy has never lost her claims to world leadership.

Too much, however, should not be made of the influence of these ethnic Italians. Useful in the occasional speculative ventures, able to whisper in the right ear, or pave the way to the right Greek or Armenian middle man, Mediterranean Italians, nevertheless, often remained uncertain whether they were Sicilians, Genoese or Venetians rather than 'Italians'. Moreover, as in other small communities in such a hot-house atmosphere, the more powerful and rich such overseas Italians became, the more time and effort they devoted to petty intellectual, political and personal squabbles and suspicions.

No better example of the power, but also the limits, of Italian communities abroad can be given than in Egypt. There, centuries of traditional contact merged into the new style which made the Italian community, in a way, patrons of the nationalist opposition to British rule. Italians, notably the '*altra sponda*' segment of the De Martino clan, held most influential positions in the Khedive's government. The Khedival family itself had the most intimate ties with Italy, and with the Savoy dynasty. In 1879, Khedive Ismail, in partial recompense of his patronage of *Aida*, went into exile in Naples. During the Libyan War, in a typical incident, the Khedive Abbas was rumoured to be coming secretly to Italy in order to discuss possible peace arrangements with Turkey. It may be learned without astonishment that it was Giacomo De Martino III whose abilities and relationships proffered themselves best to organise the meeting with Victor Emmanuel. It was arranged that King and Khedive would drive together around the grounds of a castle out of Turin. A month later, however, it was not the Khedive but Prince Fuad who turned up, and met De Martino himself in Rome. Both Giolitti and San Giuliano hoped that there might still be something to be gained from the Egyptian connection, but De Martino, with an insider's suspicion, warned against a 'double play'.[23] Fuad, who became King of Egypt in 1917, had been brought up in Naples and educated at the *Military Academy* in Turin. He kept up his contacts with Italy, first as a candidate for the title of Prince of Albania and, after his return to Egypt, using Italy as a counterbalance to Britain. When he fell ill in 1934, he was treated by his two Italian doctors who summoned a still more illustrious *professore* from a Roman clinic. In 1946 it would be Fuad's son Farouk who would offer hospitality to the exiled King Victor Emmanuel III.[24]

Despite these manifold linkages, on a personal level, and in the financial matters which inevitably lay beside, it would be a mistake to assume that there was a serious covert Italian ambition to dominate Egypt, either financially or politically. The Italian community was numerous and powerful, but also given to schism. In 1908 Primo Levi was sent by Tittoni on a special pacificatory mission to Egypt. There, he found Italians rent by a nominally political dispute in which the retiring Vice-Consul at Alexandria, the *Marchese* Di Soragna, had engaged with the Consul-General Giacomo De Martino III and other Italians, over a number of matters, including, for example, whether or not pronouncements by the local Dante Alighieri Society were radical and unpatriotic. This sort of conflict seems to have been only too common among Italians resident in foreign countries, as it also was among the smaller communities of Italians who lived in Italy's own colonies. Levi took time out in his report to preach predictable messages: Italian culture should be spread more enthusiastically; Italian trade should be favoured especially by contact with the Banco di Roma; Catholic missions could be a more useful ally if they moderated the zeal of their piety;[25] all should collaborate to the greater benefit of Italy. But, once again, it was words and not action which were most obvious.

It is also true that much Italian 'power' of the sort which Italy appeared to possess in Egypt was, in fact, predicated on Italian powerlessness. Italians were useful to the Egyptian leaders as a demonstration that not all Europeans were united in will and method with the British. Once Italy started openly to display power, either economic or political, she usually rapidly lost ground as a 'friend' of the locals. It is this process which partly explains why, contrary to Italian expectations, the local Arabs in Libya were so hostile after the invasion of 1911. The same story is repeated less dramatically elsewhere, in Montenegro, Albania and Turkey. While Italy remained entirely weak, a certain Mazzinian virginity clung both to Italians' words and to their reputation. But once Italians started to act imperially, locals soon detected Italian bombast and prepotence, and remembered also that these people were the ones whom their older masters called 'dagoes', or, in a more cultivated style, the *quantité négligeable*.

Recently Richard Webster has brilliantly exposed the detail of much of Italy's commercial interest in the Eastern Mediterranean and argued that there was an Italian *Drang nach Osten*, that Italy was 'an imperialist country in the same sense that Germany was', that twentieth-century Italian foreign policy can only be explained in terms of Italy's 'economic precariousness and imbalance' and the ambitions which this created for Italian industrialists.[26] At times Webster's brilliance seems to shade into wrong-headedness, for he fails to pay sufficient attention to the boundaries of Italian power and freedom of action. Successful in exposing the corruption of the Liberal social system and the ties which existed, even at the highest level, between business and government, Webster exaggerates the extent to which this created a foreign policy. Moreover, the size and extent of Italian investments abroad, and the profits won from them, were very limited. For most Italian businessmen, the major source of profits was not in Constantinople, but in the subsidies and protective tariffs which were offered in Rome. However much all members of the post-Risorgimento ruling classes looked after each other, Italian diplomacy depended more on lawyers and journalists than on entrepreneurs. It is a telling fact that Libya and Ethiopia, the two colonies which Italy gained in the twentieth century, were of notably little commercial value. Italian industrialists did have interests in them, but those interests were small. In the case of Libya, it is also characteristic that neither the skills of technology nor the imperatives of financial advantage led to major discovery of oil, that product which might have made the colony financially worthwhile. Italian foreign policy in both the Liberal and Fascist regimes was always more intellectual in its definition than it was commercial, was more parochial, old-fashioned, traditional than it was modern, 'imperialist', or even 'fascist'.

With the proviso that the question, 'Who is manipulating whom?', should always be asked, there is nonetheless much evidence of increasing Italian political and commercial interest in the Balkans and Asia Minor before 1914.

The major bridgehead for Italian penetration eastwards was Montenegro. The symbol of the ties between Italy and Montenegro was Queen Elena, the daughter of the ruler of Montenegro, who declared himself King Nicola in 1910. In 1903 the ambitious Venetian entrepreneur, Giuseppe Volpi, by assisting in various underhand ways the eternal *divertissements* of Crown Prince Danilo, was rewarded with the tobacco monopoly for Montenegro.[27] In the next years Volpi's enterprises spread to the more prestigious and strategically valuable areas of railway building and port construction, especially around Antivari, which, in some eyes, seemed likely to become the *entrepôt* of the Balkans. Guglielmo Marconi, himself seldom averse to financial advantage, in 1904 built a radio station at Antivari as a triumphant outpost of revived Italian science.[28] Supported also by Foscari, and with backing from leading Italian industrialists, Volpi's schemes were usually regarded benevolently by the government. While Tittoni remained Foreign Minister, Volpi could rejoice in funds both from the Banca Commerciale, from which he collected 3.4 million lire, and the Banco di Roma, which passed over 1.8 million. When Sonnino took over the government in 1909–10, Volpi's position shook while hostile investigations on the losses which he was incurring and on his methods were made by Antonio Baldacci, an expert who was himself linked to clerical financial interests. However, under San Giuliano, Volpi returned to some favour. In September 1910 publicists were talking about the advantages of Italian investment in Montenegro which would block a German or Austrian *Drang nach Süden*, and which would naturally spread peace and civilisation.[29] In 1912 the Banca Commerciale and Banco di Roma were persuaded to write off their debts from the Antivari Company which amounted to their total investment. Volpi's concern was thereupon refloated. The suspicion that Savoy money was involved was lent credence in 1913 when Volpi was formally elevated to the nobility, and could thus feel more at ease with backers like Count Ruggero Revedin, whose wife was one of Queen Elena's ladies-in-waiting. In 1914, Volpi was happily talking again about the great potential future of Montenegrin railways.

Despite Volpi's evident skills, Italian financial ventures in Montenegro failed to be very rewarding. If this was the Italian banking–military–industrial complex in action, then businessmen proved remarkably unconcerned when good money was thrown after bad. Italian diplomatists were usually anxious to participate in railway schemes not so much because of financial advantage, nor even really for strategic gain, but because such participation was part of the obligation and reward of being a Great Power. Antivari certainly was an unpromising post from which to hope to make millions. One English visitor described it as no more than 'a score of houses all told, an hotel [Volpi's famous *Hotel Marina*], and a row of wooden huts on the beach'. The old town was perched on a mountain side four miles inland, away from the malarial marshes by the bay. The Englishman found equally problematical the financial future of that section of railway line which had been constructed out of Antivari:

It is of very narrow gauge, the engines are little more modern looking than the Rocket, and the carriages are like horse-tramway-cars...I made many journeys on this line...and barely one without an incident of some kind – once the steam-pipe burst, once we ran out of fuel and the engine-driver called upon the passengers to go gathering brush wood with him, again we went off the line, and another time we were snowed up.[30]

The overwhelming impression left by Italian business involvement in Montenegro is of personal profiteering, by Volpi and Foscari, and very likely by royal personages as well. This personal character of Italo-Montenegrin financial relations is confirmed by a study of Italo-Montenegrin diplomatic relations. The fact that Montenegro was a notably unreliable friend was recognised even in Italy, especially because, in the years from 1910 to 1914, Montenegro showed markedly little desire to become an Italian vassal. King Nicola looked to Austria, France and Russia for sympathy and funds as much as he did to Italy. Contrary to the optimistic words of publicists, at the Ischl meeting with Aehrenthal from 30 August to 2 September 1910, San Giuliano revealed that Victor Emmanuel 'cared very little for his father-in-law as indeed for the whole Montenegrin royal family' but kept a certain element of relations going 'in consideration of his royal spouse whom he loved dearly'. San Giuliano and Aehrenthal also agreed that there was no need whatever to hurry plans for Balkan railways, although San Giuliano took the opportunity to make sarcastic comments about the 'few poor fishermen's huts and a Turkish fort' which made up the port of San Giovanni di Medua, a possible Albanian rival as a railhead to Antivari.[31]

San Giuliano was also unimpressed by Montenegrin suggestions, both before and during the Libyan War, that Italy sponsor a Montenegrin attack on Turkey.[32] When, in October 1912, Montenegro did attack Turkey, and thus began the Balkan Wars, Italy was responsible enough to procrastinate in the face of Montenegrin appeals for a loan.[33] Italy tried to use royal familial and financial ties with Montenegro to discourage a Montenegrin incursion into the Sandjak of Novi-Bazar. During the Scutari crisis, despite San Giuliano's repeated sardonic advice that the sure way to return Montenegro to good sense was to offer her 'a loan', that is a bribe, Montenegro made little effort to adjust its policy to Italian wishes. Worse, King Nicola was ready to offer to Austria Mount Lovcen,[34] that peak behind Antivari which Italian strategists advised must never fall into the hostile hands of a Great Power, and which would block the progress of any railway line out of Antivari.[35]

It was during the Scutari crisis also that San Giuliano began talking about the difficulty of continuing to prop up the Montenegrin dynasty, rather than allowing a union of Serbia and Montenegro, under the Serb King Peter, who was *persona grata* in Rome[36] and with Volpi. Giolitti, with his usual good sense, agreed and expressed dislike for any loan to Montenegro: 'We must seek to limit our financial involvement in Montenegro regarding it as money thrown away in complete loss.' He went on to warn that Volpi's interests there were not charitable, and were really the reverse of Italy's.[37] San Giuliano was unwilling to give up any possibility of Italian advantage and pleaded for more sympathy for Volpi, but, despite this, Italian–Montenegrin relations remained cool. In June 1913 San Giuliano advised that the Government would not object if the Banca Commerciale involved itself in a loan to Montenegro, but would 'give counsel, neither in one direction, nor the other'.[38] Railways were still a matter which could arouse Italian attention, and San Giuliano explained to Giolitti that the government must not object to Volpi (and Joel) talking to Franco-Russian financiers about the systematisation of Montenegrin railways. After all, he explained, in Montenegro, unlike in Albania, Italy had not pledged herself in any way to work with Austria. In fact, Italian interests in Montenegro clashed with Austrian, and could be harmonised more comfortably with French and Russian aims, since Austria always saw railways moving from North to South with an eventual outlet to the Aegean, while France and Russia wanted a Serb-Montenegrin outlet in the Adriatic which could benefit Italy. In passing, San Giuliano noted that a more grandiose railway or investment scheme could assist the Antivari Company which was currently 'unpopular' with King Nicola.[39] By July 1913 a new loan of 6 million francs was floated for Montenegro with Italian participation through the Società Commerciale d'Oriente, the recently reorganised company of Volpi and the Banca Commerciale.[40]

In the last months before the outbreak of the First World War, despite Volpi's optimism about the future of his companies, San Giuliano found Montenegrin conspiracies more and more tiresome. In March 1914, he was appropriately dismayed by a rumour from Tittoni that the Montenegrins were talking about a joint Franco-Austrian bank opening at Cetinje. San Giuliano at once wrote off to ask about likely Russian and Serbian reactions since, he believed, in economic and railway matters, 'our interests coincide more with Russian than Austrian aims'. Italy should be willing to work there either with French or Austrian capital but must object to the implications of Franco-Austrian collaboration.[41] San Giuliano also engaged in a number of conversations with the German ambassador, Flotow, about the possible future union of Serbia and Montenegro, which San Giuliano openly declared to be 'inevitable' on the death of King Nicola. The real purpose of such 'brutal frankness' was, however, the old one of hinting that, if Austria demanded compensation for Serbian advantage, Italy would demand compensation for Austrian advantage, and would demand it in the Trentino and Trieste.[42] Certainly no matters of trade, nor of royal relationships affected that essential base of Italian foreign policy. There the matter remained as Franz Ferdinand went to Sarajevo. Berchtold had learned enough from San Giuliano to offer Montenegro a vast loan for her support during the July Crisis. King Nicola was always loath to let such an opportunity go, but the matter was eventually swallowed up in the greater crisis.[43]

All in all, Italy's diplomatic plotting and financial involvement in Montenegro from 1903 to 1914 had been of little account, more part of the game of being a Great Power, or the intricate world of keeping government money flowing into the Italian establishment, than the heartland of national foreign policy. It is nice to note San

Giuliano pleading for greater Italian involvement in Montenegro in rivalry with Austria, while, publicly, he is asserting his 'never-to-be-forgotten' triplicism, and, privately, his fears about the 'Slav peril'. But that sort of duplicity is neither surprising nor new, and had rather more extensive play in Albania. In fact, King Nicola and his entourage were too skilled in diplomacy and peculation for Italy to do very well in Montenegro. What Italo-Montenegrin relations before 1914 indicate best is how easily inexperienced and ambitious Italians could be enticed into local affairs, which were never likely to bring advantage to any except unscrupulous individuals. In Montenegro, at least, an Italian *Drang nach Osten* was as feebly imitative and unreal as were so many other aspects of Italy's pretensions to be a Great Power.

In the other Balkan states there were also some indications of a growing Italian financial presence. In 1914, for example, German industrialists were alarmed to learn that Siemens had lost a major contract to Marconi in Greece, and that Italy had won a ship-building tender in Romania, which Germany had believed certain to be gained by German industry.[44] In Bulgaria there had been more longstanding contacts, given the tradition that Bulgarian officers received their training in Italian military academies. King Ferdinand had married a Bourbon heiress and was reported both to admire Italian fine arts and political independence.[45] Yet neither royal relationships, financial deals nor military comradeship really presented Italy with much influence in the small Balkan states. Greece, despite its use of the Marconi system, was probably Italy's most bitter diplomatic rival in 1914, saved from a serious imbroglio until 1923 mainly by the glosed tongue of Venizelos[46] and by the policing of the Greater Powers. Romania was usually a loyal and ignored associate of Italy, but not so much through economic manipulation as by the simple fact that Romania was also 'the ally or enemy' of Austria–Hungary, and cast eyes on Transylvania with the same ardour with which Italy regarded the Trentino and Trieste. Bulgaria was far more vulnerable to appeals for Slav unity than to the influence of King Ferdinand's collection of italianate *objets d'art* or of the belief that Bulgaria could challenge Serbia and defeat Austria as a new Piedmont. In the Balkans, despite the independence of her diplomacy and the effort of her finance, Italy was still the least of the Great Powers.

Of much more financial and diplomatic potential than the Balkan area was 'Asia Minor', that rump of the Ottoman Empire remaining after the Balkan Wars. This left over area, San Giuliano, for one, was convinced would soon break into its component parts. These, he was adamant, must not be taken over by small Powers as had happened to Turkey-in-the-Balkans but must be divided among the Great.

San Giuliano talked about this interesting prospect often enough before 1910. To the Istituto Coloniale, Lega Navale or Royal Geographical Society, San Giuliano had preached the need to increase Italian interest in Asia Minor. In the brief time that he was President of the Geographical Society, he did his best to hurry the lagging exploratory mission, led by naval Lieutenant Vannutelli, to the Eastern Mediterranean coasts in pursuance of what San Giuliano described as the 'applied' side of 'science' in areas where 'Italy has today and will have in the future its greatest political and economic interests'. In 1907 Vannutelli's eventual report was received: 'the Third Italy in all the pride of its renewal' had enough 'latent power and energy' to have a great commercial future in Asia Minor where ' "*audaces fortuna iuvat*" '.[47]

In fact Italian commercial and financial involvement in Turkey remained comparatively small, although it increased before the dislocation caused by the Libyan War, and was growing anew in 1913–14. Despite Italy's seat on the Ottoman Public Debt, Italians possessed less than 1% of Ottoman bonds. They also had not been involved in the profitable, but complicated, field of Turkish railway building, with the exception of their ambitions out of Antivari. Their trade with Turkey was only about 3% of their total, hardly more than their trade in the Far East. By 1914 they held fourth place behind Britain, Germany and Austria, in Turkey's overall commerce with the Great Powers, but had climbed ahead of France, which, in Asia Minor as elsewhere, preferred not so much to sell goods as to take up loans.[48]

Within these limits, there were considerable Italian interests in Turkey. Through the Società Commerciale d'Oriente, Volpi had acquired a share in the possible exploitation of the coal-mines of Eraclea, near the Black Sea, and potentially useful to an improved Turkish Black Sea fleet, and even perhaps to a completed Berlin–Baghdad railway. There were disadvantages. The Italian claims to the mines were contested by their French colleagues; and legitimate profits were distant. A semi-official propagandist writing in 1922 accompanied a text noting the ties between Mithridates and Roman Bithynia, or reporting the mission which Julius Caesar had sent there, with pictures which showed, variously: coal being carried by a primitive hand-pushed trolley and then dumped onto a small punt for transit away from the jetty; the disembarkation of construction materials for the mine on an open beach; the mine snowed up in winter; and two Italian clerks having a pleasant ride in their spare time, assisted by an escort of eight armed locals. The propagandist, not very surprisingly, had to admit that production at the mines in twenty years' operation had never risen above 1 million tons, although, he averred, it could easily be increased.[49] Volpi indeed grew so disillusioned with the mines that, in June 1912, he threatened to sell out altogether to the French; but, having displayed his patriotic and bribery skills during the negotiation of the Treaty of Lausanne, he was bailed out by the Banca Commerciale. In November 1912, the Società Commerciale d'Oriente was reorganised with Joel as President and Nogara continuing as director in Constantinople.

Another major Italian interest was held by the Ansaldo company, often the Genoese rival to Giolitti's Milanese business friends. Abdul Hamid had granted Ansaldo the contract for the naval arsenal in Constantinople, but the Young Turkish regime was not, after 1908, very enthusiastic about this, and Ansaldo's progress languished.[50] The Banco di Roma also had holdings and ambitions in Turkey, but they had been concentrated in Libya, and their failure to bring rapid financial gains put the whole Banco di Roma into crisis in 1912–14. Naturally Italy's shipping lines and merchant marine also favoured developing trade with Turkey although they were as much attracted by the government subsidies which were traditionally offered beforehand in Rome.

In Turkey thus, as in Montenegro, Italian financial interests were mainly in the hands of, or linked to, a few key persons, Volpi, Nogara, Joel, and their friends and contacts. There is no particular evidence that these men gained much legitimate return from investment in Turkey. Subsidies, bribes, insider speculations and *backsheesh* were another matter. But, in Italy's 'preparations' for a great future in the Eastern Mediterranean, it was the Italian government, and especially the Foreign Ministry of Antonino Di San Giuliano, not the financial world, which made the pace.

Despite his re-ordering of the commercial services, and his

memoranda expressing the belief that business must be diplomacy's 'secular arm', San Giuliano's first months in office merely preserved the continuity of Italian policy towards Turkey. Throughout 1910, first in Albania and then in Libya, San Giuliano was anxious to assert that Italy wanted to see retained the *status quo* in all the Ottoman Empire. A responsible Great Power's task was tirelessly to transmit restraining and hortatory words to Young Turk governments in Constantinople.[51]

In April 1911 San Giuliano sent Giolitti a memorandum arguing that German, French and British power was assisted by the foreign investment policies of those countries, and that now was the time for Italy also to join in this activity. The Italian government must accept its obligation generously to provide capital with 'the stimulation to act'.[52] But this repetition of San Giuliano's old assertions led nowhere in the greater crisis developing in Libya. Commercial policy in Turkey became instead the sort of obscure process in 'subventioning' which marked the Theodoli mission on the outbreak of the Libyan War. San Giuliano also provided De Martino in Constantinople with last minute funds, presumably to be disbursed to potential spies and other friends in Turkey who might assist a rapid peace, or protect Italian interests in the interim.[53]

Whether or not because of these preparations, as the colonial war proceeded in Libya, Italian commercial agents, especially Nogara, who remained in Constantinople, were able to sound the terrain for Italian peace moves.[54] It was certainly Volpi's contacts with Nogara, as well as his experience and ability in distributing subventions, which encouraged Giolitti to appoint him one of the negotiators who began meeting the Turks in Switzerland in July. In indirect assistance, the Italian government continued to arrange for money to reach Nogara or his agents in Constantinople.[55]

Rhetoric meanwhile began to talk about what would happen when peace was made in Libya. San Giuliano told the Chamber of Deputies that he hoped 'the great events in the Mediterranean' had restored to all Italians 'the profound conviction' that Italy must have a colonial policy based on 'adequate and effective means'.[56] At the Istituto Coloniale, Bettòlo, the new president, reminded his listeners that 'maritime power' was 'the index and the instrument of the expansionist strength of the country'. To aid this growth of naval strength, Bettòlo also set up a most complicated set of sub-committees to concentrate on every conceivable area of Italian emigration or commerce. Rather as in the governmental processes of a university department of the 1970s there were not enough zealous members to go round and there had to be considerable doubling up. The membership of the sub-committee on Turkey ought not to have gladdened Giolitti's heart, as the chairman was Andrea Torre, and Foscari, Theodoli and A. Martini-Marescotti were the other members.[57]

In the area of policy, however, it was Austria which recalled Italian attention to basic issues in Turkey. On 13 August 1912 Berchtold, anxious about the deteriorating situation in the Balkans, tried to revive a united Concert attitude to the question of the survival or reform of Turkey.[58] Italy reacted a little slowly to Berchtold's schemes, fearing as usual that Austria might be trying to steal a march in Albania,[59] but San Giuliano and Giolitti eventually agreed that Italy must not be left out of any conference which might occur. Great Power discussions about the reform of Turkey might encourage a peace in Libya, and San Giuliano also worried how plans about 'decentralisation' from Constantinople could be utilised by Italy in her 'temporary' occupation of the Dodecanese. Italy, he wrote mechanically, naturally favoured the postponement of the collapse of the Ottoman Empire, which could still have years of vitality.[60]

The Libyan War having been concluded, Italian communities could resume an orthodox life in the Balkans and Asia Minor. Italian trade in the Eastern Mediterranean, struck down during the war, began rapidly to recover. San Giuliano hastened formally to wish these returning interests 'a prompt and general revival'.[61] The conclusion of the talks in Switzerland, if precipitated more by events in the Balkans than by his financial skills, released Volpi to resume his speculations. Nogara too now took over from Theodoli on the Ottoman Public Debt, and was soon being used by Giolitti to make contacts with and pass bribes to Arabs unwilling passively to accept Italian government in Libya.[62] The new-style ambassador, Camillo Garroni, the agent of Giolittian political and Genoese commercial interests, at last reached Constantinople. Under the tuition of Nogara, Volpi and Garroni, the seeds of Italian commercial advantage in Turkey would be nurtured more solicitously than ever before.

Diplomatic events also revived Italian independence. The Triple Alliance was renewed, without Italy having to make any special pledges about the Dodecanese, and with Berchtold, pre-occupied by events in the Balkans, no longer mentioning the nasty prospect that the Austrian interpretation of Article VII might carry as far as the advantages which Italy had won, however temporarily, in the Eastern Mediterranean. The summoning of the Ambassadors' Conference in London also promised diplomatic opportunity and advantage if Italy could find the right mixture of bravado and legerdemain.

The various sections of the De Martino family were soon involved in new plans for Turkey. Giacomo De Martino III was sent on a private visit to London in order to sound out what advantages in Asia Minor Italy might hope to win by accepting British strategists' objections to Italy's prolonged retention of the Dodecanese.[63] The Egyptian, De Martino Bey, meanwhile arrived in Italy in search of funds for the Khedive. If Italy could raise the money, De Martino promised monetary guarantees from the Khedive's rights to tariffs in Konia and Angora, and intimated that there were further 'noteworthy and advantageous' concessions which could be wrung from Turkey. San Giuliano was very interested, and was willing for Pacelli to raise the funds, even if this meant the Banco di Roma, given its past record and its current doubtful financial position, would soon be appealing again to the national treasury. Giolitti however, was more impressed by Stringher's advice from the Banca d'Italia that floating a loan would not be expedient. 'I understand how the conclusion of this loan could help our future relations with Turkey', he wrote, 'but at this moment it is not very advisable to take capital away from the Italian market.'[64] Confronted by Giolitti's opposition, De Martino Bey had to take his loan schemes elsewhere.

Despite this, San Giuliano was devoting more and more attention to claims which Italy might want to present to Turkey in recompense for the evacuation or retention of the Dodecanese. The German ambassador was told that the Triple Entente now counted on the collapse of Asiatic Turkey and wanted all Aegean islands to go to Greece in order to destroy a potential Triple Alliance base for naval or commercial interest. From Anglo-French talk about a Mediterranean accord San Giuliano had detected some sort of Triple Entente agreement on spheres of interest in Asia Minor. France could not be denied Syria, if she regarded such a denial as a *casus belli*, but neither Italy nor, hopefully, Germany and Austria, could stand by and let the Mediterranean become 'a French lake'.[65] At the same time Barrère was treated to one of San Giuliano's familiar tirades against Greece, and then told bluntly that Italy must have a share in any breakup of Asia Minor.[66] To Vienna, San Giuliano changed tack slightly, declaring that Russia lay behind the Greek insistence on annexing the Aegean islands. Italy did not want to encourage the collapse of the Ottoman Empire, but the Triple Alliance must plan out its policies on this eventuality well beforehand.[67] San Giuliano thereupon explained to Jagow, quite falsely, that it was Berchtold who was trying to push the Ambassadors' Conference into a wholesale discussion of the future of Asia Minor.[68]

Having made it seem as though others had unleashed a storm over Asia Minor, San Giuliano took the opportunity to move from general comments to particular ones. In passing, he reminded Giolitti that the Triple Entente was 'preparing an active and ambitious policy in the Eastern Mediterranean, and for the partition of Asiatic Turkey, [believing] that they can count on the support of the Quadruple alliance of the Balkan states'.[69] On 21 January he explained to Giolitti that he had instructed Garroni to make plain Italy's opposition to the dismemberment of Turkey. However, he now had little hope that the collapse of Turkey could be avoided. To safeguard Italian interests 'in the day of the *Débâcle*' an urgent series of provisions 'of a political and economic character' must be taken. Remembering the abortive affair of the Egyptian loan, he admitted that Italy had now reached a stage in which she must accept the rules of the game as played by really Great Powers. Launching into familiar themes he noted:

Among the most effective means of all is being militarily strong by land and sea, and having public opinion morally prepared to follow, without sentimentality, the policy rooted in a cold calculation of our interests.

Because of this it was

absolutely necessary to construct in Asiatic Turkey a network of economic interests and acquired rights, by means of concessions, loans, diverse undertakings etc...not only in that part of Asiatic Turkey to which we can perhaps one day put forth claims for territorial dominion but also in other parts as eventual objects of exchange.

Even if it was for the moment unpopular, this forward policy must be pursued in Turkey. Diplomatically, the best collaborators would be Germany and Austria, although Italy could not surrender to Austria one jot or tittle of her claims to equality in Albania, Montenegro or Balkan railway affairs.[70]

This memorandum, with its admission of future territorial claims on Asia Minor, was a remarkably frank statement by San Giuliano of the extent of his ambitions in the area. Without waiting for comment from Giolitti, San Giuliano asked Garroni for suggestions how best to mark out the Italian sphere in Asia Minor. Italy must have equality with others, he opined:

so that in case of partition we can raise territorial claims with the least probability of intransigent resistance.

Garroni should favour all Italian economic interests, setting down clearly

the means and persons on which and through which to act, preferred undertakings, initiatives, and localities, [the style of] cooperation of the various Italian public bodies, as well of our capitalists, banks etc, the shipping lines to construct, all in all an organic and constant programme.[71]

It was a little precipitate and ingenuous so to advise an ambassador whose experience ought to have taught him more than a San Giuliano would ever know about modern capitalism. San Giuliano seems to have been reacting so urgently both because he could not keep believing in Italy's good luck in still occupying the Dodecanese, and because he had misread the war situation in the Balkans. Although there is something unreal about this sudden glow of enthusiasm for Asia Minor, neither San Giuliano, nor Nogara and his friends, were likely to abandon an issue once raised. It was true that the Italian Chamber of Commerce in Constantinople complained that Italian government assistance to them was minimal,[72] but businessmen often cried poor. Whether helped by Garroni and the Italian government, or simply reclaiming business opportunities lost in the Libyan War and now available, especially while Austria's line to Constantinople was blocked by the Balkan Wars, a network of Italian interests did begin to appear in Asia Minor. As was customary in Italy, publicists did even better than businessmen. Luigi Federzoni, scenting sensations which would be useful politically in the coming general elections, accompanied the Duke of the Abruzzi on a naval cruise in the Eastern Mediterranean.

Any surrender of the Dodecanese, Federzoni described, would be the waste of 'the precious blood of the fallen' and of the achievements of the interim Governor, Ameglio, who had 'an authentically Roman soul and mind'. The Duke himself reported, less rhetorically, on the sound mining prospects of Anatolia.[73]

In the next months San Giuliano continued to press on his diplomats the crucial significance of Asia Minor 'in the perhaps not far off day of the liquidation of the ...sick man' of Europe. San Giuliano reiterated two basic themes. French rivalry, as indicated for example by the recent French movement of its fleet to the Mediterranean, or by French reminders that Italy was pledged to leave the Dodecanese, could only be countered by persuading Germany to treat Italy seriously, since Italy 'will not make any more *giri di walzer*'.[74] (In passing San Giuliano added that the Triple Alliance should favour Turkey rather than Greece which was bound to be 'in the opposite camp to ours'.)[75] Concerning Austria, the message was a little different. Italy should stay close to Austria, and even be kind to her, because the results of the Balkan Wars were affecting Austria worse than any other Power, since they were strategically benefitting Austria's rivals, Italy and Russia. Italian protestations of loyalty might restrain Austria from a *coup de main* in the Balkans, and, as well, if the Austrian war party did predominate, Italian steadfastness would help Italy the better to remind Austria of the true implications of Article VII of the Triple Alliance. In less intricate language, San Giuliano explained to the Chamber of Deputies:

we did not wish only to assure Italy's position in the Mediterranean through the occupation of Libya, but we wanted beyond that to show to the world and ourselves that Italy could resolve by herself and by her own efforts alone the first major problem of international relations placed before her...If by the force of events, against our will and against the will of our allies and all the Great Powers, there must occur, sooner or later, territorial changes in the Mediterranean, Italy cannot remain a passive spectator [of this event].

At this stage, the Chamber broke out into shouts of '*Bravo*' and '*Benissimo*' and there was general applause. San Giuliano was then allowed to return to his accustomed comments, to his rejection of the idea that anyone (that is, France) could call the Mediterranean '*mare nostrum*', to his predictions about the coming struggle of the nations, until he reached a triumphant conclusion:

In half a century of struggle to raise herself from her unhappy past condition to her present grandeur which is [only] a preparation for a still more radiant future, [Italy] has revealed herself not only with the thought and work of a few individuals which can vanish but with the virile *virtù* of the whole nation which [always] remains.[76]

It was in this mood of heightened patriotism that San Giuliano made his obscure and perhaps rash plans during the Scutari crisis.

Meanwhile, the financial pot was beginning to simmer nicely in Constantinople. In early April 1913, San Giuliano wanted to nominate both Volpi and Nogara to the International Financial Commission due to begin sitting in Paris with the task of defining the economic implication of the Balkan Wars, that is, really, to insure that, despite the collapse of Turkey-in-Europe, the Great Powers' financial rewards would survive unabated in Asia Minor. Giolitti, at a moment in which he was doubtless unimpressed by speculation in Montenegro, baulked at the nomination of Volpi, but eventually accepted it when San Giuliano agreed to drop Nogara on the grounds that the Società Commerciale d'Oriente was about to clinch a deal with the Turkish government. San Giuliano reiterated to Giolitti Italy's need to be represented by people like Volpi, 'of *souplesse* and elasticity of mind', who understood the complications of the Balkans and the 'often complex relations [there] between political and economic interests and between politicians and financiers.'[77]

What was happening in Constantinople was that Nogara, working with an Armenian intermediary, had been able to set up a dummy Ottoman corporation, the Società Anonima Ottomana, with money from the Banca Commerciale. This, Nogara explained to Joel, would be 'an instrument in this work of economic penetration in Asia Minor', which he had marked down as the whole area from Alexandretta to Smyrna.[78]

At this stage, the Germans, prodded by their Embassy in Constantinople, asked just what the Italians thought that they were doing.[79] Perhaps this German question had been inspired by the latent war of imperialist industrialists, but Italian diplomats were often not averse to encouraging greater attentiveness to themselves by this sort of pinpricking. Indeed, in the summer of 1913, the concern which Italy provoked from Britain on the Dodecanese and Mediterranean questions, and from Germany on Asia Minor, was a testimony to the successful independence of San Giuliano, and in striking contrast to the usual bland contempt which met the plotting of the 'beggars of Europe'. As far as Italy was involved, negotiating about spheres in Asia Minor was just about the best of all possible worlds. Italian 'enterprises', despite Nogara's efforts, remained far more impressive on the drawing boards than in reality. But, once having attracted the attention of Germany, Italy could go through a predictable gamut of protestations of loyalty to the Triple Alliance, and appeals for sympathy and support against Austria, France and Britain. Italy, in other words, could put herself in the unusual and enjoyable situation of being able to make the Triple Alliance work actively for her. Most significant of all, the more Austria was inveigled into ventures which had received Italian approval, the more difficult Austria would find it to act by herself in the Balkans, and, just conceivably, the nearer Italy would move to that longed for moment of being able in Vienna to plead for the application of Article VII with German backing.

The Germans began by pointing out that Nogara's conversations might be intruding into that area of Southern Anatolia reserved to Germany. San Giuliano, in January, had envisaged just this circumstance. Italian financial operations, he then thought, might reach into the spheres of others in order 'to be an eventual object of exchange'. San Giuliano had then predicted to Garroni that Italy would have to be prepared to confront 'the interests and aspirations of Powers stronger than us' by which he seems to have meant specifically Germany.[80] It is thus not surprising that San Giuliano had well rehearsed arguments ready for Flotow's enquiry. It was a difficult matter, San Giuliano said, and he was embarrassed because Asia Minor was regarded as a question of such importance by Giolitti. Having asserted his virtue, and anyhow pointed out the limits of his personal responsibility, San Giuliano became more specific. Naturally, he did not favour the collapse of Turkey, but it must be recognised that this eventuality was not likely to be distant. Then, France would take Syria and, he had always thought, Germany would want Northern Anatolia as far as some point south of Smyrna. Could not Italy, which must not allow the Mediterranean balance to be altered to her disadvantage, be fitted in between? Italy could try to protect herself by appealing to the Triple Entente, although, of course, San Giuliano would not want such a drastic reversal of policy. Else, Italy, Germany and Austria could reach an understanding about Asia Minor, and even about the whole Mediterranean.[81]

Thus the ostensibly embarrassed San Giuliano had turned the charge that Nogara had been caught with his fingers in the till at Constantinople into a discussion how Italian interests in the whole East Mediterranean might best be defended or asserted. It was a breathless *tour de force* to risk treating the abrupt Germans so cynically, and Bollati from Berlin hastened to warn of the serious damage which could be inflicted on Italo-German relations since Germany would defend her interests in Asia Minor 'with all means and at whatever cost'.[82]

San Giuliano had prepared suitably marshy ground to meet such a German cavalry charge. Jagow wrote back to Flotow of his 'astonishment' at Nogara's negotiations, and at San Giuliano's blatantly 'political' rather than economic ends; but San Giuliano showed no sign of weakening or mortification. Nogara, he remarked brazenly, had not worked under any official commission from Italy, yet Italy had believed that sphere of Asia Minor to be open to penetration.[83] When no-one objected to this falsehood, San Giuliano was soon convinced that his policy was not a perilous one. The Austrians, obligingly, took the moment to offer Italy participation in a possible Balkan railway construction, and to reach a general economic accord in Albania.[84] On 10 June Bollati was able to report that the Germans were willing to talk about a Triple Alliance agreement in Asia Minor. Germany, it seemed, might even be willing to renounce to Italy spheres in the hinterlands from the gulfs of Adalia and Cos. San Giuliano jubilantly underlined clauses of this despatch and sent it off to Giolitti, who, in turn, noted that the concession was useful whether it be financially exploited or not. Who knew what was possible in future exchange or compensation? 'It is,' the Prime Minister noted confidently, 'a good result which we have obtained.'[85] Soon Stringher of the Banca d'Italia, and King Victor Emmanuel III were also privy to these ambitions that Italy look for 'the opportunity to follow up with banking enterprises as well as commercial and industrial initiatives the aims of foreign policy...in Asia Minor'.[86] Garroni, in Constantinople, kept matters on the boil by repeatedly reporting the 'disastrous' condition of Turkey:

The Ottoman Empire because of its heterogeneous ethnic composition, because of the disorder of its own administration, [and] of its inability to reform will not be able for long to resist that slow process of its disintegration.

It would be risky to set a definite date but Turkey unquestionably was 'moving towards its complete collapse'.[87]

San Giuliano's brief stop-over in Kiel *en route* to Stockholm on 2–3 July 1913 not only ensured Italo-German agreement in restraining a possible Austrian move against Serbia, but also produced a secret settlement of respective Italian and German *'zones de travail'* in Asia Minor.[88] Italy's interfering persistency continued to bring rewards.

Back home in Rome, San Giuliano, confronted by stronger British warnings on the Dodecanese, was now ready to talk about handing them back, at some future date. In any case, perhaps there were greater interests for which to play, foreshadowing the *débâcle*, 'perhaps not far off', of Asiatic Turkey. 'There,' he warned, 'we must hasten to affirm ourselves by a serious economic activity in the zone which is the least difficult to reserve to Italy.'[89]

It was an opportune moment for De Martino to sit down and write a full scale report to San Giuliano about the Turkish situation and the related question of the Dodecanese. Russia, with her eyes on Armenia, and France, with her general contestation of Italian influence in the Levant, which she regrettably viewed 'in a sharply political way', were the most unpleasant problems. Italy must try to hang on to 'some solid vestige' in the Dodecanese in order to ingratiate herself with Turkey, and to block France.[90] No doubt needing little reminding of the continued delicacy of Italy's occupation of the Dodecanese, San Giuliano, often from Fiuggi during the hot summer days, continued to try to jog the arm of businessmen and bankers. No, Giolitti, would not oppose a possible 'private' visit of Luzzatti to Constantinople; yes, Joel was ready to pledge Italian capital for a possible Adalian railway line; but then there was the further problem of the opposition of Tedesco, the Minister of the Treasury, to the export of capital.[91] Could not this be got around? Was it not also laudable that the Navy Minister favoured a new, subsidised shipping line from Italy to Asia Minor.[92]

Gradually, the generic desire in the *Consulta* that Italy favour commercial and cultural penetration of all kinds into Asia Minor was being concentrated into this possibility of a railway concession on the coast of Southern Anatolia. On 19 August Nogara received preliminary authorisation for the Società Commerciale d'Oriente to study the feasibility of constructing a railway, although not yet also a port, without which the value of the railway would remain not only hypothetical but practically minimal. It was characteristic of the Italians that the railway should not be in the 'zone of work' settled in the meeting with the Germans at Kiel, and of the Turks that the new concession should conflict with a concession granted a decade before to a British company and described by Sir Edward Grey as 'so to say, our ewe lamb' in the area.[93] Moreover, the plot was thickening still further, because Austria, despite her involvement in the Balkans, now was openly developing an interest in Asia Minor.[94]

Austrian attention had shifted to Asia Minor at about the same time as Italy's – in January–February 1913. A secret Austrian mission in the spring had duly reported favourably on commercial, archaeological, and even colonial prospects in Southern Anatolia. Austria thereupon declared her intention to open a consulate in Adalia and, on 5 August, Italy was told of this Austrian 'interest'.[95] Austria, too, it now turned out, was interested in railway development.

The almost exact parallel of Austrian and Italian policies in Asia Minor raises many questions about secret knowledge and competition between the two. But, so far as archival evidence goes, the parallel was created almost automatically by the nature of diplomacy, and by the desire of the two weakest Great Powers to be involved in any strategic, commercial or territorial profits which could be made from what both Vienna and Rome believed to be 'the not far-off collapse' of Asiatic Turkey.

What was certain was that playing diplomatic games to create spheres of interest in Asia Minor would require a very cool head. San Giuliano was soon aware of Turkey's cleverness in offering Italy a railway concession which conflicted with Britain, but he readily understood that Italy had a strong negotiating card in her 'temporary' occupation of the Dodecanese.[96] In this regard, Italy would need to work fast in case British hostility became too peremptory.[97] In this event, San Giuliano mused, Italy would not be able to sustain her position in Asia Minor, since it would be against the wish of every Power except Germany. Italy, he therefore advised, should seek some sort of arrangement with Austria, although the danger of Austrian *faits accomplis* should never be ignored. The Austrians, he noted piously, did not always mean what they said. With this reservation, the 1906 Anglo-Franco-Italian treaty on Ethiopia, which San Giuliano had negotiated as ambassador in London, would make a good model for a settlement in Asia Minor. Then, in Asia Minor, Libya, Somalia, Eritrea and Ethiopia, Italy would have 'a colonial dominion' sufficient for her economic potentialities.[98] San Giuliano also spelled out to the King, who was upset by the Hohenlohe decrees, that these negotiations in Asia Minor were a tactical affair. 'As soon as the situation is delineated better,' he explained,

and the accords are made with Germany and Austria in Asia Minor, we must at once attempt to complete them by accords with France and England.[99]

San Giuliano had not forgotten that there were 'friends' and 'allies'. Nor did he disregard other norms of Italian diplomacy. Germany, he soon suggested innocently, must talk to the Austrians on Italy's behalf, since unilateral discussions between Rome and Vienna sometimes developed an uncomfortable and unfortunate atmosphere.[100]

In the meantime, San Giuliano was hardly acting in a way which deserved Austrian trust. Meditating on the reliability of promises from Stringher and Joel for greater support, San Giuliano noted again Italy's need to intensify her 'economic activity in that region of Asia Minor which could, with the least difficulty...become Italian'. As for the Austrian ally, Italy was glad to welcome her presence in Asia Minor, as long as it was understood that Italy had 'some rights already acquired'. 'Naturally', Italy would be willing to grant Austria a sphere, but, in such a division: 'we must search to have the biggest and best part, and possibly...give to Austria-Hungary the zone which would most put her into conflict with the Triple Entente'. This involvement of Austria would 'introduce into the Mediteranean a new political and military factor opposed to French or Franco-English hegemony'. French 'prepotence' would be checked, and the Triple Alliance 'cemented'.[101] The extent of San Giuliano's diplomatic scheming is sometimes alarming, and it is hard to reconcile his competition against Austria in the Balkans with his statement that even an Austrian military presence might be conceivable in Asia Minor. Anything, it seemed, even Austrian military collaboration, could be useful to keep the wheels turning in Asia Minor, to make sure that Italy was not omitted from the list of the beneficiaries of the defunct Turkish Empire. A resurrected Goldoni might have found San Giuliano's Italy an easy object of satire in an updated version of *The Servant of Two Masters*.

Both Germany, which was most suspicious of bilateral Italo-Turkish deals, and Britain, which at last had discovered that Italy's railway plans conflicted with the concession granted between Smyrna and Aidin, bombarded Rome with requests for a clarification of Italian policies. To the French, it was obvious that Italy could not possibly be planning economic penetration for any other than political motives. Behind this Italian ambition, Paris remarked fearfully, must lie the hand of Germany.[102]

Italy's insistence on intruding into Asia Minor had thus, predictably and deservedly, aroused the suspicion of all Powers. But for the Powers so much stronger than Italy, it was difficult to decide how to turn suspicion into action or retribution. None of the Powers, except perhaps France, was easily able to comprehend that Italy was being as coolly cynical as she really was. Rodd, for example, remained ingenuous enough to report that there was nothing 'unlawful' about the planned Italian railway, whatever that meant.[103] Not until 18 October did Grey spell out the fact that the British government was 'unable to contemplate any compromises' on the Smyrna–Aidin affair.[104] And then, Italy at once regarded this not as a firm statement, but as a parameter within which to bargain for Italian rights. German diplomats in other reports about Italy were almost as baffled, and were astonished to discover that Italian claims were not put forward with the tacit support of Britain and France, or of Austria.[105] Once this was apparent, Germany began hinting at Constantinople that the Turks need not treat Italian pretensions with too much sympathy[106] but, like Britain, Germany was unwilling to bring her opposition into the open.

Indeed, when San Giuliano found that his patrons were a little lukewarm about his policies, he merely argued that Italy step up her economic action in Asia Minor. He endorsed, for example, a suggestion by De Martino that visits by the Italian navy should be organised to ports which might be part of any allotted sphere.[107]

He also at once reproached Britain with his dismay that she should appear to block Italian economic development. How could Italy be responsible over the Dodecanese, or in a possible Mediterranean agreement, if Britain was too legalistic about the Smyrna–Aidin railway?[108] Indubitably, as San Giuliano had already many times repeated, if Britain insisted, and Italy had to hand over the Dodecanese to Greece, then it was Turkey which would suffer, and Turkey which would reject the hand of friendship from London (and Rome) and thus fall completely under German influence.[109]

For the Germans, San Giuliano had other arguments ready. Italy was a liberal country, with a parliament and a free public opinion. The Hohenlohe decrees had struck at the base of Italo-Austrian relations and thus at the Triple Alliance. Could not Germany help San Giuliano to placate his public opinion by favouring compensation to Italy in Asia Minor? Certainly, Germany must not support Austria ahead of Italy, especially if it was true, as was rumoured, that any Austrian railway concessions would aim to be linked up to the Berlin–Baghdad railway.[110]

Some commentators have accepted this last rumour as true,[111] although it seems doubtful if it was so. In fact the Austrians were appealing to Berlin for support against Italy since 'the Monarchy ...cannot possibly admit that Italy should acquire a large territory in Anatolia without getting some compensation'.[112] Not surprisingly the Germans were as embarrassed by this appeal to be the patrons of Vienna, as they were by Rome's importunities. In the next year as well, they remained generally unhelpful in the face of appeals from their 'noble second' for assistance in Turkey.

San Giuliano's policy in Turkey was bolder than in other areas, perhaps because Italy had least to lose in any real sense in Asia Minor. Convinced that Turkey must collapse soon, sensing his 'laws of history' in action, San Giuliano moved forward in order to be ready for that day. He ignored German hints, and instead brought Italy's diplomatic support behind a Russian request to be admitted into the Council of the Ottoman Public Debt.[113] He even contested Giolitti's opposition to his idea that Italy should sell a warship to Turkey. To his Prime Minister's comment that this would win Italy the undying enmity of the Greeks, San Giuliano replied that Italy had earned this anyhow because of Albania and the Dodecanese, but that it should be recalled that among 'the Greek characteristics is volubility'.[114]

When Germany started talking about Italian concessions to Austria in Asia Minor, San Giuliano remarked that the concessions might better be made by Germany. Such a 'sacrifice would not to be too great if it assured concord between Italy and Austria'. Privately he added that if Italy was driven to grant a concession to Austria, a territory might be found which could embroil Austria with Germany.[115] In fact, despite this talk about an arrangement with Austria, there was little likelihood of it coming early to fruition while San Giuliano could believe or hope that Italy was winning the battle of economic penetration in Asia Minor. The only way in which Italy could be checked was if Britain or Germany or both[116] denounced Italian conspiracies. This neither Power was able or willing to do. On the Smyrna–Aidin railway, for example, the British Foreign Office had feebly accepted the conclusion that: 'the Italians have in this case cards which neither we nor the Company can trump'.[117] In Asia Minor, as in the Dodecanese and South Albania, San Giuliano was demonstrating, in the general circumstances of 1913, that, if Italy was cynical enough, the Concert of the Great Powers could be held to ransom by the weakest of their number. Although he was somewhat alarmed by his Foreign Minister's strategems, Giolitti did not call San Giuliano up short. Indeed, in December 1913, Cabinet approved 'special expenses' of 400,000 lire for the Foreign Ministry to spend on Italian 'interests' in Asia Minor. And Giolitti reminded the parsimonious Tedesco that he should bear Italy's needs in mind.[118]

San Giuliano had done his best to drive home any possible Italian advantage, while Italy was still favoured by the tense international situation during the Balkan Wars. But, as peace returned to most of the Balkans, as Germany and Austria began to have time to assess the new diplomatic situation, and as domestic conflict increased in Italy, the opportunities began to be more limited.

Joel and Nogara, accompanied by De Martino, went to London in January 1914 for private talks on the Smyrna–Aidin railway. After weeks of hard bargaining, they were able to initial a preliminary agreement with the British on 6 March.[119] A more detailed settlement was signed on 19 May. The Italian negotiators had been assisted by the usual barrage of Italian diplomatic flack, pleas that Britain state in Constantinople at least that she did not oppose an Italian presence in Asia Minor, warnings about Germany, and even statements that Italy would 'go it alone'.[120] San Giuliano declared bluntly to Imperiali that:

Our supreme aim is to obtain fully public concessions in Asia Minor...at this moment it is less unfortunate to displease Grey than to [annoy] the Ottoman government.[121]

Confronted with this style of intransigence, Britain made no attempt to call Italy's bluff, despite the admission in London that Italian claims were 'purely political'.[122] Grey fell back into the weak stance that the British government would not interfere one way or the other in Italian negotiations with the Smyrna–Aidin company.[123] The ewe lamb would, it seemed, have to be sacrificed to Britain's importunate client. Only the strong voice of Crowe could be heard countering this variety of appeasement. In minute after minute, he condemned Grey and Nicolson for their weakness in dealing with Italy; Britain must understand that it was foolish to play into the hands of people 'incapable of straightforwardness'.[124]

Blithely unaware or insensible of this sort of attitude, San Giuliano continued to argue that Italy must participate in the 'contest' of economic penetration into Turkey, 'with calm and prudence, without rashness, arrogance or exaggeration', but 'at any cost'.[125] In negotiating with Britain he had the much exploited advantage that he could always say, or, better, get Imperiali to say, that Italy would not evacuate the Dodecanese without compensation.[126] But, in other areas, the Italian position was deteriorating.

Turkish politicians had been happy to accept Italian bribes and other overtures while it seemed that it was Italy alone which prevented the Dodecanese from being handed over to Greece. In 1914, the London Conference of Ambassadors having been completed, the situation began to change. Italy's occupation became much more equivocal, and was perhaps the major surviving factor stopping the islands simply being returned to Turkey. Therefore, Turkish enthusiasm for an Italian economic presence waned. Many of the 'small interests', which San Giuliano so zealously advocated, had not clinched their deals in Constantinople by July 1914. There was every sign that Turkey needed to learn nothing about the value of procrastination and obfuscation in dealing with the least of the Great Powers.

The charity of Italy's allies was also wearing thin in 1914. The

Germans had been rather taken aback by the stubbornness with which San Giuliano attacked the interests of the British Smyrna–Aidin company. Germany showed no interest in sponsoring a serious Italo-British conflict which, they rightly saw, was unlikely, whatever San Giuliano said.[127] Indeed, in many a despatch there is implied a German awareness that Italy was persistently bluffing, and an astonishment that the other Powers did not call that bluff. In the last months before the war, new German patronage of Greece also undermined Italo–German relations. Perhaps, too, the German coolness to Italy indicated a deepening and genuine German suspicion of an Italian intrusion into Asia Minor[128] and a reluctance to see the easy promises of 1913 turned into anything like reality – a development which might threaten Germany's paramount position as a railway builder in the Ottoman Empire. German industrialists had not been pleased in the early months of 1914 to lose contracts to Italian rivals both in Greece and Romania, and they probably overestimated the likelihood that Italian intrusion into Asia Minor could challenge German hegemony.

Austrian wishes had never accorded very well with Italian in Asia Minor, but the devotion of Austrian attention to the area was sporadic. San Giuliano grew practised in uttering, without challenge, fair words in Vienna to the effect that Italy, in pursuing her interests, was also pursuing those of Austria–Hungary.[129] However, the publicity given to the Smyrna–Aidin agreement recalled Austrian notice to the fact that Italy might be stealing a march in Turkey. The Austrians remembered that they had unfinished negotiations with Italy about 'spheres of interest' in Asia Minor, and began to ask what had happened to these.[130] San Giuliano at once fell into the ancient groove of his negotiating method, protesting his innocence in Berlin, but also warning the Germans that Britain regarded Austria as an extension of Germany in Asia Minor. Would it not therefore be better for all concerned if it was Germany which made room for Austria, handing over 'a small strip' for penetration by Vienna?[131]

San Giuliano found that these ploys were not recieved with great sympathy in Berlin. It was Germany's coolness which ensured that, at the Abbazia meeting with Berchtold, there was the embarrassment of bilateral Italo-Austrian discussions about Asia Minor. San Giuliano had tried to undermine the Austrian position by spreading wholly false rumours that it was Britain which really objected to an Austrian penetration of Asiatic Turkey; and he managed to get away from Abbazia without the Austrians calling this bluff, although Berchtold was dismayed by Italy's attitude, especially as he, too, now had learned belatedly to mouth words about 'the not too far off collapse' of the Ottoman Empire.[132]

In addition to diplomatic difficulties, there were also financial ones. The manifest troubles of the Italian economy in 1913 had rendered dubious San Giuliano's frequent statements about Italy's great economic progress. Tedesco, the Minister of the Treasury in Giolitti's government, was particularly appalled by the financial strategems of Giolitti and San Giuliano. 'In the Ministry of Foreign Affairs,' he noted, 'it is believed that a grand policy is made with grand means, and there is no thought for the fact that financially speaking Italy is neither France, nor England, nor Germany.'[133] Stringher of the Banca d'Italia was also growing worried lest Italy be overextended in Albania and Asia Minor, where there was so little return. Joel of the Banca Commerciale was still interested in the area, but very much on the grounds that it should be the government which shouldered the financial burdens and dangers. The Società Commerciale d'Oriente, he stated, should be treated the same way as the Antivari company in 1909,[134] a not very happy parallel given the 6 million lire absorbed by that institution. The Banco di Roma, which had been the junior partner to the Banca Commerciale in bailing out the Antivari company,was badly placed to help this time. Still absorbing its losses in Libya, the Banco di Roma was rumoured to be about to close its office in Constantinople, or even to collapse altogether, although the irrepressible Nogara said all that it needed was government funds, and then profits would soon follow.[135] Casting doubt on this forecast were a series of major engineering and archaeological surveys of the Adalia region, which reported the obvious: that immense labour and investment would be needed before any return could be hoped for in Asia Minor.

Despite such depressing news, San Giuliano did not alter his policy. Giolitti, while he retained power, could always be convinced of the value of government loans to subsidiaries of the Banca Commerciale, which could be described as working in the 'national interest'.[136] Salandra came into office with the reputation of being perhaps the strongest supporter in the country of private enterprise,[137] although that did not necessarily mean the Banca Commerciale, 'Giolitti's bank', since, after San Giuliano's death, Salandra would seek to undermine the Banca Commerciale as part of his general campaign to overturn *giolittismo*. San Giuliano's independent position in the Salandra Cabinet, and Salandra's initial lack of confidence in leading another interim administration, did not make this potential rivalry a problem for the moment. Graver issues were the continued failure of the Powers to be generous patrons of Italy, recurrent reports from Garroni of Turkish aggrievement over Italy's policies which led to the sacrifice of Turkey 'to Italian interests', and of Turkish resentment that Italy was being so openly ambitious in Asia Minor.[138] In June, there were even rumours that Hungarian capital might be intending to intrude into Southern Anatolia.[139] Garroni, too, had grown irritated and cynical enough to pick up an earlier comment by San Giuliano that the best way to enhance Italian interests in Asia Minor would be by a renewed war between Greece and Turkey.[140] In the meantime, San Giuliano was reduced to the ancient expedient of an appeal to Britain to hasten the Turkish government into granting concessions to Italy. If Italy did not get them, Italy could not evacuate the Dodecanese. 23 July 1914 was not a good day for Imperiali to pick for such discussions, if he really expected much British sympathy.[141]

Generally, San Giuliano had grown alarmed enough at the deterioration of Italy's position to have produced for Salandra a full-scale memorandum about the links between banking and Italian foreign policy. These links, he said, were now 'indispensable for the international life of Italy'. France, Germany and Austria were all thoroughly familiar with the economic side of foreign policy. But, the trouble was that Italian banks were 'immature, modest, timid and relatively poor' and needed to be 'driven on' by the government. Of the available banks, the Banca d'Italia was 'weak', the Banco di Roma in financial trouble, and Credito Italiano was beginning its investments in South America, so, San Giuliano added defensively to his new Prime Minister, he had relied most on the Banca Commerciale, given Joel's 'open and enlightened mind'. But, San Giuliano noted self-righteously and in an obvious appeal to Salandra's anti-Giolittian prejudices, Italy should not rely on one bank alone. Therefore, there should be revived sympathy for the Banco di Roma which needed all the help it could get to defend Italian interests in

Asia Minor, and notably in Ethiopia, where 'without the existence of. . . economic interests we risk seeing our territorial rights reduced to a *mere railway*'.[142]

These luxuriant hopes soon withered before the cruel blast of the July Crisis and the World War. By 5 August a Consul in Anatolia was already reporting the new difficulties of economic operations, even though Turkish entry into the war still lay more than two months ahead. The Turkish army had taken over the administration in the Aidin *vilayet*, and any businessman could be despoiled without hope of compensation. 'Here laws or binding treaties no longer exist.'[143] The Italian card-house in Asia Minor had been built on even less secure foundations than elsewhere.

Both San Giuliano, until his death, and then his successors, would dream of using the war to reconstruct an Italian presence in Asia Minor. By 1917 San Giuliano's old associate in Eritrea, Leopoldo Franchetti, had become a belated convert to the idea that it was in Asia Minor that the final solution to all Italy's demographic colonial problems could be found.[144] An Italian sphere, and later a mandate, were included on the varying lists of Italian war aims. Yet, except among enthusiasts, with the war, Asia Minor fell back into the perspective of general Italian interests. Especially for San Giuliano, the paramount need remained to regain the Trentino and Trieste. Concern for Asia Minor survived because Italy always found the gravest difficulty in abandoning any claim once launched, and because Italy continued her 'temporary occupation' of the Dodecanese.[145] It was only the triumphs of Kemal Atatürk in 1920–1 which ended almost all Italian ambitions in Asia Minor, although Volpi, told by Ciano in 1938 of Italy's intentions to seize Albania, still remembered enough about the fruitfulness of the Eraclea coal mine to ask why should not Italy invade Turkey as well?[146]

What then can be made of Italy's pre-1914 version of a *Weltpolitik*? Though limited mainly to the classical *mare nostrum*, Italy did make considerable effort to extend her interests in the Balkans and Eastern Mediterranean during the last years before 1914. San Giuliano, who, more than anyone, directed this effort, was convinced of the necessity for Italian policy to be assisted by the 'secular arm'[147] of business. Spurred on by the resulting government encouragement, some Italian businessmen, Volpi, Nogara, Foscari and Joel, agents or directors of great banks both liberal and clerical, sometimes with heavy industry as well behind them, did try to beat out an Italian road to the East. Yet, matters are far out of perspective if this process is seriously paralleled to Germany. To begin with, planned business ventures in Turkey were usually far from realised ones; as Garroni once remarked innocently to the Turkish Minister of Public Works: 'making a survey does not necessarily mean building a railway'.[148] For Volpi, Nogara and their associates, business activities in Turkey rarely meant completing anything. Profit lay more in the creation of companies, in building paper houses of trade and industry, which could match San Giuliano's diplomatic paper houses of 'zones of work' and 'spheres of influence'. There is little evidence that in Asia Minor Italian industry was, in any serious way, the puppet master of Italian diplomacy. Most industrialists, indeed, were growing more timid in 1914 as Italy's general diplomatic and economic prospects deteriorated. No wonder that a Nationalist like Corradini could complain that it was 'plutocratic pacifism' which was to blame for still desiring the survival of Turkey.[149]

In the nineteen-twenties, the writer of a pro-Fascist survey of 'Moslem Italy' declared: 'Reality teaches that in no field of national life do economic facts exceed in importance political ones...The same...[is true] of colonial matters.'[150] Fascist theory perhaps explained this ostentatious rejection of Marxism, and yet, as far as Italy was concerned, it made much sense. In the last years before the First World War, there was no industrialist-dictated '*svolta imperialistica*' or Italian 'grab for world power', unless these terms are defined very narrowly. Italian imperialism, or San Giuliano's expansionism, was not made in newly industrialised Milan, Turin or Genoa so much as it was made in Rome by the '*rivoluzione mancata*' which was the Risorgimento. Italy wholeheartedly joined in and sometimes even led the 'glamorous'[151] contest of the Great Powers to divide Turkey because Italy had defined herself and been defined as a Great Power.

In retrospect, what is most distinctive about Italian policy in the Eastern Mediterranean from 1912 to 1914 is not its domestic impulsion, nor even San Giuliano's sometimes frantic and always unprincipled efforts to establish an Italian presence, but rather the latitude allowed to Italy by her more powerful 'allies and friends'. No doubt San Giuliano was convinced that the 'contest' of the nations, which he had first learned about at Catania University so many years before, was likely to be unleashed, and unleashed soon, in the Levant. In result, he probably did less than any other European statesman to seek genuine ways to allow the Ottoman 'Sick Man of Europe' time to recuperate. It is curious and even startling to hear an Italian Foreign Minister talking gaily about the advantages of a Graeco-Turkish war. Yet, what is still more striking, is the topsy-turvy state of the Concert when Italy could oppose the ambition of both Britain and Germany at the same time. The insistent question arises why, at least on paper, was Italy allowed to get away with so much? Why was San Giuliano's adventurism not called short by the magisterial rebuke of one of Italy's diplomatic betters? Why was not San Giuliano's constant and outrageous duplicity not exposed by the Germans who perceived it, or by the British, among whom Crowe certainly did?

The answer to these questions, and the explanation of the extent of Italian intrusion into Asia Minor in 1913–14 lies in the threat to the major Powers of the continuing Balkan Wars, and the opportunity which the resultant need for restraint by the major Power permitted to Italy, if she was willing to be unscrupulous enough. Turkey, as well, had very special reasons for not objecting while Italy cast a lascivious eye over her body in 1913.

But, in 1914, matters had started to change. Italy did manage to impose her own version of the Smyrna–Aidin concession onto the British company, but the legal status of Italian penetration into Turkey remained highly doubtful. Certainly there was little sign of Italy being herself able, or being allowed by the Turks, to begin actual railway building. From Germany, Italy faced always greater resistance to her attempt to define a lasting sphere in Asia Minor; and Austrian interest, if never whole-hearted, was growing more and more suspicious of Italy. It was always true that the Powers, except France, were inclined to overestimate Italy, and none was willing openly to condemn Italian intrusion into Asia Minor, even in 1914. But, by then, there was every sign that the climate for Italian adventurism was becoming less favourable than before.

San Giuliano may have realised this. Although, in the July Crisis, he continued with his pushing and prodding in Asia Minor, he never entirely lost his sense of perspective. However involved he had been in the complexities of the diplomatic game, in all the Eastern Mediterranean, in Asia Minor, in the Dodecanese, in Albania or

Montenegro, however hard he had played it, however wanton and aggressive had been some of his words, his mind remained cool enough to realise that, if there was a major crisis, what Liberal Italy perforce must consider first was not a *Weltpolitik*, nor a rebuilding of a Roman Empire, but rather the completion of the Risorgimento in Trento and Trieste. Well before Mussolini, Italian diplomatists knew of the value and attraction of theoretical pretensions, or what would soon be called propaganda, no matter how unmatched by facts. Unlike their Fascist successors, the diplomats of Liberal Italy neither forgot, nor ultimately were given the opportunity to forget, the difference between rhetoric and reality. In fact, of course, a real 'contest of the nations' was not brewing in Asia Minor but in Europe. In face of that contest, San Giuliano soon recalled that Italian ambition must needs tailor itself to Italian strength, and to the manipulative skills of Italian diplomats.

San Giuliano's epilogue. The realities of European war 28 June to 16 October 1914

It may seem curious to call the July crisis and the first months of World War I an epilogue. Yet, for the foreign policy of Antonino Di San Giuliano, and for the traditions of diplomacy in Liberal Italy, a real European crisis and a real European war were disasters, talked about before, but, in reality, unlooked for. So much of Italian policy in the last years had been a conjuring trick, the sort of sleight of hand which was encouraged by Italy's role as the least of the Great Powers; but, from August 1914, conjuring tricks were unlikely any longer to be good enough. All the other Great Powers had gone to war. The simple corollary was that Italy, as a Great Power, must also, sooner or later, enter the war. For this task perhaps she would have to rely on the King and his generals, given the ultimate realities enunciated by Victor Emmanuel III some years before:

I am more than ever convinced of the utter worthlessness of treaties or any agreements written on paper. They are worth the value of the paper. The only real strength lies in bayonets and cannon.[1]

Yet, a reliance on bayonets and cannon was not a comfortable prospect in Liberal Italy, for bayonets and cannon had seldom brought military triumph, and an Army, wasted by the conflict in Libya and the continued need for 'pacification' there, was hard to regard as likely to be an immaculate agent of an ever victorious foreign policy.

It was also regrettably true that the Army was needed at home. In the very summer of 1914 the Liberal regime was endangered by social crisis in 'Red Week', the days which followed widespread strikes and demonstrations on 7 June. Salandra stolidly ordered the intervention of the Army, and 10,000 troops were used in the Emilia alone 'to restore order'.[2] Both Italy's foreign and domestic record suggested that, if the international crisis was, at last, to be the prophesied Darwinian 'contest of the nations', then Italy should, with trepidation and common sense, fall back on the arts of diplomacy to identify the most rewarding and rewarded moment of intervention in the war. To minds as lucid as those of Giolitti or San Giuliano, war made it starkly evident that Italy must seek to book the cheapest possible passage to greatness; for the least of the Great Powers, there was no other attractive and sensible variety of war, although Salandra would soon fatuously depict a war effort of *sacro egoismo*, a war when '*L'Italia farà da sè*'.

On 28 June 1914 it was not yet apparent that these questions of war and peace were hanging over Italy, and San Giuliano performed the obsequies of the assassination at Sarajevo with due decorum. Putting aside his joyful sarcasm about the Villa d'Este in his telephone conversation with Salandra, San Giuliano formally told the Senate that Italy deplored the Sarajevo crime: 'The Italian people, whose heart always beats for any human misadventure, and is never insensible before any human pain'[3] sent appropriate good wishes to the Austrian people. The Senate rose as a mark of respect, and, after a brief reconvention in July, both Chambers were adjourned, and did not assemble again until December. As was true of the decision to go to Libya, the choices of the *intervento* were to be made by Italian parliamentarians but not by the Italian parliament. Moreover, San Giuliano's position was not to be cribbed or confined by advice from his Prime Minister, as it had been in 1911. Salandra's mind lacked the cutting edge of Giolitti's, and, in any case, frightened by 'Red Week', and soon ambitious to use the opportunity proffered to destroy the 'parliamentary dictatorship' of his predecessor, Salandra concentrated on domestic affairs,[4] and let San Giuliano expertly run foreign policy. More than ever before in his career, San Giuliano 'made policy' in the July crisis, and was hindered only by illness. Through the hot summer days, San Giuliano rarely bothered to come to Rome, but nursed his weakening heart and his diplomatic schemes at Fiuggi.[5] Occasionally the King was consulted, but Victor Emmanuel also did not like Roman summers, and was often away in Piedmont. Giolitti, with notable discretion, and notable reliance on San Giuliano, spent his summer out of Italy altogether, in London and Paris. What decisions Italy made in July 1914 were made by Antonino Paternò Castello Di San Giuliano.

San Giuliano's first diplomatic reaction to the assassination of

Franz Ferdinand took place, naturally enough, within the context of current diplomacy. The assassination of an Archduke was not in itself regarded as likely to produce a sea-change in the diplomatic situation. But that diplomatic situation was bad enough; Aliotti continued to advise that the total collapse was near for William of Wied's regime in Albania,[6] the Greeks still had not left Northern Epirus, Austria seemed always on the point of acting on her own accord to prevent any Serb or Montenegrin advantage in Northern Albania, or to stop a Serb–Montenegrin union. These were problems which had confronted Italy for over a year, most graphically during the Scutari Crisis in April 1913. Then, later, and in June–July 1914, Italian policy was both to offer Austria, and to threaten her, with Italian collaboration or parallel action. On the very day of Franz Ferdinand's death, San Giuliano wrote to Avarna, as he had written before:

It must not be believed that Italy is not ready to act with determination in order to safeguard her own Adriatic interests should Austria–Hungary take the grave decision to proceed to a territorial occupation. Italian public opinion would be the first not to permit the balance of the Adriatic to be disturbed to our disadvantage.[7]

He followed this up the next morning with another complaint to Vienna against the tendency for Austria no longer to take seriously Italy's 'parallel interest' in Southern Albania against the Greeks.[8] There were even weird rumours that Austria was showing untoward interest in Ethiopia[9] (where Martini used the opportunity to appeal to Salandra against Foreign Ministry interference, and request that all 'indigenous' Ethiopian questions pass through the Ministry of Colonies).[10]

Barrère, a little optimistically, reported that Franz Ferdinand's death had soon been greeted with joy in Rome, given the '*caractère de véritable religiosité*' of Italian patriotism at that moment.[11] But, at first, the Triple Alliance seemed to be functioning in a reasonable way. From Bollati, San Giuliano learned that Zimmermann, the German Under-Secretary of State, also did not regret the death of the Archduke who had wanted to improve the lot of the Slavs in the Habsburg Empire, and persecute Hungarians and Italians. 'For the moment,' Bollati noted,

Zimmermann detects as the principal danger that the legitimate indignation breaking out in Austria–Hungary against Serbia could lead to measures too severe and provocative for the neighbouring Kingdom. And he foresees for the German government a continuous and laborious task of restraining the Cabinet in Vienna from compromising decisions.[12]

To an Italian ear this sounded like a better promise than Italy had heard for some time of a restoration of the working of the Triple Alliance in the Balkans. Therefore, on 1 July, San Giuliano's first assessment to his ambassadors of the meaning of the Sarajevo crime was by no means pessimistic. The new heir to the throne, Archduke Charles, married to an Italian Bourbon princess, might well be willing to encourage an improvement in Austro-Italian relations.[13]

There the situation remained for the next few days. A little ominous was Avarna's revelation of deepening Austrian hostility against Serbia, and against Russia as well,[14] but there was still no sign of violent crisis. San Giuliano spent his time in the familiar and agreeable task of suggesting to Salandra that conciliation was the best way to confront Italy's domestic problems,[15] and, on the diplomatic front, declaring, yet again, that Italy wanted the Powers to preserve William of Wied on his throne, so that there should not be a direct Austro-Italian confrontation in Albania.[16] San Giuliano checked the temperature of Austria's Balkan policy on 4 July by mentioning again to Avarna and Bollati his 'preoccupation' with rumours of Austria's possible intentions towards Albania, regarding Mount Lovcen, or towards a possible Serb–Montenegrin union, or perhaps Serbia alone as a result of the Sarajevo crime. He had been irritated by Mérey's unseemly and 'jocular' criticism of Italian policy in Albania: 'If in Vienna there is suspicion of Italy, in Italy there is suspicion of Austria.' On a customary tack, San Giuliano added that he was 'now almost alone in believing in the good faith of the Austro-Hungarian government'. His conclusion was also not new:

It seems to me with regard to this danger that it is necessary to recall the attention of Germany which perhaps has still not completely taken into account the gravity of the danger which is threatening the Triple Alliance.[17]

Germany greeted this accustomed Italian technique with accustomed promises, framed in general terms, by Zimmermann on 5 July, that Germany would hold back Austria from any Balkan coups.[18] In agreement with the Romanians, whose position as an associate member of the Triple Alliance with *terra irredenta* in the Habsburg Empire bore many parallels to Italy, San Giuliano, on 6 July, strongly advised restraint on Serbia, and continued to suggest that the same be done in Vienna, by working through Berlin.[19] At the same time, he tried to keep up the Italian position in Asia Minor, and Ethiopia, and told Rodd, on 7 July, that new Graeco-Turkish hostility could produce further unfortunate delays in the Italian evacuation of the Dodecanese.[20]

These policies may have been well-tried and indeed clever, but other events were beginning to make them irrelevant. On 5 July, unbeknown to the Italians, the Kaiser gave Austria the 'blank cheque' for decisive action against Serbia, and his advice was backed by Bethmann Hollweg that same afternoon. Despite Zimmermann's words to Rome, Germany was certainly not going to restrain Austria, at least in direct confrontation with Serbia. On 7 July the Austro-Hungarian joint council of ministers met to consider Germany's proffered support. Berchtold advised of a potential further problem:

We have now to reckon once again with Italy and Rumania; and here, in accord with the Berlin cabinet, it seemed to him better to act, and to wait for requests for compensation later.[21]

Berchtold's decision, and indeed his very language, treating Italy and Romania as similar powers, destroyed at a stroke all San Giuliano's efforts of the past three years to assert, by diplomatic action within the Triple Alliance, Italian rights as a Great Power. Once again, in a decisive moment for Austria, Italy was to be ignored, as she had been in the Bosnia–Herzegovina crisis, despite the insistence then, and later, that Italian membership of the Triple Alliance could not survive another Austrian *coup de main*. This was not a very surprising policy from Austria. What is a little surprising in July 1914 is the abrupt German abandonment of the pretence of equal treatment for Italy and Austria which she had so often adopted in the past eighteen months. Whether caused by the emotional impact of the Sarajevo crime, or a testimony to Germany's disgust at Italian hostility to Greece, or newly demonstrating her ancient contempt for the likely military qualities of the 'Southern partner', or just a sudden decisive weariness with Italian importunities and diplomatic 'dishonesties', Germany's abandonment of Italy throughout the July Crisis is most striking, and most strikingly different from anything that had gone before. In 1908 Austria had annexed Bosnia–Herzegovina in defiance of Germany (and Italy);[22] in 1914 Austria was encouraged, and even propelled to act against Serbia by direct German behest. The norms of the Triple Alliance were thus destroyed.

San Giuliano, of course, knew nothing of these decisions, and indeed was talking privately of the great value of Germany in holding Italy and Austria apart:

partly agreeing and partly disagreeing now with us, now with Austria in order to preserve a balance, the breaking of which would perhaps endanger European peace.[23]

However, the Sarajevo crisis, added to what was still seen in Rome as the graver continuing problem in Albania, stimulated San Giuliano to ponder generally Italian membership of the Triple Alliance. Jagow had been giving perplexing advice to Bollati, confirming Zimmermann's earlier statement that Germany 'always gave and will continue to give counsels of moderation to Austria–Hungary with respect to her action toward Serbia' but then had added, personally speaking, that he believed that Austria could not be too 'submissive...confronted by a Serbia sustained and driven on by the provocative support of Russia', and had stated, in a foreboding manner, 'a really energetic and coherent action by Austria–Hungary would not lead to a conflict'.[24] Flotow, the German ambassador, who, also nursing an illness not improved by the Roman summer, was sharing the same hotel with San Giuliano at Fiuggi, was equally discomforting.[25] On 9 July, he spoke 'very confidentially' to San Giuliano about the prospect of an Austrian seizure of Mount Lovcen. San Giuliano naturally replied that Italy was 'resolutely contrary' to such an act; but 'Flotow then went on in such a way', San Giuliano recorded,

as to produce in me the impression that the cession to Italy of a part of the Italian provinces ruled by Austria would be a very difficult matter, but not at all impossible in exchange for a proportionate and effective support, perhaps even military, of Italy to Austria.

That sounded the most fascinating possibility and San Giuliano at once expressed interest, and had Flotow helpfully agree that any future negotiations should be conducted through Berlin, rather than bilaterally between Rome and Vienna. Sensing dangers as well as opportunities, and never a simple-minded devotee of the proprieties of alliance, San Giuliano, when Flotow had left, secretly leaked the news to his ambassadors in Cetinje, Belgrade and St Petersburg, warning them of possible surprise Austrian military action against Mount Lovcen, and declaring that Serbia and Montenegro should be clear that their union could only proceed 'in a slow and imperceptible fashion' so that Austria could not have a pretext for action.[26]

San Giuliano's version of the meeting may be doubted. In his account, Flotow asserted that it was San Giuliano who raised the prospect of cession in the Trentino, and even that San Giuliano had threatened to go to war against Austria, after calling Serbia and Russia on to Italy's side,[27] if Austria moved towards Mount Lovcen. So unabashed a threat was not very much in character, but certainly Flotow's report cannot have encouraged any German reconsideration of their failure to consult Italy about events so far in the Sarajevo crisis.

Although concentrating more on the prospect of Serb–Montenegrin union, or an Austrian move against Mount Lovcen than on any avenging of Franz Ferdinand, San Giuliano half sensed that a real crisis was in the wind, in all probability because of information culled from Flotow, while he and San Giuliano took the Fiuggi waters together. Avarna and Bollati too were warning fearfully of the gravity of Austro-Italian dissidence, and of the new strength of German support for Austria's quarrel with Serbia.[28] Then, on 14 July, San Giuliano was given further depressing information from Flotow that William of Wied intended to abandon Albania.[29] San Giuliano had never ceased privately to believe that eventually William must go, but at this moment the threat to Italian interests from Greece had never been greater and Italy was in an awkward position to push ahead with her own interests in Albania. Whether impressed by this, and by the recurrent rumours of a general Balkan crisis, or impelled by the relative quiet and comfort of Fiuggi, San Giuliano, on 14 July, settled down to write to Bollati a long analysis of the present state of the Triple Alliance. It was, he noted, a perplexing task, since so many Italian aims were incomplete or under challenge. Italo-Austrian relations had deteriorated sadly since 1913, when, by his own effort and that of Giolitti, they had reached a zenith of friendliness. Austrian policy, exemplified in the Hohenlohe decrees, and in Albania, and confirmed at the Abbazia meeting, had destroyed this idyll, and now German intervention was needed to restore it, or at least to preserve a modicum of tolerance. What could be done in Albania? It could be divided directly between Italy and Austria, but this would be expensive and difficult for Italy, and would altogether ruin her relationship with the small states of the Balkans. Perhaps Austria and Greece could divide Albania, or Austria could take territory in the North, and Valona become the capital of a smaller autonomous state in the South? But if so, Italy must be compensated by territorial concession of 'Italian lands' within the Habsburg Empire. Moreover, there were further threats in the Balkans: Serb–Montenegrin union, an Austrian move against Mount Lovcen, or Austro-Serb conflict as a result of Franz Ferdinand's assassination. 'All our policy', San Giuliano emphasised, 'must aim to hinder again on this occasion Austrian territorial aggrandisement without corresponding adequate territorial compensation in our favour.' Italy would find it unacceptable if, under the impulse of what should have been the long dead principles of the Divine Right of Kings, Austria presented Serbia with 'demands incompatible with the Liberal principles of our civil legislation'.

With these problems in mind, San Giuliano surmised that 'it seems...possible, and perhaps even probable that in the not too far off future, we shall have to leave the Triple Alliance'. But, for now, Italy could not take so grave a step. The Central Powers had the stronger armies, and wars were decided on land. France would not treat Italy in a dignified manner, if she learned that Italy was divorced from her allies. Therefore, before abandoning the Triple Alliance, Italy must reinforce herself militarily and economically, and advantageously settle her differences with France and Britain in the Dodecanese, Libya and Ethiopia. Time was on Italy's side; Russia was growing stronger; Romania would become an ever more doubtful ally of the Central Powers; Spain was gravitating towards the Entente. Britain would become more radical and pacifist, but would always resist a dominating Power, that is Germany, given her naval concentration. 'The prognosis' San Giuliano decided,

is therefore reserved for the future, and I do not at all exclude the probability of our leaving the Triple Alliance in some years, in order to join the other bloc or to stay neutral, but today I would consider it a serious and dangerous mistake to weaken without absolute necessity the reciprocal bonds between us and our allies, and I believe it therefore necessary and urgent that Germany works to make compatible both the defence of our interests and our loyalty to the Triple Alliance.[30]

For all its characteristic imprint of San Giuliano's subtleties, his preference for complexities to clarity, for dark to light, and despite the half-hints that San Giuliano did know something of the 'blank cheque'[31] and was pondering how it could be adjusted to Italy's benefit, nonetheless the very drafting of the despatch indicated an Italian sensing that this was a crisis moment for the Triple Alliance. Presumably thinking that Austria was only contemplating some *coup de main* in the Balkans with German support, and not tolerating or encouraging general war, San Giuliano was emphasising that Italy must be treated as an equal Great Power, and that far and away the best solution to any new Balkan imbroglio would be for Germany to persuade Austria finally to compensate Italy from Habsburg lands. His comments about leaving the Triple Alliance, if qualified by the phrase 'in some years', also revealed his suspicion that this sort of compensation was unlikely. Deep in San Giuliano's mind lay the policy used at Scutari of putting off, and therefore avoiding, Austrian action by raising complications, but San Giuliano was none too confident a repetition of the diplomatic filibuster would work this time. Naturally, and, from Italy's point of view, appropriately, San Giuliano went on talking about compensation, especially the ancient chance of regaining the *terra irredenta*, but in the next days it gradually became apparent that it was not only a Balkan *coup de main* which was being planned by the Central Powers.

While the diplomatic conflict slowly unfolded, there were new references to the possibility that Germany would sponsor the completion of the Risorgimento. On 16 July, Flotow, who was still sipping Fiuggi water, offered Berlin the advice that Italy should be mollified by compensation from within the Austrian Empire. Two days later, the suggestion was passed on to Vienna, although no greater pressure was put on the 'noble second' to appease Italy.[32]

In Rome, information was not as readily at hand as it was in Fiuggi. Neither Salandra nor De Martino had yet comprehended clearly what sort of Balkan crisis was brewing. De Martino wrote to Fiuggi explaining Salandra's doubts and fears about an expedition against Albania, where there might be serious opposition. To De Martino it seemed therefore that preventative action would be best, and Italy must take Valona as well as the island of Saseno, but this act should be negotiated first with Austria.[33] De Martino evidently still expected no more than an Austrian coup in the Balkans, and was ready to seek Italian compensation in Albania, and ignore the ancient requirement of Trento and Trieste.

But San Giuliano had begun to see that this was not just another Balkan crisis. Again it was his intimacy with Flotow at Fiuggi which, by 16 July, had revealed that Austria would be ready to use force against Serbia if necessary. San Giuliano had this information cabled to his ambassadors in Vienna, Berlin, St Petersburg and Belgrade, adding bluntly that Italy opposed any Austrian territorial aggrandisement and would 'do all possible to prevent it'.[34] On 17 July he further told St Petersburg (and Bucharest) that 'from a most authoritative source' (that is, presumably, Flotow) he had learned that Austria 'supported by Germany' intended to pose unacceptable conditions to Serbia, and then use the pretext to attack her. San Giuliano appealed both to Russia and to Romania to make their opposition wholly plain in Berlin and Vienna.[35] And, the next day, he wrote firmly to Bollati, saying that any Austrian occupation *'dans les régions des Balcans'* whether 'temporary or permanent' would give Italy a perfect right to invoke Article VII of the Triple Alliance.[36]

San Giuliano's policy at this time has been deemed by Albertini one of 'utter, unreserved surrender to the Central Powers',[37] but it was scarcely so. Rather, both with propriety and skill, San Giuliano had asked for diplomatic reward, and indeed the very greatest diplomatic reward which Italy could ever hope for, but also had tried to use Italy's international contacts to avert the still only shadowy dangers of a real war.

Certainly, Austria understood the difference between likely Italian policy in peace and in war. On 15 July, still with some respect for diplomatic niceties, Berchtold cabled Mérey ordering him to release to San Giuliano Austria's ultimatum against Serbia one day before it was delivered. But, on 20 July, with the crisis worse, and with Russian intervention probable, Berchtold altered his instructions. Italy should now be told of the ultimatum only the day after it was sent.[38] By this decision, Austria indicated her unreserved determination to crush Serbia and definitely broke her relationship with Italy. On 3 August Salandra, for one, maintained that, had Italy been told beforehand, she would have been obliged to march with Austria, although he added that Italy would have had to agree to the terms of the ultimatum,[39] a very large reservation.

Having recognised the danger of general war, Italian policy in the days which followed sought ways of avoiding a conflict, although this peacemaking was hindered by San Giuliano's debilitating illness, and by his preference for reticence rather than open honest dealing. There have been many bitter criticisms of San Giuliano's failure fully to declare his hand in the week after 20 July, but most are posited on an absurd over-estimation of Italian strength and ability to act openly. There is no evidence that Germany and Austria would have been stopped by a clearer Italian stance; in fact the evidence about the ultimatum is all to the contrary. Moreover, wars do not usually break out without there also being a chance for a diplomatic solution. While this chance remained, any sensible Italian Foreign Minister had to cover Italy from the dangerous prospect of a diplomatic compromise, or, worse still, an Austro-German diplomatic victory. With this result, not just the expansionist policies of 1912–14 would have fallen into ruin, but the very existence of Italy might have been threatened. Italy could not simply declare her diplomatic hostility to the Central Powers, without, what would in fact have been impossible, a permanent diplomatic guarantee from the Triple Entente. If Serbia was diplomatically castrated, then an exposed Italy could be the next on Austria's, and perhaps even on Germany's list. To be an international Galahad is not only difficult, but positively dangerous if the only means possessed are those which Italy had in July 1914.

Within the bounds created by such a scenario, San Giuliano did try to exercise diplomatic restraint. His discovery of Romania in the July crisis and in subsequent weeks is striking and important. Berlin and Vienna were showered with advice that their policies would estrange both Italy and Romania, their only current allies.[40] San Giuliano also made efforts to alert the other Powers to the European danger. On 22 July, for example, he again told Austria confidentially that he knew that Russia would not accept an Austrian move against Serbia. That same day, he also informed the British ambassador, Rodd, that, 'in constant touch' with the Austrian Embassy, he had found that the Austrian terms to Serbia would be unacceptable, and that the Austrian war party aimed at crushing Serbia totally.[41] Barrère had been given the same news in more general terms the day before.[42]

But there were risks for Italy which San Giuliano was still not willing to run. Although he constantly emphasised that it was 'public opinion' and Italy's Liberal constitution which would find intolerable an Austrian *coup de main* in the Balkans, with the despatch of the Austrian note on 23 July, San Giuliano at once requested that Italy's prefects check any popular demonstrations against the ultimatum.[43] He had also already appealed to Britain, as the least involved Great Power, to act jointly with Italy to avert a war. He told Rodd, on 22 July, that it was 'impossible to foresee' whether the *casus foederis* of the Triple Alliance would arise but that, in the meantime, it would be ideal

to examine if, in hypothetical case, England and Italy could imitate the custom of English M.P.s 'to pair', that is that a liberal and a conservative swear reciprocally to the respective parties to absent themselves at the same time.

This would have been an ideal solution for Italy, with the prospect of damage to Austria and to France at the same time, at no cost to Italy. Notably, San Giuliano's telegram was not sent to Tittoni in Paris. But, when Rodd's despatch finally reached London on 27 July, San Giuliano's suggestion evoked the contemptuous but accurate minute: 'A pair of Italy and Great Britain would hardly balance.'[44]

With the despatch of the Austrian ultimatum, and clear advice from Avarna that Austria was making ready to go to war against Serbia,[45] San Giuliano began further preparations. De Martino was instructed to bring the Prime Minister, Salandra, up to date with the crisis, and to point out to him that Article VII forbade even a temporary occupation in the Balkans without mutual agreement beforehand.[46] On the morning of 24 July, telegrams were sent to Vienna, Berlin and St Petersburg asserting that Italy was not formally bound to join the Triple Alliance in any Balkan conflict.[47]

Despite his illness, San Giuliano returned briefly to Rome, where, later on 24 July, he and Salandra met Flotow, and again made the Italian position quite plain. San Giuliano declared bluntly that a European war would be the direct result of 'an act of provocation and aggression by Austria', and then matched these ominous words by the more familiar theme that only compensation from Austria itself could be a possible means for the Italian government to overcome the objections of 'public opinion' to 'a war fought in the interests of Austria'.[48]

San Giuliano had thus not entirely abandoned his dual policy, and certainly not summarily rejected Italian membership of the Triple Alliance. If there was going to be a diplomatic solution to the crisis, it was still possible that Italy would not be too humiliated. Yet, if there was to be a European war, San Giuliano's policy was undoubtedly leading Italy towards neutrality, at the very least. Indicative is a letter drafted by San Giuliano to the King on 24 July which, in its invocation of constitutional proprieties, gave every sign of being a preparation for a public declaration in the days to come. San Giuliano began by noting that neither he nor Salandra had said anything which restricted Italian freedom of action in the Balkans. Both he and Salandra, confronted by an 'Austrian initiative', were 'convinced that it...[would] be very difficult, perhaps impossible, certainly dangerous, to drag Italy into taking part in an eventual war caused by Austria, and made in the interests of Austria'. Italy must inform her allies of this, persuade them to accept her definition of Article VII, and 'assure ourselves of eventual compensation for any Austrian territorial aggrandisement at all'. Compensation must be clearly marked out, in addition, because of an 'eventual, but not probable' Italian entry into the war, the timing of which could be decided by Italy alone. A general assessment of the relation of Balkan events to Italy's interests elsewhere was also urgently required.[49]

Constitutional forms having been observed in the conversations with Salandra, and in the letter to the King, San Giuliano hastened back to Fiuggi on the evening of 25 July.[50] From there, he explained to Salandra the next day that health reasons kept him away from Rome, but also that it was pleasant to be far from journalists and 'public opinion'. San Giuliano still dreamed of circumstances by which benefit might be extracted for Italy: 'Immediate decisions are not at all necessary' he remarked,

rather they would be extremely dangerous; for the moment, everybody, at home and abroad, should be left in uncertainty about our attitudes and our decisions in order to try to get some positive advantage. For the first time since the Kingdom of Italy has existed, a German Minister of Foreign Affairs says that it is the right moment to have the Trentino...As for demonstrations against the war in association with Austria it seems to me that they can be of more use than harm to our negotiations, but we cannot reassure public opinion and say that we shall not make war at any cost, because in that case we shall not get anything anywhere. Therefore, in my opinion, we must work in silence, speak little, not be too hasty, and stay away from Rome as much as possible.[51]

San Giuliano was not thus spelling out his policies to his Prime Minister, or even to himself. While 'decisions' were avoided it was still possible to imagine the presence, or the promise of the presence in war of Italian forces alongside her Triple Alliance partners. Underlining what had always been true for him and for his predecessors' foreign policy, San Giuliano had reminded Salandra that, if there was the opportunity, Italian diplomacy must concentrate on winning the Trentino. Yet San Giuliano's policy was now leading to a situation where this would occur by an intervention on the victorious side after an initial declaration of neutrality. Perhaps because of the native Italian politician's contempt for the military, perhaps out of realistic assessment of Italian armed might, perhaps from the experience of Libya, San Giuliano better than most European statesmen in July 1914 rejected the 'short-war illusion', and began to understand that a war could be long, and offer to Italy many useful and exploitable complications.

By 26 July San Giuliano had also begun to think more coherently about mediation. At first, with hardly unreasonable realism, San Giuliano did not perceive how little Italy could bring the greater Powers to peace if they were decided against it. He had tried to keep in contact with Britain, and, on 25 July, he asked Imperiali to tell Grey that Italy favoured a peace initiative, but was in a very delicate position towards Germany.[52] In fact, Britain was doing little to associate with Italy in an attempt at compromise; Imperiali was even having difficulty arranging appointments with Grey, as good an indication as any of the limitations of Italy's role as a Great Power.[53] In Rome, too, Rodd was hardly useful in stimulating London to an awareness of Italy's needs and interests. He was personally anxious that both Britain and Italy stay out of a war, unless a Great Power was to be utterly overthrown, but his diary also tells of his personal involvement in his tour of the art collections of Montecatini, Pescia, Prato and Florence, and contains the characteristic summer 1914 complaint that it was unreasonable for a crisis to occur just as he was due to go on leave.[54]

On 26 July San Giuliano informed the King, rather generally, that personally he favoured a compromise action in association with Britain,[55] but, the next day, he appealed yet again to Germany, as a matter 'of the...highest urgency', to persuade Vienna to think about compensation for Italy in the Trentino, since Italy certainly did not intend herself to negotiate directly with Vienna. Public pressures, he urged, were so great that, if there was no such step, Italy would not only see the Triple Alliance shattered, but also might be 'driven...to make war against Austria'.[56] These words were also sent to Avarna in Vienna. It was already becoming likely that, when Italy did intervene in the war, it would be alongside her 'friends' and against her 'allies'.

Events had once again forced San Giuliano to leave Fiuggi for Rome, where, on 27 July, both Barrère and Rodd received the impression that the Italian decision now heavily depended on Britain. San Giuliano told Rodd that, in Austria, there had been '*le triomphe de l'imbecilité*'.[57] As a last minute attempt to avoid disaster, in the early morning of 28 July 1914, San Giuliano launched his own peace effort, suggesting the re-assembly of the London Conference of ambassadors.[58] He also manifested again his total support for any British peace move.[59] But it was too late to hope for much by then, and it is significant that Imperiali was again unable to see Grey on 28 July, and had to make do with a meeting with Nicolson in the morning, and Grey's private secretary, Tyrrell, in the evening.[60] Events had outrun the always dubious likelihood that any action by Italy would stop a general war. On 29 July first Germany, and then Russia, declared their intention to begin general mobilisation. The die was cast.

In passing it should be asked what responsibility did Italy bear for the breakdown of the mechanisms of peace? In the long term, San Giuliano's Italy did undoubtedly contribute to the crisis. In Libya, Asia Minor and Albania, Italian policy, although posited on the continuance of peace, had scarcely aided the cause of peace or conciliation. Italian leaders had never wholly subscribed to the theory that 'might was right', but they had been zealots of an Italian version of that theory, that diplomatic finesse could conjure up 'right'. Under San Giuliano's guidance, it was by craft that the least of the Great Powers played the diplomatic game, and it had played it without giving quarter. In this sense, Italian policies contributed to the general instability of the international system in 1914.

In the short term, Italy was too weak, and too dependent on peace, to sponsor the outbreak of war. All San Giuliano's policies in the July Crisis sprang from a sensitive comprehension of this weakness, either in real war, or even if there were a major diplomatic compromise. Only in one very indirect manner can grounds be seen for asking whether Italy contributed more directly to the coming of war. It is still striking how rapidly and dramatically the Triple Alliance collapsed in the July Crisis. The pinion of the Southern element of the Triple Alliance lay in what one day would be called the Rome–Berlin axis, that is, in the relationship between Germany and Italy. During the Balkan troubles of 1913, Italo–German ties had played at least some part in putting off crises, in avoiding a general war. Although the end of the Balkan wars did gradually produce a cooling of Italo–German friendship, nonetheless, as late as May 1914, the Italian Chief of General Staff, Pollio, was happily promising his allies Italian troops, perhaps even for the Eastern Front, and certainly had learned to use Germanic language about the attractions of preventive war against Russia.[61]

In the July Crisis, the German leadership made only the most belated and half-hearted attempt to appeal to this past cooperation. Was it that Germany recognised that Italy and Austria were incompatible allies, and that, having punted on Austria, it was useless to have much more to do with Italy? Perhaps this was so, although there were currents of Italo–Austrian collaboration which could have been better exploited. Was the German military–industrial complex antagonised by Italian importunities in Asia Minor or by her recent financial deals in Romania and Greece? Or was it something more simple and more general?

The German leadership in the July Crisis contained many 'lovers of Italy', who admired the Roman Empire and the Renaissance, but who believed, in their hearts, that in A.D. 1914 there was death in Venice, and there were beggars in Rome. The Kaiser himself, von Moltke, and Bethmann Hollweg held these views. So too, with more experience, did the Secretary of State, Jagow, a man who had served as ambassador in Rome, who had 'much feeling for Italian art' and was 'delicate' and 'sensitive'.[62] German policies to Italy, or non–policies, in the July Crisis were dictated, like so many other aspects of German policy at that time, by a sense of relief from a cutting of the Gordian knot, by a disastrous attitude, certainly never subscribed to by a San Giuliano, that it was time to get down to basics. Forgetful that diplomacy, and, for that matter, peace and humanity, are a patchwork woven with many threads, the German leadership knew now that Italy was a complicated and complicating country, and remembered only Bismarck's dictum: 'as to Italy she does not count'. For foreign powers of probity and 'idealism', it is always thus tempting to grow weary of Italy, suddenly to perceive Italian weakness, and to move straight from an over-estimation of Italian strength, significance and value to a peremptory abandonment of her altogether, except as a state which one day may be taught probity and idealism by foreign tutors. In the July Crisis, Germany was bent on war, or, just possibly, a total diplomatic victory. For neither of these eventualities did Germany make much effort to see how Italy could remain in the Triple Alliance, or preserve some shreds of respectability as the least of the Great Powers.

With Austria, Russia and Germany mobilising, Italy was thus left to work out her own position. By 29 July Italian 'public opinion' was aroused to the July Crisis. For some days, most newspapers of the 'parties of order' – Nationalists, clericals and even some Liberals – had favoured Italian entry into the war alongside the Central Powers. Nationalist spokesmen worried lest irredentist 'sentimentality' prevent Italy from military triumph. As late as 29 July, for example, Sonnino, with his usual narrow devotion to 'honour', was writing that Italy 'must keep scrupulous and loyal faith to the alliances and to [other] undertakings made'.[63] It was the parties of the moderate Left, Republicans, Socialists like Bissolati, and anti-clericals, who already favoured a war on the other side. Although no radical, the Minister of Colonies, Ferdinando Martini, shared these pro-French sympathies. On 27 July he complained to Salandra that Italian foreign policy was too pro-Austrian; and, the next day, probably influenced by Barrère, he suggested that Italy could find a legal basis for a declaration of neutrality by reference to the 1902 Prinetti–Barrère accords.[64] Not surprisingly, San Giuliano rejected such fatuous advice, which would have meant a tame Italian acceptance of a virtual French protectorate. San Giuliano had not been converted to Francophilia, and, on 3 August, was still saying that what would be best would be for both Austria and France to be beaten. The Italian Navy had equally not given up thought of France as a possible enemy, and, on 28 July, Italo-French relations were tender enough for Barrère to make an estimation of the strength of Italian forces, even though he denied that there was any serious indication that they were about to be deployed against France.[65]

Yet, any discussion of Italian 'public opinion' in the July crisis is largely irrelevant, because it was San Giuliano who made Italian foreign policy at that moment. There is no sign that he was even particularly impressed by the complaint of the Minister of War, Grandi, on 26 July, about the lack of expenditure on the Italian Army which rendered it, in the Minister's opinion, hardly strong enough for domestic purposes.[66] San Giuliano decided his policy in diplomatic and not military terms, yet his decisions were sensible, and were made from within Italian tradition. For Italian foreign policy in July 1914, there was no need to ask 'who rules in Rome?' The answer certainly was San Giuliano, if often not in Rome, but in Fiuggi.

Throughout the last days of the July Crisis, the multiple lines of San Giuliano's policies continued, although they were scarcely gauged important by the other Great Powers. San Giuliano pledged Italian sympathy for any potential peace moves, be they San Giuliano's own suggestion of a revived London Conference of Ambassadors, or Grey's plan, or even the brief and abortive intimation that Germany and Austria might favour conciliation. In particular, San Giuliano formally hoped for some agreement between Italy's two great patrons, an agreement which would prevent war, and ideally deny a diplomatic triumph either to Austria or France. As he telegraphed Imperiali on the morning of 28 July:

It must be understood that for whatever peace initiative on which England and Germany are agreed Your Excellency is authorised in advance to associate us at once without awaiting instructions.

Late that night, San Giuliano was also still trying to resuscitate the idea that Germany work on Austria to grant concessions to Italy.[67] With rather more chance of being listened to, he carefully kept in contact with Bucharest, so that both Italy and Romania could agree to deny that Austria's actions constituted a *casus foederis* for the Triple Alliance.[68] Nor did he abandon Italy's particular interests in the Balkans, extracting a promise from the Austrians on 29 July that they did not intend to occupy Mount Lovcen.[69]

But Italy's chance of having a serious impact on the July Crisis had by now disappeared. Italy's choice between war and neutrality had become a domestic one, of relevance basically only to Italy.

What that choice would be was quite evident by 29 July, despite the continuance of diplomatic forms, and the need for certain constitutional proprieties to be observed. Already, on the morning of 29 July, San Giuliano had informed his ambassadors in Berlin and Vienna, for their personal information, that Italy could not take part in an 'unjustified war', for which Austria was 'responsible'. He also told his allies quite plainly that, unless there was some last-minute compromise, British intervention was certain.[70]

Therefore, Liberal Italy began the due processes of its decision-making. King Victor Emmanuel returned to Rome from Piedmont on the evening of 28 July, but left again the next morning, as if to demonstrate that the great crisis moment was not yet. However, after an appeal by Martini to Salandra, the King was called back to Rome on 30 July.[71] Barrère, often such an impertinent patron or opponent of Italian politicians, was now confident or sensible enough to lie low, and not obtrude French influence on the Italian decision.[72] The Cabinet met on 31 July. Although voices had continued to pour into Salandra's ears,[73] complaints against San Giuliano's 'levity' and unnecessary subtlety, now even Martini had to admit that 'San Giuliano...[made] a most systematic and lucid report of the international situation'. The Foreign Minister declared that: 'fortunately the *casus foederis* does not exist; neither the spirit nor the letter of the Triple Alliance force us to join in this case with Germany and Austria'.[74] By the evening, both Barrère and Rodd were aware that Italy was certain to declare her neutrality.[75]

San Giuliano's anxiety not to commit Italy unnecessarily led to a further day's delay, much to the disgust of Martini, but, on 2 August, Italy's declaration of neutrality was drafted, and was formally published on the morning of 3 August. Forced by the great crisis to choose between her friends and her allies, Italy had certainly not chosen her allies.

Critics of San Giuliano remained. Andrea Torre, for one, maintained that Salandra had agreed when he had remarked that San Giuliano's policies had been 'a complete failure'. Sonnino worried how Italy would preserve her greatness, and complained naively that Italy would have been 'more honourable' if she had acted with the Triple Alliance.[76] But, more perspicaciously, the great names of Italian diplomacy associated themselves with the government's decision. The aged Visconti Venosta telegraphed his approval of

395

neutrality. Giolitti, who by staying out of Italy throughout the crisis was available, uncommitted in an emergency, to return with new policies, found no reason to abandon his confidence in San Giuliano, and also telegraphed his approval, adding that Italy must now move close to Britain with whom she must 'stay friends'. He wrote privately to San Giuliano congratulating him on his policy during the crisis and remarking on his ability to see questions from every side.[77] None mentioned any other than legal and diplomatic factors in applauding the decision. While Nationalists and men of honour were expending rhetoric on the concept *'dura lex, sed lex'*, those favouring neutrality might also have noted not only Italy's military weakness, but also that her harvest was not yet complete and was ten percent less than average, and that the social crisis of June had thrown into more than usual disarray Italy's essential imports of raw materials, from coal to wool. Still more alarming from a social point of view was the lot of hundreds of thousands of Italian emigrants, resident in the belligerent countries, and who, terrified by the onset of war and the sudden obviousness that they were aliens, flooded back to Italy in August, their wages left behind in transit, their savings frozen or lost in Europe's tottering banks.[78] But Italian diplomacy was not posited on such social problems.

Both Giolitti, in a letter to Salandra on 5 August,[79] and San Giuliano himself, in addressing Cabinet on 31 July, used the expression 'fortunately' to qualify the reasons for Italy's decision. Is this then evidence that there could have been another decision, if only Germany and Austria had not acted so brutally? And is there any evidence for Salandra's alleged statement that San Giuliano's policies had been a 'complete failure', that his triplicism from 1912 to 1914 had not only been mistaken, but positively dangerous for Italy's ultimate interests?

It is always difficult to answer hypothetical questions about San Giuliano's foreign policies, because usually there were so many currents running at the same time in different possible directions. Suffice it to say that, for the weakest of the Great Powers, 'clarity' and 'idealism' hardly made a desirable or successful foreign policy. It remains ironical that for Italian foreign as well as for domestic policies, critics were men like Martini, Sonnino or Albertini, who, piously regretting the tawdry machinations of a San Giuliano or a Giolitti, themselves enunciated policies from the Right, of a nationalist and domestic hostility to socialism and even to clericalism which were the most wildly unrealistic in the mass age of the twentieth century. Strictly limited to foreign policy, the complaint of Martini for example, which was echoed by Albertini in the *Origins of the War of 1914*,[80] that San Giuliano lacked 'idealism', was matched only by the ridiculous suggestion that Italy acquire idealism by referring her legal position to the Prinetti–Barrère accords. The clarity of Prinetti's policies was hardly self-evident; and certainly any such admission in July 1914 must have carried for Italy the positive danger of Austrian attack. After all, although the Italian government had no definite information, diplomatic caution was right in a world where the Austrian Chief of General Staff could seriously advocate preventative war against Italy. Standing foursquare for . . . something or other, for National Grandeur, or for Liberty, or so that it could be said '*Italia farà da sè*', was not realistic when Italy was a Great Power in name and tradition, and not in substance.

It is also not true that San Giuliano, beneath his caution and complexity, did not comprehend the great lines of Italian policy. On 3 August he told Malagodi, with a wholly accurate estimation of Italy's strategic weakness: 'Our decision depended necessarily on that of England. Besides, it is a case of *force majeure*.'[81] He also showed no sign of letting a great decision cloud his understanding that complications, and potentialities, remained. There were still 'friends' and still 'allies', if new words were perhaps needed to describe them. As San Giuliano said cynically but realistically to Malagodi some weeks later: 'The ideal for us would be that Austria is beaten on the one hand and France on the other.'[82] It was an ideal which should have been shared by any Italian Foreign Minister who aimed at a justification by diplomacy of Italy's role as a Great Power.

Even before neutrality was formally proclaimed, San Giuliano had remembered that Italy had a number of policies at stake. On 31 July, for example, he had turned back to the Dodecanese question, telling Imperiali to ask Grey to favour an Italian concession in Asia Minor. San Giuliano regretted that Britain had not treated Italy well there, perhaps because of the 'accidental' occupation of the Dodecanese. But Italy was still most anxious to keep the closest contacts with Britain[83] in the Eastern Mediterranean. San Giuliano also took the time to remind Salandra that government influence be used to persuade Italian banks to make more money available for

Italian concerns in Albania, and, on 7 August, wrote again to Stringher about the Vismara concession, which was, he said, so important to Italy 'for reasons of international policy'.[84] But, if San Giuliano kept an eye on these minor issues, and some Italian publicists dreamed still more remotely, for example, of winning Italy the Portuguese colonies,[85] the greater question was the war, and the state of the Triple Alliance.

With hindsight, Italy's move from neutrality to eventual intervention on the Entente side seems almost inevitable. Both San Giuliano and Salandra perhaps in their hearts agreed,[86] but both went out of their way in the next weeks not to commit Italy too dangerously. Although San Giuliano was less affected than most European statesmen by the contemporary illusion that the war would be short, or the fear that, if it were not, it would bring social revolution in its train, nonetheless, he was most anxious to state in August 1914 that Italy had declared her neutrality, no more and no less.

For the eager Martini the Triple Alliance was finished, since Germany and Austria had launched 'an iniquitous, abominable... [and] unjust' war,[87] but, for San Giuliano, however he may have shared fears about the arrogance of victorious Austrians,[88] matters were more complicated. A victory by the Central Powers was possible and even probable, since both the *Consulta* and Italy's military chiefs had advised for years that Germany's army was sharply superior to any other in Europe. In these circumstances, a sensible Italian Foreign Minister would be wise not to expose Italy too far. Already, on 2 August, with neutrality not yet officially announced, San Giuliano had been at pains to emphasise to Berlin that Italy was not leaving the Triple Alliance. Victor Emmanuel, too, was encouraged to reply calmly to an impetuous request by the Kaiser for Italian solidarity with her allies.[89] San Giuliano even went out of his way to acknowledge old diplomatic priorities, for example, the Austrian declaration that they did not intend to annex Mount Lovcen,[90] as though, in the practice of Italian diplomacy, the peacetime procedures continued. On 6 and 7 August San Giuliano exerted what pressure he could to encourage Albania and Montenegro to remain neutral, and therefore, potentially, under Italian influence. In the first major naval incident of the war in the Mediterranean, Italy allowed the *Goeben* and the *Breslau* to sail from

Messina harbour en route to Turkey, where in the next months they would play a crucial role in driving Turkey into the war on the side of Central Powers. It was perhaps just as well that Italy did not know Jackie Fisher's advice that the Commander in Chief of the British Mediterranean fleet should have sunk the ships at Messina: '*as if international law mattered a d...n!!*' and that then 'the Italians would have loved him forever!'[91]

Towards the Entente Powers, San Giuliano was also cautious. On 5 August Sazonov, the Russian Foreign Minister, approached Italy with the prospect of the domination of the Adriatic, the annexation of the Trentino, and perhaps more, if she joined the Entente side.[92] Two days later, Carlotti was predicting as well that the Entente would not oppose Italian wishes in the Aegean or in Anatolia.[93]

San Giuliano reacted very cautiously to these attractively wild but dangerously vague offers. Certainly he understood that, for a Power of Italy's real strength, it would be most important in war to have any terms of intervention as concrete as possible. But they would also need to be terms offered by the winning side. Both San Giuliano and Salandra agreed to reply only generally to the Russian suggestions, and to emphasise the importance of Italy's friendship with Britain. To begin with, Rodd was an easier and more reliable man to deal with than were Barrère or Krupenski.[94] Furthermore, London was always regarded by Italy as a more hopeful negotiating place than Paris or St Petersburg. It was an ideal moment to start talking about the 'traditional friendship'.[95] Also significant was the unspoken assumption that the Entente, or rather Britain, could win the naval war, and that France and Russia could lose the land campaign. Both the war, and a peace, carried dangers for Italy; in these perplexing circumstances, an evocation of Italy's ties with Britain could still offer some protection from Austrian ire should the course of the war turn out to be as brief as many predicted.

San Giuliano had assimilated readily the basic rule of diplomacy in wartime: now 'cannon speak', and not diplomacy.[96] But, of course, it was more difficult than that. By 9 August Rodd reported, accurately, that there was a growing feeling that Italy would have to enter the war, or she would be left out of account.[97] This was a most unpleasant prospect for the Italian ruling classes which continued generally to believe that since all the other Great Powers were making war, Italy would not be a Great Power unless she made war too. The problem which remained was when? As San Giuliano's successors found in May 1915, and as Mussolini would find in 1940, detecting the moment, and even the side, from which to fire the shot before last in a war, is by no means easy.

Resisting the contemporary fears that the war could be over before Italy had time to get in even one shot, San Giuliano's predictable first counsel was for caution. It should not be forgotten, he reminded the King, that wars also require soldiers: 'What Italy needs now politically is a prudent reserve, and militarily a rapid preparation which is as little apparent as possible.'[98] San Giuliano's advice was presumably directed mainly at Salandra, and, behind him, at Martini and the interventionists, as the King, who, perhaps fearing revolution, was rumoured to be a prey 'to nerves'[99] and continued to behave with strict constitutional propriety in what would become his familiar pattern of belief that legality eliminated responsibility. In case Salandra did not understand, on 11 August he was gently reminded of San Giuliano's special place in his Cabinet, and of the traditional mortality of non-Giolittian Prime Ministers: 'In general,' San Giuliano noted coolly, 'I think (as does Giolitti) that one should speak as little as possible of foreign affairs in Cabinet.'[100]

In his letter to the King on 10 August, San Giuliano had also emphasised 'for now' the necessity for Italy to repair her relations with Germany and Austria.[101] Resisting even the interesting prospect of Lord Alfred Rothschild telling Imperiali that he favoured Italian intervention,[102] San Giuliano continued to reply blandly to Entente allurements. Grey was particularly helpful, resisting any temptation to put untoward pressure on Italy, and assuring Imperiali that Britain recognised that any decision must be made by Italy on her own part.[103] San Giuliano thus was able to strive to repair his line to Berlin, and even to Vienna. On 10 August he spoke to Flotow, generally, but as though Italy was still interested in an eventual accord with the Central Powers, after Austria had made a suitable offer in the Trentino. San Giuliano also declared that Austro-Italian collaboration in the future of Albania was essential.[104] He received Avarna, who had come back to Rome to resign, and, with the help of the King, instead persuaded the ambassador to return to his post lest Italo-Austrian relations be damaged.[105] By 7 August he had already explained to Salandra that the result of the war could not yet be foreseen, and he repeated the warning on 13 August.[106] In the next weeks, as the armies prepared for what would become the Battle of the Marne, San Giuliano saw no reason to change these cautious opinions.

Yet San Giuliano had begun to prepare Italy, not necessarily for auction to the highest bidder, but rather to the bidder who was going to win. On 11 August he transmitted to Imperiali a list of Italian requirements, which the ambassador communicated to Grey the next day. The threads of Italian ambition might have been predicted: Italy must get the Trentino and Trieste; beyond that, the future status of Valona must be clear; the Dodecanese could be surrendered, although Italy would want some *lien* on them, and, if Turkey entered the war on the other side, Italy would want a share in any division of Turkey's Mediterranean provinces; in any circumstance, Italy must keep her economic concessions in Adalia; Italy would need a war indemnity, and a pledge by the Entente both to defend the eventual peace settlement and to avoid any separate peace.[107]

The omission in these 'terms' of very detailed requests in the Adriatic and in Africa have often been commented on unfavourably by patriotic Italian historians, who have believed that the demands were not high enough. Other commentators have seen them as evidence of San Giuliano's greater commitment to the Eastern Mediterranean than to the Adriatic. Perhaps there is some point in the latter argument, but it is also necessary to emphasise that San Giuliano certainly did not regard his list as definite war entry terms, and what is perhaps most striking about them, and indeed about San Giuliano's whole attitude since he had learned of the Austrian ultimatum to Serbia, is that number one priority for Italy remained to obtain the Trentino and Trieste, 'to complete the Risorgimento'. But San Giuliano had other motives, also, in his approach to London. With considerable perspicacity, he had detected that, for the Entente, Germany and not Austria was the main enemy, a potentially dangerous division for Italy. After all, it was only on 12 August that Britain and France had finally declared war on Austria. San Giuliano's 'terms' were therefore followed up by a suggestion to Imperiali to encourage a Triple Entente naval attack on Austria. Grey should be told secretly, San Giuliano advised, that 'the Austrian fleet in the Adriatic is a very strong reason in favour of us remaining neutral'. Such an attack would have strategic advantages, but, as San Giuliano continued to point out until his death, an Anglo-French fleet in the Adriatic would be the best guarantee for Italy that her immediate interests would be achieved, however the war ended.[108] Austria would then be as much the real enemy of Britain and France as Germany already was.

The Italian Foreign Minister had other problems to confront while he waited for the situation on the battlefield to develop. Tittoni, for example, who was yet again making apparent his willingness to return as Foreign Minister, had to be put in his place.[109] San Giuliano went on acting so secretly, and with such anxiety that his left hand did not know what his right hand was doing, that Imperiali protested that his policy in London was hindered because he was not kept informed about what San Giuliano was causing to be said in other capitals.[110] San Giuliano meanwhile found it worthwhile to remind Salandra again that 'rapid' military preparations were necessary,[111] although, as a Foreign Minister, he continued to make no effort himself to have contact with the Chiefs of Staff or Service Ministers, or to unite military and diplomatic policy.

Salandra felt no particular loyalty to his Foreign Minister, but he had not yet seen any reason for decisive action. His political friends, Sonnino and Fusinato, still favoured the Triple Alliance, as did Bertolini who was particularly dangerous as the possible successor to San Giuliano in a new Giolitti government.[112] In contrast, Martini breathed hot for the Entente, and pressure from 'public opinion' also leaned that way.[113] But Salandra was a little embarrassed by the number of politicians and diplomats offering themselves as replacements for San Giuliano, whose health became critical at the end of August. Neither the Powers on the battlefield, nor Giolitti on the domestic front, had yet declared themselves. Salandra therefore awaited events, and abided by San Giuliano's reiterated emphatic advice: 'Italy cannot *break* with Austria and Germany if she does not have the certainty of victory. *That is not heroic, but it is wise and patriotic.*'[114] By 18 August Grey, again demonstrating his sensitivity to Italy's position and the wisdom of San Giuliano's advice that negotiations be restricted to London, had accepted that Italy would not do anything decisive until the progress of the war was more certain.[115] To assist this clarity of vision, Imperiali was reminded of the tantalising prospect that Britain would be willing to offer Italy financial assistance on favourable terms once she decided to intervene.[116]

San Giuliano enjoyed these days of waiting, as he rebutted or asked for amplification of the offers and suggestions which were made to Rome. Encouragingly, it was becoming clearer that it had been an illusion to believe that the war would be short. The first weeks had favoured Germany rather than France, but, in contrast to the long and widely-held Italian belief that the land war would see an easy Germany victory, in mid–August this was no longer certain in San Giuliano's eyes. The Foreign Minister appealed for patience; to be able to intervene, to pick accurately which way events were flowing, to prepare an ideal future, San Giuliano mused: 'time can be the decisive factor'. It was too soon to break with Germany and Austria 'or accentuate their hostility. Therefore calm, caution, secrecy.'[117]

In the next fortnight Germany's failure to win the war outright, at one blow, became clear, as the French held on the Marne, and, by mid–September, the German armies had been driven back to before Rheims. During these weeks, the changing war situation dominated Italian diplomacy, as half-hints turned into definite suggestions, and definite suggestions into plans for later policy. For a mind like San Giuliano's, remaining very alive while his body collapsed, nothing could have been a more pleasant task. There would be time for Italy to be needed, for the least of the Great Powers to count. In these circumstances he told his Prime Minister with only partial irony: 'to be Italian Minister of Foreign Affairs is wholly delightful; such is the deference [which I receive] from every side'.[118]

But San Giuliano did not want Italy to leap from the frying pan of neutrality into the fire of intervention, just because it looked cooler there for the moment. Even after the Battle of the Marne, he continued to warn that Germany had great reserves and, despite a momentary setback, would not give up easily.[119] And there were so many strands which had to be woven together before intervention should be consummated.

One interesting strand was Romania, Italy's small 'Latin sister' in the Balkans. San Giuliano had long been aware of the potential value of Romania as another irredentist state, attached to the Triple Alliance. That Romania could balance Greece and perhaps the Slav states of the Balkans was another matter of interest and attraction.[120] San Giuliano had thus made a considerable effort to identify Italy's and Romania's stances during the July Crisis, but, in August, he had done nothing further while he waited to see what would happen on the Eastern front. But, by the beginning of September, with the Battle of the Marne, and Russian advances into Galicia, secret negotiations began in Bucharest. San Giuliano promoted the impression that Romania would follow Italy into the war when she chose to intervene, and on 23 September reached an agreement on cooperation with Romania.[121] Despite pledged secrecy in Bucharest, San Giuliano at once instructed Imperiali to leak the news to Grey, noting that it could 'strengthen our position for obtaining larger concessions in imminent important negotiations'.[122]

San Giuliano had thus not given up his customary duplicity, especially when enjoying the unusually privileged position of being a Great Power able to patronise a small Power with similar interests. Italy could only gain from the Italo-Romanian agreement, but San Giuliano's good sense and dishonesty were wasted by his successor. The blinkered 'probity' of Sonnino did not help him understand the advantages of a client–supporter, and in 1915 he made no effort to use the September 1914 agreement.[123] It is also ironical that Romania's Prime Minister, Ion Bratianu, who after San Giuliano's death became Europe's most 'skilled operator' in a diplomatic style which would have been envied by Ostap Bender, in August 1916 painstakingly selected the 'right moment' for Romanian intervention, which proved so disastrous that Falkenhayn's armies occupied Bucharest less than one month later.[124] In admiring the most skilled of San Giuliano's operations it is worth recalling Bratianu, and noting how difficult it was to choose the opportune occasion to enter the First World War, and how advantageously timed for his patriotic reputation was San Giuliano's death in October 1914.

Apart from Romania, the other Balkan area in which San Giuliano believed preparation to be necessary was Albania. Sonnino, for example, having recovered from his loyalty to the Triple Alliance during the Battle of the Marne, by September 1914 was pressing for an Italian expedition to Valona which would protect and assert Italian interests in Albania against Austria, Greece and any other possible rivals.[125] Preparation for military action in Albania had been part of San Giuliano's policy in Albania for a long time and had again been mentioned by De Martino during the July Crisis. But San Giuliano had always regarded the threat of action as more advantageous than the action itself. In August–September 1914 he continued this well-worn policy,[126] rejecting a military operation because of its openness, and the difficulty of explaining it in Vienna. By the beginning of October, even San Giuliano seems to have accepted the need for military action, especially to rebuke the Greeks who continued to expand their occupation of the Epirus.[127] He received approval from London for such an action, promising to consult neither Germany nor Austria – a safe undertaking because he had already approached the Central Powers and received their consent.[128] It must remain doubtful whether San Giuliano would have in fact acted, but, a fortnight after his death, on 30 October 1914, Italian sailors occupied the island of Saseno off Valona.[129] The city itself was seized on 25 December and remained under Italian occupation throughout the war.[130]

Another perplexing area for San Giuliano was Asia Minor, where, after the arrival of the *Goeben* and *Breslau* at Constantinople, Turkish intervention on the side of the Central Powers had become only a matter of time.[131] In his despatches, Garroni left it in no doubt that the Germans were complete masters in Constantinople, and reminded San Giuliano and Salandra that, if Italy was to enter the war against Germany and Austria, then it would be very likely that she would fight against Turkey too.[132] Although San Giuliano did not hesitate to open consideration of that interesting prospect in his negotiations with the Triple Entente,[133] the die for Turkey was not formally cast until after San Giuliano's death. From August to October 1914 San Giuliano's policy in Constantinople advocated quiescence, until Italy could see more definitely what was going to happen. But Italy's interests in Asia Minor had certainly not been forgotten.

In Ethiopia there were continued rumours of troubles approaching for Italian interests as Emperor Lij Yasu moved to consolidate his throne by a military adventure, which would probably be directed against Italy's colonies. Certainly, there was little doubt that there would be the gravest problems if Italy joined the Triple Alliance and Lij Yasu could rely on the sympathy of Britain and France. Ethiopia was hardly a decisive interest in any Italian policy; San Giuliano's main task with regard to Ethiopia remained to assert the authority of the *Consulta* over the ambitions of Martini and the Ministry of Colonies. But the violent intentions of Lij Yasu, and continuing rumours of activity by Austrian agents hostile to Italy, added a further dimension to possible negotiation of Italian intervention.[134]

Less apparent among San Giuliano's preparations were military ones. Rather than emphasising these, he confined himself to general assertions such as, for example, those made to Rodd, that Italy was 'making good' her military deficiencies 'every day'.[135] At the same time, he did not forget his appeals for 'decisive' Anglo-French naval action in the Adriatic against Austria.[136] San Giuliano has been criticised for his continued 'unreal' diplomatising, pursued without consideration of the state of Italy's armies. The criticism is just, although San Giuliano's behaviour was hardly surprising given the functioning of civil–military relations in Liberal Italy. In any case, it was rather more Salandra's task to see that military preparations were being made. After August 1914 there was some effort to prepare Italy's army and navy for an intervention,[137] but little could be done about continuing military pre-occupation in Libya, Eritrea and, for that matter, at home, 'preserving order'. Salandra showed an alarming willingness to listen to friends who told him that the real problem had been the failure of Giolittian administration in past years.[138] That such stories did nothing to make better Italy's likely achievement in real war did not matter, when what was becoming really important to Salandra, Sonnino, Albertini and their colleagues was the chance to dismantle Giolitti's political system, and bring Italy a more austere domestic order, which would avoid intellectually and socially dangerous compromises with Catholics and Socialists.

San Giuliano stood apart from all this in his illness, in his past and surviving relationship with Giolitti, and in the personal attacks which continued to be made against him by Sonnino, Andrea Torre and Martini.[139] While Salandra remained reluctant to commit himself to sacking San Giuliano, an action which carried the possible international danger of seeming decisive to Germany and Austria, and the more immediate domestic danger of arousing Giolitti, San Giuliano was able to remain the despot of Italian foreign policy. But there was every reason why his rule should be restricted to diplomacy. It was not a little appropriate that in the very last days of San Giuliano's life, there should be a crisis at the Ministry of War, where Grandi was driven from office after a public campaign against him by the friends of Salandra, and by more private attacks by the associates of the Chief of General Staff, Cadorna. The appointment of Zupelli on 11 October was, to some extent, another blow against the Giolittian system, a public rebuke for the 'inefficiency' and 'unpreparedness' of the Giolittian army. But, as Zupelli's main qualification was that he was acceptable to Cadorna, it was also a first step towards a reassertion of the *Statuto* and of the supremacy in Liberal Italy of soldiers over civilians in war-time.[140] The fall of Grandi ought not to have been comforting for San Giuliano, but the Foreign Minister did not live to find out his own fate if ever the Giolittian structure was successfully undermined.

At the end of August, Italy's ambassador in Berlin, Riccardo Bollati, briefly visited Rome. On his return to Berlin, he wrote to his triplicist friend and colleague, Avarna, in Vienna, that he had received a 'disastrous' impression of the state of Italian opinion. From then on, he continued to predict that Italy would intervene on the Entente side, and to bemoan the way in which he and Avarna were kept in ignorance by San Giuliano of Italy's real policies.[141]

After the initial efforts in the July Crisis and in early August 1914 to persuade Austria to offer concessions to Italy in the Trentino, Germany abandoned a formally active policy towards Italy until after San Giuliano's death.[142] What policy there was, was unofficial. The Central Powers were now weakly represented in Rome. Flotow was regarded in Berlin as a lightweight and a neurotic; the strong-willed Austrian ambassador, Mérey, had had a nervous collapse as a result of the war, becoming, in a colleague's words an 'hysterical old maid', and on 14 August had been replaced by the smoother Macchio who, however, proved a weak ambassador, objecting to German pressure that Austria yield to Italy, but seeing few ways around the Austro-Italian antipathy.[143] Imperial Germany characteristically confused its own policy by encouraging unofficial agents to visit Italy. Bülow was notably pressing in his attentions, and, more quietly, financial agents of Ballin and Stinnes also worked on Italian 'opinion'.[144]

San Giuliano was naturally delighted that Italy could arouse these efforts at seduction. Whatever Bollati's feeling of hopelessness, San Giuliano continued to try to keep alive the attentions of the Central Powers. There was always the chance to score points from Austria, for example, when Italy declared that she had agreed formally to protect Russian subjects in Turkey, because of Russia's friendly attitude during the Libyan War.[145] But San Giuliano was not anxious to burn his boats with the Central Powers, and especially did not want to renounce potential German pressure against Austria in Italy's favour, pressure which still might render it conceivable that Italy could be given Trieste and the Trentino.

There might yet be plenty of time and opportunity. On 29 August San Giuliano confirmed Italian neutrality, declaring that the war was likely to last some time.[146] Over the next six weeks he continued to remind Berlin of Austria's stubborn hostility to Italy, and refusal to defer to her wishes in Albania, the Trentino and even Ethiopia. But he also occasionally talked in words which might win favour in Berlin. The last good example of this was on 6 October when San Giuliano, from his bed set up in the *Consulta*, received Flotow. With the open cynicism which he often directed at the German Ambassador, San Giuliano remarked that he wanted a war which Germany won and Austria lost. He mentioned again the Slav danger, which, he said, Italy must oppose in the Adriatic, even if Austria was unwilling or unable to do so. Personally speaking, he continued to favour neutrality, as he thought Italy needed 'ten years' before her economic development would allow her to join the great contest of the nations. But, with familiar innocence, he added that pressures for intervention were strong, and Germany must come up with an offer soon.[147]

There is no particular reason to give great credence to what San Giuliano said. In particular, his rhetoric about the Slav peril seemed always designed for listeners who believed in it rather than having any strong relation to his policy to Russia, that '*grande impotenza*' of his old joke.[148] Yet, the words did have a significance. Bollati was both right and wrong in detecting a continued Italian drift towards intervention on the Entente side. San Giuliano himself favoured the drift, but, on his death-bed, he had still not decided that the drift was strong enough to move the Italian ship of state. There would need to be further, more detailed, and more drawn-out discussion of the prize that Italy would obtain.

If Italy, although not denouncing the Triple Alliance, adopted a low profile in negotiations with the Central Powers from August to October 1914, talks with the Triple Entente, or rather with Britain, were much more serious. Excitement among the Italian ruling classes about the continuing war was growing. Although fears remained that such a terrible conflict could release social pressures which would in turn topple Italy's dynasty[149] and the whole Liberal political and social system, among the anti-Giolittian conservatives in Salandra's government exaltation increased with the thought that this war might be the chance to destroy Giolitti. Already, in the first days of the conflict, Salandra had explained to his friend, Sonnino:

I only had the modest intentions of putting the State back on its feet [after it had been] weakened by ten years of ruinous policies; but now I must enter into history.[150]

For Salandra, whose previous modest claims to greatness were a predictable university chair, and the title of being the first mainland Southerner to be Italian Prime Minister, these were great hopes indeed. But Salandra remained oppressed by his fear of social revolution and by his conviction that any decisive move on his part would be countered by a more decisive one from Giolitti.

Salandra's friends and allies were more anxious for action. Sonnino, who had coupled his initial view that 'honour' should drive Italy into the war on the Triple Alliance side with the remark that if she did not join in, it would be 'the end of a great policy for Italy',[151] was impressed by the Battle of the Marne. By late September, admitting that winter must necessarily delay armed action, Sonnino nonetheless began, with his usual tidiness of mind, to set dates for Italian 'readiness'. February 1915 seemed to him a time when the snows would be melting.[152] Martini, *Corriere della Sera*, and the strange *de facto* alliance of conservatives, republicans and even revolutionaries, who favoured Italian war entry as a way of defeating Giolitti, all saw the Battle of the Marne as confirmation of their belief that Italy must join the war as soon as possible.[153] Even Ettore Ferrari, the Grand Master of Italian Free Masonry, on 6 September, communicated to Salandra via Martini Masonry's view that 'Right' lay on the Triple Entente side, and that Italy should soon 'choose the moment in which...[her] cooperation should become a fact'. Ferrari declared that Masonry would do all it could to prepare Italian consciousness.[154]

The course of the war, and the continuance of Salandra in office, was having a gradual effect on the loyalty to Giolitti of some of his more ambitious followers. If this was indeed 'a moment in History', then many an individual, his career in the balance, began to have second thoughts on the advisability of supporting neutralism and missing out on greatness. It was Mussolini, one of Giolitti's political enemies, who provides the most famous example of this position.

Abandoning orthodox socialism he joined the war party in October 1914 largely because of its intellectual prestige. War could be a great moment for revolution, but also perhaps a great moment for '*professore* Mussolini'.[155] But similar influences were also felt by more respectable politicians.[156] The King, still behaving with safely austere constitutional propriety,[157] began to consider what it would be like to be a soldier monarch. Although his puny stature made more sensible a concentration on his accustomed frugal dinners at the *Quirinale*, Victor Emmanuel talked to Salandra about the Savoyard tradition of a King leading his own armies. Perhaps a time was coming when he could rebut the cartoonists' image of him as a helmet with boots sticking out. The King promised that he would accept the decision of the government 'whatever it will be', but, after the Battle of the Marne, the Savoy dynasty saw more advantages in intervention than in neutrality.[158]

Before these burgeoning hopes of his enemies, Giolitti remained curiously passive. By late August, he was aware of the Government's drift towards intervention, but merely noted that the right moment for Italy would rather be when she was stimulated by some 'new facts' relevant to 'the defence of our vital interests'.[159] One of the reasons for Giolitti's restraint must have been his reliance on San Giuliano, if perhaps cynically leavened by an expectation that San Giuliano did not have long to live, or that, if he did live, Salandra would sooner or later make a move against his Foreign Minister which Giolitti could then use to provoke a government crisis.

This is conjecture; but certainly in his last weeks of life and in his 'war preparations' San Giuliano remained loyal to his Giolittian traditions and made no effort to involve Salandra or his Cabinet colleagues, let alone 'public opinion', in his policies. Despite his own deep involvement in Free Masonry,[160] San Giuliano was not even impressed by his Grand Master's declaration for the Entente. For the Foreign Minister, more than ever, foreign policy was a mental exercise to be performed in his own mind.

San Giuliano's original 'list of terms' to the Entente on 11 August had naturally not been followed up in any serious way, since he had been awaiting the course of the war. He had allowed his ambassadors to ruminate, especially to the sympathetic Grey[161] or to the hasty Sazonov, but, throughout August, San Giuliano made no further effort to seek out what Italy would obtain from the Entente. He

continued to derive malicious pleasure from diverting the importunities of the French and Russian representatives in Rome, and grew
monotonous in his blatantly cynical advice that the best way to
impress Italy was for an Anglo-French fleet to sink Austrian ships
in the Adriatic. But, words aside, San Giuliano made plain that he
did not regard the military situation as yet decisive and that, if
anything, the prolongation of the war was increasing the need for
Italy to maintain her neutrality.[162] Salandra, he suggested, should
keep a tighter rein on 'the press', and, San Giuliano was implying,
on his impertinent friends as well.[163] Rodd, on 27 August, wrote
home regretfully to London that, despite 'public opinion', it seemed
likely that Italy would remain neutral for some time.[164]

Nor did the Battle of the Marne impel San Giuliano much nearer
a decision. Rather, on 17 September, it was Imperiali who tried to
provoke a definite statement from Rome, warning that Tyrrell had
said that, if Italy did not intervene, her interests might receive little
attention at the peace table.[165] San Giuliano's first reaction was only
to remind Imperiali about the advantages of Anglo-French naval
action against Austria. After all, it was still necessary, he noted,
savouring the opportunity for brutal frankness, 'to create the *casus
belli*'.[166]

But the war situation, and the fact that it could be argued that
it was Britain which had taken the initiative, always a circumstance
desired in San Giuliano's diplomacy,[167] made the Foreign Minister
reluctant to see all contacts abandoned. So, after an eager British
agreement to the suggestion that Italy would need the assistance of
a war loan, and further warnings against inaction from Tyrrell,[168]
on 25 September, San Giuliano made a new statement of Italian
terms.[169] The price had gone up, if not wildly. What was more
notable was a greater clarity about Italian ambition, especially in the
Adriatic. Italy's border with whatever state existed there in the future
must reach Dante's River Quarnaro in Istria, and the Dalmatian
Islands must go to Italy. Albania could be divided by Serbia and
Greece, but Italy must retain 'unrestricted sovereignty' over
Valona. There were also further interests which concerned Italy in
Asia Minor and in Africa, where financial, and perhaps territorial,
concessions must be made, although this would be better ascertained
when, for example, Turkey's position in the war was decided. San
Giuliano added, in conclusion, his favoured and important themes

of an Anglo-French naval strike against Austria, and the definite settlement of a loan on generous terms to Italy.

This initiative has brought much praise of San Giuliano from Italian historians whether patriotic or more realistic. Vigezzi, for example, has seen this 'culmination' of San Giuliano's policies as a reasonable set of demands by Italy which would not have led her into future dissidence with her neighbours.[170] Such praise is hardly justified, although San Giuliano had made a judicious assessment of Italy's likely future needs. He had not overlooked the fact that Italy had interests in the Adriatic, in the Eastern Mediterranean, and in Africa; and he had also seen that the Adriatic ambitions were the most significant. Still more important was his emphasis on a loan, and on decisive Anglo-French naval commitment to a war not only against Germany, but also against Austria. In contrast to the woolly mixture of 'honour' and ambition which Sonnino and Salandra would display in 1915, San Giuliano had made an accurate judgement of the bases of Italian foreign policy.

How serious and decisive was this initiative meant to be? Was it a dying man's sketched masterpiece for his successors to fill out, or another San Giuliano despatch, hardly more significant than a thousand others? It is difficult to give too decided a response to this question. Evidence in favour of the argument that Italy had moved definitively towards the Triple Entente can be found, for example, in a conversation which De Martino had with Martini, on 24 September, in which the Secretary-General stated that 'the moment is coming near in which... our intervention is not only justified but necessary'.[171] This was in striking contrast to views expressed earlier by De Martino[172] and it was unusual for him to differ greatly from San Giuliano. On the other hand, in talking to the interventionist Martini, De Martino, with the bureaucratic expertise of a Southerner, may have been preparing the way for his personal transformation from being the nominee of San Giuliano to being the agent of Sonnino. Despite the attacks on his neutralism in August–September 1914, De Martino was able to remain Secretary-General of the Foreign Ministry until 1920, that is until the clear mind of Giolitti returned one last time to direct Italian foreign policy.

It is important to note that, after the declaration of neutrality, there is no evidence that San Giuliano had ever rejected the argument that, eventually, Italy must enter the war on the Entente side. More earnest neutrality, even trimming to the side of the Central Powers, had only been encouraged by the war situation, by San Giuliano's deepening belief that the war was going to last, and by a native Italian diplomatic good sense which suggested that it was unwise not to hear what all sides were offering. But there is also much about the despatch of 25 September which does not denote ultimate decision. In form, in any case, it was very little more than a request for the ambassadorial opinions of Carlotti and Tittoni, and San Giuliano usually asked his ambassadors for their views when he was not intending to act, rather than *vice versa*. Moreover, the telegram was not sent to Imperiali in London, where Italy intended to carry out her negotiations. When San Giuliano did speak to Rodd about the matter two days later, he made clear that no date had been set, although the British ambassador optimistically predicted that San Giuliano had committed himself further than ever before.[173]

Similarly questionable for a Power contemplating joining the Triple Entente was San Giuliano's use of phrases about 'countering Slav encroachment' to explain Italy's Adriatic ambitions. Perhaps the progress of Russian armies against Austria in Galicia had finally changed San Giuliano's mind about the *'grande impotenza'*, but also present in this usage of a German catchcry was San Giuliano's knowledge that, after his initial enthusiasm, Sazonov more than anyone else had cooled to the idea of Italian intervention. In the pattern of her diplomacy, Italy had begun negotiations by emphasising potential disunity between the Powers with whom she was negotiating, from which divisions there might accrue hidden gains and escape clauses.

San Giuliano thus had moved nearer intervention. Having received predictable replies from Carlotti and Tittoni, on 29 September, he suggested to Salandra the need

to hasten the signature of the London agreement and to concentrate all our effort to assure ourselves the best possible diplomatic and military situation in order to achieve the great national aim, that is to give to Italy her natural borders.[174]

Yet, even in this statement, ambiguities remained. San Giuliano still did not mention war, and Italy's 'natural borders' meant merely the taking of Trentino and Trieste; Valona, Asia Minor and the rest, even the Dalmatian islands were excluded. Considering how physically painful it must now have been for San Giuliano to prepare any diplomatic communication, perhaps he was just using short-hand. But there is still one further question: why this apparently but not definitely decisive move towards intervention just at the time of the year when the weather made most unlikely Italian military action against Austria for the next four or five months?

On this equivocation, and on his past style as a negotiator, doubts must remain about the extent of San Giuliano's commitment. Although he had stated to Salandra that 'an agreement' should urgently be made in London, he took no steps forward himself. Although he told Imperiali that the British should curb Pan-Slav propaganda, he concentrated instead, in the days which followed, on Italy's direct interests in the Balkans, by paving the way for an expedition to Valona where he did not forget Italy's conflict with Greece,[175] nor the lingering usefulness to Italy of possible support or sympathy from Germany in the Balkans.

On 12 October San Giuliano held his last important political discussions before his death. Russia had not yet destroyed Austrian armies in Galicia, and San Giuliano grew a little cooler in his enthusiasm for the Entente. Again emphasising Italy's financial problems, he spoke about his fear of the sacrifices which would be asked of Italian families in war-time. To enter such a conflict, Italy would have to have legitimate reasons, which could be seconded by a loan, and she was concerned by the 'Slav peril' in the Adriatic.[176] As Rodd confided, perhaps a little wearily, to his diary:

We went over all the old ground again, and he begged me to put before Grey the necessity of getting things into a shape in which they could rapidly mature if and when the occasion arises.

Despite his illness, San Giuliano's reasoning had been as 'clear and flexible' as ever.[177]

That same day, San Giuliano also saw Malagodi for the last time, and again talked about the requirement that Italy eventually confront Austria. But he stressed: 'for the moment we must still wait. The war will not end so soon'. The state of the Italian Army, and winter in which Southern Italian troops could not fight an Alpine war, were good enough extra reasons to procrastinate. In future military action, Italy must work out her collaboration with Russia, as it would be Italy and Russia who would carry on the land war against Austria (and, he no doubt implied, what better way to arrest the Slav peril than to cooperate with Italy). In sum, although Italy formally had 'not...entered the path of negotiations', there were 'conversations' which should continue and even reach a conclusion at some time so long as it occurred in London, and not in Paris or Rome where there were too many rumours, too much public opinion.[178] These were appropriately opaque last words for San Giuliano's diplomacy, as he moved towards intervention with half-hints and with a constant awareness of, and delight in, complexities and unforeseen eventualities. San Giuliano's only further experience now was death.

But in this he made one last compromise. Malagodi, before being received by San Giuliano, who was propped up on cushions in his study, had bumped into a priest going out. Malagodi thought this might be confirmation of the malicious rumour spreading in Rome that San Giuliano's notorious atheism was weakening. San Giuliano, as usual alert to his visitor's secret thoughts, at once declared, with an extravagant cynicism, that the priest was 'a fine source of information who explains many things'.[179] At the same time, he scribbled out in a failing hand a poem about his own coming funeral and the reactions which his colleagues would have.[180]

These were almost his last attempts at cynicism. In the next hours his health worsened drastically, and San Giuliano died at 2 p.m. on 16 October. A colleague spread the rumour that his last words were '*Italia, Italia grande*'.[181] But San Giuliano's mind had rested not only on the body politic, but also on his soul; *in extremis*, he, who had never taken communion or been confessed before, took the precaution of confession, anointment with holy oil, and even a hastily composed blessing from the new Pope, Benedict XV. Martini was left to ponder in his diary whether San Giuliano was trying to please some of his fanatically religious female relations, or whether there was something more to the dying man's final change of course:

A sudden repentance? A doubt at the last hour?...A stout desire to avoid posthumous polemics so that it could not be said that a Minister of the King of Italy, a *Cavaliere* of the *Annunziata* had died an unbeliever in a state palace?

Martini's malice towards his old companion of the Commission on Eritrea had not altogether been dissipated, even by the unattested information from De Martino that San Giuliano thought Martini would be his best successor.[182] Or had San Giuliano made one last sarcastic joke after all?

The gentlemanly Rodd was more generous in his assessment of the dead Foreign Minister. San Giuliano had, he remembered, 'a very plastic mentality'. San Giuliano did intend that Italy should eventually join the Triple Entente, but would have been a difficult and elusive factor in the conduct of negotiations.[183] Perhaps a better, if indirect, testimony of the damage done to Italian foreign policy by the death of San Giuliano was that Salandra, acting as interim Foreign Minister, on 18 October, uttered the notorious phrase '*sacro egoismo*' which would dog Italian ambition to Versailles and beyond. And when it was announced that it would be Sonnino who would be the new Foreign Minister, Rodd recorded his delight to the Foreign Office. Sonnino was 'absolutely straight' and the negotiations of Italy's entry into the war would now be so much easier without the conniving of San Giuliano.[184] 'Honour', 'honesty', 'straightness', these were the last qualities which Italian foreign policy needed, if it was also to have ambition. And Sonnino certainly still wanted Italy to have 'a great policy', still saw the very justification of the dynasty and the Liberal state in this 'great policy'. As he would tell Bülow, with his usual misplaced honesty, in February 1915, the choice for his Italy was 'either war or revolution'.[185]

Apart from the mistakes of his successors, the eulogy which San Giuliano would have most enjoyed was published in the *Rivista Coloniale*. There it was stated that an English journalist had declared that San Giuliano had pursued a policy to obtain Italian supremacy in the Mediterranean, and had done it with such ability and subtlety that it was likely to succeed. San Giuliano had been, with Grey, one of Europe's greatest diplomatists.[186]

Of course, San Giuliano was also very lucky. He had died before making a drastic mistake, when the three alternatives of a Triple Entente victory, a Central Power victory or a peace of exhaustion, all seemed possible in Rome,[187] and when, therefore, there was still not an urgent need for him to make a decision. Had he lived, given the domestic pressures in Italy, he must soon either have been driven from the Cabinet, or forced to choose between intervention and neutrality. Had he made a right choice then, sooner or later, while the Liberal regime survived, even Giolitti would have wanted to assert Italy's Great Power status and take her into the war. There is no evidence that San Giuliano or Giolitti, for all their skill, subtlety and cynicism would have been any better at picking the right moment to enter the great conflict decisively than were Sonnino and Salandra in 1915, or Bratianu in 1916, or Mussolini in 1940.

Thus admiration for San Giuliano's sheer diplomatic *finesse* must be countered with reaffirmation of the absurdity of Liberal Italy's pretensions as a Great Power, and of the tragedy which these brought to Italian society. But a historian cannot change the past; he can only describe it. Given the norms of Liberal Italy, its very cultural and social basis, and given the Foreign Minister's own acceptance of these norms and their culture, then San Giuliano's foreign policy had been brilliantly successful from July to October 1914. Whatever his past triplicism, he had seen that Trento and Trieste were the real ambitions of a Liberal state. He had perceived that a non-belligerent's policy in war should be tailored to the war situation. He had predicted, earlier than most, that the war would be long. He had realised the problem of Italian military deficiencies, and, however ignorant and contemptuous he may have been of all military matters, he had tried to encourage Salandra to see that it was the present state of the Army which was important to Italy, not recriminations about its past. He had seen that Italy must encourage her allies to fight her war against Austria, and not just their war against Germany. And he had made clear that Italy would need financial aid to fight at all. San Giuliano had alienated neither the Triple Entente nor the Central Powers, and had managed even to get away with talking openly to Britain and France about his fears of the Slav peril. He had not forgotten that Greece should be reminded that it was a small Power, and that there were exciting possibilities near the horizon in Turkey, and more distantly in Ethiopia. For the ambitions of Italian foreign policy, San Giuliano, working by himself, more surely than ever before July 1914, had done his sums and got them right. And then he had died before plans on paper had to be turned into something in practice, before Italy really would experience 'the great contest of the nations'. No wonder there is a Viale Antonino Di San Giuliano outside the Farnesina in Rome today.

Conclusion

In April 1911 Giovanni Giolitti declared that all his governments aimed merely to see an Italy which was 'calm, prosperous and great'.[1] Two years later, Filippo Tommaso Marinetti and his Futurists demanded that 'the word ITALY dominate over the word LIBERTY' and that national foreign policy become 'cynical, crafty and aggressive'.[2] To some analysts, it is the difference between these two remarks, the contrast of the peaceable, if perhaps corrupt, liberalism of Giolitti, and the strident, irrational nationalism of some intellectuals which is the best evidence that Liberal Italy was, by 1914, headed for collapse and the degradation of fascism.

However, a detailed study of Italian foreign policy in the last years before 1914 reveals more continuity and consensus about diplomatic ambitions than might have been expected from these contrasting words. For, in 1913, San Giuliano's foreign policy was 'cynical, crafty and aggressive', just as much as San Giuliano's and many of his colleagues' definition of domestic policies sprang from an ideal that 'Italy', national unanimity behind the existing ruling class, surpass 'Liberty', with its horrid prospect that, via socialism, the 'terrible masses' were entering history and could in no way be diverted. What made Liberal foreign policy distinguishable from fascism-to-come was not its intention, but rather a combination of accident, opportunity and professionalism.

What are the most basic characteristics of Italian diplomacy from 1910 to 1914? Firstly, its dishonesty, the fact that it was crafted from an ideal or an idea, from the myth of the Risorgimento or the myth of Rome; secondly that it was in fashion: that Italy, the least of the Great Powers, tried and was permitted to behave internationally as did the more genuine Great Powers, whose strength was based on the sinews of military, naval or industrial might and not merely on an idea of greatness. It is also notable that, just before 1914 in contrast to just before 1939, Italian diplomacy, despite a participation in the arms race, despite Pollio's blithe advocacy of total war against

Turkey, or even preventive war alongside Germany, was posited essentially on peace, on the belief that Europe was confronting an 'unending period of peace'. Belief was not credulity; San Giuliano, that master of peacetime duplicity, went on detecting that sooner or later, 'in ten years' time' or some such, would occur 'the great contest of the nations', for which, ideally, he was honing the iron of Italian readiness.

In this ambiguity lies one of the attractions of a study of Italian foreign policy before 1914. Any student must be struck by the ability of Giolitti, his coolness, his sense of reality, his balance, if also wondering about his parochialism and his age in the modern world. Also remarkable is the sense of ambiguity, bathos, and failure of San Giuliano, that aristocrat who 'knew his times'. One reason why Italian diplomacy obtained certain superficial successes from 1910 to 1914 was precisely because the masters of Italian diplomacy were equivocal about it, and, even while they strove to conjure up a third Rome, nonetheless comprehended that this was a labour of Sisyphus, and one which, if ever a real test was demanded, would lead to Lissa, Adowa or Caporetto.

There lay the final problem. How could Italy manage to *fare da sè* when it had not made itself, when its 'unity' was based on a political and not a social revolution, when the Piedmontese Giolitti, wanting to damn his rival Salandra, could think of no better expletive than to call him a *'pugliese'*, a man from Apulia, who was thus naturally a liar and a cheat?[3] How could the Italy which imported its coal, or which did not find oil in Libya, fuel a modern navy? How could a state dependent on domestic repression and police action use its Army to conquer living-space? How could the poverty of Italy be transmuted into the industrial–military base of a Great Power? The foreign policy of Liberal Italy was more covert, more hesitant, more verbally restrained than that of Fascist Italy, but it was not different in kind; instead, from the Risorgimento to the fall of fascism, Italy pursued the foreign policy of the least of the Great Powers. John Bright classically described the diplomacy of Victorian England as 'a gigantic system of out-relief for the British aristocracy'. His comment could be adapted to the Italian context, for Italy's pretensions to be a Great Power were a luxury which provided a gigantic system of out-relief for those social and regional groups which made the Italian Risorgimento and which, with some additions, went on governing Italy from 1860 to 1945.

The Ten Commandments for Italians abroad

1   The *patria* is one only. Your *patria* is Italy. No other country can be loved by you like Italy.

2   Never speak the name of the *patria* without reverence, exalting the glories of your Italy which is one of the most ancient, noble and civilised nations in the world, be strengthened by those traditions and those energies, to which are entrusted her best fortunes. Do not complain if you have abandoned her to look somewhere else for what she could not give you.

3   Remember solemnly to celebrate national festivals. Lend a helping hand without stint whenever the *patria* is threatened. On this occasion and in all those relevant to the aspirations, the prestige and the dignity of the *patria*, forget your political party, your religious beliefs, and remember only that you are an Italian. Take the opportunity to mix among your co-nationals, educated and ignorant, rich and poor, Southern and Northern, conservative and progressive and treat them all as brothers, and refresh their spirit talking with them about the land in which you were born.

4   Honour the official Representatives of your Country. Offending them, you offend a little the *patria*; respect them even if sometimes they do not please you. Tolerate their defects, appreciate their qualities, do not put snags in their path, help them, if you can, in their useful activities.

5   Do not give up your Italian citizenship, cancelling in yourself the consciousness and the sentiment of being an Italian. Do not flee for lust in material gains from the duties related to your citizenship; do not evade military service; do not refuse to pay taxes. Do not camouflage with a barbaric transcription your name and surname; do not corrupt by means of words, methods of speech and foreign pronunciation, the usages and customs of the country in which you are a guest.

6   Do not undermine because of mere jealousy the authority and prestige of your co-nationals who occupy important positions. Do not oppose them out of a malign spirit of hostility or from blind partisanship. Contribute generously and in proportion to your means, the mite needed by Italian groups of charity and mutual aid. Work for peace, bring together enemies, do not provoke schisms, party wars, polemics, fights, which, damaging the Italian name, weaken the authority of our associations.

7   Do not take fellow citizens away from the *patria*, allowing your descendants to lose their *italianità* and be absorbed by the people among whom you have emigrated.

Educate your sons in the cult of Italy. Oblige them to speak, read and write their paternal language and to study the history of Italy; preferably send them to Italian schools; buy good Italian books. Try to spread among foreigners the knowledge of Italy, the love for its culture and language.

8   Be proud to declare yourself, always, on every occasion, an Italian by origin and sentiment, and be respectful without servility among those who give you hospitality.

9   Do not prefer foreign products; but try to buy and get others to buy, use and get used always goods and commodities which have been produced and manufactured in Italy.

In the price of any object made in Italy and bought abroad, there is included a tiny, invisible contribution which multiplied by the millions of Italian emigrants, assures a conspicuous income to the national agriculture and industries.

If, on the contrary, you buy or consume foreign products, you are refusing as an adult thus to repay as it is your duty to the *patria*, what you were loaned when you were an infant, when you were nourished without profit, in the only hope then of receiving in compensation, the work of your arms and your brain.

10   Do not desire foreign women; but by preference marry an Italian. With her and by her you can preserve in your sons the blood and the language of your fathers even if your destiny drives you and your descendants to remain far from the *patria*.

Published in *RC*, VII, 25 Dec. 1912.

Pro-memoria on our politico–military situation

The internal crisis of Turkey, and especially the last events occurring in Albania, which have enormously worsened the politico–military situation of the enemy Empire, impels us, as far as I can see, to act again in the Aegean.

I do not know well our situation with respect to the friendly and allied Powers because I have not been sent sufficient communications, and I do not know what are the reasons which paralyse our action in the Eastern Mediterranean. I imagine that the interest of those Powers which have invested enormous capital in Turkey counsel them to keep alive and possibly unharmed at least the trunk of the debtor, while the repetition of our blows could cause her collapse. It would be useless for me to say that our interests must be safeguarded before those of others, for it is not certain on this point that I will be allowed to attract the government's attention. Yet I can say that, given the present situation of Turkey, her collapse is probable even without action on our part. And then I ask myself: why should we not exploit the opportunity? Yet we must also be aware that if Turkey, through foreign gold or the support of the Powers, succeeds in staying on her feet, despite sudden blows and old frictions, to us can only come the greatest damage through the prolongation of this war which eventually will demand a summoning of greater effort compared to what we would need now to attack her in such a way as to force her to secure a peace in order to save herself from total ruin.

At the beginning, it could not be in our interest for the empire to collapse while we were not in a position to achieve further gains, since we were busy with the occupation of Libya, which not only seemed, but indeed was, easy. But at present, after our victories and thanks to other events which more or less derive from them, our politico–military situation is changed. Without intending it, we have lit a fire which threatens to spread, and we cannot by our wish alone regard our action as limited to Libya.

We thought from the beginning, and we had reason to think it, that we had against us only the Turks, but we have had in fact against us first the Arabs, and then the Western Powers.

In Libya we have had only victories, but for various reasons progress occurs only slowly, and will continue to occur slowly until the Arabs are paid. Only a person who refuses to believe the evidence of his eyes can say that the Turks could succeed in expelling us from the conquered territory, and indeed they are the sort of people who do not want to look and who pretend not to believe in the importance of our latest and really fine victories. It is clear that in Africa there are not nor can there be decisive battles. Even if all the [local tribesmen] whom we have against us from Tobruk to Buchamez, retreated, and we had no one against us, at the first important move towards the interior we would find ourselves back with the same problem, because money will still flow in.

The losses endured by the Arabs in various engagements are enormous, but they are only affected for a few days by the injury inflicted, then they are once again not concerned about it: to fight is their life, and also they are paid for it.

The goods necessary for their livelihood: grain and livestock they have. Indeed rather more livestock than usual because there are no exports; they will eventually be destroyed it is true, but for now and for some time still they will be able to bear, I won't say with *virtù*, but with Moslem indifference, the wretchedness and all the devastation of war.

They have plenty of arms; munitions too. And there is perhaps no material easier to transport and to smuggle than cartridges.

Hence it is not in Libya that a solution can be reached. The disintegration will come, but when? They will fight on and on, and presumably we shall kill many other hundreds and thousands of Arabs. But the Turks with their unlimited funds will always be safely based out of reach.

The situation, from one moment to another, can change to our advantage: I would like to be able to establish this, but I cannot believe it.

And, in the last analysis, when not even one more Turk remains in Libya and the Arabs surrender, Turkey would still not recognise, or so I believe, our decree of sovereignty. But would the Powers recognise it? I do not know. From one angle, this decree was necessary and, after the boldness of the conquest, any other decision would have been inadequate. Certain issues need to be resolved at once. The occupation of Bosnia and of Herzegovina by Austria was in substance an annexation. But how many hundreds of millions has our neighbouring Empire had to waste in order to transform it into an annexation *de iure*? And what dangers has she had to confront.

It is said justly that our splendid and successful expedition has provoked discomfort and danger for all Europe. But it is quite obvious that the die is cast, and I cannot see the end of discomfort and danger while we continue to adopt guerilla tactics in Libya, while we continue to occupy the islands of the Southern Aegean, and keep ourselves at Stampalia, and in the Central Aegean. In short, we are in suspense waiting for some favourable event to turn up which can change the situation radically to our advantage. Now of favourable events, I forsee only two: victories in Libya or the collapse of Turkey. Victories make no impression either on Turkey or on others. There remains the collapse. If it must come, I repeat, why shouldn't we take advantage of it? And if we must regard it as certain and soon, why should we wait to strike? Certainly if all the Great Powers were in agreement and intended to stop us, *then we must stop, and it would not be a humiliation to do so before what would really be force majeure* [in original underlined probably by Giolitti]. But allow me to doubt that, breaking out of that circle of dumb hostility in which the Great Powers are constrained, there could be an accord between them. Moreover, they have proclaimed their neutrality, as long as we promise to respect the Balkan peninsula in its present state. In any case, while we are waging war against Turkey, can we be held back from an action which would greatly improve our position, and which militarily and politically seems naturally indicated: i.e. *the conquest of Smyrna*? [underlining probably by Pollio]. I am not briefed, as I have already said, about the international situation, and therefore I cannot give a definite answer. But, on the other hand, in war, political and military action are so inextricably mixed that it is impossible to separate them, and therefore I still believe myself competent *to counsel that we take Smyrna* [Pollio underlining].

It would be a serious affair, difficult, but not beyond our means and our capacity for war. It is a strange war that we are fighting, and it is impossible not to recognise the difficulties which our diplomacy has had to combat, and does combat in another campaign full of perils. But at the stage in which we find ourselves should we really worry, if we seriously make war against Turkey, that the Western Powers will send their fleets against us or will invade Italy? If this is not a danger, and if there is only the threat that they will look for compensation, and at the expense of Turkey, before they come running to assist the 'quarry' should we not go ahead! Austria can then move against the Sandjak of Novi Bazar, but what does it matter to us if she returns there?

Austria can aim at Albania – and this would be more serious. But would the Albanians remain tranquil while their country is used as compensation? I do not believe it. Can a German intervention in the Mediterranean be imagined when it would leave her at the mercy of the English fleet? And can we turn England into an enemy when we have shown so much courtesy to her, even suspending our naval action to give the royal yacht peace and quiet on its voyage to India?

There is one more issue to appraise and one which I believe can grant us a certain freedom of action. And that is the attitude of the little Balkan states whom, I am sure, only want a word to ally themselves sooner or later with us.

But setting aside all these considerations, I must return to my own field of expertise. And, staying there, I must by necessity solemnly re-affirm that there is nothing that has more importance and more weight in politics than energetic military action. And, in the final analysis, I add that, if it should unfortunately be necessary to renounce in fact the Smyrna expedition, which anyhow ought to be preceded by the taking of Chios, it is indispensable, absolutely, whatever is the outcome of diplomatic negotiations, whatever is the fate which awaits Turkey, that we at least give the impression that we have decided to take Smyrna. The Turks have assembled there an army. It would be really most unfortunate if, encouraged by our inaction, they sent these troops, for example to Albania, where they could be used to clean up the situation that we have not created, but which – still I believe – can only bring us advantages and even great advantages, especially if the fire spreads into Macedonia and if the little Balkan states begin to make trouble.

Appendix II

The Eastern question – and this is my conclusion – has lasted for centuries. It is possible that now, finally, it will be resolved and that the humiliation of having the Turks in Europe will end. However I unswervingly believe that, in the present historic moment, Italy, after what she has done and what she has said, must not fall into a position of sheathing her sword, but rather must go forward and take for herself an equal position along with the other competitors, invoking that renewed energy which has been released by her re-awakened powers, and by that faith which she now has in herself after the deeds which she has done in a manner up to the standard of any Great Power whatever.

Lt.-Gen.
Chief of General Staff of Army
(signed) A. POLLIO

CG, 22/59, C/5, 29 June 1912.

San Giuliano's poem about his funeral ceremony

In pugliese Salandra, in meneghino
Marcora, narreranno le mie gesta.
Leggendo il funerale del cugino,
Giovannino dirà: Che bella festa!

Sosterrà De Martino che son morto
perché son nato, ahimè, di venerdì;
inventerà mia nuora in modo accorto
virtú del nonno ad educar Niní.

Torre dirà che la mia colpa vera
fu non aver seguito i suoi consigli.

Penserà Merey: 'Morir debbo anch'io,
dei fratelli siamesi è questo il fato';
Garbasso prima dell'estremo addio
'Agli atti' la mia morte ha già passato.

Di poche anime buone il passeggero
rimpianto forse aleggerà per poco
sopra le pieghe del mio drappo nero,
e tra le faci del funereo loco

tremolerà per l'aleggiar gentile
forse la fiamma allor di qualche face,
e spirerà sulla mia spoglia umile
un'aura cheta di serena pace.

Sulla mia bara mesti e addolorati
i farmacisti deporranno i fiori;
e così si vedrà che vi son cuori
nel dolce italo suol memori e grati.

E quando poscia dai registri loro
mireranno che perdita avran fatto
allora tutti esclameranno in coro:
'Peccato che sia morto un sí bel matto!'

Un bel discorso farà Borsarelli
Scriverà Falbo una necrologia;
ai funerali penserà Bruschelli,
e a farsi dar denari l'Albania.

Appendix III

E l'asinello dalla lunga coda
dai dolci occhi velati di mestizia
raglierà forte, si che ognuno l'oda:
'Spento è colùi che mi rendea giustizia'.

Salandra in the dialect of Puglia, Marcora [the President of the Senate] in Milanese will relate my history. Reading about the funeral of his 'cousin', Johnny [Giolitti, also a wearer of the collar of the Annunziata, and therefore 'cousin' of the King] will say: 'What a fine *festa!*' De Martino will argue that I died because I was born, alas, on a Friday. My daughter-in-law will shrewdly invent virtues of grandpa to educate my little Tony [his heir, the new Antonino].

[Andrea] Torre will say that my real trouble was that I did not follow his advice. Mérey will think: 'I, too, must die. This is the fate of Siamese twins' [a reference to the fact that Italy and Austria were either 'allies or enemies'].
Garbasso [the *capo di gabinetto*] already before the final adieu will have transferred my death to the historical section. The passing sorrow of a few good people will perhaps last for a while above the folds of my funeral pall, and in between the lights of the funeral place perhaps will gently tremble the flame of some other torch and will breathe over my humble remains a silent aura of serene peace. On my bier, sorrowful and saddened, the chemists will leave flowers and so it will be seen that in the sweet soul [soil] of Italy there are hearts which are respectful and grateful. And when afterwards beside their account books, they contemplate what monetary loss they will have, then they will all exclaim together: 'What a shame that such a fine fool is dead'. [All this is a reference to San Giuliano's long need for constant medication to stay alive.]

Borsarelli will make a fine speech, Falbo [a journalist] will write an obituary. Bruschelli [San Giuliano's private secretary] will contemplate funerals and Albania will ask for money. And the little donkey with the long tail with its sweet eyes veiled by sadness, will bray, loudly, yes so that everyone hears him: 'Dead and gone is he who rendered me justice!'

Quoted from L. Androvandi Marescotti, *Guerra diplomatica* (Milan, 1936), pp. 51–2.

Abbreviations used in the notes and bibliography

ACS	Archivio Centrale dello Stato
AG	Archivio di gabinetto, 1910–14
AHR	*American Historical Review*
AR	Archivio riservato di gabinetto, 1906–10
ASMAE	Archivi storici del Ministero degli Affari Esteri
BD	*British Documents* (ed. Gooch and Temperley)
BP	Bertie Papers
BS	*Balkan Studies*
BSGI	*Bollettino della Società geografica italiana*
CAB	British Cabinet Papers, 1902–15
CB	Carte Brusati
CD	*Atti parlamentari, Camera dei deputati*
CEH	*Central European History*
CG	Carte Giolitti
CHJ	*Cambridge Historical Journal*
CHR	*Catholic Historical Review*
CID	Committee of Imperial Defence
CM	Carte Martini
CP	Confidential Print
CR	*Contemporary Review*
CS	Carte Salandra (ACS)
CSG	Carte Di San Giuliano
CS(L)	Carte Salandra (Lucera)
CT	Carte Torre
DDF	*Documents diplomatiques françaises*
DDI	*Documenti diplomatici italiani*
DGP	*Die Grosse Politik*
DGPS	Direzione generale di pubblica sicurezza
EHR	*English Historical Review*
GP	Grey Papers
HJ	*Historical Journal*
HP	Hardinge Papers
HT	*History Today*
IQ	*Italian Quarterly*
JAH	*Journal of African History*
JCEA	*Journal of Central European Affairs*
JCH	*Journal of Contemporary History*

Abbreviations

JEH	Journal of Economic History
JMH	Journal of Modern History
JSH	Journal of Social History
LP	Lansdowne Papers
MAE P	Archivio politica, Ministero degli affari esteri
NA	Nuova Antologia
NP	Nicolson Papers
NRS	Nuova Rivista Storica
OUA	Oesterreich-Ungarns Aussenpolitik
PCG	Presidenza del consiglio, gabinetto, atti
PP	Past and Present
PRO	Public Record Office
RC	Rivista Coloniale
RDM	Revue des deux mondes
RH	Revue historique
RHD	Revue d'histoire diplomatique
RHMC	Revue d'histoire moderne et contemporaine
RP	Rodd Papers
RSC	Rivista di Storia Contemporanea
RSI	Rivista Storica Italiana
RSPI	Rivista di Studi Politici Internazionali
RSR	Rassegna Storica del Risorgimento
RSS	Rivista Storica del Socialismo
SC	Storia Contemporanea
SEER	Slavonic and East European Review
SP	Sonnino papers
SS	Studi Storici

Select Bibliography

The bibliography is divided into:
I. Unpublished sources
II. Documentary collections
III. Primary sources: Italy
IV. Secondary sources: Italy
V. Primary sources: other countries
VI. Secondary sources: other countries

I. UNPUBLISHED SOURCES

Archivi storici del Ministero degli Affari Esteri files
    Archivio riservato di gabinetto, 1906–10
    Archivio di gabinetto, 1910–14
    Archivio politica, 1910–14
British Foreign Office files 371 PRO
Ministero Interno: Direzione generale di pubblica sicurezza: ufficio riservato ACS
Presidenza del consiglio, gabinetto, atti 1910–14 ACS
Carte Ameglio ACS
Carte Bergamini S. Giovanni in Persiceto
Bertie Papers PRO
Carte Brusati ACS
Carte San Giuliano ASMAE
Carte Giolitti ACS
Grey Papers PRO
Hardinge Papers Cambridge University Library
Carte Martini ACS
Nicolson Papers PRO
Rodd Papers courtesy Francis, 2nd Baron Rennell of Rodd
Carte Salandra ACS
Carte Salandra Lucera
Sonnino Papers Microfilm, University of Sydney
Carte A. Torre ACS

II. DOCUMENTARY COLLECTIONS

British Documents on the Origins of the War, 1898–1914, ed. G. P. Gooch and H. Temperley
    (11 vols, London, 1926–38)
I documenti diplomatici italiani, 4th. series, vol. XII; 5th series, vol. I, ed. A. Torre (Rome,
    1954, 1964)

431

Bibliography

Documents diplomatiques françaises (1871–1914) 2nd and 3rd series (Paris, 1929–55)

Die Grosse Politik der europäischen Kabinette, 1871–1914, ed. J. Lepsius, A. Mendelssohn Bartholdy, F. Thimme (40 vols, Berlin, 1922–7)

Oesterreich–Ungarns Aussenpolitik, 1908–14, ed. L. Bittner and H. Uebersberger (8 vols, Vienna, 1930)

Trattati e convenzioni fra il Regno d'Italia e gli altri stati, vols. 22–3 (Rome, 1930)

Atti Parlamentari, discussioni 1848–1948, Camera dei deputati e Senato (Rome)

Annuario dell'Italia all'estero e delle sue colonie, 1911–14 (Rome, 1911–14)

Annuario diplomatico del Regno d'Italia (Rome, 1909, 1926)

Annuario Massonico del Grande Oriente d'Italia, 1911–14 (Rome, 1911–14)

Libro d'Oro della Nobiltà Italiana, vols I–III (Rome 1910–1915)

Relazione Generale della R. Commissione d'Inchiesta sulla Colonia Eritrea (Rome, 1891)

III. PRIMARY SOURCES: ITALY

Abbott, C. F., *The Holy War in Tripoli* (London, 1912)

Albertini, L., *Venti anni di vita politica* (5 vols., Bologna, 1950–3)

Albertini, L., *Epistolario 1911–1926,* vol. I (Milan, 1968)

Aldrovandi Marescotti, L., 'Al principio della guerra mondiale (giugno–novembre 1914)', *NA,* f 1515, 16 April 1935

Aldrovandi Marescotti, L., *Guerra diplomatica: ricordi e frammenti di diario 1914–1919* (Milan, 1936)

Aldrovandi Marescotti, L., *Nuovi ricordi e frammenti di diario* (Milan, 1938)

Amendola, E. K., *Vita con Giovanni Amendola* (Florence, 1960)

Antongini, T., *D'Annunzio* (London, 1938)

Artom, I. and E., *Iniziative neutralistiche della diplomazia italiana nel 1870 e nel 1915, documenti inediti,* ed. A. Artom (Rome, 1954)

Avarna Di Gualtieri, C., *L'ultimo rinnovamento della triplice (5 dicembre 1912)* (Milan, 1924)

Avarna Di Gualtieri, C., 'Il carteggio Avarna-Bollati, luglio 1914-maggio 1915', *RSI,* LXI–LXII (1949–1950)

Bachi, R., *L'Italia economica nell'anno 1913* (Città di Castello, 1914)

Bachi, R., *L'Italia economica nell'anno 1915* (Città di Castello, 1916)

Bagot, R., *My Italian Years* (London, 1911)

Bagot, R., *The Italians of Today* (London, 1912)

Barclay, T., *The Turco-Italian War and Its Problems* (London, 1912)

Barzilai, S., *Vita internazionale* (Florence, 1911)

Barzilai, S., *Vita parlamentare* (Rome, 1912)

Barzilai, S., *Dalla Triplice Alleanza al conflitto europeo: discorsi parlamentari e scritti vari* (Rome, 1914)

Barzilai, S., *Luci ed ombre del passato: memorie di vita politica* (Milan, 1937)

Bergamini, A., 'La "Dante Alighieri" in Sardegna e i suoi presidenti', *NA,* f 1849, Jan. 1955

Bernotti, R., *Cinquant'anni nella Marina militare* (Milan, 1971)

Bertolini, P., 'Diario (agosto 1914-maggio 1915)', *NA,* f 1221, 1 Feb. 1923

Bezzi, E., *Irredentismo e interventismo nelle lettere agli amici, 1903–1920,* ed. T. Grandi and B. Rizzi (Trento, 1963)

Bissolati, L., *La politica estera dell' Italia dal 1897 al 1920: scritti e discorsi* (Milan, 1923)

Blaserna, P. (ed.), *Cinquanta anni di storia italiana* (3 vols, Milan, 1911)

Bolla, N., *Il segreto di due re* (Milan, 1951)

Bono, S., 'Lettere dal fronte libico (1911–1912)', *NA*, f 2052, Dec. 1971

Bonomi, I., *La politica italiana da Porta Pia a Vittorio Veneto, 1870–1918* (Turin, 1946)

Booth, C. D. and I. B., *Italy's Aegean Possessions* (London, 1928)

Bovio, G., *Il secolo nuovo* (Rome, 1923)

Brancaccio, N., *In Francia durante la guerra* (Milan, 1926)

Cadorna, L., *Altre pagine sulla grande guerra* (Milan, 1925)

Cadorna, L., *Lettere famigliari*, ed. R. Cadorna (Milan, 1967)

Caniglia, B., *Italia e Albania (ottobre 1914–agosto 1920): studio storico-politico-economico* (Rome, n.d.)

Cantalupo, R., *L'Italia musulmana* (Rome, 1928)

Cantalupo, R., *Ritratto di Pietro Lanza di Scalea* (Rome, 1939)

Cantalupo, R., *Fuad, primo re d'Egitto* (Milan, 1940)

Cirmeni, B., 'L'intesa italo-russa e la Triplice Alleanza', *NA*, f 910, 16 Nov. 1909

Colajanni, N., *Gli avvenimenti di Sicilia e le loro cause* (Palermo, 1894)

Conti, E., *Dal taccuino di un borghese* (Cremona, 1946)

Cora, G., 'Belgrado 1914', *RSPI*, VIII (1941)

Corradini, E., *Il Nazionalismo italiano* (Milan, 1914)

Corradini, E., *Discorsi politici (1902–1924)* (Florence, 1925)

Crespi, A., 'Two years of Italian imperialism', *Fortnightly Review*, XCV, 1 June 1914

Curàtolo, G. E., *Francia e Italia: pagine di storia 1849–1914* (Turin, 1915)

De Benedetti, M., 'Il Monumento a Vittorio Emanuele II a Roma', *NA*, f 947, 1 June 1911

De Biase, C., 'La neutralità italiana (luglio–ottobre 1914): da un carteggio inedito Salandra–Di San Giuliano', *Quaderni di cultura e di storia sociale* III (1954)

De Biase, C., 'Il "Diario" del ministro Vincenzo Riccio (1915)', *NA*, f 1860, 1868, Dec. 1955, Aug. 1956

De Bono, E., *Nell'esercito nostro prima della guerra* (Milan, 1931)

De Bono, E., *La guerra come e dove l'ho vista e combattuta io* (Milan, 1935)

De Bosdari, A., *Delle guerre balcaniche della Grande Guerra e di alcuni fatti precedenti ad esse* (Milan, 1927)

De Cesare, R., 'Emilio Visconti Venosta: storia e ricordi'. *NA*, f 1031, 1 Jan. 1915

De' Luigi, G., *Il Mediterraneo nella politica europea* (Naples, n.d.)

De Martino, G. [II], *Cirene e Cartagine: note e impressioni della carovana De Martino–Baldari, giugno–luglio 1907* (Bologna, 1908)

De Martino, G. [II], *La Somalia nostra* (Bergamo, 1913)

De Martino, G. [III] 'Ricordi di carriera: la mia missione a Costantinopoli per la guerra di Libia', *Rassegna di Politica Internazionale*, IV (1937)

De Roberto, F., *The Viceroys*, trans. A. Colquhoun (London, 1962)

De Roberto, F., *Catania* (Bergamo, 1907)

De Roberto, F., *L'imperio* (Milan, 1929)

De Rossi, E., *La vita di un ufficiale italiano sino alla guerra* (Milan, 1927)

Di San Giuliano, A., *La questione elettorale in Italia sunto in due conferenze orali* (Catania, 1876)

Di San Giuliano, A., *Sulla ferrovia circumetnea: lettera ai consiglieri comunali di Catania* (Catania, 1882)

Bibliography

Di San Giuliano, A., *Discorso politico tenuto all' Arena Pacini* (Catania, 1882)

Di San Giuliano, A., *Discorso politico pronunziato al banchetto offertogli da alcuni amici elettori* (Catania, 1886)

Di San Giuliano, A., *Conferenza sul tema il partito progressista costituzionale e le classi lavoratrici* (Milan, 1890)

Di San Giuliano, A., *Le condizioni presenti della Sicilia: studii e proposte* (Milan, 1894)

Di San Giuliano, A., 'I fini della nostra politica coloniale', *La Riforma Sociale*, III (1895)

Di San Giuliano, A., 'La crisi dell'Africa italiana', *NA*, f 576, 16 Dec. 1895

Di San Giuliano, A., *Lettere sull'Albania* (Rome, 1903)

Di San Giuliano, A., 'L'emigrazione italiana negli Stati Uniti d'America', *NA*, f. 805, 1 July 1905

[Di San Giuliano, A.], 'The influence of the Far Eastern War on the European situation', *National Review*, 77, Nov. 1905

Durham, M. E., *High Albania* (London, 1909)

Durham, M. E., *The Struggle for Scutari* (London, 1914)

Einaudi, L., *Cronache economiche e politiche di un trentennio (1893–1925)*, vol. III (1910–1914) (Turin, 1960)

Fazio, G., *Essenza e fattori della grandezza marittima* (Rome, 1904)

De Frenzi, G., (i.e. Federzoni, L.), *Per l'italianità del 'Gardasee'* (Naples, 1909)

De Frenzi, G. (i.e. Federzoni, L.), *L'Italia nell'Egeo* (Rome, 1913)

Federzoni, L., *La Dalmazia che aspetta* (Bologna, 1915)

Federzoni, L., *Paradossi di ieri* (Milan, 1926)

Federzoni, L., *Italia di ieri per la storia di domani* (Milan, 1967)

Frassati, A., *Giolitti* (Florence, 1959)

Foscari, P., *Per l'Italia più grande: scritti e discorsi*, ed. T. Sillani (Rome, 1928)

Franchetti, L., *Mezzogiorno e colonie*, ed. V. Zanotti-Bianco (Florence, 1950)

Franchetti, L., 'L'Italia e l'Asia Minore', *NA*, f 1087, 1 May 1917

Fusinato, G., *Pasquale Stanislao Mancini* (Turin, 1889)

Galli, C., *Diarii e lettere: Tripoli, 1911; Trieste, 1918* (Florence, 1951)

Galli, C., 'Il marchese Di San Giuliano e la neutralità nel '14', *NA*, f 1867, July 1956

Garronne, G. and E., *Lettere e diarii di guerra 1914–1918*, ed. V. and A. Galante Garronne (Milan, 1974)

Gayda, V., *La crisi di un impero (pagine sull'Austria contemporanea)* (Turin, 1913)

Gentile, S. C., 'Il personale del Ministero degli affari esteri', *Rivista d'Italia*, IV (1901)

Giolitti, G., *Memorie della mia vita* (Milan, 1922)

Giolitti, G., *Memoirs of my Life* (London, 1923)

Giolitti, G., *Discorsi extraparlamentari* (Turin, 1952)

Giolitti, G., *Discorsi parlamentari* (4 vols, Rome, 1954)

Giolitti, G., *Quarant'anni di politica italiana dalle carte di Giovanni Giolitti*, ed. P. D'Angiolini, G. Carocci, C. Pavone (3 vols, Milan, 1962)

Golzio, F. and Guerra, A. (eds.), *La cultura italiana del '900 attraverso le riviste*, vol. V (Turin, 1962)

Gray, E. M., *The Bloodless War* (New York, 1916)

Graziani, R., *Ho difeso la patria* (Cernusco sul Naviglio, 1948)

Guariglia, R., *Ricordi, 1922–1946* (Naples, 1949)

Guariglia, R., *Primi passi in diplomazia e rapporti dall'ambasciata di Madrid, 1932–1934*, ed. R. Moscati (Naples, 1972)

Bibliography

Guicciardini, F., 'Impressioni di Tripolitania', *NA*, f 679, 1 April 1900

Guicciardini, F., 'Impressioni d'Albania', *NA*, f 708, 709, 16 June, 1 July 1901

Guicciardini, F., 'Impressioni di Macedonia', *NA*, f 773, 774, 1 March, 16 March 1904

Guicciardini, F., 'Serbia e Grecia in Albania', *NA*, f 984, 16 Dec. 1912

Guicciardini, F., *Cento giorni alla Consulta: diario e ricordi*, ed. P. Guicciardini (Florence, 1943)

Irace, T. *With the Italians in Tripoli: the authentic history of the Turco-Italian war* (London, 1912)

'Justus', V. *Macchi di Cellere all'ambasciata di Washington: memorie e testimonianze* (Florence, 1920)

Labriola, A., *Storia di dieci anni, 1899–1909* (Milan, 1910)

Labriola, A., *Le tendenze politiche dell'Austria contemporanea* (Naples, 1911)

Labriola, A., *La guerra di Tripoli e l'opinione socialista* (Naples, 1912)

Lago, M., *Angelo Zanelli* (Rome, 1911)

Lanciani, R., *La distruzione di Roma antica* (new ed., Milan, 1971)

Lapworth, C., *Tripoli and Young Italy* (London, 1912)

Lega Navale Italiana, *Italia Marinara* (Rome, 1947)

'Legatus', 'S.E. Sir James Rennell Rodd', *NA*, f 898, 16 May 1909

Levi, P. (L'Italico), *Luigi Orlando e i suoi fratelli: per la patria e per l'industria italiana* (Rome, 1898)

Levi, P., *Missione nell'Africa settentrionale, giugno-luglio 1908* (Rome, 1908)

Licata, G., *Notabili della Terza Italia: in appendice carte di Salvago Raggi e altri inediti* (Rome, 1968)

Limo, G. ('Argus'), *Le idealità della Lega Navale Italiana e il 'Mare Nostrum'* (Rome, 1903)

Lodi, L., *Venticinque anni di vita parlamentare: da Pelloux a Mussolini* (Florence, 1923)

Luciolli, M., *Palazzo Chigi: anni roventi* (Milan, 1976)

Luzzatti, L., *Memorie, Vol III, 1901–1927*, ed. E. and F. de Carli and A. de Stefani (Milan, 1966)

Lyttelton, A. (ed.), *Italian Fascisms from Pareto to Gentile* (London, 1973)

Malagodi, O., *Imperialismo: la civiltà industriale e le sue conquiste, studii inglesi* (Milan, 1901)

Malagodi, O., *Conversazioni della guerra, 1914–1919*, vol. I, ed. B. Vigezzi (Milan, 1960)

Mantegazza, V., *La Turchia liberale e le questioni balcaniche* (Milan, 1908)

Mantegazza, V., *La Grande Bulgaria* (Rome, 1913)

Mantegazza, V., *Il Mediterraneo e il suo equilibrio* (Milan, 1914)

Mantegazza, V., *Italiani in Oriente: Eraclea* (Rome, 1922)

Martini, F., *Nell'Affrica Italiana: impressioni e ricordi* (rev. ed., Milan, 1895)

Martini, F., *Lettere, 1860–1928* (Milan, 1934)

Martini, F., *Diario, 1914–1918*, ed. G. De Rosa (Milan, 1966)

Marvasi, R., *Così parlò Fabroni* (Rome, 1914)

Mayor Des Planches, E., 'Re Vittorio Emanuele II alla vigilia della guerra del settanta (con documenti inediti)', *NA*, f 1154, 16 April 1920

McClure, W. K., *Italy in North Africa: an account of the Tripoli enterprise* (London, 1913)

McCullagh, F., *Italy's War For a Desert: being some experiences of a war correspondent with the Italians in Tripoli* (London, 1912)

Medici Del Vascello, L., *Per l'Italia!* (Bari, 1916)

Melegari, G., 'L'Imperatore Nicolò II e la sua politica: ricordi ed impressioni', *NA*, f 1233, 1 Aug. 1923

Bibliography

Merlika Kruja, E., 'La libertà albanese e la politica italiana dal 1878 al 1912', *Rivista d'Albania*, IV (1942)

Michels, R., *L'imperialismo italiano: studi politico-demografici* (Milan, 1914)

Michels, R., *Political parties* (New York, 1962)

Moneta, E. T., *Le guerre, le insurrezioni e la pace nel secolo decimonono: compendio storico e considerazioni* (2 vols, Milan, 1905)

Mosca, G., *Italia e Libia: considerazioni politiche* (Milan, 1912)

Nasi, N., *Memorie: storia di un dramma parlamentare* (Grottaferrata, 1951)

Nitti, F. S., *Scritti politici* (6 vols, Bari, 1959–67)

Occhini, P. L., 'Enrico Corradini, africanista', *NA*, f 1532, 16 Jan. 1936

Orlando, V. E., 'Dante e il Piemonte', *NA*, f 1813, May 1952

Orlando, V. E., *Memorie, 1915–1919*, ed. R. Mosca (Milan, 1960)

Orlando, V. E., *Discorsi parlamentari* (4 vols. Rome, 1965)

Ostler, A. *The Arabs in Tripoli* (London, 1912)

Page, T. N., *Italy and the World War* (London, 1921)

Pansa, M., 'Ricordi di vita diplomatica, 1884–1914', ed. E. Serra, *NA*, f 1921–4, Jan.–April 1961

Paoli, R., *Nella colonia Eritrea: studi e viaggi* (Milan, 1908)

Papafava, F., *Dieci anni di vita italiana (1899–1909): cronache* (2 vols., Bari, 1913)

Papini, G., *Passato remoto (1885–1914)* (Florence, 1948)

Paulucci Di Calboli, G., 'Antonino Di San Giuliano', in Confederazione fascista dei professionisti e degli artisti, *Celebrazioni Siciliane*, part I (Urbino, 1939)

Paulucci Di Calboli, G., 'Il marchese Di San Giuliano', *NA*, f 1628, 16 Jan. 1940

Peano, L., *Ricordi della guerra dei trent'anni, 1915–45* (Florence, 1948)

Piazza, G., *La nostra terra promessa: lettere dalla Tripolitania marzo–maggio 1911* (Rome, 1911)

Piazza, G., *Alla corte di Menelik: lettere dall'Etiopia* (Ancona, 1912)

Piazza, G., *La fiamma bilingue: momenti del dissidio ideale, 1913–1923* (Milan, 1924)

Ramaciotti, G., *Tripoli: a narrative of the principal engagements of the Italo-Turkish war* (London, 1912)

Rava, L., *Per la 'Dante Alighieri' (trenta anni di propaganda) Discorsi e ricordi 1900–1931* (Rome, 1932)

Riccio, V., *Saggi biografici* (Milan, 1924)

Rodd, J. R., 'The Italian people', *Proceedings of the British Academy*, IX (1920)

Rodd, J. R., *Social and diplomatic memories*, (3 vols, London, 1922–5)

Rodd, J. R., *Rome of the Renaissance and today* (London, 1932)

Romei Longhena, G. G., 'Ricordi della corte di Abdul Hamid', *NA*, f 1517, 1 June 1935

Sailer, E., 'Come impedimmo l'aggressione etiopica nel 1914', *NA*, f 1525, 1 Oct. 1935

Salandra, A., *La neutralità italiana (1914): ricordi e pensieri* (Milan, 1928)

Salandra, A., *L'intervento (1915): ricordi e pensieri* (Milan, 1930)

Salandra, A., *Italy and the Great War, From Neutrality to Intervention* (London, 1932)

Salandra, A., 'Corona governo e parlamento', ed. G. B. Gifuni, *La Politica Parlamentare*, X (1957)

Salazar, F. Z., *Margherita of Savoy, First Queen of Italy: her life and times* (London, 1914)

Salvemini, G., *Come siamo andati in Libia e altri scritti dal 1900 al 1915*, ed. A. Torre (Milan, 1963)

Scalabrini, G. B., *Trent'anni di apostolato: memorie e documenti*, ed. A. Scalabrini (Rome, 1909)

Bibliography

Scalia, G. (ed.), *La cultura italiana del 1900 attraverso le riviste Vol. IV*, '*Lacerba*', '*La Voce*' (*1914–1916*) (Turin, 1961)

Scarfoglio, E., *La guerra della sterlina contro il marco vista dall'Italia* (Rome [1915])

Scaroni, S., *Con Vittorio Emanuele III* (Milan, 1954)

Sforza, C., 'Sonnino and his foreign policy', *CR*, CXXXVI (1929)

Sforza, C., 'War Legends: I Italy and the Triple Alliance. II The Roman Catholic Church and the Entente', *CR*, CXLII (1932)

Sforza, C., *Europe and the Europeans: a study in historical psychology and international politics* (London, 1936)

Sforza, C., *L'Italia dal 1914 al 1944 quale io la vidi* (Milan, 1944)

Sforza, C., *Costruttori e distruttori* (Rome, 1945)

Sforza, C., *Italy and Italians* (London, 1948)

Soleri, M., *Memorie* (Rome, 1949)

Solmi, A., *Discorsi sulla storia d'Italia* (Florence, 1933)

Solmi, A. (ed.), 'Carteggio tra Salandra e Sonnino nella prima fase della neutralità italiana', *NA*, f 1510, 16 Feb. 1935

Sonnino, S., 'L'Africa italiana – appunti di viaggio', *NA*, f 435, 1 Feb. 1890

Sonnino, S., 'Beatrice', *NA*, f 1198, 16 Feb. 1922

Sonnino, S., *Discorsi parlamentari* (3 vols, Rome, 1925)

Sonnino, S., *Diario*, ed. B. F. Brown and P. Pastorelli (3 vols, Bari, 1972)

Sonnino, S., *Scritti e discorsi extraparlamentari, 1870–1922*, ed. B. F. Brown (2 vols, Bari, 1972)

Strong, S. A., 'The exhibition illustrative of the provinces of the Roman Empire at the Baths of Diocletian, Rome', *Journal of Roman Studies*, I (1911)

Sulliotti, A. I., *In Albania: sei mesi di regno da Guglielmo di Wied a Essad Pascià, da Durazzo a Vallona* (Milan, 1914)

Tamaro, A., *L'Adriatico – Golfo d'Italia – L'italianità di Trieste* (Milan, 1915)

Theodoli, A., 'La preparazione dell'impresa di Tripoli: ricordi di una missione in Turchia', *NA*, f 1496, 16 July 1934

Theodoli, A., *A cavallo di due secoli* (Rome, 1950)

Tittoni, T., *Due anni di politica estera, 1903–5: discorsi pronunciati al Senato del Regno ed alla Camera dei Deputati* (Rome, 1906)

Tittoni, T., *Sei anni di politica estera, 1903–9: discorsi pronunciati al Senato del Regno ed alla Camera dei Deputati* (Rome, 1912)

Tittoni, T., *Italy's foreign and colonial policy: a selection from the speeches delivered in the Italian parliament during his six years in office, 1903–1909*, trans. B. Quaranta Di San Severino (London, 1915)

Tittoni, T., *Il giudizio della storia sulla responsabilità della guerra* (Milan, 1916)

Tittoni, T., 'L'Italia nella Guerra dell'Intesa', *NA*, f 1067,1 July 1916

Tittoni, T., 'La responsabilità della guerra', *NA*, f 1072, 16 Sept. 1916

Tittoni, T., 'I rapporti economici tra gli alleati dopo la guerra', *NA*, f 1088, 16 May 1917

Tittoni, T., 'Giuseppe Saracco', *NA*, f 1189, 1190, 1 Oct., 16 Oct. 1921

Tittoni, T., 'Tunisia-Tripolitania e l'Italia', *NA*, f 1249, 1 April 1924

Tittoni, T., 'Ricordi personali di politica interna', *NA*, f 1369, 1370, 1 April, 16 April 1929

Tittoni, T., *Nuovi scritti di politica interna ed esterna* (Milan, 1930)

Todd, M. L., *Tripoli the Mysterious* (London, 1912)

Bibliography

Trevelyan, G. M., 'Englishmen and Italians: some aspects of their relations past and present', *Proceedings of the British Academy*, IX (1919)

Turati, F., *Discorsi parlamentari* (3 vols, Rome, 1950)

Underwood, F. M., *United Italy* (London, 1911)

Vannutelli, L., *Sguardo retrospettivo sulla mia vita nella marina* (Rome, 1959)

Varè, D., *Laughing Diplomat* (London, 1938)

Varè, D., *Twilight of the Kings* (London, 1948)

Varè, D., *The Two Impostors* (London, 1949)

Villari, L. (ed.), *The Balkan Question: the present condition of the Balkans and of European responsibilities by various writers* (London, 1905)

Villari, P., 'Dove andiamo?' *NA*, f 535, 1 Nov. 1893

Villari, P., *Scritti e Discorsi per la 'Dante'* (Rome, 1933)

Vivante, A., *Irredentismo adriatico*, Florence, 1912

Volpi, G., 'Ricordi e orizzonti balcanici', *Rassegna di Politica Internazionale*, IV (1937)

Wright, H. C. S., *Two Years under the Crescent* (London, 1913)

XXX, 'La Federazione dell'italianità', *NA*, f 885, Nov. 1908

XXX, *L'Adriatico: studio geografico, storico e politico* (Milan, 1914)

Zimmern, H., *Italy of the Italians* (rev. ed. London, 1914)

Zimmern, H., *Italian Leaders of Today* (London, 1915)

IV. SECONDARY SOURCES: ITALY

Abrate, M., *La lotta sindacale nella industrializzazione in Italia, 1906–1926* (Turin, 1967)

Alberti, A., *L'Opere di S.E. il Generale Pollio e l'esercito* (Rome, 1923)

Alberti, A., *Il generale Falkenhayn: le relazioni tra i capi di S.M. della Triplice* (Rome, 1924)

Alberti, M., *L'irredentismo senza romanticismi* (Como, 1936)

Albertini, A., *Vita di Luigi Albertini* (Rome, 1945)

Albertini, L., *The Origins of the War of 1914*, trans. I. M. Massey (3 vols, London, 1952–7)

Alcock, A. E., *The History of the South Tyrol Question* (Geneva, 1970)

Allain, J-C., 'Les débuts du conflit italo-turc: octobre 1911–janvier 1912 (d'après les archives françaises)', *RHMC*, XVIII (1971)

Andrè, G., *L'Italia e il Mediterraneo alla vigilia della prima guerra mondiale*, vol. 1 (Milan, 1967)

Aquarone, A., 'La politica coloniale italiana dopo Adua: Ferdinando Martini, Governatore in Eritrea', *RSR*, LXII (1975)

Ara, A., 'La questione dell'Università italiana in Austria', *RSR*, LX (1973)

Ara, A., *Ricerche sugli austro-italiani e l'ultima Austria* (Rome, 1974)

Arè, G., *Economia e politica nell'Italia liberale (1890–1915)* (Bologna, 1974)

Arè, G. and Giusti, L., 'La scoperta dell'imperialismo nella cultura italiana del primo novecento', *NRS*, LVIII–LIX (1974–5)

Arfé, G., *Storia del socialismo italiano (1892–1926)* (Turin, 1965)

Askew, W. C., *Europe and Italy's Acquisition of Libya, 1911–12* (Durham, N.C., 1942)

Askew, W. C., 'The Austro-Italian antagonism, 1896–1914' in L. P. Wallace and W. C. Askew (eds.), *Power, Public Opinion and Diplomacy. Essays in Honor of Eber Malcolm Carroll* (Durham, N.C., 1959)

Barclay, G. St J., *The Rise and Fall of the New Roman Empire: Italy's bid for world power, 1890–1943* (London, 1973)

Bibliography

Barié, O., 'La "politica nazionale" del *Corriere della Sera* dalla crisi del 1908 alla guerra di Libia', *Il Risorgimento*, XX (1968)

Barié, O., 'La "politica nazionale" del *Corriere della Sera* dalla guerra di Libia alla Grande Guerra', *Il Risorgimento*, XX (1968)

Barié, O., *Luigi Albertini* (Turin, 1972)

Belloni, C., *Dizionario storico dei banchieri italiani* (Florence, 1951)

Bertoldi, S., *Vittorio Emanuele III* (Turin, 1970)

Bonelli, F., *Lo sviluppo di una grande impresa in Italia, la Terni dal 1884 al 1962* (Turin, 1975)

Borgata, G., *Quadro delle società azionarie italiane alla vigilia della crisi europea* (Rome, 1916)

Bosworth, R. J. B., 'Sir Rennell Rodd e l'Italia', *NRS*, LIV (1970)

Bosworth, R. J. B., 'Britain and Italy's acquisition of the Dodecanese, 1912–1915', *HJ*, XIII (1970)

Bosworth, R. J. B., 'The opening of the Victor Emmanuel Monument', *IQ*, XVIII (1975)

Bosworth, R. J. B., 'The Albanian forests of Signor Giacomo Vismara: a case study of Italian economic imperialism during the Foreign Ministry of Antonino Di San Giuliano', *HJ*, XVIII (1975)

Cafagna, L., *The Industrial Revolution in Italy, 1830–1914* (London, 1971)

Caizzi, B., *Camillo e Adriano Olivetti* (Turin, 1962)

Caliaro, M. and Francesconi, M., *L'Apostolo degli Emigranti Giovanni Battista Scalabrini, Vescovo di Piacenza, la sua opera e la sua spiritualità* (Milan, 1968)

Candeloro, G., *Storia dell'Italia moderna Vol. VII: la crisi di fine secolo e l'età giolittiana* (Milan, 1974)

Caracciolo, A., *Roma capitale* (Rome, 1974)

Caracciolo, M., *L'Italia e i suoi alleati nella Grande Guerra* (Milan, 1932)

Carazzi, M., *La Società Geografica Italiana e l'esplorazione coloniale in Africa (1867–1900)* (Florence, 1972)

Carocci, G., *Giolitti e l'età giolittiana: dall'inizio del secolo alla prima guerra mondiale* (Turin, 1961)

Carrà, A., 'Correnti di opinione in Sicilia sull'impresa libica', *Storia e Politica*, V (1966)

Carrà, A., *La Sicilia orientale dall'Unità all'impresa libica* (Catania, 1968)

Carrié, R. Albrecht-, 'Italian colonial policy, 1914–1918', *JMH*, 18 (1946)

Casalegno, C., *La Regina Margherita* (Turin, 1956)

Castronovo, V., *La stampa italiana dall'unità al fascismo*, Bari, 1970

Castronovo, V., *Economia e Società in Piemonte dall'unità al 1914* (Milan, 1969)

Catalano, F., *Luigi Luzzatti, la figura e l'opera* (Milan, 1965)

Cataluccio, F., *Antonio Di San Giuliano e la politica estera italiana dal 1900 al 1914* (Florence, 1935)

Cataluccio, F., *Italia e Francia in Tunisia (1878–1939)* (Rome, 1939)

Cataluccio, F., *La politica estera di E. Visconti Venosta* (Florence, 1940)

Cataluccio, F., *La 'Nostra Guerra': L'Italia nella guerra mondiale* (Rome, 1940)

Cataluccio, F., 'Lotte e ambizioni di Antonio Di San Giuliano', in M. M. Libelli (ed.), *Studi in onore di Niccolò Rodolico* (Florence, 1944)

Cataluccio, F., 'La formazione culturale e politica di A. Di San Giuliano', *NA*, f 2025, Nov. 1969

Chabod, F., 'Considerazioni sulla politica estera dell'Italia dal 1870 al 1915', in G. Pepe (ed.), *Orientamenti per la storia d'Italia nel Risorgimento* (Bari, 1952)

Chabod, F., *Storia della politica estera italiana dal 1870 al 1896*, vol. I, part II (Bari, 1965)

439

Bibliography

Cian, V., *Luigi Federzoni, profilo* (Piacenza, 1924)

Ciasca, R., *Storia coloniale dell'Italia contemporanea da Assab all'Impero* (Milan, 1938)

Cilibrizzi, S., *Storia parlamentare politica e diplomatica d'Italia da Novara a Vittorio Veneto* (8 vols, Naples, 1939–52)

Clough, S. B., *The Economic History of Modern Italy* (New York, 1964)

Colapietra, R., *Leonida Bissolati* (Milan, 1958)

Collotti, F. (ed.), *Storiografia del Risorgimento triestino* (Trieste, 1955)

Consiglio, A., *Vita di Vittorio Emanuele* (Milan, 1950)

Coppa, F. J., 'Giolitti and the Gentiloni pact between myth and reality', *CHR*, LIII (1967)

Coppa, F. J., 'The Italian tariff and the conflict between agriculture and industry: the commercial policy of Liberal Italy, 1860–1922', *JEH*, XXX (1970)

Coppa, F. J., 'Economic and ethical liberalism in conflict: the extraordinary liberalism of Giovanni Giolitti', *JMH*, 42 (1970)

Coppa, F. J., *Planning, Protectionism and Politics in Liberal Italy: Economics and politics in the Giolittian age* (Washington, D.C., 1971)

Corselli, R., *Cadorna* (Milan, 1937)

Croce, B., *A History of Italy 1871–1915* (Oxford, 1929)

Cunsolo, R. S., 'Libya, Italian Nationalism and the revolt against Giolitti', *JMH*, 37 (1965)

D'Alessandro, A., 'Il Banco di Roma e la guerra di Libia', *Storia e Politica*, VII (1968)

De Agostini, E., *La Reale Società Geografica Italiana e la sua opera dalla fondazione ad oggi (1867–1936)* (Rome, 1937)

De Biase, C., 'Antonio Salandra', *Archivio Storico Pugliese*, VII (1954)

De Biase, C., 'La crisi del governo italiano del marzo 1914', *NA*, f 1897, Jan. 1959

De Biase, C., *La rivelazione di Giolitti del dicembre 1914* (Modena, 1960)

De Biase, C., 'Le trattative con l'Austria alla vigilia dell'intervento', *Osservatore politico letterario*, 1 (1961)

De Biase, C., 'Concezione nazionale e concezione democratica dell'intervento italiano nella prima guerra mondiale', *RSR*, LI (1964)

De Biase, C., *L'Aquila d'Oro: storia dello Stato Maggiore Italiano (1861–1945)* (Milan, 1970)

De Chaurand De Saint Eustache, F., *Come l'esercito italiano entrò in guerra* (Milan, 1929)

Decleva, E., *Da Adua a Sarajevo: la politica estera italiana e la Francia 1896–1914* (Bari, 1971)

Decleva, E., *L'Italia e la politica internazionale dal 1870 al 1914: l'ultima fra le grandi potenze* (Milan, 1974)

De Felice, R., *Mussolini il rivoluzionario 1883–1920* (Turin, 1965)

Degl'Innocenti, M., *Il socialismo italiano e la guerra di Libia* (Rome, 1976)

De Grand, A. J., 'The Italian Nationalist Association in the period of Italian neutrality August 1914–May 1915', *JMH*, 43 (1971)

Del Boca, A., *Gli italiani in Africa orientale: dall'unità alla marcia su Roma* (Bari, 1976)

De Rosa, G., *Filippo Meda e l'età liberale* (Florence, 1959)

Di Giamberardino, O., *L'ammiraglio Millo dall'impresa dei Dardanelli alla passione Dalmatica* (Livorno, 1950)

Dore, G., *La democrazia italiana e l'emigrazione in America* (Brescia, 1964)

Dore, G., 'Some social and historical aspects of Italian emigration to America', *JSH*, 2 (1968)

Esposito, R. F., *La Massoneria e l'Italia dal 1800 ai nostri giorni* (Rome, 1956)

Fatica, M., 'Bilancio di contributi recenti sulle origini e i fini dell'intervento italiano nella prima guerra mondiale', *Critica Storica*, V (1966)

Bibliography

Ferraris, L. V., 'L'amministrazione centrale del Ministero degli Esteri italiano nel suo sviluppo storico (1848–1954)', *RSPI*, XXI (1954)

Foerster, R. F., *The Italian Emigration of Our Times* (Cambridge, Mass., 1919)

Gabriele, M., 'Origini della convenzione navale italo-austro-germanica del 1913', *RSR*, LII (1965)

Gabriele, M., *Le convenzioni navali della Triplice* (Rome, 1969)

Gaeta, F., *Nazionalismo italiano* (Naples, 1965)

Gaeta, F. (ed.), *La stampa nazionalista* (Rocca San Casciano, 1965)

Galante Garrone, A., *I radicali in Italia (1849–1925)* (Milan, 1973)

Gallavresi, G., *Italia e Austria (1859–1914)* (Milan, 1922)

Ganapini, L., *Il nazionalismo cattolico: i cattolici e la politica estera in Italia dal 1871 al 1914* (Bari, 1970)

Garzia, I., 'Le origini dell'art. 15 del Patto di Londra', *Storia e Politica*, XIV (1975)

Gentile, E., '*La Voce* e l'età giolittiana', *SC*, II (1971)

Gentile, E., 'La politica di Marinetti', *SC*, VII (1976)

Gerschenkron, A., 'Notes on the rate of industrial growth in Italy, 1881–1913', *JEH*, XV (1955)

Giannini, A., *I rapporti italo-inglesi* (Milan, 1940)

Giannini, A., *L'Albania dall'indipendenza all'unione con l'Italia (1913–1939)* (Milan, 1940)

Giannini, A., *L'ultima fase della questione orientale (1913–1939)* (Milan, 1941)

Giuffrida, R., *Il Banco di Sicilia* (Palermo, 1971)

Glanville, J. L. *Italy's Relations with England, 1896–1905* (Baltimore, 1934)

Gottlieb, W. W., *Studies in Secret Diplomacy During the First World War* (London, 1957)

Grassi, F., 'L'industria tessile e l'imperialismo italiano in Somalia (1896–1911)', *SC*, IV (1973)

Gregori, F., *La vita e l'opera di un grande vescovo: mons. Giov. Battista Scalabrini (1839–1905)* (Turin, 1934)

Halpern, P. G., *The Mediterranean Naval Situation, 1908–1914* (Cambridge, Mass., 1971)

Hentze, M., *Pre-Fascist Italy: the rise and fall of the parliamentary regime* (London, 1939)

Hess, R. L., 'Italy and Africa: colonial ambitions in the First World War', *JAH*, IV (1963)

Hess, R. L., *Italian Colonialism in Somalia* (Chicago, 1966)

Hollis, C., *Italy in Africa* (London, 1941)

Hughes, H. S., *The United States and Italy* (rev. ed., Cambridge, Mass., 1965)

Istat, *Compendio delle statistiche elettorali italiane dal 1848 al 1934* (2 vols, Rome, 1946–7)

Jemolo, A. C., *Church and State in Italy, 1850–1950* (Oxford, 1960)

Joll, J., *Intellectuals in Politics: three biographical essays* (London, 1960)

Katz, R., *The Fall of the House of Savoy: a study in the relevance of the commonplace or the vulgarity of history* (London, 1972)

Lavagetto, A., *La vita eroica del capitano Bottego (1893–1897)* (Milan, 1934)

Leti, G., *Carboneria e massoneria nel Risorgimento italiano: saggio di critica storica* (Bologna, 1925)

Levra, U., 'Repressione e progetti reazionari dopo i tumulti del '98', *RSC*, IV (1975)

Levra, U., *Il colpo di stato della borghesia* (Milan, 1975)

Lodolini, E., 'Mediterraneo, Adriatico, Intervento nella politica del partito mazziniano italiano (1900–1918)', *RSR*, XXXVIII (1951)

Longhitano, R., *Antonino Di San Giuliano* (Rome, 1954)

Lo Presti, S., *Memorie storiche di Catania: fatti e leggende* (Catania, 1957)

441

Bibliography

Lowe, C. J., 'Britain and Italian intervention, 1914–1915', *HJ*, XII (1969)

Lowe, C. J. and Marzari, F., *Italian Foreign Policy, 1870–1940* (London, 1975)

Luzzatto, G., *L'economia italiana dal 1861 al 1914*, Vol 1, (*1861–1894*) (Milan, 1963)

Macartney, M. H. H. and Cremona, P., *Italy's foreign and colonial policy, 1914–1937* (London, 1938)

McLean, D., 'British finance and foreign policy in Turkey: the Smyrna–Aidin railway settlement 1913–14', *HJ*, XIX (1976)

Malatesta, A., *Ministri, deputati, Senatori dal 1848 al 1922* (3 vols, Milan, 1940)

Malgeri, F., *La guerra libica (1911–1912)* (Rome, 1970)

Maltese, P., *La terra promessa: la guerra italo-turca e la conquista della Libia 1911–1912* (Milan, 1968)

Manzotti, F., *La polemica sull'emigrazione nell'Italia unita fino alla prima guerra mondiale* (Milan, 1962)

Manzotti, F., *Il socialismo riformista in Italia* (Florence, 1965)

Mazzetti, M., 'Recenti studi italiani di storia militare', *SC*, I (1970)

Mazzetti, M., 'L'Italia e le convenzioni militari segrete della Triplice Alleanza', *SC*, I (1970)

Mazzetti, M., 'Spese militari italiane e preparazione nel 1914', *Clio*, VIII (1972)

Mazzetti, M., 'L'Italia e la crisi albanese del marzo-maggio 1913', *SC*, IV (1973)

Mazzetti, M., *L'esercito italiano nella triplice alleanza* (Naples, 1974)

Miccichè, G., *Dopoguerra e fascismo in Sicilia* (Rome, 1976)

Michel, E., *Esuli italiani in Tunisia (1815–1861)* (Milan, 1941)

Miège, J-L., *L'imperialisme colonial italien de 1870 à nos jours* (Paris, 1968)

Milanini Kemény, A., *La società d'esplorazione commerciale in Africa e la politica coloniale (1879–1914)* (Florence, 1973)

Milza, P., 'Les rapports économiques franco-italiens en 1914–1915 et leurs incidences politiques', *RHMC*, XIV (1967)

Ministero Della Guerra, Ufficio Storico, *L'esercito italiano nella grande guerra (1915–1918)*, vol. I (Rome, 1927)

Minniti, F., 'Esercito e politica da Porta Pia alla Triplice Alleanza', *SC*, IV (1973)

Missori, M., *Governi, alte cariche dello stato e prefetti del regno d'Italia* (Rome, 1973)

Mola, A. A., *Stampa e vita pubblica di provincia nell'età giolittiana* (Milan, 1971)

Mola, A. A. (ed.), *L'età giolittiana* (Bologna, 1971)

Mola, A. A., *Storia della Massoneria italiana dall'Unità alla Repubblica* (Milan, 1976)

Molinelli, R., 'Per una storia del nazionalismo italiano', *RSR*, L (1963)

Molinelli, R., 'Nazionalisti cattolici e liberali (Il Nazionalismo italiano dal congresso di Roma a quello di Milano)', *RSR*, LII (1965)

Molinelli, R., 'Il Nazionalismo italiano e l'impresa di Libia', *RSR*, LIII (1966)

Molinelli, R., 'I Nazionalisti italiani e l'intervento a fianco degli imperi centrali', *RSR*, LIX (1972)

Monteleone, R., 'Iniziative e convegni socialisti italo-austriaci per la pace nel decennio prebellico', *RSR*, X (1967)

Monticone, A., 'Salandra e Sonnino verso la decisione dell'intervento', *RSPI*, XXIV (1957)

Monticone, A., *Nitti e la grande guerra, 1914–18* (Milan, 1967)

Monticone, A., *La Germania e la neutralità italiana, 1914–1915* (Bologna, 1971)

Mori, G., 'Le guerre parallele. L'industria elettrica in Italia nel periodo della grande guerra (1914–1919)', *SS*, XIV (1973)

Bibliography

Mori, R., 'La penetrazione pacifica italiana in Libia dal 1907 al 1911 e il Banco di Roma', *RSPI*, XXIV (1957)

Mosca, O., *Volpi di Misurata* (Rome, 1928)

Moscati, A., 'Pelloux, presidente del consiglio', *RSR*, LV (1968)

Neppi Modona, G., *Sciopero, potere politico e magistratura 1870–1922* (Bari, 1969)

Odenigo, A., *Piero Foscari: una vita esemplare* (Rocca San Casciano, 1959)

Pastorelli, P., 'L'Albania nel Patto di Londra', *Clio*, V (1969)

Pastorelli, P., *L'Albania nella politica estera italiana 1914–1920* (Naples, 1970)

Paternò Castello Di Carcaci, F., *I Paternò di Sicilia* (Catania, 1936)

Pepe, A., *Storia della CGdL dalla fondazione alla guerra di Libia, 1905–1911* (Bari, 1972)

Pepe, A., *Storia della CGdL dalla guerra di Libia all'intervento, 1911–1915* (Bari, 1971)

Pescosolido, G., 'Il dibattito coloniale nella stampa italiana e la battaglia di Adua', *SC*, IV (1973)

Peteani, L., *La questione libica nella diplomazia europea* (Florence, 1939)

Piccioli, A., *La pace di Ouchy* (Rome, 1935)

Pierotti, M., *L'Istituto Coloniale Italiano, sue origini, suo sviluppo* (Rome, 1922)

Pincherle, M., 'La preparazione dell' opinione pubblica all'impresa di Libia', *RSR*, LVI (1969)

Pinzani, C., 'I socialisti italiani e francesi nel periodo della neutralità italiana (1914–1915)', *SS*, XV (1974)

Piscitelli, E., 'Francesco Crispi, Primo Levi e "la Riforma" ', *RSR*, XXXVII (1950)

Po, G., *Il Grande Ammiraglio Paolo Thaon di Revel* (Turin, 1936)

Pryce, R., 'Italy and the outbreak of the First World War', *CHJ*, XI (1954)

Rainero, R., *L'anticolonialismo italiano da Assab ad Adua (1869–1896)* (Milan, 1971)

Renzi, W. A., 'Italy's neutrality and entrance into the Great War: a re-examination', *AHR*, LXXIII (1967–8)

Renzi, W. A., 'The Entente and the Vatican during the period of Italian neutrality, August 1914–May 1915', *HJ*, XIII (1970)

Restifo, G., 'L'esercito italiano alla vigilia della grande guerra', *SS*, XI (1970)

Rochat, G., 'La preparazione dell'esercito italiano nell'inverno 1914–15 in relazione alle informazioni disponibili sulla guerra disposizione', *Risorgimento*, XIII (1961)

Rochat, G., 'L'esercito italiano nell'estate 1914', *NRS*, XLV (1961)

Rochat, G., *Il colonialismo italiano* (Turin, 1974)

Romano, S. F., *Storia dei fasci siciliani* (Bari, 1959)

Rota, E., 'I movimenti pacifisti dell'800 e '900 e le organizzazioni internazionali' in *Questioni di storia contemporanea* (Milan, 1952)

Rusinow, D. L., *Italy's Austrian Heritage, 1919–1946* (Oxford, 1969)

Sabbatucci, G., 'Il problema dell'irredentismo e le origini del movimento nazionalista in Italia', *SC*, I–II (1970–1)

Salata, F., 'Ministeri degli affari esteri del Regno d'Italia: Il Marchese di San Giuliano' *Storia e politica internazionale*, II (1940)

Salomone, A. W., *Italy in the Giolittian Era: Italian democracy in the making, 1900–14* (Philadelphia, 1945; new ed. 1960)

Salvatorelli, L., *La Triplice Alleanza, storia diplomatica 1877–1912* (Rome, 1939)

Salvatorelli, L., 'Giolitti', *RSI*, LXII (1950)

Salvemini, G., 'Pasquale Villari', *NRS*, II (1918)

Bibliography

Salvemini, G., *La politica estera italiana dal 1871 al 1915*, ed. A. Torre (Milan, 1970)

Sandonà, A., *L'irredentismo nelle lotte politiche e nelle contese diplomatiche italo-austriache* (3 vols, Bologna, 1932–8)

Scheider, W., 'Fattori dell'imperialismo italiano prima del 1914–15', *SC*, III (1972)

Schmitt, B., 'The Italian documents for July 1914', *JMH*, XXXVII (1965)

Sciacca, L., *Catania com'era* (Catania, 1974)

Segrè, C. G., *Fourth Shore: the Italian colonization of Libya* (Chicago, 1974)

Serra, E., *Camille Barrère e l'intesa italo-francese* (Milan, 1950)

Serra, E., 'Vittorio Emanuele III diplomatico', *NA*, f 1824, 1952

Serra, E., *L'Intesa Mediterranea del 1902: una fase risolutiva nei rapporti italo-inglesi* (Milan, 1957)

Serra, E., 'Giuseppe Tornielli Brusati di Vergano', *Storia e Politica*, II (1963)

Serra, E., 'La coerenza di Salvemini', *NA*, f 2035, 1970

Sertoli Salis, R., *Le isole italiane dell'Egeo dall'occupazione alla sovranità* (Rome, 1939)

Sillani, T. (ed.), *L'Italia di Vittorio Emanuele III, 1900–1925* (Rome, 1926)

Sillani, T. (ed.), *La Libia in venti anni di occupazione, studi e documenti* (Rome, 1932)

Sillani, T. (ed.), *L'Italia e il Levante, studi e documenti* (Rome, 1934)

Sillani, T. (ed.), *L'Italia e l'Oriente medio ed estremo, studi e documenti* (Rome, 1935)

Silva, P., *L'Italia fra le grandi potenze (1882–1914)* (Rome, 1931)

Silvestri, M., 'La politica estera del Regno d'Italia', *Storia e Politica*, III (1964)

Smith, D. Mack, *Italy, a Modern History* (rev. ed., Ann Arbor, 1969)

Smith, D. Mack, *Le guerre del Duce* (Bari, 1976)

Solari, L., *Marconi nell'intimità e nel lavoro* (Milan, 1940)

Solmi, A., 'Le Origini del Patto di Londra', *Politica*, XVII (1923)

Solmi, A., 'La guerra libica e il Dodecanneso nei documenti segreti della diplomazia russa', *Politica*, XVIII–XIX (1923–4)

Spadolini, G., *Giolitti e i cattolici, 1901–1914 con documenti inediti* (Florence, 1960)

Spadolini, G., 'Giolitti e il Parlamento', *NA*, f 2012, Aug. 1968

Spadolini, G., 'Ricordo di Mario Toscano (con una nota biobibliografica))', *NA*, f 2014, Oct. 1968

Spadolini, G., *Il Mondo di Giolitti* (Florence, 1970)

Spinazzola, V., *Federico De Roberto e il verismo* (Milan, 1961)

Stickney, E. P., *Southern Albania or Northern Epirus in European International Affairs, 1912–1923* (Stanford, 1926)

Swire, J., *Albania: the rise of a kingdom* (London, 1929)

Taccari, M., *I Florio* (Caltanissetta, 1967)

Tadini, G., *Il Marchese Di San Giuliano nella tragica estate del 1914* (Rome, 1945)

Tamagna, F., *Italy's Interests and Policies in the Far East* (New York, 1941)

Tamborra, A., 'The Rise of Italian industry and the Balkans (1900–1914)', *Journal of European Economic History*, 3 (1974)

Thayer, J. A., *Italy and the Great War: politics and culture, 1870–1915* (Madison, 1964)

Tommasini, F., *L'Italia alla vigilia della guerra: la politica estera di Tommaso Tittoni* (5 vols, Bologna, 1934–41)

Tommasini, F., 'La conferenza d'Algeciras e l'Italia', *NA*, f 1517, 1 June 1935

Torre, A., 'Origini dell'accordo tripartito per la Abissinia', *NA*, f 1534, 16 Feb. 1936

Torre, A., 'La preparazione diplomatica dell'impresa libica', *Rassegna di Politica Internazionale*, XIV–XV (1936–7)

Bibliography

Torre, A., 'Il Mediterraneo alla vigilia della guerra 1914–1918', *NA*, f 1602, 16 Dec. 1938

Torre, A., 'L'impresa libica e un mancato accordo mediterraneo', *Storia e Politica Internazionale*, 1 (1939)

Torre, A., 'Italia e Albania durante le guerre balcaniche', *Rivista d'Albania*, 2–4 (1940)

Torre, A., *Alla vigilia della guerra mondiale, 1914–18* (Milan, 1942)

Torre, A., 'Il Marchese di San Giuliano fra la neutralità e l'intervento', *Nova Historia*, 22–5 (1954)

Torre, A., 'Ricordo di Antonino Di San Giuliano', *NA*, f 1849, Jan. 1955

Torre, A., 'Il progettato attacco austro-ungherese alla Serbia del luglio 1913' in *Studi Storici in onore di Gioacchino Volpe per il suo 80° compleanno*, vol. II (Florence, 1958)

Torre, A., 'Il primo conflitto mondiale 1914–18' in *La politica estera italiana dal 1914 al 1943* (Turin, 1963)

Torre, A., 'L'azione di San Giuliano nel luglio 1914', *Clio*, V (1969)

Torre, A., 'Dimostrazioni antiaustriache del maggio 1914 in un carteggio di Sangiuliano–Salandra' in L. Montagna (ed.), *Studi storici in memoria di Leopoldo Marchetti* (Milan, 1969)

Torre, A., 'La posizione dell'Italia fra gli alleati nella prima guerra mondiale', *RSR*, LVI (1969)

Torrey, G. E., 'The Rumanian-Italian agreement of 23 September 1914', *SEER*, XLIV (1966)

Toscano, M., *Il Patto di Londra* (Bologna, 1934)

Toscano, M., *Pagine di storia diplomatica contemporanea*, vol. 1 (Milan, 1963)

Toscano, M., 'Le origini diplomatiche dell'art.9 del patto di Londra relativo agli eventuali compensi all'Italia in Asia Minore, *Storia e Politica*, IV (1965)

Toscano, M., 'Rivelazioni e nuovi documenti sul negoziato di Londra per l'ingresso dell'Italia nella prima guerra mondiale', *NA*, f 1976–9, Aug.–Nov. 1965

Toscano, M., *Storia diplomatica della questione dell'Alto Adige* (Bari, 1967)

Toscano, M., 'Imperiali e il negoziato per il patto di Londra', *Storia e Politica*, VIII (1968)

Treves, P., *L'idea di Roma e la cultura italiana del secolo XIX* (Milan, 1962)

Ufficio Storico Della R. Marina, *La Marina italiana nella grande guerra*, vol. 1 (Florence, 1935)

Ullrich, H., *Le elezioni del 1913 a Roma: i liberali fra massoneria e vaticano* (Milan, 1972)

Valeri, N., *Giovanni Giolitti* (Turin, 1971)

Valiani, L., 'Recenti pubblicazioni sulla prima guerra mondiale', *RSI*, LXXII (1960)

Valiani, L., 'Il partito socialista italiano dal 1900 al 1918', *RSI*, LXXV (1963)

Valiani, L., 'Le origini della guerra del 1914 e dell'intervento italiano nelle ricerche e nelle pubblicazioni dell'ultimo ventennio', *RSI*, LXXVIII (1966)

Valiani, L., 'Italian-Austro-Hungarian negotiations, 1914–1915', *JCH*, 1 (1966)

Valiani, L., 'Italia ed Austria 1866–1915 nella storiografia italiana', *Storia e Politica*, XII (1973)

Valori, F., 'Il cinquantennio dell'impresa libica', *NA*, f 1931, Dec. 1961

Varley, D. H., *A bibliography of Italian colonisation in Africa with a section on Abyssinia* (London, 1936)

Vidal, C., 'Le duel diplomatique Poincaré-Tittoni, 1909–1914', *RSR*, XXXVIII (1951)

Vigezzi, B., 'I problemi della neutralità e della guerra nel carteggio Salandra–Sonnino (1914–1917)', *NRS*, XLV (1961)

Vigezzi, B., 'Il suffragio universale e la 'crisi' del liberalismo in Italia (dicembre 1913–aprile 1914)', *NRS*, XLVIII (1964)

Vigezzi, B., 'La neutralità italiana del luglio-agosto 1914 e il problema dell'Austria-Ungheria', *Clio*, 1 (1965)

Bibliography

Vigezzi, B., *L'Italia di fronte alla prima guerra mondiale*, vol. 1 (Milan, 1966)

Vigezzi, B., *Da Giolitti a Salandra* (Florence, 1969)

Vigezzi, B., 'L'opinione pubblica italiana e la Francia nell'estate 1914', *NRS*, LIX (1975)

Vigezzi, B., *Giolitti e Turati: un incontro mancato* (2 vols, Milan, 1976)

Vitale, E., *La riforma degli istituti di emissione e gli 'scandali bancari' in Italia, 1892–1896* (3 vols, Rome, 1972)

Volpe, G., *L'Italia nella triplice alleanza, 1882–1915* (Milan, 1939)

Volpe, G., *Vittorio Emanuele III* (Milan, 1939)

Volpe, G., *Il popolo italiano tra la pace e la guerra (1914–1915)* (Milan, 1940)

Volpe, G., *L'impresa di Tripoli, 1911–1912* (Rome, 1946)

Watson, C. Seton-, *Italy from Liberalism to Fascism, 1870–1925* (London, 1967)

Webster, R. A., 'From Insurrection to Intervention: the Italian crisis of 1914', *IQ*, V (1961)

Webster, R. A., 'Autarky, expansion and the underlying continuity of the Italian State', *IQ*, VIII (1964)

Webster, R. A., *L'imperialismo industriale italiano 1908–1915: studio sul prefascismo* (Turin, 1974)

Webster, R. A., *Industrial Imperialism in Italy 1908–1915* (Berkeley, 1975)

Whittam, J., *The Politics of the Italian Army, 1861–1918* (London, 1977)

Wollemborg, L., *Politica estera italiana, anteguerra e guerra (1882–1917)* (Rome, 1938)

Zaghi, C., *L'Africa nella coscienza europea e l'imperialismo italiano* (Naples, 1973)

Zazo, A., *La politica estera del regno delle due Sicilie nel 1859–60* (Naples, 1940)

V. PRIMARY SOURCES: OTHER COUNTRIES

Asquith, H. H., *The Genesis of the War* (London, 1923)

Asquith, H. H., *Memories and Reflections, 1852–1927* (2 vols., London, 1928)

Barrère, C., 'L'Italie e l'agonie de la paix en 1914', *RDM*, 95, 1 Oct. 1926

Barrère, C., 'Les responsabilités du Prince de Bülow', *RDM*, 101, 1 May 1931

Barrère, C. 'Le prélude de l'offensive allemande de 1905', *RDM*, 102, 1 Feb. 1932

Barrère, C., 'Souvenirs diplomatiques – la chute de Delcassé', *RDM*, 103, 1 Jan. 1933

Barrère, C., 'Lettres à Delcassé', *Revue de Paris*, XLIV (1937)

Barrère, C., 'Diplomatic recollections: the conference of Saint Jean de Maurienne', *National Review*, 110 (1938)

Boyle, C. S. C., 10th. Earl of Cork and Orrey, *My Naval Life, 1886–1941* (London, 1942)

Bülow, B. H. von, *Memoirs* (4 vols, London, 1930–2)

Burian, S., *Austria in Dissolution* (London, 1925)

Cambon, P., *Correspondence, 1870–1924* (3 vols, Paris, 1946)

Chamberlain, J. A., *Seen in Passing* (London, 1937)

Chirol, V., *Fifty Years in a Changing World* (London, 1927)

Churchill, W. S., *The World Crisis* (6 vols, London, 1923–31)

Conrad von Hötzendorf, F., *Aus meiner Dienstzeit, 1906–1918* (5 vols, Vienna, 1921–3)

Djemal Pasha, A., *Memories of a Turkish Statesman 1913–1919* (London, n.d.)

Ernst, O. (ed.), *Franz Joseph as Revealed by His Letters* (London, 1927)

Esher, R., *Journals and Letters* (4 vols, London, 1934–8)

Lloyd George, D., *War Memoirs*, vol. 1 (London, 1938)

Goschen, E., 'Lettere a Maria Pansa (1914–1924)' ed. E. Serra, *NA*, f 1935, 1962

Bibliography

Gregory, J. D., *On the Edge of Diplomacy: rambles and reflections, 1902–1928* (London, 1928)

Grey, E., *Twenty-five Years, 1892–1916* (2 vols, London, 1925)

Haldane, R. B., *Before the War* (London, 1920)

Hardinge, C., *Old Diplomacy* (London, 1947)

Hoyos, A., 'Russia's pre-war policy', *CR*, CXXXV (1929)

Hohler, T., *Diplomatic Petrel* (London, 1942)

Kann, R. A., 'Emperor William II and Archduke Franz Ferdinand in their correspondence', *AHR*, LVII (1952)

Laroche, J., *Quinze ans à Rome avec Camille Barrère, (1898–1913)* (Paris, 1948)

Lennox, A. G. (ed.), *The Diary of Lord Bertie of Thame, 1914–18*, vol. I (London, 1924)

Levine, I. D. (ed.), *The Kaiser's Letters to the Tsar* (London, 1924)

Lichnowksy, K. M., *Heading for the Abyss* (London, 1928)

Loiseau, C., 'Ma mission auprès du Vatican (1914–1918)', *RHD*, LXXIV (1960)

Lützow, H. von, *Im diplomatischen Dienst der K.U.K. Monarchie* (Munich, 1971)

Marder, A., *Fear God and Dread Nought: the correspondence of Admiral of the Fleet, Lord Fisher of Kilverstone* (3 vols, London, 1952)

McKenna, S., *Reginald McKenna, 1863–1943, A Memoir* (London, 1948)

Nicholas, Prince of Greece, *Political Memoirs, 1914–1917: pages from my diary* (London, 1928)

Nekludoff, A., *Diplomatic Reminiscences, 1911–17* (London, 1920)

Paléologue, M., *The Turning point: three critical years, 1904–6* (London, 1935)

Petrie, C., *The Life and Letters of the Right Hon. Sir Austen Chamberlain*, vol. I (London, 1939)

Poincaré, R., *The Origins of the War* (London, 1922)

Poincaré, R., *Memoirs* (4 vols, London, 1926–30)

Rodd, J. R., *Frederick Crown Prince and Emperor* (London, 1888)

Rodd, J. R., *The Customs and Lore of Modern Greece* (Chicago, 1938)

Rumbold, H., *The War Crisis in Berlin, July–August 1914* (London, 1940)

Steed, H. Wickham, *Through Thirty Years 1892–1922: a personal narrative* (2 vols, London, 1924)

Tcharykov, N. V., 'Sazonoff', *CR*, CXXXIII (1928)

Tcharykov, N. V., 'Reminiscences of Nicholas II', *CR*, CXXXIV (1928)

Tirpitz, A. von, *My Memoirs* (2 vols, London, n.d.)

Vansittart, R. G., *The Mist Procession* (London, 1958)

Viviani, R., *As We See It: France and the truth about the war* (London, n.d.)

VI. SECONDARY SOURCES: OTHER COUNTRIES AND GENERAL

Abrams, L. and Miller, D. J., 'Who were the French colonialists? A reassessment of the *parti colonial*, 1890–1914' *HJ*, XIX (1976)

Ahmad, F., *The Young Turks: the Committee of Union and Progress in Turkish politics 1908–1914* (Oxford, 1969)

Anderson, E. N., *The First Moroccan Crisis, 1904–1906* (Chicago, 1930)

Anderson, M. S., *The Eastern Question, 1774–1923* (London, 1966)

Andrew, C. M., *Théophile Delcassé and the Making of the Entente Cordiale: a reappraisal of French foreign policy, 1898–1905* (London, 1968)

Bibliography

Andrew, C. M. and Kanya-Forstner, A. S., 'The French "Colonial Party": its composition, aims and influence, 1885–1914', *HJ*, XIV (1971)

Andrew, C. M. and Kanya-Forstner, A. S., 'The French Colonial Party and French colonial war aims, 1914–1918', *HJ*, XVII (1974)

Balfour, M., *The Kaiser and His Times* (London, 1964)

Barnes, H. E., *The Genesis of the World War* (New York, 1927)

Berghahn, V. R., *Germany and the Approach of War in 1914* (London, 1973)

Bestuzhev, I. V., 'Russian foreign policy, February–June 1914', *JCH*, I (1966)

Binion, R. *Defeated leaders: the political fate of Caillaux, Jouvenel and Tardieu* (New York, 1960)

Blaisdell, D. C. *European Financial Control in the Ottoman Empire* (New York, 1929)

Bridge, F. R., '*Tarde venientibus ossa*: Austro-Hungarian colonial aspirations in Asia Minor 1913–14', *Middle Eastern Studies*, 6 (1970)

Bridge, F. R., *From Sadowa to Sarajevo: the foreign policy of Austria-Hungary, 1866–1914* (London, 1972)

Bridge, F. R., *Great Britain and Austria–Hungary 1906–1914: a diplomatic history* (London, 1972)

Butterfield, H., 'Sir Edward Grey in July 1914', *Historical Studies*, V (1965)

Cairns, J. C., 'International politics and the military mind: the case of the French republic, 1911–1914', *JMH*, 25 (1953)

Carrié, R. Albrecht-, 'Revisionism revisited', *JCEA*, XVI (1956–7)

Chickering, R., *Imperial Germany and a World Without War* (Princeton, 1975)

Churchill, R. S., *Winston S. Churchill*, vols. I–II (London, 1966–7)

Clarke, I. F., *Voices Prophesying War 1763–1984* (London, 1970)

Collins, D. H., 'The Franco-Russian alliance and Russian railways 1891–1914', *HJ*, XVI (1973)

Cooper, M. B., 'British policy in the Balkans, 1908–9', *HJ*, VII (1964)

Crankshaw, E., *The Fall of the House of Habsburg* (London, 1963)

Dakin, D., *The Greek Struggle in Macedonia 1897–1913* (Salonika, 1966)

Dangerfield, G., *The Strange Death of Liberal England, 1910–1914* (New York, 1965)

Edwards, E. W., 'The Franco-German agreement on Morocco, 1909', *EHR*, LXXVIII (1963)

Ekstein, M., 'Sir Edward Grey and Imperial Germany in 1914', *JCH*, 6 (1971)

Epstein, K., *Matthias Erzberger and the Dilemma of German Democracy* (New York, 1959)

Eubank, K., *Paul Cambon: Master Diplomatist* (Norman, Oklahoma, 1960)

Farrar, L. L., *The Short-War Illusion* (Santa Barbara, 1973)

Fay, S. B., *The Origins of the World War* (2 vols., New York, 1929)

Feis, H., *Europe, the World's Banker 1870–1914* (New Haven, 1930)

Fischer, F., *Germany's Aims in the First World War* (London, 1967)

Fischer, F., *War of Illusions* (London, 1975)

Geiss, I., 'The outbreak of the First World War and German war aims', *JCH*, I (1966)

Geiss, I. (ed.), *July 1914: the outbreak of the First World War* (London, 1967)

Girault, R., 'Sur quelques aspects financiers de l'alliance franco-russe', *RHMC*, XVIII (1961)

Haggie, P., 'The Royal Navy and war planning in the Fisher era', *JCH*, 8 (1973)

Hale, O. J., *Publicity and Diplomacy: with special reference to England and Germany, 1890–1914* (New York, 1940)

Hanak, H., 'A lost cause: the English Radicals and the Habsburg Empire, 1914–1918', *JCEA*, XXII (1963–4)

Bibliography

Heilbronner, H., 'The merger attempts of Serbia and Montenegro, 1913–1914', *JCEA*, XVIII (1958–9)

Helmreich, E. C., *The Diplomacy of the Balkan Wars, 1912–1913* (Cambridge, Mass., 1938)

Hess, R. L., *Ethiopia* (Ithaca, 1970)

Hinsley, F. H., *Power and the Pursuit of Peace* (Cambridge, 1963)

Howard, H. N., *The Partition of Turkey: a diplomatic history, 1913–1923* (New York, 1966)

Jarausch, K. H., *The Enigmatic Chancellor: Bethmann Hollweg and the hubris of Imperial Germany* (New Haven, 1973)

Jaszi, O., *The Dissolution of the Habsburg Monarchy* (Chicago, 1961)

Jesman, C., *The Russians in Ethiopia: an essay in futility* (London, 1958)

Joll, J., *1914: the unspoken assumptions* (London, 1968)

Kautsky, K., *The Guilt of William Hohenzollern* (London, n.d.)

Kennedy, P. M., 'The development of German naval operations plans against England, 1896–1914', *EHR*, LXXXIX (1974)

Kitchen, M., *The German Officer Corps, 1890–1914* (Oxford, 1968)

Lafore, L., *The Long Fuse: an interpretation of the origins of World War I* (London, 1966)

Langhorne, R., 'The Naval question in Anglo-German relations, 1912–1914', *HJ*, XIV (1971)

Leon, G. B., 'Greece and the Albanian question at the outbreak of the First World War', *BS*, II (1970)

Lewis, B., *The Emergence of Modern Turkey* (London, 1961)

Mackintosh, J. P., 'The role of the Committee of Imperial Defence before 1914', *EHR*, LXXVII (1962)

Marcus, H. G., *The Life and Times of Menelik II: Ethiopia 1844–1913* (Oxford, 1975)

Marder, A. J., *From Dreadnought to Scapa Flow: the Royal Navy in the Fisher era, 1904–1919* (3 vols, London, 1961–)

May, A. J., 'The Novibazar railway project', *JMH*, 10 (1938)

May, A. J., 'Trans-Balkan railway schemes', *JMH*, 24 (1952)

May, A. J., *The passing of the Habsburg Empire, 1914–1918* (2 vols, Philadelphia, 1966)

Mayer, A. J., 'Internal causes and purposes of war in Europe, 1870–1956: a research assignment', *JMH*, 41 (1969)

Meyer, H. C., 'German economic relations with Southeastern Europe, 1870–1914', *AHR*, LVII (1951)

Michon, G., *The Franco-Russian Alliance, 1891–1917* (London, 1929)

Mommsen, W. J., 'Domestic factors in German foreign policy before 1914', *CEH*, VI (1973)

Monger, G., *The End of Isolation: British foreign policy, 1900–7* (London, 1963)

Mortimer, J. S., 'Commercial interests and German diplomacy in the Agadir crisis', *HJ*, X (1967)

Moseley, P. E., 'Russian policy in 1911–12', *JMH*, 12 (1940)

Nicolson, H., *Sir Arthur Nicolson, Bart. First Lord Carnock* (London, 1930)

Platt, D. C. M., *Finance, Trade and Politics in British Foreign Policy 1815–1914* (Oxford, 1968)

Poidevin, R., 'Les intérêts financiers français et allemandes en Serbie de 1895 à 1914', *RH*, CCXXXII (1964)

Prevelakis, E., 'Eleatherios Venizelos and the Balkan Wars' *BS*, VII (1966)

Pribram, A. F., *The Secret treaties of Austria–Hungary 1879–1914* (2 vols, Cambridge, Mass., 1920–1)

Bibliography

Pribram, A. F., *Austria-Hungary and Great Britain, 1908–1914* (London, 1951)

Raditsa, B., 'Venizelos and the struggle around the Balkan Pact', *BS*, VI (1965)

Raffalovitch, A., *'L'abominable venalité de la presse! d'après les documents des archives Russes (1897–1917)*(Paris, 1931)

Redlich, J., *Emperor Francis Joseph of Austria: a biography* (Hamden, Conn., 1965)

Remak, J., 'The healthy invalid: how doomed the Habsburg Empire?', *JMH*, 43 (1971)

Renouvin, P., *The Immediate Origins of the War (28 June–4 August 1914)* (New Haven, 1928)

Rogger, H., 'Russia in 1914', *JCH*, I (1966)

Rohl, J. C. G., 'Admiral von Müller and the approach of war, 1911–1914', *HJ*, XII (1969)

Sarkissian, A. O. (ed.), *Studies in Diplomatic History and Historiography in Honour of G. P. Gooch* (London, 1961)

Schmitt, B., *The Annexation of Bosnia, 1908–1909* (Cambridge, 1937)

Silberstein, G. E., *The Troubled Alliance: German–Austrian relations 1914 to 1917* (Lexington, 1970)

Silberstein, G. E., 'The High Command and diplomacy in Austria–Hungary, 1914–1916', *JMH*, 42 (1970)

Skendi, S., *The Albanian National Awakening 1878–1912* (Princeton, 1967)

Sousa, N., *The Capitulatory Regime of Turkey: its history, origin and nature* (Baltimore, 1933)

Steinberg, J., 'The Kaiser's navy and German society', *PP*, 28 (1964)

Steinberg, J., *Yesterday's Deterrent: Tirpitz and the birth of the German battle fleet* (London, 1965)

Steiner, Z., *The Foreign Office and Foreign Policy 1898–1914* (Cambridge, 1969)

Stieve, F., *Isvolsky and the World War* (London, 1926)

Stone, N., 'Conrad von Hötzendorf, Chief of Staff in the Austro-Hungarian Army', *HT*, XIII (1963)

Stone, N., 'Army and Society in the Habsburg monarchy, 1900–1914', *PP*, 33 (1966)

Stone, N., 'Moltke–Conrad: relations between the Austro-Hungarian and German General Staffs, 1909–1914', *HJ*, IX (1966)

Stone, N., 'Hungary and the crisis of July 1914', *JCH*, I (1966)

Taylor, A. J. P., *Rumours of War* (London, 1952)

Taylor, A. J. P., *The Struggle for Mastery in Europe, 1848–1918* (Oxford, 1954; new ed., London 1971)

Taylor, A. J. P., *The Habsburg Monarchy, 1809–1918* (rev. ed., Harmondsworth, 1964)

Taylor, A. J. P., *Politics in Wartime and Other Essays* (London, 1964)

Thaden, E. C., 'Charykov and Russian foreign policy at Constantinople in 1911', *JCEA*, XVI (1956–7)

Thaden, E. C., 'Montenegro: Russia's troublesome ally, 1910–1912', *JCEA*, XVIII (1958–9)

Thaden, E. C., *Russia and the Balkan Alliance of 1912* (Philadelphia, 1965)

Tilley, J. and Gaselee, S., *The Foreign Office* (London, 1933)

The History of the 'Times', vols. III–IV (London, 1947–52)

Trebilcock, C., 'Legends of the British armament industry 1890–1914: a revision', *JCH*, 5 (1970)

Trevelyan, G. M., *Grey of Fallodon* (London, 1937)

Trumpener, U., 'German military aid to Turkey in 1914: an historical re-evaluation', *JMH*, 32 (1960)

Trumpener, U., 'Turkey's entry into World War I: an assessment of responsibilities', *JMH*, 34 (1962)

Bibliography

Trumpener, U., 'Liman von Sanders and the German-Ottoman alliance', *JCH*, 1 (1966)

Trumpener, U., *Germany and the Ottoman Empire 1914–1918* (Princeton, 1968)

Vagts, A., *The Military Attaché* (Princeton, 1967)

Valiani, L., *The End of Austria–Hungary* (London, 1973)

Wanks, S., 'The appointment of Count Berchtold as Austro-Hungarian Foreign Minister', *JCEA*, xxiii (1963–4)

Watson, D. R., 'The making of French foreign policy during the first Clemenceau ministry 1906–1909', *EHR*, lxxxvi, 1971

Weber, E., *The Nationalist revival in France, 1905–1914* (Berkeley, 1959)

Wertheimer, M., *The Pan-German League, 1890–1914* (New York, 1924)

Williamson, S. R., 'Influence, power and the policy process: the case of Franz Ferdinand, 1906–1914', *HJ*, xvii (1974)

Zeldin, T., *France 1848–1945: Vol. 1, Ambition, Love and Politics* (Oxford, 1973)

Zeman, Z. A. B., *The Breakup of the Habsburg Empire, 1914–1918: a study in national and social revolution* (London, 1961)

Zilliacus, K., *The Mirror of the Past* (London, 1944)

VII. JOURNALS AND NEWSPAPERS

Avanti!

Bollettino della Società geografica italiana

Corriere della Sera

Lega Navale

Nuova Antologia

La Riforma Sociale

Rivista Coloniale

La Stampa

The Times

La Tribuna

L'Unità

Notes

CHAPTER 1. SOCIETY AND POLITICS IN LIBERAL ITALY

1 A. Gramsci, *Selections from the Prison Notebooks* (London, 1971), pp. 89–90.
2 Tancredi's famous comment in G. Di Lampedusa, *The Leopard* (London, 1963), p. 28.
3 S. Romano, *Crispi: progetto per una dittatura* (Milan, 1973), p. 88.
4 F. S. Nitti, *La decadenza dell'Europa* (Florence, 1922), p. 178.
5 N. Kogan, *The Politics of Italian Foreign Policy* (London, 1963), p. 4.
6 G. Mori, 'Le guerre parallele: l'industria elettrica in Italia nel periodo della grande guerra (1914–1919)', *SS*, XIV (1973), pp. 294, 317.
7 *OUA*, 3, 2438, 31 Jan. 1911, Mérey to Aehrenthal; for further comments on the military insufficiency of lines in this area see F. De Chaurand De Saint Eustache, *Come l'esercito italiano entrò in guerra* (Milan, 1929), p. 121; the standard, English-language economic history of Italy is S. B. Clough, *The Economic History of Modern Italy* (New York, 1964).
8 Rolling-stock had been allowed to run down before the railways were nationalised, on generous terms, in 1905. See A. Papa, *Classe politica e intervento pubblico nell'età giolittiana: la nazionalizzazione delle ferrovie* (Naples, 1973).
9 There is a standard history F. Bonelli, *Lo sviluppo di una grande impresa in Italia: la Terni dal 1884 al 1962* (Turin, 1975).
10 See the tables in A. J. P. Taylor, *The Struggle for Mastery in Europe, 1848–1918* (London, 1971), pp. xxvii–xxix; L. Cafagna, *The Industrial Revolution in Italy, 1830–1914* (London, 1971), pp. 37–8, 47–8.
11 P. G. Halpern, *The Mediterranean Naval Situation, 1908–1914* (Cambridge, Mass., 1971), pp. 161–2, 190.
12 For some examples see the delightful N. Stone, *The Eastern Front, 1914–1917* (London, 1975).
13 K. H. Jarausch, *The Enigmatic Chancellor: Bethmann Hollweg and the hubris of Imperial Germany* (New Haven, 1973), pp. 18–19.
14 Cited by R. J. B. Bosworth, 'The British press, the Conservatives and Mussolini, 1920–1934', *JCH*, 5 (1970), p. 167.
15 Taylor, *op. cit.*, p. 283.
16 M. Mazzetti, *L'esercito italiano nella triplice alleanza* (Naples, 1974), p. 212.
17 F. R. Bridge, *Great Britain and Austria–Hungary 1906–1914: a diplomatic history* (London, 1972), p. 146.
18 A. Lyttelton (ed.), *Italian Fascisms from Pareto to Gentile* (London, 1973), pp. 213–14.
19 *CD*, XXIII, xiii, 7 June 1911, p. 15348; cf. also AG, 23/207, 15 Jan. 1911, San Giuliano to P. Levi requesting a general effort by Italian diplomats in 1911 to rebut foreign denigration of Italy, and especially to deny allegations about the insalubriousness of Rome, which might restrain tourists from joining the *Cinquantennio* celebrations.

20 RP, 27 Nov. 1911, Rodd to Grey. Rodd was often puzzled by the 'mercurial temperament' of Southerners or Latins. He also noted patronisingly that San Giuliano was 'in spite of his Sicilian origin,...eminently level-headed'; CP, 9860/277, 15 Oct. 1910, Rodd to Grey.

21 See generally the over-intellectualised and rather unsatisfactory P. Treves, *L'idea di Roma e la cultura italiana del secolo XIX* (Milan, 1962). Treves' biases include a dislike of the 'pseudoradicalism' of Mack Smith and A. J. P. Taylor, whom he finds guilty of being 'substantially "anti-Italian"', p. 5 fn. 7.

22 F. Chabod, *Storia della politica estera italiana dal 1870 al 1896*, vol. I (Bari, 1965), pp. 230–1. Chabod's whole section on the 'idea of Rome' pp. 215–373 is masterly.

23 Cited by A. Caracciolo, *Roma capitale* (Rome, 1974), pp. 38, 111.

24 Chabod, *op. cit.*, vol. I, p. 297.

25 See R. J. B. Bosworth, 'The opening of the Victor Emmanuel monument', *IQ*, XVIII (1975), pp. 78–87.

26 Gramsci, *op. cit.*, p. 68.

27 A good example of a forerunner of Fascist cries for 'Tunis, Jibuti, Corsica and Nice' is G. E. Curàtolo, *Francia e Italia: pagine di storia, 1849–1914* (Turin, 1915).

28 O. Malagodi, *Conversazioni della guerra, 1914–1919* (Milan, 1960), vol. I, p. 20.

29 For a version in English see C. J. Lowe and F. Marzari, *Italian Foreign Policy 1870–1940* (London, 1975), pp. 373–4.

30 For the origins of Italian colonialism see R. Ciasca, *Storia coloniale dell'Italia contemporanea* (Milan, 1938); A. Del Boca, *Gli italiani in Africa orientale* (Bari, 1976); R. L. Hess, *Italian Colonialism in Somalia* (Chicago, 1966).

31 See G. Pescosolido, 'Il dibattito coloniale nella stampa italiana e la battaglia di Adua', *SC*, IV (1973), pp. 675–712; R. Rainero, *L'anticolonialismo italiano da Assab ad Adua (1869–1896)* (Milan, 1971).

32 A. Aquarone, 'La politica coloniale italiana dopo Adua: Ferdinando Martini', *RSR*, LXII (1975), pp. 449–83. Aquarone notes (p. 453) that King Umberto himself blocked any real chance of abandonment of the colony.

33 See U. Levra, *Il colpo di stato della borghesia* (Milan, 1975). Levra makes the point that the reaction had commenced under Pelloux's predecessor, Di Rudinì.

34 The classic explanation of this thesis is A. W. Salomone, *Italy in the Giolittian Era* (Philadelphia, 1945).

35 *Quarant'anni di politica italiana dalle carte di Giovanni Giolitti*, vol. I (1885–1900), ed. P. D'Angiolini; vol. II (1901–9), ed. G. Carocci; vol. III (1910–28), ed. C. Pavone (Milan, 1962).

36 G. Spadolini, *Il mondo di Giolitti* (Florence, 1970), pp. 327–39. For the less savoury side of Tittoni, rumoured to involve even the encouragement and/or concealment of murder see R. Marvasi, *Così parlò Fabroni* (Rome, 1914).

37 V. Vailati, *Badoglio risponde* (Milan, 1958), p. 241.

38 See the cartoon collection E. Gianeri, *Il piccolo re: Vittorio Emanuele nella caricatura* (Turin, 1946).

39 *OUA*, 3, 2755, 14 Oct. 1911, Mérey to Aehrenthal; F. Martini, *Diario, 1914–1918*, ed. G. De Rosa (Milan, 1966), pp. 16–31, 53–4, 126.

40 *OUA*, 2, 2134, 26 April 1910, Mérey report.

41 AG, 27/347, 24 Aug. 1913, King Victor Emmanuel III to San Giuliano.

42 *OUA*, 3, 2755, 14 Oct. 1911, Mérey to Aehrenthal.

43 There is a dreadful eulogy of the Duke, collecting some of his speeches, E. M. Gray (ed.), *Il Duca d'Aosta cittadino della riscossa italica* (Milan, 1931). A good example of the hostility with which the King pursued the Aostas may be found in his efforts to hinder the Duchess of Aosta from engaging in active Red Cross service in Libya in October 1911. See F. Malgeri, *La guerra libica* (Rome, 1970), p. 151.

44 C. Casalegno, *La Regina Margherita* (Turin, 1956), p. 170.

45 Victor Emmanuel's stature was also offensively exposed by his mother's ostentatious love of mountaineering. See her preference for the purity of the mountains, compared to the evils of parliament, *ibid.*, p. 179. For Margherita's intellectual circuit there is material in English in J. A. Thayer, *Italy and the Great War: politics and culture, 1870–1915* (Madison, 1964), pp. 43–5, 202; The best, if rather pop, study of Victor Emmanuel is S. Bertoldi, *Vittorio Emanuele III* (Turin, 1970). Less useful is R. Katz, *The Fall of the House of Savoy* (London, 1972).

46 See files in AG, 22/158.

47 CB, 9, vi.2.34, 8 Oct. 1912, Leonardi Cattolica to Brusati. The Naval Minister apologised for not passing on sufficiently exact accounts of the progress of the Libyan War, explaining, interestingly, that he had not wanted too much publicity, nor to involve Victor Emmanuel too much when the King was so often absent from Rome. He promised that future bulletins would be more detailed and extensive. cf. also 29 Oct. 1911, Pollio to Brusati lamenting that the King did not involve himself more in the war. Brusati also kept detailed reports on 'subversives', being, with appropriate traditionalism, rather more hostile to Republicans than to Socialists e.g. 12, report of the Republican Congress of 16 to 18 May 1914.

48 Bertoldi, *op, cit.*, p. 287. The King also was said to read all diplomatic despatches, see *OUA*, 3, 2884, 7 Dec. 1911, Mérey to Aehrenthal.

49 The best study of parliament in the period remains the descriptive and patriotic S. Cilibrizzi, *Storia parlamentare politica e diplomatica d'Italia da Novara a Vittorio Veneto* (8 vols, Naples, 1939–52), vol. iv covers the years 1909–14.

50 There is a good example in March 1914 when Federzoni asked about the 'systematic persecution' of Italians in Fiume, see CSG, 5, [March 1914], San Giuliano to Avarna, and his consuls in Fiume and Budapest.

51 See e.g. AG, 8/24; 24/226.

52 For an analysis of Giolitti's reputation in historiography see R. J. B. Bosworth, 'The English, the historians and the *età giolittiana*', *HJ*, xii (1969), pp. 353–67, or, more generally, A. W. Salomone (ed.), *Italy from the Risorgimento to Fascism* (N.Y., 1970).

53 Vailati, *op. cit.*, p. 242.

54 The figures and their importance are contested. See M. Mazzetti, 'Spese militari italiane e preparazione nel 1914', *Clio*, viii (1972), pp. 423–48; G. Restifo, 'L'esercito italiano alla vigilia della grande guerra', *SS*, xi (1970), pp. 783–93; G. Rochat, 'L'esercito italiano nell'estate 1914', *NRS*, xlv (1961), pp. 295–348. For a new, English language account of the Army see J. Whittam, *The Politics of the Italian Army, 1861–1918* (London, 1977).

55 E. De Bono, *Nell'esercito nostro prima della guerra* (Milan, 1931), pp. 150–1, 159. E. De Rossi, *La vita di un ufficiale italiano sino alla guerra* (Milan, 1927), pp. 40, 51. cf. Socialists' advocacy of reform of the matrimonial system in the Army, F. Turati, *Discorsi parlamentari* (Rome, 1950), vol. ii, pp. 1027–9.

56 De Rossi, *op. cit.*, pp. 33, 38–9. As far as the alcoholic proclivities of the Italian Army are concerned, still the most delightful source is E. Lussu, *Sardinian Brigade* (New York, 1967), e.g. pp. 37–8.

57 De Rossi, *op. cit.*, p. 44.

58 De Bono, *op. cit.*, p. 23. Caneva, born in Udine in 1845, joined the Italian Officer Corps in 1867.

59 De Rossi, *op. cit.*, pp. 72–3. Pollio's predecessor Saletta had been, oddly, the first Piedmontese Chief of General Staff.

60 Spingardi was an up-to-date War Minister in his advocacy of shooting and gymnastics. See De Chaurand, *op. cit.*, p. 105. For Cadorna's background see R. Corselli, *Cadorna* (Milan, 1937), pp. 13–16.

61 De Bono, *op. cit.*, p. 135.

62 De Rossi, *op. cit.*, pp. 59–60.

63 Rochat, *op. cit.*, p. 319.

64 Malagodi, *op. cit.*, vol. I, p. 174.

65 E. De Bono, *La guerra come e dove l'ho vista e combattuta io* (Milan, 1935), p. 22.

66 CB, 10, VI.4.36, 19 Aug. 1911, Giolitti to Spingardi.

67 Malagodi, *op. cit.*, vol. I, p. 199. The alternative Army story about politicians complained that legislation for the Army was always brought forward in June or July when the deputies were most anxious to get off on their holidays. De Chaurand, *op. cit.*, p. 67.

68 De Bono, *Nell'esercito nostro*, p. 189. cf. also the Army's dislike of 'publicity' and 'civilian interference' during the Libyan campaign e.g. CB, 10, VI.5.37, 24 Jan. 1912, Spingardi to Pollio.

69 Martini, *op. cit.*, pp. 99–100. A detailed analysis of budgetary information in R. Bachi, *L'Italia economica nell'anno 1913* (Città di Castello, 1914), p. 215 reveals that only about one-sixth of the Ministry of War's vote was devoted to 'armaments', even if that was defined very generously to include the building of fortifications and any 'works' done by the Artillery or Engineers. In comparison, one-twelfth of the total Army vote went on new mounts and forage for the cavalry, and more than one-tenth on the *carabinieri*, the domestic police, which was a semi-militarised organisation.

70 Cited by C. De Biase, *L'Aquila d'oro: storia dello stato maggiore italiano (1861–1945)* (Milan, 1970), p. 203.

71 De Rossi, *op. cit.*, p. 66.

72 R. Graziani, *Ho difeso la patria* (Cernusco sul Naviglio, 1948), pp. 10–11.

73 De Biase, *op. cit.*, pp. 206–7.

74 A. A. Mola, *Storia della Massoneria italiana dall' Unità alla Repubblica* (Milan, 1976), pp. 295–312.

75 Pescosolido, *op. cit.*, pp. 703–4.

76 Mazzetti, *op. cit.*, p. 427.

77 D. Mack Smith, *Victor Emanuel, Cavour and the Risorgimento* (London, 1971), pp. 329–30.

78 S. Bernotti, *Cinquant'anni nella Marina militare* (Milan, 1971), pp. 21–4.

79 L. Vannutelli, *Sguardo retrospettivo sulla mia vita nella marina* (Rome, 1959), pp. 37, 47, 52–5, 64, 76–7.

80 Each has a patriotic biographer: O. Di Giamberadino, *L'ammiraglio Millo* (Livorno,

1950); G. Po, *Il Grande Ammiraglio Paolo Thaon Di Revel* (Turin, 1936) (p. 249 lists his many relations who held high office gracefully in Piedmont).

81 e.g. M. Gabriele, *Le convenzioni navali della Triplice* (Rome, 1969), p. 93.

82 *Ibid.*, pp. 21–2 also gives the list of possible bases. A naval writer summed up forward defence under the slogan 'Rome must defend itself at Carthage'.

83 For the complicated story of corruption see U. Spadoni, 'Linee di navigazione e costruzioni navali alla vigilia dell'inchiesta parlamentare sulla marina mercantile italiana (1881–82)', *NRS*, LVII (1973), pp. 313–72.

84 G. Fazio, *Essenze e fattori della grandezza marittima* (Rome, 1904), pp. 15, 24, 30.

85 Eulogies of the Florio family are still appearing in Sicily, see M. Taccari, *I Florio* (Caltanissetta, 1967), a study issued under the auspices of the Regional Union of Commerce, Industry, Artisan Work and Agriculture. For a less official and more penetrating account see Webster, *op. cit.*, p. 130. Webster (p. 300) is mistaken in stating Pietro Di Scalea was the son of Giulia Florio. In fact, Giulia had married Prince Di Trabia, the head of the Lanza family and Pietro's uncle. This and other genealogical information may be culled from *Libro d'Oro della Nobiltà Italiana*, vol. III (Rome, 1914).

86 L'Italico (i.e. P. Levi), *Luigi Orlando e i suoi fratelli* (Rome, 1898), p. 24. Both Luigi Orlando and Benedetto fled for sanctuary to Malta after the failure of the uprising.

87 *Ibid.*, pp. 125, 154.

88 e.g. see E. Piscitelli, 'Francesco Crispi, Primo Levi e "La Riforma"', *RSR*, XXXVII (1950), pp. 411–17.

89 G. Dore, *La democrazia italiana e l'emigrazione in America* (Brescia, 1964), e.g. see pp. 69–95.

90 Webster, *op. cit.*, p. 303; in 1912, the SNGI paid 10%, Bachi, *op. cit.*, p. 174.

91 Webster, *op. cit.*, pp. 305–9.

92 A. J. P. Taylor, *Essays in English History* (Harmondsworth, 1976), p. 15.

93 Robert Michels, in his famous contemporary analysis, noted regretfully that Italian capitalists still preferred state investment to speculation. R. Michels, *L'imperialismo italiano: studi politico-demografici* (Milan, 1914), p. 99.

94 A. Pepe, *Storia della CGdL dalla fondazione alla guerra di Libia, 1905–1911* (Bari, 1972), pp. 378–80.

95 *Ibid.*, p. 468; M. Abrate, *La lotta sindacale nella industrializzazione in Italia 1906–1926* (Turin, 1967), pp. 99–100.

96 E. Conti, *Dal taccuino di un borghese* (Cremona, 1946), p. 65.

97 *Ibid.*, pp. 2, 17.

98 *Ibid.*, pp. 82, 91–2.

99 *Ibid.*, pp. 92–3, 96–7.

100 *Ibid.*, pp. 100, 103.

101 Webster, *op. cit.*, p. 147.

102 So rather naively writes F. J. Coppa, *Planning, Protectionism and Politics in Liberal Italy* (Washington, D.C., 1971), p. 73.

103 *Ibid.*, pp. 73–82.

104 Naturally landowners, especially in the North, had good reason to fear the deterioration of the 'social question' as sharecroppers and agricultural labourers began to unionise. See the classic R. Zangheri (ed), *Lotte agrarie in Italia 1901–26: La*

Federazione nazionale dei lavoratori della terra (Milan, 1960). There are some useful comments in English in P. Corner, *Fascism in Ferrara 1915–1925* (Oxford, 1975), pp. 1–18. Landowners had formed their own 'employer union' in Ferrara province as early as 1901.

105 P. Togliatti, *Lectures on Fascism* (London, 1976), p. 31.

106 Mola, *op. cit.*, pp. 238, 253, 258, 271, 286–7. See also G. Leti, *Carboneria e massoneria nel Risorgimento italiano* (Bologna, 1925).

107 Mola, *op. cit.*, p. 365. For Chiaraviglio's business activities in the iron industry, see Webster, *op. cit.*, p. 147.

108 Togliatti, *op. cit.*, p. 32 (Togliatti compares this purpose with the same usefulness to many Italians of the Partito Nazionale Fascista).

109 Quoted by R. F. Esposito, *La Massoneria e l'Italia dal 1800 ai nostri giorni* (Rome, 1956), p. 152.

110 The Church was especially affronted when the Jew, Nathan, became mayor of Rome. Catholic organs talked about the reign of Anti-Christ. See Mola, *op. cit.*, p. 265. The Church was also not delighted by the fact that one Jew, Luzzatti, succeeded another, Sonnino, as Prime Minister in 1910.

111 General Ameglio, the military governor of the Dodecanese Islands after 1912 was a notable exponent of the Masonry of Palazzo del Gesù. Esposito, *op. cit.*, pp. 161–2.

112 For an English language summary see F. J. Coppa, 'Giolitti and the Gentiloni pact between myth and reality', *CHR*, LIII (1967), pp. 217–28.

113 Mola, *op. cit.*, pp. 307–11.

114 Esposito, *op. cit.*, p. 173.

115 H. Ullrich, *Le elezioni del 1913 a Roma* (Milan, 1972), provides full details.

116 L. Ganapini, *Il nazionalismo cattolico* (Bari, 1970), pp. 212–13.

117 For a general and favourable account see A. Galante Garrone, *I radicali in Italia (1849–1925)* (Milan, 1973).

118 e.g. CG, 14/19, 22 April 1913, Giolitti to Fusinato.

119 See the extraordinary E. A. and L. T. Mowrer, *Umano and the Price of Lasting Peace* (New York, 1973), pp. 31, 88, 132–3.

120 G. Bovio, *Il secolo nuovo* (Rome, 1923), pp. 163, 202–11; 252, 259–272.

121 e.g. E. T. Moneta, *Le guerre, le insurrezioni e la pace nel secolo decimonono* (2 vols, Milan, 1905); see also the very general E. Rota, 'I movimenti pacifisti dell'800 e '900 e le organizzazioni internazionali', in *Questioni di storia contemporanea* (Milan, 1952), pp. 1963–2018.

122 R. Chickering, *Imperial Germany and a World Without War* (Princeton, 1975), p. 288. Chickering's is the most recent account of the German and French peace movements.

123 Malgeri, *op. cit.*, pp. 69–96, noting also the opposition of Ojetti, Einaudi and the doubts of conservatives like Martini, Luzzatti and Mosca. Salvemini's usually accurate polemics about Libya have been collected in G. Salvemini, *Come siamo andati in Libia*, ed. A. Torre (Milan, 1963); or, with domestic reference, see G. Salvemini, *Il ministro della mala vita*, ed. E. Apih (Milan, 1966).

124 e.g. see E. Amendola Kühn, *Vita con Giovanni Amendola* (Florence, 1960), pp. 295–303.

125 F. Papafava, *Dieci anni di vita italiana (1899–1909)* (Bari, 1913), vol. II, p. 481.

126 The most recent study is M. Degl'Innocenti, *Il socialismo italiano e la guerra di Libia* (Rome, 1976).

127 R. Monteleone, 'Iniziative e convegni socialisti italo-austriaci per la pace nel decennio prebellico', *RSS*, x (1967), pp. 1–42.

128 Degl'Innocenti, *op. cit.*, pp. 151–2.

129 *Ibid.*, pp. 36–41.

130 *Ibid.*, p. 47.

131 The best study of the emigration phenomenon remains R. F. Foerster, *The Italian Emigration of Our Times* (Cambridge, Mass., 1919).

132 e.g. see Michels, *op. cit.*, p. 6.

133 For the debate in general see F. Manzotti, *La polemica sull'emigrazione nell'Italia unita* (Milan, 1962).

134 Degl'Innocenti, *op. cit.*, p. 206.

135 e.g. see G. Papini, 'La vita non è sacra' in G. Scalia (ed.), *La cultura italiana del '900 attraverso le riviste* (Turin, 1961), vol. IV, pp. 205–8.

136 O. Malagodi, *Imperialismo* (Milan, 1901), e.g. pp. vi–vii.

137 G. Giolitti, *Discorsi extraparlamentari* (Turin, 1952), p. 261.

138 G. Piazza, *La fiamma bilingue* (Milan, 1924), p. 52.

CHAPTER 2. NEW POLITICAL PRESSURE GROUPS AND FOREIGN POLICY

1 e.g. P. L. Occhini, 'Enrico Corradini africanista', *NA*, f 1532, 16 Jan. 1936, pp. 196–7. cf. E. Corradini, *Discorsi politici (1902–1924)* (Florence, 1925), pp. 249–62.

2 In English, see the useful collection of extracts from Corradini's writings in A. Lyttelton (ed.), *Italian Fascisms from Pareto to Gentile* (London, 1973), pp. 135–63.

3 J. A. Thayer, *Italy and the Great War: politics and culture, 1870–1915* (Madison, 1964) provides a challenging introduction to the pre-1914 Italian intellectual world. For Pascoli in particular see p. 242. For a good example of Pascoli's style of rhetoric by 1911 see R. J. B. Bosworth, 'The opening of the Victor Emmanuel monument', *IQ*, XVIII (1975), p. 82.

4 Corradini's speech on his return in 1909 was characteristically addressed to the Dante Alighieri Society in Milan. See Corradini, *op. cit.*, pp. 73–87. The venue, Milan, Italy's industrial capital, was also significant of Corradini's (and Nationalism's) close relationship to the Italian business world.

5 Papini, himself a Florentine, later recalled how shocked he had been, as a boy, by Adowa. He also had a characteristic reaction to Rome, on a first visit there in 1901. He found too many tourists: 'The foreigners dominated: Palazzo Farnese and Villa Medici were in French hands, Palazzo Venezia had fallen to hated Austria; Germany had dared to plant its Embassy on the Campidoglio...My proud heart of a twenty-year-old Italian suffered all this in silence.' G. Papini, *Passato remoto (1885–1914)* (Florence, 1948), pp. 59–61, 99–102.

6 F. Gaeta, *Nazionalismo italiano* (Naples, 1965), pp. 118–19.

7 R. Molinelli, 'I Nazionalisti italiani e l'intervento a fianco degli imperi centrali', *RSR*, LIX (1972), pp. 197–205.

8 It is typical of the looseness of Italian political groupings that the figure is sometimes given as 6 and sometimes as 4. The list of deputies given follows that in R. Molinelli,

'Nazionalisti cattolici e liberali (Il Nazionalismo italiano dal congresso di Roma a quello di Milano)', *RSR*, LII (1965), pp. 368–9. Cf. also R. S. Cunsolo, 'Italian Nationalism and the revolt against Giolitti', *JMH*, 37 (1965), p. 205 fn. 82.

9 V. Cian, *Luigi Federzoni, profilo* (Piacenza, 1924), pp. 7–19.

10 For the money see Molinelli, 'Nazionalisti cattolici e liberali', p. 366. For the scandals R. Marvasi, *Cosí parlò Fabroni* (Rome, 1914).

11 G. De Frenzi, *Per l'italianità del 'Gardasee'* (Naples, 1909), p. 43.

12 *Ibid.*, pp. 63–9; cf. also L. Rava, *Discorsi e scritti per la 'Dante'* (Rome, 1932), pp. 37–42.

13 e.g. L. Federzoni, *Paradossi di ieri* (Milan, 1926), pp. 41–72.

14 For an exhaustive study of the Rome elections see H. Ullrich, *Le elezioni del 1913 a Roma* (Milan, 1972).

15 Now available in English is the delightful period piece L. Barzini, *Peking to Paris: a journey across two continents in 1907* (London, 1972).

16 Federzoni, *Paradossi di ieri*, pp. 11–12.

17 G. De Frenzi, *L'Italia nell'Egeo* (Rome, 1913), p. 113.

18 A. A. Mola, *Storia della Massoneria italiana dall'Unità alla Repubblica* (Milan, 1976), pp. 306–12.

19 Molinelli, 'Nazionalisti Cattolici e Liberali', p. 371.

20 Note *Giornale d'Italia*'s reaction to the 1913 election campaign. Ullrich, *op. cit.*, pp. 40–3.

21 The family was one of those whose title of nobility was worth the price of a good cigar; despite the resonant name, the family had been ennobled by King Victor Emmanuel II. For some of Medici's speeches (in language not so different from San Giuliano), see L. Medici del Vascello, *Per l'Italia!* (Bari, 1916).

22 L. Tosi, 'Romeo A. Gallenga Stuart e la propaganda di guerra all'estero (1917–1918)', *SC*, II (1971),

23 If hagiography is preferred, see A. Odenigo, *Piero Foscari: una vita esemplare* (Rocca San Casciano, 1959). For his speeches (and a eulogy – preface by Federzoni) P. Foscari, *Per l'Italia più grande*, ed. T. Sillani (Rome, 1928).

24 G. D'Annunzio, *La nave* (Rome, 1939), p. 70.

25 For the Nationalists' debate about irredentism, see R. Molinelli, 'I Nazionalisti italiani e l'intervento', pp. 188–95.

26 L. Albertini, *Epistolario, 1911–1926* (Milan, 1968), vol. I, p. 14.

27 M. Lago, *Angelo Zanelli* (Rome, 1911).

28 e.g. his extraordinary tirade, L. Villari, *The Liberation of Italy, 1943–7* (Appleton, Wisconsin, 1959).

29 Cunsolo, *op. cit.*, p. 29.

30 For an exhaustive study of the origins of irredentism see A. Sandonà, *L'irredentismo nelle lotte politiche e nelle contese diplomatiche italo-austriache* (3 vols., Bologna, 1938).

31 G. Sabbatucci, 'Il problema dell'irredentismo e le origini del movimento nazionalista in Italia', *SC*, I (1970), pp. 469–71.

32 C. Seton-Watson, *Italy from Liberalism to Fascism* (London, 1967), p. 102.

33 Z. Sternhell, 'Paul Déroulède and the origins of modern French nationalism', *JCH*, 6 (1971), pp. 46–70.

34 For his account of this episode see G. Giuriati, *Con D'Annunzio e Millo in difesa dell'Adriatico* (Florence, 1954).

35 e.g. DGPS, 3/6, 18 Dec. 1910, Luzzatti to Prefects; 3/7, 19, 20, 21 April 1911, memos on VIIIth Congress of Trento and Trieste Association held in Rome; CS(L), C. 2. 42/5, 26 March 1914, San Giuliano to Salandra.

36 e.g. *OUA*, 2, 2135, 26 April 1910, Mérey report.

37 C. Galli, *Diarii e lettere* (Florence, 1951), pp. 144–5.

38 Even a pro-irredentist source admits that, in Trieste, irredentists were only 2% of the population, M. Alberti, *L'irredentismo senza romanticismi* (Como, 1936), p. 32.

39 E. Apih, *Italia fascismo e antifascismo nella Venezia Giulia (1918–1943)* (Bari, 1966), p. 15.

40 Sabbatucci, *op. cit.*, p. 479.

41 San Giuliano exchanged letters of textual criticism with learned professors about the *Divine Comedy*. F. Cataluccio, 'Lotte e ambizioni di Antonio Di San Giuliano', in M. M. Libelli (ed), *Studi in onore di Niccolò Rodolico* (Florence, 1944), pp. 46–7; cf. also S. Sonnino, 'Beatrice', *NA*, f 1198, 16 Feb. 1922, pp. 318–36; V. E. Orlando, 'Dante e il Piedmonte', *NA*, f 1813, May 1952, pp. 3–26.

42 CSG, 4, 11 July 1913, Boselli to San Giuliano.

43 Sabbatucci, *op. cit.*, p. 480.

44 Villari had an English wife. The English translation of P. Villari, *Life and Times of Savonarola* (London, 1888), is dedicated to 'the Right Hon. William Ewart Gladstone, Champion of Italian freedom, Master of Italian learning'. His son was Luigi, the Nationalist and Fascist. It is characteristic of the ambiguity of P. Villari's liberalism that Gaetano Salvemini would also regard him as a 'spiritual father' because of his interest in the Southern question. See G. Salvemini, 'Pasquale Villari', *NRS*, II (1918), pp. 113–39.

45 P. Villari, 'Dove andiamo?', *NA*, f 535, 1 Nov. 1893, pp. 5–24.

46 P. Villari, *Scritti e discorsi per la 'Dante'* (Rome, 1933), p. xix.

47 Sabbatucci, *op. cit.*, p. 486.

48 From his speech in November 1896, when accepting the Presidency, Villari, *Scritti*, p. 4.

49 *Ibid.*, p. 5.

50 From his speech to the tenth Dante Congress in Messina, 24 Oct. 1899, *ibid.*, p. 77. It was ironical that within a year King Umberto was assassinated by an Italian anarchist, having returned home from life in an emigrant community in Patterson, New Jersey.

51 Rava, *op. cit.*, pp. 69–73.

52 These details are provided by the *Annuario dell'Italia all'estero e delle sue colonie*, (published by the Istituto Coloniale Italiano, Rome, 1911), pp. 438–44.

53 MAE P 675/884, 23 Dec. 1913, Sanminiatelli to San Giuliano.

54 For the polite contacts between Boselli and San Giuliano see AG, 7/43, 31 Aug. 1911, Boselli to San Giuliano.

55 *BSGI*, IV s, 9, April 1908, pp. 425–51.

56 E. De Agostini, *La Reale Società Geografica Italiana e la sua opera dalla fondazione ad oggi (1867–1936)* (Rome, 1937), p. 36. There is a detailed study of the early history of the Society, M. Carazzi, *La Società Geografica Italiana e l'esplorazione coloniale in Africa 1867–1900* (Florence, 1972).

57 De Agostini, *op. cit.*, pp. 12–14.

58 CD, xx, 2nd Sesssion, iv, 25 April 1899, p. 3423. A. Lavagetto, *La vita eroica del capitano Bottego (1893–1897)* (Milan, 1934). The biography appeared in a cheap series of 'Green books', put out by Mondadori; 1934 was a suitable moment to revive an imperial hero.

59 BSGI, IV s, 7, June 1906.

60 BSGI, IV s, 9, March 1908.

61 The latter was formally accorded membership on 1 July 1912 on the motion of San Giuliano, seconded by Scalea, BSGI, v s, 1, 1 July 1912.

62 BSGI, IV s, 9, March 1908.

63 De Agostini, *op. cit.*, p. 36.

64 Lega Navale Italiana, *Italia Marinara* (Rome, 1947), p. 5.

65 G. Limo, *Le idealità della Lega Navale Italiana e il 'Mare Nostrum'* (Rome, 1903), pp. 45–59.

66 Lega Navale Italiana, *op. cit.*, pp. 6–7.

67 G. Limo, *La guerra del 190...* (La Spezia, 1899); cf I. F. Clarke, *Voices prophesying war 1763–1984* (London, 1970), p. 45.

68 Limo, *L'idealità della Lega Navale Italiana* pp. 13, 20, 38.

69 e.g. G. Fazio, *Essenza e fattori della grandezza marittima* (Rome, 1904).

70 R. Bernotti, *Cinquant'anni nella Marina militare* (Milan, 1971), pp. 23–4.

71 R. Bonelli, *Lo sviluppo di una grande impresa in Italia* (Turin, 1975), pp. 64–5, 96–7.

72 M. Pierotti, *L'Istituto Coloniale Italiano, sue origini, suo sviluppo* (Rome, 1922), pp. 15–16. For the French group, see the rival opinions of C. M. Andrew and A. S. Kanya-Forstner, 'The French "Colonial Party": its composition, aims and influence, 1885–1914', *HJ*, XIV (1971); 'The French Colonial Party and French colonial war aims, 1914 1918', *HJ*, XVII (1974); L. Abrams and D. J. Miller, 'Who were the French colonialists? A reassessment of the *parti colonial*, 1890–1914', *HJ*, XIX (1976).

73 P. G. Halpern, *The Mediterranean Naval Situation, 1908–1914* (Cambridge, Mass., 1971), pp. 154–5.

74 *Ibid.*, p. 197.

75 F. Martini, *Fra un sigaro e l'altro* (Milan, 1930). For his career as a lyricist, see M. Carner, *Puccini: a critical biography* (London, 1974), p. 197.

76 A. Aquarone, 'La politica coloniale italiana dopo Adua: Ferdinando Martini Governatore in Eritrea', *RSR*, LXII (1975), p. 470.

77 CM, 11/56 includes printed monthly booklets on the Asmara meeting. This information is taken from the booklet for June 1905.

78 *Ibid.*, booklets for July, Aug., Sept., 1905.

79 R. Paoli, *Nella colonia Eritrea: studi e viaggi* (Milan, 1908), pp. 88–9.

80 CM, 11/56 booklet for October 1905, listing the motions approved at the Congress.

81 Pierotti, *op. cit.*, pp. 9–10.

82 Pierotti, *op. cit.*, p. 9.

83 Being Governor of the Somaliland was a somewhat barren task. Despite his colonialist training, in office, De Martino II's major ambition seems to have been to build himself a new Residence, which, he noted solemnly, would reinvigorate Italy's 'pacific influence' in the colony. CB, 10, VI.4.36, 16 May 1911, De Martino II to San Guiliano. cf. also R. L. Hess, *Italian Colonialism in Somalia* (Chicago, 1966), p. 107. De Martino was, almost inevitably, involved in dispute with the

representatives of the Italian military in the colony, and pursued by charges of corruption.

84 *RC*, I, May 1906, preface.

85 E. Catellani, 'L'Italia dopo la Conferenza di Algeciras: l'equilibrio del Mediterraneo e il sistema delle alleanze', *RC*, I, May 1906. Catellani was a professor from the University of Padua.

86 *RC*, I, May 1906, p. 61.

87 E. Mayor des Planches, 'Gli Stati Uniti e l'emigrazione italiana', *RC*, I, May 1906, pp. 75–82. His article was a tacit endorsement of the views expressed a year before by San Giuliano about the experience of Italian migrants in the U.S.

88 *RC*, III, Jan.–June 1907, report of a meeting of the Istituto Coloniale of 28 April 1907, p. 488. At the meeting of 7 March 1907, San Giuliano had urged members to see to it that Italy 'safeguard and intensify' her actions in areas of national interest, threatened by 'foreign rivalry'.

89 *RC*, IV, July–Dec. 1907, p. 162.

90 *RC*, V, March–April 1908, pp. 161–76. De Martino further wrote up his ideas about this journey, G. De Martino, *Cirene e Cartagine: note e impressioni della carovana De Martino-Baldari, giugno-luglio, 1907* (Bologna, 1908).

91 *RC*, V, March–April 1908, pp. 302–5.

92 *Ibid.*, p. 305.

93 *RC*, V, Oct. 1908, pp. 478–93.

94 See report by XXX, 'La federazione dell'italianità', *NA*, f 885, 1 Nov. 1908, pp. 139–45, 'XXX' was either Tittoni or a source inspired by him.

95 *RC*, V, Nov.–Dec. 1908, pp. 694–5.

96 *Ibid.*, pp. 704–24.

97 Indeed 1907 brought no revival to a traditional commercial–colonialist group which had been lingering on since 1896. See A. Milanini Kemeny, *La società d'esplorazione commerciale in Africa e la politica coloniale (1879–1914)* (Florence, 1973). This group, under the Milanese, Pippo Vigoni, had been an early rival in colonialist sponsorship with the Geographical Society. In 1899 its name was changed to the Società Italiana di Esplorazioni Geografiche e Commerciali. It was largely moribund by 1911, although it did not disappear until 1928 when it was absorbed into the Istituto Coloniale Fascista, the reorganised version of the Istituto Coloniale. Pippo Vigoni attended the Asmara Conference.

98 *RC*, VI, Jan.–June 1909, p. 359. By the end of 1909, formally there were 500 members, although there were doubts whether many members had in fact renewed their subscriptions.

99 *RC*, rev. s., I, 25 March 1910, did note a need for a more 'practical' approach which would give greater consideration to trade, and a committee was set up under De Martino II to pursue the problems of Italian commerce, especially with the Near East. Maggiorino Ferraris and Foscari of the business interest, Fusinato, Cappelli and Torre for the politicians, Maraini and Vico Mantegazza for the intellectuals were made members of the committee, but *Rivista Coloniale* gives few details of its later activities.

100 *RC*, VI, Jan.–June 1909.

101 *Corriere della Sera*, 5 June 1911.

102 *Corriere della Sera*, 1 May 1911.

103 *Avanti!*, 5 June 1911.

104 See for example the moderate tone of Giolitti's speech inaugurating the Victor Emmanuel monument, making much of Italy's constitutional liberties and the need for social and economic progress. CG, 37/151.

105 PCG, 16/2/758, 19 Nov. 1910, Fusinato to Luzzatti.

106 e.g. MAE P, 131/17, 21 Oct. 1911, Fusinato to San Giuliano; 130/17, 13 Dec. 1911, Fusinato to San Giuliano; 177/17/86, 24 Jan. 1912, Fusinato to San Giuliano; 675/844, 14 April 1914, Primo Levi to Pellegrini.

107 e.g. note his eulogy of the founder of the Triple Alliance G. Fusinato, *Pasquale Stanislao Mancini* (Turin, 1889).

108 Pierotti, *op. cit.*, p. 15.

109 De Martino II himself was now inclined to believe that Italy's present ambitions were satisfied. See *RC*, 2 s, VIII, 1–15 March 1913; G. De Martino, *La Somalia nostra* (Bergamo, 1913).

110 *RC*, 2 s, VII, 25 Oct. 1912, p. 286.

111 *Ibid.*, p. 288.

112 See Appendix 1.

113 *RC*, 2 s, IX, 15 June 1914.

114 S. Scaroni, *Con Vittorio Emanuele III* (Milan, 1954), p. 92.

CHAPTER 3. THE MAKING OF A FOREIGN MINISTER: ANTONINO DI SAN GIULIANO

1 D. Mack Smith, *Italy, a Modern History* (rev. ed., Ann Arbor, 1969), p. 293, cf. also the hostile comments in L. Albertini, *The Origins of the War of 1914* (3 vols. London, 1952–7). e.g. vol. II, p. 245 sums up San Giuliano's policy as one of 'utter, unreserved surrender to the Central Powers'.

2 C. Galli, *Diarii e Lettere* (Florence, 1951), p. 229.

3 A. Torre, 'Il marchese di San Giuliano fra la neutralità e l'intervento', *Nova Historia*, 22 (1954), p. 106.

4 F. Salata, 'Ministri degli affari esteri del regno d'Italia: Il Marchese Di San Giuliano', *Storia e Politica Internazionale*, II (1940) p. 24.

5 San Giuliano can still be attacked for not being nationalist enough. See P. Pastorelli, *L'Albania nella politica estera italiana, 1914–1920* (Naples, 1970), pp. 14–15.

6 For a full genealogy of the family see F. Paternò Castello Di Carcaci, *I Paternò Di Sicilia* (Catania, 1936).

7 F. De Roberto, *I viceré* (new ed., Milan, 1976); cf. also *L'imperio* (Milan, 1959).

8 i.e. 'Berets and hats can never come together.' Quoted from S. F. Romano, *Storia dei fasci siciliani* (Bari, 1959), p. 100.

9 L. Sciacca, *Catania com'era*, Catania, 1974, pp. 134–7; S. Lo Presti, *Memorie storiche di Catania, fatti e leggende*, Catania, 1957, pp. 203–6.

10 F. Cataluccio, 'La formazione culturale e politica di A. Di San Giuliano', *NA*, f 2025, 1969, p. 305.

11 *Ibid.*, pp. 304–5.

12 A. Torre, 'Ricordo di Antonino Di San Giuliano', *NA*, f 1849, 1955, p. 31.

13 F. Martini, *Diario 1914–1918* (Milan, 1966), p. 184.

14 D. Varè, *Laughing Diplomat* (London, 1938), p. 61.

15 Cataluccio, *op. cit.*, pp. 307–8.

16 *Ibid.*, pp. 308–9.

17 *Ibid.*, pp. 310–12.

18 A. Paternò Castello Di San Giuliano [sic], *La questione elettorale in Italia sunto in due conferenze orali* (Catania, 1876).

19 Sciacca, *op. cit.*, p. 45.

20 A. Paternò Castello Di San Giuliano, *Sulla ferrovia circumetnea: lettera ai consiglieri comunali di Catania* (Catania, 1882).

21 A. Di San Giuliano [sic], *Discorso politico tenuto all' Arena Pacini, domenica 3 settembre 1882* (Catania, 1882).

22 *CD*, xv, vii, 19 Feb. 1884, p. 6255.

23 *CD*, xv, ii, 3 March 1883, pp. 1640–1.

24 *Ibid.*, p. 1662, 16734.

25 *CD*, xv, xvi, 17 Feb. 1886, pp. 16871–3, 16881–2.

26 G. Neppi Modona, *Sciopero, potere politico e magistratura, 1870–1922* (Bari, 1969), pp. 11–12, 42–3.

27 A. Di San Giuliano, *Discorso pronunziato al banchetto offertogli da alcuni amici elettori del 1° collegio di Catania* (Catania, 1886).

28 Romano, *op. cit.*, pp. 47–8, 52.

29 A. Carrà, *La Sicilia orientale dall' Unità all'impresa libica* (Catania, 1968), p. 131; An '*Associazione dei Contadini*' had also been established in Catania province in November 1888 (p. 141).

30 *Ibid.*, pp. 73–4.

31 A. Di San Giuliano, *Conferenza sul tema il partito progressista costituzionale e le classi lavoratrici* (Milan, 1890). Apart from the obvious invocation of the new age in the *Carmen Saecularis*, San Giuliano also was exhibiting the usual width of culture of Italian politicians. Only weeks before, an important discovery of the 'Acta' of the Secular Games of 17 B.C. had been made during building operations on the Tiber embankment. The Accademia dei Lincei entrusted the task of the explanation of the find to Theodore Mommsen. That year at Wiesbaden, San Giuliano would have another author apart from Goethe to help him meditate on parallels between Italy and Germany. See E. Fraenkel, *Horace* (Oxford, 1966), pp. 366–7.

32 E. Vitale (ed.) *La riforma degli istituti di emissione e gli 'scandali bancari' in Italia, 1892–1896* (Rome, 1972), vol. III, pp. 365–6.

33 Romano, *op. cit.*, p. 53.

34 F. Cataluccio, 'Lotte e ambizioni di Antonio Di San Giuliano', in M. M. Libelli (ed.) *Studi in onore di Niccolò Rodolico* (Florence, 1944), pp. 51–2.

35 Romano, *op. cit.*, pp. 349–50.

36 *Ibid.*, pp. 113–14. De Felice declared 'I am a socialist because knowledge [*scienza*] is socialist.'

37 U. Levra, *Il colpo di stato della borghesia* (Milan, 1975), pp. 339–40. This occurred after an incident in the Chamber during which Bissolati knocked down Sidney Sonnino with a blow on the head.

38 G. Miccichè, *Dopoguerra e fascismo in Sicilia 1919–1927* (Rome, 1976), pp. 132–3. In

fact the Fascists had some trouble destroying the hegemony of De Felice Giuffrida and his successors in Catania in 1920–2.

39 A. Di San Giuliano, *Le condizioni presenti della Sicilia: studii e proposte* (Milan, 1894), pp. 7, 12–13, 213–21.

40 *CD*, XVIII, 1st Session, vi, 25 April 1894, pp. 8094–7.

41 He learned from these experiences that 'the defence of the country must not be neglected at any cost'. Cataluccio, 'La formazione culturale e politica di A. Di San Giuliano', p. 313.

42 In one moment of conventional wisdom he argued that Italy should have diplomatic representation in Teheran since all the other Great Powers, and even Romania and Holland did. *CD*, XV, iii, 14 March 1883, pp. 1964–5.

43 *CD*, XV, viii, 4 April 1884, pp. 7098, 7105.

44 G. Dore, *La democrazia italiana e l'emigrazione in America* (Brescia, 1964), pp. 48, 72–4.

45 Di San Giuliano, *Discorso pronunziato al banchetto offertogli da alcuni amici elettori del 1° collegio di Catania*, pp. 24–7.

46 Di San Giuliano, *Conferenza sul tema il partito progressista costituzionale e le classi lavoratrici*, pp. 16–19.

47 *CD*, XVI, 4th Session, iii, 14 May 1890, pp. 2849 50.

48 A. Del Boca, *Gli italiani in Africa orientale* (Bari, 1976), pp. 439–45.

49 R. Rainero, *L'anticolonialismo italiano da Assab ad Adua (1869–1896)* (Milan, 1971), pp. 247–50.

50 F. Martini, *Nell'Affrica Italiana: impressioni e ricordi* (Milan, 1895), pp. 15, 332. Martini's spelling of 'Affrica' was deliberate on the grounds that this was a more accurate version than the accustomed 'Africa'.

51 *Ibid.*, p. 50.

52 *Relazione generale della R. Commissione d'Inchiesta sulla Colonia Eritrea* (Rome, 1891), pp. 8–9.

53 *Ibid.*, pp. 204–5 cited by Rainero, *op. cit.*, p. 262.

54 C. G. Segrè, *Fourth Shore* (Chicago, 1974), pp. 13–15.

55 *CD*, XVII, vi, 23 March 1892, pp. 7260–1; XVIII, vi, 2 May 1894, pp. 8297–301.

56 A. Di San Giuliano, 'La crisi dell'Africa italiana', *NA*, f 576, 16 Dec. 1895, pp. 606–10; 'I fini della nostra politica coloniale', *La Riforma Sociale*, III (1895), pp. 310–23; published also in *Bollettino della Società Africana d'Italia*, 14 (1895), pp. 17–31; S. Sonnino, L'Africa italiana-appunti di viaggio', *NA*, f 435, 1 Feb. 1890, pp. 425–65.

57 Di San Giuliano, 'La crisi dell'Africa italiana', p. 627.

58 *CD*, XIX, 1st Session, iii, 20 March 1896, pp. 3534, 3536–7.

59 *CD*, XIX, 1st Session, vii, 30 Nov. 1896, pp. 7760–1; XX, 1st Session, i, 18 May 1897, pp. 781–94.

60 A. Aquarone, 'La politica coloniale italiana dopo Adua: Ferdinando Martini Governatore in Eritrea', *RSR*, LXII (1975), pp. 465–70.

61 Segrè, *op. cit.*, p. 14.

62 R. Longhitano, *Antonino Di San Giuliano* (Rome, 1954), p. 94.

63 *CD*, XX, 2nd Session, iii, 4 March 1899, pp. 2601–2.

64 *CM*, 13, 24 Dec. 1899, San Giuliano to Martini.

65 G. Candeloro, *Storia dell'Italia moderna*, vol. VII (Milan, 1974), pp. 144–5.

66 F. Cataluccio, 'Lotte e ambizioni di Antonio Di San Giuliano', p. 49.

67 *La Tribuna*, 6 Nov. 1904.

68 F. Cataluccio, *Antonio Di San Giuliano e la politica estera italiana dal 1900 al 1914* (Florence, 1935), p. 6.

69 *CD*, XIX, 1st Session, vi, 29 June 1896, p. 6817.

70 *CD*, XX, 2nd Session, i, 15 Dec. 1898, p. 996.

71 E. Decleva, *Da Adua a Sarajevo* (Bari, 1971), p. 169.

72 A. Di San Giuliano, *Lettere sull'Albania* (Rome, 1903); see also V. Castronovo, *La stampa italiana dall'unità al fascismo* (Bari, 1970), pp. 171–3.

73 F. Guicciardini, 'Impressioni d'Albania', *NA*, f 709, 1 July 1901, pp. 28, 53, 56.

74 Di San Giuliano, *Lettere sull'Albania*, pp. 16–18, 37, 81.

75 *Ibid.*, p. 10.

76 *Ibid.*, p. 89.

77 F. Cataluccio, 'Lotte e ambizioni di Antonio Di San Giuliano', p. 49.

78 N. Nasi, *Memorie: storia di un dramma parlamentare* (Grottaferrata, 1951), p 382, fn. 1.

79 Torre, 'Ricordo di Antonino Di San Giuliano', p. 34.

80 F. Manzotti, *La polemica sull'emigrazione nell'Italia unita fino alla prima guerra mondiale* (Milan, 1962), pp. 159–65. He notes that he had found no mention by Giolitti in his papers of the emigration problem.

81 A. Di San Giuliano, 'L'emigrazione italiana negli Stati Uniti d'America', *NA*, f 805, 1 July 1905, pp. 88, 92, 103–4.

82 L. Lodi, *Venticinque anni di vita parlamentare* (Florence, 1923), p. 88.

83 *DDF*, 2 s, VI, 356, 26 April 1905, Barrère to Delcassé, MAE P, 208/24, 1 Nov. 1905, Lanza to Tittoni.

84 MAE P, 208/24, 2 Dec. 1905, Silvestrelli to Tittoni; 209/24, 28 Dec. 1905, Silvestrelli to San Giuliano; 5 Jan. 1906, Silvestrelli to San Giuliano.

85 E. Serra, *Camille Barrère e l'intesa italo-francese* (Milan, 1950), pp. 48–51, 199.

86 L. Albertini, *Venti anni di vita politica*, vol. 1, part 1 (Bologna, 1950), p. 253.

87 Cataluccio, *Antonio Di San Giuliano*, pp. 31–2.

88 e.g. MAE P, 209/24, 11 April 1906, Lanza to Guicciardini.

89 e.g. MAE P, 209/24, 6 April 1906, Tornielli to Guicciardini.

90 M. Mazzetti, *L'esercito italiano nella triplice alleanza* (Naples, 1974), pp. 212–15.

91 *CD*, XX, 2nd Session, i, 28 Nov. 1898, pp. 270–1.

92 AR, 1/64, 2 Nov. 1908, Tittoni to San Giuliano.

93 AR, 2/103, 1 June 1908, San Giuliano to Tittoni.

94 MAE P, 492/121, 5 Nov. 1909, San Giuliano to Tittoni.

95 AR, 2/103, 12 Oct. 1908, San Giuliano to Tittoni.

96 AR, 2/103, 1 June 1908, San Giuliano to Tittoni.

97 Cataluccio, *Antonio Di San Giuliano*, p. 35.

98 AR, 1/5, 3 Oct. 1907, San Giuliano to Tittoni.

99 MAE P, 491/121, 10 Oct. 1907, San Giuliano to Tittoni.

100 e.g. MAE P, 491/121, 25 Nov. 1908, San Giuliano to Tittoni; 492/121, 14 June 1909, San Giuliano to Tittoni.

101 MAE P, 492/121, 15 Dec. 1909, San Giuliano to Guicciardini. The despatch is cited at length in F. Tommasini, *L'Italia alla vigilia della guerra: la politica estera di Tommaso Tittoni* (Bologna, 1934–1941), vol. V, pp. 209–11.

CHAPTER 4. THE *CONSULTA*: THE BUREAUCRATS
OF FOREIGN POLICY

1   S. Scaroni, *Con Vittorio Emanuele III* (Milan, 1954), p. 66.
2   G. Rumi, *Alle origini della politica estera fascista, (1918–1923)* (Bari, 1968), p. 281.
3   R. Guariglia, *Primi passi in diplomazia e rapporti dall' ambasciata di Madrid 1932–1934*
    (Naples, 1972), pp. 11–12.
4   G. Licata, *Notabili della Terza Italia* (Rome, 1968), pp. 255–6.
5   V. Mantegazza, *La Turchia liberale e le questioni balcaniche* (Milan, 1908), pp. xxxix–xl.
    The ambassador involved was Bollati, the post Athens.
6   D. Varè, *The Two Impostors* (London, 1949), pp. 69–71.
7   D. Varè, *Laughing Diplomat* (London, 1938), p. 61.
8   *Ibid.*, p. 49.
9   *Punch*, 14 Nov. 1923.
10 Varè, *Laughing Diplomat*, p. 62.
11 Varè, *The Two Impostors*, pp. 55–6.
12 Guariglia, *op. cit.*, p. 4.
13 Officially Italy did not possess ambassadors but 'Envoys Extraordinary' and 'Ministers
    Plenipotentiary'. In 1907 salaries were:
> Envoys Extraordinary and Ministers Plenipotentiary
> 1st class   15,000 lire
> 2nd class   9,000 lire
> Counsellors 1st class   6,000 lire
> Counsellors 2nd class   5,000 lire
> 1st Secretaries   4,000 lire
> 2nd Secretaries   3,000 lire
> 3rd Secretaries   2,500 lire
> *Consular Service*
> Consuls-General 1st class   9,000 lire
> Consuls-General 2nd class   6,000 lire
> Consuls 1st class   5,000 lire
> Consuls 2nd class   4,000 lire
> Vice-Consuls 1st class   3,000 lire
> Vice-Consuls 2nd class   2,500 lire

Figures from *Bollettino del Ministero degli Affari Esteri*, Rome, 1908.
14 Guariglia, for example, was able to mobilise in his favour one uncle who was a
    general, another who was a deputy, Minister and important spokesman on foreign
    affairs. An earlier relation had worked for the Bourbon Ministry of Foreign Affairs
    before transferring to the Italian after 1860. A cousin had joined the diplomatic
    service and been posted to the Paris Embassy where his career was cut short by a
    fatal fall from a horse. Guariglia, *op. cit.*, pp. 4–5, 9. The examination process was
    remarkably similar under the Fascists. See M. Luciolli, *Palazzo Chigi: anni roventi*
    (Milan, 1976), pp. 11–14.
15 Licata, *op. cit.*, pp. 238–41, 251–4.
16 A. Theodoli, 'La preparazione dell'impresa di Tripoli', *NA*, f 1496, 16 July 1934,
    pp. 240–1; Mayor devoted some of his retirement to the appropriate task of being

a monarchist historian. E. Mayor des Planches, 'Re Vittorio Emanuele II alla vigilia della guerra del settanta (con documenti inediti)', *NA*, f 1154, 16 April 1920, pp. 337–54.

17 e.g. see F. J. Coppa, *Planning, protectionism and politics in Liberal Italy* (Washington D.C., 1971), p. 26; R. A. Webster, *L'imperialismo industriale italiano 1908–1915* (Turin, 1974), pp. 146–7, 205–6.

18 Mantegazza, *op. cit.*, p. xxi. Imperiali had the problem of dealing with the French ambassador, Constans, of Boulanger crisis fame, and a formidable expert in imperialism, colonialism and peculation.

19 P. A. Allum, *Politics and society in post-war Naples* (Cambridge, 1973), p. 14; F. Gilbert, 'Ciano and his Ambassadors' in G. A. Craig and F. Gilbert (eds), *The Diplomats, 1919–39* (Oxford, 1953), pp. 512–36.

20 C. Sforza, *L'Italia dal 1914 al 1944* (Milan, 1944), p. 16.

21 These details have been culled from the *Annuario diplomatico del regno d'Italia* (Rome, 1909).

22 Characteristic was the fact that Avarna was married to a Dolgorouky. Italian diplomats usually seem to have been less eagerly sought on the international aristocratic marriage market than their colleagues from other countries.

23 M. Pansa, 'Ricordi di vita diplomatica, 1884–1914', *NA*, f 1924, April 1961, p. 533.

24 Melegari has left no memoirs except a chatty invocation of the joys of court life, G. Melegari, 'L'Imperatore Nicolò II e la sua politica: ricordi ed impressioni', *NA*, f 1233, 1 Aug. 1923, pp. 193–206.

25 In 1914 Tittoni even made himself available to be the new leader of the 'constitutional opposition' in case Giolitti drifted too far to the left. L. Albertini, *Epistolario, 1911–1926* (Milan, 1968), vol. I, p. 229. Salvago Raggi claimed that Fusinato had told him 'that Tommaso Tittoni was interested in only three people: Tommaso, Tittoni and Tommaso Tittoni'. Licata, *op. cit.*, p. 435.

26 C. Galli, *Diarii e lettere* (Florence, 1951), p. 46.

27 Guariglia, *op. cit.*, pp. 31–2.

28 Varè, *Laughing Diplomat*, pp. 61–2.

29 There is a poor and favourable biography by R. Cantalupo (pseud. Legatus), *Vita diplomatica di Salvatore Contarini* (Rome, 1947). Contarini was launched into the Ministry by Rudinì whose secretary he became. Nonetheless Contarini was an early enthusiast for the Crispian version of Africanism (pp. 31–2).

30 Luciolli, *op. cit.*, p. 53.

31 Varè, *Laughing Diplomat*, pp. 227–8; Galli, *op. cit.*, p. 46.

32 In July 1914 Fasciotti picked a bad moment apparently to plot that his achievements in the diplomatic, political and economic world be consummated by elevation to the Embassy at Constantinople. See CB, 10, VII.1.41, 11 July 1914, Fasciotti to Brusati.

33 Cerruti's Hungarian actress wife has left memoirs of their life in the inter-war period, E. Cerruti, *Ambassador's wife* (London, 1952).

34 Guariglia, *op. cit.*, p. 22.

35 R. Guariglia, *Ricordi 1922–1946* (Naples, 1949), p. 9.

36 L. V. Ferraris, 'L'amministrazione centrale del Ministero degli Esteri italiano nel suo sviluppo storico (1848–1954)', *RSPI*, XXI (1954), p. 653.

37 Varè, *Laughing Diplomat*, p. 274; Webster, *op. cit.*, pp. 300–1; There is a poor eulogy R. Cantalupo, *Ritratto di Pietro Lanza Di Scalea* (Rome, 1939) pp. 17–18 where Scalea is described as 'magnificent gentleman, supremely elegant...tall, slender, strong, [with] a superb Lombard face'. For Scalea's post-war career see G. Miccichè, *Dopoguerra e fascismo in Sicilia 1919–1927* (Rome, 1976), pp. 146–7, 201 n. 140.

38 In this capacity, see his patriotic comments about the triumph of 'the symbolic eagle of Rome' in the Italian colonies. P. Lanza Di Scalea, 'La politica coloniale', in T. Sillani (ed), *L'Italia di Vittorio Emanuele III 1900–1925* (Rome, 1926), p. 174.

39 Ferraris, *op. cit.*, p. 611. It was not unusual for Scalea to be handed responsibility for the more obscure, technical areas of Italian policy cf. AG, 8/24, 7 June 1911, San Giuliano to Manfredi.

40 For the De Martinos of Tunis see E. Michel, *Esuli italiani in Tunisia (1815–1861)* (Milan, 1941), pp. 21, 98, 369.

41 Licata, *op. cit.*, p. 242; P. Levi, *Missione nell' Africa settentrionale, giugno–luglio 1908* (Rome, 1908), pp. 13, 47.

42 R. Cantalupo, *Fuad, primo re d'Egitto* (Milan, 1940) hints at the reasons for these royal friendships.

43 A. Zazo. *La politica estera del regno delle due Sicilie nel 1859–60* (Naples, 1940), pp. 222 3, 357–8.

44 CB, 10, VI.4.36, 30 Jan. 1910, De Martino to Brusati. De Martino said Tittoni's choice would produce only 'a sale of smoke without the least practical result'. See also P. Levi, *op. cit.*, pp. 25–6 praising De Martino who held 'many strings to his bow', and was 'step by step' restoring Italian influence in Egypt.

45 G. De Martino, 'Ricordi di carriera: la mia missione a Costantinopoli per la guerra di Libia', *Rassegna di Politica Internazionale*, IV (1937), 255–7.

46 Galli, *op. cit.*, p. 47.

47 E. Piscitelli, 'Francesco Crispi, Primo Levi e "La Riforma"', *RSR*, XXXVII (1950), pp. 411–12.

48 G. Pescosolido, 'Il dibattito coloniale nella stampa italiana e la battaglia di Adua', *SC*, IV (1973), p. 688 fn. 28.

49 P. Levi, *Luigi Orlando e i suoi fratelli; per la patria e per l'industria italiana* (Rome, 1898). Levi also looked for profits from a textile company which, after 1898, speculated, somewhat fruitlessly, in the Italian Somaliland. F. Grassi, 'L'industria tessile e l'imperialismo italiano in Somalia (1896–1911)', *SC*, IV (1973), p. 713.

50 Ferraris, *op. cit.*, p. 608.

51 F. Gregori, *La vita e l'opera di un grande vescovo: mons. Giov. Battista Scalabrini (1839–1905)* (Turin, 1934), pp. 10–11.

52 G. B. Scalabrini, *Trent'anni di apostolato: memorie e documenti* (ed. A. Scalabrini) (Rome, 1909), p. 5.

53 R. Molinelli, 'Nazionalisti cattolici e liberali (Il Nazionalismo italiano dal congresso di Roma a quello di Milano)', *RSR*, LII (1965), p. 36. L. Ganapini, *Il nazionalismo cattolico* (Bari, 1970), pp. 186–224.

54 Quoted by Ganapini, *op. cit.*, pp. 57–8. Also quoted on the leading page of Angelo Scalabrini's edition of his brother's work, Scalabrini, *op. cit.*

55 Ferraris, *op. cit.*, pp. 452–61.

56 *Ibid.*, pp. 429–30.

57 Giacomo Malvano, served under ten different tenures of the Foreign Ministry and eight different Foreign Ministers; Riccardo Bollati worked under three.

58 Ferraris, *op. cit.*, pp. 612–13.

59 e.g. Mantegazza, *op. cit.*, pp. xiii–xiv; *CD*, XXIII, xix, 22 Feb. 1913, San Giuliano speech p. 23315.

60 Guariglia, *Primi passi*, p. 21; cf. Galli, *op. cit.*, pp. 13–14 commenting on how Squitti, his predecessor in Trieste, had managed to breach the 'hermetically sealed' diplomatic service.

61 Luciolli, *op. cit.*, p. 18.

62 Guariglia, *op. cit.*, pp. 24–5 says that there was only one typewriter in Imperiali's chancellery in London, and only one set of trousers to be shared by the needy attachés; cf. also Pansa, *op. cit.*, p. 369; D. Varè, *Laughing Diplomat*, pp. 49–50.

63 PCG, 13/1, 27 May 1914, San Giuliano to Salandra.

64 There are examples in the archives of money going to Mantegazza (which perhaps helps to explain why he was clear in his mind that San Giuliano was a better Foreign Minister than Tittoni), and oddly enough to Federzoni. AG, 23/210, Aug. 1911; 22/158, 21 July 1913, San Giuliano to Mattioli (the Minister of the Royal Household) and 21 July 1913, Mattioli to San Giuliano. See also V. Mantegazza, *Il Mediterraneo e il suo equilibrio* (Milan, 1914), pp. 106–13. Bettòlo wrote a preface to this book.

65 Both Avarna and Pansa, for example, obviously believed it was demeaning to be too close to the press. AG, 25/231, 28 Nov. 1911, Avarna to San Giuliano; 28 Nov. 1911, Pansa to San Giuliano.

66 See Fasciotti's complaints about the minimal funds available. AG, 8/26, 5 July 1911. The Libyan War did increase the Ministry's desire to improve contacts with the foreign press. See AG, 10/63a.

67 Examples are Reginald Harris of the *Standard*, Leo Maxse of the *National Review*, an Arab nationalist paper in Cairo and *Le Gaulois*. AG, 28/376; 8/26; 25/233; 8/23.

68 D. Varè, *Laughing Diplomat*, pp. 68–9; cf. also Albertini, *op. cit.*, vol. I, p. 145. Bertolini had allegedly told Barzini that Giolitti underestimated the value of the press and that the *Ufficio Stampa* was simply ridiculous.

69 DGPS, 3/7, 19–21 April 1911.

70 AG, 7/43b, March 1911, San Giuliano to Giolitti.

71 *Corriere della Sera*, 18, 20, 24, 25 July 1911.

72 DGPS, 2B/5(i), 27 March 1911, San Giuliano memorandum.

73 MAE P, 676/844, 19 Dec. 1912, De Facendis to San Giuliano.

74 PCG, 10/3, 21 Feb. 1913, San Giuliano to Giolitti; 9/2, 9 May 1913, San Giuliano to Giolitti; 13 May 1913, Giolitti to San Giuliano; CG, 19/45, 6 April 1913, San Giuliano to Giolitti.

75 PCG, 9/2, 11 Oct. 1913, San Giuliano to Giolitti reported that the Ministry had 60,153.58 lire left of its Albanian fund of 250,000 lire. San Giuliano suggested that he be permitted to talk to Tedesco about the subvention being raised to 400,000 lire.

76 SP, 54, Oct. 1913, De Martino memorandum. cf. also Ferraris, *op. cit.*, pp. 614–15.

77 AG, 19/116, 17 Feb. 1914, De Martino memorandum.

78 e.g. CSG, 5, 20 March 1914, San Giuliano to De Martino.

79 The Abbazia meeting produced embarrassing questions not only from Federzoni,

but also from San Giuliano's ancient rival, De Felice Giuffrida. S. Cilibrizzi, *Storia parlamentare, politica e diplomatica d'Italia* (Naples, 1939–52), vol. IV, p. 326.

80 L. Tosi, 'Romeo A. Gallenga Stuart e la propaganda di guerra all'estero (1917–1918)', *SC*, II (1971), pp. 519–20, 525–7.

81 AG, 2/14, 16 Nov. 1910, San Giuliano memorandum.

82 PCG, 15/2, 23 April 1911, San Giuliano to Giolitti.

83 Ferraris, *op. cit.*, pp. 612–14.

84 e.g. see the series of letters in 1914 by Primo Levi offering support for the agencies of the *Reale Museo Commerciale di Venezia*, and the *Società Commerciale d'Oriente*, AG, 29/387.

85. MAE P, 675/844, 5 Nov. 1913, San Giuliano to Joel.

86 PCG, 9/2, 9 May 1913, San Giuliano to Giolitti.

87 AG, 19/117 bis, 30 April 1914, De Martino memorandum.

88 R. L. Hess, 'Italy and Africa: colonial ambitions in the First World War', *JAH*, IV (1963), pp. 105–26; cf. also Varè, *The Two Impostors*, p. 45.

CHAPTER 5. HOW ITALY WENT TO LIBYA

1 Tittoni did serve in the first Fortis Ministry until December 1905.

2 CS(L), 3/88, Diary entry, 31 March 1910. Salandra even thought that Tittoni may have been part of the pro-French plot and had been rewarded with the Paris Embassy as a consequence (Diary entry, 6 April 1910). There is no other evidence for this. Tittoni's posting to Paris seems more a neat act of revenge by San Giuliano than a reward. The diary entries however give an unusual glimpse into Salandra's personal animus and willingness to believe that failure sprang from involved personal conspiracies.

3 S. Cilibrizzi, *Storia parlamentare politica e diplomatica d'Italia* (Naples, 1939–52), vol. IV, pp. 25–6. There were rumours of shady international financial dealings around the Prime Minister's family. See C. Licata, *Notabili della Terza Italia* (Rome, 1968), pp. 337–8, 343.

4 L. Luzzatti, *Memorie* (Milan, 1966), vol. III, pp. 288–9.

5 *Ibid.*, vol. III, pp. 288–9, 293–4, 327, 495–9, 510–1; F. Martini, *Diario, 1914–1918* (Milan, 1966), p. 81.

6 Luzzatti, *op. cit.*, vol. III, p. 326.

7 *Ibid.*, vol. III, p. 309. Luzzatti, typically, had been one of the sponsors of a *Comitato Italiano Ottomano*. In 1910 he was a Vice-President of the Istituto Coloniale although he was not prominent at meetings.

8 AR, 5/180, 2 April 1910, report of San Giuliano–Bethmann Hollweg talk.

9 *Ibid.*, 3 April 1910, San Giuliano to Pansa.

10 AG, 2/14/32, 21 April 1910, L. Ricci to San Giuliano; 1 May 1910, San Giuliano to Ricci.

11 e.g. AR, 5/181, 19 June 1910, San Giuliano to Tittoni. The British ambassador, Rodd, thought Barrère's obduracy had made his position 'very difficult'. RP, 27 June 1910, Rodd to Hardinge.

12 RP, 27 June 1910, Rodd to Hardinge.

13 *OUA*, 2, 2135, 26 April 1910, Mérey to Aehrenthal. For Mérey, see H. von Lützow,

Im diplomatischen Dienst der k.u.k. Monarchie (Munich, 1971), pp. 192–3, alleging that Mérey wanted to treat Italy 'like a conquered land'.

14 AR, 5/180, 4 June 1910, San Giuliano to his major ambassadors; FO 371/905/16364, 6 May 1910, Villiers minute on Rodd to Grey.

15 For typical comments at the time, with a major impact on subsequent historiography e.g. G. Salvemini, *La politica estera italiana dal 1871 al 1915*, (ed. Augusto Torre) (Milan, 1970), pp. 374–9. cf. *OUA*, 3, 2246, 5 Sept. 1910, Ambrozy to Aehrenthal; 2251, 12 Sept. 1910, Aehrenthal to Ambrozy.

16 AR, 5/117, 25 April 1910, Avarna to San Giuliano. Conrad, the Austrian Chief of General Staff, continued to be very pessimistic about the likelihood of Italian military loyalty to Austria. cf. *OUA*, 3, 2404, 3 Jan. 1911, Conrad to Aehrenthal.

17 AG, 3/21 bis, 11 May 1910, San Giuliano to Avarna.

18 AR, 5/117, 11 May 1910, San Giuliano to Avarna.

19 *Ibid.*, 5/205, 22 Sept. 1910, San Giuliano to Avarna, Pansa. It was characteristic that all such complaints were also sent on to Berlin with the usual ambition there of scoring points off Austria, and perhaps being able to request German good offices to restrain Austria in any serious dispute. cf. also *OUA*, 3, 2256, 24 Sept. 1910, Ambrozy to Aehrenthal.

20 e.g. *ibid.*, 5/201, 7 Aug. 1910, San Giuliano to Avarna, promising that naval manoeuvres near Venice would be conducted cautiously.

21 DGPS, 3/6, 18 Dec. 1910, Luzzatti to prefects.

22 Salvemini, *op. cit.*, p. 377.

23 F. R. Bridge, *From Sadowa to Sarajevo* (London, 1972), p. 330.

24 MAE P, 190/20, 10 Oct. 1910, Melegari to San Giuliano; 7 Dec. 1910, Imperiali to San Giuliano.

25 For the issue see generally W. C. Askew, 'The Austro-Italian antagonism, 1896–1914', in L. P. Wallace and W. C. Askew (eds.) *Power, Public Opinion and Diplomacy* (Durham, N.C., 1959), pp. 172–221.

26 AR, 5/180, 3 April 1910, San Giuliano to Pansa.

27 MAE P, 128/17, 12 July 1910, San Giuliano to Imperiali.

28 *Ibid.*, 128/17, 30 July 1910, Mayor des Planches to San Giuliano. The ambassador said that the idea had come from Primo Levi.

29 *Ibid.*, 128/17, 2 Dec. 1910, San Giuliano to Mayor des Planches.

30 *CD*, XXIII, ix, 30 Nov. 1910, pp. 10079–10089. Tittoni had the further motivation for interest in Libya in his links to the Banco di Roma.

31 *Ibid.*, pp. 10164–6.

32 *Ibid.*, pp. 10170–80.

33 Most Italian attention focused on Tripoli, but it is more convenient to use 'Libya' either to mean Tripoli, or the eventual combination of Tripoli, Cyrenaica and more uncertainly, the internal *vilayet* of Fezzan.

34 Both States were interested in possible penal settlements (in the style of Britain's colonies in Australia). They also saw themselves as possible successors to the failing Portuguese Empire. See R. Ciasca, *Storia coloniale dell'Italia contemporanea da Assab all' Impero* (Milan, 1938), pp. 16–17. Ciasca also notes the interest in Libya of Rome, Venice, Genoa, Florence, the Knights of Malta and some priests from the Genoese Republic, and then the Kingdom of Sardinia in the 1820s and 1830s (pp. 309–10).

35   *Ibid.*, p. 311. Ciasca assumes that Salisbury actually offered Libya. W. L. Langer, *European alliances and alignments, 1871–1890* (new ed. New York, 1964), p. 160 is more doubtful about the concreteness of this offer.

36   Italy rejected the British suggestion of a condominium in Egypt, but did take Massawa on the Red Sea and begin her imperial career as a sort of junior partner in the British Empire. See A. Ramm, 'Great Britain, and the planting of Italian power in the Red Sea, 1868–1885', *EHR*, LIX (1944), pp. 211–36.

37   W. C. Askew, *Europe and Italy's acquisition of Libya, 1911–12* (Durham, N.C., 1942), pp. 12–14.

38   See A. F. Pribram, *The Secret Treaties of Austria-Hungary, 1879–1914* (Cambridge, Mass., 1920–1), vol. II, pp. 110–15.

39   See *DDF*, 2 s, i, 17; cf. also E. Serra, *Camille Barrère e l'intesa italo-francese* (Milan, 1950), pp. 86–100 for a detailed account of the negotiations. Even Visconti Venosta, the Coriolanus of Italian foreign policy, can be found admitting in 1899 that Italy could have colonies after suitable development of her economy and public will. F. Cataluccio, *La politica estera di E. Visconti Venosta* (Florence, 1940), pp. 80–1.

40   *BD*, VII, 4, 1 Jan. 1902, Currie to Lansdowne. The major monograph on the subject is E. Serra, *L'Intesa Mediterranea del 1902: una fase risolutiva nei rapporti italo inglesi* (Milan, 1957). Serra's argument that the agreement was 'a decisive phase in Italo-English relations' relies very much on Italian rather than British evidence.

41   G. Giolitti, *Memoirs of My Life* (London, 1923), p. 227.

42   *BD*, I, 360, 7 March 1902, Lansdowne to Currie. In return the British were secretly shown the text of the 1900 Barrère–Visconti Venosta letters. The British themselves secretly showed the text of their agreement to the Germans. See *CP*, 8181/150, 18 March 1902, Lansdowne to Lascelles.

43   Serra, *L'Intesa Mediterranea*, pp. 197–8. Serra notes naively that Cranborne's remarks were technically correct but 'inexact in substance'.

44   *DDF*, 2 s, ii, 313; Serra, *Camille Barrère*, pp. 127–65 gives the standard account of the agreement.

45   Pribram, *op. cit.*, vol. I, pp. 232–5.

46   The standard account is F. Tommasini, *L'Italia alla vigilia della guerra* (Bologna, 1934–41), vol. v, pp. 477–503.

47   e.g. typically M. Toscano, *Il Patto di Londra* (Bologna, 1934), p. 22 thought foreign statesmen had been mistaken in not recognising Italy's 'historic mission', but that success in Libya had brought a progressive 'spiritual awakening'. cf. also in more detail L. Peteani, *La questione libica nella diplomazia europea* (Florence, 1939).

48   F. Cataluccio, *Antonio Di San Giuliano e la politica estera italiana* (Florence, 1935), p. 50.

49   G. De Martino, *Cirene e Cartagine* (Bologna, 1908), p. 162.

50   T. Sillani (ed.), *La Libia in venti anni di occupazione* (Rome, 1932), pp. 19, 23.

51   The Fascist regime was more interested in drilling for water than for oil. See C. G. Segrè, *Fourth Shore* (Chicago, 1974), pp. 115, 183; D. Mack Smith, *Mussolini's Roman Empire* (London, 1976), p. 122. Italy's main 'mineral' exploitation in Libya to 1945 was of the salt-pans near Tripoli. P. Maltese, *La terra promessa* (Milan, 1968), pp. 367–8. He notes that even Volpi made a financial loss out of Libya.

52   The basic sources on the Banco di Roma are R. Mori, 'La penetrazione pacifica

italiana in Libia dal 1907 al 1911 e il Banco di Roma', *RSPI*, XXIV, pp. 102–18; A. D'Alessandro, 'Il Banco di Roma e la guerra di Libia', *Storia e Politica*, VII (1968), pp. 491–509; F. Malgeri, *La guerra libica, 1911–1912* (Rome 1970), pp. 16–19.

53 D'Alessandro, *op. cit.*, p. 496. The Bank's presence at Tangiers fulfilled a right acquired by the Italian government at the Algeciras Conference.

54 *Ibid.*, p. 498.

55 e.g. *ibid.*, pp. 502–5; Malgeri, *op. cit.*, p. 18. Malgeri's evidence that the Bank's action was directed by the government is only a claim in 1915 by the Bank on the Italian government for damages suffered in the Italo-Turkish war.

56 T. Tittoni was of course from 1903 the most blatant evidence that Giolitti was willing to 'transform' Catholics. G. Spadolini, *Giolitti e i cattolici, 1901–1914* (Florence, 1960), pp. 38–45. Ernesto Pacelli was the uncle of a rising young priest who would later become Pope Pius XII.

57 Mori, *op. cit.*, p. 104.

58 *Ibid.*, pp. 107–10.

59 Malgeri, *op. cit.*, p. 27.

60 A copy of this report exists in the Torre papers, 3/7, 6 Feb. 1911, Pestalozza to San Giuliano. I have not been able to locate it in the AS MAE. A Fascist source admits that pre-1911 Libyan trade figures are 'uncertain'. Sillani (ed.), *op. cit.*, p. 126; cf. also Malgeri, *op. cit.*, p. 27.

61 Mori, *op. cit.*, pp. 110–13; Malgeri, *op. cit.*, pp. 20–1.

62 MAE P, 7/1/1, 8 Nov. 1910, Pestalozza to San Giuliano.

63 *Ibid.*, 7/1/1, 3 Dec. 1910, Mayor des Planches to San Giuliano.

64 W. C. Askew, *Europe and Italy's Acquisition of Libya, 1911–1912*, p. 40; G. Piazza, *La nostra terra promessa* (Rome, 1911), pp. 62–8 has a sensational report of a meeting with an unrepentant Guzman.

65 Characteristically the British Foreign Office ignored quite detailed reports from Rodd about the deterioration of Italo-Turkish relations, and concentrated, out of habit, on the ambassador's comments about Italo-Austrian relations. e.g. FO 371/1133/459, 31 Dec. 1910, Rodd to Grey.

66 MAE P, 128/17, 7 Dec. 1910, San Giuliano to Mayor des Planches; *OUA*, 3, 2348, 2355, 2356, respectively 6, 7, 8 Dec. 1910, all Mérey to Aehrenthal.

67 e.g. *ibid.*, 128/17, 9 Dec. 1910, San Giuliano to Mayor des Planches.

68 *Ibid.* 128/17, 29 Dec. 1910, San Giuliano to Mayor des Planches.

69 Quoted from A. Lyttelton (ed.), *Italian Fascisms from Pareto to Gentile* (London, 1973), pp. 146–7.

70 R. Molinelli, 'Il nazionalismo italiano e l'impresa di Libia', *RSR*, LIII (1966), p. 288.

71 Giolitti, *op. cit.*, p. 259 notes reasonably that, by July, public opinion was nearly unanimous in its desire to act in Libya.

72 Molinelli, *op. cit.*, p. 285.

73 F. Gaeta, *Nazionalismo italiano* (Naples, 1965), p. 94.

74 Cited *ibid.*, p. 96.

75 R. S. Cunsolo, 'Libya, Italian Nationalism and the revolt against Giolitti', *JMH*, 37 (1965), p. 188.

76 *Ibid.*

77 Malgeri, *op. cit.*, p. 47. Frassati intervened with San Giuliano personally to get

government backing for Bevione's visit AG, 23/192, 1 March 1911, Frassati to San Giuliano; 7 March 1911, San Giuliano to Prefect in Turin. Piazza illustrated the Francophobe side of Italy's drive to Libya, by reaching it via Tunis and not hesitating to make many pointed comments about the continued relevance of 1881. Piazza, *op. cit.* The fullest account of opinion and the Libyan campaign is in Maltese, *op. cit.*

78 Castronovo, *La Stampa italiana dall' Unità al fascismo*, p. 192.

79 M. Pincherle, 'La preparazione dell'opinione pubblica all'impresa di Libia', *RSR*, LVI (1969), p. 466. Bevione often wrote directly on the orders of Frassati. See p. 469.

80 Malgeri, *op. cit.*, p. 39. On 8 January 1911, *Giornale d'Italia* declared Italy needed an 'open and decisive' policy in Libya. Pincherle, *op. cit.*, p. 454; J. L. Miège, *L'imperialisme colonial italien de 1870 à nos jours* (Paris, 1968), p. 91.

81 e.g. R. Molinelli, 'Nazionalisti cattolici e liberali (Il Nazionalismo italiano dal congresso di Roma a quello di Milano)', *RSR*, LII (1965), pp. 355–78; Gaeta, *op. cit.*, p. 126 notes splits in the group's attitude to the Balkan Wars.

82 See classically in G. Carocci, *Giolitti e l'età giolittiana* (Turin, 1961), p. 139; cf. Malgeri, *op. cit.*, pp. 54–5.

83 Cited Malgeri, *op. cit.*, pp. 98 9.

84 AG, 7/43b, 1 April 1911, San Giuliano to Giolitti.

85 DGPS, 2B/5 (1), 27 March 1911, San Giuliano memorandum.

86 San Giuliano's own respect for public opinion was no doubt hardly increased by finding that the old leader of the Sicilian *fasci* around Catania, Giuseppe De Felice Giuffrida, now campaigned for the Libyan War in his paper *Corriere di Catania*. Malgeri, *op. cit.*, pp. 64–5. Italian Socialists were, of course, by no means united in their opposition to the war.

87 *CD*, XXIII, iii, 7 June 1911, pp. 15348–56.

88 Von Lützow, *op. cit.*, p. 130.

89 F. Guicciardini, 'Impressioni di Tripolitania', *NA*, f 679, 1 April 1900, pp. 402, 421–2.

90 It is this speech which is emphasised in the standard history of the Italian parliament, a history written in the Fascist era from a nationalist viewpoint. Cilibrizzi, *op. cit.*, vol. IV, pp. 158–9. Foscari's speech became something of a piece of nationalist mythology. It was included in a short collection of Foscari's more 'luminous' pieces, published on his death in 1928 to celebrate one of the first great patriots 'in the years of our passion', as Luigi Federzoni described it in a pious introduction. See P. Foscari, *Per l'Italia più grande*, T. Sillani (ed.) preface by L. Federzoni (Rome, 1928), pp. 3–5, 87–113. The main speaker against the war was the Arabist deputy for Rome, Livio Caetani. See Maltese, *op. cit.*, p. 53.

91 *Corriere della Sera*, 8 June 1911.

92 *Ibid.*, 9 June 1911. The editorial was again written by Torre. On 10 June he once again attacked San Giuliano for failing completely to reply satisfactorily to Guicciardini's charges. In August, in urging immediate action, Torre reverted to the familiar theme that if Italy failed to act, she would become merely 'a maritime Switzerland'. CT, 1/4, 25 Aug. 1911, A. Torre to Albertini.

93 M. Degl'Innocenti, *Il socialismo italiano e la guerra di Libia* (Rome, 1976), p. 65.

94 *Corriere della Sera*, 12 June 1911.

95 *RC*, VI, 10 June 1911.

96 *Corriere della Sera*, 12 June 1911.

97 For Giolitti's own comments see Giolitti, *op. cit.*, pp. 233–4.

98 G. Salvemini, *Il ministro della malavita* (Milan, 1966), p. 236; for Giolitti's programme, see Giolitti, *Discorsi parlamentari* (Rome, 1954), vol. III, p. 1366–9; 1370–5. It was in his speech of 8 April that Giolitti boasted of having relegated Karl Marx to the attic.

99 See generally A. Pepe, *Storia della CGdL dalla fondazione alla guerra di Libia, 1905–1911* (Bari, 1972); G. Arfé, *Storia del socialismo italiano (1892–1926)* (Turin, 1965), pp. 146–8.

100 Pepe, *op. cit.*, pp. 423–8.

101 *Ibid.*, pp. 465–6.

102 Quoted *ibid.*, p. 468.

103 A. Pepe, *Storia della CGdL dalla guerra di Libia all'intervento 1911–1915* (Bari, 1971), p. 122.

104 See Castronovo, *op. cit.*, pp. 187–194.

105 Giolitti, *Memoirs of my life*, p. 224; cf. Malgeri, *op. cit.*, pp. 97–9.

106 In June 1911 Tittoni had sent the patriotic *feste* a message about 'the flame' roused by them in every heart. See also MAE P, 493/121, 29 Jan. 1911, Tittoni to San Giuliano, report warning Italy of the new dangers of expansionist France in North Africa which was deliberately aiming against Italy. San Giuliano took the unusual step of having the report printed and circulated. San Giuliano was perhaps the most conservative member of Giolitti's new reforming Cabinet. This is no doubt more evidence of the lingering monarchical assumptions about the making of foreign policy in Liberal Italy. But as these assumptions were so strong it is not really good evidence of Giolitti's cynicism. Tittoni and Guicciardini were also not social radicals.

107 MAE P, 670/844, 30 March 1911, Mayor des Planches to San Giuliano. No doubt Mayor believed that such disinterested action would naturally be rewarded with special Italian privileges in Albania.

108 *Ibid.*, 670/844, 3 April 1911, Squitti to San Giuliano.

109 *Ibid.*, 670/844, 13 April 1911, Avarna to San Giuliano.

110 e.g. *ibid.*, 671/844, 18 May 1911, Pansa to San Giuliano; 26 May 1911, Imperiali to San Giuliano.

111 *Ibid.*, 671/844, 26 April 1911, Giolitti to San Giuliano; 12 May 1911, San Giuliano to Mayor des Planches; or e.g. DGPS, 3/7, 19–21 April 1911, report on 7th Congress of Trento and Trieste Association.

112 *Ibid.*, 129/17, 6 March 1911, San Giuliano to Mayor des Planches. cf. also AG, 41/638, 7 April 1911, San Giuliano to Mayor des Planches.

113 MAE P, 129/17, 7 June 1911, Mayor des Planches to San Giuliano.

114 *Senate*, XXIII, viii, 15 June 1911.

115 viz. Giolitti's calmness in his speech of 14 July, on provisions for the city of Rome. Giolitti, *Discorsi parlamentari* vol. III pp. 1436–7; or still more graphically his address at the opening ceremonies of the Victor Emmanuel monument. See generally, R. J. B. Bosworth, 'The opening of the Victor Emmanuel monument', *IQ*, XVIII (1975), p. 85.

116 CG, 13/13, 1 July 1911, San Giuliano to Giolitti. See Malgeri, *op. cit.*, pp. 100–1.

117 FO 371/1134/27882, 3 July 1911, Rodd to Grey. See also Malgeri, *op. cit.*, pp. 117–18.

118 FO 371/1250/29707, 28 July 1911, Grey to Rodd.
119 CG, 22/59, c/1, 26 July 1911, Imperiali to San Giuliano. The words Imperiali used to describe the meeting were different from Grey's, but the apparent impact was the same. Imperiali remained optimistic about British moral support as the crisis deepened e.g. AG, 23/188, 7 Sept. 1911, Imperiali to San Giuliano.
120 *Ibid.*, 22/59, c/1, 28 July 1911, Avarna to San Giuliano.
121 De Martino, 'Ricordi di carriera', pp. 254–5.
122 *Ibid.*, pp. 255–6.
123 *Ibid.*, p. 257.
124 C. Galli, *Diarii e lettere*, pp. 45–6.
125 AG, 7/43b, 22 July 1911, San Giuliano to Giolitti. The increase in the Prime Minister's attention to foreign affairs and in the information which he sought and received is one of the most notable features of the whole Libyan crisis, and casts grave doubts on any theory that he may have been manipulated by San Giuliano.
126 This has been published in *Dalle carte di Giovanni Giolitti: Quarant'anni di politica italiana*, vol. III, ed. C. Pavone (Milan, 1962), pp. 52–6; see also Malgeri, *op. cit.*, pp. 100–1.
127 MAE P, 13/1/1, 29 July 1911, San Giuliano to Avarna, Pansa.
128 *Ibid.*, 672/844, 5 Aug. 1911, San Giuliano to Melegari.
129 *Dalle carte di Giovanni Giolitti*, vol. III, pp. 57–9.
130 CG, 17/38, 13 Aug. 1911, Scalea to San Giuliano; cf. Malgeri, *op. cit.*, pp. 102–3.
131 MAE P, 13/1/1, 11 Aug. 1911, De Martino to San Giuliano.
132 *Ibid.*, 13/1/1, 15 Aug. 1911, De Martino to San Giuliano.
133 AG, 22/184, 21 Aug. 1911, De Martino to San Giuliano. San Giuliano minuted sagely that his own visits to Libya suggested to him that military victory might not be as easy as De Martino thought.
134 MAE P, 130/7, 1 Sept. 1911, De Martino to San Giuliano.
135 Malgeri, *op. cit.*, p. 103; AG, 22/184, 31 Aug. 1911, San Giuliano to Giolitti.
136 CG, 23/60, 17 Aug. 1911, Marro to Pollio; 22/59, c/3, 23 Aug. 1911, Marro to Pollio; MAE P, 13/1/1, 19 Sept. 1911, De Martino to San Giuliano.
137 CG, 22/59, c/1, 27 Aug. 1911, Melegari to San Giuliano.
138 *Ibid.*, 13/13, 30 Aug. 1911, San Giuliano to Giolitti.
139 *Ibid.*, 22/59, c/1, 31 Aug. 1911, San Giuliano to Giolitti enclosing Tittoni's despatch of 25 Aug.; cf. also a longer similar despatch 22/59, c/1, 7 Sept. 1911, Tittoni to San Giuliano.
140 *Ibid.*, 13/13, 31 Aug. 1911, San Giuliano to Giolitti; cf. F. Malgeri, *op. cit.*, p. 103.
141 *Dalle carte di Giovanni Giolitti*, vol. III, pp. 59–60.
142 CG, 22/59, c/2, 13 Sept. 1911, San Giuliano memorandum.
143 AG, 22/184, 15 Sept. 1911, San Giuliano to Victor Emmanuel III.
144 *Ibid.*, cf. CG, 25/64, 15 Sept. 1911, San Giuliano to Giolitti.
145 Malgeri, *op. cit.*, p. 132.
146 France's ally, Russia, was reported to be likely to 'remain passive' before Italian action, and then help Italy reach a settlement. AG, 22/158, 18 Sept. 1911, San Giuliano to Victor Emmanuel III.
147 *Ibid.*, 7/43b, 21 Sept. 1911, San Giuliano to Giolitti, Victor Emmanuel III.

148   Malgeri, *op. cit.*, pp. 127–8.

149   CG, 18/43/5, 21 Sept. 1911, San Giuliano to Galli; AG, 22/184, 21 Sept. 1911, San Giuliano to Giolitti.

150   CG, 16/28, 24 Sept. 1911, San Giuliano to Victor Emmanuel III; Malgeri, *op. cit.*, pp. 136–7.

151   Malgeri, *op. cit.*, pp. 127–8.

152   CG, 17/36, 24 Sept. 1911, San Giuliano to Avarna and others. The territory was now not described as Tripoli but 'Tripolitania and Cyrenaica'.

153   *Ibid.*, 17/36, 24 Sept. 1911, San Giuliano to Avarna; *OUA*, 3, 2653, 26 Sept. 1911, Aehrenthal to Mérey.

154   *Ibid.*, 17/36, 24 Sept. 1911, San Giuliano to Pansa.

155   *Ibid.*, 22/59, c/1, 26 Sept. 1911, San Giuliano to Avarna.

156   AG, 22/162, 25 Sept. 1911, San Giuliano to De Martino.

157   Malgeri, *op. cit.*, pp. 139–40; 155–60.

158   *DDF*, 2 s, xiv, 89, 20 July 1911, Barrère to De Selves.

159   RP, 3 August 1911.

160   In the final crisis, on 20 Sept., Sonnino notably spoke out in favour of war. S. Sonnino, *Scritti e discorsi extraparlamentari, 1870–1922* (Bari, 1972), vol. II, pp. 593–9.

161   Malgeri, *op. cit.*, p. 148.

162   CM, 13, 3 Sept. 1911, Giolitti to Martini.

163   B. Croce, *A History of Italy 1871–1915* (Oxford, 1929), p. 261; *Storia d'Italia dal 1871 al 1915* (Bari, 1967), p. 247.

164   It is surprising how commonly the theory of a '*svolta*' in 1911 is accepted at face value. Perhaps one of the greatest contributors to later analyses was the brilliant contemporary work R. Michels, *L'imperialismo italiano* (Milan, 1914). Yet Michels' assumptions that Italian policies in Africa and China had only been favoured by tiny factions, and that, before 1911, Italy was substantially 'immune' to imperialism, regarded by friends of peace as 'an impregnable fortress of justice, the only one which the ferocious imperialist tempest was still not able to destroy' (pp. 1–2) is hardly borne out by modern research on Italy, and is not backed by any understanding of the limitations and opportunities allowed by Italy's role as the least of the Great Powers.

165   Recent research about the origins of the Ethiopian war has demonstrated the profundity of ambition to take Ethiopia among orthodox diplomatic agents in Fascist Italy. They were indeed very often men trained in their attitude to Empire in San Giuliano's Ministry. This does not mean that diplomats necessarily felt enthusiasm for Mussolini's methods. See R. De Felice, *Mussolini il duce: gli anni del consenso, 1929–1936* (Turin, 1974), pp. 597–9. De Felice (pp. 602–3) cites major advice from Scalea when Minister of Colonies in 1925 to prepare 'militarily and diplomatically' for the eventual dismemberment of Ethiopia.

CHAPTER 6. HOW ITALY STAYED IN LIBYA

1   F. Malgeri, *La guerra libica (1911–1912)* (Rome, 1970), p. 165.

2   There is excellent evidence of San Giuliano's preoccupation with the immediate rather than the long-term in AG, 22/158, 27 Sept. 1911, San Giuliano to King Victor Emmanuel III.

3   For a survey see W. C. Askew, *Europe and Italy's Acquisition of Libya* (Durham, N.C., 1942), pp. 100–3. The Libyan War precipitated an enormous list of publications from various 'overseas correspondents' glad to have a job, and usually anxious to report as sensationally as possible. Most were hostile to Italy.

4   See maps in R. Ciasca, *Storia coloniale dell'Italia contemporanea* (Milan, 1938).

5   Malgeri, *op. cit.*, pp. 167–70.

6   It was typical that by January 1912 40% of Italian casualties had come from cholera and other diseases, and not from actual fighting, *ibid.*, p. 166.

7   Askew, *op. cit.*, pp. 6–7. Tripoli and Cyrenaica sent six deputies to the Turkish Chamber, but Turkey as a whole, despite minimal expense on administration, made a financial loss from the *vilayets*.

8   So Marinetti called war in the Futurist Manifesto of 1909. See English translation in A. Lyttelton (ed.) *Italian Fascisms from Pareto to Gentile* (London, 1973), p. 212. In 1913 Papini, with a typical effort to go rhetorically one better, in a parody of the eucharist, proclaimed 'blood is the wine of strong peoples...' See G. Papini, 'La vita non è sacra', in G. Scalia (ed.), *La cultura italiana del '900 attraverso le riviste*, vol. IV (Turin, 1961), p. 207.

9   S. Bono, 'Lettere dal fronte libico (1911–1912)', *NA*, f 2052, Dec. 1971, pp. 530–1.

10 See Malgeri, *op. cit.*, pp. 283–92.

11 R. Molinelli, 'Nazionalisti, cattolici e liberali (Il Nazionalismo italiano dal congresso di Roma a quello di Milano)', *RSR*, LII (1965), p. 355.

12 C. Galli, *Diarii e lettere* (Florence, 1951), p. 104; for some of Sonnino's criticisms see S. Sonnino, *Scritti e discorsi extraparlamentari 1870–1920* (Bari, 1972), vol. II, pp. 1605–6 arguing that special recognition should not be given to the Caliphate; pp. 1607–8 defending Italy against France in the *Carthage* and *Manouba* incidents.

13 e.g. L. Albertini, *Epistolario, 1911–1926* (Milan, 1968), vol. I, pp. 15–16.

14 *Ibid.*, 4 Nov. 1911, Barzini to Albertini complaining that Giolitti hindered journalists from reporting the war. 'Rome is the incubus of this expedition' by the fault of 'Giolitti who cares little for soldiers and much for socialists; the King who is timid in nature ['*statura*', punning on Victor Emmanuel's lack of height] and humanitarian by organic weakness... The Chief of Staff who reads 'Adowa' in every word which reaches him' (pp. 23–9). In a letter, 28 Nov. 1911, Albertini to D'Annunzio, Albertini noted his good impressions of Barzini's reports (p. 38).

15 Tittoni at least made Albertini's agents in Paris believe that he preferred a stronger policy. e.g. Albertini, *Epistolario*, vol. I, pp. 94–5, 97, 113–14.

16 *CD*, XXIII, xv, 28 March 1912, pp. 18660–2; 18664. San Giuliano's old radical enemy from Catania, N. Colajanni, also criticised the government's failure to prepare the expedition better.

17 V. Castronovo, *La stampa italiana dall'Unità al fascismo* (Bari, 1973).

18 L. Ganapini, *Il nazionalismo cattolico* (Bari, 1970), pp. 172–4.

19 *Ibid.*, p. 187.

20 *Ibid.*, pp. 184–5, 188–9. By 1913 *Civiltà Cattolica* believed that the war had revived the 'religious spirit' as soldiers had to see the need for divine help. G. De Rosa, *Il movimento cattolico in Italia: dalla restaurazione all'età giolittiana* (Bari, 1970), p. 334.

21 Ganapini, *op. cit.*, pp. 197–9 notes for example that in Bologna, the Catholic Electoral Association declared that there was virtually no difference between Catholicism and Nationalism; cf. also De Rosa, *op. cit.*, pp. 339, 347.

22 R. De Felice, *Mussolini il rivoluzionario, 1883–1920* (Turin, 1965), p. 115.

23 G. Arfé, *Storia del socialismo italiano* (Turin, 1965), p. 160. Turati's embarrassment was evident in his speech to the Chamber of 23 February. See F. Turati, *Discorsi parlamentari* (Rome, 1951), vol. III, pp. 1069–81. In conclusion (p. 1081) he too accepted a familiar metaphor, that the real problem for Italy was that she was still 'in the delicate period of [her] economic and civil adolescence'; cf. Giolitti, who, speaking that same day, was at pains to argue that he had entered the war not from enthusiasm, but 'for reason, cold reason'. G. Giolitti, *Discorsi parlamentari* (Rome, 1954), p. 1441.

24 The major study is M. Degl'Innocenti, *Il socialismo italiano e la guerra di Libia* (Rome, 1976), which is very critical of Italian socialism's failure to detect the '*svolta imperialistica*' of the ruling classes.

25 A. Pepe, *Storia della CGdL dalla guerra di Libia all'intervento* (Bari, 1971), p. 87.

26 E. Amendola Kühn, *Vita con Giovanni Amendola* (Florence, 1960), pp. 295–7, 300–2.

27 G. Carocci, *Giolitti e l'età giolittiana* (Turin, 1961), p. 146. For some reluctant comments on the Prime Minister's spryness, see Albertini, *Epistolario*, vol. I, p. 137. Giolitti, who had met Volpi and Bertolini in Turin, seemed to them like a 'young man...vigorous, gay, he has a crystalline clarity of views [and] an unshakeable faith in complete success...at the hotel...he went up the stairs two at a time like a youth going to an assignation'.

28 Galli, *op. cit.*, p. 113; A. Theodoli, 'La preparazione dell'impresa di Tripoli: ricordi di una missione in Turchia', *NA*, f 1496, 16 July 1934, p. 240; J. C. Allain, 'Les débuts du conflit italo-turc: octobre 1911–janvier 1912', *RHMC*, XVIII (1971), p. 107.

29 *The Times*, 29 Sept. 1911.

30 A. J. Marder (ed.), *Fear God and Dread Nought: the correspondence of Admiral of the Fleet, Lord Fisher of Kilverstone* (London, 1952), vol. II, p. 394.

31 *The Times*, 1 Nov. 1911. The last volume of what Trevelyan viewed as his epic on the Risorgimento, *Garibaldi and the Making of Italy*, was first published in 1911. When Italy was fighting on the same side as Britain in the First World War, Trevelyan recorded, by contrast, that Italians 'above all...[are]...fond of children'. G. M. Trevelyan, *Scenes from Italy's War* (London, 1919), p. 10.

32 FO 800/64, GP, 4 Sept. 1911, Rodd to Grey.

33 The Foreign Office even seems to have forgotten what the French thought it knew about the Prinetti–Barrère exchanges. See FO 800/173, BP, 25 Sept. 1911, Bertie to Nicolson.

34 FO 371/1251/38072, 29 Sept. 1911, minutes by Nicolson, Grey.

35 FO 371/1251/38157, 29 Sept. 1911, Grey to Rodd; CG, 23/60, 29 Sept. 1911, Imperiali to San Giuliano.

36 Characteristic of much of Liberal England was Grey's method. He simply showed

a despatch listing Italian complaints to Barbour of *The Times. BD*, IX, i, 256, 30 Sept. 1911, Rodd to Grey; 264, 2 Oct. 1911, Grey to Rodd; CG, 12/10, 4 Oct. 1911, Imperiali to San Giuliano.

37 *Dalle carte di Giovanni Giolitti*, vol. III, ed. C. Pavone (Milan, 1962), p. 64, 2 Oct. 1911, Giolitti to Victor Emmanuel III.

38 2 undated memoranda, probably from early October 1911, AG 7/43c; 4/30 bis.

39 CG, 14/17/1, 2 Oct. 1911, Tittoni to San Giuliano.

40 CG, 15/25 bis, 27 Sept. 1911, Avarna to San Giuliano.

41 GC, 22/59, c/3, 29 Sept. 1911, Avarna to San Giuliano; *OUA*, 3, 2670, 29 Sept. 1911, Aehrenthal to Ambrozy.

42 CG, 22/59, c/3, 1 Oct. 1911, San Giuliano to Pansa and others.

43 CG, 15/25, 2 Oct. 1911, Avarna to San Giuliano; *OUA*, 3, 2683, 1 Oct. 1911, Aehrenthal to Ambrozy (and Berlin).

44 CG, 15/25, 2 Oct. 1911, San Giuliano to Avarna; *OUA*, 3, 2706, 4 Oct. 1911, Aehrenthal to Ambrozy.

45 CG, 14/17/2, 3 Oct. 1911, Avarna to San Giuliano; 20/47, 4 Oct. 1911, Avarna to San Giuliano, *OUA*, 3, 2713, 5 Oct. 1911, Aehrenthal to Ambrozy.

46 See F. Malgeri, *op. cit.*, pp. 301–3; *Dalle carte di Giovanni Giolitti*, vol III, 2 Oct. 1911, Giolitti to Victor Emmanuel III; 2 Oct. 1911, Victor Emmanuel III to Giolitti; 6 Oct. 1911, San Giuliano to Giolitti; 6 Oct. 1911, Giolitti to Leonardi Cattolica, pp. 64–8.

47 CG, 20/47, 8 Oct. 1911, San Giuliano to Giolitti; *OUA*, 3, 2738, 10 Oct. 1911, Aehrenthal to Mérey.

48 AG, 4/30 bis, 14 Oct. 1911, Avarna to San Giuliano.

49 Theodoli, *op. cit.*, pp. 242–9.

50 A copy of the decree is in Malgeri, *op. cit.*, p. 398.

51 CG, 14/17/5, 10 Oct. 1911, San Giuliano to Pansa and others.

52 *Ibid.*, 14/17/6, 10 Oct. 1911, San Giuliano to Pansa and others.

53 e.g. MAE P, 131/17, 19 Oct. 1911, San Giuliano to Pansa and others; 30 Oct. 1911, Tittoni to San Giuliano.

54 CG, 14/17/10, 14 Oct. 1911, Avarna to San Giuliano.

55 e.g. *ibid.*, 14/17/10, 13 Oct. 1911, San Giuliano to Pansa and others; 14 Oct. 1911, San Giuliano to Melegari; 14/17/9, 14 Oct. 1911, Tittoni to San Giuliano.

56 *Ibid.*, 14/17/18, 22 Oct. 1911, San Giuliano to Pansa.

57 *Ibid.*, 14/17/22, 27 Oct. 1911, San Giuliano to Avarna.

58 e.g. C. Seton-Watson, *Italy from Liberalism to Fascism* (London, 1967), p. 308; cf. Malgeri, *op. cit.*, pp. 313–15.

59 *Dalle carte di Giovanni Giolitti*, vol. III, p. 70, 25 Oct. 1911, Giolitti to Victor Emmanuel III.

60 AG, 4/30 bis [5 Nov. 1911], memorandum. Italy did agree that it might still be possible to recognise the 'spiritual authority' of the Caliph. There is a copy also in Malgeri, *op. cit.*, pp. 398–9.

61 e.g. *BD*, IX, i, 301, 6 Nov. 1911, Grey to Rodd.

62 MAE P, 132/17, 17 Nov. 1911, Zaccagnini to Primo Levi.

63 See generally M. S. Anderson, *The Eastern Question 1774–1923: a study in international relations* (New York, 1966), pp. 288–90; A. J. P. Taylor, *The Struggle for Mastery in*

Europe 1848–1918 (new ed., London, 1971), pp. 474–6; E. C. Thaden, 'Charykov and Russian foreign policy at Constantinople in 1911', *JCEA*, xvi (1956–7), pp. 25–44.

64 Thaden, *op. cit.*, p. 36 notes that the Italians, when reminded of the fact, had promised to keep their part of the Racconigi agreement, i.e. they would not block any Russian restoration of her rights of passage through the Straits. For Tittoni and Izvolsky, see C. Vidal, 'Le duel diplomatique Poincaré-Tittoni, 1909–1914', *RSR*, xxxviii (1951), pp. 691–2.

65 AG, 24/222, [Nov. 1911], San Giuliano to Tittoni; 'Legatus' [R. Cantalupo], *Vita di Salvatore Contarini* (Rome, 1947), p. 42.

66 F. R. Bridge, *From Sadowa to Sarajevo* (London, 1972), pp. 336–7. Bridge at times exaggerates the ingenuousness of Aehrenthal's motives.

67 Malgeri, *op. cit.*, p. 319; Conrad had repeated his military advice as late as 15 November. See also *OUA*, 3, 3056, 6 Dec. 1911, Mérey to Aehrenthal noting Italian pleasure given that Conrad's opinions had been 'most precisely' known in Rome.

68 CG, 15/25 bis, 11 Dec. 1911, San Giuliano to Pansa, Avarna. San Giuliano continued to have cause to complain about the abrupt hostility of Mérey, e.g. AG, 25/246, 24 Dec. 1911, San Giuliano to Avarna.

69 It is odd to find no mention of this version in the latest Italian account of the incident. E. Decleva, *Da Adua a Sarajevo: la politica estera italiana e Francia, 1896–1914* (Bari, 1971), p. 411. The French military by now believed that Italy could not win the war on the front in Libya and must either extend the sphere of action, or be driven to peace by Great Power intervention. Allain, *op. cit.*, pp. 110–15.

70 At least so F. S. Nitti, then Minister of Commerce, later maintained. No archival evidence has yet appeared to support his claims. See Malgeri, *op. cit.*, p. 329, fn. 84.

71 MAE P, 177/17/86, 19 Jan. 1912, Tittoni to San Giuliano. The Poincaré government had only taken office on 12 January; Poincaré became President in February 1913; for an account of the pleasant exchanges with Kiderlen Wächter, see AG, 26/287, 21 Jan. 1912, San Giuliano to Avarna, Pansa.

72 *DDF*, 3 s, i, 503, 22 Jan. 1912, Poincaré to Barrère; 506, 23 Jan. 1912, Poincaré to Barrère. Poincaré had taken matters into his own hands as Prime Minister and not left them to the Foreign Minister.

73 FO 800/52, GP, 24 Jan. 1912, Bertie to Grey.

74 *DDF*, 3 s, i, 516, 25 Jan. 1912, P. Cambon to Poincaré. Cambon's views reflected those of the British Foreign Office.

75 MAE P, 177/17/86, 19 Jan. 1912, San Giuliano to Tittoni.

76 *Ibid.*, 177/17/86, 24 Jan. 1912, San Giuliano to Tittoni.

77 Malgeri, *op. cit.*, p. 329.

78 Decleva, *op. cit.*, pp. 413–16.

79 O. Malagodi, *Conversazioni della guerra*, vol. 1 (Milan, 1960), p. 20 cf. also MAE P, 60/9, 1 March 1912, Tittoni to San Giuliano. That old quietist Tittoni now said that the sincerity of French friendship to Italy should always be doubted and that Crispi had been correct when he argued that conservative government in France brought the prospect of war with Italy.

80 e.g. MAE P, 647/844, 11 Feb. 1912, Avarna to San Giuliano anxiously giving assurances that Austria's Eastern policy was essentially peaceful and did not depend simply on Aehrenthal's personality.

81 e.g. *ibid.*, 674/844, 21 Feb. 1912, Avarna to San Giuliano warning that the Austrian General Staff was very concerned by the Albanian situation and was sending reinforcing troops to Dalmatia; 23 Feb. 1912, San Giuliano to Avarna promising that Italy would do all possible to stop volunteers from trying to assist the Albanian independence movement.

82 S. Cilibrizzi, *Storia parlamentare politica e diplomatica d'Italia* (Naples, 1939–52), vol. IV, p. 198.

83 CG, 12/11, 12 Oct. 1911, Stringher to Schwabach.

84 e.g. CG, 17/40, 17 Feb. 1912, Volpi to Giolitti; 17/41, 21 Feb. 1912, Volpi to Giolitti. For Nogara and Volpi's dealings in Constantinople see A. Piccioli, *La pace di Ouchy* (Rome, 1935), pp. 18–25, 28–37.

85 *DDF*, 3 s, ii, 69, 20 Feb. 1912, Poincaré note.

86 *BD*, IX, i, 370, 28 Feb. 1912, Grey to Bertie and others; FO 371/1531/9001, 29 Feb. 1912, Rodd to Grey. The unanimity of the ambassadors undoubtedly reflected their reading of the impact of the *Carthage* and *Manouba* incidents.

87 FO 371/1531/9286, 3 March 1912, Rodd to Grey.

88 CG, 17/41, 29 Feb. 1912, Nogara to Volpi.

89 *Ibid.*, 17/41, 10 March 1912, Nogara to Volpi.

90 e.g. MAE P, 134/17, 3 March 1912, Carlotti to San Giuliano, Carlotti also forwarded a number of reports from his military attaché about Turkish military strength. e.g. 7 March 1912, Carlotti to San Giuliano on the situation at Smyrna; 20 March 1912, on the position at Rhodes.

91 Malgeri, *op. cit.*, p. 351 fn. 41; R. A. Webster, *L'imperialismo industriale italiano* (Turin, 1974), p. 443 dismisses him as 'a noted expert in international law', now a 'Giolittian deputy'.

92 MAE P, 177/17/86, 24 Jan. 1912, Fusinato to San Giuliano.

93 *RC*, VII, 8, 25 April 1912.

94 CG, 17/41, 11 March 1912, Fusinato to Giolitti.

95 *Ibid.*, 22/59/C/4, 18 March 1912, Leonardi Cattolica to Giolitti.

96 Malgeri, *op. cit.*, p. 336; AG, 10/63c, 22 March 1912, Pansa to San Giuliano. R. Katz, *The Fall of the House of Savoy* (London, 1972), p. 199.

97 Nicolson told Lowther, the British ambassador in Constantinople, of his annoyance at Imperiali's frequent interviews of this nature. FO 800/193A, Lowther Papers, 1 April 1912, Nicolson to Lowther. cf. also FO 371/1254/13892, 29 March 1912, Grey to Rodd.

98 CG, 24/62/2, 3 April 1912, Avarna to San Giuliano.

99 *Ibid.*, 24/62/2, 8 April 1912, San Giuliano to Avarna, Pansa. In the month before, there had been further exchanges about the renewal of the Triple Alliance, but Italy had kept to the policy of procrastination until the end of the war.

100 *Ibid.*, 24/62/2, 10 April 1912, San Giuliano to Avarna.

101 e.g. AG, 7/43c, 28 May 1912, Torretta to Di Scalea.

102 CG, 24/62/2, 28 April 1912, San Giuliano to Pansa and others.

103 *BD*, IX, i, 393, 19 April 1912, Rodd to Grey.

104 e.g. FO 371/1531/17083, 19 April 1912, Nicolson memorandum; FO 800/180, BP, 16 May 1912, Bertie to Nicolson.

105 FO 371/1533/21265, 17 May 1912, Delmé-Radcliffe to Grey.

106   CG, 17/40, 27 July 1912, Giolitti to Leonardi Cattolica. Once again in fact there had been pre-planning, 22/59/C/4, 6 July 1912, Leonardi Cattolica to Giolitti.

107   *CD*, XXIII, xvii, 21 June 1912, pp. 214–21.

108   CG, 22/59/C/5, 29 June 1912, Pollio to Giolitti. See translation Appendix II. For an example of Pollio's complaints about being leashed in by politicians see CB, 9, VI.3.35, 4 May 1912, Pollio [to Brusati].

109   Malgeri, *op. cit.*, p. 342, fn. 20.

110   CG, 18/43/9, 13 May 1912, Giolitti to Volpi.

111   *Ibid.*, 17/41, 3 May 1912, San Giuliano to Giolitti; 4 May 1912, Garbasso to De Martino complaining especially of the hopelessness of using other Great Power ambassadors to make peace feelers. In November 1912, Garbasso became San Giuliano's *capo di gabinetto*, replacing De Martino who was promoted to Secretary-General.

112   *ibid.*, 18/43/9, 20 June 1912, Volpi to Giolitti. Volpi also reported to the King and was, in turn, spied on by royal agents. See CB, 9, VI.2.34, 6 June 1912, Volpi to Brusati; 16 June 1912, 'XO' to Brusati.

113   MAE P, 137/17, 18 June 1912, Carlotti to San Giuliano.

114   *Ibid.*, 136/17, 19 June 1912, Stringher to San Giuliano. Joel of the Banca Commerciale Italiana had also continued to sound Italy's case in financial circles. AG, 16/97 bis, 28 May 1912, Joel to San Giuliano.

115   CG, 17/41, 10 July 1912, Volpi to Giolitti. Joel had received his information from the Director-General of the Deutsche Bank whose letter of 8 July 1912 was forwarded to Giolitti.

116   Nogara had wanted London, and Giolitti had, sensibly enough, rejected a Turkish suggestion of Vienna. *Ibid.*, 17/40, 1 July 1912, Nogara to Volpi; Malgeri, *op. cit.*, p. 140.

117   A. Salandra, *La neutralità italiana*, (1914) (Milan, 1935), p. 140.

118   e.g. Malgeri, *op. cit.*, p. 350.

119   e.g. CG, 17/40, 17 July 1912, San Giuliano to Fusinato remarking that Giolitti had 'naturally' shown him Fusinato's reports.

120   *Dalle carte di Giovanni Giolitti*, vol. III, 19 July 1912, San Giuliano to Giolitti, p. 73; CG, 21/48/2, 2 Aug. 1912, San Giuliano to Giolitti.

121   A. Torre, 'Ricordo di Antonino Di San Giuliano', *NA*, f 1849, Jan. 1955, p. 34 recalls that San Giuliano stoically turned down a generous suggestion from Giolitti that he take time off to go to Catania. San Giuliano believed that 'the interests of the country' required that he stay in Rome. Many letters in this period appear to indicate exceptional personal warmth between the two men.

122   CG, 21/48/2, 1 Aug. 1912, Nogara to Volpi remained pessimistic about Turkish intentions.

123   e.g. typically MAE P, 672/844, 28 July 1912, San Giuliano to Carlotti noting that Squitti, the Italian Minister in Cetinje, had told Prince Nicola to abstain as far as possible from any provocative action towards the Turks.

124   CG, 11/1, 22 July 1912, Fusinato to Giolitti.

125   *Ibid.*, 21/48/2, 6 Aug. 1912, Giolitti to San Giuliano.

126   *Ibid.*, 21/48/2, 9 Aug. 1912, San Giuliano to Pansa; 11 Aug. 1912, San Giuliano to Giolitti. Giolitti had thought it was Marschall, but was corrected by San Giuliano.

127 Bridge, *op. cit.*, pp. 344–5; CG, 21/48/2, 17 Aug. 1912, San Giuliano to Giolitti; 18 Aug. 1912, Giolitti to San Giuliano.

128 e.g. CG, 21/48, 6 Aug. 1912, San Giuliano to Giolitti. San Giuliano was also worried lest the military get above themselves and risk another Adowa in Libya, 21/48/2, 5 Aug. 1912, San Giuliano to Giolitti; 7 Aug. 1912, Giolitti to San Giuliano.

129 *Ibid.*, 21/48/2, 9 Aug. 1912, Bertolini to Giolitti.

130 Albertini, *Epistolario.* vol. I, p. 130.

131 *Ibid.*, vol. I, pp. 139–40, 29 Aug. 1912; cf. pp. 143–6. According to Barzini, Fusinato said that the annexation had been a mistake, and Bertolini that Giolitti did not realise the value of the press.

132 CG, 21/48/3, 12 Sept. 1912, Spingardi to Giolitti; 21/48/2, 18 Aug. 1912, Giolitti to San Giuliano.

133 Characteristically Italian agents abroad, whether official or unofficial, had tried to exploit Great Power fears of these events to Italy's advantage. e.g. *ibid.*, 21/48/3, 14 Sept. 1912, Imperiali to San Giuliano; 19 Sept. 1912, Volpi to Giolitti reporting on Joel's activities in Berlin.

134 *Ibid.*, 21/48/4, 1 Oct. 1912, San Giuliano to Giolitti.

135 *Ibid.*, 21/48/4, 1 Oct. 1912, Volpi to Giolitti.

136 *Ibid.*, 21/48/4, 2 Oct. 1912, Giolitti to Volpi; 2 Oct. 1912, Italian memorandum to the Turks.

137 *Ibid.*, 21/48/4, 3 Oct. 1912, Giolitti to San Giuliano, cf. 3 Oct. 1912, Victor Emmanuel III to Giolitti approving the idea, but wondering about the Austrian reaction.

138 *Ibid.*, 21/48/4, 4 Oct. 1912, San Giuliano to Giolitti (in two different telegrams).

139 *Ibid.*, 21/48/4, 8 Oct. 1912, Nogara to Volpi.

140 *Ibid.*, 21/48/4, 12 Oct. 1912, Giolitti to Bertolini.

141 Albertini, *Epistolario*, vol. I, p. 161.

142 CG, 21/48/4, 12 Oct. 1912, Giolitti to Bertolini; 12 Oct. 1912, Italian memorandum.

143 *Ibid.*, 21/48/4, 14 Oct. 1912, San Giuliano to Giolitti.

144 FO 371/1525/43188, 16 Oct. 1912, Volpi to Giolitti.

145 CG, 21/48/4, 16 Oct. 1912, Volpi to Giolitti.

146 For the text see Malgeri, *op. cit.*, pp. 402–5.

147 San Giuliano protested to Barrère about French tardiness, CG, 26/73, 20 Oct. 1912, San Giuliano to Tittoni.

148 *Ibid.*, 21/48/4, 18 Oct. 1912, Giolitti to Bertolini.

149 e.g. L. Albertini, *Epistolario*, vol I, pp. 161–2; see generally Malgeri, *op. cit.*, pp. 388–9.

150 MAE P, 139/17, 31 Oct. 1912, San Giuliano to Italian diplomatic agents abroad.

CHAPTER 7. THE POLITICS OF ALLIANCE:
ITALY IN THE TRIPLE ALLIANCE, 1912–1914

1 Cited L. Albertini, *The Origins of the War of 1914* (London, 1952–7), vol. II, p. 9.

2 *CD*, XXIII, ix, pp. 10170–2, San Giuliano speech, 2 Dec. 1910.

3 A. F. Pribram, *The Secret Treaties of Austria-Hungary 1879–1914* (Cambridge, Mass., 1920–1), vol. I, p. 15.

4   The best example of this is San Giuliano's major biographer, F. Cataluccio, *Antonio Di San Giuliano* (Florence, 1935), pp. 83–4.

5   L. Salvatorelli, *La Triplice Alleanza* (Rome, 1939), p. 15.

6   e.g. G. Volpe, *L'Italia nella Triplice Alleanza* (Milan, 1939), p. 16. In English these arguments are endorsed by W. C. Askew, 'The Austro-Italian antagonism, 1896–1914', in L. P. Wallace and W. C. Askew (eds), *Power, Public Opinion and Diplomacy* (Durham, N.C. 1959), pp. 172–221.

7   F. R. Bridge, *From Sadowa to Sarajevo* (London, 1972) pp. 310–79 for the best recent summary of Austrian foreign policy in the period.

8   For the various terms see Pribram, *op. cit.*

9   e.g. see A. J. P. Taylor, *The Struggle for Mastery in Europe* (new ed., London, 1971), pp. 312–23.

10 Salvatorelli, *op. cit.*, pp. 239–240.

11 B. H. von Bülow, *Memoirs* (London, 1930–2), vol. II, p. 571.

12 It was Bülow on whom German diplomacy relied in the *intervento* to try to use his numerous friendships to win back Italy to the Triple Alliance cause. See B. Vigezzi, *Da Giolitti a Salandra* (Florence, 1969), pp. 208–9. It was of course often true that European diplomats and politicians, with their classical scholarship, and awareness of the cultural greatness of Italy, over-valued Italian power, in contrast to soldiers who knew more of the likely military performance of Italy at the moment. cf. N. Stone, 'Conrad von Hötzendorf, Chief of Staff in the Austro-Hungarian Army', *HT*, XIII (1963), p. 483 for comments on the difference between Conrad and Aehrenthal in this regard.

13 Pribram, *op. cit.*, vol. I, pp. 241–3 (see also Bridge, *op. cit.*, p. 439).

14 J. A. Thayer, *Italy and the Great War; politics and culture* (Madison, 1964), p. 148.

15 E. Apih, *Italia, fascismo e antifascismo nella Venezia Giulia (1918–1943)* (Bari, 1966), p. 15.

16 G. Gallavresi, *Italia e Austria (1859–1914)* (Milan, 1922), pp. 267, 273.

17 R. A. Webster, *L'imperialismo industriale italiano* (Turin, 1974), pp. 307–10, 575–83.

18 See L. Federzoni introduction to P. Foscari, *Per l'Italia più grande: scritti e discorsi* (Rome, 1928), pp. 3–5.

19 R. Monteleone, 'Iniziative e convegni socialisti italo-austriaci per la pace nel decennio prebellico', *RSS*, x (1967), p. 15.

20 R. De Felice, *Mussolini il rivoluzionario* (Turin, 1965), pp. 62–8 for an account of Mussolini's equivocal relationship with irredentism, C. Battisti and the respectable intellectuals of *La Voce*, while living in the Trentino in 1909.

21 D. Varè, *Laughing Diplomat* (London, 1938), p. 34.

22 e.g. after the Messina earthquake in December 1908, or during the Libyan War. Bridge, *op. cit.*, pp. 312, 336. After the event, Giolitti would claim that Italy renewed the Triple Alliance so readily in 1912, largely to ensure that any negotiations were over before Franz Joseph died. F. Martini, *Diario, 1914–18* (Milan, 1966), p. 29; cf. also San Giuliano's fear of Franz Ferdinand, AG, 22/184, 15 Sept. 1911, San Giuliano to King Victor Emmanuel III.

23 e.g. see F. S. Nitti, *Il capitale straniero in Italia* (Bari, 1915), or E. M. Gray, *The Bloodless War* (New York, 1916), and see Webster, *op. cit.*, pp. 232–3.

24 E. Grey, *Twenty-five years, 1892–1916* (London, 1925), vol. I, p. 6.

25 The figures are adapted from R. Bachi, *L'Italia economica nell'anno 1915* (Città di Castello, 1916).

26 Vigezzi, *op. cit.*, p. 18.

27 Webster, *op. cit.*, pp. 204–8.

28 Cited by Vigezzi, *op. cit.*, p. 206.

29 Webster, *op. cit.*, pp. 170–1.

30 See generally *ibid.*, especially pp. 116–55.

31 e.g. J. R. Rodd, *Social and diplomatic memories* (London, 1922–5), vol. III, p. 164.

32 AR, 5/201, 7 Aug. 1910, San Giuliano to Avarna.

33 AG, 7/43b, 31 Jan. 1911, Avarna to San Giuliano.

34 AR, 5/205, 23 April 1911, San Giuliano to Avarna.

35 *Ibid.*

36 Typical is MAE P, 670/844, 24 April 1911, Mayor des Planches to San Giuliano reporting an Albanian's opinion that Austrian policy in Albania thought of benefitting the locals via schools etc. while Italian policy was too self-interested. The despatch was scored with underlining by San Giuliano.

37 C. Avarna Di Gualtieri, *L'ultimo rinnovamento della triplice (5 dicembre 1912)* (Milan, 1924), pp. 48–9, but cf. Mérey's interest in alliance renewal in January 1911 e.g. *OUA*, 3, 2408, 10 Jan. 1911, Mérey to Aehrenthal.

38 Albertini, *op. cit.*, vol. I, p. 426 says in July 1911; G. Salvemini, *La politica estera italiana dal 1871 al 1915* (Milan, 1970), pp. 381–2 says in August, but cf *OUA*, 3, 2584, 8 Aug. 1911, Mérey to Aehrenthal.

39 e.g. Bridge, *op. cit.*, p. 335.

40 F. Malgeri, *La guerra libica* (Rome, 1970), pp. 111, 124.

41 CG, 22/59, C/2, 13 Sept. 1911, San Giuliano memorandum.

42 *Ibid.*, 15/25 bis, 27 Sept. 1911, Avarna to San Giuliano.

43 Cited by Bridge, *op. cit.*, p. 336.

44 e.g. his musings on Article VII, CG, 15/25 bis, 22 Nov. 1911, Avarna to San Giuliano.

45 *Ibid.*, 9 Dec. 1911, Pansa to Giolitti.

46 *Ibid.*, 11 Dec. 1911, San Giuliano to Pansa, Avarna.

47 *Ibid.*, 13 Dec. 1911, Avarna to San Giuliano.

48 *Ibid.*, 15 Dec. 1911, Pansa to San Giuliano. He added on 17 Dec. that Bethmann Hollweg shared his view that the renewal should be attempted only given the decline in Franz Joseph's health.

49 MAE P, 98/15, 13 Dec. 1911, Tittoni to San Giuliano.

50 CG, 15/25, 17 Jan. 1912, Avarna to San Giuliano; 20 Jan. 1912, Pansa to San Giuliano.

51 *Ibid.*, 15 March 1912, San Giuliano to Avarna, Pansa; 2 April 1912, Pansa to San Giuliano. The Austrians seem to have believed Germany was very serious at this time *OUA*, 4, 3375, 15 March 1912, Aehrenthal to Mérey.

52 MAE P, 674/844, 10 May 1912, San Giuliano to his ambassadors.

53 Malgeri, *op. cit.*, p. 315.

54 MAE P, 137/17, 6 July 1912, Avarna to San Giuliano. cf. Bridge, *op. cit.*, pp. 339–42.

55 Askew, *op. cit.*, p. 198; AG, 26/287, 23 Oct. 1912, San Giuliano to Pansa.

56 AG, 10/63d, 6 Nov. 1912, San Giuliano to Carlotti.

57 CG, 12/9, 1 Nov. 1912, San Giuliano to Avarna, Pansa.

58 *Ibid.*, 29/88, 7 Nov. 1912, San Giuliano to Giolitti; *DGP*, 33, 12382, 13 Nov. 1912, Jagow to Bethmann Hollweg. San Giuliano had already preached to Giolitti about the menace of Austria's attitude to Serbia e.g. AG, 10/63d, 6 Nov. 1912, San Giuliano to Bollati; 7 Nov. 1913, San Giuliano to Bollati.

59 *DGP*, 33, 12416, 23 Nov. 1912, Kiderlen Wächter to Jagow.

60 CG, 12/9, 14 Nov. 1912, San Giuliano to Giolitti.

61 *Ibid.*, 22/56, 15 Nov. 1912, San Giuliano to Giolitti; 16 Nov. 1912, San Giuliano to Giolitti; 19 Nov. 1912, San Giuliano to Avarna, Pansa.

62 *DGP*, 33, 12452, 26 Nov. 1912, 12460, 27 Nov. 1912, Jagow to Bethmann Hollweg.

63 MAE P, 100/15, 26 Nov. 1912, Avarna to San Giuliano; 29 Nov. 1912, Italian Consul in Trieste to Avarna.

64 CG, 12/9, 30 Nov. 1912, San Giuliano to Bollati.

65 *DGP*, 33, 12484, 2 Dec. 1912, Jagow to Bethmann Hollweg; CG, 16/34, 4 Dec. 1912, San Giuliano to Avarna and others.

66 *DDF*, 3 s, v, 34, 10 Dec. 1912, Barrère to Poincaré; Scalea told Rodd FO 371/1384/55337, 15 Dec. 1912, Rodd to Grey, that Italy disliked the reappointment of Conrad. Italy had already stated to Russia that she believed the Racconigi pact to be still operative, AG, 10/63d, 7 Nov. 1912, Torretta to San Giuliano.

67 e.g. see J. C. G. Röhl, 'Admiral von Müller and the approach of war, 1911–14', *HJ*, XII (1969), pp. 661–2; F. Fischer, *War of Illusions* (London, 1975), pp. 161–9.

68 AG, 26/287, 22 Nov. 1912, Pansa to San Giuliano.

69 G. Rochat, 'L'esercito italiano nell'estate 1914', *NRS*, XLV (1961), pp. 317–18.

70 M. Mazzetti, *L'esercito italiano nella triplice alleanza* (Naples, 1974), pp. 265–88; It is not really very helpful to remark as does A. Alberti, *Il generale Falkenhayn: le relazioni tra i capi di S.M. della Triplice* (Rome, 1924), pp. 79–80 on this legal emphasis always on the (unknown) clauses of the *casus foederis*.

71 M. Gabriele, *Le convenzioni navali della Triplice* (Rome, 1969), p. 285.

72 In fact, the Italian delegate, Conz, was in first Berlin, and then Vienna, during the most tense days of the Scutari crisis. *Ibid.*, pp. 360–75.

73 For the agreement see *Trattati*, vol. 22, pp. 354–9.

74 Gabriele, *op. cit.*, p. 397.

75 Mazzetti, *L'esercito italiano nella triplice alleanza*, pp. 394–5, 405; M. Mazzetti, 'L'Italia e le convenzioni militari segrete della Triplice Alleanza', *SC*, I (1970), p. 402.

76 *Ibid.*, pp. 379, 389–90, 393.

77 Rochat, *op. cit.*, pp. 324–5.

78 Note royal attention to such matters CB, 10, VI.4.36, 30 Oct. 1910, Spingardi to Tedesco; 16 Feb. 1912, Spingardi to Pollio.

79 e.g. *OUA*, 3, 2438, 31 Jan. 1911, Mérey to Aehrenthal.

80 CS, 2/16, 27 March 1914, Thaon di Revel to Salandra.

81 Gabriele, *op. cit.*, pp. 394–6.

82 *Ibid.*, pp. 250–1.

83 Rochat, *op. cit.*, pp. 319–320.

84 CS, 4/30, 26 July 1914, Grandi to Salandra.

85 Rochat, *op. cit.*, p. 321.

86 Mazzetti, *L'esercito italiano nella triplice alleanza*, pp. 28–9 emphasises that Conrad, on the Austrian side, was not precisely informed about the diplomatic details of the

Triple Alliance, but Mazzetti's point is reduced in significance, by the very different role of the Army in the power structure of Italy compared to Austria–Hungary.

87 S. Skendi, *The Albanian National Awakening 1878–1912* (Princeton, 1967), pp. 460–1.

88 MAE P, 671/844, 26 April 1911, Ministry of Interior to San Giuliano; cf. also 674/844, 23 Feb. 1912, San Giuliano to Avarna.

89 Skendi, *op. cit.*, p. 291.

90 AR, 5/205, 23 April 1911, San Giuliano to Avarna.

91 MAE P, 671/844, 9 June 1911, San Giuliano to Avarna; 10 June 1911, Avarna to San Giuliano. San Giuliano, not averse to scoring points on his own, duly thanked Aehrenthal for his reasonableness, as the *Consulta* had had no success in trying to explain Italy's problem to Mérey; 10 June 1911, San Giuliano to Avarna.

92 *Ibid.*, 672/844, 28 July 1912, San Giuliano to Carlotti. e.g. cf. 672/844, 17 July 1912, San Giuliano to ambassadors.

93 *Ibid.*, 674/844, 11 Feb. 1912, Avarna to San Giuliano. San Giuliano had requested this confirmation after reports from the Italian consul on Corfu of increasing Austrian 'propaganda activity' in Albania.

94 *Ibid.*, 675/844, 16 Aug. 1912, Carlotti to San Giuliano. For the Austrian move see Bridge, op. cit., pp. 344–5.

95 CG, 21/48/2, 17 Aug. 1912, San Giuliano to Giolitti. San Giuliano went on to explain also that the decentralisation proposals might have relevance to the Dodecanese. Although Italy would return these to Turkey after the Libyan War, it would be opportune to exert an Italian influence over the type of Turkish administration.

96 MAE P, 676/844, 10 Dec. 1912, Avarna to San Giuliano.

97 Bridge, *op. cit.*, p. 348.

98 FO 371/1384/55337, 15 Dec. 1912, Rodd to Grey.

99 *DGP*, 34, i, 12521, 9 Dec. 1912, Jagow to Foreign Ministry.

100 e.g. *ibid.*, 12552, 17 Dec. 1912, Jagow to Bethmann Hollweg; 12574, 21 Dec. 1912, Jagow to Bethmann Hollweg; 12798, 5 Feb. 1913, Benckendorff and Hindenburg to Bethmann Hollweg.

101 CSG, 1, [Jan. 1913], San Giuliano to Imperiali.

102 *Ibid.*, [Feb. 1913], San Giuliano to Avarna.

103 AG, 16/97 ter, [San Giuliano] memorandum, 14 Feb. 1913.

104 M. Mazzetti, 'L'Italia e la crisi albanese del marzo-maggio 1913', *SC*, IV (1973), pp. 220–1; in English, see the relevant chapter entitled 'Montenegro versus Europe' in E. C. Helmreich, *The Diplomacy of the Balkan Wars, 1912–1913* (Cambridge, Mass., 1938).

105 *DGP*, 34, ii, 13001, 21 March 1913, Flotow to Foreign Ministry; FO 371/1800/13038, 21 March 1913, Rodd to Grey.

106 *DGP*, 34, ii, 12990, 17 March 1913, Tschirsky to Bethmann Hollweg.

107 CSG, 1, [Jan. 1913], San Giuliano to Avarna; M. Mazzetti, 'L'Italia e la crisi albanese', pp. 221–2.

108 CG, 19/45, 20 March 1913, Giolitti to San Giuliano. Also *Dalle carte di Giovanni Giolitti* (Milan, 1962), vol. III, (ed. C. Pavone), p. 82.

109 CG, 19/45, 20 March 1913, San Giuliano to Giolitti.

110 *Ibid.*, 20 March 1913, San Giuliano to Giolitti; 22 March 1913, San Giuliano to

Giolitti. Mazzetti, 'L'Italia e la crisi albanese', p. 225 has convincingly dated this letter.

111 Mazzetti, 'L'Italia e la crisi albanese', p. 226 sees this as a victory for San Giuliano, contrasting it with G. Giolitti, *Memorie della mia vita* (Milan, 1922), pp. 299–300 which describes 'perfect unanimity' at the time between San Giuliano and Giolitti. Yet Giolitti's subsequent backing down, and the excellent relations which he maintained with San Giuliano until 1914 make it more likely that Giolitti's first fears of Italy being involved in a general war on Austria's side resulted from a lack of detailed knowledge of the London Conference by a Prime Minister, who was, after all, concentrating on preparing elections.

112 CG, 19/45, 21 March 1913, San Giuliano to Giolitti; *DGP*, 34, ii, 13001, 21 March 1913, Flotow to Foreign Ministry. San Giuliano leaked the news of Giolitti's objections to Flotow, saying also that he had not told Mérey. Presumably both pieces of information were meant to encourage Germany to restrain Austria.

113 *Ibid.*, 22 March 1914, Giolitti to San Giuliano; San Giuliano to Giolitti.

114 CSG, 2, 22 March 1913, San Giuliano to major ambassadors; San Giuliano to Carlotti; cf. also *DGP*, 34, ii, 13011, 23 March 1913, Flotow to Foreign Ministry.

115 CG, 19/45, 28 March 1913, Giolitti to San Giuliano.

116 *Ibid.*, 28 March 1913, San Giuliano to Giolitti; Giolitti to San Giuliano.

117 *DGP*, 34, ii, 13068, Flotow to Foreign Ministry. CSG, 2, April 1913 memorandum; 1 April 1913, San Giuliano to Tittoni. San Giuliano was still encouraging this, FO 371/1801/17605, 18 April 1913, Grey to Rodd.

118 MAE P, 677/844, 5 April 1913, Bollati to San Giuliano.

119 e.g. *DGP*, 34, ii, 13076, 31 March 1913, Flotow to Bethmann Hollweg.

120 CG, 19/45, 8 April 1913, San Giuliano to Giolitti.

121 Mazzetti, 'L'Italia e la crisi albanese', pp. 234–6.

122 AG, 27/314, 7 April 1913, San Giuliano to Giolitti.

123 CG, 19/45, 11 April 1913, San Giuliano to Giolitti.

124 CSG, 2, [April 1913], San Giuliano to Carlotti.

125 *Ibid.*, 14 April 1913, San Giuliano to Bollati; 20 April 1913, San Giuliano to Imperiali.

126 *Ibid.*, 23 April 1913, San Giuliano to his major ambassadors and to the ministers in Belgrade and Cetinje.

127 *Ibid.*, [April 1913] San Giuliano to Bollati; *DGP*, 34, ii, 13210, 26 April 1913, Flotow to Foreign Ministry.

128 CSG, 2, 29 April 1913, San Giuliano to his major ambassadors; *DGP*, 34, ii, 13244, 28 April 1913, Flotow to Foreign Ministry.

129 *Ibid.*, 25 April 1913, San Giuliano to Imperiali.

130 Bridge, *op. cit.*, pp. 351–2.

131 CSG, 2, [April 1913], San Giuliano to his major ambassadors; Mazzetti, 'L'Italia e la crisi albanese', p. 242; cf. FO 371/1771/19973, 28 April 1913, Grey to Rodd for very similar advice given by Imperiali to the Ambassadors' Conference. *DGP*, 34, ii, 13260, 2 May 1913, Jagow to Foreign Ministry.

132 MAE P, 677/844, 30 April 1913, Carlotti to San Giuliano; Imperiali to San Giuliano.

133 Mazzetti, 'L'Italia e la crisi albanese', pp. 247–8, 251–3. On 5 May Pollio was still trying to elucidate just what the Army was meant to be preparing for.

134 *Ibid.*, pp. 249–250.

135　MAE P, 677/844, 30 April 1913, Bollati to San Giuliano; 1 May 1913, Avarna to San Giuliano.

136　*Ibid.*, 1 May 1913, Tittoni to San Giuliano.

137　Mazzetti, 'L'Italia e la crisi albanese', p. 255. Avarna described his own discussions with Berchtold about military cooperation in Albania as 'academic'.

138　*Ibid.*, pp. 256–61. cf. also *DDF*, 3 s, vi, 471, 3 May 1913, Pichon to P. Cambon.

139　e.g. *DDF*, 3 s, vi, 483, 4 May 1913, Pichon to P. Cambon.

140　A. I. Sulliotti, *In Albania: sei mesi di regno* (Milan, 1914), pp. 5, 20.

141　MAE P, 677/844, 5 May 1913, Bollati to San Giuliano.

142　FO 371/1818/20802, 5 May 1913, Rodd to Grey. It is notable, that, shortly later, the semi-official propagandist V. Mantegazza, *Il Mediterraneo e il suo equilibrio* (Milan, 1914), pp. 258–60 also maintained that Italian readiness to go to Valona had caused the Austrian passion against Scutari 'to die down'.

143　FO 371/1801/21878, 8 May 1913, Rodd to Grey.

144　*DGP*, 34, ii, 13277, 6 May 1913, Flotow to Foreign Ministry.

145　C. Galli, *Diarii e lettere* (Florence, 1951), p. 167.

146　e.g. see C. De Biase, *La rivelazione di Giolitti del dicembre 1914* (Modena 1960); B. Vigezzi, 'Le "rivelazioni" di Giolitti del 9 dicembre 1914 e i rapporti con Salandra', *NRS*, xlv (1961). For a basic summary of the diplomacy of the incident see A. Torre, 'Il progettato attacco austro-ungherese alla Serbia del luglio 1913' in *Studi Storici in onore di Gioacchino Volpe per il suo 80° compleanno* (Florence, 1958), vol. ii, pp. 997–1018.

147　The two relevant telegrams have been published in *Dalle carte di Giovanni Giolitti*, vol. iii, nos. 109, 110, pp. 90–1.

148　e.g. CS, 1/5, 6 July 1913, De Martino to San Giuliano. On Austria's position see Bridge, *op. cit.*, pp. 353–7; cf. in contrast Torre's belief that Italy did perhaps persuade Germany to restrain Austria. Torre, *op. cit.*, p. 1018. Zimmermann deprecated the significance of the affair CS, 1/5, 11 Aug. 1913, Bollati to San Giuliano.

149　e.g. see F. Guicciardini, 'Serbia e Grecia in Albania', *NA*, f 986, 16 Jan. 1913; Victor, 'Montenegro ed Austria-Ungheria', *NA*, f 993, 1 May 1913.

150　e.g. *DGP*, 35, 13437, 28 June 1913, Flotow to Bethmann Hollweg; 13568, 19 July 1913, Flotow to Bethmann Hollweg.

151　Bridge, *op. cit.*, pp. 359–360.

152　CS, 1/5, 19 Oct. 1913, San Giuliano to Avarna, Bollati.

153　CSG, 4, 21 Oct. 1913, San Giuliano to Bollati; *DGP*, 36, i, 14187, 21 Oct. 1913, Zimmermann to Tschirsky.

154　Bridge, *op. cit.*, pp. 361–2.

155　CSG, 4, 1 Nov. 1913, San Giuliano to Avarna.

156　*DGP*, 36, ii, 14195, 21 Oct. 1913, Benckendorff and Hindenburg to Bethmann Hollweg.

157　CSG, [Nov. 1913], San Giuliano to Tittoni; San Giuliano to major ambassadors.

158　CG, 22/59/C/3, 8 Nov. 1913, San Giuliano to Giolitti; 13 Nov. 1913, Millo to San Giuliano.

159　e.g. see *DGP*, 36, ii, 14236, 4 Jan. 1914, Jagow to Tschirsky.

160　Given the nature of these, it is not astonishing that contemporaries believed the Italians to be 'most unpopular' in Montenegro. M. E. Durham, *The Struggle for Scutari* (London, 1914), p. 97.

161 Webster, *op. cit.*, pp. 387–90.

162 *Ibid.*, pp. 392–5.

163 A. J. May, 'Trans-Balkan railway schemes', *JMH*, 24 (1952), p. 352 cf. also the same author's 'The Novibazar railway project', *JMH*, 10 (1938).

164 A. Di San Giuliano, *Lettere sull'Albania* (Rome, 1903), p. 10.

165 *Ibid.*, p. 8.

166 AG, 15/94 bis, 4 April 1913, [San Giuliano] to Giolitti. cf. M. E. Durham, *High Albania* (London, 1909), pp. 9–10 for wholly accurate comments on the consular contest in bribery, and the cynicism of Albanian attitudes to such 'subventioning'.

167 AG, 15/94 bis, 31 March 1913, San Giuliano to Bianchi.

168 *Ibid.*, 6 April 1913, San Giuliano to Giolitti; 15 April 1913, San Giuliano to Ministry of Treasury.

169 e.g. PCG, 9/2, 5 May 1913, Stringher to San Giuliano; 9 May 1913, San Giuliano to Giolitti.

170 *Ibid.*, 9 May 1913, San Giuliano to Giolitti.

171 e.g. MAE P, 674/844, 28 Feb. 1912, Labia to San Giuliano; 675/844, 9 July 1913, Labia to San Giuliano.

172 *Ibid.*, 675/844, 13 June 1911, Labia to San Giuliano. The figures cited were:

	1902 %	1909 %	1910 %
Imports			
Austria	43	36	39
Italy	8	11	19
Britain	22	23	11
Turkey	15	23	26
Exports			
Austria	48	41	61
Italy	18	32	16
Turkey	15	12	18

173 Askew, 'The Austro-Italian antagonism, 1896–1914', p. 205 citing 26 May 1911, Bilinski to Aehrenthal. This trade position is also accepted by Vigezzi, *Da Giolitti a Salandra*, p. 18.

174 Galli, *op. cit.*, pp. 167–9.

175 MAE P, 675/844, 12 July 1913, San Giuliano to Consuls in Scutari, Durazzo, Valona.

176 PCG, 9/2, 28 July 1913, San Giuliano to Giolitti.

177 See in general R. J. B. Bosworth, 'The Albanian forests of Signor Giacomo Vismara: a case study of Italian economic imperialism during the Foreign Ministry of Antonino Di San Giuliano', *HJ*, XVIII (1975), pp. 571–86.

178 MAE P, 675/844, 19 Feb. 1914, Galli to San Giuliano. The concessionaire was to be a Signor Giannelli. It is a little confusing to find Galli and subsequently the *Consulta* filing him as Signor Germanico, when it seems that was the street in which Signor Giannelli lived!

179 Sulliotti, *op. cit.*, p. 139.

180 J. Swire, *Albania* (London, 1929), pp. 57–8 reveals that Primo Dochi's eclectic career had included a stint as a priest in Newfoundland and India, before he became Abbot

of the Mirditi in 1888. After that he collaborated with the Austrians in introducing his version of an Albanian alphabet into their schools.

181 *Ibid.*, p. 200.

182 e.g. Bosworth, 'The Albanian forests of Signor Giacomo Vismara', pp. 577–8. Bib Doda had also been in touch with Scalabrini, mutual respect being rooted perhaps in mutual catholicism. Moreover, if Bib Doda received 300,000 lire to buy arms, he was willing to become a pro-Italian client. See AG, 26/307, 27 Nov. 1912, Scalabrini memorandum.

183 CS, 8/63, 23 March 1914, San Giuliano to Salandra.

184 MAE P, 675/844, 3 Aug. 1913, Primo Levi memorandum. cf. Levi's bluntness, 29 Oct. 1913, Primo Levi memorandum, which noted that an Italo-Austrian economic accord in Albania was best kept secret as it would be so difficult to apply; *DGP*, 36, ii, 14432, 4 April 1914, Flotow to Bethmann Hollweg.

185 *Ibid.*, 678 bis/29, 25 Sept. 1913, Galli to San Giuliano.

186 PCG, 9/2, 11 Oct. 1913, San Giuliano to Giolitti.

187 MAE P, 675/844, 5 Nov. 1913, San Giuliano to Joel.

188 PCG, 13/1, 14 Feb. 1914, Colosimo to San Giuliano.

189 CS, 8/63, 17 March 1914, [De Martino] report. Galli, too, now rejoiced in the *Consulta's* greater generosity. Galli, *op. cit.*, p. 207.

190 MAE P, 675/844, 15 April 1914, Pellegrini (of *Reale Museo Commerciale di Venezia*) to Primo Levi; 7 April 1914, Galli to San Giuliano; 14 April 1914, Primo Levi to Pellegrini.

191 *Ibid.*, 8 June 1914, Galli to San Giuliano.

192 AG, 19/117 bis, 18 April 1914, Aliotti to San Giuliano; 30 April 1914, De Martino *pro-memoria*.

193 CSG, 5, [May 1914], San Giuliano to Aliotti.

194 CS (L), C.2.42/26, 25 May 1914, San Giuliano to Salandra. San Giuliano explained to the Powers that he could not recall Aliotti as it would make the consul 'the most popular man in Italy', e.g. *DGP*, 36, ii, 14470, 2 June 1914, Flotow to Foreign Ministry.

195 Martini, *op. cit.*, p. 90.

196 Bosworth, 'The Albanian forests of Signor Giacomo Vismara', pp. 584–5.

197 *Dalle carte di Giovanni Giolitti*, vol. III, pp. 97–100; e.g. S. Sonnino, *Diario 1914–16* (Bari, 1972), vol. II, pp. 3–4.

198 e.g. CM, 13, 20 May 1914, Scarfoglio to Martini.

199 e.g. CSG, 5, 20 March 1914, San Giuliano to De Martino; cf. also *DGP*, 36, ii, 14414, 11 Feb. 1914, Flotow to Bethmann Hollweg; 14444, 20 May 1914, to Foreign Ministry. CS, 5/42, 29 June 1914, Aliotti to San Giuliano.

200 *DGP*, 36, ii, 14373, 23 April 1914, Flotow to Bethmann Hollweg.

201 *DGP*, 36, ii, 14463, 30 May 1914, Flotow to Foreign Ministry. FO 371/1895/24734, 2 June 1914, Rodd to Grey. Italy also appealed significantly to Russia, *DGP*, 36, ii, 14484, 9 June 1914, Flotow to Bethmann Hollweg.

202 PCG, 13/1, 21 Feb. 1914, San Giuliano to Giolitti forwarding November 1913 report from Major Egidi. The Major also found in Albania a struggle of 'subsidies' between Italy and Austria which, he believed, Italy must win. Albania naturally enough, was a great source of *bon-mots* among the international diplomatic community. One good

story was that the entire Wied family was habitually bereft of intelligence, as only thus could be explained Prince William's acceptance of the Albanian throne. P. Cambon, *Correspondence 1870–1922* (Paris, 1946), vol. III, 3 Feb. 1914, letter to his brother Jules.

203 e.g. MAE P, 100/15; 102/15.

204 A. Ara, 'La questione dell' Università italiana in Austria', *RSR*, LX (1973), pp. 52–88, 252–80.

205 MAE P, 101/15, 17 June 1913, Avarna to San Giuliano.

206 e.g. *ibid.*; see also AG, 13/81, 26 June 1913, Thaon di Revel to San Giuliano. cf. also generally Galli, *op. cit.*, pp. 1–44.

207 CSG, 3, 11 July 1913, Boselli to Foreign Ministry. San Giuliano's minute for De Martino suggested an approach to Stringher.

208 Ara, *op. cit.*, p. 259. Hohenlohe had also consistently opposed the establishment of any Italian faculty at Trieste.

209 MAE P, 102/15, 24 Aug. 1913, San Giuliano to Avarna.

210 *DGP*, 39, 15747, 10 Sept. 1913, Hindenburg to Bethmann Hollweg.

211 MAE P, 102/15, 31 Aug. 1913, Avarna to San Giuliano, 29 Aug. 1913, Avarna to San Giuliano.

212 *Ibid.*, 30 Aug. 1913, San Giuliano to Avarna.

213 *Ibid.*, 19 Sept. 1913, San Giuliano to Avarna, Bollati.

214 e.g. PCG, 9/4, 27 Sept. 1913, Giolitti to San Giuliano; cf. also 6 Dec. 1913, San Giuliano to Giolitti asking for pressure to be put on Stringher to finance an Italian bank at Trieste.

215 MAE P, 102/15, 27 Sept. 1913, Bollati to San Giuliano.

216 CSG, 4, 23 Oct. 1913, San Giuliano to Avarna.

217 *Ibid.*, [Oct. 1913], San Giuliano to Bollati, Avarna; 28 Oct. 1913, San Giuliano to De Martino; CG, 22/49, 7 Nov. 1913, Giolitti to San Giuliano.

218 *DGP*, 39, 15752, 9 Nov. 1913, Flotow to Bethmann Hollweg. San Giuliano could adduce different conclusions from the same evidence. In February 1914 he was appealing to the Germans that they take Italy more seriously because of the 'variegated' Austrian Army would not be able to withstand a strong Slavic push. 15840, 26 Feb. 1914, Flotow to Bethmann Hollweg.

219 N. Stone, 'Moltke–Conrad: Relations between the Austro-Hungarian and German General Staffs, 1909–14', *HJ*, IX (1966), p. 214.

220 CSG, 5, 3 April 1914, San Giuliano to Avarna, Bollati; *DGP*, 34, i, 15542, 15543, 9 April 1914, Flotow to Bethmann Hollweg.

221 CS (L), C.2.42/5, 26 March 1914, San Giuliano to Salandra. The Austrians countered by talking about the danger of anti-Italian demonstrations e.g. *DGP*, 39, 15723, 5 April 1914, Flotow to Bethmann Hollweg. San Giuliano had rejected the initial Austrian idea that the meeting be held at Fiume, AG, 29/380, 30 March 1914, San Giuliano to Avarna.

222 CS (L), C.2.42/8, 20 April 1914, San Giuliano pro-memoria. Despite the fact that the 1913 Austrian government had budgeted for an Italian law faculty to be established at Trieste in 1914–16, progress had again been vetoed by Hohenlohe.

223 *Ibid.*

224 *DGP*, 39, 15727, 15728, 17 April 1914, Flotow to Bethmann Hollweg. Cf. A. Salandra, *La neutralità italiana (1914)* (Milan, 1928), pp. 26–7.

225 AG, 17/105 bis, 15 April 1914, Bollati to San Giuliano.

226 *DGP*, 39, 15729, 20 April 1914, Tschirsky to Bethmann Hollweg. The Austrian analysis of the Abbazia meeting is surprisingly unaware of the extent of possible Italian objections to Austrian moves in Northern Albania. When meeting different select audiences, San Giuliano remained characteristically willing to call Serbia, Austria's 'new Piedmont'.

227 e.g. FO 371/1894/18041, 21 April 1914, Rodd to Grey; *DGP*, 39, 15730, 20 April 1914, Flotow to Bethmann Hollweg.

228 e.g. CSG, 5, 13 May 1914, San Giuliano memorandum.

229 *DGP*, 34, i, 13331, 12 May 1914, Flotow to Bethmann Hollweg.

230 *Ibid.*, 39, 15731, 27 April 1914, Flotow to Bethmann Hollweg. Flotow, with his usual willingness to call a spade a spade, replied that it was rather Italy's expansionist policies in the Mediterranean which had undermined her relations with Britain.

231 AG, 29/380, 15 June 1914, San Giuliano to Avarna, Bollati, Carlotti; *DGP*, 36, ii, 14494, 13 June 1914, Flotow to Jagow.

232 *DGP*, 36, ii, 14507, 20 June 1914, Flotow to Bethmann Hollweg; cf. 14499, 16 June 1914, Tschirsky to Foreign Ministry.

233 Mazzetti, *L'esercito italiano nella triplice alleanza*, pp. 405–9.

234 The (unsuccessful) negotiations with Barrère are the most obvious parallel, although in June 1914 Rodd was also engaged in discussions with the *Consulta*, on how to export to Britain Sir Henry Layard's collection of Renaissance paintings. FO 800/65, GP, 1 July, 9 July, 20 July, 4 Aug. 1914, Rodd to Grey.

235 As narrated by Salandra, *op. cit.*, p. 16.

CHAPTER 8. THE POLITICS OF FRIENDSHIP: ITALY,
THE TRIPLE ENTENTE AND THE SEARCH FOR A NEW
MEDITERRANEAN AGREEMENT, 1911–1914

1 G. Rochat, 'L'esercito italiano nell'estate 1914', *NRS*, XLV (1961), p. 324.

2 O. Malagodi, *Conversazioni della guerra 1914–1919* (Milan, 1960), vol. I, pp. 16–17.

3 It is odd to find in 1976 school exercise books printed in Italy which include Corsica in the detail of the 'geography of Italy', while adding parenthetically that Corsica belongs 'politically' to France.

4 G. Salvemini, *La politica estera italiana dal 1871 al 1915* (Milan, 1970), pp. 47–8.

5 R. Michels, *L'imperialismo italiano* (Milan, 1914), p. 158.

6 Note AG, 22/162, 31 Aug. 1911, San Giuliano to Melegari in which San Giuliano agreed that sooner or later Italy and Russia would have to unite to block an Austrian advance in the Balkans, but that this could only be at a time when both Powers were much stronger militarily. In 1914, Giolitti predicted that Russia would be the Power to collapse under the strain of war. Malagodi, *op. cit.*, vol. I, p. 86.

7 B. H. von Bülow, *Memoirs* (London, 1930–2), vol. IV, p. 125.

8 A. Torre, 'Ricordo di Antonino Di San Giuliano', *NA*, f 1849 (1955), p. 41.

9 For Izvolsky, see F. Stieve, *Izvolsky and the World War* (London, 1926).

10 E. Serra, *Camille Barrère e l'intesa italo-francese* (Milan, 1950), p. 233.

11 MAE P, 60/9, 29 Jan. 1911, Tittoni to San Giuliano.

12 P. Milza, 'Les rapports économiques franco-italiens en 1914–1915 et leurs incidents

politiques', *RHMC*, xiv (1967), pp. 33–4. Milza provides the following comparison of Italian trade with France and Germany.

Year	Italian imports (in millions of lire)		Total
	From France	From Germany	
1887	320	165	1,740
1898	118	185	1,544
1908	242	549	3,137
1913	283	612	3,645

Year	Italian exports		Total
	To France	To Germany	
1887	400	115	1,162
1898	151	186	1,351
1908	164	275	1,830
1913	231	343	2,711

(pp. 36–7) with Austria the 1913–14 figures were imports 265m lire, exports 222 m.

13 *Ibid.*, p. 38 cites the relative figures for 1911–12 as French concerns 32m lire, British 6m, German 3m, others 2m.

14 The culmination of this banking duel was in December 1914 when French money and skills helped the establishment of the Banca Italiana di Sconto, the *'banca italianissima'*, quite rightly noted by Webster as an indication that, on this level too, Salandra intended to wipe out the whole Giolittian system. R. A. Webster, *L'imperialismo industriale italiano* (Turin, 1974), p. 170.

15 V. Castronovo, *La stampa italiana dall'Unità al fascismo* (Bari, 1973), pp. 210–11. *L'Idea Nazionale* also received money from Dante Ferraris whose business ties were more with Germany, though with the usual combination of admiration and competition.

16 Milza, *op. cit.*, pp. 69–70.

17 Although reviewing the complaints at his insurance scheme from foreigners, Giolitti notes that these came from 'Austrian, Hungarian, English, German and French companies' which had owned 'three-fifths' of the Italian businesses. Writing of course in the 1920s, well after the event, Giolitti alleges that the most brusque opponent of his scheme was the Austrian ambassador, Mérey. G. Giolitti, *Memoirs of my life* (London, 1923), pp. 233–4.

18 S. Scaroni, *Con Vittorio Emanuele III* (Milan, 1954), p. 32, and see generally R. J. B. Bosworth, 'The Opening of the Victor Emmanuel monument', *IQ*, xviii (1975).

19 See R. Katz, *The Fall of the House of Savoy* (London, 1972), p. 199. The scholarly, coin-collecting, and parsimoniously bourgeois King was also hardly *simpatico* to King Edward VII of England.

20 D'Annunzio also often found France a useful haven from his numerous creditors in Italy. See A. J. Rhodes, *The Poet as Superman* (London, 1959), pp. 127–9.

21 A. Lyttelton (ed.) *Italian Fascisms* (London, 1973), p. 16.

22 Rochat, *op. cit.*, p. 302.

23 Quoted by Webster, *op. cit.*, p. 164.

24 *Ibid.*, p. 171.

25 e.g. CS, 2/16, 27 March 1914, Thaon di Revel to Salandra; April 1914, Thaon di Revel to Salandra in which he seemed to envisage even England as a possible enemy.

26 *Ibid.*, 15 July 1914, Thaon di Revel to Salandra.

27 Webster, *op. cit.*, p. 168.

28 CS, 2/16, 30 July 1914, Thaon di Revel to Salandra, enclosing copy of 25 July 1913 report by Leonardi Cattolica.

29 PCG, 5/523, 6 July 1912, Tittoni to San Giuliano. A similar Italian organisation was set up in March 1913 under the aged Visconti Venosta. Its membership did not contain many from the heart of Italian foreign policy making elite. The most notable figures were Barzilai, Bissolati, Maggiorino Ferraris, Luzzatti, Martini, Orlando, Pirelli and Ponti. For the complete list see E. Decleva, *Da Adua a Sarajevo* (Bari, 1971), p. 461, fn. 135.

30 Webster, *op. cit.*, p. 167 points out the relationship between Ansaldo and Paul Clemenceau, the brother of Georges. In 1913 Paul Clemenceau became one of the council of administration of *Nobel italiana*

31 Decleva, *op. cit.*, pp. 413–14, 416 and *passim*.

32 *Ibid.*, p. 432.

33 Serra, *Camille Barrère*, pp. 110–11, 294.

34 M. Mazzetti, 'Recenti studi italiani di storia militare', *SC*, 1 (1970), p. 153.

35 For the latest state of play see W. A. Renzi, 'Mussolini's sources of financial support, 1914–1915', *History*, 56, 187 (1971), especially pp. 190–4. See also R. De Felice, *Mussolini il rivoluzionario* (Turin, 1965), pp. 300–3.

36 D. Mack Smith, *Italy, a Modern History* (Ann Arbor, 1959), pp. 265–6 argues this case, paralleling it to 1936–9.

37 B. Caizzi, *Camillo e Adriano Olivetti* (Turin, 1962), pp. 17–18, 53, 65.

38 One eminent milord, Lord Esmé Howard, later preferred the Fascist regime to its Liberal predecessors because Mussolini had taught the Italians no longer to spit in public. E. Howard, *Theatre of Life* (London, 1936), vol. 1, p. 608.

39 See generally R. J. B. Bosworth, 'The English, the historians and the *età giolittiana*', *HJ*, XII, pp. 358–9.

40 See G. M. Trevelyan, *Scenes from Italy's war* (London, 1919), p. 14. cf. also generally 'Englishmen and Italians: some aspects of their relationship past and present', *Proc. Brit. Acad.*, IX (1919), pp. 91–108; *The Historical causes of the present state of affairs in Italy* (London, 1923).

41 H. Wickham Steed, *Through thirty years 1892–1922* (London, 1924), vol. 1, p. 135.

42 A. Albertini, *Vita di Luigi Albertini* (Rome, 1945), pp. 39–44.

44 Malagodi, *op. cit.*, vol. 1, p. 152.

45 In 1911 San Giuliano himself was still on the committee of the Anglo-Italian Literary Society, and in May was sent an essay in English on Petrach which, he wrote back politely, he would read with interest, See AG, 8/26.

46 J. A. Thayer, *Italy and the Great War, politics and culture* (Madison, 1964), p. 208.

47 CS, 2/16, 1 Aug. 1914, Thaon di Revel to Salandra. Always implicit is the perennial Italian fear that a superior fleet could detach Sicily from the very shaky union. Nelson

had of course done this in the war against Napoleon. The Americans, or at least, Lucky Luciano, had similar ideas in the war against Hitler.

48 FO 371/469/10712, 25 Feb. 1908, minute by Hardinge on despatch Lascelles to Grey. For these assumptions see generally, R. J. B. Bosworth, 'The traditional friendship: a study of British foreign policy towards Italy, 1902–1915' (unpublished Cambridge Ph.D. thesis, 1971).

49 Z. Steiner, *The Foreign Office and Foreign Policy, 1898–1914* (Cambridge, 1969), pp. 122–4.

50 See generally P. G. Halpern, *The Mediterranean Naval Situation* (Cambridge, Mass., 1971), pp. 71–5.

51 e.g. CAB, 38/21/26, 4 July 1912, CID meeting.

52 CAB, 38/21/27, 11 July 1912, CID meeting.

53 MAE P, 493/121, 16 Sept. 1912, Imperiali to San Giuliano.

54 In a way Italian diplomacy 1935–40 is very similar to 1911–14. The most important difference is that the wire to London was broken by the Ethiopian War and intervention in Spain, and that Mussolini did not recognise this and did not treat seriously enough Chamberlain's efforts to renew it.

55 *DDF*, 2 s, ii, 312, 29 June 1902, Barrère, to Delcassé.

56 *Ibid.*, 329, 10 July 1902, Barrère to Delcassé, enclosed the text of the letters exchanged. (See also 310, 28 June 1902, Barrère to Delcassé).

57 *Ibid.*, 2 s, vi, 99, 17 Feb. 1905, Barrère to Delcassé.

58 Bertie and Rodd had been rivals in 1903 for the Rome Embassy, which Bertie had then used as an essential stepping stone to his appointment to Paris. Rodd was rusticated to Stockholm and had to wait until 1908 to get the Rome post. See R. J. B. Bosworth, 'Sir Rennell Rodd e l'Italia', *NRS*, LIV (1970), pp. 422–5.

59 R. Croft-Cooke, *The unrecorded life of Oscar Wilde* (London, 1972), pp. 75–6.

60 C. Barrère, 'L'Italie et l'agonie de la paix, en 1914', *RDM*, 35, 1 Oct. 1926, p. 554.

61 For examples of Rodd's publications, see Bosworth, 'Sir Rennell Rodd e l'Italia', pp. 420–1.

62 FO 800/64, GP, 16 Oct. 1911, Rodd to Grey, (*BD*, ix i 286).

63 FO 800/351, NP, 17 Oct. 1911, Rodd to Nicolson.

64 *DDF*, 2 s, xiv, 475, 25 Oct. 1911, Barrère to De Selves.

65 FO 800/64, GP, 25 Oct. 1911, Rodd to Grey, (*BD*, ix i 296).

66 *DDF*, 2 s, xiv, 490, 28 Oct. 1911, P. Cambon to De Selves.

67 FO 800/64, GP, 14 Nov. 1911, Rodd to Grey, (*BD*, ix i 308).

68 FO 371/1135/49052, 27 Nov. 1911, Rodd to Grey.

69 CG, 14/17/4, 8 Oct. 1911, San Giuliano to Imperiali.

70 Barrère had openly told San Giuliano so. MAE P, 177/17/86, 24 Jan. 1912, San Giuliano to Tittoni.

71 FO 800/64, GP, 5 Feb. 1912, Rodd to Grey, (*BD*, ix i 368).

72 *DDF*, 3 s, i, 516, 25 Jan. 1912, P. Cambon to Poincaré.

73 *DDF*, 3 s, ii, 58, 17 Feb. 1912, Barrère to Poincaré.

74 e.g. see *DDF*, 3 s, ii, 181, 218, 219, 264, 280 and G. Andrè, *L'Italia e il Mediterraneo alla vigilia della prima guerra mondiale*, vol. 1 (Milan, 1967), p. 22, fn. 31 bis.

75 e.g. MAE P, 60/9, 1 March 1912, Tittoni to San Giuliano; or AG 9/58, 24 May 1912, Tittoni to San Giuliano; See also Andrè, *op. cit.*, p. 28 fn. 43.

76 *BD*, x, ii, 419, 13 April 1912, Rodd to Grey.

77 Andrè, *op. cit.*, p. 38 fn. 57.

78 RP Diary, May 1912.

79 FO 371/1383/21920, 24 May 1912, Grey to Bertie and minutes.

80 e.g. *BD*, x, ii, 392, 2 June 1912, Kitchener to Grey; MAE P, 136/17, 5 June 1912, Grimani (Italian Consul-General in Cairo) to San Giuliano. Hardinge in India was also unhappy; see HP, 92, 3 June 1912, Nicolson to Hardinge; 7 Aug. 1912, Hardinge to Nicolson.

81 *DDF*, 3 s, iii, 15, 17 May 1912, P. Cambon to Poincaré.

82 *BD*, ix, i, 408, 6 June 1912, Grey to Bertie.

83 e.g. *BD*, x, ii, 396, 24 June 1912, Rodd to Grey: *DDF*, 3 s, iii, 190, 10 July 1912, Barrère to Poincaré; 213, 20 July 1912, Barrère to Poincaré.

84 Andrè, *op. cit.*, pp. 52–4 (note p. 53 fn. 85 that San Giuliano had implied that the most appropriate evidence of French sympathy to Italy would be assistance in concluding the Libyan War).

85 *Ibid.*, pp. 65–6. The journalist responsible was Lucien Wolf, a strong Italophobe, possibly in the pay of the Turks.

86 *Ibid.*, pp. 69, 74.

87 *DDF*, 3 s, iii, 403, 15 Sept. 1912, Poincaré to Laroche.

88 Andrè, *op. cit.* pp. 88–90.

89 FO 371/1369/40008, 20 Sept. 1912, Grey to Dering.

90 FO 371/1369/40422, 21 Sept. 1912, Grey to Bertie.

91 Andrè, *op. cit.*, pp. 99–100.

92 *Ibid.*, pp. 99, 101.

93 *Ibid.*, p. 101.

94 *DDF*, 3 s, iv, 214, 21 Oct. 1912, P. Cambon to Poincaré.

95 *DDF*, 3 s, iv, 454, 30 Sept. 1912, Laroche to Poincaré. Rodd also reported this. The King as well liked the idea. FO 371/1384/46352, 27 Oct. 1912, Rodd to Grey.

96 *DDF*, 3 s, iv, 243, 244, 25 Oct. 1912, Poincaré to P. Cambon, Barrère.

97 *DDF*, 3 s, iv, 285, 30 Oct. 1912, P. Cambon to Poincaré.

98 FO 800/64, GP, 30 Oct. 1912, Grey to Rodd.

99 Andrè, *op. cit.*, pp. 109–14.

100 *DDF*, 3 s, iv, 437, 12 Nov. 1912, Barrère to Poincaré.

101 *BD*, x, ii, 424, 10 Nov. 1912, Rodd to Grey.

102 *DDF*, 3 s, iv, 497, 20 Nov. 1912, Barrère to Poincaré; Andrè, *op. cit.*, p. 118.

103 AG, 9/58, 27 Nov. 1912, San Giuliano to Giolitti.

104 Andrè, *op. cit.*, pp. 125–7.

105 *BD*, x, ii, 427, 23 Nov. 1912, Rodd to Grey; AG, 10/63b, 24 Nov. 1912, San Giuliano to Imperiali.

106 Andrè, *op. cit.*, p. 124.

107 *DDF*, 3 s, iv, 560, 25 Nov. 1912, Barrère to Poincaré.

108 *BD*, x, ii, 428, 6 Dec. 1912, Rodd to Grey.

109 FO 371/1384/53326, 9 Dec. 1912, Rodd to Grey.

110 FO 800/361, NP, 10 Dec. 1912, Rodd to Nicolson. At the same time Barrère also reminded his government of the problem, *DDF*, 3 s, v, 34, 10 Dec. 1912, Barrère to Poincaré.

111 FO 371/1383/51092, 20 Dec. 1912, Grey to Rodd, Crowe minute. FO 371/1384/52344, 8 Dec. 1912, Rodd to Grey, minute.
112 *DDF*, 3 s, v, 81, 17 Dec. 1912, de Gondrecourt to Millerand.
113 *BD*, x, ii, 429, 20 Dec. 1912, Grey to Rodd.
114 *Ibid.*, 434, 6 Feb. 1913, Rodd to Grey.
115 *Ibid.*, 434, 6 Feb. 1913, Rodd to Grey; 435, 13 Feb. 1913, Grey to Rodd.
116 *Ibid.*, 436, 437, 15 Feb. 1913, Rodd to Grey; 4 March 1913, Grey to Rodd. *DDF*, 3 s, v, 437, 20 Feb. 1913, Barrère to Jonnart; 27 Feb. 1913, Jonnart to Barrère.
117 *CD*, XXIII, xix, 22 Feb. 1913, pp. 23315–20.
118 *Senate*, XXIII, xiii, 8 March 1913. The parliamentary debates on foreign affairs from 1912 to 1914 were extraordinarily patriotic, with enthusiasm for Italy's new nationalism by no means only coming from Foscari, Federzoni and the Nationalists.
119 e.g. Andrè, *op. cit.*, pp. 147–59.
120 CSG, 1, 28 Feb. 1913, San Giuliano to Tittoni.
121 AG, 16/97 ter, 14 Feb. 1913, [San Giuliano] memo.
122 CB, 10, VII.1.41, 26 May 1913, Cadorna to Pollio.
123 J. C. Cairns, 'International politics and the military mind: the case of the French Republic, 1911–1914', *JMH*, 25 (1953), p. 278.
124 It is also significant that in April 1913 San Giuliano and Giolitti combined to dissuade Fusinato from abandoning negotiations at the Hague on compensation for the *Carthage* and *Manouba* and *Tavignano* incidents. Fusinato really was a confirmed triplicist, but San Giuliano believed such petulance would put Italy outside the pale of the civilised world 'as rebels to that institution of international peace and civilisation'. CG, 14/19, 24 April 1913, San Giuliano to Giolitti.
125 *Ibid.*, 22/59/D, 10 Sept. 1913, San Giuliano to Giolitti.
126 Andrè, *op. cit.*, pp. 179, 187.
127 *DDF*, 3 s, viii, 339, 16 Oct. 1913, Barrère to Pichon.
128 *Ibid.*, 368, 21 Oct. 1913, Barrère to Pichon.
129 *Dalle carte di Giovanni Giolitti*, ed. C. Pavone, vol. III (Milan, 1962), pp. 92–4.
130 *Ibid.*, pp. 94–5.
131 Andrè, *op. cit.*, pp. 198–200; *DDF*, 3 s, viii, 368, 21 Oct. 1913, Barrère to Pichon.
132 Andrè, *op. cit.*, pp. 210–13.
133 CSG, 4, 1 Nov. 1913, San Giuliano to Avarna.
134 *Ibid.*, 1 Nov. 1913, San Giuliano to Martin Franklin.
135 CG, 11/1, 2 Nov. 1913, San Giuliano to Giolitti.
136 Andrè, *op. cit.*, pp. 221–4.
137 *DDF*, 3 s, viii, 399, 29 Oct. 1913, P. Cambon to Pichon; *BD*, x, i, 152, 22 Oct. 1913, Grey to Bertie.
138 Andrè, *op. cit.*, p. 233 fn. 64. See *DDF*, 3 s, viii, 557, note about the Triple Alliance.
139 Andrè, *op. cit.*, pp. 235–8; Decleva, *op. cit.*, pp. 437–8.
140 See generally *CD*, XXIV, i, debates on 27 Nov., 11 Dec. 1913.
141 *CD*, XXIV, i, 16 Dec. 1913. San Giuliano repeated this phrase in the Chamber to great applause. cf. also *Dalle carte di Giovanni Giolitti*, vol. III, p. 96, fn. 1.
142 CSG, 4, [Dec. 1913], San Giuliano memorandum.
143 *Ibid.*, [Nov. 1913], San Giuliano note.
144 CG, 15/91, 11 Dec. 1913, Giolitti to San Giuliano.

145 Andrè, *op. cit.*, pp. 246–8.
146 MAE P, 60/9, 28 Nov. 1913, Bordonaro to San Giuliano.
147 CSG, 4, [Dec. 1913], San Giuliano to Tittoni. cf. *DDF*, 3 s, viii, 612, 11 Dec. 1913, Doumergue to P. Cambon and others.
148 FO 371/1662/58081, 16 Dec. 1913, Rodd to Grey, forwarding a letter by Capt. W. H. Boyle of 13 December (*BD*, x, xii, 439). cf. also FO 371/2005/16931, 11 April 1914, Rodd to Grey sending another report from Boyle that it would be easy to overrate Italian naval efficiency.
149 *DDF*, 3 s, viii, 591, 6 Dec. 1913, Pichon to P. Cambon; 601, 9 Dec. 1913, P. Cambon to Pichon; 618, 12 Dec. 1913, P. Cambon to Pichon.
150 FO 800/64, GP, 8 Dec. 1913, Rodd to Grey.
151 FO 800/65, GP, 10 Jan. 1914, Imperiali to Grey and minute.
152 FO 371/2004/7779, 17 Feb. 1914, Rodd to Grey.
153 AG, 17/106, 16 Jan. 1914, Albertini to Imperiali. Albertini was at the time very critical of San Giuliano's triplicism.
154 *DDF*, 3 s, ix, 117, 20 Jan. 1914, Barrère to Doumergue.
155 *Ibid.*, 324, 18 Feb. 1914, Barrère to Doumergue.
156 Rochat, 'L'esercito italiano nell' estate 1914', p. 518.
157 See *Dalle carte di Giovanni Giolitti*, vol. iii, pp. 101–3.
158 For typical complaints by Federzoni that San Giuliano's policy was not forward enough see *CD*, xxiv, ii, 25 Feb. 1914.
159 FO 371/2005/14630, 30 March 1914, Grey to Bertie, Rodd.
160 *BD*, x, ii, 444, 27 April 1914, Rodd to Grey.
161 *Senate*, xxiv, i, 8 April 1914.
162 CSG, 5, 25 April 1914, San Giuliano to Tittoni; AG, 19/117 bis, 1 May 1914, San Giuliano to Bollati and others.
163 As San Giuliano later labelled it, *Senate*, xxiv, i, 26 June 1914.
164 CSG, 5, 1 May 1914, San Giuliano to Imperiali. cf. Andrè, *op. cit.*, pp. 260–3.
165 For text see *Trattati*, vol. 23, pp. 171–3.
166 *BD*, x, ii, 445, 446 both 6 May 1914, Grey to Rodd; Andrè, *op. cit.*, pp. 268–9.
167 FO 371/2005/23578, 17 May 1914, Crowe minute, (*BD*, x, ii, 449 partially).
168 CS(L), C.2. 42/19, 19 May 1914.
169 Andrè, *op. cit.*, p. 277.
170 *Ibid.*, p. 279; *BD*, x, ii, 450, 4 June 1914, Grey to Rodd.
171 Andrè, *op. cit.*, pp. 280–2.
172 *DDF*, 3 s, 415, 20 June 1914, Barrère to Doumergue.
173 FO 371/2005/29914, 29 June 1914, Nicolson note.
174 Andrè, *op. cit.*, p 286.
175 *DDF*, 3 s, x, 467, 1 July 1914, P. Cambon to Viviani.
176 *Ibid.*, 445, 27 June 1914, Barrère to Doumergue.
177 FO 371/2005/31565, 6 July 1914, Rodd to Grey. San Giuliano had still not given up his ambition also to include Spain. L. Albertini, *The Origins of the War of 1914* (London, 1952), vol. i, p. 570, believes San Giuliano was not 'thoroughly in earnest'. He does not say why.
178 Andrè, *op. cit.*, p. 295.
179 Scaroni, *op. cit.*, p. 134.

CHAPTER 9.'*UN CLIENTE MALEDUCATO*': ITALY IN THE
DODECANESE AND ETHIOPIA, 1912–1914

1 A. J. P. Taylor, *The Struggle for Mastery in Europe, 1848–1918* (Oxford, 1954), p. xxiii and fn. 4.

2 Formally Rhodes is not one of the Southern Sporades or Dodecanese group. The main islands of the group eventually taken were Carpathos, Leros, Calymnos, Patmos, Cos, Symi, Chalki, Nisyros, Telos, Cassos, Castellorizzo, Stampalia and Rhodes. For a geographical description from a strongly Graecophile source see C. D. and I. B. Booth, *Italy's Aegean possessions* (London, 1928). The Booths (p. 291) contrast the sad fate of the Greeks of the Dodecanese to those under benevolent British rule in Cyprus. The traditional Italian account is R. Sertoli Salis, *Le isole italiane dell'Egeo dall'occupazione alla sovranità* (Rome, 1939) which asserts briefly that Italian behaviour throughout was 'correct and legitimate' (p. 20).

3 e.g. MAE P, 134/17, 20 March 1912, Carlotti to San Giuliano forwarding his military attaché's report that Rhodes was most vulnerable to serious attack. In November 1911, Spingardi had been thinking generally about the attractions of the 'Aegean Islands' as possible future bases for air-ships. See CB, 10, VI.5.37, Nov. 1911, Spingardi to Brusati.

4 CG, 24/62/2, 8 April 1912, San Giuliano to Avarna, Pansa; 10 April 1912, San Giuliano to Pansa.

5 Indeed to Germany and Austria, San Giuliano had made his denials even before acting. See *ibid.*

6 AG, 7/43 c, 28 May 1912, Torretta to Scalea. Torretta, who had a *Chargé's* enthusiasm for improved relations with the country in which he was stationed, may have been exaggerating.

7 *DDF*, 3 s, iii, 17, 17 May 1912, Sainte-Aulaire to Poincaré.

8 *Ibid.*, 9, 15 May 1912, Poincaré note.

9 FO 371/1535/18780, 20 May 1912, DMO memorandum and minute.

10 Minute on FO 371/1535/21770, 18 May 1912, Lowther to Grey. For a general assessment of British policy see R. J. B. Bosworth, 'Britain and Italy's acquisition of the Dodecanese, 1912–1915', *HJ*, XIII (1970), pp. 683–705.

11 FO 800/356, NP, 23 May 1912, Nicolson to Bertie.

12 *Ibid.*, 24 May 1912, Bertie to Nicolson; *DDF*, 3 s, iii, 33, 24 May 1912, Poincaré to Cambon.

13 FO 371/1535/23344, 31 May 1912, Admiralty to Foreign Office.

14 *BD*, IX, i, 430, 29 June 1912, Admiralty to Foreign Office.

15 *BD*, IX, i, 439, 6 Aug. 1912, Grey to Rodd.

16 MAE P, 154/17, 10 June 1912, Tittoni to San Giuliano. Tittoni noted his agreement given Britain's objections to an Italian occupation.

17 *DDF*, 3 s, iii, 110, 16 June 1912, Barrère to Poincaré.

18 AG, 10/63b, 20 May 1912, Pansa to San Giuliano.

19 *Ibid.*, 9/57, 23 May 1912, San Giuliano to Avarna; Avarna to San Giuliano; 10/63b, 27 May 1912, Avarna to San Giuliano.

20 *Ibid.*, 9/57, 24 May 1912, Avarna to San Giuliano.

21 *Ibid.*, 10/63b, 28 May 1912, San Giuliano to Avarna.

22 *Ibid.*, 10/63b, 30 May 1912, Pansa to San Giuliano; 31 May 1912, Avarna to San Giuliano.

23 *Ibid.*, 10/63b, 23 June 1912, Avarna to San Giuliano; CG, 24/62/2, 25 June 1912, San Giuliano to Avarna.

24 AG, 25/247, 27 June 1912, San Giuliano to Avarna, Pansa.

25 e.g. CG, 11/1, 23 July 1912, Giolitti to [San Giuliano]; 27 July 1912, Giolitti to Volpi.

26 e.g. G. Jaia, 'L'Isola di Rodi', *RC*, v, July, Aug., Sept., Nov. 1912, pp. 735–74, 874–889, 966–1003, 1081–114.

27 e.g. MAE P, 154/17, 3 July 1912, Ameglio to Giolitti; 19 Sept. 1912, Ameglio to San Giuliano. There is also a considerable file of local exercises in nationalism in the Ameglio papers which are at the ACS. V. Mantegazza, 'Le dodici isole e Chio – le loro antiche autonomie', *NA*, f 973, 1 July 1912, pp. 141–50 already also demanded that Turkey must eventually give Italy valid guarantees of her treatment of the Greek population. By 1 Nov. the Royal Geographical Society had decided to send a mission to investigate the geological possibilities of the islands 'conscious of [Italy's] own real civilising mission'. See *BSGI*, v, i, 1 Nov. 1912, and A. Martelli, 'Ricerche geologiche e geografico-fisiche nelle Sporadi meridionali', *BSGI*, v, i, Dec. 1912, pp. 1297–324.

28 MAE P, 137/17, 5 July 1912, Avarna to San Giuliano.

29 CG, 11/1, 20 July 1912, Fusinato, Volpi, Bertolini to Giolitti.

30 *Ibid.*, 21/48/2, 12 Aug. 1912, De Martino memorandum. De Martino was also spending his time happily encouraging more reliable government subsidies to Italian shipping lines to Egypt and the Eastern Mediterranean. AG, 10/59, 6 June 1912, De Martino to G. Abignente.

31 CG, 21/48/2, 7 Aug. 1912, Giolitti to San Giuliano.

32 *Ibid.*, 21/48/2, 17 Aug. 1912, San Giuliano to Giolitti; 18 Aug. 1912, Giolitti to San Giuliano.

33 See FO 371/1536/39010, 16 Sept. 1912, Bertie to Grey; *DDF*, 3 s, iii, 429, 19 Sept. 1912, P. Cambon to Poincaré.

34 CG, 21/48/4, 1 Oct. 1912, San Giuliano to Giolitti.

35 e.g. *DDF*, 3 s, iv, 91, 8 Oct. 1912, Poincaré to his ambassadors in London, Vienna, Berlin.

36 FO 371/1526/43550, 16 Oct. 1912, minute on Lowther to Grey.

37 FO 371/1521/49523, 20 Nov. 1912, Rodd to Grey; 50358, 23 Nov. 1912, Bertie to Grey.

38 MAE P, 154/17, 25 Oct. 1912, Imperiali to San Giuliano; 27 Oct. 1912, Carlotti to San Giuliano.

39 FO 371/1521/50979, 28 Nov. 1912, Grey to Rodd; *BD*, IX, ii, 382, 13 Dec. 1912, Grey to Rodd.

40 There is of course much continuity to be found in Italian foreign policy. San Giuliano would not have been surprised to learn that his disciple, Sforza, was the first Great Power Foreign Minister to abandon the Greeks in Asia Minor after the First World War. Nor would he have been surprised at least by the intention of the Corfu Incident, despite the common argument that this was a Mussolinian coup. It is notable that the Italian ambassador in Athens in 1924, the appropriately named Giulio

Cesare Montagna, who was perhaps the most exuberant advocate of Italian action, was a career diplomat, Minister in Teheran during San Giuliano's ministry.

41 MAE P, 676/844, 10 Dec. 1912, Avarna to San Giuliano.

42 *Ibid.*, 14 Dec. 1912, San Giuliano to De Facendis; 16 Dec. 1912, San Giuliano to Carlotti.

43 e.g. *Ibid.*, 31 Dec. 1912, San Giuliano to Carlotti.

44 CSG, 1, 7 Jan. 1913, San Giuliano to De Martino; *BD*, IX, ii, 474, 9 Jan. 1913, Grey to Rodd.

45 *BD*, IX, ii, 483, 10 Jan. 1913, Rodd to Grey.

46 *Ibid.*, 509, 15 Jan. 1913, Rodd to Grey; San Giuliano said much the same to Barrère if also emphasising the identity of views between Italy and Austria. *DDF*, 3 s, v, 219, 15 Jan. 1913, Barrère to Poincaré.

47 *DGP*, 34, 12686, 13 Jan. 1913, Jagow to Bethmann Hollweg.

48 CSG, 1, [Jan. 1913], San Giuliano to Bollati.

49 *Ibid.*, 16 Jan. 1913, Giolitti to San Giuliano. San Giuliano at once relayed this suggestion to London and Constantinople. 16 Jan. 1913, San Giuliano to Garroni, Imperiali.

50 *Ibid.*, [Jan. 1913], San Giuliano to his major ambassadors.

51 *Ibid.*, [Jan. 1913], San Giuliano to Imperiali.

52 e.g. *Ibid.*, [Jan. 1913], San Giuliano to Avarna; *DGP*, 34, i, 12713, 21 Jan. 1913, Jagow to Foreign Ministry.

53 FO 371/1801/17062, 17 April 1913, Grey to Bertie; /17496, 15 April 1913, Sir Henry Jackson note.

54 *BD*, IX, ii, 874, 23 April 1913, Grey to Elliot and others.

55 FO 800/366, NP, 13 May 1913, Nicolson to Cartwright.

56 De Bosdari had admirable qualifications for an Italian diplomat. He had been San Giuliano's *Chargé* at the Embassy in London, where, by his own account, he had done much of the work. When stationed in Budapest he had had articles published on Dante in the respectable local paper, *Pester Lloyd*. See A. De Bosdari, *Delle guerre balcaniche, della grande guerra e di alcuni fatti precedenti ad esse* (Milan, 1927), pp. 32–3, 35.

57 e.g. CG, 11/1, 28 Feb. 1913, De Bosdari to San Giuliano; MAE P, 156/17, 9 April 1913, De Bosdari to San Giuliano; cf. De Bosdari, *op. cit.*, p. 75.

58 De Bosdari, *op. cit.*, p. 77. In eastern Albania where Italian interests were not involved, San Giuliano was by no means anti-Greek, and can be found telling the Germans of the advantages of saving Greece from the Triple Entente by persuading Austria not to be too insistent that Janina go to Albania. CSG, 2, 16 March 1913, San Giuliano to Bollati.

59 See MAE P, 161/17.

60 PCG, 9/2, 16 March 1913, Chief of General Staff *pro-memoria*; 1 April 1913, Chief of General Staff and Colonial Office *pro-memoria*; 5 April 1913, Thaon di Revel to Minister of Marine; 12 April 1913, Spingardi to San Giuliano.

61 CSG, 2, 20 April 1913, San Giuliano to Imperiali; *DGP*, 34, ii, 12 April 1913, Flotow to Foreign Ministry.

62 PCG, 9/2, 20 April 1913, San Giuliano to ambassadors in London, Paris, Vienna, Berlin; *DGP*, 34, ii, 13192, 22 April 1913, Flotow to Bethmann Hollweg.

63   *DGP*, 34, ii, 13287, 10 May 1913. San Giuliano again suggested that there could be compromise on Albania's border near Janina but that Austria did not favour it. Flotow's despatches in this period show an honest bafflement at the twists of Italian policy. See nos. 13293, 13301.

64   FO 371/1818/21566, 7 May 1913, Grey to Rodd.

65   FO 371/1772/22548, 13 May 1913, Rodd to Grey; cf. *BD*, IX, ii, 966, 8 May 1913, Rodd to Grey; 982, 13 May 1913, Grey to Rodd.

66   *DDF*, 3 s, vi, 634, 28 May 1913, Pichon to P. Cambon; *BD*, IX, ii, 1012, 28 May 1913, Grey to Bertie.

67   FO 371/1764/25846, 2 June 1913, Grey to Rodd.

68   e.g. *DDF*, 3 s, vii, 67, 10 June 1913, Pichon to P. Cambon. According to De Bosdari, P. Cambon persistently leaked information to the Greeks about Italian aims in the Dodecanese. See De Bosdari, *op. cit.*, p. 75.

69   FO 371/1801/27482, 16 June 1913, Grey to Bertie, Buchanan.

70   *BD*, IX, ii, 1070, 19 June 1913, Dering to Grey; CP, 10431/247, 19 June 1913, Dering to Grey.

71   *DGP*, 35, 13640, 17 June 1913, Flotow to Bethmann Hollweg; 13462, 28 June 1913, Flotow to Foreign Ministry.

72   *BD*, IX, ii, 1142, 14 July 1913, Grey to Cartwright, Rodd; FO 371/1806/33976, 17 July 1913, Grey to Cartwright and others.

73   *DGP*, 35, 13657, 12 July 1913, Flotow to Foreign Ministry; 13660, 19 July 1913, Flotow to Foreign Ministry.

74   AG, 15/94 bis, 17 July 1913, San Giuliano to Giolitti; also CG, 29/90.

75   AG, 28/370, 17 July 1913, San Giuliano to Giolitti; cf. also SP, reel 54, 24 July 1913, San Giuliano to Giolitti.

76   AG, 16/94 ter, 22 July 1913, De Martino to San Giuliano.

77   *Ibid.*, 16/97 bis, 27 July 1913, San Giuliano to De Martino. He also chose this moment again to appeal to his ambassadors for their advice. 28/370, 26 July 1913, San Giuliano to his major ambassadors and to De Bosdari.

78   *BD*, IX, ii, 1187, 30 July 1913, Grey to Bertie, Buchanan.

79   *Ibid.*, 1190, 31 July 1913, Grey to Cartwright, Rodd; 1202, 5 Aug. 1913, Grey to Cartwright and others; AG, 15/94 bis, 2 Aug. 1913, San Giuliano to Giolitti.

80   *DGP*, 35, 13676, 2 Aug. 1913, Flotow to Foreign Ministry; cf. his urgent advice to Imperiali that Italy should not receive any blame for the failings of the Ambassadors' Conference. AG, 28/370, 5 Aug. 1913, San Giuliano to Imperiali.

81   MAE P, 155/17, 7 Aug. 1913, De Bosdari to San Giuliano; AG, 15/94 bis, 11 Aug. 1913, De Bosdari to San Giuliano; cf. Garroni's advice that Italy should divert all French pressure. Any retreat on the Dodecanese, he said, would be undignified. AG, 28/370, 4 Aug. 1913, Garroni to San Giuliano.

82   FO 371/1802/36930, 11 Aug. 1913, Grey to Rodd.

83   *BD*, X, i, 145, 12 Aug. 1913, Grey to Rodd. The French no doubt were hardly pleased to learn from their secret service on 10 Aug. that San Giuliano had said that if the Ambassadors' Conference failed all blame should be made to fall on France. *DDF*, 3 s, vi, 594, 10 Aug. 1913, Pichon to P. Cambon. Cambon was naturally pleased by Grey's show of firmness. *DDF*, 3 s, viii, 19, 12 Aug. 1913, P. Cambon to Pichon.

84   AG, 4/31, 19 Aug. 1913, San Giuliano *pro-memoria*; also CG, 29/90. San Giuliano

did now approach De Bosdari to investigate further Greek intentions towards the Triple Alliance. MAE P, 155/17, 19 Aug. 1913, San Giuliano to De Bosdari.

85 AG, 16/97 bis, 18 Aug. 1913, Rodd to San Giuliano forwarding 14 Aug., Grey to Rodd.

86 *BD*, ix, ii, 1255, 2 Sept. 1913, Rodd to Grey.

87 *BD*, x, i, 146, 8 Sept. 1913, Rodd to Grey.

88 Giolitti himself was probably sincere in this. See CG, 19/46, 21 Aug. 1913, Giolitti to San Giuliano taking the San Giuliano memorandum of 19 Aug. at face value.

89 *BD*, x, i, 148, 13 Sept. 1913, Grey to Bertie; *DDF*, 3 s, vii, 163, 18 Sept. 1913, de Fleuriau to Pichon.

90 e.g. *DGP*, 36, 13902, 20 Aug. 1913, Jagow to the Kaiser; 13841, 8 Sept. 1913, Jagow to Flotow; 13843, 10 Sept. 1913, Jagow to Wangenheim; 13848, 10 Sept. 1913, Benckendorff and Hindenburg to Bethmann Hollweg, raising and then discounting the idea that Giolitti could be running a rival foreign policy in Turkey behind his Foreign Minister's back.

91 CG, 22/59/D, 10 Sept. 1913, San Giuliano to Garroni (copy forwarded to Giolitti).

92 *BD*, x, i, 151, 15 Oct. 1913, Dering to Grey.

93 CG, 22/59/C/3, 8 Nov. 1913, San Giuliano to Giolitti.

94 *DDF*, 3 s, viii, 471, 10 Nov. 1913, Barrère to Pichon; 13991, 18 Nov. 1913, Flotow to Bethmann Hollweg.

95 CSG, 4, [Dec. 1913], San Giuliano to Imperiali.

96 *DDF*, 3 s, viii, 538, 27 Nov. 1913, P. Cambon to Pichon.

97 *BD*, x, i, 168, 11 Dec. 1913, Grey to Rodd.

98 FO 371/1804/55760, 12 Dec. 1913, Grey to Cartwright and others.

99 *DGP*, 36, ii, 14205, 15 Dec. 1913, Flotow to Foreign Ministry; 14211, 18 Dec. 1913, Flotow to Bethmann Hollweg.

100 CSG, 4, 24? Dec. 1913, San Giuliano to ambassadors to Great Powers. San Giuliano was again abetted by De Martino who spent Christmas Day producing a memorandum arguing that although Italy could not make political gain out of the Dodecanese, she must make economic.

101 CG, 15/21, 27 Dec. 1913, Aldrovandi to San Giuliano.

102 *Ibid.*, 15/21, 28 Dec. 1913, San Giuliano to Tittoni.

103 *Ibid.*, 15/21, 29 Dec. 1913, Bollati to San Giuliano; CSG, 4, 30 Dec. 1914, San Giuliano to Bollati.

104 FO 371/1844/58267, 30 Dec. 1913, Mallet to Grey.

105 CSG, 4, 31 Dec. 1913, San Giuliano to ambassadors to Great Powers.

106 CG, 12/6, 2 Jan. 1914, San Giuliano to Giolitti.

107 FO 371/2112/107, 1 Jan. 1914, Rodd to Grey; CSG, 5, 3 Jan. 1914, San Giuliano to Imperiali. The message was repeated to all Italy's major ambassadors. AG, 17/106, 7 Jan. 1914, San Giuliano circular.

108 e.g. AG, 17/106, 9 Jan. 1914, San Giuliano to ambassadors to Great Powers and Turkey. San Giuliano even made repeated complaints at the time that Lichnowsky, the German ambassador in London, was too lukewarm in supporting the Italian case. Italy actually got Lichnowsky to agree to change the phrasing of one of his statements to Grey. See *ibid.*, 11 Jan. 1914, San Giuliano to ambassadors to Great Powers; 12 Jan. 1914, San Giuliano to Imperiali.

109 *Ibid.*, 17/106, 4 Jan. 1914, Ministry of War to San Giuliano saying Italian expenses during the occupation of the Dodecanese were 16,480,338.35 lire; 5 Jan. 1914, Ministry of Colonies to San Giuliano listing Turkish officers who had come to Cyrenaica since 1912 (although the last example cited was in June 1913).

110 FO 371/2112/2179, 11 Jan. 1914, Rodd to Grey.

111 e.g. *DDF*, 3 s, ix, 84, 14 Jan. 1914, P. Cambon to Doumergue. Izvolsky alleged that the French even contemplated war to remove the Italians. F. Stieve, *Izvolsky and the World War* (London, 1926), p. 161.

112 *DDF*, 3 s, x, 48, 30 March 1914, J. Cambon to Doumergue.

113 C. De Biase, 'La crisi del governo italiano del marzo 1914', *NA*, f 1897, Jan. 1959, pp. 67–8.

114 AG, 17/106, 20 Jan. 1914, San Giuliano to Garroni.

115 CSG, 5, 25 Jan. 1914, San Giuliano to Imperiali; also AG, 17/106.

116 *BD*, x, i, 217, 28 Jan. 1914, Grey to Rodd.

117 FO 371/2112/4568, 2 Feb. 1914, Grey to Goschen; /5179, 4 Feb. 1914, Rodd to Grey; AG, 17/106, 27 Jan. 1914, San Giuliano to Imperiali; 3 Feb. 1914, San Giuliano to Imperiali; *DGP*, 36, ii, 14262, Jagow to Lichnowsky; 14277, 2 Feb. 1914, Flotow to Foreign Ministry, AG, 29/300, 4 Feb. 1914, San Giuliano to Imperiali. San Giuliano was duly attacked in the Chamber on 6 Feb. by Federzoni because of the content of the British note. 19/117, 6 Feb. 1914, copy of Federzoni interrogation.

118 FO 371/2118/10127, 6 March 1914 for the agreement.

119 AG, 17/106, 6 March 1914, De Martino to Imperiali.

120 CSG, 5, 15 March 1914, San Giuliano to Garbasso; 20 March 1914, San Giuliano to De Martino. It is interesting to speculate how much San Giuliano's interest in 'public opinion' was in fact produced by Federzoni's untoward questions in the Chamber.

121 CSG, 5, [May 1914], San Giuliano to Imperiali.

122 O. Di Giamberardino, *L'ammiraglio Millo dall'impresa dei Dardanelli alla passione Dalmatica* (Livorno, 1950), pp. 13–31.

123 P. G. Halpern, *The Mediterranean Naval Situation, 1908–1914* (Cambridge, Mass., 1971), pp. 216–17.

124 e.g. G. A. Rosso, *I diritti d'Italia oltremare* (Rome, 1916), p. 86.

125 For an explication by a semi-official publicist of the government position see V. Mantegazza, *Il Mediterraneo e il suo equilibrio* (Milan, 1914). There is a preface by Bettòlo and Mantegazza waxes eloquent about the battle of the races in the crucial naval area of the Aegean.

126 e.g. MAE P, 460/97, 12 June 1914, San Giuliano to De Bosdari. De Bosdari later alleged that he had seen signs of this already in October 1913. De Bosdari, *op. cit.*, p. 92.

127 SP, reel 47.1, 23 June 1914, *pro-memoria*.

128 *DDI*, 5 s, i, 474, 28 Aug. 1914, Imperiali to San Giuliano; 497, 29 Aug., San Giuliano to Imperiali.

129 *Ibid.*, 803, 25 Sept. 1914, San Giuliano to Tittoni, Carlotti.

130 For a brief summary of subsequent developments see Bosworth, 'Britain and Italy's acquisition of the Dodecanese, 1912–1915', pp. 704–5.

131 For a fascinating account of Menelik's Ethiopia see H. G. Marcus, *The Life and times*

of Menelik II: Ethiopia 1844–1913 (Oxford, 1975); there is also a contemporary Nationalist Italian account by that indefatigable traveller to areas of Italian interest, G. Piazza, *Alla corte di Menelik* (Ancona, 1912).

132 FO 800/133, LP, 14 Oct. 1903, Bertie to Lansdowne.

133 For a detailed account of the negotiation of this treaty see R. J. B. Bosworth, 'The traditional friendship: British foreign policy towards Italy, 1902–1915' (unpublished Cambridge Ph.D., 1971), pp. 75–88, and for the treaty terms, pp. 342–50.

134 For the last days of Menelik, a story which combines the barbarous grandeur of Macbeth and King Lear see Marcus, *op. cit.*, pp. 232–61.

135 PCG, 9/17, 21 July 1913, San Giuliano to Giolitti with enclosures.

136 e.g. FO 371/1572/31574, 24 July 1913, F.O. memorandum.

137 FO 371/1572/50679, 4 Nov. 1913, Grey to Dering.

138 AG, 16/97 ter, 22 Aug. 1913, San Giuliano to Garroni.

139 SP, reel 50.6, 2 Oct. 1913, Bertolini to San Giuliano.

140 MAE P, 751/1145, 11 Oct. 1913, Colli to San Giuliano.

141 PCG, 9/17, 6 Nov. 1913, Imperiali to San Giuliano.

142 FO 371/1572/51992, 11 Nov. 1913, Grey to Dering.

143 PCG, 9/17, 17 Nov. 1913, Bertolini to San Giuliano. Agnesa wrote an accompanying *pro-memoria*.

144 SP, reel 50.6, 26 Nov. 1913, Bertolini to San Giuliano.

145 FO 371/1572/55130, 6 Dec. 1913, Rodd to Grey; MAE P, 754/1145, 5 Dec. 1913, Imperiali to San Giuliano, and undated note San Giuliano to Bertolini.

146 PCG, 9/17, 8 Dec. 1913, San Giuliano to Giolitti forwarding earlier correspondence with Imperiali. He had commissioned a full-scale investigation of Italy's legal position in Ethiopia see AG, 29/379, undated memorandum by G. Ciamarra.

147 FO 371/1572/55401, 4 Dec. 1913, Nicolson minute; /58089, 22 Dec. 1913, Rodd to Grey.

148 FO 371/1878/1238, 9 Dec. 1913, Thesiger to Grey.

149 MAE P, 751/1145, 16 Jan. 1914, Colli to San Giuliano; 18 Jan. 1914, Colli to San Giuliano.

150 *Ibid.*, 754/1145, 18 Jan. 1914, Ministry of Colonies to San Giuliano. With the addition of the area around Lake Tsana, it was noted, 'Eritrea would become one of the best European colonies in Africa.'

151 *Ibid.*, 754/1145, 20 Jan. 1914, San Giuliano to Imperiali.

152 *Ibid.*, 754/1145, 19 Feb. 1914, San Giuliano to Tittoni, Imperiali.

153 AG, 19/113, 7 March 1914, Pollio to San Giuliano; 8 March 1914, San Giuliano to Pollio.

154 MAE P, 751/1145, 9 March 1914, San Giuliano to Salvago Raggi; 12 March 1914, Bertolini to San Giuliano; 23 March 1914, Martini to San Giuliano; 31 March 1914, De Martino note.

155 Kitchener in Egypt was worried by the troop moves, Rodd in Rome was not. FO 371/1878/15884, 4 April 1914, Kitchener to Grey; /18238, 22 April 1914, Rodd to Grey.

156 MAE P, 752/1145, 3 April 1914, San Giuliano to Imperiali, Tittoni; 10 April 1914, San Giuliano to Salvago Raggi.

157 *Ibid.*, 20 May 1914, Martini to San Giuliano. Martini also showed appropriate interministerial rivalry, repeatedly attacking the reports of Colli, the *Consulta's*

official, and praising Salvago Raggi, the Colonial governor. See also CS, 2/14, 30 June 1914, Martini to Salandra.

158 MAE P, 752/1145, 9 June 1914, San Giuliano to Salvago Raggi.
159 CS, 8/63, 11 June 1914, San Giuliano to Salandra.
160 Marcus, *op. cit.*, p. 276.
161 FO 371/2171/38844, 12 Aug. 1914, Grey to Rodd.

CHAPTER 10. PREPARING TO DIGEST SOME SPOILS: ITALIAN POLICY TOWARDS TURKEY, 1912–1914

1 E. Decleva, *Da Adua a Sarajevo* (Bari, 1971), p. 278.
2 There is a most entertaining, popular account of the Great Power effort: P. Fleming, *The Seige at Peking* (London, 1959), pp. 177–94.
3 F. M. Tamagna, *Italy's Interests and Policies in the Far East* (New York, 1941), pp. 5–6.
4 T. Sillani (ed.), *L'Italia e l'Oriente medio ed estremo* (Rome, 1935), p. 73.
5 e.g. see L. Gramatica, 'Le Missioni cattoliche nell' Oriente medio ed estremo', in Sillani (ed.), *op. cit.*, pp. 88–110.
6 J. P. Diggins, *Mussolini and Fascism: the view from America* (Princeton, 1972), p. 12.
7 A good example is the innocuous memoirs of the man sent to be ambassador in Washington in 1913, 'Justus', *V. Macchi di Cellere all'ambasciata di Washington* (Florence, 1920). The chief of the Macchi family in the 1920s held the appropriate post at court of Master of Ceremonies.
8 R. F. Foerster, *The Italian Emigration of Our Times* (Cambridge, Mass., 1919), p. 229.
9 R. Michels, *L'imperialismo italiano* (Milan, 1914), p. 103.
10 G. Dore, *La democrazia italiana e l'emigrazione in America* (Brescia, 1964), p. 200.
11 For a survey of emigrant politics see *ibid.*, pp. 204–32.
12 AG, 23/207, 4 Jan. 1911, P. Levi to San Giuliano. Levi, ironically given later 'assimilation' policies, suggested that Australia might be a more satisfactory venue for Italian emigrants.
13 This, the most famous of emigrant songs, and many other poignant examples of this 'foreign policy of the poor' can be found in A. V. Savona and M. L. Straniero (eds.), *Canti dell'emigrazione* (Milan, 1976).
14 L. Ganapini, *Il nazionalismo cattolico* (Bari, 1970), p. 213.
15 A. Theodoli, *A cavallo di due secoli* (Rome, 1950), pp. 23–5, 31–45, 52–3.
16 *Ibid.*, pp. 59–67 (cf. F. Malgeri, *La guerra libica* (Rome, 1970), pp. 304–7). There is also the separately published account A. Theodoli, 'La preparazione dell'impresa di Tripoli', *NA*, f 1496, 16 July 1934, pp. 239–49.
17 Theodoli, *A cavallo di due secoli*, pp. 69–70. It is most appropriate that today a Theodoli represents international petrol companies in Rome.
18 R. A. Webster, *L'imperialismo industriale italiano* (Turin, 1974), p. 454; cf. also A. Piccioli, *La pace di Ouchy* (Rome, 1935), pp. 18–25.
19 N. Sousa, *The capitulatory regime of Turkey* (Baltimore, 1933), p. 76; D. C. Blaisdell, *European Financial Control in the Ottoman Empire* (N.Y., 1929), pp. 1–2. It was the Italians who in 1892 first advocated that the presidency of the council of the Debt should be a revolving office (p. 121). This was always likely to be regarded in Italy as a pleasing admission of her rights to be accepted as a Great Power.

20 On occasion, San Giuliano was perfectly willing to complain about the politics of such expatriates. e.g. *OUA*, 3, 3082, 9 Dec. 1911, Mérey to Aehrenthal.

21 Foerster, *op. cit.*, pp. 210–16.

22 G. G. Romei Longhena, 'Ricordi della corte di Abdul Hamid', *NA*, f 1517, 1 June 1935, pp. 359–60; R. Cantalupo, *Fuad, primo re d'Egitto* (Milan, 1940), p. 77.

23 CB, 9, VI.2.34, 17 May 1912, De Martino to Brusati; VI.7.39, 17 June 1912, memorandum; cf. also P. Levi, *Missione nell'Africa settentrionale* (Rome, 1908), p. 13; C. Masi, 'L'Italia e il Levante nella storia politica e diplomatica contemporanea (1815–1934)', in T. Sillani (ed.), *L'Italia e il Levante* (Rome, 1934), pp. 64–5, 70–1.

24 Cantalupo, *op. cit.*, pp. 51–7, 195–6.

25 P. Levi interestingly took it upon himself to recommend this to the Provincial Mother in Cairo, to the local friars, and their superior in Rome, given what he described as Pius X's position. It is very doubtful if many priests or nuns would have been over-impressed with this sort of paternal advice from an old friend of Crispi. P. Levi, *op. cit.*, pp. 167–9. De Martino was still embroiled in the problem on the morrow of his transfer to Constantinople. See CB, 10, VI.4.36, 17 April 1911, De Martino to San Giuliano.

26 R. A. Webster, *Industrial Imperialism in Italy, 1908–1915* (Berkeley, 1975), pp. 3, 51.

27 Webster, *L'imperialismo industriale italiano*, pp. 380–94.

28 F. R. Bridge, *From Sadowa to Sarajevo* (London, 1972), p. 267; L. Solari, *Marconi nell'intimità e nel lavoro* (Milan, 1940), p. 121.

29 e.g. E. C. Cagli, 'L'opera degli italiani nel Montenegro', *NA*, f 929, 1 Sept. 1910, pp. 51–73.

30 J. Cary, *Memoir of the Bobotes* (London, 1964), pp. 20–5.

31 *OUA*, 2, 2244, Report of San Giuliano–Aehrenthal talks.

32 e.g. *OUA*, 3, 2456, 20 Feb. 1911, Mérey to Aehrenthal; E. C. Helmreich, *The Diplomacy of the Balkan Wars, 1912–1913* (Cambridge, Mass., 1938), pp. 84–5.

33 AG, 26/311, 8 Oct., 20 Oct. 1912, Squitti to San Giuliano; 21 Oct. 1912, San Giuliano to Squitti.

34 Helmreich, *op. cit.*, p. 317. For the Montenegrin loan see AG, 28/366, 369.

35 C. Galli, *Diarii e lettere* (Florence, 1951), pp. 206–7.

36 AG, 28/366, 10 April 1913, San Giuliano to Avarna.

37 *Ibid.*, 364, 15 April 1913, Giolitti to San Giuliano; *Dalle carte di Giovanni Giolitti*, vol. III (ed. C. Pavone) (Milan, 1962), pp. 86–8.

38 AG, 28/362, 12 June 1913, San Giuliano to Imperiali.

39 PCG, 9/2, 9 June 1913, San Giuliano to Giolitti. cf. CG, 22/55, 16 June 1913, Joel to Giolitti.

40 AG, 28/363, 21 July 1913, Joel to P. Levi.

41 *Ibid.*, 380, 19 March 1914, San Giuliano to Squitti; 20 March 1914, San Giuliano to Tittoni, Avarna, Squitti.

42 e.g. AG, 29/380, 4 April, 9 April 1914, both San Giuliano to Avarna, Bollati; cf. also H. Heilbronner, 'The merger attempts of Serbia and Montenegro, 1913–1914', *JCEA*, XVIII (1958–9), p. 285. Volpi, with his usual business acumen, also had fingers in Serb pies, and no doubt believed that he could survive the loss of the patronage of Crown Prince Danilo.

43 Heilbronner, *op. cit.*, p. 291.

44 F. Fischer, *War of Illusions* (London, 1975), pp. 293–4.

45 V. Mantegazza, *La Grande Bulgaria* (Rome, 1913), pp. 193, 219.
46 For an admirable later example, see Venizelos' comment 'You are a Great Power and Greece is a little State' and the plea for sympathy which followed O. Malagodi, *Conversazioni della guerra* (Milan, 1960), vol. I, p. 181.
47 *BSGI*, 7, June 1906 reporting meetings of 1, 6 May 1906; L. Vannutelli, 'Nella Turchia Asiatica', *BSGI*, 8, March 1907, pp. 201–29. There is also a brief account in L. Vannutelli, *Sguardo retrospettivo sulla mia vita nella marina* (Rome, 1959), pp. 56–7.
48 H. N. Howard, *The partition of Turkey* (reprint, New York, 1966), pp. 48–50; Blaisdell, *op. cit.*, pp. 123–4.
49 V. Mantegazza, *Italiani in Oriente, Eraclea* (Rome, 1922), pp. 49, 67, 83, 87, 91, 105, 156.
50 Webster, *L'imperialismo industriale italiano*, pp. 424–6.
51 e.g. *OUA*, 2, 2167, 12 May 1910, Mérey to Aehrenthal.
52 PCG, 15/2, 23 April 1911, San Giuliano to Giolitti.
53 AG, 22/162, 25 Sept. 1911, San Giuliano to De Martino.
54 CG, 17/41, 26 Jan. 1912, Nogara to Volpi who sent it on to Giolitti; 17 Feb. 1912, Volpi to Giolitti promising to make this standard practice.
55 *Ibid.*, 17/41, 3 May 1912, San Giuliano to Giolitti.
56 *CD*, XXIII, xvii, 21 June 1912, p. 21421.
57 *RC*, VII, 25 June 1912.
58 Bridge, *op. cit.*, pp. 344–5.
59 This is simply asserted as Austria's motive by A. Torre, 'Italia e Albania durante le guerre balcaniche', *Rivista d'Albania*, II (1940), p. 180.
60 CG, 21/48/2, 17 Aug. 1912, San Giuliano to Giolitti; 18 Aug. 1912, Giolitti to San Giuliano.
61 MAE P, 139/17, 31 Oct. 1912, San Giuliano to his diplomatic agents.
62 *Dalle carte di Giovanni Giolitti*, vol. III, p. 77.
63 CSG, I, 7 Jan. 1913, San Giuliano to De Martino.
64 *Dalle carte di Giovanni Giolitti*, vol. III, pp. 78–9.
65 *DGP*, 34, i, 12686, 13 Jan. 1913, Jagow to Bethmann Hollweg.
66 *DDF*, 3 s, v, 219, 15 Jan. 1913, Barrère to Poincaré; cf. FO 371/1764/2913, 15 Jan. 1913, Rodd to Grey. San Giuliano earned the minute 'very pig-headed' from Vansittart in the Foreign Office.
67 CSG, I, [8] Jan. 1913, San Giuliano to Avarna.
68 *DGP*, 34, i, 12701, 18 Jan. 1913, Jagow to Foreign Ministry. cf. RP, c/3, 19 Jan. 1913, Rodd to Grey in which Rodd learned from Jagow that San Giuliano had been 'taking the name of Germany and Austria in vain' over the Eastern Mediterranean Question.
69 CG, 15/25, 21 Jan. 1913, San Giuliano to Giolitti.
70 PCG, 9/1, 21 Jan. 1913, San Giuliano to Giolitti.
71 AG, 29/402, 23 Jan. 1913, San Giuliano to Garroni.
72 MAE P, 160/17, 19 Feb. 1913, Garroni to San Giuliano.
73 L. Federzoni, *L'Italia nell'Egeo* (Rome, 1913), pp. vi, 126.
74 e.g. AG, 16/97 ter, 14 Feb. 1913, [San Giuliano] memorandum.
75 AG, 27/312, 17 March 1913, San Giuliano to his major ambassadors.
76 *CD*, XXIII, xix, pp. 23315–18, 22 Feb. 1913. In his corresponding speech to the Senate,

San Giuliano rebuked the doubts of a colleague. 'No, Hon. Carafa d'Andria, the great memories of a great people must not embalm them. You embalm bodies not living things; and the great memories of Italy and of Rome are living things when in fact we know how to use them to drive us to enlightened and prudent action, to persevering and constant action, when they do not serve as a pretext for soaring rhetoric but as a spur to works worthy of our history.' *Senate*, XXVIII, xiii, 8 March 1913, p. 9979.

77 *Dalle carte di Giovanni Giolitti*, vol. III, pp. 85–9.

78 AG, 27/335, 21 April 1913, Nogara to Joel; 13/3, 14 May 1913, Volpi to San Giuliano.

79 *DGP*, 37, ii, 15046, 22 May 1913, Jagow to Flotow. The claim in Fischer, *op. cit.*, p. 301 that it was Germany which initiated the Triple Alliance discussions on Turkey is thus true only in the most restricted sense.

80 AG, 29/402, 23 Jan. 1913, San Giuliano to Garroni. His despatch noted that, in a Turkish collapse, Armenia would go to Russia, South Mesopotamia and Arabia to Britain, and Syria to France. The only Power seriously involved in Turkey, to which San Giuliano did not designate territory was Germany.

81 *DGP*, 37, ii, 24 May 1913, Flotow to Bethmann Hollweg.

82 PCG, 9/1, 26 May 1913, Bollati to San Giuliano.

83 *DGP*, 37, ii, 15049, 1 June 1913, Flotow to Bethmann Hollweg.

84 CG, 22/55, 6 June 1913, De Martino memorandum.

85 *Ibid.*, 17/37, 10 June 1913, Bollati to San Giuliano; 11 June 1913, San Giuliano to Giolitti.

86 PCG, 9/1, 28 June 1913, San Giuliano to Giolitti, Garroni (there is also a copy in SP, reel 54).

87 MAE P, 160/17, 24 June 1913, Garroni to San Giuliano; 26 June 1913, Garroni to San Giuliano.

88 *DGP*, 37, ii, 15053, 8 July 1913, Jagow to Flotow; 16 July 1913, Jagow to Bollati. For the official side see CB, 7, IV.12.28.

89 AG, 15/94 bis, 17 July 1913, San Giuliano to Giolitti.

90 *Ibid.*, 16/97 ter, 22 July 1913, De Martino report.

91 PCG, 9/1, 18 July 1913, Garroni to San Giuliano; 20 July 1913, Giolitti to San Giuliano; 25 July 1913, San Giuliano to Giolitti; 26 July 1913, Giolitti to San Giuliano; SP, 54, 24 July 1913, San Giuliano to Giolitti.

92 PCG, 9/1, 11 Aug. 1913, Millo to Giolitti; 30 Aug. 1913, Giolitti to Millo; San Giuliano, P. Levi and Nogara were still advocating the subsidies in September, 22 Sept. 1913, San Giuliano to Giolitti.

93 Cited by D. C. M. Platt, *Finance, Trade and Politics in British Foreign Policy 1815–1914* (Oxford, 1968), p. 207. Even Mario Toscano admitted that the British company's rights were judicially sound. M. Toscano, *Gli accordi di San Giovanni di Moriana* (Milan, 1936), p. 14. For the Italian version of the zone, see PCG, 9/1, 31 Aug. 1913, Garroni to San Giuliano.

94 See the aptly titled F. R. Bridge, '*Tarde venientibus ossa*: Austro-Hungarian colonial aspirations in Asia Minor 1913–14', *Middle Eastern Studies*, 6 (1970), pp. 319–30.

95 AG, 15/94 bis, 5 Aug. 1913, Avarna to San Giuliano.

96 *Ibid.*, 16/97 bis, 1 Aug. 1913, San Giuliano to Garroni. Joel was more concerned. CG, 29/90, 10 Aug. 1913, San Giuliano to Giolitti.

97 AG, 4/31, 19 Aug. 1913, San Giuliano *pro-memoria*.

98 CG, 29/93, 21 Aug. 1913, San Giuliano to Giolitti, AG, 16/97 bis, 22 Aug. 1913, San Giuliano to Garroni.

99 AG, 27/347, 24 Aug. 1913, San Giuliano to King Victor Emmanuel III; cf. 24 Aug. 1913, King Victor Emmanuel III to San Giuliano warning that Italy's 'needs' in the Mediterranean carried her 'naturally towards concert with France and England'.

100 *DGP*, 37, ii, 15058, 22 Aug. 1913, Flotow to Bethmann Hollweg.

101 CG, 22/59/D, 10 Sept. 1913, San Giuliano to Garroni.

102 FO 371/1844/40922, 5 Sept. 1913, Marling to Grey; *DDF*, 3 s, vii, 130, 9 Sept. 1913, De Manneville to Pichon; 132, 9 Sept. 1913, De Billy to Pichon.

103 FO 371/1844/43546, 23 Sept. 1913, Rodd to Grey. Vansittart's tougher mind did explain in a note that the Italian government was willing to persuade its subjects to 'try on' anything, no matter how dubious, 45086, 27 Sept. 1913, Rodd to Grey, Vansittart note.

104 FO 371/1844/46976, 18 Oct. 1913, Grey to Dering.

105 e.g. *DGP*, 37, ii, 15061, 27 Sept. 1913, Benckendorff and Hindenburg to Bethmann Hollweg.

106 MAE P, 160/17, 14 Oct. 1913, San Giuliano to Bollati.

107 CSG, 4, 22 Oct. 1913, De Martino memorandum.

108 *Ibid.*, 27 Oct. 1913, San Giuliano to Imperiali. The French were warned that a press quarrel might ensue. Nov. 1913, San Giuliano to Tittoni.

109 FO 371/1844/56128, 6 Dec. 1913, Rodd to Grey admitted ruefully that Italy had used the Dodecanese 'for a lot of purposes'.

110 CSG, 4, [Nov. 1913], De Martino memorandum.

111 Webster, *L'imperialismo industriale italiano*, pp. 477, 437–532 has rich and fascinating detail on commercial aspects of Italian policy in Asia Minor.

112 Cited by Bridge, '*Tarde venientibus ossa*', p. 323.

113 *DGP*, 37, ii, 15265, 20 Nov. 1913, Flotow to Bethmann Hollweg.

114 AG, 13/81, 17 Nov. 1913, San Giuliano to Garroni; cf. 14 Nov. 1913, San Giuliano to Giolitti; 15 Nov. 1913, Giolitti to San Giuliano.

115 CSG, 4, [24 Nov. 1913], San Giuliano to Bollati, Avarna, Garroni. cf. PCG, 9/1, 22 Nov. 1913, Flotow to San Giuliano; 24 Nov. 1913, San Giuliano to Giolitti.

116 Note Kühlmann's suggestion that Germany make plain to Britain that she was carrying no brief for Italy in the continuing Smyrna–Aidin affair. *DGP*, 37, ii, 15081, 29 Nov. 1913, Kühlmann to Bethmann Hollweg.

117 D. McLean, 'British finance and foreign policy in Turkey: the Smyrna-Aidin railway settlement 1913–14', *HJ*, xix, 1976, p. 525.

118 PCG, 9/1, 13 Dec. 1913, Giolitti to Tedesco. San Giuliano was also growing alarmed at the new restraint being shown in Italian banking circles towards Italian expansionism. See *Dalle carte di Giovanni Giolitti*, vol. iii, pp. 96–7.

119 FO 371/2118/10127 provides the details.

120 e.g. FO 371/2117/4556, 1 Feb. 1914, Mallet to Grey in which Mallet even notes that a breakdown in the traditional friendship could affect British interests in the Red Sea.

121 AG, 17/106, 3 Feb. 1914, San Giuliano to Imperiali.

122 McLean, *op. cit.*, p. 527.

123 e.g. *DDF*, 3 s, ix, 84, 14 Feb. 1914, P. Cambon to Doumergue.

124 FO 371/2113/5554, 30 Feb. 1914, Rodd to Grey.

125 CSG, 5, [Jan. 1914], San Giuliano memorandum.

126 *Ibid.*, 3 Jan. 1914, San Giuliano to Imperiali. There was another example of San Giuliano's nervousness in the last stage of negotiations with the Smyrna–Aidin Company reminiscent of the final days of the negotiation of the Treaty of Lausanne. San Giuliano, and Joel, were willing to accept a compromise whereby some British delegates entered the board to build the new Smyrna–Aidin line. It was once again the clear-minded Giolitti who opposed this idea on the grounds that it would destroy at a stroke the 'political value' of the scheme. See PCG, 13/3, 2 March 1914, Giolitti to San Giuliano.

127 e.g. *DGP*, 36, ii, 14242, 4 Jan. 1914, Flotow to Bethmann Hollweg; Flotow developed the theme that it was Italian intransigence which was driving Britain more securely into the arms of France. See AG, 17/106, 9 Jan. 1914, San Giuliano to his major ambassadors.

128 e.g. a representative of the Deutsche Bank in Constantinople alleged that Italy intended soon to establish a real colony in Asia Minor. *DGP*, 37, ii, 15102, 29 Jan. 1914, Mutis to Bethmann Hollweg. The German business community was usually markedly hostile to Italian policies towards Turkey.

129 e.g. CSG, 5, 6 Jan. 1914, San Giuliano to Avarna.

130 It was now that Berchtold remarked bitterly '*tarde venientibus ossa*'. See Bridge, *op. cit.*, pp. 326–7.

131 *DGP*, 37, ii, 15107, 19 March 1914; 15108, 21 March 1914; 15111, 3 April 1914, all Flotow to Bethmann Hollweg.

132 CS(L), C.2.42/8, 20 April 1914, San Giuliano pro-memoria; Bridge, *op. cit.*, p. 327.

133 *Dalle carte di Giovanni Giolitti*, vol. III, p. 97.

134 PCG, 13/3, 6 March 1914, Joel to San Giuliano; 11 March 1914, San Giuliano to Giolitti.

135 CS, 8/63, 29 May 1914, Garroni to San Giuliano.

136 PCG, 13/3, 11 March 1914, San Giuliano to Giolitti.

137 G. Carocci, *Giolitti e l'età giolittiana* (Turin, 1961), p. 166.

138 MAE P, 4 June 1914, Garroni to San Giuliano. cf. *DGP*, 36, ii, 14469, 30 May 1914, Flotow to Bethmann Hollweg.

139 AG, 15/94 bis, 9 June 1914, De Lucchi (Fiume) to San Giuliano.

140 MAE P, 460/97, 14 June 1914, Garroni to San Giuliano; cf. AG, 17/106, 3 Feb. 1914, San Giuliano to Imperiali.

141 FO 371/2119/33783, 23 July 1914, Grey to Rodd. cf. FO 371/2136/32381, 16 July 1914, Government of India report about Italian meddling in the Gulf of Aden which produced a minute by Crowe that nothing else could be expected of Italians, and Sir Arthur Nicolson, the Permanent Under-Secretary, was now irritated enough with Italy to agree.

142 CS, 8/63, 11 June 1914, San Giuliano to Salandra cf. also PCG, 13/1, 10 July 1914, San Giuliano to Salandra with the usual plea that capital be found for Balkan railway investment.

143 MAE P, 168/17, 5 Aug. 1914, Carletti to Garroni, forwarded to Rome 6 Aug.

144 L. Franchetti, 'L'Italia e l' Asia Minore', *NA*, f 1087, 1 May 1917.

145 e.g. SP, reel 47: 1, 19 Nov. 1914, Ministry of the Navy to Sonnino.

146 D. Mack Smith, *Le guerre del Duce* (Bari, 1976), p. 203. Volpi, by then, had risen to the appropriate office of President of Confindustria.

147 San Giuliano repeated his metaphor in direct reference to the Società Commerciale d'Oriente, MAE P, 675/844, 5 Nov. 1913, San Giuliano to Joel.

148 Djemal Pasha, *Memories of a Turkish statesman* (London, n.d.), p. 77.

149 E. Corradini, *Discorsi politici* (Florence, 1925), p. 170. The reason, Corradini said sadly, was that Turkey was such a good area for business.

150 R. Cantalupo, *L'Italia musulmana* (Rome, 1928), p. 154.

151 M. S. Anderson, *The Eastern Question* (London, 1966), p. 263 wisely explains many of the Turkish ventures of the Great Powers by this adjective. Britain and Germany may have begun worrying, before 1914, about the oil deposits of the area, but, for Italy, it was the 'glamour', the 'contest' which was the most important. cf. M. Kent, *Oil and Empire* (London, 1976). There is no evidence, however, that Italy saw the Turkish Empire as a source of oil for her armies or industry.

CHAPTER 11. SAN GIULIANO'S EPILOGUE. THE REALITIES OF EUROPEAN WAR 28 JUNE TO 16 OCTOBER 1914

1 Cited by W. A. Renzi, 'Italy's neutrality and entrance into the Great War: a re-examination', *AHR*, LXXIII (1967–8), p. 1414.

2 See generally L. Lotti, *La settimana rossa* (Florence, 1965).

3 *Senate*, XXIV, i, 29 June 1914, p. 679.

4 e.g. see his own comments A. Salandra, *La neutralità italiana* (Milan, 1928), p. 107; or CS, 8/62, in which on 30 June 1914 Salandra received a long detailed list of subversive press and other organisations in Italy. Included, characteristically as subversives, were Anarchists, Syndicalists, Socialists, Republicans and Clericals.

5 e.g. CS(L), C.2.42/30, 1 July 1914, San Giuliano to Salandra saying that the heat prevented him from appearing in the Chamber. Typically, and in contrast to his always polite correspondence with Giolitti, San Giuliano told Salandra quite firmly what he should do.

6 e.g. CS, 5/42, 29 June 1914, Aliotti to San Giuliano; *DDI*, 4 s, XII, 18.

7 *DDI*, 4 s, XII, 3, 28 June 1914, San Giuliano to Bollati, Avarna, Aliotti.

8 *Ibid.*, 8, 29 June 1914, San Giuliano to Avarna.

9 *Ibid.*, 10, 29 June 1914, Cerrina (Governor of Eritrea) to San Giuliano; 26, 30 June 1914, Bollati to San Giuliano. These fears of Austrian penetration of Ethiopia continued throughout the July Crisis.

10 CS, 2/14, 30 June 1914. Martini to Salandra.

11 *DDF*, 3 s, X, 460, 30 June 1914, Barrère to Viviani; cf. also his later memories C. Barrère, 'L'Italie e l'agonie de la paix en 1914', *RDM*, 35, Oct. 1926, pp. 545–61.

12 *DDI*, 4 s, XII, 25, 30 June 1914, Bollati to San Giuliano.

13 *Ibid.*, 39, 1 July 1914, San Giuliano to Avarna and others.

14 *Ibid.*, 52, 2 July 1914, Avarna to San Giuliano.

15 CS(L), C.2.42/31, 2 July 1914, San Giuliano to Salandra. In contrast, at the same time, Luigi Albertini was trying to stiffen the government against yielding to obstructionism in the Chamber, an interesting sidelight to Albertini's later role as

the major historian of the July Crisis. See L. Albertini, *Epistolario 1911–1926* (Milan, 1968), vol. I, pp. 244–5, 247.

16 *DDI*, 4 s, XII, 54, 57, both 3 July 1914, San Giuliano to Bollati and others.

17 *Ibid.*, 77, 4 July 1914, San Giuliano to Avarna, Bollati.

18 *Ibid.*, 78, 5 July 1914, Bollati to San Giuliano.

19 *Ibid.*, 89, 6 July 1914, San Giuliano to Fasciotti; 90, 6 July 1914, San Giuliano to Cora. Cora, the Italian *Chargé* in Belgrade, later wrote his memoirs of these days. G. Cora, 'Belgrado 1914', *RSPI*, VIII (1941), pp. 513–30, mainly concentrating on personal impressions which he gained from playing bridge with the famous Russian Minister, Hartwig. Cora does recall the importance for Italy at the time of Mount Lovcen.

20 FO 371/2119/32141, 6 July 1914, Rodd to Grey; FO 371/1880/31558, 6 July 1914, Rodd to Grey; FO 800/65, GP, 7 July 1914, Rodd to Grey.

21 Cited by L. Valiani, 'Italian-Austro-Hungarian negotiations 1914–1915', *JCH*, I (1966), p. 114.

22 F. R. Bridge, *From Sadowa to Sarajevo* (London, 1972), p. 303 underlines Aehrenthal's failure then to inform Germany of his plans.

23 O. Malagodi, *Conversazioni della guerra* (Milan, 1960), vol. I, p. 11. San Giuliano also made some sensible remarks about the need not to get out of perspective the personal influence and ambition of Franz Ferdinand (pp. 10–11).

24 *DDI*, 4 s, XII, 123, 9 July 1914, Bollati to San Giuliano.

25 Salandra, *op. cit.*, pp. 74–5.

26 *DDI*, 4 s, XII, 124, 9 July 1914, San Giuliano to Avarna and others.

27 *DGP*, 34, i, 15555, 10 July 1914, Flotow to Bethman Hollweg.

28 e.g. *DDI*, 4 s, XII, 133, 9 July 1914, Bollati to San Giuliano; 154, 11 July 1914, Avarna to San Giuliano; 169, 12 July 1914, Bollati to San Giuliano saying that the Austrian ambassador in Berlin, Szögyény was talking about the possibility of the 'cession' to Italy of Valona and 'all its surrounding territory'.

29 *Ibid.*, 200, 14 July 1914, San Giuliano to Avarna, Bollati.

30 *Ibid.*, 225, 14 July 1914, San Giuliano to Bollati.

31 These are denied by Valiani, *op. cit.*, p. 115.

32 L. Albertini, *The Origins of the War of 1914* (London, 1953), vol. II, pp. 231–4.

33 MAE P, 675/844, 18 July 1914, De Martino to San Giuliano. cf. *DDI*, 4 s, XII, 286, 16 July 1914, Aliotti to San Giuliano saying that armed Italo-Austrian intervention in Albania would at least have a salutary effect on Greece.

34 *DDI*, 4 s, XII, 272, 16 July 1914, San Giuliano to Avarna and others.

35 *Ibid.*, 311, 17 July 1914, San Giuliano to Avarna and others.

36 *Ibid.*, 334, 18 July 1914, San Giuliano to Bollati.

37 Albertini, *The Origins*, vol. II, p. 245.

38 Valiani, *op. cit.*, p. 116.

39 Malagodi, *op. cit.*, vol. I, p. 17.

40 e.g. *DDI*, 4 s, XII, 346, 18 July 1914, San Giuliano to Avarna; 393, 21 July 1914, San Giuliano to Fasciotti.

41 *Ibid.*, 418, 22 July 1914, San Giuliano to Avarna; FO 371/2188/33328, 22 July 1914, Rodd to Grey.

42 *DDF*, 3 s, X, 546, 21 July 1914, Barrère to Bienvenu-Martin.

43 CS(L), C.12/21, 23 July 1914, De Martino to Salandra.

44 FO 371/2158/33981, 22 July 1914, Rodd to Grey; *DDI*, 4 s, XII, 424, 22 July 1914, San Giuliano to Avarna and others. Valiani, *op. cit.*, p. 115 wrongly says that San Giuliano told the Russian ambassador Krupenski: 'we can assist Serbia, within certain limits, by diplomatic methods; but we shall certainly not go to war with Austria to save her'. In fact San Giuliano made this remark to the Serbian *Chargé*, an entirely different matter.

45 *DDI*, 4 s, XII, 448, 23 July 1914, Avarna to San Giuliano.

46 *Ibid.*, 449, 450, 23 July 1914, both San Giuliano to De Martino.

47 *Ibid.*, 457, 24 July 1914, San Giuliano to Avarna, Bollati, Carlotti.

48 *Ibid.*, 488, 24 July 1914, San Giuliano to Bollati, Avarna.

49 The original is available CS(L), C.2.42/37; see also Salandra, *op. cit.*, pp. 78–80; B. Vigezzi, *L'Italia di fronte alla prima guerra mondiale* (Milan, 1966), vol. I, pp. 8–9.

50 *DDI*, 4 s, XII, 525, 25 July 1914, San Giuliano to Salandra.

51 *Ibid.*, 560, 26 July 1914, San Giuliano to Salandra.

52 *Ibid.*, 502, 25 July 1914, San Giuliano to De Martino.

53 *Ibid.*, 503, 25 July 1914, Imperiali to San Giuliano.

54 e.g. RP, Diary entry for 26 July 1914, which contains the first serious mention by Rodd of the July Crisis. Rodd also feared war would help socialism and revolution – see his entry for 3 July.

55 *DDI*, 4 s, XII, 551, 26 July 1914, San Giuliano to King Victor Emmanuel III.

56 *Ibid.*, 575, 27 July 1914, San Giuliano to Bollati, Avarna.

57 RP, Diary entry for 27 July 1914; cf. also *DDF*, 3 s, XI, 153, 159 both, 27 July 1914, Barrère to Bienvenu-Martin. It was on this day that Austria began enrolling 'volunteers' to fight in Albania with the obvious implication that they would be unlikely to leave. See F. Fischer, *War of Illusions* (London, 1975), p. 407.

58 *DDI*, 4 s, XII, 621, 28 July 1914, San Giuliano to his ambassadors to the Great Powers.

59 FO 371/2159/34474, 28 July 1914, Rodd to Grey.

60 *DDI*, 4 s, XII, 625, 655, both 28 July 1914, Imperiali to San Giuliano. The importance of the Italian initiative on 28 July has been greatly exaggerated by Albertini, as also has been his criticism of San Giuliano for not doing it earlier. See Albertini, *The Origins*, vol. II, pp. 418–21. cf. also G. Tadini, *Il Marchese Antonino di San Giuliano nella tragica estate del 1914* (Rome, 1945), pp. 49–50, who is one of the few Italian historians willing to admit the limitations imposed on Italy's initiative given that Britain persisted in regarding her as a *quantité négligeable.*

61 Fischer, *op. cit.*, p. 401.

62 H. von Lützow, *Im diplomatischen Dienst der k.u.k. Monarchie* (Munich, 1971), p. 116.

63 R. Molinelli, 'I Nazionalisti italiani e l'intervento a fianco degli imperi centrali', *RSR*, LIX (1972), p. 199; S. Sonnino, *Diario* (Bari, 1972), vol. II, p. 8. See also in general B. Vigezzi, 'I problemi della neutralità e della guerra nel carteggio Salandra-Sonnino (1914–1917)', *NRS*, XLV (1961). Vigezzi has subsequently published an exhaustive account of Italian public opinion and foreign policy from July to October 1914. Vigezzi, *L'Italia di fronte alla prima guerra mondiale*. Vigezzi remarks elsewhere on the lack of enthusiasm for war of Italian capitalism. See B. Vigezzi, *Da Giolitti a Salandra* (Florence, 1969), p. 99.

64 CS(L), C.2.44/5, 27 July 1914, Martini to Salandra; /6, 28 July 1914, Martini to Salandra.

65 *DDF*, 3 s, XI, 194, 28 July 1914, Barrère to Bienvenu Martin.

66　CS, 4/30, 26 July 1914, Grandi to Salandra.

67　e.g. *DDI*, 4 s, XII, 639, 28 July 1914, San Giuliano to Imperiali and others; 658, 28 July 1914, San Giuliano to Bollati, Avarna.

68　e.g. *ibid.*, 661, 28 July 1914, San Giuliano to Bollati, Avarna, Fasciotti; 700, 29 July 1914, Fasciotti to San Giuliano.

69　*Ibid.*, 697, 29 July 1914, Imperiali to San Giuliano; *DDF*, 3 s, XI, 237, 29 July 1914, Barrère to Bienvenu-Martin.

70　*DDI*, 4 s, XII, 682, 29 July 1914, San Giuliano to Bollati, Avarna; 705, 29 July 1914, San Giuliano to Bollati, Avarna.

71　F. Martini, *Diario 1914–1918* (Milan, 1966), p. 6.

72　*DDF*, 3 s, XI, 321, 30 July 1914, Barrère to Viviani.

73　Perhaps San Giuliano's most bitter critic was Andrea Torre, Rome correspondent of *Corriere della Sera*. It is interesting to speculate how much Albertini's arguments about San Giuliano in *The Origins of the War of 1914* owe to Torre's letters and reports during the July Crisis. e.g. see Albertini, *Epistolario*, vol. I, pp. 218, 219, 251–3.

74　Martini, *op. cit.*, p. 7.

75　*Ibid.*, p. 8. cf. *DDF*, 3 s, XI, 411, 31 July 1914, Barrère to Viviani; FO 371/2159/34933, 31 July 1914, Rodd to Grey; J. R. Rodd, *Social and Diplomatic memories* (London, 1925), vol. III, pp. 208–9.

76　Albertini, *Epistolario*, Vol. I, pp. 253–4; Sonnino, *op. cit.*, vol. II, pp. 8–12. Fusinato of the Istituto Coloniale, and one of the negotiators of the Treaty of Lausanne also disliked the compromises of Italian policy, although asking Salandra not to reveal to San Giuliano that he had written. Fusinato's mind seems to have been disturbed by the 'great crisis', the 'collapse' of the Triple Alliance and the 'danger' of revolution. On 22 September 1914 he committed suicide.

77　CS(L), C.1.2/35, 1 Aug. 1914, Visconti Venosta to Salandra; /36, 2 Aug. 1914, Ruspoli to Salandra; Giolitti continued to resist suggestions that he take power. For his reasons see A. Frassati, *Giolitti* (Florence, 1959), pp. 10–1.

78　G. Volpe, *Il popolo italiano tra la pace e la guerra (1914–15)* (Milan, 1940), pp. 29–30, 43–8; For the harvest see Martini, *op. cit.*, p. 196. The 'glorious summer' of 1914 had been a wet one in Italy.

79　CS(L), C.1.2/40, 5 Aug. 1914, Giolitti to Salandra.

80　Albertini, *The Origins*, vol. II, p. 322, complains that San Giuliano (and Salandra) moved Italy towards intervention by the 'back streets' and not the 'high road'. cf. *Corriere della Sera*'s advice of 31 July that Italy could still side with Austria. In a letter to his wife on that day Albertini asserted another position i.e. that 'woe' would come to any Power which did not join the war. See Vigezzi, *L'Italia di fronte alla prima guerra mondiale*, p. 199.

81　Malagodi, *op. cit.*, vol. I, p. 17. On 27 July W. S. Churchill's first notices to the Royal Navy urged them to be ready for combat between the Triple Entente and the Triple Alliance. R. Churchill, *Winston S. Churchill* (London, 1967), vol. II, p. 708. Martini also was talking about the vulnerability of Italian coastal cities to a British fleet. Martini, *op. cit.*, pp. 11–12.

82　Malagodi, *op. cit.*, p. 20. cf. also *DDI*, 5 s, i, 54, 55, 4 Aug. 1914, San Giuliano to Salandra. cf. Vigezzi, *Da Giolitti a Salandra*, pp. 41–8. Note also A. J. P. Taylor, *The First World War* (Harmondsworth, 1966), p. 89 remarking with much sense that

France wanted Italy to join the war on the Entente side after August 1914 essentially in order that Italy be weakened by the process of war.

83   *DDI*, 4 s, XII, 876, 1 Aug. 1914, San Giuliano to Imperiali.

84   PCG, 13/1, 5 Aug. 1914, San Giuliano to Salandra; 9 Aug. 1914, Salandra to Rubini (note also 10 Aug. 1914, Rubini to Salandra asking, innocently, why San Giuliano liked to communicate via Salandra rather than directly with his Cabinet colleague). MAE P, 678 bis/29, 7 Aug. 1914, San Giuliano to Stringher.

85   G. Del Re, 'Le Colonie portoghesi: ripercussioni della grande guerra', *RC*, IX, Aug.–Sept. 1914, pp. 34–46.

86   L. Aldrovandi Marescotti, 'Al principio della guerra mondiale (giugno–novembre 1914)', *NA*, f 1514, 16 April 1935, p. 483; Malagodi, *op. cit.*, pp. 181–91. Any apparent differences between San Giuliano and Salandra seem to have been the result either of wishful thinking by interventionists like Martini, or because San Giuliano did not like revealing his own mind too closely even to the Prime Minister.

87   Martini, *op. cit.*, p. 14. Martini wanted Italy to mobilise as did Andrea Torre, who hoped openly that San Giuliano would be sacked or would die. Albertini, *Epistolario*, vol. I, pp. 256–8.

88   Martini, *op. cit.*, p. 19.

89   *DDI*, 5 s, i, 3, 2 Aug. 1914, San Giuliano to Bollati; Vigezzi, *L'Italia di fronte alla prima guerra mondiale*, vol. I, pp. 38–9.

90   *DDI*, 5 s, i, 71, 5 Aug. 1914, San Giuliano to Salandra.

91   *Ibid.*, 92, 6 Aug. 1914, San Giuliano to De Facendis; 104, 7 Aug. 1914, San Giuliano to Aliotti; A. J. Marder, *From Dreadnought to Scapa Flow* (London, 1965), vol. II, p. 32.

92   *DDI*, 5 s, i, 65, 5 Aug. 1914, Carlotti to San Giuliano.

93   *Ibid.*, 107, 7 Aug. 1914, Carlotti to San Giuliano.

94   Martini, *op. cit.*, p. 14 with Salandra telling Martini to strengthen his contacts with Rodd, rather nicely matched by FO 371/2163/37527, 8 Aug. 1914, Rodd to Grey, alleging quite incorrectly that Martini had great influence, and would be a better man to work through than San Giuliano.

95   *DDI*, 5 s, i, 34, 8 Aug. 1914, Salandra to Imperiali; FO 371/2161/35721, 4 Aug. 1914, Rodd to Grey. Rodd was also attractive because of his own initial aversion to the war. His acceptance that Italy and Britain might 'pair', and then, once the war started, his alarmist reports that Italy was about to be bought by the Central Powers did not improve his reputation in London. Typical is a minute by Grey's secretary, Tyrrell, sarcastically doubting a report from the 'minor poet'. FO 800/65, GP, 8 Sept. 1914, Rodd to Grey.

96   *DDI*, 5 s, i, 54, 4 Aug. 1914, San Giuliano to Salandra. Note also San Giuliano's sensible comments about Switzerland, and about his own health.

97   FO 800/65, GP, 9 Aug. 1914, Rodd to Grey.

98   *DDI*, 5 s, i, 166, 10 Aug. 1914, San Giuliano to King Victor Emmanuel III.

99   Albertini, *Epistolario*, vol. I, pp. 256–8; it is interesting at the time to find Victor Emmanuel's *homme de confidence*, the British military attaché, Delmé-Radcliffe, opening an optimistic correspondence with Grey about the prospect that Italy would fight 'for humanity'. See FO 800/107, GP, 7, 9 Aug. 1914, Delmé-Radcliffe to Grey.

100 See Vigezzi, *L'Italia di fronte alla prima guerra mondiale*, vol. I, p. 59.

101   *DDI*, 5 s, i, 166, 10 Aug. 1914, San Giuliano to King Victor Emmanuel III.

102   *DDI*, 5 s, 155, 9 Aug. 1914, Imperiali to San Giuliano. Apparently fearing that his Foreign Minister had not got the message, 315, 18 Aug. 1914, Imperiali to San Giuliano reiterated the usefulness of the sympathy of the House of Rothschild and suggested that Alfred Rothschild be sent a formal note of thanks for it. But San Giuliano rejected the idea, 358, 20 Aug. 1914, San Giuliano to Imperiali. Naturally Martini was also made aware of the Rothschild offer. Martini, *op. cit.*, p. 34.

103   FO 371/2164/37805, 11 Aug. 1914, Grey to Rodd. Imperiali, for his part, had reminded San Giuliano that Turkey seemed likely to enter the war, which would mean the final break-up of the Ottoman Empire, in which Italy should secure her interests. *DDI*, 5 s, i, 167, 10 Aug. 1914, Imperiali to San Giuliano.

104   DDI, 5 s, i, 172, 10 Aug. 1914, San Giuliano to Avarna, Bollati; 11 Aug. 1914, San Giuliano to Avarna, Bollati.

105   Salandra, *op. cit.*, pp. 148–9.

106   *DDI*, 5 s, 119, 7 Aug. 1914, San Giuliano to Salandra; 230, 13 Aug. 1914, San Giuliano to Salandra.

107   *Ibid.*, 201, 11 Aug. 1914, San Giuliano to Imperiali; FO 371/2171/38844, 12 Aug. 1914, Grey to Rodd.

108   *DDI*, 205, 12 Aug. 1914, San Giuliano to Imperiali. More explicitly see 241, 14 Aug. 1914, San Giuliano to Tittoni.

109   e.g. *Ibid.*, 5 s, i, 217, 12 Aug. 1914. San Giuliano to Salandra. cf. CS, 1/5, 15 Aug. 1914, Tittoni to Salandra. Also note Tittoni's modest revelation that he would be in Rome, and that he greatly respected Salandra, a statement made immediately after the death of his dear friend San Giuliano CS(L), C.1.4/18, 18 Oct. 1914. Salandra was a little acerbic in his comments on Tittoni's 'availability' in March 1914. See Salandra, *op. cit.*, p. 143.

110   *DDI*, 5 s, i, 242, 14 Aug. 1914, Imperiali to San Giuliano cf. also 265, 15 Aug. 1914, San Giuliano to Salandra advising against conversations with Barrère or Krupenski because of their habitual 'lack of reserve'.

111   *Ibid.*, 219, 12 Aug. 1914, San Giuliano to Salandra.

112   Sonnino, *op. cit.*, vol. II, p. 14; P. Bertolini, 'Diario (Agosto 1914–Maggio 1915)', *NA*, f 1221, 1 Feb. 1923, pp. 213–15. Agreement between Bertolini and Sonnino seemed especially ominous to Salandra. For his own sarcastic comments about Bertolini see Salandra, *op. cit.*, pp. 140–1. CS(L), 1–2/72, 73, 13 Aug. 1914, Fusinato to Salandra. Fusinato may also have seen himself as a possible triplicist Foreign Minister. See /83, 16 Aug. 1914, Fusinato to Salandra. According to Orlando the neutralist Bertolini was still a possible candidate for the *Consulta* in November. V. E. Orlando, *Memorie* (Milan, 1960), p. 28.

113   Vigezzi, *L'Italia di fronte alla prima guerra mondiale*, vol. I, passim. Guicciardini was another possibility as Foreign Minister. See Sonnino, *op. cit.*, vol. II, p. 13.

114   *DDI*, 5 s, i, 281, 16 Aug. 1914, San Giuliano to Salandra.

115   *Ibid.*, 317, 18 Aug. 1914, Imperiali to San Giuliano; FO 371/2171/40193, 17 Aug. 1914, Rodd to Grey; 18 Aug 1914, Grey to Rodd.

116   *DDI*, 5 s, i, 370, 21 Aug. 1914, Imperiali to San Giuliano.

117   *Ibid.*, 230, 13 Aug. 1914, San Giuliano to Salandra.

118   Malagodi, *op. cit.*, vol I, p. 22.

119 *Ibid.*, p. 20.
120 e.g. CG, 15/25, 21 Jan. 1913, San Giuliano to Giolitti.
121 *DDI*, 5 s, i, 773, 23 Sept. 1914, Fasciotti to San Giuliano.
122 *Ibid.*, 796, 25 Sept. 1914, San Giuliano to Imperiali; cf. G. E. Torrey, 'The Rumanian-Italian agreement of 23 September 1914', *SEER*, XLIV (1966), p. 415. Rodd as usual did what San Giuliano wanted him to do, and duly instructed London of the increased value to the Triple Entente of Italy and Romania acting together. FO 800/65, GP, 21 Oct. 1914, Rodd to Grey.
123 Torrey, *op. cit.*, pp. 419–420.
124 G. E. Torrey, 'Rumania and the belligerents 1914–1916', *JCH*, I (1966), pp. 171–91.
125 Sonnino, *op. cit.*, vol. II, pp. 15, 18–20.
126 e.g. *DGP*, 36, ii, 14550, 29 Aug. 1914, Tschirsky to Foreign Ministry; 14551, 31 Aug. 1914, Flotow to Foreign Ministry; *DDI*, 5 s, i, 642, 10 Sept. 1914, San Giuliano to Avarna, Bollati; 723, 17 Sept. 1914, San Giuliano to Imperiali, Tittoni, Carlotti.
127 Salandra, *op. cit.*, p. 65 emphasises that the Greeks were a real problem for Italy. The Greeks also had been 'insulting' in their press about Italian neutrality. A. De Bosdari, *Delle guerre balcaniche, della grande guerra e di alcuni fatti precedenti ad esse* (Milan, 1927), pp. 104–5.
128 *DDI*, 5 s, i, 886, 5 Oct. 1914, Bollati to San Giuliano; FO 371/2009/55845, 6 Oct. 1914, Grey to Rodd; /57096, 7 Oct. 1914, Rodd to Grey.
129 Familiarity with Saseno revealed that it had no supplies of running water although Italian propagandists continued to speak of it as the 'Gibraltar' of the Adriatic. e.g. A. I. Sulliotti, *In Albania: sei mesi di regno* (Milan, 1914), p. 149.
130 Whether from traditional anti-clericalism or not, Italian politicians had a preference for dealing with Albania on especially holy days. Mussolini's invasion in 1939 occurred on Good Friday as a Fascist expansion of the Christmas Day occupation in 1914. In these last days of his life, San Giuliano did not forget to keep up pressure on banks and state industrial concerns to finance Vismara, whose chances of cropping his trees had again deteriorated with the onset of war. See e.g. MAE P, 678 bis/29, 26 Aug. 1914, Rubini to San Giuliano; 6 Sept. 1914, Bianchi to San Giuliano and R. J. B. Bosworth, 'The Albanian forests of Signor Giacomo Vismara', *HJ*, XVIII (1975), pp. 584–5.
131 See generally U. Trumpener, 'Turkey's entry into World War I: an assessment of responsibilities', *JMH*, XXXIV (1962); W. W. Gottlieb, *Studies in Secret Diplomacy during the First World War* (London, 1957).
132 e.g. CS, 4/31, 24 Sept. 1914, Garroni to San Giuliano.
133 e.g. *ibid.*, 24 Aug. 1914, San Giuliano to Garroni.
134 e.g. see *DDI*, 5 s, i, 429, 466, 504, 534, 546, 550, 567, 591, 625, 655, 660, 676, 693, 697; CM, 13, 25 Aug. 1914, Salandra to Martini; 3 Sept. 1914, Salvago Raggi to Martini. Martini, *op. cit.*, pp. 59, 85.
135 FO 371/2171/42189, 22 Aug. 1914, Rodd to Grey.
136 *Ibid.*, /42189, 25 Aug. 1914, Rodd to Grey.
137 G. Rochat, 'La preparazione dell'esercito italiano nell'inverno 1914–15 in relazione alle informazioni disponibili sulla guerra disposizione', *Risorgimento*, XIII (1961), p. 12 notes that Cadorna had provided a detailed war plan against Austria by 1 September 1914. See also generally Vigezzi, *L'Italia di fronte alla prima guerra mondiale*,

vol I, pp. 65–75. cf. *DDI*, 5 s, i, 468, San Giuliano to Salandra in which San Giuliano again suggested more rapid military preparations and that from Cadorna's *pro-memoria* it was evident that Italian forces at present were not such as to be able to decide the war.

138 e.g. Sonnino, *op. cit.*, vol. II, pp. 15–19.

139 Torre had added De Martino to the list of those whom he wanted removed from office. He said that De Martino was 'a Levantine, that is a man *without principle*, without character, facile in lying and dissimulation, a player with words, shrewd in deceitful expedients'. Albertini, *Epistolario*, vol. I, pp. 276–7; cf. also pp. 282–3 for Sonnino's continuing attacks on San Giuliano.

140 Vigezzi, *L'Italia di fronte alla prima guerra mondiale*, vol. I, pp. 724–5.

141 C. Avarna Di Gualtieri, 'Il Carteggio Avarna-Bollati, luglio 1914-maggio 1915', *RSI*, LXI (1949), pp. 249–65. See especially Bollati's letters 31 Aug. 1914, 24 Sept. 1914, 9 Oct. 1914. Pessimism and timidity were not new qualities in the character of Riccardo Bollati. Over a decade before, he explained to an intrepid lady British visitor that he had accepted a posting to Cetinje because it was nearer Rome than Buenos Aires and regretted: 'Nothing bites you, everything bites me. Your method of seeing lands is undoubtedly the best, but I am satisfied with what I can see from the windows of the best hotel'. M. E. Durham, *Twenty years of Balkan tangle* (London, n.d.), p. 43.

142 A. Monticone, *La Germania e la neutralità italiana: 1914–1915* (Bologna, 1971), p. 40.

143 Valiani, *op. cit.*, pp. 119–20. San Giuliano said Macchio was 'as sweet as honey' Malagodi, *op. cit.*, vol. I, pp. 9, 23; Von Lützow, *op. cit.*, p. 225.

144 Monticone, *op. cit.*, pp. 50–5.

145 *DDI*, 5 s, i, 443, 25 Aug. 1914, San Giuliano to Avarna, Bollati.

146 *Ibid.*, 495, 29 Aug. 1914, San Giuliano to Avarna, Bollati and his other ambassadors.

147 Monticone, *op. cit.*, pp. 45–6.

148 Malagodi asked him about this on 12 September given Russia's able military effort so far, and San Giuliano, if admitting that Russia had done better than he had expected, certainly made no mention of concern about a Slav peril. Malagodi, *op. cit.*, vol. I, p. 21.

149 Avarna Di Gualitieri, *op. cit.*, pp. 256–7 provides the example of Avarna who, distraught and confused, but worried above all that the Savoy dynasty survive, began to wonder if after all that Italy should join the Triple Entente and denounce the Triple Alliance. cf. also the open comments of Sonnino, *op. cit.*, vol. II, p. 89, entry for 16 Feb. 1915.

150 A. Solmi, 'Carteggio fra Salandra e Sonnino nella prima fase della neutralità italiana', *NA*, f 1510, 16 Feb. 1935, p. 487. By 29 October Salandra believed that Italy must win territorial advantage from the war, or her monarchical institutions would be overthrown. See Bertolini, 'Diario (Agosto 1914–Maggio 1915)', p. 217.

151 Sonnino, *op. cit.*, vol. II, p. 9.

152 e.g. Solmi, *op. cit.*, p. 491, 24 Sept. 1914, Sonnino to Salandra.

153 Once again an immense wealth of detail about the state of public opinion in September and October 1914 can be found in Vigezzi, *L'Italia di fronte alla prima guerra mondiale*, vol. I, especially part II; part III chs III–IV.

154 CS(L), C.2.44/9, 11 Sept. 1914, Martini to Salandra.

155 R. De Felice, *Mussolini il rivoluzionario* (Turin, 1965), pp. 256–87.

156 e.g. A. Monticone, *Nitti e la grande guerra, 1914–18* (Milan, 1961), pp. 6–8; Orlando, *op. cit.*, p. 283.

157 Albertini, *Epistolario*, vol. I, pp. 276–7. De Martino had told him 'the King is a true constitutional sovereign; he thinks as his ministers think'.

158 Martini, *op. cit.*, pp. 103–4.

159 L. Peano, *Ricordi della guerra dei trent'anni, 1915–1945* (Florence, 1948), pp. 17–18.

160 Note Salandra's heavy emphasis on this, Salandra, *op. cit.*, pp. 138–9.

161 Imperiali had again become notably effusive about his 'friend' Grey. San Giuliano may have been more impressed to learn *DDI*, 5 s, i, 474, 28 Aug. 1914, Imperiali to San Giuliano that both Grey and Churchill had talked about Britain's willingness to waive her old objections to Italian retention of the Dodecanese. cf. 497, 29 Aug. 1914, San Giuliano to Imperiali.

162 *Ibid.*, 468, 27 Aug. 1914, San Giuliano to Salandra; 478, 28 Aug. 1914, San Giuliano to Imperiali; 495, 29 Aug. 1914, San Giuliano to his ambassadors.

163 *Ibid.*, 479, 28 Aug. 1914, San Giuliano to Salandra.

164 FO 371/2008/43868, 27 Aug. 1914, Rodd to Grey. cf. 'Un ex-diplomatico', 'La neutralità italiana', *NA*, f 1025, 1 Sept. 1914, pp. 90–9 suggesting that neutrality was useful in allowing foreigners to detect Italy's real value, and that Carducci had been right to say that Italy should be considered above all.

165 *DDI*, 5 s, i, 710, 17 Sept. 1914, Imperiali to San Giuliano.

166 *Ibid.*, 726, 17 Sept. 1914, San Giuliano to Imperiali.

167 FO 371/2008/50148, 16 Sept. 1914, Rodd to Grey has evidence that San Giuliano was trying to prompt a British initiative by talking about Italy's objections to the Adriatic falling under complete Slav domination; and also about Italy's need for a war loan.

168 *DDI*, 5 s, i, 750, 19 Sept. 1914, San Giuliano to Imperiali; 758, 21 Sept. 1914, Imperiali to San Giuliano. The French were also hinting at loans which could be made available to Italy, 772, 22 Sept. 1914, Ruspoli to San Giuliano.

169 *Ibid.*, 803, 25 Sept. 1914, San Giuliano to Tittoni, Carlotti.

170 Vigezzi, *L'Italia di fronte alla prima guerra mondiale*, vol. I, pp. 109–10.

171 Martini, *op. cit.*, p. 121.

172 e.g. Albertini, *Epistolario*, vol. I, pp. 280–1. On 21 September A. Torre still believed the *Consulta* to be 'strongly triplicist'.

173 FO 371/2171/53584, 27 Sept. 1914, Rodd to Grey.

174 *DDI*, 5 s, i, 842, 29 Sept. 1914, San Giuliano to Salandra.

175 *Ibid.*, 855, 30 Sept. 1914, San Giuliano to Imperiali; 873, 3 Oct. 1914, San Giuliano to Imperiali.

176 *Ibid.*, 937, 12 Oct. 1914, San Giuliano to Imperiali.

177 RP, Diary entry, 12 Oct. 1914.

178 Malagodi, *op. cit.*, vol. I, pp. 22–4.

179 *Ibid.*, p. 22.

180 A. Torre, 'La posizione dell'Italia fra gli alleati nella prima guerra mondiale', *RSR*, LVI (1969), p. 536. (See Appendix III for the text).

181 L. Lodi, *Venticinque anni di vita parlamentare* (Florence, 1923), p. 173.

182 Martini, *op. cit.*, pp. 185–7. Martini also gives a vivid description of the torment evident on San Giuliano's corpse pp. 184–5.

183 RP Diary entry, 18 Oct. 1914; Rodd, *op. cit.*, vol. III, pp. 220–4.

184 FO 800/65, GP, 7 Nov. 1914, Rodd to Grey, 14 Nov. 1914, Rodd to Grey.
185 Sonnino, *op. cit.*, vol. II, p. 89.
186 *RC*, IX, 30 Oct. 1914.
187 Note De Martino's understanding of this in his major report to Sonnino. SP, 47:1, 30 Nov. 1914.

CONCLUSION

1 G. Giolitti, *Discorsi parlamentari* (Rome, 1954), vol. III, p. 1375.
2 E. Gentile, 'La politica di Marinetti', *SC*, VII (1976), p. 420.
3 O. Malagodi, *Conversazioni della guerra 1914–1919* (Milan, 1960), vol I, p. 57.

Index

Abbas II, Khedive, 344
Abbazia meeting, 249–51, 292, 371, 383
Abdul Hamid I, Sultan, 343, 353
Abruzzi, Luigi Amedeo, Duke of the, 15, 175, 358–9
Adalia, 314, 323, 324, 328, 362, 363 4, 371, 401
Adler, Viktor, 203, 260
Adowa, 11–12, 13, 24, 27, 39, 40, 55, 57, 58, 66, 67, 78, 83, 84, 86, 89, 112–14, 116, 136, 137, 142, 159, 163, 166, 192, 257, 329, 419
Aehrenthal, Alois von, 128, 130, 160, 162, 174–6, 180–1, 183, 198, 201, 207, 209, 211, 213, 221, 247, 280, 348
Aero Club of Italy, 110
Africa, North, see Libya
Agadir Crisis, 151–2, 163, 208
Agnesa, Giacomo, 58, 60, 125, 332
Aida, 344
Aidin, 373
Albania, 326, 335, 345, 379, 383; Italian ambitions in, 46–7, 51, 64, 87, 121, 123, 135, 189, 195, 254, 257, 284, 290, 294, 309, 311–16, 318, 328–30, 346, 349, 351, 354–5, 358, 367–8, 371, 373, 375, 382–6, 391, 398, 400, 404, 411; San Giuliano and, 87, 88; Albanian Office, 125, 240; Libyan War and, 151, 175; Triple Alliance and, 199, 208, 214, 220–35, 237–8, 240–6, 250–1, 253, 311, 312, 362; Italo-Albanians, 220; Greece and, 307–8, 311–16, 318, 321, 323, 326–7
Albertini, Luigi, 45, 143, 144, 148, 168, 194, 196, 206, 264–5, 291, 386, 396–7, 406
Alexandra, Queen, 70
Alexandretta, 360
Algeciras Conference, 63, 67, 90–1, 127, 200, 257, 300
Algeria, 10
Aliotti, Carlo, 244–5, 251, 379

Ameglio, Giovanni, 263, 305, 359
Amendola, Giovanni, 35, 171
Anatolia, 359, 361, 364, 372, 373, 399
Ancona, Eugenio Alfonso, Duke of, 15
Anglo-Franco-Italian agreement of 1906, 329, 331–4, 365
Angora, 356
Ansaldo, 30, 259, 261, 353
Antivari (place and Company), 225, 227, 236, 347–9, 350, 352, 371
Aosta, Emanuele Filiberto, Duke of, 15, 52, 55, 129
Arctic Ocean, 52
Armenia, 363
Army, 16; weakness of, 2–3; Ministry of War and, 19; domestic role, 20–4, 31, 32–3, 219, 377, 394, 419; expenditure on, 20–1, 23; foreign policy and, 22, 312, 318, 418–9; big business and, 30; San Giuliano and, 74, 390; Triple Alliance and, 91, 199–200, 208, 216–22, 229–30, 232, 249, 252, 261, 280, 292, 392; colonies and, 125, 329; war and, 131, 157, 400, 402–3, 406–7, 413–4, 417; Libya and, 141, 143, 145, 158–9, 161, 162, 166–8, 171, 176, 178, 182, 189, 192, 194, 215; France and, 261–2, 282; Ethiopia and, 333, 335
Artom, Ernesto, 65
Asia Minor, see Turkey
Asmara, 58, 59, 63, 89, 108, 113, 133, 329
Assab, 11
Assicurazioni Generali, 59
A.N.I. (Associazione Nazionalista Italiana), see Nationalist Association
Argentina, 50, 54, 105, 337–9
Australia, 83, 337
Austria–Hungary, 91, 198, 251, 348, 352; Risorgimento and, 1, 9; rivalry with Italy, 3–5, 10–11, 31, 57, 63, 87–8, 121, 127, 130–2, 196–201, 204–5, 209–11, 213–15, 217–38, 240–1, 243–6, 248–51, 253–8, 260–1, 264–5, 267–8, 270–1,

Austria–Hungary (*cont.*)
276–7, 279–80, 283–4, 286–8, 290–4,
296–8, 301–2, 304–7, 311–13, 315–16,
318, 321, 323, 327–8, 337, 349, 350–1,
355–9, 361–8, 370–2, 375; Italian
irredentism and, 28, 46–9, 122, 128–9,
131, 174, 178, 192, 201–3, 207–8, 210,
212, 215, 233, 246–7, 249, 252, 255,
264, 284–5; Libyan War and, 140–1,
151–3, 155–7, 160–3, 171, 174–9, 181,
183–4, 186–9, 191, 193–5, 301; July
Crisis and, 328, 379–89, 391–7; First
World War and, 397–408, 411–14, 417
Auteri Berretta, Giovanni, 86
Avanti!, 64, 170
Avarna, Giuseppe, Duke of Gualtieri,
96–7, 101, 103, 130, 161, 162, 174–5,
176, 178, 181, 186, 207, 209–12, 214,
215, 221, 234, 247, 248, 287, 303–4,
379–80, 383, 388, 391, 400, 407

Baccarini, Alfredo, 75
Badoglio, Pietro, 109
Bakunin, Michael, 105
Baldacci, Antonio, 347
Ballin, Albert, 407
Banca Commerciale Italiana, 25, 59, 125,
206, 242, 243, 259, 261, 343, 347,
349–50, 353, 360, 371–2
Banca d'Italia, 49, 51, 59, 125, 140, 184,
185, 238, 242, 245, 356, 362, 371–2
Banca Italiana di Sconto, 206
Banca Romana, 206
Banco di Roma, 12, 43, 91, 134, 139–41,
157, 169, 174, 206, 335, 340–1, 345,
347, 353, 356, 371–2
Banco di Sicilia, 107, 185
Bank of Ethiopia, 139
Bank Scandals, 4, 16, 78, 206
Baratieri, Oreste, General, 84
Barrère, Camille, 90–1, 127, 129, 136–8,
152, 155–6, 157, 160, 163, 174, 178,
184, 195, 199, 208, 216, 219, 248, 257,
258, 263, 266–7, 269–73, 277–82,
284–8, 291–2, 294, 296, 303, 306, 322,
357, 379, 387, 391, 393, 395, 397, 399
Barrès, Maurice, 261
Barzilai, Salvatore, 49, 161
Barzini, Luigi, 168
Bava Beccaris, Fiorenzo, 55

Belgium, 4, 341
Benedict XV, Pope, 100, 415
Benghazi, 112, 142, 156, 165
Berchtold, Leopold von, 69, 191, 214–15,
220, 223, 225, 229, 233, 248, 249–51,
292, 304, 305, 350, 355–7, 370–1, 381,
386
Bergamini, Alberto, 45, 87, 143, 144
Bergamo, Adalberto Luitpoldo, Duke of,
15
Bergson, Henri, 261
Bernini, Gian Lorenzo, 95
Bertie, Francis, 182, 270, 275, 306, 329
Bertolini, Pietro, 31, 190, 192, 193, 331–2,
333, 402
Besso, Marco, 63
Bethmann Hollweg, Theobald von, 6,
128, 130, 132, 207, 214, 381
Bettòlo, Giovanni, 56–7, 60, 65, 85, 156,
354
Bevione, Giuseppe, 44, 143, 144
Bianchi, Riccardo, 238
Bib Doda, Prince, 241–2
Bismarck, Otto von, 7, 75, 77, 198, 313,
393
Bissolati, Leonida, 35, 170, 203, 393
Bizerta, 87, 88, 135
Blanc, Alberto, 103
Boer War, 165, 173
Bollati, Riccardo, 54, 102, 103, 111,
116–17, 118, 191, 227, 251, 285–7, 295,
362, 379–80, 382–3, 386, 407–8
Bonghi, Ruggero, 50
Bonnefon Craponne, Luigi, 29, 149–50
Bonomi, Ivanoe, 170
Borden, Robert, 268
Borghese, Scipione, 42–3, 52, 54
Borgnini, Giuseppe, 81
Borsarelli Di Rifreddo, Luigi, 60, 123
Boselli, Paolo, 49, 51–2, 62, 64, 85
Bosnia–Herzegovina (crisis), 28, 40, 63,
67, 92, 127, 130, 133, 156, 165, 172,
177, 198, 200, 208, 221, 228, 230, 238,
240, 242, 245, 381
Bottego, Vittorio, 53
Boué de Lapreyère, Augustin, 262
Boulanger, Georges, 47
Bovio, Giovanni, 34
Boyle, William H. D., 290
Bratianu, Ion, 404, 417

Brazil, 337–8
Breslau, 398, 405
Bright, John, 419
Britain, 3–4, 81, 90, 92–3, 128–9, 131,
  197, 199–200, 205, 208, 210–11, 217,
  228, 230, 241, 261, 265–6, 270, 329,
  331–3, 335, 340, 345, 352, 354, 356,
  361, 364–71, 375, 419; Italian navy and,
  24, 93, 218, 255, 262, 266, 268–9, 274,
  298, 301–2, 311, 319, 327, 401–2,
  411–12; Ottoman Empire and, 123;
  Libyan War and, 135–7, 140–1, 151–4,
  157, 167, 171–3, 179, 182, 184, 187–8,
  193, 209; Triple Entente and, 256, 264,
  267–8, 300; failed Mediterranean
  agreement and, 270–81, 286, 290–1,
  293–7; Dodecanese and, 301–3, 305–6,
  310, 313–14, 318–22, 324–8, 360, 363,
  367; July crisis and, 384, 387, 390–1,
  395–6; First World War and, 399,
  401–2, 405, 408, 411, 413–14, 417
Brusati, Ugo, 16, 229
Bulgaria, 205, 233, 315, 351
Bülow, Bernhard von, 200, 206, 256, 271,
  287, 407, 416

Cadorna, Luigi, 22, 166, 283, 406–7
Cadorna family, 21
Caetani, Leone, 42
Cafiero, Carlo, 105
Cafiero, Ugo, 105
Cambon, Jules, 325
Cambon, Paul, 182, 272–3, 275, 277, 278,
  288, 290, 296, 311, 322
Canada, 83
Caneva, Carlo, 21, 166
Canevaro, Felice Napoleone, 54, 64
Caporetto, Battle of, 22, 51, 124, 419
Cappelli, Raffaele, 54, 64, 185
Carabinieri, 21, 76
Carducci, Giosuè, 16, 40, 42, 49, 50
Carlotti, Andrea, 100, 103–4, 185, 190,
  191, 221, 306, 312, 399, 413
Carthage, 10, 61, 62, 135
Carthage (and *Manouba* incidents), 34,
  122, 181–3, 185, 213, 262, 273, 282,
  293
Cassaro, Antonio Statella di, 71
Catholics, *see* Vatican
Cavagnari, Carlo, 134

Cavour, Camillo (Benso di), 1, 2, 9, 12,
  68, 116, 126, 256
Central Powers, *see* Triple Alliance,
  Germany, Austria–Hungary
Cerruti, Vittorio, 108
Chamber of Commerce, Rome, 340–3;
  Constantinople, 343, 358
Chamber of Deputies, 252, 288, 342; role
  of, 17, 18, 20, 43, 108; San Giuliano
  and, 75, 78–9, 81–4, 89, 94, 132–5, 190,
  196, 281–2, 288–9, 333, 354, 359–60,
  378; Libya and, 141, 142, 146–8, 150,
  154, 169, 186, 194; Balkan Wars and,
  233
Charles, Archduke, 380
Charles-Albert, 12, 95
'Charykov Kite', 179–80
Chiang Kai-Shek, 106
Chiaramonte Bordonaro, Antonio, 55,
  108, 109, 287
Chiaraviglio, Mario, 31
China, 106, 156, 330, 337
Chios, 304
Churchill, Winston Spencer, 268, 328
Ciano, Galeazzo, 101, 106, 373
Cirmeni, Benedetto, 55, 263, 289
Civiltà Cattolica, 33, 169
Clemenceau, Georges, 262
Clemenceau, Paul, 262
Clement XII, Pope, 95
clericals, *see* Vatican
coal, 2–3, 319, 342, 352–3, 373, 396, 419
Colajanni, Napoleone, 31, 76, 83
Colli Di Felizzano, Giuseppe, 331
Colonna Di Cesarò, Giovanni Antonio,
  65
C.I.D., 274
Comte, Auguste, 73, 76
Confederazione Generale del Lavoro, 28,
  36, 170
Confindustria, 28–9, 149–50
Congo, 52
Congress of Berlin, 135, 165, 300
Congress of Italians Abroad (First), 62–3
Congress of Italians Abroad (Second),
  64–5, 66, 148, 185, 263
Conrad von Hötzendorf, Franz, 131, 181,
  196, 204, 209, 211, 212, 215–17, 219,
  249, 252
Constans, Ernest, 342

Constantine I, King, of Greece, 234, 313
Contarini, Luigi, 107
Contarini, Salvatore, 59, 68, 107–9, 112, 117, 154, 158, 180
Conti, Ettore, 29–30
Coppola, Francesco, 45
Corfu Channel, 231, 311, 312–13
Corradini, Enrico, 37, 39–42, 51, 59, 62, 142–4, 168, 338, 374
Corriere della Sera, 45, 64, 119, 121, 122, 143, 148, 149, 154, 168, 169, 265, 409
Corsica, 47, 255, 257
Corti, Luigi, 135
Cos, Gulf of, 362
Cranborne, James Gascoyne-Cecil, Viscount, 137
Credaro, Luigi, 31
Credito Italiano, 372
Crespi, Silvio, 60, 63
Crete, 5, 165, 308
Crimean War, 179
Crispi, Francesco, 8, 9, 11–12, 24, 27, 36, 45, 47, 75, 78, 81, 83–4, 89, 98, 101, 103, 111, 113–16, 127, 145, 154, 169, 198, 256–8, 266
Croce, Benedetto, 32, 164, 260
Crowe, Eyre, 270, 280–1, 293–5, 324, 369, 375
Cyprus, 137, 308, 310
Cyrenaica, *see* Libya

Daily Graphic, 275
Dalmatia, 49, 88, 201–2, 212, 220, 247, 411, 413
Danilo of Montenegro, Crown Prince, 236, 347
D'Annunzio, Gabriele, 16, 39–40, 44–7, 143, 260
Dante Alighieri (ship), 5, 51
Dante Alighieri Society, 32, 42, 49–54, 57, 61, 63, 66, 67, 128, 138, 179, 247, 345
Dardanelles, The, 184, 186–8, 213, 217, 300, 301, 303, 308, 310, 327
De Amicis, Edmondo, 76
De Bosdari, Alessandro, 312, 318
De Felice Giuffrida, Giuseppe, 36, 77–9, 83–6
Delcassé, Théophile, 257
Delmé-Radcliffe, C., 54, 188, 265

De Marinis, Errico, 55, 133–5, 148
De Martino (family), 344, 356
De Martino Bey, 356
De Martino, Giacomo I, 111–12
De Martino, Giacomo II, 54, 59, 60–2, 64–5, 84, 112, 125, 138, 265
De Martino, Giacomo III, 54, 60, 71, 99, 108, 109, 111–13, 116–18, 122–3, 125–6, 154–5, 158–9, 162, 165, 195, 244, 276, 305, 317, 318, 323, 327, 333, 342, 344–5, 354, 356, 363, 366, 368, 385, 388, 404, 412, 414
De Martino, *Pasha*, Giacomo, 111
Déport, 261
Depretis, Agostino, 2
Dering, Herbert G., 276
De Roberto, Federico, 70, 74, 77
Déroulède, Paul, 47
De Tocqueville, Alexis, 79
Diaz, Armando, 68, 166
Di San Giuliano, *see* San Giuliano
Di Soragna, Marchese, 345
Dodecanese Islands (Aegean Islands), 43, 108; Italian ambitions in, 53, 254; Italian occupation of, 122, 188, 195, 213, 222, 224, 231, 246, 253, 263, 277, 283–4, 290, 294, 301–29, 335, 355–6, 358–9, 360, 364, 367–9, 372–3, 375, 384, 397, 401; Italian seizure of, 187, 213, 274, 300, 363–4
Dogali, 163
Doumergue, Gaston, 291, 293
Dreikaiserbund, 267
Dreyfus, Alfred, 47
Durazzo, 221, 240, 241, 244, 246, 251

Edward VII, King, 70, 129
Egypt, 16, 111–13, 135, 137, 166, 167, 172, 177, 225, 266, 274, 275, 291, 303, 306, 312, 326, 330, 343–5, 356–7
Einaudi, Luigi, 32, 338
Elba, 3, 218
Elena, Queen, 13, 15, 148, 260, 347
Emigration, 4, 27, 36–7, 50–2, 56, 59, 60, 62–3, 65, 80–3, 89, 114, 117, 126, 139, 142, 144, 148–9, 194–5, 205, 338–9, 344, 396
Ems telegram, 269
Entente Cordiale, *see* Triple Entente, Britain, France

Eraclea, 254, 342, 352–3, 373
Eritrea, 12, 27, 54, 58, 80–1, 84–5, 87, 93,
    109, 113, 125, 134, 329–33, 335, 365,
    373, 406
Essad Toptani Pasha, 242, 245
Ethiopia (Abyssinia), 109, 339, 379; Italian
    ambitions in, 11, 12, 47, 52, 54, 59, 65,
    82–4, 115, 135–6, 195, 254, 291, 294,
    296, 322, 326, 329–36, 346, 365, 373,
    381, 384, 405, 408, 417
Étienne, Eugène, 57, 63
Evans, Arthur, 306

Facta, Luigi, 110
Falkenhayn, Erich von, 404
Fanfani, Amintore, 73
Farnese Palace, 129
Farouk, King, 345
Fasciotti, Carlo, 108
Fashoda, 269
Federzoni, Luigi, 18, 24, 32, 41–4, 48, 54,
    65, 108, 123, 143–4, 288, 292, 358–9
Ferdinand II, 71, 111
Ferdinand IV, 10
Ferdinand, King 'Foxy' of Bulgaria, 351
Ferrari, Ettore, 409
Ferraris (family), 55
Ferrero, Guglielmo, 145
Ferri, Enrico, 56
Fezzan (Libya), 191, 306
Fisher, Jackie, 172, 399
Fiuggi, 119, 155, 318–19, 363, 382–3,
    385–6, 389, 391, 394
Fiume, 28, 47, 49, 105, 202, 263
Florio, Giulia, 26
Florio, Ignazio, 26, 60, 63
Florio, Vincenzo, 25
Florio (family), 25, 29
Flotow, Hans von, 228, 231, 232, 247,
    251, 252, 313, 315, 319, 322–3, 350,
    361–2, 382–3, 385–6, 388, 400, 407–8
Forges-Davanzati, Roberto, 45
Fortis, Alessandro, 31, 89, 91, 127, 133,
    185, 263
Foscari, Piero, 44, 48, 55, 60, 63, 120, 147,
    202, 236, 244, 345–8, 355, 373
France, 15, 63, 87, 90, 91, 127–9, 197,
    200, 206, 302, 348, 352; Risorgimento
    and, 1, 10; rivalry with Italy, 10–11,
    57, 62–3, 73–4, 80, 87–8, 119, 199–200,

208, 210–11, 216–19, 222, 235, 241,
    255–70, 285, 329, 331–3, 335, 340,
    342–3, 350, 353–4, 356, 359, 361, 363,
    365–6, 372, 375; Italian navy and, 24–5,
    57, 218, 262, 268–9, 276, 283, 311, 359,
    393, 401–2, 411–12; Ottoman Empire
    and, 123; Libyan War and, 135, 137–9,
    140–1, 146, 151–2, 154, 157, 160, 163,
    167, 171–2, 174, 178–9, 181–4, 188,
    193, 195, 212, 214, 277; failed
    Mediterranean agreement and, 270–3,
    275–87, 290–6; Dodecanese and, 303,
    306, 309, 314–15, 317, 320, 323, 325,
    335–6, 363; July Crisis and, 384, 393–5;
    First World War and, 397, 399, 401–3,
    405, 411–12, 417
France (ship), 262
Francesco II, King, 111
Franchetti, Leopoldo, 55, 60, 61, 82–4,
    112, 151, 373
Franco, Francisco, 106
Fransoni, Francesco, 107
Franz Ferdinand, Archduke, 57, 128, 204,
    212, 215, 232, 247, 252–3, 296, 300,
    328, 335, 350, 379, 384
Franz Joseph, 16, 128, 202, 211, 212, 233
Frassati, Alfredo, 144, 289
Frederick, Archduke, 260
Free Masons, 24, 31–3, 42–3, 49, 74, 100,
    104, 133, 330, 341, 409–10
Fuad, Prince and King, 344–5
Fuga, Ferdinando, 95
Fusinato, Guido, 31, 64, 65, 149, 185–7,
    190–2, 402
Futurists, 7, 418

Gallenga Stuart, Romeo, 44, 65
Galli, Carlo, 68, 154, 158, 159, 161, 165,
    240–1, 243, 244
Galli, Roberto, 134
Gallina, Giovanni, 102, 103
Gambetta, Léon, 47, 263
Garbasso, Carlo, 189
Garibaldi, Giuseppe, 1, 8, 9, 27, 46, 50,
    72, 111, 172, 260
Garibaldi, Menotti, 50
Garibaldi, Ricciotti, 151, 220
Garroni Carbonara, Camillo Eugenio,
    101, 104, 121, 153–4, 159, 321, 323,
    331, 355, 357–8, 361–2, 372, 374, 405

Gasparri, Pietro, 106
Gaulois, 289
Gazzetta del Circolo di Cittadini, 74
Genoa, Ferdinando, Duke of, 15
Gentiloni Pact of 1913, 32, 43, 114–15, 169–70
Germany, 1, 3–4, 31, 52, 55, 82, 86, 91, 93, 122, 127–8, 256–9, 263–4, 267–70, 274, 280, 301, 329, 340, 346, 351, 352, 374; Italian navy and, 25; Triple Alliance and, 128–30, 197–201, 203–7, 209, 211, 213–18, 222–7, 230, 232–5, 241, 243, 245–6, 248–9, 251–3, 261, 270, 272, 278, 283, 285–7, 290–1, 293, 295, 298, 307, 309–11, 313–16, 318–19, 321, 323, 325, 327–8, 335, 354, 357–70, 373, 375, 419; Libyan War and, 136, 140–1, 151–2, 156–8, 160, 162–3, 171, 174, 176–7, 181–84, 186–90, 193, 214; July Crisis and, 296, 328, 379, 381–3, 385–7, 389–96; First World War and, 398, 400–3, 405, 407–8, 412–14, 417
Giolitti, Federico, 30
Giolitti, Giovanni, 38, 72, 85, 91, 101, 107, 120, 256–7, 330, 332; domestic affairs and, 12–13, 17, 19–20, 30–1, 33, 35, 37, 41–6, 49–50, 64, 66, 69, 78–9, 89, 101, 108–9, 119, 120–1, 123, 125, 127–8, 142, 144–5, 149–50, 185, 204, 206, 220, 259, 261, 263–5, 299, 325, 349, 368, 371–2, 400, 406–9, 418–19; Libyan War and, 13, 34, 44, 65, 137, 142–9, 151–71, 173–4, 176–9, 183, 186–7, 190–4, 208, 269, 342, 344, 354; Army and, 22–3; Triple Alliance and, 48, 203, 209–14, 217–19, 221–2, 225–8, 231–3, 235, 237–8, 243, 248, 253, 262, 284–5; Triple Entente and, 265; failed Mediterranean agreement and, 278–9, 285, 288–9; Dodecanese and, 304–5, 310, 316–17, 319, 321–3; Asia Minor and, 354–8, 360, 362–3, 367–8; July Crisis and, 378, 396; First World War and, 406, 409–10, 416
Giornale d'Italia, 42, 43, 45, 87, 117, 143, 168
Giovinezza, 49
Giuriati, Giovanni Battista, 47
Gladstone, William Ewart, 50
Goeben, 398, 405

Gramsci, Antonio, 1
Grandi, Domenico, 219, 394, 406
Gray, Ezio Maria, 204
Great Britain, *see* Britain
Greece, 132, 140, 253, 284, 323, 372, 375, 379, 383, 403–5, 411, 414, 417; Balkan Wars and, 217, 220, 222, 228, 232–5; Central Powers and, 245–6, 250–1, 318, 321, 325, 327–8, 351, 370, 384, 392; Dodecanese and, 301, 305–8, 310–17, 319, 322, 324, 326, 356–7, 359, 367, 369, 381
Grey, Edward, 7, 69, 153, 172–3, 184, 204, 229, 267, 269, 272–8, 280–1, 291–3, 295–6, 302–3, 308–9, 311, 313, 315, 318–22, 326–7, 331–3, 364, 366, 369, 390–1, 394, 397, 400–2, 410, 414, 416
Guariglia, Raffaele, 98, 106, 109–10
Guesde, Jules, 261
Guicciardini, Francesco, 7, 60, 87, 92, 93, 104, 110, 127, 128, 144, 146–8, 150, 168–9, 186, 220
Gustav V, King of Sweden, 89
Guzman (incident), 141

Habsburg Empire, *see* Austria–Hungary
Hague, The, Court of Disputes at, 182, 183, 248
Hague Peace Conference, 34
Hardinge, Charles, 7, 118, 267, 270
Harrar, 53
Haus, Anton, 218
Hegel, Georg Wilhelm, 80, 260
Hodeida, 141
Hohenlohe Decrees, 14, 122, 202, 234, 247–9, 253, 284–5, 287, 365, 367, 383
Hohenlohe, Konrad von, 202, 247, 252
Hugo, Victor, 47

Ibrahim Pasha, 141–2, 158
L'Idea Nazionale, 32, 40–1, 43, 119, 142, 168, 259
Imbriani-Poerio, Matteo Renato, 46, 47
Imperiali, Guglielmo, 60, 101, 104, 128, 137, 152–3, 172–3, 224, 228, 268–9, 275–8, 287, 289, 291–5, 303, 305–6, 308–9, 313, 315, 318–20, 322–3, 326–8, 331, 342, 369, 372, 390–1, 394, 397, 400–2, 411, 413–14

India, 7, 272, 274, 301
Insabato, Enrico, 146
irredentism, 42, 46–50, 57, 88, 128–30,
  175, 201–3, 207–8, 210, 215, 233–4,
  236, 246–7, 255, 264, 385; Nationalist
  Association and, 41, 44, 66, 85, 143–5,
  161, 393
Ismail Kemal, Vlora, 220, 238, 242
Ismail, Khedive, 344
Isonzo River, 130, 210, 254
Istituto Agricolo Coloniale, 61
Istituto Coloniale Italiano, 53, 57–68, 89,
  108–10, 112–14, 125, 133, 138, 147–9,
  185, 244, 263, 317, 352, 354
Istria, 49, 201, 411
Izvolsky, Alexander Petrovich, 138, 180,
  256

Jagow, Gottlieb von, 69, 171, 213, 215,
  226, 229, 295–6, 310, 357, 362, 382, 392
Japan, 25
Jaurès, Jean, 260
Joel, Otto, 190, 206, 243, 259, 343, 349,
  353, 360, 363, 365, 368, 371, 373
Jones, Martina Potter-, 338
Journal of Roman Studies, The, 271
Juba River, 53

Kemal Atatürk, 373
Kiderlen Wächter, Alfred von, 182, 213
Kiel Canal, 24, 56, 268
Kitchener, Horatio Herbert, 274
Koch, Ottaviano Armando, 106
Konia, 356
Krupenski, Anatol Nicholaievich, 184,
  256, 399
Krupp, 261
Kühlmann, Richard von, 277

Labia, Natale, 240
Labriola, Antonio, 100
Lago, Mario, 45, 59, 108, 109, 154, 158
Lake Chad, 166
Lansdowne, Henry, Fifth Marquess of,
  173, 195, 267, 271, 275
Lanza Di Scalea, Pietro, 26, 30, 54, 55, 60,
  62, 109–11, 123, 154, 158, 164, 222, 338
Lanza Di Scordia, Giuseppe, Prince of
  Trabia, 55, 105, 106
Lanza (family), 25–6, 78

Laroche, Jules, 278
Lateran Pacts, 114
Lauro, Achille, 110
Lausanne, Treaty of, 65, 190–4, 216,
  305–6, 308, 318, 322, 325, 326, 353
Layard, Henry, 271
Lazarrini, Giuseppe, 327
Lega Franco-Italiana, 262
Lega Navale, La, 56, 352
Leonardi Cattolica, Pasquale, 32, 176, 186,
  188, 262
Levi, Primo, 27, 45, 54, 58–61, 63, 113,
  117, 118, 125, 242–3, 339, 345
Libya, 27, 258, 266, 269, 272, 275, 289,
  294, 297, 326, 329–31, 340, 346, 353–4,
  384, 390–1, 419; Italian ambitions in,
  13, 59–60, 62, 115, 134–64, 185, 206;
  Libyan War, 14, 29, 65–6, 108, 118,
  121–2, 127, 131, 165–83, 185–90,
  192–5, 198, 208–9, 212–13, 215–16,
  221–3, 237, 267, 270–1, 277, 281–2,
  297, 300, 305, 342, 349, 352, 355, 358,
  407; after 1912, 219, 306, 310, 312,
  314–16, 322, 335
Lichnowsky, Karl Max von, 223
Lij Yasu, Emperor, 330, 332–3, 335, 405
Limo, Giovanni, 55–6
Lissa, Battle of, 24, 163, 166, 419
Litta, Eugenia, 337
Lloyd of Austria, 28
Lloyd George, David, 291
Lotta di Classe, La, 170
Loubet, Émile, 262
Lovcen, Mount, 249, 251, 349, 380,
  382–4, 394, 398
Löwenthal von Linau, Heinrich, 244
Lützow, Heinrich von, 130
Luzzatti, Luigi, 94, 127–8, 150, 185, 338,
  363

Macchio, Karl von, 407
Macedonia, 5, 221
Mafia, 110
Malagodi, Olindo, 37, 255, 397, 414–15
Malaparte, Curzio, 40
Malgeri, Francesco, 183
Mallet, Louis, 302
Malta, 34, 47, 71, 139, 140, 142, 218, 266,
  274, 298
Malvano, Giacomo, 102, 116

Mancini, Pasquale Stanislao, 11, 103, 115
Manzoni, Alessandro, 50
Manzoni, Gaetano, 117, 124, 330–1
Marconi, Guglielmo, 347, 351
Marcora, Giuseppe, 31
Marescotti, A. Martini-, 355
Margherita, Queen of Italy, 15–16, 23, 40, 52, 70
Maria, Empress of Russia, 70
Maria Pia, Queen of Portugal, 16
Marinetti, Filippo Tommaso, 7, 40, 168, 260, 418
Marne, Battle of, 328, 401, 403–4, 409–11
Marschall von Bieberstein, Adolf, 190, 209, 213
Martini, Ferdinando, 31, 54, 58, 60, 62, 64, 81–5, 125, 133–4, 185, 329, 330, 333, 339, 393, 395–6, 400, 402, 405–6, 409, 412, 415
Marx, Karl, 73, 79, 260
Massawa, 11, 81, 82
Maurras, Charles, 261
Mayor des Planches, Edmondo, 61, 101, 132, 135, 141, 151, 153
Mazzini, Giuseppe, 1, 8, 34, 46, 203
Mazzinians, 8–9, 33–4, 201, 255, 338
McKenna, Reginald, 268
Meale, Gaetano, 34
Medici del Vascello, Luigi, 44
Melegari, Giulio, 102, 159, 312
Melegari, Luigi Amedeo, 102
Menelik II, Emperor, 12, 83, 329–30, 332
Mentana, 163
Mensdorff Pouilly Dietrichstein, Albert, 223, 315
Mercatelli, Luigi, 159
Meréy, Kajetan von Kapos-Mére, 129–30, 177, 183, 213–15, 225–8, 231, 233, 248, 263, 297, 304, 380, 386, 407
Merry del Val, Raffaele, 23
Mesopotamia, 53
Messaggero, Il, 122
Metternich, Klemens von, 5
Michels, Roberto, 256
Mill, J. S., 73, 76
Millo, Enrico, 24, 188, 217, 235, 327
Milza, Pierre, 259
Ministry of Colonies, 19, 117, 125, 188, 193, 379
Mirditi, 241–2

Moltke, Helmuth von, (elder), 3
Moltke, Helmuth von, (younger), 7, 216, 219, 392
Moneta, E. T., 34–5
Montenegro, 15, 16, 241, 260, 398; Libyan War and, 151; Balkan Wars and, 193, 220–4, 226–8, 230–2, 235–7; union with Serbia, 249–50, 379, 383–4; Italian economic interests in, 345–51, 353, 358, 360, 376
Morin, Enrico Costantino, 55
Moro, Aldo, 73, 283
Morocco, 10, 52, 136–8, 151–2, 154–5, 157, 160, 163, 165, 174, 178, 181, 208, 258, 267, 269, 270, 272–3
Morpurgo, Elio, 65
Mussolini, Benito, 32, 34, 37–8, 40–1, 45–6, 59, 65, 68, 73, 95, 98, 106–9, 111–12, 115, 119, 126, 154, 170, 203, 263, 298, 339, 376, 400, 409–10, 417
Mussolini, Vittorio, 40

Nasi, Nunzio, 31, 55
Nathan, Ernesto, 31, 32, 43, 49–50, 60
Nationalist Association, 18, 37, 39–48, 51–2, 57, 68, 108, 240; Army and, 24; domestic role of, 32, 64, 170; foreign policy and, 54, 66, 202, 247, 266, 299, 300, 328, 374; Libyan War and, 65, 142–5, 147–8, 150–1, 153–4, 161–3, 167–8, 183, 193–4, 213; Foreign Ministry and, 98, 110, 115, 122, 249; San Giuliano and, 120–1, 142, 288; France and, 261–3; July Crisis and, 393, 396
Navy, 44; energy needs, 3; rivalry with Austria, 5, 57, 131, 267; Ministry of, 19; domestic role of, 20, 24–5, 32; expenditure on, 20–1, 24–5; foreign policy and, 56, 318, 327–8, 366; San Giuliano and, 74; Libyan War and, 159–60, 162, 176, 182, 184–5, 186–7, 304; Triple Alliance and, 207, 216–17, 225, 229, 235, 268, 283, 288, 325; Britain and, 255, 266, 268–9, 290, 298, 319; France and, 261–2, 267–9, 275–6, 282, 359, 393; First World War and, 401–2, 406, 411–12
Navy League (Austrian), 57

Navy League (Lega Navale), 25, 53, 55–7, 61, 65–8, 89, 156
Navy League (German), 55
Nice, 47, 255, 257, 298
Nicola I, King of Montenegro, 13, 227, 236, 347–51
Nicolson, Arthur, 173, 267, 270, 272, 274, 279, 296, 302, 311, 320, 369, 391
Nitti, Francesco Saverio, 2, 73, 204
Nobel, 261
Nogara, Bernardino, 184, 190–1, 342–3, 353–5, 358, 361–2, 364, 368, 371, 373–4
Novi-Bazar, Sandjak of, 130, 189, 349
Nuova Antologia, 147

Olivetti, Camillo, 263
Oriani, Alfredo, 40
Orlando, Luigi, 27
Orlando, Paolo, 27
Orlando, Vittorio Emanuele, 27, 73
Orlando (family), 25–7
Osservatore Romano, 169, 202, 340
Ottoman Empire, *see* Turkey
Ottoman Public Debt, 339–43, 352, 355, 367

Pacelli, Ernesto, 139, 157, 356
Pan German League, 52, 122
Pansa, Alberto, 102, 159, 161, 181, 212
Pan-Slavs, 122, 414
Panther, 151–2
Paoli, Renato, 59
Papacy, *see* Vatican
Papini, Giovanni, 40, 168
Pascoli, Giovanni, 39
Paternò Castello (family), 76, 338
Paternò Di Manchi Di Bilici, Gaetano, 105
Patria degli italiani, La, 338
Pelloux, Luigi, 12, 23, 54, 56, 79, 85, 87, 169, 185
Perrone, 259
Pestalozza, Giulio, 140–1
Peter I, King of Serbia, 349
Philippines, 341
Piazza, Giuseppe, 44, 143
Pichon, Stephen-Jean-Marie, 262, 288
Pirelli, Giovanni Battista, 60
Pisacane, Carlo, 1
Pistoia, Filiberto Lodovico, Duke of, 15

Pittoni, Valentino, 203
Poincaré, Raymond, 182, 257, 273, 275–6, 278–9, 285, 301, 303, 306
Pollio, Alberto, 21, 22, 162, 189, 216–19, 229, 252, 261, 283, 292, 333, 392, 418
Pompilj, Guido, 108–9
Portuguese colonies, 398
Prevesa, 175
Prezzolini, Giuseppe, 40
Pribram, Alfred F., 196
Primo Dochi, 241
Prinetti, Giulio, 13, 103, 112–13, 127, 136–8, 152, 155–7, 160, 173, 174, 178, 195, 199, 208, 216, 257, 266–7, 269–71, 273, 275, 278, 280, 282, 284, 292, 298, 393, 397
Puccini, Giacomo, 58

Quarnaro, 49, 263, 411

Racconigi, 138, 157, 180, 195, 200, 201, 256
Ragusa (Dubrovnik), 46
Railways, 112, 194; Cavour and, 1, 2–3; *Circumetnea*, 74; San Giuliano and, 75; Albania and, 88, 125, 238, 241, 358, 362; Libya and, 140; Sir Edward Grey and, 204; Montenegro and, 236–7, 347–50, 352; Asia Minor and, 291, 292, 314, 321, 352; Smyrna–Aidin Railway Company, 321, 323, 326–7, 366–70, 374; Ethiopia and, 335, 373; Berlin to Baghdad, 352, 367; Turkey and, 363–4, 366–70, 374–5
Rattazzi, Urbano, 16
Rava, Luigi, 42, 51, 54, 60
Reale Museo Commerciale di Venezia, 244
Rechid Pasha, 192
'Red Week', 19, 30, 219, 377
Regno, Il, 39
Renaud di Falicon, Emilio, 55
Resto del Carlino, 42
Revedin, Count Ruggero, 347
Rheims, 403
Rhodes, island of, 43, 187, 300–2, 308, 317, 328
Riforma, La, 45, 113
Rivista Coloniale, 59–60, 65, 416
Rocco, Alfredo, 41, 108

Rochefort, Henri, 47
Rodd, Sir James Rennell, 7–8, 129, 152,
  163, 172, 184, 188, 222, 230, 231, 248,
  263, 270–5, 277–81, 285, 287, 290–1,
  293, 295–6, 306, 308–9, 314, 319–20,
  322–4, 326, 332, 366, 381, 387–8,
  390–1, 395, 399, 406, 411, 413–14, 416
Romania, 205, 232, 351, 370, 380–1, 384,
  386–7, 392, 393, 403–4
Rome, idea of, 5–6, 8–9, 13, 38, 46, 60,
  63–5, 67, 77, 86–8, 103, 135, 139,
  143–4, 147, 151, 165, 200, 229, 246,
  282, 307, 340, 343, 359, 374, 376, 419
Rosmini, Antonio, 50
Rosso, Augusto, 105, 106, 109
Rothschild, Alfred, Lord, 400
Royal Commission of 1890 (on Eritrea),
  81–3
Royal Commission of 1907 (on Foreign
  Ministry), 98–9
Royal Commission of 1913 (on Foreign
  Ministry), 110
Royal Italian Geographical Society, 42,
  52–5, 58, 61, 66–8, 89, 110, 113, 114,
  125, 352
Rubattino Shipping Company, 25
Rudinì, Antonio Starrabba Di, 50, 78, 81,
  83, 84, 103, 107, 111, 115, 329
Ruspoli, Camillo, 44, 60
Ruspoli, Mario, 285, 287
Russell, John, 74
Russia, 4, 7, 82, 122, 131, 200, 210,
  216–18, 223–4, 226, 228, 251, 256, 267,
  270, 279, 289, 300, 310, 312, 315, 318,
  329, 340, 343, 348, 350, 357, 359, 363,
  380, 382–4, 386, 391, 393, 399, 404,
  407–8, 411, 413–14; Racconigi
  Agreement, 137–8, 157, 180, 200;
  Libyan War and, 154, 159, 177,
  179–80, 184, 187–8, 193, 212, 301

Saffi, Aurelio, 46
Salandra, Antonio, 17, 19, 20, 30, 58, 60,
  62, 64, 65, 73, 85, 109, 118, 127, 206,
  218–19, 232, 242, 252–3, 262, 266, 292,
  295, 325, 333, 371–2, 377–9, 385–6,
  388–90, 393, 395–400, 402, 405–6,
  409–14, 416–17, 419
Salata, Francesco, 68
Saletta, Tancredi, 91, 199, 216

Salisbury, Robert Gascoyne-Cecil, Third
  Marquess of, 7, 200, 326
Sallier de la Tour, Giuseppe, 102, 103
Salvago Raggi, Giuseppe, 54, 55, 100,
  103, 125, 330–1, 333
Salvatorelli, Luigi, 197
Salvemini, Gaetano, 35, 149, 171, 196
San Giovani di Medua, 349
San Giuliano, Antonino Di (Senior),
  70–1
San Giuliano, Antonino Paternò Castello
  Di, 9–10, 67–9, 127, 259, 271, 329–33,
  337, 347–9, 365, 418–19; Triple
  Alliance and, 14, 128–32, 197–8, 203–4,
  206–10, 212, 214–17, 219–20, 222–35,
  237–8, 240–2, 244–54, 262, 303, 307,
  350–1, 363; southern background, 15,
  30, 37, 69–79, 85–6, 111, 190, 258, 299;
  Chamber of Deputies and, 18, 49,
  74–6, 83–6, 89, 133–5, 141–2, 169, 196,
  281–2, 284, 354, 359–60; domestic
  affairs and, 19–20, 30–1, 75–9, 83–5, 89,
  112, 142, 144, 263, 325, 338, 371, 378;
  Army and, 22, 333, 406, 414, 417;
  political pressure groups and, 49, 53–5,
  58–65; Libyan War and, 65, 132–5,
  138, 140–5, 147–8, 150–2, 154–63, 166,
  168–9, 171–95, 344; background in
  diplomacy, 80–94; Foreign Ministry
  and, 96–7, 99, 101–9, 112–15, 118–26,
  155, 158; July Crisis and, 255, 296, 350,
  375, 377–80, 382–97; Triple Entente
  and, 256, 258, 265–6, 269; failed
  Mediterranean agreement and, 270,
  273, 275–81, 284–9, 291–7; Dodecanese
  and, 300, 302, 304–5, 306, 308–23,
  326–8, 335–6; First World War and,
  335, 397–408, 410–13, 415–17; Asia
  Minor and, 352–62, 364–76; death of,
  415–16
San Giuliano, Benedetto Orazio Di, 27,
  71, 73, 75
San Giuliano, Benedetto Di (son of
  Antonino), 190
Sanminiatelli, Donato, 51
Santi Quaranta, 312
Saracco, Giuseppe, 185
Sarajevo, 253, 328, 335, 350, 378, 380–3
Sardegna, 24
Saseno, 307, 313, 385, 405

Sazonov, Sergei, 69, 229, 399, 410, 413
Scalabrini, Angelo, 54, 60, 63, 114–15, 125, 240
Scalabrini, Giovanni Battista, 114
Scalabrinian Missionary Brothers, 339
Scalea, *see* Lanza Di Scalea, Pietro
Schleswig-Holstein, 243
Schnaebele (incident), 269
Schneider-Creusot Company, 261
Scutari (incident), 223–4, 227–8, 230–3, 237–8, 240–2, 243–4, 253, 312, 313, 349, 360, 379, 385
Senate, 17, 282, 293, 337, 378
Serbia, 205, 216, 251, 351, 363–4, 411; Balkan Wars and, 214–15, 220, 222–4, 228, 231–7, 312, 315; union with Montenegro, 249–50, 350, 379; July Crisis and, 380–4, 386–8, 401
'Serb War Scare', 232–4
Sicilian *fasci*, 11, 50, 78–9, 83, 190
Siemens Company, 351
Sighele, Scipio, 42
Sillitti, Luigi, 107
Silvestrelli, Giulio, 90
Smyrna, 189, 193, 302, 360, 361
Socialists, 16, 133, 259, 263, 339; colonialism and, 11–12, 82–3; Army and, 23; Navy and, 24, 56–7; big business and, 28–30; church and, 32, 33; internationalism and, 34, 35; foreign affairs and, 35, 202–3, 260, 292; emigration and, 37; nationalism and, 40, 50, 57, 64, 66, 142; San Giuliano and, 69, 75–80, 85, 94, 190; Foreign Ministry and, 100, 115, 122; Libya and, 144, 148–9, 161, 169–70; July Crisis and, 393, 397; First World War and, 406, 410
S.P.D. (German Socialist Party), 203
Società Africana d'Italia, 133
Società Anonima Ottomana, 360
Società Anonima La Siderurgica Italiana, 56
Società Commerciale d'Oriente, 184, 243, 343, 350, 352, 360, 364, 371
Società di Navigazione Generale Italiana, 25, 27–8, 60, 85
Somaliland (Benadir), 11, 53, 54, 60, 64, 81, 112, 125, 331, 365
Sonnino, Giorgio, 55, 58, 60, 62

Sonnino, Sidney, 23, 43, 45, 49, 55–6, 60, 85, 87, 90, 93, 94, 110, 127, 143, 146, 148, 156, 168, 194, 264, 347, 393, 395–6, 402, 404, 406, 409, 412, 416–17
Sorel, Georges, 261
South America, 34, 40, 142, 372
Spain, 73, 82, 293, 341, 384
Spencer, Herbert, 73, 74
Spingardi, Paolo, 31, 32, 162, 176, 192, 226, 312
Stampa, La, 44, 143, 144, 158, 263, 289
Stampalia, Island of (Astropalia), 187, 300, 302
Starace, Achille, 149
Stinnes, Hugo, 407
Stringher, Bonaldo, 49, 51, 59, 60, 63, 64, 184, 185, 190, 238, 245, 259, 356, 362, 365, 371, 398
Stylos, Cape, 313, 327
Sudan, 291
Suez, 301, 303
Sweden, 89, 233
Switzerland, 31, 128, 190–2, 200, 304, 305, 354–5
Syria, 309, 357, 361

Taliani del Marchio, Francesco Maria, 106
Tavignano, 182–3
Taylor, A. J. P., 28, 299
Tedesco, Francesco, 121, 363, 368, 371
Terni, 3–4, 29, 56
Thaon di Revel, Paolo, 24–5, 54–5, 184, 217–18, 262, 266, 312
Theodoli, Alberto, 176, 341–3, 354–5
Thesiger, Wilfred, 332
Ticino, Canton, 298
Tien-tsin, 337
Tierra del Fuego, 52
Times, The, 172, 264
Tittoni, Romolo, 43, 139, 343
Tittoni, Tommaso, 12–13, 15, 19, 36, 42, 62, 89–93, 101, 103, 112, 115, 121, 127, 133–4, 137–9, 141, 145, 148, 150, 157, 160, 168–9, 174, 180, 185, 201, 212, 229–30, 256–8, 273, 275, 279, 282, 284, 289, 301, 303, 323, 341, 345, 350, 388, 402, 413
Tobruk, 156, 271–2
Toeplitz, Giuseppe, 259
Togliatti, Palmiro, 31

Tolomei, Enrico, 49
Torre, Andrea, 31, 44–5, 60, 65, 121, 148, 206, 355, 395, 406
Torre, Augusto, 68
Toscano, Mario, 68
Transylvania, 351
Trento (Trentino), 34, 210; in Habsburg Empire, 9, 201; Italian ambitions towards, 11, 46, 49–50, 129, 174, 178, 192, 203, 206, 228, 246, 249, 251, 255, 257, 350–1, 373, 376, 383, 386, 389–90, 399–401, 407–8, 413, 417
Trento and Trieste Association, 44, 49, 57, 120, 249
Trevelyan, George Macaulay, 172, 264
Treves, Claudio, 37
Tribuna, La, 44, 45, 122, 143, 144, 206, 255
Trieste, 5, 28, 122, 129, 201; in Habsburg Empire, 9, 131, 203, 207, 247–50, 252, 284; Italian ambitions towards, 11, 46–9, 174, 178, 192, 202–4, 206, 212, 228, 240, 246, 251, 254–5, 257, 263, 350–1, 373, 376, 386, 401, 408, 413, 417; Slav outpost, 256
Triple Alliance, 30, 36, 80–1, 123, 128–9, 131, 172, 174–5, 182, 196–8, 201–4, 207–8, 254, 256, 259, 267, 270, 273–4, 285–8, 291, 295, 297–302, 309–11, 313, 319, 357, 361, 365; (1882), 10, 198–9, 201; military arrangements, 91, 199–200, 216–19, 229, 252, 261–2, 266, 268, 272, 288, 292, 325, 356; (1887), 136, 199; (1902), 137, 199, 200; (1912), 155–6, 160–1, 181, 195, 199, 209–16, 222, 269–70, 274–5, 277–8, 280, 289, 294, 356; Article VII, 174, 186, 188, 209, 212, 228–9, 288, 301, 303–4, 306, 316, 328, 356, 359, 361, 386, 388–9; Balkan Wars and, 222, 226, 228, 231–5, 240, 248, 253, 279–81, 283, 308, 310–11, 318, 321; in 1914, 236, 243, 250–2; July Crisis and, 255, 380–1, 384–6, 388–92, 394–5; First World War and, 398, 400, 402, 404–5, 408, 413, 416–17
Triple Entente, 3, 123, 129, 131, 172, 174, 184, 195–6, 200, 210–11, 217, 226, 231–2, 254, 256, 258, 264, 266–7, 270, 273, 281, 285, 287, 291, 294, 297–9, 310, 315–16, 327–8, 335–6, 357, 365,

387, 398–9, 401–2, 405, 407–10, 412–13, 416
Tripoli, *see* Libya
Tsana, Lake, 254, 291, 296, 326, 331–3
Tunis, 10, 40, 47, 54, 62, 71, 86, 111, 135, 138, 140–2, 146, 155, 166–7, 172, 177, 181, 199, 255, 257, 275, 293–4, 312, 343
Turati, Filippo, 33, 36, 170, 203
Turkey, 140, 220–1, 232, 235, 257, 273, 284, 293–4, 302, 304, 335, 346, 353, 370, 399; Italian ambitions towards, 11, 16, 53, 87, 123, 133, 138, 159, 204–5, 234, 248, 254, 300–1, 306–7, 309–14, 316–28, 330–1, 333, 336, 340–3, 346–7, 352, 354–6, 358–76, 381, 391–2, 397, 401, 405, 407, 411, 413, 417; possible collapse of, 86, 88, 128, 132, 135–6, 138, 151, 165, 175, 179–80, 192, 224, 250, 267, 270, 282–5, 288, 290–2, 301, 310–11, 317, 321, 355, 357, 360, 362–3, 366, 371; Libyan War and, 132–5, 140–1, 146–8, 151–4, 156–8, 161–2, 164–5, 167, 173–80, 182–93, 209, 211, 276, 301, 305–6, 308, 349, 354
Tyrrell, William, 291, 391, 411

Uccialli, Treaty of (1889), 83
Udine, Umberto Filippo, Prince of, 15
Ufficio Stampa, 120, 122–4
Umberto I, King, 12, 15, 70, 81, 133
Unione Operaia, 77, 87
Unità, L', 35
United States, 25, 61, 77, 83, 86, 89, 140, 205, 263, 337–9, 341

Valona, 87–8, 222, 229, 230–1, 240–1, 245, 307, 384–5, 401, 404–5, 413–14
Vannutelli, Lamberto, 351
Vansittart, Robert, 302, 306
Vanvitelli, Luigi, 95
Varè, Daniele, 60, 96, 98, 104–5, 120, 203, 246
Varese, 221
Vatican, 1, 6, 32, 109, 186; Giolitti and, 13; Army and, 23–4; domestic affairs and, 33, 43, 49, 260, 265, 343; San Giuliano and, 74; nationalism and, 113, 202, 340; Libya and, 139–40, 169–70, 206; Albania and, 238, 240; in Pacific and Indian Oceans, 337; Turkey and,

Vatican (*cont.*)
340–3, 345; July Crisis and, 393, 397;
First World War and, 406
Venezia Giulia, 46, 49, 202
Venezian, Giacomo, 49
Venizelos, Eleutherios, 235
Versailles Conference, 7, 416
Victor Emmanuel II, 15, 97, 102–3, 265
Victor Emmanuel III, 13–17, 20–1, 31, 35,
54–5, 58, 62, 67–8, 85, 91, 95, 103, 111,
131, 148, 160–1, 173, 176, 178, 186,
188, 217, 219–20, 225–6, 250, 255,
259–60, 265, 284, 286, 288, 292, 298,
316–17, 341, 344–5, 348, 362, 365,
377–8, 389–91, 395, 398, 400, 410
Victor Emmanuel Monument, 8, 45, 59,
64, 66, 67, 144, 146, 148
Victoria, Princess, 70
Victoria, Queen, 260
Vigezzi, Brunello, 412
Villa d'Este, 378
Villari, Luigi, 45
Villari, Pasquale, 31, 32, 45, 50, 55
Visconti Venosta, Emilio, 12, 65, 87,
90–1, 101, 115, 127, 136, 198, 257, 395

Visconti Venosta, Enrico, 101
Visconti Venosta, Giovanni, 101
Visconti Venosta (family), 105
Vismara, Giacomo, 241–3, 245, 398
Volpi, Giuseppe di Misurata, 44, 60, 63,
68, 184, 189–90, 192, 236, 343, 347–50,
352–5, 360, 373–4

Wangenheim, Hans von, 190, 191, 213
Webster, Richard, 346
Weithword, Bianca, 338
Wilde, Oscar, 271
William II, Kaiser, 16, 91, 186, 209, 213,
217, 233, 234, 246, 250, 260, 285, 381,
392, 398
William of Wied, 235, 245, 246, 379–80,
383
Wilson, Henry, 302

Yemen, 54

Zanardelli, Giuseppe, 12, 56, 85, 137
Zanardelli (Consulta's cat), 96
Zimmermann, Arthur, 287–8, 379–82
Zupelli, Vittorio, 407